FOR THE
GLORY OF GOD

FOR THE GLORY OF GOD

HOW MONOTHEISM LED TO REFORMATIONS, SCIENCE, WITCH-HUNTS, AND THE END OF SLAVERY

Rodney Stark

PRINCETON UNIVERSITY PRESS
PRINCETON AND OXFORD

Published by Princeton University Press, 41 William Street,
Princeton, New Jersey 08540
In the United Kingdom: Princeton University Press,
3 Market Place, Woodstock, Oxfordshire OX20 1SY

Library of Congress Cataloging-in-Publication Data

Stark, Rodney.
For the glory of God : how monotheism led to reformations, science,
witch-hunts, and the end of slavery / Rodney Stark.
p. cm.
Includes bibliographical references and index.
ISBN 0-691-11436-6 (alk. paper)
1. Monotheism—History. 2. Reformation. 3. Religion and science—
History. 4. Witchcraft—History. 5. Slavery—Religious aspects—History.
I. Title.
BL221 .S747 2003
291.1′4—dc21 2002031746

British Library Cataloging-in-Publication Data is available

This book has been composed in Sabon with Centaur Display

Printed on acid-free paper ∞

www.pupress.princeton.edu

Printed in the United States of America

10 9 8 7 6 5 4 3 2 1

Contents

Illustrations

Acknowledgments

In the first volume of this two-volume work, I thanked a long list of colleagues whose friendship and advice I value. Here I will limit myself to several people who made important contributions to the present volume.

John A. Auping, S.J., of the Universidad IberoAmericana, Mexico, aroused my interest in abolition and Christianity when he graciously sent me a copy of his book *Religion and Social Justice*. Later he shared with me a rare seventeenth-century manuscript concerning the role of Catholic orders in opposing the enslavement of Indians. Then he read and carefully criticized a draft of Chapter 4.

Marion S. Goldman of the University of Oregon convinced me to include the "theory" that deviance creates social solidarity among the faulty explanations of the witch-hunts I expose in Chapter 3.

David Martin of the London School of Economics gave me the benefit of his immense knowledge of European religious history as well as his sociological insights.

Not only did Jeffrey Burton Russell of the University of California, Santa Barbara, make many very useful suggestions, but I was greatly reassured when my chapter on the witch-hunts passed his expert judgment with only positive comments.

Arthur Wu of the Duvall Institute has done his best to make me into a passable medievalist.

As for Brigitta van Rheinberg, editor of religion and history at Princeton University Press, when advised by both Martin and Russell that this book will be controversial and will provoke some hostile reviews, she wrote to me, "Well, that's one of the reasons I look forward to publishing it! It's time that some of the standard assumptions get questioned and turned around." No author could ask for more.

Finally, this is the third time I have had the privilege to be edited by Lauren Lepow, Princeton's Senior Editor, and I have run out of superlatives to describe the immense talent and care she brings to a book.

Corrales, New Mexico
April 15, 2002

FOR THE
GLORY OF GOD

Inspiration. To many Christians, this sandstone formation near Colorado Springs is not only the amazing result of erosion but a monument to the beauty of God's creation. Taoist monks have found it a very special place for meditation, and some New Age sorcerers think it marks a mystical vortex that amplifies all spells. © E. O. Hoppé/CORBIS.

Introduction

Dimensions of the Supernatural

Uncommon things must be said in common words.
—*Coventry Patmore*

Just as many religions teach that human culture was a gift from the Gods, many social scientists propose that religion is so basic to culture that without it "humanity could not have emerged from its pre- or proto-human condition."[1] Even if one doubts that humans were actually taught by various Gods how to build fires or grow maize, and takes a more limited view of the role of religion in the evolution of culture, it is obvious that ideas about the supernatural have profoundly influenced life in "advanced" as well as in less "sophisticated" societies, and that *monotheism* may well have been the single most significant innovation in history.

How, when, or even where belief in One God first occurred will probably never be known, but the dramatic results can be seen in virtually every aspect of the cultures and histories of the great monotheisms. Had the Jews been polytheists, they would today be only another barely remembered people, less important but just as extinct as the Babylonians. Had Christians presented Jesus to the Greco-Roman world as "another" God, their faith would long since have gone the way of Mithraism. And surely Islam would never have made it out of the desert had Muhammad not removed Allah from the context of Arab paganism and proclaimed him as the only God. Having embraced monotheism and the inherent duty to missionize, these three faiths changed the world.

This is not to suggest that the three great monotheisms are essentially the same, or that they have had a similar impact on history. As will be seen, Judaism, Christianity, and Islam differ in many important ways that have produced rather different historical consequences. For one thing, Jews have seldom had the power to directly determine events. As for the two powerful monotheisms, consider that Christianity was able to stimulate the rise of science while Islam could not. On the other hand, Islam produced no witch-hunts. However, even these differences illustrate the larger truth: that religion has played a leading role in directing the course of history.

Unfortunately, in today's intellectual environment, that simple and obvious statement is widely regarded as both unfortunate and false. Proponents of this revisionist claim overcome its inherent contradiction by assigning many of the most unfortunate aspects of history to religious causes, while flatly denying even the most obvious and overwhelming evidence that religion was the basis for any of the "good" things that have come to pass. For example, it is argued that Christianity played no significant role in sustaining the abolitionist cause but was a major factor in justifying slavery.

Of course, most of those who sustain and repeat such historical falsifications do not mean to mislead—they, too, have been misled. Were that not so, it would have been futile to write this book. But I cling to the belief that many readers respect the authority of evidence and will honor my search for what really happened and why.

The overall purpose of this book is to show how ideas about God have shaped the history and culture of the West, and therefore of the world—including both "good" and "bad" consequences. My method is to closely examine four major historical episodes, each of which was sustained by people who believed they were acting for the glory of God. I use the word "episode" to emphasize that this is *not* a "history of ideas." In every instance, the ideas are treated as a component of human action, of human organizations, or of social movements.

The first episode is, eventually, the Protestant Reformation. I inserted the word "eventually" here to alert readers that the reforming impulse is an aspect of all religious organizations, and that the Reformations of the sixteenth century had their beginnings as far back as, perhaps, the second century. As is explained in Chapter 1, theological disputes, especially those assuming the existence of One True God, inevitably result in religious sects and reformations. The chapter examines this process in pre-Christian times, in Judaism, in the early Church, and in Islam. Then I trace many centuries of failed efforts to reform the Catholic Church and show how that frequently resulted in the appearance of popular, "heretical" movements. Finally arriving in the sixteenth century, I formulate and test a new explanation as to why Protestantism succeeded in some places and not others. An additional purpose of the chapter is to provide an outline of European religious history that will place the remaining three chapters within a coherent context.

The second episode is the rise of science. Chapter 2 shows that there was no "scientific revolution" that finally burst through the superstitious barriers of faith, but that the flowering of science that took place in the sixteenth century was the normal, gradual, and direct outgrowth of Scholasticism and the medieval universities. Indeed, theological assumptions unique to Christianity explain why science was born only in Christian Europe. Contrary to the received wisdom, religion and science not only were compatible; they were inseparable. Hence the last portion of the chapter demonstrates that the battle over evolution is not a conflict between religion and science but between True Believers on both sides.

Chapter 3 shows that the commitment of Christian theologians to reason, which sustained the rise of science, also resulted in tragedy when applied to the question, "Why does non-Church magic work?" Thus Chapter 3 examines how the answer to this question caused generations of clearheaded, decent Europeans (including some celebrated for their contributions to the rise of science) to engage in witch-hunting. Having dispatched eight popular explanations of why the witch-hunts took place, I propose a new theory to explain the variations in where and when witch-hunts occurred.

As it happened, some of the very same people who were active in witch-hunting played leading roles in declaring that slavery was an abomination in the eyes of God. It was that conclusion, and only that conclusion, that enabled the West to abolish slavery. In fact, slavery was abolished in much of the non-Western world only because of Western pressure and interference—and slavery continues in some non-Christian areas. Chapter 4 shows why Christians reached this profoundly important conclusion and Muslims did not. The chapter also illustrates that it was vital to the subsequent success of the abolition movements that they were able to utilize the resources of the churches.

Although each of these four episodes was of long duration, each is closely associated with the sixteenth century. It was in 1517 that Luther nailed his Ninety-five Theses to the door of the Castle Church in Wittenberg. In 1543 Copernicus published *De revolutionibus orbium coeles-*

tium. It was during the latter half of the sixteenth century that the witch-hunts reached their height, and it was in 1510 that King Ferdinand initiated the Atlantic slave trade when he authorized the importation of African slaves to mine gold in the Spanish New World. Consequently, the chapters usefully expand upon one another, and many people make repeated appearances.

Finally, in a brief postscript, I sum up my efforts to create a sociology of Gods, showing that images of Gods, rather than ritual behavior, are the fundamental aspect of religion.

The remainder of this introduction will be devoted to defining and illustrating some key concepts that are basic to the subsequent chapters.

Godly and Godless Religions

Religion consists of *explanations* of *existence* based on *supernatural assumptions* and including statements about the *nature* of the *supernatural* and about *ultimate meaning.*

Ultimate meaning concerns the fundamental point and *purpose of being*. Does life have meaning? Why are we here? What can we hope? Why do we suffer? Does justice exist? Is death the end?

Supernatural refers to *forces or entities* (conscious or not) that are *beyond or outside nature* and which can suspend, alter, or ignore physical forces. ***Gods*** are a particular form of the supernatural consisting of *conscious supernatural beings.*

Notice that the definition of religion leaves room for "Godless" religions, such as the elite forms of Confucianism and Taoism wherein the supernatural is conceived of as a *supernatural* ***essence***—an underlying mystical force or principle governing life, but one that is *impersonal, remote, lacking consciousness, and definitely not a being*. As explained in the *Lao-tzu*, the Tao is a cosmic essence, the eternal Way of the universe that produces harmony and balance. Although the Tao is said to be wise beyond human understanding and "the mother of the universe," it is also said to be "always nonexistent," yet "always existent," "unnameable" and "the name that can be named." Both "soundless and formless," it is "always without desires." Finally, the sage is advised to make no effort to understand the Tao, which is how such an understanding will be achieved. Little wonder that the Tao inspires meditation and mysticism, but not worship.

Religions based on essences are not found only in the East. Many Western intellectuals, including some theologians and even bishops, propose an image of "God" as impersonal and unconscious as the Tao. Supernatural essences may be ideal objects for meditation and mystical contemplation by intellectuals, but Godless religions fail to appeal to the general public, and therefore the popular forms of Confucianism and Taoism include a substantial pantheon of Gods. This split has existed for millennia. The Chinese philosopher Xun-zi (*ca. 215 B.C.E.*)* taught that the truly educated know that although religious rituals can be beautiful and inspiring, they are but products of the human imagination: "They are done merely for ornament." However, "the common people regard them as [involving the] supernatural."[2]

Why do most people prefer a Godly religion? Because Gods are the only plausible sources of many things people desire intensely. It must be recognized that these desires are not limited to tangibles. Very often it is rewards of the spirit that people seek from the Gods: meaning, dignity, hope, and inspiration. Even so, the most basic aspect of religious activity consists of exchange relations between humans and Gods; people ask of the Gods and make offerings to them. Indeed, it is believed that Gods, unlike unconscious essences, set the terms for such exchanges and communicate them to humans. Thus while Godless religions rest upon the results of human meditation and speculation—upon wisdom—Godly religions rest upon ***revelations***, on *communications believed to come from the Gods*. Consequently, the intellectual advocates of Godless religion devote themselves to seeking enlightenment through meditation, while the intellectuals in Godly religions devote their efforts to understanding the full implications of revelations: ***theology*** consists of *explanations that justify and specify the terms of exchange with Gods, based on reasoning about revelations*. That is, theologians attempt to expand understanding of divine concerns and desires, and to extend the range of instances to which they apply, by tracing the logical implications of revelations. Indeed, the authority of the Mishnah rests on the Jewish belief that revela-

* Because this book meanders over more than two thousand years of history, it seemed appropriate to ease the burden on readers by providing the dates for every significant person mentioned in the text who lived and did his or her primary work before 1930. Dates will be placed at the first substantial reference to the person, not at the first mention if it is only incidental. As in this instance, it is now conventional to use B.C.E. (Before the Common Era) rather than B.C. All years not identified as B.C.E. belong to the era that was once designated as A.D.

Chinese Gods. The elite forms of Taoism, Confucianism, and Buddhism are "Godless," but the popular forms of these religions are bursting with Gods. Here are just a few of them, their statues lining the walls of the Temple Loong Wah. © Underwood & Underwood/CORBIS.

tions are granted to scholars through their close study of the Torah. A classic example of the theological process is the evolution of elaborate Christian doctrines concerning Mary despite how little is actually said about her in the New Testament. Many similar results of theological inquiry play important roles in the subsequent chapters.

Religious Practice

Not only does religion consist of a certain kind of beliefs about the meaning of life and about the nature of the supernatural; *all* other aspects of religion *are derivative* of these beliefs, especially those about the supernatural: the forms and motives of rites, rituals, prayers, sacrifices, and even mystical experiences are determined by the nature of the *object* to which they are directed. Thus religious ***practice*** includes *all activities performed for religious motives* or purposes; only when we know what religion *is*, can we distinguish actions and feelings that are religious rather than otherwise. A High Mass and a Nazi Party rally both qualify as rites, and both can inspire deep emotions in participants. Only by noting which is grounded in supernatural assumptions and which is not, can we effectively distinguish them. In similar fashion, William James (*1842–1910*) rejected the idea of "religious sentiments" or "religious emotions" as having a distinct psychology. Rather, what can be identified as "religious fear, religious love, religious awe, religious joy, and so forth" are nothing more (or less) than natural emotions "directed to a religious object"—objects being religious because they involve "the divine."[3] Hence my references to religious rites, for example, mean rites that are performed for religious motives or purposes. Applying the adjectival form of "religion" as a modifier makes it possible to incorporate all aspects of religion and of the religious life without the use of more complex definitions.

Although I define religion as a set of beliefs, religions exist outside of sacred texts only as *social or collective phenomena*. Purely idiosyncratic faiths are found only, and then very rarely, among the mad, or (perhaps) singular prophets—even ascetic hermits pursue a collective faith. One reason religions are social is that it is a difficult task to create a plausible and satisfying religious culture, and therefore any given religion (even those attributed to a single founder) is usually the product of many contributors. For this same reason, religions are most effectively sustained by dedicated specialists. The second reason religions are social is that the universal problem of religion is *confidence*—the need to convince people that its teachings are true and that its practices are effective. Since the ultimate proofs of religious claims typically lie beyond direct examination, it is through the testimony of others that people gain confidence in a religion. Organized religious groups maximize the opportunity for people to reassure one another that their religion is true. Among followers of Godly religions, in addition to asserting their personal certainty about otherworldly rewards, people often enumerate miracles—how they recovered from cancer, how they overcame alcoholism or drug abuse, how they became reliable and faithful spouses, how they survived a catastrophic accident, or how their prayers for a dying child were answered. Thus do people demonstrate that a religion "works," that its promises come true.

Magic

While all religions offer answers to questions of ultimate meaning (even if only to say that life is without meaning), magic does not. As Emile Durkheim (*1858–1917*) noted, magic is concerned not with the meaning of the universe but with "technical and utilitarian ends," and hence "it does not waste its time in speculation."[4] Or, as John Middleton put it, "Magical beliefs and practices are particularly significant in being mainly instrumental, with little expressive content."[5] Thus magic is excluded by the definition of religion since it does not concern itself with ultimate meaning and typically does not offer explanations even of its own mechanisms, let alone of more profound matters. In addition, magic is essentially Godless.

Magic refers to all efforts to *manipulate or compel* supernatural forces *without reference to a God or Gods* or to *matters of ultimate meaning*. Put another way, magic is *limited to impersonal conceptions of the supernatural*, what the celebrated Bronislaw Malinowski (*1884–1942*) described as a "mystic, impersonal power." He went on to describe the nearly "universal idea found wherever magic flourishes" that there exists "a supernatural, impersonal force."[6]

Summing up more than a century of anthropological studies of magic, Middleton pointed out:

> [T]he realm of magic is that in which human beings believe that they may directly affect nature and each other, for good or for ill, by their own efforts (even though the precise mechanism may not be understood by them), as distinct from appealing to divine powers by sacrifice or prayer.[7]

Of course, Middleton did not mean to place in the magical realm just any or even most human efforts to affect nature or one another. He assumed his readers understood that, just as rain dances differ from irrigation projects, only efforts involving a resort to supernatural means constitute magic. What is important is that these efforts are not directed toward a God, albeit they are efforts to manipulate supernatural forces.

Because the distinction between religion and magic is of such major importance in this book, especially in Chapters 2 and 3, it will be helpful to expand on these matters. When a Catholic wears a Saint Christopher's medal to ensure a safe journey, that is *not* magic because the power of the medal is attributed to the patron saint whose powers, in turn, are granted by a God. The medal is intrinsic to an exchange with a God. But when devotees of the New Age place "mystic" crystals under their pillows to cure a cold, this *is* magic because no appeal has been made to a God. The same applies to astrology. The conclusion that tomorrow is not an auspicious day for travel, for example, is not a message from a God but a calculation concerning the location of heavenly bodies relative to one's birth date. Magic deals in impersonal supernatural forces, often in the belief that such forces are *inherent properties* of particular objects such as planets or crystals, or of words, especially written or spoken formulas and incantations. Ruth Benedict (*1887–1948*) distinguished religion and magic in this way, proposing that the former involves "personal relations with the supernatural," while the latter deals with "mechanistic manipulation of the impersonal."[8]

Admittedly, the most sophisticated form of magic, known as *sorcery*, may sometimes involve supernatural creatures having some degree of consciousness. That is, sometimes sorcerers do attempt to compel certain primitive spiritual entities such as imps and demons to perform certain services. Even so, it still remains possible to "distinguish between magic and religion on the basis of the criterion of compulsion."[9] As Benedict put it, "*Magic* is mechanical procedure, the compulsion of the supernatural."[10] Compulsion assumes supernatural beings of extremely limited capacity—it is quite inconceivable even to compel the small Gods of polytheistic systems, let alone omnipotent beings. Hence compulsion of spiritual entities remains within the realm of magic, but exchanges with the Gods shift the activity into the realm of religion. Max Weber (*1864–1920*) made this same point when he noted that "those beings that are worshipped and entreated religiously may be termed 'gods,' in contrast to the 'demons,' which are magically coerced and charmed."[11]

Dualistic Monotheism

Not only can religions be separated into the Godless and the Godly; there is enormous variation within the latter category: from religions that believe in flocks of tiny Gods who are everywhere, to religions that believe in One God who is everywhere. However, although monotheism means belief in only one God, in none of the great monotheisms—Judaism, Christianity, or Islam—is there only *one* supernatural *entity.* In each, God is surrounded by "a cloud of beings."[12] As Herbert Spencer (*1820–1903*) pointed out:

> Another fact to be noted respecting the evolution of monotheisms out of polytheisms . . . is that they do not become complete; or at least do not maintain their purity . . . [for example] the Hebrew religion, nominally monotheistic, retained a large infusion of polytheism. Archangels exercising powers in respect to their respective spheres, and capable even of rebellion, [a]re practically demi-gods . . . [Christian] trinitarian[ism] is partially polytheistic . . . Nay, even belief in a devil, conceived as an independent supernatural being, implies surviving polytheism.[13]

If we ignore his questionable evolutionary assumptions, Spencer surely was correct, and his mention of a devil acknowledges that there is a clear distinction among the various additional supernatural beings within the great monotheisms between those regarded as good and those who are evil. Therein lies the limiting principle of monotheism.

In practice, absolute monotheism is possible *only* when the supernatural is conceived of not as a *being* but as an *essence*, as an impersonal, remote, divine principle such as the Tao. If there is only one supernatural *being*, such a God would of necessity be *irrational* and *perverse*; one God of infinite scope must be responsible for *everything*, evil as well as good, and thus must be dangerously capricious, shifting intentions unpredictably and without reason. Within the confines of absolute monotheism, the only alternative to such a fearsome God is a divine essence that is responsible for *nothing*, being utterly remote from human concerns. But such nonbeings have little to offer most people and never supplant supernatural beings, except among small elites.

This necessarily limits monotheism since, in order for a divine being to be rational and benign, it is necessary for the religious system to postulate the existence of other, if far lesser, beings. That is, *evil* supernatural beings such as Satan are essential to the most rational conception of divinity. Thus Judaism, Christianity, and Islam are ***dualistic monotheisms***—each teaches that, in addition to a supreme divine being, *there also exists at least one evil, if less powerful, supernatural being.* As Jeffrey Burton Russell put it, "Dualism posits two opposite powers of good and evil, attributing evil to the will of a malign spirit."[14] The principle of dualism reflects the necessity either to conceive of a single divine essence that is above the question of good or evil by virtue of being remote from any exchanges with humans (the Tao), or to admit the existence of more than one supernatural being.

Because evil supernatural beings cannot be trusted and may do serious harm to humans, people will prefer conceptions of Gods wherein the good ones are far more powerful than the wicked ones. Hence entirely symmetrical dualism is rare and tends to be limited to good and evil essences, although some faiths have sustained conceptions of an evil being nearly as powerful as the good one—the Cathars being an example (Chapter 1). Usually, however, evil is not accorded full Godhood—Yahweh, Jehovah, and Allah merely tolerate lesser evil beings.

As was demonstrated in the first of these volumes,* and will be again throughout this book, monotheism has immense capacities to mobilize human action—capacities far beyond those found in polytheism or in Godless religions. However, precisely because the Gods of monotheism ask so much, some humans are always tempted to soften and weaken their conception of God until it fades into an undemanding, unconscious, essence. Thus, for example, when Protestant academics hailed Paul Tillich's proposal that God is only a psychological construct, the "ground of our being,"[15] they banished the possibility of miracles and otherworldly rewards and settled for an essence that is no more Godlike than the Tao. Like the Tao, figments of human psychology ask nothing and give nothing. Thus recent history shows that even within a monotheistic tradition, religious groups that succumb to the temptation to dispense with Gods as conscious beings soon find that their membership dwindles to a few intellectuals as most of their rank-and-file members shift to Godly faiths.[16]

If the most basic aspect of any religion is its conception of the supernatural, then the most basic aspect of social scientific studies of religion is a

* *One True God: Historical Consequences of Monotheism* (Princeton: Princeton University Press, 2001).

sociology of Gods. Yet this is the topic that has received the least attention. Instead, for several generations nearly everyone in the field accepted Durkheim's assertion that religion is not about the supernatural at all, but only about rites and rituals. As will be seen throughout the book, and at length in the postscript, Durkheim was wrong. The contrasts already drawn between supernatural *beings* and unconscious, impersonal, vaguely supernatural *essences* reveal that different conceptions of the supernatural have dramatically different effects on the human experience. Even within Godly religions, compare the social implications of belief in a pantheon of undependable and often immoral Gods with those of belief in a supreme being who imposes moral obligations on humans. As will be seen, the consequences of these and other such differences in how the supernatural is conceived are decisive.

Conclusion

Although much of this book is devoted to history, my aims are those not of a historian but of a social scientist—which is what I am. In recent years I have turned to assembling and analyzing historical materials to expand the applications of original sociological theories that, in turn, are meant to illuminate the history. This approach involves synthesizing the work of many historians, not to produce a history, but to construct "cases" suitable for analysis. Hence although I have taken pains to offer a clear overall picture of each of the four episodes, I have eliminated some interesting aspects because they were irrelevant to the analysis.

As is necessary for anyone writing a historical study of any substantial scope, I have relied mainly on "secondary" sources: I am indebted to hundreds of fine specialists who have educated me about the many special topics involved. A very rewarding by-product of that fact has been the opportunity to acquire and read a substantial library of books and essays by historians, many of them very gracefully written.

Having said these agreeable things about my debts to historians, I must also register some of my disappointments. Foremost, of course, are the many efforts to dismiss the role of religion in producing "good" things such as the rise of science or the end of slavery, and the corresponding efforts to blame religion for practically everything "bad." Of course, I was prepared for this when I began. What I was not prepared for was how many of the historians I read to write these studies expressed militant anti-Catholicism, and how few of their peers have taken exception to the litany of contemptuous, anti-Catholic comments, delivered without any trace of self-consciousness. Of course, no reputable, recent historians actually use such self-incriminating words as "papists," or "Romanism." Instead, they substitute intellectualized equivalents such as "enemies of reason," "benighted scholastics," "fanatical friars," and adjectives such as "sinister," "brutal," "uncomprehending," "cruel," "repressed," and "totalitarian."

Far more pernicious, however, are the many silences and omissions that distort scholarly comprehension of important matters. Among the many glaring examples to be revealed is that vigorous efforts by sixteenth-century popes to halt slavery were effectively "lost" from the record until the past decade or so, as will be clear in Chapter 4.

But perhaps the most serious harm is done unintentionally by honorable scholars. Although most living historians are probably not prejudiced against Roman Catholics, or at least not more so than against members of any other faith, most hold false views that they do not know to have been the product of the anti-Catholicism of previous generations. For example, aside from a few specialists, most historians still seem to assume that the Spanish Inquisition burned large numbers of heretics, witches, Marrano Jews, and other deviants in public autos-da-fé, and that to have fallen into the hands of the inquisitors was an almost certain sentence of death. All false! As will be seen, especially in Chapter 3, Spanish inquisitors seldom had anyone burned, and the typical sentence they meted out was mild in the extreme: for those convicted of witchcraft, in Spain it was usually sufficient to say they were sorry.

I am not and have never been a Roman Catholic. When I note virtues that many historians have misrepresented or ignored in their writings about Catholicism, I deny acting as an apologist. Indeed, sincere Catholics will find much to be uncomfortable about when reading some of the chapters that follow, and I have written some unpleasant things about Protestants, Jews, Muslims, heretics, skeptics, and pagans too. It is, of course, easy to find fault. Sad to say, in today's intellectual climate it takes much greater courage to praise. I hope that I measured up.

Finally, because this is a work of social science, not philosophy, I have taken pains neither to imply nor to deny the existence of God. This is a matter beyond the scope of science. Consequently, my personal religious views are of concern only to me.

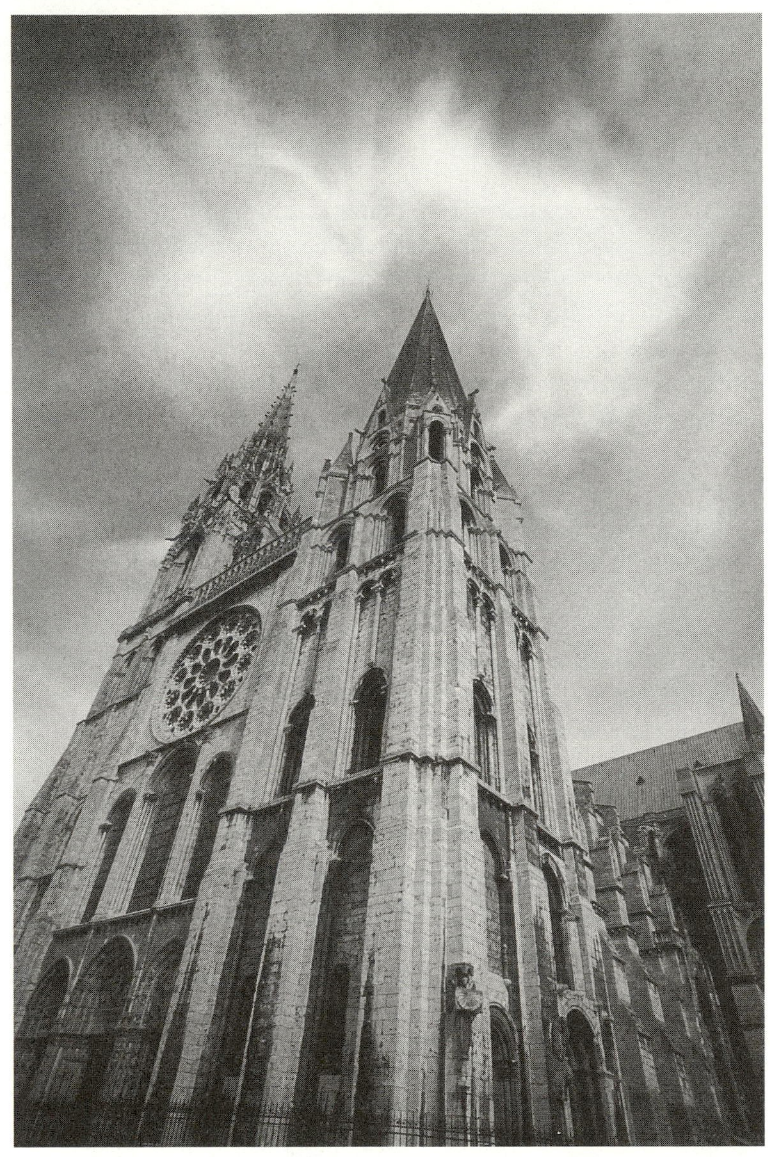

Grand Illusion. Built between 1120 and 1170, the Chartres Cathedral and the many similar medieval structures give false testimony that this was an Age of Faith and of Catholic unity. In truth, the average medieval European seldom attended mass, and the Church itself was bitterly divided between those wanting a more intense faith and those content that the tithes kept coming. © Craig Aurness/CORBIS.

 I

God's *Truth*: Inevitable Sects and Reformations

Here I stand. I cannot do otherwise, so help me God. Amen.
—*Martin Luther*

Every October, Lutheran churches around the world celebrate Reformation Sunday in remembrance of the religious drama played out by Martin Luther and his opponents in Germany during the sixteenth century.

Most people still use the term "Reformation" this way, but that definition has become much too narrow. Even the most partisan Lutheran historians no longer ignore the English Reformation, nor do they any longer dismiss Calvinism as a mere aftermath. Instead, they acknowledge the diversity of the Reformation even in Germany. Respectable reference works also reflect this expansion of the subject: *The Oxford Dictionary of World Religions* defines the "Reformation" as "Movements for reform in the Christian Church in the West, which took place in the early 16th century."[1]

But this definition is also out-of-date. Many contemporary scholars now refuse to restrict the Reformation to sixteenth-century events, noting that Jan Hus was burned for precipitating a Bohemian Reformation long before Luther was born—hence the title of James Tracy's recent book: *Europe's Reformations, 1450–1650*. But even Tracy's time frame ignores the fact that John Wyclif planted the seeds of the English Reformation during the fourteenth century. Moreover, historians have begun to expand the Reformation to include early medieval "heresies" as well as efforts at reform that developed within the Church as early as the eleventh and twelfth centuries.[2]

However, even this greatly increased scope is inadequate. In this chapter I will define a ***reformation*** *as efforts to restore or renew* standards of religious belief and practice to a more *demanding* level, *within* a religious organization. Although reformations begin as efforts *within* a religious organization, if they are thwarted they will often be *externalized*, thereby becoming *sects*—groups offering *high-intensity religious alternatives* to the conventional religious bodies. Thus defined, reformations have occurred not only in Christianity but in Judaism and Islam, and in less dramatic fashion within polytheisms as well, and sect movements are endemic in all forms of religion. Moreover, not only have reformations taken place in past times; they can be observed even today—albeit on a smaller scale. However, the early and medieval Christian Church was unusually prone to reformations as well as to sect formation because these phenomena are *chronic*, *inevitable*, and extremely *bitter* whenever efforts are made to sustain a religious *monopoly*.

Seen from this perspective, Marcion may have attempted the first reformation of the Christian Church way back in the second century and, having failed, formed an early and important sect. To amplify this assertion, an overview of what follows may be useful. I will argue that religious diversity is a fundamental feature of societies, reflecting the fact that people differ in the level of intensity they seek in religion. Where free to do so, this diversity of taste will manifest itself in a diversity of organized religious options. However, if organizational diversity is suppressed, the demand for high-intensity religion will serve as the mainspring for reformation, as those committed to high standards will be forced to work from within. But when efforts at reform fail, they will tend to erupt as external challenges to the prevailing establishment.

This definition of reformations provides for the fact that they may or may not succeed—Hus failed and so did Luther. That is, Luther may in some sense have reformed Christianity, but he did not reform the Roman Catholic Church—that was accomplished by the Counter-Reformation. Luther's efforts at reformation were thwarted, and what he actually did was to create a new sect. He differed from Hus only in that his movement survived, and so did he. Consequently, I will credit Luther with initiating the "Protestant Reformation," thus reminding readers that Luther did not reform the Catholic Church, but that instead he established the Protestant alternative to the Roman Catholic Church. In addition to attempting to explain why reformations occur, this chapter also explores the conditions under which sect movements and attempts at reformations attract widespread public support, devoting extended analysis to the rise of Protestantism.

However, the chapter is of much greater scope than would be needed simply to trace the gathering of religious dissatisfactions and pressures that burst forth in the "Protestant Reformation." A principal aim is also to provide an outline of medieval European religious history to serve as an adequate context for the subsequent chapters. In doing so, I attempt to dispel a number of incorrect, but widely believed, claims about what went on and why. Three especially important examples of these *incorrect* claims are:

1. That the medieval period was an Age of Faith during which the average person was deeply religious.
2. That the great medieval sect movements were expressions of lower-class suffering and antagonism.
3. That the Roman Catholic Church, especially at the parish level, tended to be dominated by religious fanatics who tried to impose repressive and unnatural morality on the laity.

In addition to these, the chapter confronts at least a dozen other significant misconceptions about religion in medieval Europe, but it will be adequate to consider them as they arise.

I begin by explaining some simple, but very fundamental, social scientific principles that will be applied in subsequent sections and will be useful in other chapters as well.

Religious Diversity

In much previous work I have demonstrated that pluralism is the natural or normal[3] religious state of affairs—that in the *absence of repression*, there will be multiple religious organizations.[4] One reason for pluralism is that in any normal population people seem to differ according to the intensity of their religious desires and tastes. That is, some people are content with a religion that, although it promises less, also requires less. Others want more from their religion and are willing to do more to get it. Max Weber expressed this point by noting that "in every religion . . . people differ greatly in their religious capacities"; hence in every society some people qualify as "religious virtuosi."[5] Building on this observation, I have proposed that the religious diversity in all societies is rooted in social *niches*, groups of people sharing particular preferences concerning religious intensity. I argue that these niches are quite stable over time and quite similar in their fundamental outlook across societies and history.[6]

Put another way, in all societies people can be ranked according to the intensity of their religious concerns and tastes, and hence in the level of demands they are willing to fulfill to satisfy their needs. Most people want some intensity in their religion and will accept some costs, but not too much of either. Some people will have little religious interest and will prefer to be involved as little as possible. But in any society, as Weber noted, some people will aspire to a high-intensity faith. Given the diversity of religious *demand*, other things being equal there will be a corresponding diversity in religious *supply*: hence pluralism, the existence of multiple religious organizations. Thus in any society where diversity is not suppressed by force, the religious spectrum will include a full range of religious organizations, from some that demand little and are in a very low state of tension with their surroundings to some that offer very high-intensity faith. Enrollment in these groups will tend to resemble a normal curve, with the moderate faiths commanding the largest followings.[7]

Even in very small, very "primitive" societies, pluralism exists in the distinct totemic cults, each with its separate initiations and rites. In these societies, of course, individuals lack an opportunity to choose, and therefore the totemic cult groups probably tend to be similar in their level of intensity, although they may differ considerably from time to time because even here individual levels of religiousness will vary. However, in somewhat more complex cultures, religious pluralism will be quite evident because religious choices are "not inescapably prescribed by tribal or family adherence," but take on "a voluntary, personal" aspect.[8] Indeed, in polytheistic societies where the Gods are conceived of as specialized and of small scope, pluralism flourishes since it takes a substantial pantheon of such Gods to satisfy the range of things humans seek from supernatural beings, and people patronize particular deities as they see fit. Thus any ancient Roman, Greek, or Egyptian city sustained separate temples devoted to each of a score or more major Gods, with a scattering of temples to lesser deities.[9] Within monotheism, however, the diversity of religious desires and tastes results not in a diversity of Gods but in a diversity of *groups*, differing in their approaches to the *same* God.

Just as religious "consumers" differ in the intensity they desire from religion, the primary basis for the diversity of religious organizations, in both polytheistic and monotheistic settings, is the level of intensity and sacrifice imposed on members. As Benton Johnson noted in his seminal essay, religious bodies "range along a continuum from complete rejection to complete acceptance of the [cultural and social] environment in which [they] exist."[10] This has come to be known as the "church-sect dimension," *churches* being religious bodies in a low state of tension, *sects* being bodies in a high state of tension. The level of tension between a religious group and the rest of society translates directly into the costs imposed on membership: sects ask far more of their members in terms of sacrifice and the intensity of their commitment.

But why will they do it? Why will people choose to pay high religious costs? For centuries, starting with the earliest founders of the field, social scientists have answered that question by invoking abnormal psychology: ignorance, fear, anxieties, illusions, and, when more intense levels of faith are involved, mental pathology. On April 6, 1723, in one of his celebrated *Cato's Letters*, John Trenchard characterized piety as a common form of madness, "doubtless [caused by] a fever in the head . . . The enthusiast heats his own head by extravagant imaginations, then makes . . . God to be the author of his hot head . . . because he takes his own frenzy for inspiration." More than two centuries later, Gordon W. Allport, Harvard psychologist and one of the founders of the Society for the Scientific Study of Religion, allowed that mature adults could share his very mild ("intrinsic") religiousness, so long as they continued to have constructive doubts, but he dismissed stronger affirmations of faith as "primitive credulity," and as "childish, authoritarian, and irrational."[11] At the time, this was the conventional view, and it is still held by many social scientists despite overwhelming evidence to the contrary. Thus it came as a shock, even an affront, when in 1972 the late Dean Kelley, a distinguished liberal Protestant clergyman and Director for Civil and Religious Liberty for the National Council of Churches, published *Why Conservative Churches Are Growing*.

Kelley had wanted the title "Why Strict Churches Are Strong," but the publisher overruled him in favor of one more apt to provoke attention. The task he set himself in the book was to explain why, in an era when membership in the liberal Protestant churches such as the Methodists, Episcopalians, and United Church of Christ was rapidly declining, "strict" groups such as the Southern Baptists, Seventh-day Adventists, Mormons, and Assemblies of God were growing rapidly. His conclusion can be expressed in simple economics. Price, or cost, is only one factor in assessing an exchange; quality is the other, and combined they yield an estimate of *value*. Therein lies the key to the appeal of more demanding religious groups: despite being expensive they can offer greater value; indeed, they are able to do so partly *because* they are expensive. That is, religions that ask more from their members are thereby enabled to give them more—in worldly as well as spiritual rewards.

Initially, Kelley's work was almost universally rejected,[12] and he was subjected to considerable personal abuse.[13] But the liberal churches continued to decline and the conservative churches continued to grow, and by now objective social scientists agree that Kelley was right. A persuasive empirical and theoretical literature confirms that, within limits, higher-tension faiths offer a far more rewarding experience to members than do permissive, low-cost faiths.[14] This is not to suppose that one day most people will belong to high-tension sects. Most people will usually prefer a somewhat more moderate level of tension. However, it does mean that very low-tension faiths will fail (if permitted by the state to do so), and that sects will always enjoy a substantial appeal and will be able to generate the highest levels of member commitment. This, combined with the tendency of higher-tension groups to drift toward lower tension, makes the formation of new sects inevitable. Moreover, where sect formation is prevented, high levels of religious dissatisfaction and angry demands for religious reform are to be expected.

These tendencies are not peculiar to the United States, or to Christianity, or to modern times. They are universal. That high-tension sects abound within monotheism is easily demonstrated. Not so obvious is that this is true within polytheism as well.

Sects within Polytheism

Our impression of Greco-Roman polytheism has been badly distorted by the depiction of the Gods in the *Iliad* and the *Odyssey*. Here, the Gods of Olympus are represented as superior to humans *only* in their powers,[15] having the same ethical and moral shortcomings as do mortals, hence their constant intrigues, outrageous behavior, and selfish pursuits. This prompted Xenophanes (*ca. 570–480* B.C.E.) to complain that "Homer. . . ascribed to the gods all things that among men are a shame and a reproach—theft and adultery and deceiving one another."[16] Indeed, while these stories of heroic deeds and the Gods were popular in ancient times, they were not religious texts. Consequently, to depend upon Homer for

Ungodly Hangover. The Gods of antiquity were not morally edifying examples. Here, in this sixteenth-century painting by Girolamo Mocetto, the God Bacchus is depicted as suffering from have drunk too much wine. © Historical Picture Archive/CORBIS.

our impressions of Greek religion is tantamount to basing our depiction of Christianity on Arthurian legend rather than the New Testament. This is not to say that the actual Grecian religious texts, such as those compiled in the Orphic Rhapsodies, present an attractive picture of the Gods—Zeus is reported to have raped his mother, who thereupon bears his daughter

Persephone, whom Zeus then rapes to sire Dionysos, and so on. What is so different from Homer's tales is that in these accounts the Gods do not devote themselves so fully to trivial concerns. Rather, issues of death, afterlife, justice, penance, and sacrifice are central themes.[17]

Contrary to common images of Greek and Roman religious practice as consisting mainly of feasting as a tribute to philandering Gods, and the making of votive offerings in pursuit of favors from fickle deities, the concept of "sin" was highly developed among some groups in classical times, as was the idea of penance. Thus some of the religious groups and organizations offered extremely demanding, costly, high-tension faiths. Among the more demanding and austere of these were the groups associated with **Orpheus** and **Pythagoras**. Walter Burkert noted that, in contrast with many other Greek religions whose origins are unknown, Orpheus and Pythagoras were the "founders of sects."[18]

The identity of Orpheus is unknown, and the name is probably a pseudonym. He is presented as a singer and poet, and the works attributed to him go back as far as the middle of the sixth century B.C.E. However, Pythagoras (*ca. 580–500 B.C.E.*) was undoubtedly a historical figure. He was born in Samos and recruited followers to his religious views in southern Italy. Both faiths stressed the individual's responsibility to pursue moral perfection, and Burkert linked this to the fact that these were among the earliest Grecian religions to rely mainly on the written rather than the spoken (and memorized) word: "The new form of transmission introduces a new form of authority to which the individual, provided that he can read, has direct access without collective mediation."[19]

E. O. James argued that the Orphics represented the "first really serious attempt in Greece to make human destiny depend upon character and conduct in the present state of existence."[20] But the Pythagorean view was quite similar, holding that life on earth was punishment for sins in former lives. Thus both faiths imposed quite stringent ascetic demands upon those who would belong, for both taught that one must suffer punishments in this life as atonement so that one might enter "a festive existence" in the afterlife rather than "suffer terrible things" that are in store for "evildoers."[21] Thus for both Orphics and Pythagoreans, "as one rises or goes to bed, puts on shoes or cuts one's nails, rakes the fire, puts on a pot or eats, there is always a rule to be observed, something wrong to be avoided."[22] Orphics observed elaborate dietary restrictions: they ate no meat, eggs, or beans, and they drank no wine. Suicide was prohibited, and so were various forms of sexual expression—indeed, many adherents embraced celibacy. Some of the most devout Orphics became wandering beggars. Pythagorean asceticism was quite similar. They, too, observed extensive dietary laws, wore white garments, obeyed elaborate rules concerning ordinary daily activities, and did not speak in the dark; husbands as well as wives were forbidden extramarital sex.

It must not be supposed that these were merely obscure, strange sects, very out of keeping with "normal" Greek religions. They were but two of many high-tension religious groups that flourished in the classical world—indeed, the similarities to Judaism are many. Moreover, many other large pagan religious groups in the Greco-Roman world made significant, if less stringent, demands upon their followers. Devotees of Isis were bound by an elaborate code of conduct. For example, Tran Tam Tinh reported that female members were expected to observe frequent days of chastity, and that annually all devotees were expected to plunge into nearly frozen rivers and then crawl "on their bleeding knees around the temple of Isis."[23] Initiates into the cult of Mithra were "expected to obey strong rules of purity and to oppose evil in the world."[24] That religions impose demands is entirely in keeping with an observation frequently confirmed in my previous empirical studies: people tend to value a religion in terms of what it costs, and if most people find some religions too expensive, most do not value faiths that cost little or nothing.

Sect Formation in Monotheism

Within polytheism, the diversity of religious preferences is met through the formulation or importation of new religions devoted to *new* Gods—thus did Isis migrate to Rome from Egypt. But within monotheism, unmet religious desires are satisfied by the formation of new *groups* devoted to the *same* God. Usually, new groups are formed by persons seeking a higher-intensity faith; hence most new groups are sects.

One of the cherished achievements of the scientific study of religion was to recognize and explain why religious bodies have a tendency to move from higher to lower levels of tension with their sociocultural environments: that is, sects tend to become churches.[25] As this occurs, those followers with a strong preference for higher-tension religion will tend to drop out, and some of them are apt to form a new sect to replace their original affiliation—often claiming that theirs is the authentic group, rather than the more "worldly" parent body.

There are several reasons for the transformation of sects into churches. It is often the case that the majority of second- and third-generation members do not share the same desire for a high-tension faith that shaped the founding generation. There would be a significant tendency in this direction simply from regression to the mean—the founding generation will have been selected for their unusually high-tension religious preferences, and, because socialization is always imperfect, some of their children will have far less intense religious preferences.[26] Moreover, unless the group is extremely stigmatized and isolated, external societies always offer very high levels of temptation to assimiliate, as was demonstrated by the Jews of western Europe subsequent to their emancipation early in the nineteenth century.[27] Another mechanism involves social mobility resulting in subsequent generations' enjoying substantially higher status than did the founders. Other things being equal, because of their high levels of demand, high-intensity faiths are relatively more costly for the privileged. For example, an austere religion is much less a matter of choice for those unable to afford luxury, but the wealthy must resist temptation to limit themselves to plain living. To recognize this is *not* to assume that ascetic groups appeal primarily to the less fortunate. As will be seen, many (perhaps most) ascetic movements have considerably *over*recruited persons of privilege—indeed Buddha was a prince before founding his monastic order, and, of his first 60 members, at least 55 were from "prominent families."[28] As another example, of 483 ascetic Catholic saints who lived between 500 and 1500, 75 percent were from the nobility (22 percent from royalty), and another 14 percent were from wealthy families.[29]

Another factor in sect transformation is that by somewhat reducing an initial high level of intensity, religious groups can grow more rapidly, since they can appeal to a larger segment of the population. This often proves to be a strong inducement, especially to ambitious clergy. Moreover, by reducing their intensity, groups can reduce the level of tension and conflict they may experience with outsiders, which often proves attractive as well.[30]

Unfortunately, for generations most social scientists claimed that sect formation is not motivated by doctrinal disputes, as these are merely masks for more basic, "material" motives. For example, in *The Social Sources of Denominationalism*, the classic work wherein appears the first statement of a theory of the transformation of sects into churches, H. Richard Niebuhr (*1894–1962*) began with bitter criticism of the "orthodox interpretation [that] looks upon the official creeds of the churches as containing the explanation of . . . the prevailing differences."[31] Doctrinal differences are never basic; "these differences ha[ve] their roots in more profound social divergences." Thus did Niebuhr dismiss the claims by various Christian groups that their differences were of doctrinal origins, citing "the universal human tendency to find respectable reasons for a practice desired from motives quite independent of the reasons urged,"[32] for the fact is that "theological opinions have their roots in the relationship of the religious life to the cultural and political conditions prevailing in any group of Christians."[33] Thus "the sect has ever been the child of an outcast minority, taking its rise in the religious revolts of the poor."[34]

But, as will be seen, most of the great sect movements in European history were not "revolts of the poor." To the contrary, these movements were sustained by the privileged, and the poor seldom played any significant role at all. While it would be absurd to deny that material factors influence doctrinal disputes or indeed the formulation of doctrines, it is equally absurd to suppose that people don't "really" care about doctrines, and that such disputes have no reality. Most instances of religious dissent make no sense at all in terms of purely material causes; they become coherent only if we assume that people did care about the central focus of their dispute. Consequently, we must acknowledge the role of theology and of revelations in creating doctrinal disputes. When many individuals pore over scriptures in search of deeper understanding or clearer interpretations, it is inevitable that some will arrive at different conclusions. Disputes over the interpretation of scripture have often split religious communities having no detectable social or material differences to sustain a schism, theological faculties being a common example.[35] By the same token, while most revelations merely confirm the prevailing orthodoxy,[36] even some of these may include differences in emphasis or interpretation and thus produce schisms—this being the origin of several early Christian groups such as the Montanists and the Manichaeans.

The transformation of sects into churches and the formation of new sects can be observed in all historical instances of monotheism.

Early Jewish Sects

If ever there was a single Jewish faith, it fragmented in very early times, as the books of Ezra and Nehemiah attest. The Talmud notes the existence of twenty-four disputatious Jewish theological factions and sects. However, beginning in about the second century (B.C.E.), Jewish religious life in Israel was dominated by three groups, each appealing to one of the three primary niches of religious demand. Ranged from lowest to highest intensity, these were the Sadducees, the Pharisees, and the Essenes.[37]

Most of the high priests and a majority in the Sanhedrin were **Sadducees**. Later in the chapter, I explain that religious establishments are very prone to drift toward laxity, and clearly that was the case here. The faith of the Sadducees was as much a philosophy as a religion. They rejected many basic supernatural tenets of Jewish tradition. They denied the resurrection of the dead and claimed that the soul does not exist, and therefore "after death one expects to suffer nothing, either bad or good . . . and . . . man passes into non-existence."[38] They also asserted that "there is no angel or spirit" (Acts 23:8), and this has been interpreted as a denial of revelations.[39] There is evidence that the Sadducees were also lax about the Law, especially as it pertained to divorce and to intermarriage, and Helmut Koester concluded that "they had been assimilated to the culture of Hellenism in their personal style of life."[40] As for their philosophical orientation, Josephus (37–95) compared the Sadducees to the Epicurean school of Greek philosophy.[41] An apt modern comparison might be with the liberal branch of American Episcopalianism.

The **Pharisees** were "the leaders of the masses" and exponents of conventional Judaism.[42] They affirmed the traditional Jewish beliefs and practices and voiced strong objections to the laxity of many members of the religious establishment. But while being fully observant of the Law and expressing their belief in revelation and resurrection, they did not advocate asceticism and were content to lead normal lives.

In keeping with the fundamental principle propelling all sect movements, the **Essenes** denounced both Pharisees and Sadducees for failing to live up to the Law, having drifted into worldliness and apostasy. The Essenes pursued a highly ascetic, often communal, lifestyle in accord with the minutiae of the Law as they interpreted it, and were given to apocalyptic concerns about the battle between Good and Evil—many of their views being based on revelations as well as theology.[43] Thus they provided a suitable outlet for those preferring a very intense faith—the "religious virtuosi." [44]

The Essenes stood as an external challenge to conventional Judaism and especially to the religious establishment. However, given the prevailing freedom to openly dissent, the Essenes were not forced to try to achieve the reformation of a monolithic Judaism by working from within. Instead, they served as a religious escape valve.

Many scholars have assumed that class differences played a major role in the origins and membership of these three movements: that the Sadducees were of the upper class, and the Pharisees of the solid middle or possibly upper middle class, while the Essenes embodied proletarian protest and alienation.[45] Not so! As Albert Baumgarten has convincingly demonstrated, the Essenes "were not lower class dissidents, shunned by the ruling powers." The Pharisees "were not an alienated and underemployed intelligentsia searching for a place in society." Rather, all three groups were firmly rooted in the "economic, social and educational elite . . . who could afford the 'luxury' of indulgence in affairs of the spirit."[46] In fact, of the three, the Essenes produced the most sophisticated and complex scriptures and commentaries. Here were real differences in religious tastes and convictions, not mere religious masks for material concerns.

Early Christian Sects

Christianity began to fragment within a few years following the Crucifixion. By about the year 180 (when I estimate the entire Christian population to have numbered no more than 100,000), Irenaeus published *Against Heresies*, a five-volume attack on nearly two dozen groups that adhered to "incorrect" doctrines. A few years later Hippolytus issued *The Refutation of All Heresies*, an expanded catalog of heresy listing nearly fifty examples of nonconformity. Of course, some of those listed were not really groups but only heretical writings by a lone author.[47] But of the actual groups, some were based primarily on theological disputes, others involved new revelations, and, of course, social and material factors had some influence on them all. It will be useful to examine an early Christian sect based on theological disagreements with the emerging establishment and then a sect based on new revelations, both of them demanding a return to a more ascetic faith.

Marcion (*ca. 85–160*) founded one of the first important Christian sects.[48] Despite having acquired immense wealth prior to adopting a religious life, Marcion held that salvation is to be gained only through very rigorous asceticism. Not only did the Marcionites stress celibacy and renounce marriage, but they even held procreation in contempt. Therefore, according to Tertullian, the Marcionites offered baptism only to the unmarried who could be expected to be celibate, delaying it until the death-bed for everyone else.[49] This mention of Tertullian serves to remind us that, as with nearly all early Christians who were subsequently classified as heretics, Marcion's writings did not survive, and we know his views only through the attacks on him written by his enemies. Thus despite the fact that Marcion opposed sex even for procreation, Hippolytus claimed he mainly attracted people "of a sensual mode of life, inasmuch as he himself was one of lustful propensities."[50] This soon became a standard tactic in Christian controversial rhetoric.[51] As Paul Johnson explained, "The sects which attracted the largest followings were, as a rule, the most austere and God-fearing; but, being the most successful, they had to be the most bitterly assailed on moral grounds."[52] It was subsequently written of the Arians that their "women were immoral," and that among the Manichaeans, "no chastity whatever is to be found."[53]

The truth was, of course, quite different. Marcion's real "sins" were not those of immorality; they were theological, involving a truly radical challenge to conventional Christianity. In the context of the complicated efforts by second-century Church leaders to meet Jewish criticisms concerning whether Jesus fulfilled prophesies of the Messiah, Marcion's close study of scripture convinced him that the God of the Jews and the Father of Christ are not the same God.[54] Hence Christianity is not related to Judaism at all, and the Old Testament is without validity. So, when he compiled and disseminated his version of a Christian "Bible," Marcion included only the Gospel of Luke and ten letters of Paul. This was an elegant solution to the vexing problem of contradictions between the Old Testament and Christian doctrine and turned out to have great appeal to many Christians without Jewish backgrounds—especially in the East, where eventually the movement blended into Manichaeism. At first, Marcion directed his writings to the Church fathers in Rome, hoping they would see the wisdom of his suggested theological and moral reforms. Instead, Marcion's views aroused their immediate and bitter opposition. Indeed, "materialist" expectations to the contrary, when they dismissed him as a heretic, the Church fathers refunded an enormous endowment that Marcion had donated to the Church. Thereafter, Marcion began a new Christian sect movement—his reformation was externalized.

Montanus (*second century*) was a contemporary of Marcion, but the basis of his very influential sect movement was revelations, not theology.[55] In very early days, Christians believed that the Second Coming was close at hand and would surely take place in the lifetime of many then living. By the second century, however, intense millenarian expectations had been greatly muted, partly because so much time had passed and partly because they were incompatible with the policies of what had become an institutionalized Church, settled in for the long haul. Montanus would have none of this. He claimed revelations from the Holy Spirit told him that the New Jerusalem would ensue in Phrygia—soon! In preparation, Christians must attempt to lead blameless lives, which meant asceticism. The Montanists were known for their frequent fasting—Hippolytus reported "meals of parched food, and repasts of radishes."[56] They also prohibited remarriage and took a very enthusiastic view of martyrdom. Like the Marcionites, the Montanists grew very rapidly for a time, even managing to convert Tertullian, the famous Church father often regarded as the first Christian theologian.

Like most religious movements, including the conventional congregations of the early Church,[57] the Montanists attracted substantially more women than men, and two of them, Priscilla and Maximilla, also had revelations and were second only to Montanus as leaders of the movement.[58] This led to many angry attacks, such as the assertion that "they magnify these wretched women above the apostles,"[59] outrage at a "prophetess" wearing "costly apparel," and claims that it was a "falsehood" to call "Priscilla a virgin."[60] Despite this, the Montanists escaped the charges of rampant sexual immorality, perhaps only because Tertullian's conversion made that quite implausible.

Both the Marcionite and the Montanist movements arose as efforts to restore Christianity to previous levels of "holiness" and served as outlets for those seeking high-intensity religion. Both were labeled heresies and made the targets of considerable antagonism. But neither was suppressed, their opponents lacking the power to do so. Thus both survived for centuries—Montanism finally being persecuted out of existence by Emperor Justinian, late in the sixth century.

Early Islamic Sects

Even now, perhaps the most prevalent Western misconception about Islam is that it is monolithic—one great unified faith. Truth is that Islam is one of "the most fractious of the world's great religions."[61] Indeed, Islamic theology is, to quote Eric Ormsby's felicitous phrase, a "contentious science."[62] For example, by the eleventh century, the Khârijî sect had split into at least twenty additional sects.[63] Even so, as with Judaism and

Christianity, sectarianism does not attract the majority, and there has always been quite as much laxity among Muslims as in the other faiths.

Islamic diversity is not the result of unusual theological tolerance. Rather, the prevailing view in nearly every religious faction has been that all the rest are sinfully wrong. As Ibn Qudama (*1154–1233*) explained, "There is nothing outside of Paradise but hell-fire; there is nothing outside of the truth but error; and there is nothing outside of the Sunna but heretical innovation."[64] Ironically, despite such strong views concerning heresy, Islamic pluralism has stemmed from the unusually close ties between religion and the state. That is, state control has not given one faction the means to suppress the others; instead, the exigencies of governance have usually imposed the need for compromise and political coalition building upon religious factions. Thus although from time to time one Islamic faction has been able to suppress all of the others within a specific political domain, more typically the need for toleration has been imposed by unyielding diversity.[65]

The early years of Islam were marked by the successive eruptions of three major sects: the Khârijî, Shīʿah, and the Sufis. Each subsequently divided and redivided into many additional sects, but it will be adequate to briefly describe the beginnings of the original movements.[66]

A battle over succession to be caliph was the proximate cause of the **Khârijî** movement. In 680 the Caliph Muʿâwiyah died. The succession of his son Yazîd was opposed by Muhammad's grandson, Husayn, with the support of the old families of Medina. When other promises of support were not kept, Husayn and his tiny band were tracked down in the desert near Karbalâ and killed. As many devout Muslims grieved over Husayn's death and grew increasingly upset at what they regarded as the worldliness and impiety of the caliphal state, Yazîd died, leaving no heir. This prompted the Khârijî (the word means rebels) to take arms against the caliphate. Far more was involved than a war of succession, however. The primary motive for rebellion, and the most enduring aspect of the Khârijî movement, was their "puritanism."[67] Contrary to the conventional view that making the profession "There is no God but Allah, and Muhammad is his Prophet" was sufficient to qualify one as a Muslim, the Khârijî demanded that faith be accompanied by righteous living. These views were infused with a militant spirit that regarded the sword as the proper instrument of truth; anyone who disagreed with them was automatically under sentence of death. In the end it was they who died by the sword; the movement was wiped out in a series of conflicts with forces of the caliphate.[68] But the sectarian impulse did not die with them. Indeed, as mentioned, they were the source of many additional sects.

The **Shīʿah** also arose in response to the death of Muhammad's grandson Husayn, and they asserted the divine right of the "Holy Family" (blood relatives of Muhammad) to rule Islam. They quickly developed an esoteric form of millenarianism. Only a true *imām* (exemplary leader) can gain true knowledge of the hidden meanings of the Qur'ān. They believed that there had been twelve *imām*s. The first eleven were known historical figures, but upon the death of the eleventh, the twelfth *imām* was said to be in concealment, where he will remain until the Day of Judgment. Expectations concerning the identity and arrival of the "hidden *imām*" have often produced intense excitement among the Shīʿah and have served to strongly reinforce commitment to more rigorous religious standards. Indeed, the Shīʿah acknowledge an obligation to attempt to convert other Muslims. Often being a minority faith, however, they also advocate the practice of concealing their affiliation in an unreceptive environment. The Shīʿah in turn have given birth to a variety of "extremist sects."[69] One of the earliest were the Ismāʿīlī, known as the Seveners because they reject the line of twelve *imām*s, claiming there have been only seven, the last of whom is hidden. Also rejecting mosques as ostentatious, they meet in houses. Another major sect originating from the Shīʿah are the Druze.

Finally, the **Sufis**. They arose late in the tenth century as a reaction "against the general worldliness that had overtaken the Muslim community" and its stress on "law and theology" rather than on asceticism, morality, and, especially, mystical experiences.[70] The word "sufi" means a wearer of wool, indicative of asceticism, and they became famous for their ecstatic and mystical activities. Many early Sufis lived as celibates, and some became hermits (perhaps inspired by Christian examples). But the movement soon rejected withdrawal from society in favor of efforts to convert others by reminding them of the urgent choice between heaven and hell. As with the Khârijî and the Shīʿah, the Sufis spawned a large family of sects and continue to do so.

Monotheism, Monopoly, and Laxity

So long as the religious situation is free from repression, the process of sect formation will provide an adequate outlet for intense religious demand, as it did among the Jews, early Christians, and Muslims, as well as in pagan societies. However, should this outlet be blocked so that there is no satisfactory option for those seeking intense religious expression, the situation becomes dangerously unstable. Pent-up religious demand will result in periodic direct *external* challenges to the religious establishment by rebellious sects, or prompt challenges from *within* as attempted reformations. To set the stage for examination of these alternatives, we must consider why monotheism leads to monopoly and why monopolies become lax.

I have written at length about why religious intolerance is inherent in monotheism.[71] Those who believe there is only One True God are offended by worship directed toward other Gods. Indeed, intolerance of idols and false Gods is specifically ordained by Jewish, Christian, and Islamic scripture. Even so, *organizational pluralism* is "normal" in each of these great monotheisms—but only so long as no single body has sufficient power to suppress the others.

There were many Judaisms because not even the Pharisees were sufficiently powerful to outlaw all other forms of Judaism. The same was true in early Christianity—the Roman elite could declare Marcionism a heresy, but they could not suppress it. The operative factor here is power. Most (if not all) factions within each faith would have been quite happy to become the only licit religious organization, for just as monotheists know the identity of the One True God, they also know the One True *Way* in which their faith should be practiced. The Essenes regarded the Pharisees and the Sadducees as disgusting sinners, almost as much of an affront to God as were pagan idolaters and unbelievers. To the Sadducees, the Pharisees were tiresome nitpickers, and the Essenes were strange fanatics—better that both be silenced. As for the Pharisees, they shared the Essenes' view of the Sadducees, and the latter's view of the former. *Whenever a group within monotheism gains sufficient power, it will seek to silence all competitors* (other things being equal).

As will be seen, leaders of well-established religious monopolies will often tolerate minor instances of religious nonconformity—individuals and small groups that do not challenge their power and position. But real threats will bring real retribution, at which point tolerance even of nonthreatening nonconformity will be withdrawn as well. For example, once its power was fully consolidated, the Roman Catholic Church ignored many charismatic "heretics" and internal reform movements for many centuries. However, these tolerant policies ceased when serious challenges to Church authority arose following the mass mobilization of intense religious sentiments in support of the Crusades.

These matters await. Here it is sufficient to see that the urge for monopoly lies within all, or nearly all, monotheistic factions. If ever such a faction gains sufficient support from the state, a religious monopoly will be imposed. Indeed, David Hume (*1711–1776*) argued that, because they prevent conflict among disputatious sects, religious monopolies are beneficial to societies, and religious elites have often been able to convince political leaders that this is true.[72] Trouble is, as Hume's friend Adam Smith (*1723–1790*) was quick to point out, religious monopolies inevitably become lazy and lax. That is one reason why they will often tolerate nonthreatening nonconformists. The basis for laxity on the part of monopolists is simply human nature. When there is no need to work hard, most people don't. So when their authority and privilege are guaranteed by the state, clergy will fail "to keep up the fervour of faith and devotion" and will give "themselves up to indolence." Often they will tend to "become men of learning and elegance," meanwhile losing the power to effectively appeal to the people, especially to those who care most about religious matters. Consequently, when challenges arise, a monopoly religion has "no other resource than to call upon the civil magistrate to persecute, destroy, or drive out their adversaries, as disturbers of the peace."[73] Thus, according to Smith, we should expect all religious establishments to resemble the Sadducees as to laxity. Indeed, because of the power and privileges of the higher clergy in religious monopolies, ambitious people will be motivated to seek such positions even when they are quite lacking in piety.

I have written about these matters at great length, and I refer those wishing fuller treatment to these publications.[74] Here my purposes will be best served by the examination of a specific case.

The "Curse" of Constantine

For far too long, historians have accepted the claim that the conversion of Emperor Constantine (*ca. 285–337*) caused the triumph of Christianity. To the contrary, he destroyed its most attractive and dynamic aspects, turning a high-intensity, grassroots movement into an arrogant institution controlled by an elite who often managed to be both brutal and lax.

Constantine did not make Christianity the official religion of the Roman Empire, nor did he ban paganism. That came later. Constantine's "favor" was his decision to divert to the Christians the massive state funding on which the pagan temples had always depended. Overnight, Christianity became "the most-favoured recipient of the near-limitless resources of imperial favour."[75] A faith that had been meeting in humble structures was suddenly housed in magnificent public buildings—the new church of Saint Peter built by Constantine in Rome was modeled on the basilican form used for imperial throne halls. A clergy recruited from the people and modestly sustained by member contributions suddenly gained immense power, status, and wealth as part of the imperial civil service. Bishops "now became grandees on a par with the wealthiest senators in [Rome]."[76] Consequently, in the words of Richard Fletcher, the "privileges and exemptions granted the Christian clergy precipitated a stampede into the priesthood."[77]

As Christian offices became another form of imperial preferment, they were soon filled by sons of the aristocracy. Thus simony became rife—an extensive and very expensive traffic in religious offices developed, involving the sale not only of high offices such as bishoprics but even of lowly parish placements. There soon arose great clerical families, whose sons followed their fathers and grandfathers into holy office. Even the papacy ran in families. To cite but a *few* examples: Pope Innocent I (401 to 417) succeeded his father, Pope Anastasius I (399 to 401); Pope Silverius (536 to 537) was the son of Pope Hormisdas (514 to 523); Pope Gregory I (590 to 604) was the great-grandson of Pope Felix III (526 to 530) and the grandnephew of Pope Agapetus I (535 to 536). Nor was this practice limited to the closing days of the empire. Pope John XI (931 to 935) was the son of Pope Sergius III (904 to 911); Pope Benedict VIII (1012 to 1024) and Pope John XIX (1024 to 1032) were brothers; Pope Benedict IX (1032 to 1044) was the nephew of both his predecessors. Many other popes were the sons, grandsons, nephews, and brothers of bishops and cardinals.[78] The significance of clerical families also shows up in the biographies of medieval saints, nearly 20 percent of whom had an immediate family member who was also a saint.[79]

As early as the Council of Sardica in 341, Church leaders promulgated rules against ordaining men into the priesthood upon their appointment to a bishopric, requiring that bishops have previous service in lower clerical office. These rules were frequently ignored—late in the fourth century Auxentius became bishop of Milan without even having been baptized. Or the rules were circumvented by a candidate's being rushed through ordination and a series of lower clerical ranks in a week or two prior to his becoming a bishop.[80] This did not always result in the elevation of an impious opportunist—Saint Ambrose (*ca. 340–397*) went from baptism, through ordination and the clerical ranks, to his consecration as a bishop, all in eight days! And, of course, despite being in a papal family, Gregory I fully deserved to go down in history as Pope Gregory the Great. But the overall result was a Church that was run by a very worldly, political, luxury-loving, and sometimes notoriously immoral hierarchy.

Constantine's lavish support of Christianity came at the expense of paganism. Unlike Christianity, the pagan temples were top-down rather than bottom-up organizations in that they were constructed and sustained by state funding and by gifts from a few very rich benefactors. Thus while Christianity had done quite well without state support, paganism collapsed rapidly without it.[81] Nevertheless, throughout the fourth century many temples did survive and Christianity coexisted with many other faiths. Had the Church been weaker, and especially had it not gained such a potent role in secular politics, the result might have been a relatively stable pluralism, expanded periodically by the formation of new brands of Christianity.[82] Instead, with the exception of Judaism, all other religions, including all new or less powerful brands of Christianity, were soon suppressed.

At first, Christian attacks on "false" religions were merely condoned by the state; it was Christian activists who did the dirty work. In particular, the rapid growth of monasticism provided local Church officials with ardent gangs to send against their opponents. Thus did the pagan poet Libanus complain to Emperor Theodosius in 390:

> You did not order the temples to be closed, but the men in black [monks] attack the temples with stones, poles and iron crowbars, or even their bare hands and feet. Then the roofs are knocked in and the walls levelled to the ground, the statues are overturned and the altars demolished. The temple priests must suffer in silence or die.[83]

Of course, pagans often responded with force and violence too. In 356 there were riots and street fighting in Alexandria, and a bishop was murdered, while in Syria another bishop was lynched by a pagan mob following the destruction of a temple.[84] However, as their numbers dwindled, pagans were increasingly the victims of Christian terrorism. Then, toward the end of the fourth century, state policies of religious toleration came to an end. Many legal penalties were imposed on religious nonconformity, and the state officially assumed responsibility for their enforcement. Finally, in 407, it was proclaimed that if any pagan images remain, "they shall be torn from their foundations," all pagan altars "shall be destroyed in all places," and any remaining temples and shrines will be confiscated "for public use."[85] This edict was no more than a cleanup measure, as by then paganism had been driven out of public expression—at least within the cities of the empire.

However, pagans were not the only, or even often the primary, enemy. The most serious threat to monopoly power was other Christians. Chief among these were the Donatists.[86]

The Destruction of the Donatists

On February 24, 303, Emperor Diocletian launched one last effort by the Roman state to suppress Christianity. He ordered that throughout the empire, all Christian churches be destroyed, all sacred objects such as communion vessels be confiscated, and all Christian scriptures be handed over and burned. In addition, all Christians were removed from public office, and various limitations were placed on their legal rights. This last persecution was doomed to failure because it assumed that Christianity, like the pagan temples, was a top-down organization that could be destroyed through an attack on its leadership and elite supporters. But for every Church leader who was imprisoned or executed for refusing to comply, there were many ready and willing to step into his place, for Christianity was, in these pre-Constantine days, still very much a bottom-up organization. Nevertheless, although a number of Church leaders were martyred, many others failed to stand firm.

In 305, with the abdication of Diocletian, the persecution ended, never to be resumed. But it left a legacy of bitterness, especially among the Christians of North Africa. At issue was the status of *traditors*[87] among the clergy, men who had not kept the faith but had meekly surrendered their scriptures and sacred vessels when asked to do so. For centuries, accounts of the Donatist movement depended entirely upon Catholic sources, principally Saint Augustine (*354–430*). But, during the past generation, long-neglected Donatist accounts have been made available.[88] These have greatly expanded the meaning of the term *traditors*. In addition to failing to resist, at least some Christian clergy, including some bishops, actively collaborated in the persecution of other Christians, apparently in an effort to gain state preference. Thus, in 304, Mensurius, the Roman Catholic bishop of Carthage, sent thugs to beat and torture members of his flock who were bringing food to their imprisoned Christian friends and relatives.

More determined Christians denounced such collaborators as unfit to hold office and declared that all sacraments performed by these clergy were invalid. This resulted in two factions: those wishing to overlook "weaknesses" during the persecution and those taking a more rigorous view of Christian duty and virtue, who came to be known as rigorists. In 311, when a new bishop of Carthage was appointed to replace Mensurius (who had died), there was an outburst of protest: first of all, because a successor was elected before rigorist bishops could arrive to take part; second, on grounds that the successor had been consecrated by a *traditor* bishop, and hence his consecration was invalid. Subsequently, under the leadership of Donatus (*?–355*), who had eventually succeeded as bishop of Carthage, the protest movement spread across North Africa, gaining particular strength in rural areas and among the Berber peoples of the high plains.

The Donatists were a classic sect. They held that martyrdom, rather than a threat to be feared, was a blessing from God, for "suffering was the way of salvation."[89] Theirs was the One True Church, its essence was purity, and there could be no salvation outside their pure brand of Christianity. Membership was sealed by baptism, but this sacrament was valid only if performed by a holy and pure giver, for one cannot receive faith and grace from someone lacking in faith, and beyond grace. In short, baptisms, weddings, last rites—all of the sacraments of the Church—meant nothing if performed by dissolute and sinful priests. As indicated, the standards for judging the virtue of clergy had expanded far beyond the issues involving the *traditors*. Thus for other Christians to join the True Church they must be rebaptized by a worthy priest. The Catholics in Rome would not hear of such a thing. All sacraments performed by a priest whose ordination was valid (bestowed by a bishop) were also valid regardless of the moral standing of that priest, or, indeed, of the ordaining bishop. That both bishop and priest might be bound for hell was irrelevant. Validity was in the office, not the person. Thus was born a conflict that has divided Christians ever since.

Eventually this dispute was brought before Constantine, and in 316 he decided against the Donatists and in favor of the Church in Rome. Thereupon came a period of mild persecution, but the Donatists endured and even gained strength. Then, in 347 Emperor Constans I was persuaded to exile Donatus and other group leaders to Gaul, where Donatus died. The surviving leaders were able to return in 361 during the brief reign of Julian the Apostate, who cared nothing about internal Christian disputes as he made vigorous, but doomed, efforts to restore paganism. Once having reestablished themselves in North Africa, Donatist leaders rapidly attracted mass support, and for the next thirty years they were the majority Christian group. Then came Saint Augustine (*354–430*).

Having renounced his youthful commitment to the Manichaeans, become a Roman Catholic, and been appointed as bishop of Hippo, Augustine soon came to be known as the "hammer of the Donatists."[90] After several years of debates and polemics, the pounding began in 412. Impelled by Augustine, imperial officials issued severe laws denying the Donatists' civil and religious rights and provided the troops to drive the Donatists from the cities, not without atrocities. Even so, the Donatists never surrendered; they persisted in many towns and rural areas until overwhelmed by Islam in the seventh century.

In my view, the special significance of the Donatist episode is that, led by Augustine, it prompted Church and state to formulate a brutal policy concerning religious dissent. Augustine asserted that all notions of freedom of conscience are heretical, and there is no scope whatsoever for minority opinions. Since the Church is the "true mother of all Christians," it has disciplinary powers to correct disobedience, hence the absolute right to call upon the authorities to act against all forms of religious nonconformity as defined by the Church. "Deviation from orthodoxy" was therefore "an offense punishable by the state," which had a God-given obligation to suppress heretics and schismatics as criminals and rebels.[91]

Shortly after these principles had been applied to the Donatists, Augustine led the way to impose them on the Pelagians, another North African Christian sect. But then, as the fifth century waned, the repression of heresy seemed to fade away. No changes were made in official Church policy, but centuries passed with little or no effort made at enforcement.

Weakness and Toleration

Beginning in the sixth century, and well into the eleventh, there were virtually no actions taken by the Church against heresy. Many historians have interpreted this as reflecting a dearth of heresies—that heresy "virtually ceased to exist" during this era.[92] Not so. There were many heresies, great and small, throughout the period. For example, in 325 the Council of Nicaea had been quick to denounce Arianism as a damnable heresy. Nevertheless, starting early in the fifth century and lasting for the next several hundred years, Arianism prevailed in all of Spain, parts of southern Gaul, and much of Italy. Most popes settled for sending them missionaries. Nor, throughout this era, was much of anything done about the open practice of paganism in huge areas of western Europe. Moreover, by the sixth century Donatism had reasserted its presence in North Africa without opposition. In addition, the entire eastern half of the empire embraced heresies, Monophysitism being a major instance. But rather than march, Rome engaged in centuries of futile efforts at theological compromise. Finally, as will be documented later, small heretical movements formed around various charismatics with new revelations during this era, to say nothing of the chronic, potential schisms that went on within the Church.

It was not a lack of heretics and schismatics but a lack of *power* that accounted for the apparent acquiescence of the Church. Although efforts to sustain religious monopolies seem limited to monotheism, that alone is insufficient, even when one faction has an overwhelming majority. In addition, *the capacity of a religious organization to sustain a monopoly depends upon the degree to which the state uses coercive force on its behalf*. Thus persecution of religious nonconformists necessitates both a theological rationale and sufficient political power.

Popes and bishops seldom had any real temporal power of their own but relied on the state to enforce the Catholic monopoly—Augustine had no troops under his command; they were imperial forces. But now the empire was gone and with it the repressive powers of the Church! Not only was there no longer a prevailing state to root out heresy; Rome had become a provincial city, far from the eastern seat of imperial power and even at a distance from the new capital in Ravenna, ruled by Arian Lombards. Worse yet, most of the rulers who assumed authority over the many fragments of the former empire in the West were not Christians of any variety, let alone supporters of the pope. They were the dreaded "barbarians." Many centuries would be required to convert even most of the barbarian nobility, and it appears that the general barbarian populations were never effectively Christianized. In fact, for a long time wise Church leaders did not even think it feasible to fully oppose popular pagan practices. In a letter dated 601 and preserved by the Venerable Bede,[93] Pope Gregory the Great advised Abbot Mellitus, "[I] have come to the conclusion that the temples of the idols among that people should on no account be destroyed." Instead, the "idols are to be destroyed" and the "the temples themselves . . . aspersed with holy water" and used as Christian shrines. By overlaying pagan festivals and sacred places with Christian interpretations, the Church made it easy to become a Christian—so easy that actual conversion seldom occurred. Instead, in customary pagan fashion, the people treated Christianity as an "add-on religion," and the popular Christianity that eventually emerged in northern and western Europe was a strange amalgam, including a great deal in the way of pagan celebrations and beliefs, some of them superficially Christianized, but many of them not Christianized at all.[94]

In addition to lacking the state support needed to reimpose its militant monopoly, in this era the Church lacked internal unity as well. Deeply rooted in the expanding monasticism, a sectarian reform movement was gathering strength.

The Two "Churches"

Among the most impressive achievements of the Roman Catholic Church are the many times it has very successfully encapsulated the sectarian impulse safely within its institutional structure. Again and again, those most dedicated to a very high-intensity faith were channeled into religious orders, thereby put in service to the Church rather than left to become its opponents.[95] In its wisdom, the Church ignored many variations in doctrine and emphasis sustained in various orders, variations that would have been sharply rebuked among the laity or even ordinary clergy. But if these tactics were invaluable as a means of preventing the eruption of sects, they were also a potent source of challenges to the internal unity of the Church. In fact, the chain of events culminating in the sixteenth-century reformations began more than a thousand years before in monastic movements for Church reform.

In the wake of Constantine's intrusion into the rise of Christianity, there soon developed two quite distinct "Churches." These can usefully be identified as the *Church of Power* and the *Church of Piety.* The former was the main body of the Church as it evolved in response to the immense power and wealth bestowed on the clergy by Constantine. In many ways the Church of Piety arose as a *reaction* to the Church of Power, being made up of those who were still committed to the moral vision of early Christianity. The Church of Piety might have been shunted aside to become an unsuccessful Christian sect but for the fact that it had a solid institutional base in monasticism, which, in turn, was sustained primarily by the nobility and upper classes.

Christian monasticism had its roots in Jewish asceticism and, probably, in the more ascetic pagan priesthoods. Although it first appeared in Egypt, where monastic Christian communities existed by the middle of the third century, the rapid expansion of monasticism across the Mediterranean coincided with the "stampede" of aristocrats into the clergy.[96] By the middle of the fourth century there were many thousands of Christian monks and nuns, most of them living in organized communities. Naturally, those living an ascetic life felt themselves to be spiritually superior to others, as was acknowledged by Catholic doctrine. However, their antagonism toward the regular clergy and, especially, the Church hierarchy had a different basis—it was not merely that these men were not leading ascetic lives, but that so many were leading dissolute lives. This was the issue that would not subside. Again and again during the next thousand years efforts were made by the Church of Piety to reform the Church of Power.

In some ways, Pope Gregory the Great (*540–604*) was an early Protestant. Although from an ecclesiastical family, he was the first monk to ascend the papal throne. And while he faced many problems during his long tenure, his efforts to reform the Church were unceasing. His initial reforms were devoted to monastic life. Early in his reign he was given a copy of Saint Benedict's (*480–547*) Rule and was so impressed by its virtues and common sense that he wrote a biography of Benedict and worked hard, with considerable success, to have his Rule adopted by the proliferating orders. Gregory also wrote a treatise on being a bishop, *Pastoral Care*. In it he stressed that bishops should be men of meditation who steeped themselves in scripture and ruled in the spirit of humility—as "a minister, not a master."[97] It was fully as virtuous and sensible as Benedict's Rule, but while the latter was entirely in keeping with the spirit of the Church of Piety, Gregory's proposals for bishops were dismissed by the Church of Power as objectionable and unrealistic.[98] The same reactions greeted Gregory's efforts to abolish simony (purchase of religious office), while simmering hostility met his appointment of monks to high offices. Thus upon Gregory's death "the Roman clergy's outraged *esprit de corps* and concern for career structure reasserted itself," and the new pope quickly replaced monks with secular clergy.[99]

Following Gregory there were some effective popes who greatly strengthened the political position of the papacy. But even popes who were personally quite pious gave little attention to such reform issues as simony and moral standards of the clergy. Consequently, by the ninth century, it would be kind to describe the moral climate of the Church of

Power as degenerate. Popes were appointed, debauched, and often murdered by the great Roman ecclesiastical families. No instance is more notorious than the "pope-making" activities of Marozia, a promiscuous and domineering daughter of the consul Theophylact. Her mother was the mistress of Pope John X (914 to 928), whom Marozia conspired to have suffocated and replaced by Pope Leo VI (928); she then replaced the latter with Pope Stephen VII (928 to 931). In her youth Marozia was the mistress of Pope Sergius III (904 to 911), who had murdered Pope Leo V (903) to gain the papal throne, and by whom she had an illegitimate son whom she managed to get elected as Pope John XI (931 to 936). But even after the chain of Marozian popes ended, things did not improve. Pope John XII (955 to 965) surpassed even most of his immediate predecessors in immorality. He assembled a harem of young women—"some accused him of converting the Lateran Palace into a brothel."[100] He also consecrated a ten-year-old bishop, had a cardinal castrated, and loudly invoked the pagan Gods when he gambled. Appropriately, it is thought that he either died at the hands of an irate husband or suffered a fatal stroke while in bed with a married woman.[101] During the "long" century between 872 and 1012, a third of all popes died violent deaths.[102] Despite the excesses of John XII, the moral climate of the Church of Power reached its nadir with the ascension of Pope Benedict IX (1032 to 1044). Only in his twenties, and lacking ordination, he succeeded two of his uncles as pope, having been elected following a lavish campaign of bribery. There followed the "spectacle of the Pope carousing and whoring his way around Rome," displaying himself as "unblushingly and arrogantly dissolute."[103] Eventually things got so bad that even the Roman aristocracy could not look the other way, and so they paid him to leave office. Keep in mind that dissolute living was not peculiar to popes or even to the hierarchy in Rome. At all levels, and everywhere, notorious clergy prospered. Indeed, many parish priests kept concubines, came to Church drunk, or didn't show up at all, and otherwise discredited their offices. Not all, of course, but perhaps the majority.[104]

Having been bought off, Benedict was succeeded by Gregory VI (1045 to 1046), who had a reputation for piety and who seemed determined to bring about reforms. The fact that he was from a Jewish family was never an obstacle to his career, and his election was greeted with joy in the monastic communities.[105] Unfortunately, there being no other way at this time, he, too, gained office by paying large bribes. At that point, the Ger-

Simony Repaid. Many popes attempted to end simony (the purchase of religious positions), and it was a major issue raised by a succession of heretics and reformers, culminating in the Protestant list of Catholic abuses. Here is how God dealt with "simonists," as described by Dante in his *Inferno* and illustrated by Gustave Doré. © Chris Hellier/CORBIS.

man King Henry III stepped in, and with him came an era of turbulent efforts to reform the Church.

Having come to Italy, Henry refused to be crowned emperor by a pope who had committed the sin of simony. He called a synod at Sutri in 1046 at which Gregory was deposed. To lead his campaign to reform the Church, Henry appointed his cousin, Bruno, bishop of Toul, as pope in 1049. Taking the name Pope Leo IX (1049 to 1054), he proceeded against the "evils" in the Church. Having called a Church council at Rheims, he demanded that "the bishops and abbots present declare individually whether they had paid any money for their office."[106] In response, some fled and were excommunicated. Many confessed and were pardoned. Next on his agenda was the issue of clerical celibacy: he relentlessly attacked incontinent priests on all appropriate occasions and filled the high administrative posts of the Church with monks. Perhaps an even more radical innovation was Leo's public preaching. Throughout his five years of office he traveled constantly, and everywhere he went he preached "eloquently to huge crowds."[107] Thus were two very crucial precedents established during Leo's reign: the involvement of secular power in matters of Church reform, and appeals to the public concerning spiritual issues.

Leo's campaign for reform was continued by Popes Victor II (1055 to 1057) and Stephen IX (1057 to 1058), followed by Pope Nicholas II (1058 to 1061), who initiated a new, and very dangerous, road to reform. Having assembled a synod at the Lateran in April 1059, Nicholas ordered the laity to *boycott* masses and other sacraments by priests who kept concubines or who had purchased their offices. Donatism was reborn, never again to be fully suppressed.[108]

Nicholas was followed by Alexander II (1061 to 1073), another powerhouse reformer who continued the efforts against simony and on behalf of clerical celibacy, and who also tried to initiate a "crusade" to drive the Muslims from Spain. This effort drew little support from the knighthood of Europe, but it, too, set a very important precedent.

Then came Gregory VII (1073 to 1085), the name taken by the famous activist monk Hildebrand upon his election. He achieved an immense triumph by imposing the authority of the papacy upon the secular state, and then threw it all away by presuming too much. Soon after becoming pope, Gregory began to feud with King Henry IV over the appointment of German bishops. Having been threatened with excommunication, Henry gathered a synod of bishops at Worms; they voted to depose Gregory, charging that he was appealing to "the vulgar crowd" by continuing Leo's call for a boycott against priests who were not celibate or who had gained office through simony. Henry further charged that the pope had "incited subjects to rebel against their prelates," and that he had given "laymen authority over priests"—claims that were essentially true.[109] However, despite their misgivings about Gregory, most of the bishops failed to back Henry. They were reinforced in their loyalty to Rome when the cathedral in Utrecht was struck by lightning, moments after an excommunicate Henry had attended Easter services. Meanwhile, many German princes saw this as an opportunity to gain greater independence, so they backed the pope—just as many of their descendants later backed Luther in similar circumstances. There was nothing else for Henry to do but to surrender, an action that culminated in the famous scene wherein Henry stood barefoot in the snow outside the Alpine castle where Gregory was staying, and begged for the pope's pardon. But in granting it, the pope angered the rebellious German princes, who believed that they had been betrayed. In the subsequent power struggle Gregory once again excommunicated Henry. This time the pope was seen as the offender and support rallied strongly to Henry, who proceeded to appoint a rival claimant to the papal throne. In the end, Rome prevailed, but with an immense loss of prestige.

However, the most significant results of Gregory's papacy were not in the secular and political sphere. They were in his vigorous efforts to shift the balance from the Church of Power to the Church of Piety. His letters were filled with implacable demands for reform. Of one bishop he wrote that he "has openly tolerated in his clergy things altogether repugnant to our commands . . . that those who had women might keep them and those who did not have them might commit the unlawful brazenness of taking them." In others he attacked simony, decreeing that "those who obtain churches by the gift of money must utterly forfeit them." And while not directly advocating the notion that sacraments administered by dissolute clergy are invalid, he demanded that they be prohibited from performing them. In one letter he wrote that priests "persisting in fornication must not celebrate the mass, but are to be driven from the choir." In another he thundered, "Nor may those who are guilty of the crime of fornication celebrate masses or minister at the altar."[110]

Gregory was a monk, as was his successor Pope Victor III (1086 to 1087), who had been abbot of Monte Cassino. Victor was followed by another monk, Pope Urban II (1088 to 1099), who was also succeeded by a monk, Paschal II (1099 to 1118). Of course, this period of monastic ascendancy reached far beyond Rome, as large numbers of cardinals and bishops were appointed from the monastic life. And these dedicated men attempted nothing less than a reformation. Ironically, by doing so, they launched a new age of heretical mass movements. Before examining these developments, we must to back up a bit.

Laxity and Tolerance

Earlier I noted that the Church refrained, during a long period, from taking any significant actions against heresy not for lack of suitable targets but for lack of sufficient power. Here it is appropriate to recognize that another factor was involved: laxity. For centuries before the ascension of Leo IX, the Church was quite lax. Although whenever they had the means to do so, even a lax hierarchy acted to protect their power, they also tended to be quite unconcerned about purely religious matters, as was typically reflected in their disregard for religious standards in their own behavior. Hence a monopoly church can be expected to *tolerate religious nonconformity that presents it with no perceived institutional threat*. An institutional threat involves the *potential reduction or elimination of the power* of a religious group. In keeping with this principle, for many centuries the Church tolerated such nonthreatening nonconformists as Jews and heretical Christians.

Many historians have noted that relations between Christians and Jews from the fifth until the end of the eleventh century were, as the distinguished Robert Chazan put it, "tranquil." He explained that despite the prevalence of anti-Semitic beliefs and practices, the "essential fact remained . . . that Jews were to be permitted to exist within Christian society and to fulfill their religious obligations as Jews."[111] Léon Poliakov, one of the most respected historians of anti-Semitism, also wrote of the "favorable status of Jews" during this era: "Kings, nobles, and bishops granted Jews a broad autonomy: thus they administered their own communities and lived according to their own laws."[112]

In this same era, the Church was also surprisingly tolerant of obvious instances of heresy that it could easily have suppressed. For example, in the eighth century a certain Aldebert attracted large crowds as he traveled in northern France proclaiming himself a saint and distributing his hair and nail clippings to his followers. He was so popular that, after the bishop of Soissons prohibited him from preaching in churches, he set up crosses in the countryside and preached beneath them to large crowds.

As Jeffrey Burton Russell reported, eventually his followers built him churches "so that his support among the population must have been wide and enthusiastic."[113] Part of Aldebert's attraction lay in his reformist views and behavior. He dressed and lived humbly and attacked the authority of the pope. After ignoring him for a long time, the Church condemned his activities at a synod conducted by Saint Boniface in 744. But Aldebert continued his ministry. So the next year a new Church council was held at which Aldebert was officially declared a heretic. But this didn't work either. So another synod was gathered, this time in Rome at the Lateran, and this time Saint Boniface demanded that Aldebert be anathematized and excommunicated, his writings consigned to the flames. But the pope took a far more lenient view, even ruling that Aldebert's writings be placed in the papal archives rather than burned. Nevertheless, Aldebert went right back to his followers. Still, the pope advised moderation and suggested a new council. There is no record that such a council ever met, nor is there any further mention of Aldebert.[114]

Given the size of Aldebert's following, his extreme claims, and his attacks on the Church, what is remarkable is not that the Church responded, but that it delayed so long and then did so little. It strikes me as nearly certain that many less prominent dissidents were ignored to such an extent that they were ignored by historians as well.

A century after Aldebert, historians did record a woman named Theuda who attracted many followers by claiming to have received special revelations from God, including the date of the Second Coming. Her appeal was not limited to the common people, as "some men in holy orders seem to have abandoned their posts to follow her as well."[115] Eventually she, too, stimulated an official response: she was forbidden to preach and may have been whipped. But a few centuries later she surely would have been burned.

The Church paid so little attention to Aldebert and Theuda for so long because they were perceived as not worth the effort required to suppress them. As Malcolm Lambert put it, during this era, "outbreaks of doctrinal dissidence that did occur were treated mildly by the authorities, presumably because they presented no significant challenge to the church."[116]

However, even very lax ecclesiastical establishments can be energized by serious threats to their monopoly. If or when such a *threat arises*, *toleration* even of nonthreatening religious nonconformity will be *withheld* or *withdrawn*. That's precisely what happened at the end of the eleventh century, with the result that violent attacks ensued against Jews, mainly in Germanic areas along the Rhine, at the same time that the "reformation" forces within the Church aroused the public against nonconformists within the clergy. The triggering event was the confrontation with the very significant religious challenge intrinsic to the Crusades.

Crusades and Reform

In 1096 marauding bands of soldiers, gathering to take part in the First Crusade, attacked the Jews in town after town along the Rhine River. In Speyer, the local bishop saved most of the Jews by taking them into his palace. When the bishop of Worms attempted to do likewise, the soldiers broke down his gate and murdered as many as five hundred Jews. The same pattern was repeated the next week in Mainz. The archbishop attempted to protect the Jews but was forced to flee for his life, and another thousand Jews died. Then on to Cologne, where the anti-Semites had been thwarted a few weeks previously when the bishop protected the Jews. This time the bishop had hidden the local Jews in several nearby villages, but they were betrayed, and hundreds were slain. Having learned from this experience, the marauders shifted their attention to smaller communities lacking a resident bishop and were able to kill several thousand Jews without encountering any ecclesiastical opposition. In all, perhaps five thousand Jews were murdered in several months by men who were preparing to march to the Holy Land.[117]

All medieval historians know the Crusades ignited a wave of Jewish massacres, but they have not really asked why. Many seem to assume that this was simply a slight increase in the normal level of anti-Semitic violence and attribute this to "war fever." Those who know that these attacks came at the end of the "tranquil centuries" have shown more curiosity. Thus Robert Chazan understood that the medieval policy of "tolerating Jews was perhaps feasible" in "untroubled times," but that toleration "was apt to disintegrate" during "periods of agitation and stress."[118] But, as I am sure Chazan understood, there had been many periods of agitation and stress during the preceding five centuries: none of these had prompted people to start killing the Jews. Why now?

Because, when a truly significant religious threat arose as Christian Europe initiated war with Islam, toleration even of nonthreatening religious nonconformity was withdrawn. As a French abbot put it, "What is the good of going to the end of the world at great loss of men and money, to fight Saracens, when we permit among us other infidels who are a thousand times more guilty toward Christ than are the Mohammedans?"[119]

During the next several centuries, large European armies marched repeatedly to fight for and to defend the Holy Land against the "enemies of Christ." Moreover, as this immense and long-lasting armed confrontation heated up, in Spain as well as Palestine, *Muslims also began to massacre Jews*. Western historians, especially textbook writers, have given considerable coverage to the fact that in 1492, the very year of Columbus's first voyage, Ferdinand and Isabella forced all Jews to leave Spain within three months, except for those willing to convert to Christianity. Almost without exception these same writers do not report that this merely reimposed the Muslim edict of 1148 that expelled all Jews from Spain, upon penalty of death, unless they embraced Islam. Indeed, twice late in the eleventh century thousands of Jews were massacred in Granada by Muslims, and anti-Semitic massacres soon became chronic in Morocco.

In *One True God*, I examined all of the known instances of lethal attacks on Jews in western Europe (and Islam), beginning with those that were an immediate response to the First Crusade and ending with those that were collateral to the Wars of Religion. The timing and locations of these episodes are consistent with my theory concerning the withdrawal of tolerance.

But it wasn't only the tranquillity of Jewish life that ended suddenly in 1096. Toleration for heresy ended then too. The extraordinary irony is that the initial campaign was against heretics *within* the Church, being the logical culmination of the vigorous efforts by a succession of reformist popes. In fact, this was the first major Christian "reformation."[120]

The Crusades were fought by volunteers. It all began when Pope Urban II, an eloquent monk, addressed a huge gathering in a field outside the French city of Clermont on November 27, 1095. Angered over recent Muslim persecutions of Christian pilgrims to the Holy Land, the pope challenged his rowdy and pugnacious listeners: "If you must have blood, bathe in the blood of the infidels . . . Soldiers of Hell, become soldiers of the living God!" In response, shouts of "*Dieu li volt!*" (God wills it!) began to spread through the crowd. Thereupon the pope raised his crucifix and roared:

> It is Christ himself who comes from the tomb and presents you with this cross . . . Wear it upon your shoulders and your breasts. Let it shine upon your arms and upon your standards. It will be to you the surety of victory or the

> palm of martyrdom. It will increasingly remind you that Christ died for you, and that it is your duty to die for him![121]

At once, the crowd began to cut up cloaks and other pieces of cloth to make crosses and to sew them on their shoulders and chests. Everyone agreed that next spring they would march to Jerusalem. And they did.

But even though thousands heard the pope speak, they were far too few to sustain the First Crusade—not only were more men needed; this was to be a very costly enterprise. Consequently, the pope initiated a preaching campaign. Thousands of preachers spread the pope's message.[122] Appearing in every hamlet, village, and town, they preached the duty to serve or help finance the liberation of the Holy Land. And, as had the pope, they did more: they stressed the *evil of nonbelief*—"bathe in the blood of the infidels," the pope had thundered to the thousands in Clermont. "Kill the unbelievers" and "avenge Christ," echoed those who preached the Crusade all across Christian Europe.[123]

Moreover, these preachers (and those who preached all of the Crusades that were to follow) were not recruited from the worldly and lax clergy who were so typical of the Church in this era, but overwhelming they were intensely pious members of religious orders.[124] And the longer they thundered about the infidel, the more they began to include as infidel *all* who were insufficiently faithful to Christ—including unworthy priests and bishops! Just as some had noted that it made no sense to march all the way to the Holy Land to rid the world of infidels while leaving behind whole communities of Jewish infidels, so, too, the revivalists preaching the Crusades began to denounce infidels within the bosom of the Church. At first, this was not the preaching of some dissenting sect; it was the exhortation of men deeply committed to Catholic orthodoxy. Indeed, the most influential of them had been specifically commissioned by Pope Urban II to preach the Crusade. Robert of Arbissel, Vitalis of Mortain, and Bernard of Tiron had each turned away from successful clerical careers to live as ascetics in the Forest of Craon. At the invitation of the pope, each emerged from seclusion to preach the First Crusade but soon turned most of his attention to denouncing the sins of the clergy in the most graphic fashion. These three, soon joined by a great many others, traveled from place to place for years, preaching against the sins of the clergy more than in support of the Crusades, never being reluctant to name dissolute local clergy. Indeed, the pope had specifically instructed them "to denounce the two great enemies, simony and clerical unchastity.

They did it vigorously, publicly, and with the usual ambivalent consequences."[125] Local clergy, even bishops, made frequent efforts to stop them because, as Marbod of Rennes argued, "revelation of the sins of churchmen to the common people would be 'not to preach but to undermine.' "[126] Despite the anger they aroused among the regular clergy, not only did these three monks survive, but each became a successful founder of a monastic order. Nevertheless, each must have ended his days knowing that he had failed to root out even most of the worst clerical offenders. By then, however, hundreds, perhaps thousands, more were preaching reform—albeit they would soon lose their freedom to do so.

Entirely in keeping with earlier papal proposals to boycott dissolute priests, the reformers began to advocate the old Donatist position that sacraments are of no value if received from unworthy priests. For example, having charged that "many clerics are hypocrites" and that even many monks pray long and loudly only to impress others, Robert of Arbissel explained that "God pays attention not to the words but to the heart of the person who prays."[127] To those committed to following in Christ's footsteps, and to those who gathered to hear them preach, legalisms concerning the validity of sacraments based on office, not character, failed to satisfy. Increasingly people asked, How can one be absolved of sins by an insincere, venal, libertine doomed to hell? Thus Church "reform and heresy were twins."[128]

The transformation of reform into heresy is well illustrated by the careers of Henry the Monk, sometimes known as the Petrobrusian, and Arnold of Brescia.[129] Henry, an ordained priest and monk, appeared in Le Mans in 1116, where he was initially welcomed by the local bishop. Henry preached a message very like that of Robert of Arbissel, attacking dissolute clergy and calling for much greater efforts on behalf of the poor. However, Henry's preaching did far more than stir up local enthusiasm; his message prompted people to turn against the local clergy. The *Gesta pontificum cenomannensium* reported that "his speech . . . turned the people against the clergy with such fury that they refused to sell them anything that they wanted to buy, and treated them like gentiles or publicans. Not content with pulling down their houses and throwing away their belongings, they stoned and pilloried them."[130]

Having been urgently summonsed home, the bishop expelled Henry from the area but had to use force to regain control of the anticlerical uprising. Subsequently, Henry preached with great effect across an area stretching from Bordeaux to Lausanne, and as time passed, he became increasingly radical. Soon he was suggesting that the Church was unnecessary, and that each individual must forge her or his own relationship with God—anticipating Luther by four centuries. Eventually Henry settled in Toulouse, where he seems to have been protected by the civil authorities. In 1145 Pope Eugenius III (1145 to 1153) sent Saint Bernard of Clairvaux and two bishops to Toulouse to preach against Henry. As a result Henry was imprisoned by the bishop of Toulouse. Nothing further is known of his fate.

In contrast, the fate of Arnold of Brescia is well known. Born into the minor nobility, he, too, was a cleric who earned a reputation for eloquence and vehemence as he attacked worldliness and advocated reform. Eventually he was driven from Rome by Pope Innocent II, which merely made him more radical, frustrated that the rhetoric of reform seemed so ineffective. Upon his return to Rome, Arnold's demands that the clergy lead lives of absolute chastity and abject poverty, and his attacks on the sins of the papacy, were so popular that the citizens drove Pope Eugenius III out of the city. With military support, the pope managed to return in 1150 but was again driven out. The election of Pope Hadrian IV (1154 to 1159) doomed Arnold. The new pope used his power of interdict to deny all sacraments to the people of Rome. The Senate gave in and withdrew its support of Arnold, whereupon in 1155 he was "hanged, burned and his ashes thrown in the Tiber."[131]

Thus concluded the era that Giles Constable called the "Reformation of the Twelfth Century." Although it ultimately failed, it had two potent consequences. First, it voided the previous general toleration of Christian nonconformity. Attacks on "sinful" clergy prompted counterattacks on clerical "heretics," since the latter now posed a very serious institutional threat to the official hierarchy. But it was the second consequence that truly changed history, as all this *public agitation* concerning reform, and its *failure* to achieve true reformation, brought forth powerful, dissenting *mass movements*.

Sectarianism Erupts

The optimism that sustained the early reformers, such as Robert of Arbissel, faded rapidly as the Church of Power began to persecute reformers as heretics. This was coincident with the end of the era of monastic popes, which, despite strenuous and consistent reform efforts for more than a century, left the Church not much different from what it had been before the tenure of Pope Leo IX. Lurid papal misbehavior may have been curtailed for a while, but simony remained rampant, as did the moral shortcomings of the local, most visible, clergy. With the ascension of Clement III (1187 to 1191), the Roman nobility were once again in control, and the Church of Power was intact. Indeed, Clement's noble family controlled the papacy for the next several generations. His nephew became Pope Innocent III (1198 to 1216) and launched the brutal suppression of the Cathars. Innocent's nephew, in turn, became Pope Gregory IX (1227 to 1241), and Innocent's grandnephew was Pope Alexander IV (1254 to 1261).

However, the demand for religious intensity and the concomitant concern for purity do not dissipate in the face of failure. If these forces cannot find a suitable outlet within a given religious organization, they will generate new organizations. When this occurs in the context of efforts to impose a religious monopoly, violent conflicts will ensue. And they did.

The Cathars

The Cathars were the first great "heretical" mass movement to erupt as the efforts to reform the Church were thwarted, although they were not the direct outgrowth of the failed reformation.[132] Instead, they began as an external sect movement that, from the start, "offered a direct, headlong challenge to the Catholic Church, which [they] dismissed outright as the Church of Satan."[133] However, the rapid growth of the Cathars can be attributed to the same widespread public discontent with the Church that had given so much impact to the ministries of Arnold and Henry.

The Cathars embraced a nearly symmetrical dualism. There are two Gods, one good, the other evil. The proof of human experience makes it certain that the Good God has no involvement in the material world, as it is tragic, brutal, and wicked. Obviously, the Evil God created and rules over this world, albeit he is a fallen angel and less powerful than the Good God. The Cathars also taught that as the creator of this corrupt world, the God of the Old Testament is the God of Evil, and, having been created from evil by evil, the material world contains absolutely nothing good; as Matt. 7:18 explains, "a corrupt tree [cannot] bring forth good fruit." That meant, of course, that Christ was not of human flesh and blood, as the Good God would hardly have immersed him in a Satanic substance. Rather, Christ was an "angel sent from God with the message of salvation which would release trapped souls from the cycles of the world. His death was therefore not a real death or the Resurrection a real resurrection."[134] To gain salvation, one must reject the evils of this world and establish a proper relationship with the Good God.

Catharism consisted of two degrees of membership. The *perfecti* (perfect) made heroic efforts to renounce the world, which meant no sex, no meat, eggs, or dairy products, no swearing of oaths, and an absolute prohibition on fighting or killing, not just humans, but animals as well. However, the regular members "remained in the world, married, had children and ate meat," and were quite prepared to fight, kill, and die for their faith.[135] The *perfecti* were not priests but merely members advanced in their pursuit of holiness, although only *perfecti* were eligible to be elected to serve as bishops. Having no priests, the Cathars also recognized no sacraments other than baptism, and this they performed without water by the laying on of hands. Of greatest importance was the fundamental doctrine that it was up to each believer to construct a relationship with the Good God through prayer, a thoroughly "Lutheran" doctrine. As will be seen, another similarity with Lutheranism was the support given the Cathars by the local nobility.

No one really knows when the Cathars began. Our earliest knowledge of them comes from Cologne in 1143, where they already had their own local bishop and a significant, if unknown, number of adherents.[136] This information was contained in a letter written in about 1144 to Saint Bernard of Clarvaux by a local prior upon the occasion of Cathars' having been denounced to the archbishop of Cologne.[137] During their hearing, the Cathar bishop and his aide frankly admitted teaching that theirs was the only true church because only they followed the example of Christ and the apostles to embrace holy poverty. Before the archbishop could take any action—and it isn't clear what he would have done—the two Cathar leaders were seized by a mob and burned, enduring "the torment of fire, not only with patience, but with joy and gladness," according to the letter to Saint Bernard. Twenty years later, five more Cathars were denounced by their neighbors in Cologne, convicted of heresy, and burned, as were a group of Cathars who were discovered living in Metz, where they "had apparently existed quietly for some time and even had a burial place of their own."[138] Meanwhile, in 1156 a group of about thirty Cathars were discovered in England, judged heretics by a tribunal of bishops, and ordered by Henry II "to be branded, stripped and whipped out of town."[139]

Although these first historical traces of the Cathars are concentrated in the Rhineland, the center of the Cathar movement was in the Languedoc area of southern France, where they were known as the Albigensians (because their headquarters was in the city of Albi). There, in contrast with the Rhineland and England, they were not at the mercy of either mobs or archbishops because their movement had become a very powerful (even dominant) local religious influence, having attracted many Catholic clergy and perhaps a majority of the local nobility. Indeed, the nobility played a prominent role, not only in founding Cathar monasteries and convents in the Languedoc, but in filling them with dedicated *perfecti*.

There has been a very spirited academic debate as to whether their extreme dualism was a Cathar invention or an import from the East, with roots in the Bogomil movement that arose in Bulgaria in the tenth century. While I admire the scholarship displayed on both sides, I confess that I care less about where these ideas came from than about where they *went*. And they went far and wide across the Languedoc, attracting a very large and dedicated following. It is impossible to say what percentage of those in the Languedoc were actual members, but clearly there was "a strong majority sentiment in favour of the Cathars."[140] Moreover, their appeal was not mainly to peasants and artisans—they greatly overrecruited affluent townspeople, Catholic clergy, and, as mentioned, the nobility.

A major factor in the support given the Cathars by the nobility was the extremely fragmented governance of the region. Just as Luther was sustained by a host of resentful and rebellious German princes of small domains, so, too, the Cathars attracted the nobility of small estate, who abounded in the Languedoc. The proliferation of nobles resulted from the practice, modeled on Charlemagne, of dividing estates among the heirs, rather than giving all to the eldest. By the year 975 there were at least 150 independent noble families in the Languedoc, which is only about the size of Vermont.[141] By the twelfth century this number had greatly increased, and castles dotted the countryside. In addition, the region had many independent, or semi-independent, towns, nearly all of them strongly fortified. Both towns and nobility chafed at paying tithes to the Church, which was regarded as an outside institution, whereas the Cathars condemned the materialism of the Catholic Church and asked for nothing in their own support.

But far more was involved in the attraction of the nobility to Catharism than an opportunity to escape taxes. Many of them rejected their privileges and took up an austere life as *perfecti*. A surviving list indicates that of all who became *perfecti* in the Languedoc during the sixty-year period ending in 1250, 15 percent were members of the nobility,[142] at least seven times the percentage of nobles in the population.[143] Most of the others were probably from affluent families, since it was often noted at the time that there was "widespread support for Catharism . . . among people in authority."[144] This pattern is consistent with many similar examples of the particular attraction that asceticism can hold for people who are born into privilege.

In any event, the widespread support of the nobility for Catharism was revealed in the most unambiguous way when it was time to fight. As a northern prince involved in the "Crusade" against the "Albigensians" complained, "The lords of the Languedoc almost all protected and harboured the heretics, showing them excessive love and defending them against God and Church."[145]

Faced with the major institutional threat posed by the Cathars, the Church responded. First came unsuccessful efforts to derail the Cathars by sending friars to preach against their heresy. When these efforts had no effect, in 1208 Pope Innocent III sought the support of the king of France and other nobles, directing that they "attack the followers of heresy more fearlessly even than Saracens since they are more evil . . . Forward then soldiers of Christ!"[146] In keeping with previous practice, the Church also circulated lurid libels concerning sexual aberrations by Cathars and their supporters, and the pope made use of these in seeking allies "to eliminate such harmful filth."[147] King Philip II of France did not respond to the pope's appeal, but several dukes and counts did, and a series of brutal battles ensued. In July 1209 Béziers fell to the papal forces, and all of its inhabitants were butchered—whether Cathars, Catholics, or Jews. But the Cathars didn't quit, and it wasn't until 1229, or perhaps even later, that the entire region had been secured from Cathar control. Of course, that left many Cathar survivors scattered here and there. To hunt them down, the Papal Inquisition was founded in 1233.

Waldensians

Meanwhile, a major reformist group had sprung up, and it proved to be even more popular and far more durable than the Cathars.[148] The Waldensians were named for a man named Waldo (or Valdes), a very rich merchant of Lyons, a city just north of the Languedoc. In 1176, inspired by hearing the life story of Saint Alexius (an heir to riches who chose poverty), Waldo gave away all his property—he actually threw substantial sums of money away in the streets. Having commissioned translations of scriptures into French so he could discover what the Gospels actually taught, he began to preach a message of apostolic poverty. Waldo rapidly attracted followers, who called themselves the Poor Men of Lyons, and who also "are described as giving up their goods and bestowing them on the poor, a fact which shows they were of some substance."[149] Indeed, at a somewhat later period, a significant number of members of the lesser nobility were among the Waldensians in Metz, and "Waldensians in Germany gained the support of the comparatively wealthy." However, as the persecution became intense, the group became more dependent on smallholders and artisans to fill its ranks.[150]

In the beginning, the Waldensians seem to have had no intention of forming a sect but saw themselves as in league with the reform movement being preached far and wide by those still within the Church. Therefore, in 1179 Waldensian representatives went to Rome to seek papal support. Instead, they aroused considerable apprehension. Walter Map, the English chronicler and gossip, observed: "They go about two by two, barefoot, clad in woolen garments, owning nothing, holding all things in common like the Apostles . . . [I]f we admit them, we shall be driven out."[151] The pope blessed their lifestyle but forbade them to preach. Of course, they didn't obey and subsequently were declared heretics by Pope Lucius III in 1184.

Initial efforts to suppress the Waldensians were hindered by the fact that, although they began in southern France and gained many followers in the Languedoc (especially in the aftermath of the Cathar suppression), their area of greatest success was along the Rhine, at a time of political breakdown and open warfare stemming from a conflict between the pope and the Holy Roman Emperor. In this confused situation, the Waldensians flourished, as the means were lacking to repress heresy. Eventually, of course, the Church and various states were able to mount bloody campaigns against the Waldensians. But although many were killed in battle and many others were executed, these efforts failed—the attacks merely drove the Waldensians into the mountains, especially into the Cottian Alps along what is now the French and Italian border. By taking advantage of very difficult mountain terrain and keeping a low profile, the Waldensians were able to avoid or withstand a series of attacks until finally, after many centuries, religious peace broke out in Europe. As Malcolm

Lambert noted, against overwhelming odds the Waldensians "outlasted all the persecutions . . . [to] link hands with the Protestant Reformation."[152] Indeed, Waldensian churches still exist.

Heresies of the Free Spirit

After the Cathars and Waldensians came wave upon wave of heretical movements. Many of these are grouped under the name "Free Spirit" to identify movements that stressed mysticism and held it possible for one to achieve true mystical union with God. It was charged that this belief was used to justify the heretical notion that, having achieved such a state of union, the individual was now free to ignore moral limits on behavior, being beyond sin. It was this claim that caused these groups to be labeled "free spirit" by their enemies.

Accounts of major "free spirit" groups, all of them written by their accusers, abound in lurid accusations of sexual impropriety, and some historians accept these as true—Gordon Leff argued that there must be "real ground" behind these charges because they were repeated so often.[153] Viewed from a wider perspective, Leff's fallacy is obvious. Charges of sexual impropriety were repeated for so long, about so many different and so many obviously innocent groups and individuals, that they lose all credibility in the absence of compelling, independent evidence. Imputation of orgies, incest, promiscuity, rape, child abuse, bestiality, and sexual acts committed on altars were the standard stuff in Church attacks on its enemies, beginning at least as far back as attacks on Marcion in the second century. Admittedly, there were probably small groups here and there through the centuries who did think of themselves as free of moral restraints and who held orgies, but they are incidental to religious history. In the instances involving the "free spirit" groups, the truth is quite the opposite. As summarized by Robert Lerner in his celebrated study, "Free spirits believed they could attain union with God on earth, but they thought they could only reach this state by means of bodily austerities and spiritual abnegation . . . their heresy was not a medieval anomaly but was closely related to the orthodox mystical movement of the later Middle Ages and grew out of a concern for a life of spiritual perfection."[154]

The late thirteenth and fourteenth centuries saw the rise of many "Free Spirit" groups. Among the more prominent were the closely connected, all-male **Beghards** and the all-female **Beguines**. These two groups appeared toward the end of the thirteenth century, taking the form of unofficial religious orders without religious vows.[155]

The English words "beg" and "beggar" derive from Beghard, and those who were known by that name were wandering, self-proclaimed "holy beggars," who often entered towns in a group shouting, "Bread for God's sake!" They dressed much like orthodox friars, but they had taken no religious vows and were under no Church authority. Indeed, they looked down on conventional monks and friars as soft and worldly, and they sometimes interrupted Church services to air their complaints. As Norman Cohn put it, "They preached much, without authorization but with considerable popular success."[156]

Most of the Beguines seem to have come from well-to-do families.[157] It was not unusual for daughters of the wealthy and the nobility to enter religious orders—most women's orders charged a substantial entry fee, often referred to as a dowry. But the women who entered the Beguines opted to retain greater independence and freedom of choice by embarking upon a religious life without actually taking vows, although they observed many of the same rules as did nuns, including chastity. Some of them were wandering beggars like their male counterparts. Most of them wore habits, and while some lived with their families, they often formed unofficial religious communities—nearly two thousand Beguines formed communities in and around Cologne late in the thirteenth century. It was probably no coincidence that Cologne is also where the Cathars were first discovered a century before. As will be pursued later in this chapter and again in Chapter 3, it was in Cologne and other cities and towns along the Rhine that weak governance facilitated all sorts of nonconformity. Through the centuries many heresies were clustered here, eventuating in Lutheranism and then Calvinism. It was here, too, that most of the fatal and prohibited attacks on Jews took place, and this is also where some of the bloodiest episodes of witch-hunting occurred.

In any event, the Church eventually condemned both the Beguines and the Beghards. In response, some of the Beghards seem to have gone underground, and many of the Beguines are thought to have joined regular orders, mainly the Franciscans and Dominicans.[158] But many Beghards and Beguines endured, others continued to join them, and so they persisted until the sixteenth century, when they blended into the "Protestant Reformation."

The Flagellants

In 1347 the bubonic plague[159] broke out in Sicily and then in several Italian port cities. Within a year it had spread across Europe, reaching England in 1349. By the time it was over in 1350, about a third of the population had died. Pope Clement VI added up reports indicating that 23,840,000 had perished, and modern historians estimate the total at 30 million.[160]

It is difficult to comprehend such a disaster. Everyone lost relatives and friends. Everyone must have wondered whether he or she would be next. Worst of all, no one knew why it was happening. Of course, various "explanations" prospered. One of the earliest and most widely accepted of these was that God was punishing humanity for its sins. Perhaps the "cure" was to be found through penance. Thus in 1348 there rapidly arose a mass movement of flagellation. Tens of thousands of Christians organized themselves in companies and began to travel from town to town, beating themselves and one another as atonement for sins. At first the Church supported the flagellants, and, in hopes of warding off the plague, Pope Clement IV ordered public flagellations in Avignon (where he was in exile from Rome). Although the flagellants did not stem the plague, they did often have rather pronounced moral effects on communities through which they passed, as locals became stricken with guilt: adulterers made public confessions; thieves returned stolen goods.[161]

Soon, however, as with the earlier reformers, the flagellants' concern with sins began to include the sins of the clergy and of the Church hierarchy. Unordained leaders of the movement began to hear confessions, grant absolution, and impose penances, while others seized churches and even stoned priests who resisted them. As Barbara Tuchman explained, "Growing in arrogance, they became overt in antagonism to the Church . . . and [soon] aimed at taking over the Church."[162] In 1349 the pope responded by condemning the flagellants as a heretical sect, whereupon many of its leaders were seized and executed.

These are only a few examples of the many movements that arose because the Church failed to reform, while insisting on its absolute religious monopoly. Beginning with the preaching of the Crusades, Europe experienced incessant outbreaks of high-intensity religious mass movements, not only until Luther's attempted reformation, but well beyond.

Many scholars, perhaps possessed of excessively active sociological imaginations, have claimed that these great heretical movements were not really about doctrines or moral concerns. Instead, they argue, the religious aspects of these movements masked their real basis, which was "class conflict." Friedrich Engels set the example followed by many others when he dismissed the religious aspects of these clashes as "the illusions of that epoch" and claimed that the "interests, requirements, and demands of the various classes were concealed behind a religious screen."[163] Getting down to cases, Engels classified the Albigensians (Cathars) as representing the interests of the town bourgeoisie against the feudal elites of Church and state, while dismissing the Waldensians as a purely "reactionary . . . attempt at stemming the tide of history" by "patriarchal Alpine shepherds against the feudalism advancing upon them."[164] Following Engels, many others have "exposed" the "materialism" behind medieval religious conflicts. Earlier, I reported how H. Richard Niebuhr made this a virtual article of sociological faith. In similar fashion, the prominent Italian historian Antonino de Stefano claimed that "at bottom, the economic argument must have constituted, more than any dogmatic or religious discussions, the principal motive of the preaching of heresy."[165] Even the distinguished Norman Cohn reduced medieval heresies to "the desire of the poor to improve the material conditions of their lives," which "became transfused with phantasies of a new Paradise."[166] It is appropriate that I confess that back when I knew far less history, I, too, expressed similar views.[167] And that's the point. These translations of faith into materialism are counterfactual.

Only the uninformed could conceive of Catharism as being a reaction by townspeople against the feudal elites of Church and state, for it was these elites who made up the backbone of the movement. It is equally absurd to reduce the Waldensians to Alpine shepherds, patriarchal or otherwise. At their peak they were an urban movement, very obviously overrecruited from among people of rank and privilege. And even after they had been driven from the cities into the mountains, the Waldensians "were not rough mountaineers but artisans, merchants, and innkeepers."[168]

Attributing the major medieval religious movements to poor peasants or proletarian townsfolk flies in the face of clear evidence of the substantial overinvolvement of the wealthy and privileged in most, if not all, of them. Moreover, even *if* it could be shown that the majority of followers in these movements were poor peasants, that carries little force when we recognize that nearly *everyone* in medieval Europe was a poor peasant. It is also essential to see that the emphasis placed on the virtues of poverty by so many of these groups was not a rationalization for *being* poor but a call for Christians to embrace "holy poverty" as the means of overcoming worldliness. The stress was on *choosing* poverty—an option not given to the poor—which may account for the special appeal of asceticism to those in a position to choose. It is frequently observed that wealth fails to satisfy many of those born into privilege, and that seems to have been especially so in this era when it was mainly the children of the upper classes who received a substantial amount of religious education (or any education), and whose interests and concerns were thereby aroused. Their instructors and personal confessors were usually selected from the Church of Piety: only they could educate, since local parish clergy were rarely more than semiliterate, if that.[169] Thus it was pious and learned monks who made so many upper-class Europeans very concerned about their salvation, as demonstrated by the immense wealth accumulated by the orders from rich benefactors seeking to avoid hell and to reduce their years of suffering in purgatory. But these efforts by the monks to arouse the upper classes also created receptive and powerful allies for reform.

Mass movements were not the only forces in this era seeking to reform the Church, nor were they the only source of serious challenges to Rome. Sheltered far from the scenes of actual religious conflict, increasing numbers throughout Europe were quietly devoting themselves to reassessing every aspect of Catholic theology. The university had been invented, and nothing was ever quiet again in the intellectual life of Christianity.

Scholarship and Heresy

The university was a Christian invention that evolved from cathedral schools established to train monks and priests.[170] The first[171] two universities appeared in Paris (where both Albertus Magnus and Thomas Aquinas taught) and Bologna, in the middle of the twelfth century. Oxford and Cambridge were founded around 1200, and then came a flood of new institutions during the remainder of the thirteenth century: Toulouse, Orléans, Naples, Salamanca, Seville, Lisbon, Grenoble, Padua, Rome, Perugia, Pisa, Modena, Florence, Prague, Cracow, Vienna, Heidelberg, Cologne, Ofen, Erfurt, Leipzig, and Rostock. There is a widespread misconception that these places were "universities" in name only, being nothing more than three or four teachers and a few dozen students. Not so. Early in the thirteenth century, Paris, Bologna, Oxford, and Toulouse probably enrolled from 1,000 to 1,500 students each—approximately 500 new students enrolled in the University of Paris every year.[172] It is estimated that during the first 150 years of their existence, European universities enrolled approximately 750,000 students—in an era when the population of London was never more than 35,000.[173]

The university was something new under the sun—an institution devoted exclusively to "higher learning." It was not a monastery or place for meditation. Rather, as Marcia L. Colish put it, "The scholastics who created this heady educational environment rapidly outpaced monastic scholars as speculative thinkers."[174] The key word here is "*speculative*." The medieval universities were unlike Chinese academies for training Mandarins or a Zen master's school. They were not primarily concerned with imparting the received wisdom. Rather, just as is the case today, faculty gained fame and invitations to join faculties elsewhere by *innovation*.

The results were entirely predictable: factions formed and reformed; new schools of thought abounded; controversy became the dominant fact of scholarly life.[175] In a world over which One True Church claimed exclusive doctrinal authority, the spirit of free inquiry cultivated in the universities made theology the *revolutionary*[176] discipline. As increasingly large numbers of learned scholars pored over scriptures in search of original insights, inevitably they often reached quite contradictory conclusions, some of which prompted serious religious conflict and dissent. Indeed, some of Europe's most important religious dissenters were university professors: John Wyclif at Oxford, Jan Hus at Prague, Martin Luther at Wittenberg. John Calvin was slated for a faculty appointment at the University of Paris when he disqualified himself by converting to Protestantism.

In this section I will limit discussion to Wyclif and Hus.

Wyclif and the Lollards

Sitting in his rooms at Oxford, John Wyclif (*1328–1384*) launched the Lollards, the first major English heretical movement.[177] He did so without possessing any "powers of personal leadership" or even any interest in "building up a new religious group."[178] Although he was ordained and accepted a parish appointment, Wyclif did not fulfill priestly duties. He used part of his parish income to hire someone else to fulfill the actual parish duties, while Wyclif used the remainder to support himself as an academic at Oxford.[179] Hence his theological views were entirely the product of academia, untempered by any practical experience.

In various ways Wyclif anticipated both Luther and Calvin. With Luther he believed in an unmediated relationship between God and the individual, and therefore that salvation did not require the intercession of the Church. With Calvin, he believed in the salvation of a predestined elect. But his primary emphasis, the one that caused him so much trouble and eventually caused so much trouble for the Church, was that the Church ought to give up its possessions and practice apostolic poverty. Moreover, since individuals must make their own peace with God, it was urgent that Bible truth be taken to them, especially to the poor. Thus he arranged for several translations to be made of the Bible into English—the first being very literal and very difficult to read, the second quite idiomatic and easily understood. Consequently, the Bible became accessible to those lacking Latin educations. In these days before the printing press, actual copies of the Wyclif translation were not abundant, nor were all that many people literate, even in English. Consequently, many Lollards memorized long sections of the Bible and transmitted them orally.

The term "Lollard" was used derisively by opponents of the group and came from the Middle Dutch "lollaert," which means a mutterer or mumbler—"mutterers of prayers" was a blanket designation for European heretical groups such as the Beghards, but came to specifically mean the English followers of Wyclif.[180] Although it is not clear that Wyclif played any direct role in the founding of the Lollards, they were his followers nonetheless, having formed in about 1380 around some of Wyclif's colleagues at Oxford. The group spread rapidly from there, finding particular support among the urban merchants and craftsmen, but also very substantial support among the gentry—including several knights of the royal household.[181] Shannon McSheffrey reported the overrepresentation of genteel women among the early Lollards, and that they often held important positions within the group.[182] Following the failed Lollard rising led by Sir John Oldcastle in 1414, the social position of Lollard recruits may have declined somewhat, but K. B. McFarlane was more of a snob than a historian when he dismissed the Lollards as "bumpkins."[183]

The Lollards attacked the Roman monopoly on ordination as unscriptural, rejected the doctrine of transubstantiation as involving idolatry and necromancy, opposed confession to a priest as unscriptural, denounced and dismissed pilgrimages, indulgences, and special prayers for the dead as unnecessary for salvation. They also denounced rules of celibacy as harmful because they were contrary to human nature, thus prompting fornication—far better that people marry. But one of their most revolutionary demands was that "the vernacular Bible should be freely placed in the hands of the laity, learned and unlearned alike."[184]

Lollard views proved to be extremely popular with the public, and extremely horrifying to the Church. When Henry IV took the throne in 1399, persecutions began. In 1401 came the first English statute providing for the burning of heretics, thus initiating a long string of Lollard martyrdoms. Still, the group held on as a substantial underground, finally to emerge in the 1520s to join with the rapidly growing group of English supporters of Luther, paving the way for the "English Reformation."

Hus and the Bohemian "Reformation"

Meanwhile, another university professor became the center of dissent.[185] Far away in Prague, Jan Hus (*1372–1415*) was greatly influenced by Wyclif's work. Like Wyclif, Hus was ordained and lived from his benefice as a pastor while continuing to teach at the university. Unlike Wyclif, Hus was no absentee but served his congregation faithfully. Indeed, his was a very special congregation, the Bethlehem Chapel, which was founded in 1391 to promote Church reform. Hus soon became a very popular pastor who preached in Czech and who instituted hymn singing by the entire congregation. Many members of the Bohemian nobility were regular attenders, and Queen Sophia made Hus her personal chaplain.

In 1401, the same year that Hus assumed the pulpit at Bethlehem Chapel, Wyclif's theological writings reached Prague. Hus eagerly embraced his positions, especially those concerning the authority of scripture and his judgments that much Church teaching was unscriptural or even antiscriptural. As Hus began to express these views from the pulpit, his popularity grew. Inevitably such radicalism got him in trouble with the local archbishop, and, having been excommunicated, Hus eventually left Prague to be sheltered in southern Bohemia by local nobility. While there he wrote a large number of treatises against various Church teachings and practices. In 1414 he was hailed before a Church council in Constance. Hus was reluctant to attend but did so when King Sigismund of Hungary gave him a safe-conduct. Having convicted him as a "Wycliffite heretic," the council chose to ignore the safe-conduct; on July 6, 1415, Hus was

Hus Betrayed. Although Jan Hus was given a safe-conduct to attend a hearing on his dissent from Church teachings, once he was in their hands, Church officials marched him to the stake, thereby igniting the Bohemian Reformation. © Archivo Iconografico, S.A./CORBIS.

burned at the stake—he prayed in a clear and steady voice until the smoke overcame him.

When the news of Hus's martyrdom reached Prague, it ignited a national revolt. The nobility of Bohemia and Moravia gathered, and five hundred of them signed a document sent to the Council of Constance proclaiming that they would fight to the last man in defense of true Christianity, and that thereafter they would obey only those Church directives as agreed with scripture—judgments concerning such agreement to be made by the faculty of the University of Prague. The council summonsed these nobles to appear before it and defend themselves on charges of heresy. None went. The council ordered the university closed. No one obeyed.

Soon the nobles and the university faculty, led by Queen Sophia, instituted a new form of communion in which the parishioners as well as the priest sipped wine from the chalice. Then, in 1420 the rapidly growing

Hussites issued the *Four Articles of Prague*. These condemned simony, asserted that scripture was the only standard of truth and practice, demanded that congregations should receive wine at communion, and required that all priests, monks, and nuns must practice apostolic poverty. In addition, many Hussites dismissed religious relics, the concept of purgatory, and the worth of masses for the dead. Indeed, most of the important elements of Lutheranism were present a century earlier in the Bohemian "Reformation," as Luther himself acknowledged. In the first of his three famous "Reformation Treatises" published in 1520, Luther noted that he had "not yet found any errors in his [Hus's] writings."[186]

Of course, it wasn't possible simply to institute these changes. Pope Martin V (1417 to 1431) proclaimed a Crusade against the heretics in Prague, and King Sigismund led a large force against them in 1420. But the impassioned Bohemians routed them. Sigismund raised another army and came again, only to have his troops flee in complete disorder when they heard that the Bohemians were near.

Unfortunately, the Hussites were as fully in the grip of monotheistic particularism as were their opponents. Having won their freedom, they turned their arms against all remaining traditional Catholics, looted and destroyed monasteries and convents, massacred monks, and forced everyone to accept the *Four Articles*. Soon their intolerance extended to one another, and brutal civil wars ensued, as did a series of utopian religious experiments, such as the communal episode at Tabor. Eventually hostilities died down, and in 1485 the Catholic and Hussite factions signed the Treaty of Kutna Hora. The result was that when Luther issued his challenges to the Church, there already existed a substantial "Protestant" Church to the east in Bohemia. This was not to last, however, as the Hussites were crushed during the Thirty Years' War—defeated at White Mountain in 1620 by Catholic Habsburg forces—although their tradition survived, embodied in the Bohemian Brethren and the Moravians.

The Lollards and the Hussites clearly demonstrated several critical features of the religious situation in medieval Europe. There was widespread demand, especially among the educated laity, for a more intense faith and agreement that the Church was often an impediment to salvation. As they had to the Cathars, Waldensians, and the various Free Spirit groups before them, large numbers flocked to the Lollards and the Hussites out of their belief that God could be known directly, and that scripture was the only basis for faith and practice. That being the case, scripture must be open to all. And all who claimed religious authority must live up to the standards set by the apostles. Briefly put, among those who cared most about such things, the medieval Church was widely regarded as a spiritual and political burden. Indeed, this popular antagonism had long been recognized by the Church—the first sentence of a bull issued by Pope Boniface VIII (1294 to 1303) read, "All history shows clearly the enmity of the laity towards the clergy."[187]

The Burdens of Late Medieval Catholicism

As the sixteenth century dawned, most sincerely religious Europeans were burdened by the rampant immorality and impiety of the Church. Many others, especially the nobility, also found the Church objectionable for entirely secular reasons. Since these factors played so important a role in what was about to occur, they must be summarized.

Immoral and Indolent Clergy

Many historians identify the period from 1447 through 1521 as the era of "Renaissance popes" and devote a great deal of attention and praise to their massive investments in building and rebuilding the Vatican, adorning it with great art, and thereby serving as the major patrons of Michelangelo, Botticelli, Raphael, and the rest. But these same popes were also among the most dissolute, rapacious, prolific, and notorious men ever to sit in the Chair of Peter.

Pope Pius II (1458 to 1464) wrote erotic poems and plays. He was followed by Paul II (1464 to 1471), the nephew of Pope Eugenius IV (1431 to 1447) and an extraordinarily self-centered, "self-indulgent hedonist."[188] Upon his election he wanted to take the name "Formosus" (Beautiful) to acknowledge his appearance but finally was pursuaded not to.[189] After Paul II came Pope Sixtus IV (1471 to 1484), who spent 100,000 ducats for his coronation tiara (more than $200 million in today's money), began the Sistine Chapel, and left the Church deeply in debt. While in office he made three of his nephews cardinals, giving one of them four bishoprics, which, in addition to several abbeys, brought him an immense income. This nephew died of "excessive living" at age twenty-eight.

Then came Innocent VIII (1484 to 1492), famous for his many illegitimate children, most of whom he managed to marry into various noble

Italian families. Perhaps bottom was reached with the election of Pope Alexander VI (1492 to 1503), a member of the Borgia family, and "the most notorious of all Renaissance popes."[190] He not only flaunted his mistresses and fathered nine illegitimate children by three women, but he was widely believed to have poisoned a number of cardinals to take their property. Moreover, Alexander encouraged local Humanists in their efforts to associate Christianity with paganism, referring to God as "Jupiter Optimus Maximus" and to the Virgin Mary as "Diana."[191] In 1503, while dining with a cardinal, the pope ingested poison apparently meant for his guest and died.[192] After this came Pope Julius II (1503 to 1513), known as *il terribile*. Nephew of Sixtus IV, Julius devoted most of his papacy to warfare, leading his troops up and down Italy while wearing armor made of silver. He was also a lavish spender (he hired Michelangelo to paint the ceiling of the Sistine Chapel) and the doting father of three daughters. Julius was succeeded by Leo X (1513 to 1521), the son of Lorenzo de' Medici. He was ordained at seven and promoted to cardinal at thirteen. He styled himself a Humanist and took a very good-natured view of Erasmus's satires of clerical immorality. It was Leo X who launched the campaign to sell indulgences that provoked Luther to write his Ninety-five Theses. And it was Leo X whose hostile response to Luther's initial concerns caused the "Protestant Reformation."

Leo was followed briefly by Pope Adrian (1522 to 1523), an "accidental" pope and a member of the Church of Piety. He was hated by the hierarchy for his austere lifestyle and offended the curia by acknowledging that the responsibility for Luther's attacks lay with "the papacy itself and the evils it had so long tolerated and encouraged."[193] But "the Curia was determined not to be reformed," and his reign was too brief to matter, as "he died unregretted in 1523, not without the usual suspicion of poison."[194] Thus Luther came forward at a time when "the Papacy . . . stood at the nadir of its reputation."[195] As for Rome itself, in 1490 more than 15 percent of its resident adult females were registered prostitutes, and the Venetian ambassador described it as the "sewer of the world."[196]

Away from Rome things weren't any better. Ludwig Pastor, the distinguished German Roman Catholic historian and the author of a fourteen-volume work on the papacy, noted that "it is a mistake to suppose that the corruption of the clergy was worse in Rome than elsewhere; there is documentary evidence of the immorality of the priests in almost every town in the Italian peninsula."[197] Moreover, just as most of the cardinals and many of the bishops were relatives of popes, the same phenomenon of clerical families and inherited positions held even at the lowest levels. For example, an examination of priests in Iberia revealed that more than 1,700 of those in the archdiocese of Braga alone were the illegitimate sons of priests.[198]

It is important to realize that charges of corruption, irreligiousness, and immorality among the clergy and the religious orders are not the work of Protestant partisans. Loyal Catholics, then and now, brought these charges. Thus in 1335 Pope Benedict XII issued several bulls ordering reforms in various monasteries, in which he enumerated a long list of immoral and irreligious activities, including these: attendance at worship services was irregular and many in attendance left early; many failed to wear their habits; most lived in luxury despite vows of poverty; and chastity was rare.[199] In similar fashion, the bishop of Torcello told the assembled College of Cardinals in 1458 that "[t]he morals of the clergy are corrupt, they have become an offense to the laity."[200] A century later Erasmus charged that "many convents of men and women differ little from public brothels."[201] Or, as the modern Catholic historian Imbert de La Tour summed up, "Read the testimonies of this time . . . what do they say? Always the same facts and the same complaints: the suppression of conventual life, of discipline, or morals . . . Monastic life had disappeared from the nunneries . . . and the great abbeys . . . [transforming] these asylums of prayer into centers of dissipation and disorder."[202]

But it was not only clerical immorality that upset the laity; absenteeism hobbled the Church as well. This was especially common among bishops, some of whom never set foot in their diocese—many simultaneously held several bishoprics. The first time one bishop of Sens was ever in his cathedral was for his own funeral. In the Languedoc early in the sixteenth century, of twenty-two bishops, only five were in residence; the rest were in Rome and had never considered living elsewhere.[203] Absentee bishops did not, of course, fail to accept their very substantial incomes; what they failed to do was spend much, if any, of it on local Church needs. Hence absenteeism was a major conduit through which funds flowed to Rome. Moreover, "absenteeism was rife" at lower levels as well.[204] Many local priests did not live in their parishes and seldom appeared—recall that Wyclif was supported at Oxford by his salary from a parish he did not actually serve. The same was true of most university faculty. In Oxfordshire alone, in 1520 more than 30 percent of the parishes had absent pastors.[205]

Despite all these defects in the Church of Power, one must not forget that the Church of Piety endured. There were thousands of devout priests, monks, and nuns. They were about to play leading roles in the formation and leadership of Protestant movements, and then finally to prevail over the Church of Power by accomplishing the Counter-Reformation.

Property, Privileges, and Exactions

To a very significant extent, corruption, especially in the orders and at the upper clerical levels, stemmed from the extraordinary affluence and privileges of the medieval Church. As an example of conspicuous wealth, when Henry VIII's agents confiscated the shrine of Saint Thomas à Becket at Canterbury, they removed 4,994 ounces of gold, 4,425 ounces of silver-gilt, 5,286 ounces of silver, and twenty-six cartloads of other treasure.[206] Even so, riches such as these were insignificant in the overall scheme of Church wealth.

The Church was by far the richest and largest landowner in Europe. The Diet of Nuremberg claimed in 1522 that the Church owned half of the wealth in Germany. Carlton Hayes, a Catholic historian, calculated that the Church owned only a third of the wealth in Germany and a fifth in France,[207] but the procurator-general of the Paris *Parlement* claimed in 1502 that when local parish holdings were included, the Church owned three-quarters of the wealth in France.[208] The Church held one-third of Italy as part of the Papal States and had huge holdings elsewhere in Italy and especially in Sicily. In Zurich in 1467, Church groups held one-third of the property, and similar proportions belonged to the Church in many other cities.[209]

The Church acquired all of this wealth and land in several ways. First, various monasteries greatly expanded their holdings simply by clearing and draining land to make it productive. Second, and far more important, through the centuries immense amounts of property had been ceded or bequeathed to the Church, especially by nobility seeking to improve their circumstances in the next world. Moreover, since the Church controlled the making and probating of wills, its agents were well placed to maximize these legacies. Finally, the Church simply seized some estates and lands through conquest—several popes, such as Julius II, maintained and used effective armies.

In addition, the Church enjoyed a major cash flow by imposing tithes on everyone from peasants to kings whenever possible. Not content with these regular collections, the Church often sustained major fund-raising drives—sales of indulgences, for example—to finance special undertakings such as the Crusades or the construction of the Sistine Chapel. However, in most places the Church paid no taxes to secular rulers and governments on its properties. This was widely resented, prompting various rulers and municipalities to attempt to impose taxes or to limit Church growth.

An additional burden was clerical privilege vis-à-vis the law. Most of the time, in most places, the Church was able to deny the right of secular courts to proceed against the clergy or members of religious orders. Such people could be tried only in Church courts, even for serious secular crimes including murder. And Church courts were notorious for imposing far more lenient sentences than those that prevailed in secular courts.

Inaccessible Penance

As will be discussed in detail in the section on Lutheranism, the Roman Catholic Church taught that although sins were forgiven if confessed to a priest in the spirit of true contrition, people were still required to do penance (usually defined as good works) to pay for their sins. And since only saints were capable of offsetting their sins with penances in this life, everyone else must anticipate a long period of suffering in *purgatory*, a less severe hell. However, the duration of one's time in purgatory could be reduced in this life by various "works" beneficial to the Church. Among these were pilgrimages to recognized sacred shrines. In 1343 the advertised value of a pilgrimage to the Castle Church in Wittenberg (and making the appropriate donation) was forty days off one's time in purgatory. By 1518 this had inflated to "127,709 years" off.[210] One could also earn time off by participating in official Crusades, or doing other services for the Church. Or one could pay for sacred services such as masses said for one's soul, or prayers by monks or nuns, after death—so much time off per mass or prayer. It was common practice for the wealthy to hire these services—Henry VII of England arranged to have ten thousand masses said for his soul, at sixpence each.[211] One might also shorten the stay in purgatory by making gifts of land or money to the Church. Eventually, the Church began to sell letters of pardon known as indulgences, which either canceled some specific sin (often in advance) or remitted some specific term in purgatory.

The sale of services for the dead and of indulgences yielded immense sums to the Church, much of it finding its way back to Rome. This antagonized kings and princes who saw very substantial local wealth being drained away by a distant, foreign power. It also upset members of the general population, who complained that for lack of means alone they were doomed to centuries of suffering, from which the Church allowed the rich to escape. Little wonder that the idea that salvation comes through faith alone, and that churchly intercession is unnecessary, was popular.

Finally, even dissolute priests generally maintained high standards for assessing sins of the laity. Manuals prepared for use by priests in the confessional directed them to be extremely inquisitive and probing, seeking out even minor sins and pursuing the most lurid details to such an extent that most people became very reluctant to undergo the ordeal, and many (probably most) didn't go to confession, despite the absolute obligation imposed by the Church to do so at least once a year.

These, then, were the burdens that played a crucial role when people began to seek the scriptural basis for the whole structure of Church exactions and intercessions.

Popular Bible Study: Vulgates and Printing

Three things made the university a hotbed of theological controversy. First, at a time when even very few parish clergy could read Latin, all university students and faculty could. Second, when no local churches and very few cathedrals possessed a copy of the Bible, all universities did. Third, many trained at universities did not become ordained or enter holy orders, so they were not under direct ecclesiastical supervision. Suddenly this dangerous mixture expanded and exploded when printing and vulgate Bibles—translations into "vulgar" languages—made it possible for hundreds of thousands of Europeans to study for themselves the meaning of scripture.

Recall that the founder of the Waldensians had the Bible translated into French so he could read it for himself, whereupon he decided that many Church teachings and practices were not in accord with scripture. That's precisely what the Church had always tried to prevent—to maintain a monopoly on scriptural interpretation, it is best to impose a monopoly on access to the scriptures. Consequently, even well-educated clergy did not read the Bible itself but learned of it through handbooks and secondary expositions. Actual study of the scriptures was reserved for specialists—until relatively modern times, even very few popes had ever read from a Bible.

The idea of translating the "holy word" into languages that could be understood by the people was regarded as heretical per se. As Pope Innocent III wrote in 1215, "the secret mysteries of the faith ought not . . . to be explained to all men in all places . . . For such is the depth of divine Scripture, that not only the simple and illiterate but even the prudent and learned are not fully sufficient to try to understand it."[212]

Ironically, the official Catholic Bible was itself a "vulgate," having been translated into Latin from Greek—an undertaking begun by Saint Jerome (*ca. 347–420*) and finished by others. At about this same time Ulfilas produced a Gothic translation—which was then associated with several centuries of heresy among the Visigoths. And that seems to have been where things stood until about the twelfth century, when growing literacy among the wealthy led some to desire access to the Bible. And just as Waldo's reading of a French translation of scripture led to the Waldensians, subsequent translations were also associated with demands for Church reforms and with the formation of heretical movements. Thus Wyclif's real contribution to dissent was to make the Bible available in English—the Lollards knew their scriptures. When threatened by Church officials for his involvement in producing English versions of the Bible, Wyclif defended himself by noting that Anne of Bohemia had commissioned both Czech and German vulgates. As Malcolm Lambert pointed out, for Anne these translations "were expensive devotional toys."[213] But they soon became much more when Jan Hus appeared on the scene.

However, even vulgates did not provide substantial access to scripture. Handwritten copies were always few, which is why some Lollards specialized in memorizing sections of the English Bible. But that soon changed.

In about 1455 Johannes Gutenberg (*1397–1468*) printed the first Bible. It was soon followed by a flood of printed books, many of them Bibles, most of them religious.[214] The invention of printing stimulated a very rapid expansion of literacy in Europe. Suddenly, people had something to read, and in their own language. Where once readers had numbered in the thousands, soon there were tens of thousands of readers, then hundreds of thousands. By 1500 at least 3 percent of Germans, about 400,000 people, could read.[215] To serve this rapidly growing audience, printers opened shops in every sizable town. Soon peddlers traveled the countryside selling books and pamphlets, with the result that huge numbers of Europeans began not only to read the Bible for themselves but to read commentaries and tracts. Sales totals were incredibly high, given the size of the literate populations—between 1517 and 1520, 300,000 copies of Luther's publications calling for Church reform were sold.[216] "For the first time in human history a great reading public judged the validity of revolutionary ideas through a mass-medium which used the vernacular languages together with the arts of the journalist and the cartoonist."[217] Or, as Paul Johnson so aptly put it, "the smell of printer's ink [was] the incense of the Reformation."[218]

Erasmus and Humanism

All discussions of the "Protestant Reformation" as well as the "Renaissance" give considerable attention to the intellectual movement known as *Humanism*. Unfortunately, the term is seldom defined and is used in a variety of somewhat unrelated ways. Sometimes, all that is meant is a movement placing an emphasis on "classical" (i.e., Greco-Roman) arts and culture in the curricula of European universities—this being the origin of the designation of some fields of study as "the Humanities." Sometimes, it means a shift of emphasis in philosophy or theology from the divine to the human, with strong connotations of skepticism. Those in this tradition are often called Renaissance Humanists.[219] Sometimes the term denotes a critical and analytical approach to scripture (whether pious or skeptical), often identified as Biblical Humanism.

The common element in all early forms of Humanism could best be identified as nostalgia. As Preserved Smith (*1880–1941*) explained, "its ideals were in the past, a restoration and not a progress. [Humanism] appealed not to reason, but to the Roman poets; not to nature, but to classic authority . . . its passionate rebellion against the rationalism of Aristotle and Aquinas forces us to consider it an artistic, emotional reaction against reason."[220] Or, as Johan Huizinga (*1872–1945*) expressed it, "All their ideas are permeated with a homesickness for the old, original purity . . . it is always striving for things of the past, a renovation, a restitution, and a restoration."[221] In the case of Renaissance Humanists, the goal was to reinstate classical arts and culture; for the majority of Biblical

Humanists, it was to restore Christianity to its earliest, pristine form, as revealed by the Bible.

In keeping with their desire to return to an earlier form of Christianity, Biblical Humanists attacked as nonbiblical many "encrustations" on the Church, such as veneration of holy relics, fast days, masses for the dead, the cult of saints, and clerical luxuries. In doing so, they paved the way for Protestantism—early in his career Luther thought of himself as a Biblical Humanist. However, some, perhaps most, of the leading Biblical Humanists of the late fifteenth and early sixteenth centuries were probably less than sincere. Their personal faith often seems hollow, their criticisms of the Church and of religion often seem too viciously gleeful, and many of them greatly valued form over content. Thus the Italian Humanist Lorenzo Valla (*1404–1457*) deemed that Saint Thomas Aquinas was an inferior theologian, not only because he stressed logic, but mainly because he wrote what Valla judged to be poor Latin.[222] These aspects of Humanism—snobbery and skepticism—were exemplified by the most famous Humanist of them all, Desiderius Erasmus (*1469–1536*).[223]

There are many reasons why Erasmus became and remains the darling of academic intellectuals. First is his impressive learning. Second, although he favored many reforms in the Church, he "was not fired by a reforming passion or zeal"—emotions that tend to put off the bookish.[224] Instead, his approach was whimsical and humorous, taking the form of scandalous, often quite salacious, parodies about priests, nuns, bishops, and monks. Third, he was a pacifist, a point greatly emphasized by modern writers.[225] Fourth, in contrast with Luther's, his religious views were vague to the point of insincerity. Fifth, he vilified the Scholastics, thus becoming a paragon in the eyes of those, such as Voltaire and Gibbon, who were determined to see Christianity as a cloak of intellectual darkness (see Chapter 2). Finally, he wrote elegant Latin.

The illegitimate son of a priest, Erasmus was born in Rotterdam. His father died when Erasmus was still a boy, and he was sent to school by guardians who also pressured him to enter the Augustinian order at Steyn, which he did reluctantly. He was ordained a priest on April 25, 1492, a hundred days before Columbus set sail, and although he never left Europe, Erasmus may have spent as much time traveling as did Columbus. Known as the "great cosmopolitan," he went to England several times, staying at both Cambridge and Oxford, and he also resided at many European universities, including Louvain, Turin, and Paris. In 1506, after a visit to Rome, Erasmus settled in Bologna and then moved to Venice.

From there, after another visit to England, in 1514 he settled in Basel. That same year his prior wrote recalling him to the monastic life in Steyn. Erasmus was appalled at the prospect. He quickly petitioned Pope Leo X, who considered himself a fellow Humanist, and asked for two dispensations: one to let him live in the world, the other to permit his dressing in nonclerical clothing. Both were granted. Meanwhile, Erasmus took up residence at Louvain. In 1521, he moved back to Basel. After Basel became Protestant, in 1529 Erasmus went to Freiburg. Eventually the Catholic theologians there accused him of being a secret skeptic, so he returned to Basel, where he died, choosing not to receive a priest to give him last rites or hear his confession.

Erasmus was the first "commercial" writer. He wrote books with the intention of earning large sums (Luther refused all royalties), and he succeeded. His first major financial success was *Adagia*, a compendium of more than three thousand proverbs and quotations from classical writers. Today, of course, such works are commonplace and confer little or no prestige upon their authors. But this was the first such book to appear from the printers' shops, and it established Erasmus as the foremost authority on these writers and their works.

However, he earned even larger royalties from his satires directed against the Church, *The Praise of Folly* and the *Colloquies*. The former depicted the clergy, including cardinals and popes, as corrupt, conniving, duplicitous, money-grabbing, sexual predators—all in good humor, of course. The latter brought more of the same. A prostitute admires monks as her best customers. A young woman is warned that if she wishes to keep her virginity, she should avoid the cloister. Undoubtedly, a major part of the book's success was due to the many ribald puns and jokes: a pregnant woman is given the blessing "Heaven grant that this burden that you carry [has] as easy an exit as it had entrance." For a few years *Colloquies* outsold every other book except the Bible. What these huge sales demonstrate is how widespread were cynical attitudes toward the Church among Europe's educated elites, including the clergy! Owen Chadwick put it well when he noted that "Erasmus expressed, and brilliantly," what educated men had been "mumbling" for years, "and educated Europe laughed. Kings and bishops, scholars and merchants, anyone with a claim to be educated, hailed him at first with amusement and then with serious approval . . . [Humanism] and Erasmian critique of the Church went hand in hand, especially among churchmen."[226]

In 1514 there appeared on the stage in Paris a skit entitled *Julius Exclusus*, in which the recently deceased Pope Julius II (he of the warlike ways and the silver armor) appears at the Pearly Gates and is denied entrance by Saint Peter. In the dispute that follows, the pope threatens to excommunicate Peter and brags that his major accomplishment in office was to raise revenues ("I invented new offices and sold them"); subsequently Julius sneers that the papacy amounted to little when Peter was pope as compared with the luxuries and power it now enjoys. The skit was nasty and rather juvenile, which is probably why it was a hit. Erasmus tried to conceal his authorship—"he always cautiously denied the fact; although he was careful to use such terms as to avoid formal denial."[227] Nevertheless, everyone knew it was his. However, despite these "subversive" activities, Erasmus was always careful to stay on the good side of Rome. He wrote only in Latin (including *Julius Exclusus*), which meant his work was accessible only to the well-educated elite—Churchmen were probably the major portion of his readers and admirers.[228] He frequently proclaimed his loyalty to the Church and asserted that his criticisms were only directed to making it better. He also had a gift for flattery. When he published his revised Greek New Testament, although it was riddled with mistakes, one error he did not make was to forget to dedicate it to Pope Leo X, who acknowledged it as one Humanist to another.

In any event, Erasmus did much to create an elite climate of opinion favorable to radical and immediate Church reforms. Of course, when the time for action came, Erasmus was unwilling to make an actual break with Rome. He had become the most famous intellectual in Europe, a correspondent of kings and cardinals—an exalted status he was loath to risk. Had he taken his stand with Luther (whom he initially praised), he and his writings would certainly have been condemned by the Church. As it was, his loyalty was initially celebrated by leading Churchmen as certain proof that Luther and his supporters were ignorant clods. Ironically, as the religious conflict continued to heat up, the Council of Trent did declare Erasmus posthumously a heretic and prohibit his works, taking the view that "Erasmus laid the egg which Luther hatched."[229] Meanwhile, of course, the Protestants condemned him as an insincere coward. It was not until the late nineteenth and early twentieth centuries that Erasmus was fully "rehabilitated" by Humanists who admired his condemnations of religion, both Protestant and Catholic.

Erasmus's unwillingness to back the "Protestant Reformation" was typical of the prominent sixteenth-century Humanists. Nearly all of them had initially hailed Luther but then had quickly run for cover. Self-preservation was only partly to blame. The fact is that they had no real interest in the emerging theological controversies that engaged Luther's attention. They thought them largely irrelevant, being about things they no longer believed in; the Humanists seem to have found Greco-Roman mythology as plausible and interesting as Christianity. Indeed, they saw the theological issues at the heart of Protestantism as of concern only to the superstitious masses. Their own aim seems to have been to limit Church "reforms" to the creation of an insiders' Church-within-the-Church; they were gadflies, not gladiators. Will Durant put it well: Erasmus was "humanism embodied—their cult of the classics and a polished Latin style, their gentlemen's agreement not to break with the Church, and not to disturb the inevitable mythology of the masses, provided the Church winked at the intellectual freedom of the educated classes and permitted an orderly, internal reform of ecclesiastical abuses and absurdities."[230] When Leo X became pope, the Humanists thought their time had come, since he styled himself a Humanist. Consistent with his Medici family background, Leo spent more on gambling than on the needs of the Church.[231] This "trifler" was impressed and amused by the Humanist gadflies—until one of them turned out to be a gladiator.

Luther's "Protestant Reformation"

Now comes Martin Luther and the great Protestant movement that arose during the sixteenth century and replaced Roman Catholicism as the Church in northern Europe. As I pointed out at the start of the chapter, this was not a successful reformation, as it resulted in a new, rather than a reformed, Church. However, the Protestant challenge did finally empower the Church of Piety to reform the Roman Catholic Church, as will be seen.

Although the story of the "Protestant Reformation" in Germany is well known, it will prove useful to emphasize particular aspects pertinent to a subsequent analysis of where and why Protestantism succeeded. Given these intentions, this is in no sense a history of the reformation in Germany. I will not examine the Peasants' Revolt, nor will I discuss the Anabaptists, and I will ignore many of Luther's outstanding colleagues and allies, including Melanchthon. The focus will be on Luther and the Church.[232]

Martin Luther was born in 1483 in Saxony, and in 1501 he enrolled in the University of Erfurt, one of the oldest and best universities in Germany. He received his bachelor's degree in 1502 and his master's in 1505. The next year he entered the Church. Like Erasmus, Luther became an Augustinian monk and then was ordained a priest in 1507. In 1505 he joined the faculty at the University of Wittenberg, where he received his doctorate in 1512, and, with several short breaks caused by his conflict with the Church, he remained at Wittenberg for the rest of his life.

In 1510 Luther was chosen by the vicar-general of the Augustinians in Germany as one of two monks to go to Rome to present an appeal concerning issues involving his order. The journey had historic consequences. Ten years later Ignatius Loyola (*1491–1556*), founder of the Jesuits, was advised not to go to Rome lest his faith be shaken by "its stupendous depravity."[233] Luther received no such advice, and, although moved by the grandeur and history of the city, he was deeply shocked by the open blasphemy and impiety of the clergy, including priests who thought it amusing to recite parodies of the liturgy while celebrating mass. This must not be dismissed as retroactive rationalizing; it was the typical response of devout travelers to Rome. For example, Erasmus reported from his visit to Rome five years before Luther that "with my own ears I heard the most loathsome blasphemies against Christ and His Apostles. Many acquaintances of mine have heard priests of the curia uttering disgusting words so loudly, even during mass, that all around them could hear."[234] And just as Erasmus remained within the Church, so, too, Luther had no thought of leaving even after seeing the worst excesses of the Roman hierarchy. Instead, as had thousands of devout Catholics during many centuries before him, he committed himself to reform.

Over the next few years, Luther was very busy as a preacher and administrator, and while his private devotional life was often stressful, his theology remained within the conventional Augustinian perspective. The "heresies" that eventually formed the basis of Lutheran dissent seem not to have been formulated until the period of intense doctrinal conflict that grew out of his attack on indulgences: the Ninety-five Theses.

The concept of indulgences is a classic instance of theological creativity, as opposed to the mere interpretation of revelations (or scriptures), and the same is true of the concept of purgatory on which indulgences were based. It all began with Saint Augustine, who deduced from passages in Maccabees (12:39–45) and 1 Corinthians (3:11–15) that upon death no one except the occasional saint goes directly to heaven. The condemned go directly to hell, but the remainder go to a slightly less painful form of hell to do penance until they are purged (hence "purgatory") of those sins that had not been offset by good works during their lifetimes. That is, a sin must be offset by sincere contrition, by confession to a priest and receipt of his absolution, and then by a sufficiency of good works. The Church taught that for nearly all people, at death their sins will greatly outweigh their good works, hence the need to suffer the terrible pains of purgatory for hundreds of thousands, perhaps millions of years before they are allowed to enter heaven.

Since time in purgatory was a substitute for good works, it followed that the more good works one accomplished, the shorter one's stay in purgatory, and someone hit upon the idea that good works of benefit to the Church counted more than other varieties. Indeed, the Church soon began to identify such works and assign them values as to time remitted from one's sentence to purgatory. For example, participation in a Crusade was rated as bringing complete remission from purgatory. This was extended to include those who gave the Church an amount sufficient to hire a crusader. As the Crusades petered out, the Church's desire for funds did not; hence it was promulgated that through donations or services to the Church everyone could "earn" an earlier release from the tortures of purgatory. Soon, the Church began to sell signed and sealed certificates of specific indulgences, some specifying a period of remission, others providing dispensations to commit or for having committed various sins. For example, large numbers of people purchased indulgences permitting them to eat prohibited foods on fast days; others bought permissions to keep ill-gotten property.

As time passed, and as the Church's financial ambitions continued to grow, an elaborate indulgence sales network of traveling monks developed. Then, in 1476, Pope Sixtus IV recognized how to greatly expand the market. Seeking funds to pay his many debts and to continue work on the Sistine Chapel, the pope authorized the sale of indulgences to the living that would shorten the suffering of their dead loved ones already in purgatory. As a sales slogan of the day put it, "The moment the money tinkles in the collecting box, a soul flies out of purgatory."[235]

From the start, some members of the Church of Piety such as Peter Abelard had questioned the validity of indulgences, as did Wyclif, Hus, and Erasmus, and the practice of selling indulgences on behalf of the dead had offended Luther for several years before he wrote his famous protest. What prompted Luther to act was a massive sales campaign launched in 1517 to peddle indulgences in Germany to fund the rebuilding of Saint Peter's basilica in Rome (it had also been secretly agreed that half of the funds were to go to the archbishop of Metz to repay the immense debts he had accrued to buy his office, as well as three other bishoprics). Johannes Tetzel (*ca. 1465–1519*), a prominent preacher of indulgences, took charge of the campaign in areas near Wittenberg. Drafts of some of his sermons have survived, and the following passage was typical: "[D]o you not hear the voices of your dead parents and other people, screaming and saying 'Have pity on me, have pity on me . . . We are suffering severe punishments and pain, from which you could rescue us with a few alms, if you would.' "[236] Luther was infuriated by this commercialized fear-mongering.

It is important to know that the Ninety-five Theses was not a general attack on Catholic doctrines or practices but was focused on indulgences. For example, Luther did not question the existence of purgatory (that came later) but only the idea that one may be released through purchase. Moreover, history has falsely interpreted Luther's act of nailing his theses to the door of the Castle Church as an act of defiance; this was the customary method for proposing a theological debate, and this particular church door was routinely used as a "bulletin board" by Wittenberg faculty.[237] Indeed, Luther did not assert that his theses were true, but proposed them as matters to be debated and assessed in the normal academic way. He also sent a copy of the theses along with a very respectful and dignified letter to the archbishop of Mainz.[238]

Although addressed to his fellow theologians and Churchmen, Luther's attack on indulgences spread with incredible rapidity. Luther himself expressed his amazement in a letter to Pope Leo X, written six months after he had nailed up his theses: "It is a mystery to me how my theses . . . were spread to so many places. They were meant exclusively for our academic circle here . . . they were written in such a language that the common people could hardly understand them. They use academic categories."[239] Luther was probably not being entirely candid, since he knew that some of his friends had translated the theses into German (and soon into French, English, and Italian), and that Europe's printers had recognized the document at once as a potential "best-seller"—it was only a modest exaggeration for Margaret Aston to claim that it was "known throughout Germany in a fortnight and throughout Europe in a month."[240] Luther had nailed up his theses on October 31, 1517—the eve of All Saints' Day. By December, at least three different printers in three different cities had produced German translations.[241] During the next several months editions appeared in many other places, including England. From these and subsequent mass communications came massive public sympathy and support.

Probably because Luther's critique became so widely known outside the Latin-reading elite, the response of the Church was angry and swift: Pope Leo X soon ordered him to Rome. Had Luther obeyed, he might well have disappeared into the footnotes of martyrdom. Fortunately for Luther, the German Elector Frederick objected to this summons (he, too, was very opposed to the sale of Roman indulgences in Germany), and it was agreed that Luther would appear instead before Cardinal Cajetan in Augsburg. Arriving on October, 7, 1518, with a safe-conduct from Frederick, Luther discovered that the cardinal had no interest whatever in discussing indulgences. To him, the entire matter concerned a challenge to the pope's authority, so he ordered Luther to retract. When Luther respectfully refused, the enraged cardinal ordered him to remain out of his sight until he was ready to recant everything unconditionally.

Soon rumors reached Luther that the cardinal was planning to violate his safe-conduct (just as had been done with Hus) and send him off to Rome in chains, there to be made an example. Friends helped Luther escape from Augsburg and flee back to Wittenberg, where the faculty rallied to his cause and petitioned Frederick to protect him. Then, after a confrontation between Luther and several theological opponents in Leipzig, in 1520 he wrote and published three famous and defiant tracts that came to be known as the "Reformation Treatises."

Written in magnificently vigorous German, Luther's first tract was *An Open Letter to the Christian Nobility of the German Nation concerning the Reform of the Christian Estate*, of which he wrote to a friend, "I am publishing a book in the German tongue about Christian reform, directed against the pope, in language as violent as if I were addressing Antichrist."[242] In the treatise he urged the secular forces to avert a potential popular uprising by intervening to reform a Church that refused to deal with the many grievances of the German people against Rome. The heart of his appeal was to German nationalism as against papal exploitation: "[W]e have the name, title and insignia of [the Holy Roman] empire, but the pope has its treasures, its authority, its law and its liberty. So the pope gobbles the kernel, and we play with the empty hulls."[243] He continued: "[E]very year more than three hundred thousand gulden find their way from Germany to Rome, quite uselessly and fruitlessly; we get nothing for it but scorn and contempt. And yet we wonder that princes, nobles, cities, endowments, land and people are impoverished!"[244] To end such "extortions," Luther proposed to establish a national church free of Rome and headed by the bishop of Mainz, and to "drive out of German lands the papal legates with their [powers and indulgences], which they sell to us for large sums of money . . . that is sheer knavery."[245] He also called for the reduction of mendicant orders, the abolition of masses for the dead, and the elimination of all "holy days" except Sundays. In addition, he proposed that priests be allowed to marry, and that no one be permitted to take binding monastic vows before the age of thirty. Furthermore, all canon law should be abolished; there should be one set of laws and one set of courts for everyone. Luther also proposed that the German Church be reconciled with the Hussites in Bohemia.

As to violent language: "Hearest thou this, O pope, not most holy, but most sinful? O that God from heaven would soon destroy thy throne and sink it in the abyss of hell! . . . O Christ, my Lord, look down, let the day of thy judgment break, and destroy the devil's nest at Rome."[246] Tens of thousands of copies quickly spread across Germany, arousing tumultuous approval.

The second tract, *The Babylonian Captivity of the Church*, was addressed to German clergy and scholars and was written in Latin. However, German translations were printed almost at once and quickly sold throughout Germany and then the rest of Europe. In it, Luther proposed a complete religious revolution. Beginning by comparing the long captivity of the Jews in Babylon to the thousand-year captivity of Christians under the papacy, Luther condemned doctrines of purgatory and transubstantiation, called for the dissolution of religious orders and the end to vows of celibacy. He ridiculed masses for the dead and indulgences and proclaimed that the Hussites were right: everyone should sip the communion wine, not just the priest. But most of all, he asserted the absolute authority of Holy Scriptures and proclaimed salvation by faith alone.

The third tract was titled *A Treatise on Christian Liberty* and clarified the ethical aspects of salvation by faith. Faith alone makes one a true Christian, and good works follow from faith. Noting the injunction in Matt. 7:20, "By their fruits ye shall know them," Luther offered a characteristic turn of phrase, "The tree bears the fruit, the fruit does not bear the tree."

Confronted with such impassioned heresy, the Church took action. On June 15, 1520, Luther's writings were officially condemned by a papal bull, and copies of his work were burned in Rome. In response, the students at Wittenberg burned tracts attacking Luther, including copies of the bull, and strong public support for Luther continued to spread rapidly.

Although the Church hierarchy in Germany was stunned by Luther's immense popularity, in January 1521, Luther was officially excommunicated by Pope Leo X.

Meanwhile, Luther was called to appear before the Imperial Diet meeting in Worms. Luther's friends did not want him to obey, fearing the worst. But Luther insisted. It was the most important decision of his life and changed the course of Western history. Luther's trip to Worms was not that of an excommunicated monk—"he was attended by a cavalcade of German knights and the streets were . . . thronged."[247] During his hearing, Luther refused to budge, closing with his immortal "Here I stand."

When a rump session of the Diet declared Luther to be an outlaw, his supporters hid him away in the Castle of Wartburg. There he began his German translation of the New Testament from Greek. Then it was back to Wittenberg, where he would soon be married and would direct the immense movement stirred by his writings and example. The nobility continued to protect him, while large numbers of Catholic priests, nuns, and monks flocked to become Lutherans, many to marry, and to staff the new church.

Few subjects are so well plowed as the evolution and intricacies of Luther's theology. But intricate theologies do not animate great social movements. Popular support requires a very clear, very appealing theme, expressible as a "slogan." This is not because the rank and file of social movements are ignorant, but because they are called to action, not to study and reflection. This is in no way to suggest that doctrine was unimportant; it was crucial. However, it was not abstruse theology that animated Luther's popular support, but a clear, simple summation of his views: that salvation is by faith alone, and therefore each individual must seek his or her own relationship with God, independent of churchly intercession, by joining the "priesthood of all believers."

Because the "Reformation" in Germany was led by trained theologians and preserved by the power of the nobility, it is easily overlooked that this was not merely an elite movement. Without the very widespread popular support that rallied almost immediately to the cause, such as the crowds demonstrating in the streets of Worms, both Luther and Lutheranism might well have perished. But, as amply demonstrated again and again by the great popularity of prior reformers and of many heretical movements, the "people" stood ready to support a more intense and accessible Christianity. Luther's call to faith was very welcome, and never before had such a call spread so far, so rapidly.

Mrs. Luther. The first generation of Lutheran clergy were mainly former Catholic priests and monks, most of whom followed Luther's example and married former nuns. Katherine von Bora (1499–1552), shown here in middle age, was the daughter of a German knight and joined the Cistercian order when she was sixteen—her aunt was the abbess. In 1522, Katherine joined a group of nuns who abandoned their cloister and took shelter at Wittenberg. She met Luther there, and they married the next year. © David Lees/CORBIS.

It is important, however, to more clearly identify the "people" who flocked to Luther's banner. They were not the "lower" classes. The peasants and laborers were hardly Christian in much of the area that came to be Protestant Europe, and to the extent that they used religion, their tastes ran to rituals and sacraments that offered quick relief in times of trouble or provided an additional edge when they sought desired outcomes.[248] Indeed, as will be seen in Chapter 3, many people used Church "magic" interchangeably with other forms of magic. No, in addition to the nobility and clergy, the "people" who first rallied to Luther's support were the prosperous, educated, urban laity, at this time a very rapidly growing social category: merchants, bankers, professionals, manufacturers, shopkeepers, students, and the guilds of skilled craftsmen.[249] Of very special importance was the immense appeal of Lutheranism to the printers, a rapidly growing group of "craftsmen intellectuals." From earliest days, Lutherans enjoyed a virtual monopoly of the printing industry.[250] Indeed, A. F. Pollard reported that "it was only with great difficulty that printers could be induced to publish works in defence of the Catholic Church."[251]

Nevertheless, there was nothing really new about Lutheranism. All of the major theological points had been expressed again and again over the centuries by reformers from the Church of Piety and by many dissident sects. Indeed, the very prominent French Humanist Jacques Lefèvre d'Etaples (*1450–1536*) anticipated by several years Luther's claim that salvation is through faith alone. Meanwhile in Basel in 1508, Thomas Wyttenbach (*1472–1526*) was instructing the young Ulrich Zwingli that the mass, indulgences, and clerical celibacy were unscriptural. Subsequently, Zwingli anticipated Luther's call for a religion based entirely on scripture and his claim that the papacy is itself unwarranted by scripture. As with scores of previous challenges to the Church of Power, Lutheranism was led by a member of the Catholic clergy who attracted many other clergy and members of religious orders to his cause. As with the Lollards and the Hussites, Lutheranism was a product of the universities. Just as the nobility had often backed religious opposition to Rome, so, too, they sustained Lutheranism; just as the informed public had rallied to many previous proponents and movements offering a direct path to salvation, they rallied to Luther. Finally, as with all previous efforts at reformation, once again the Church of Power prevailed as Luther and his supporters were externalized.

Yet there *was* something unique about Lutheranism: Martin Luther. Despite their many virtues, all previous reformers and sect leaders seem ordinary when compared with Luther, with his astonishing intellect, his magnificent prose style, his musical talent, his incredible energy, his surprising tenderness,[252] and, perhaps above all, what he might well have agreed to call his absolute pigheadedness. There he stood.

The English Reformation

Depending on one's point of view, the English either did achieve a true reformation or they merely institutionalized a heretical sect movement. I incline to the view that, although limited in area, this was a reformation.

When it was over, essentially the same Church continued, but with somewhat renewed fervor. Indeed, Henry VIII (*1491–1547*) had no intention of starting a new Church but merely meant to separate English Catholicism from Rome (to this day the Anglican Church has a legitimate claim to apostolic succession). Consequently, following the break, most of the original Roman Catholic clergy ministered to the people from the same churches and chapels. Granted that services were now in English rather than Latin, but the same sacraments were provided. As for renewed standards, for at least a brief period the moral tone of the English Church was elevated significantly. Because key features of the English Reformation will be pertinent to later analysis of the spread of Protestantism, I will summarize them briefly.[253]

The Lollards provided the opening chapter of the English Reformation. And although suppressed, they sustained an active underground that embraced Lutheranism when it first arrived in England. As A. G. Dickens explained, the importance of this "native English heresy" was that it created "popular reception-areas for the newly imported Lutheranism." Thus "the early English Protestants of the 1520s and 1530s were Lutherans."[254] The primary route of Lutheranism into England was through a group of exiled English dissenters in Antwerp, led by William Tyndale (*1494–1536*), who had met with Luther in 1524 and whose English translation of the Bible became the basis of the King James Version. Among the other leading exiles were Simon Fish, William Roye, and Jerome Barlow, all of them busy writing tracts and books expressing Protestant views, all of which found eager readers in England.[255] The exiles lived in the "English House" maintained in Antwerp by English merchants and afforded legal immunity by the local authorities. (Sadly, in 1535 Tyndale was lured beyond the boundaries of English House, seized by Catholic agents, tried as a heretic, and strangled, and his body was burned.)

The close ties between the English Reformation and the Continent are evident in the remarkable *Biographical Register of Early English Protestants c.1525–1558*.[256] This register makes it possible to locate geographically more than two thousand early Protestants. More than 70 percent of them came from a "crescent of coastal counties" with a "westward extension up the Thames" to London, "the region most closely in touch with the exiled propagandists led by Tyndale, and also with the continental world of Erasmus."[257] It is of note that this was also the wealthiest and best-educated area of England. This is no surprise since, as in Germany, the popular support for Protestantism came not from the "lower" classes, but from the literate and affluent laity—the gentry, professionals, bankers, the emerging industrialists, and merchants, especially those engaged in trade with the Continent. In 1530 Bishop Nix of Norwich complained that "such as keepeth and readeth" heretical books are "merchants . . . that hath their abiding not far from the sea."[258] Bishop Nix could as well have included the upper classes in general, as anticlerical, antipapal sentiments had "put down roots throughout the dominant classes."[259]

While the English Parliament had considerable power in the sixteenth century, the Crown was still dominant. In this instance Crown and Parliament combined to initiate the "English Reformation," although their motives and eventual aims seem to have been rather different. Many members of the House of Commons legislated against Rome out of Protestant sentiments, while Henry, having no sympathy at all for Protestant religious views, aimed merely to nationalize the Church; hence the many Protestant sympathizers in the House did not make their motivations obvious. Consequently, the Parliament that gathered in November 1529 went down in history not as the "Protestant Parliament" but as the "Reformation Parliament." First came a series of statutes curtailing ecclesiastical privileges such as the clergy's right to probate all wills and their imposition of death taxes, and prohibiting them from holding more than one benefice at a time. To the last of these measures, Parliament attached a clause denying the pope's power to authorize anything "contrary to the present Act." Next came legislation requiring that when accused of a felony, all clerics under the rank of subdeacon must be tried in a civil, not an ecclesiastical, court; that "annates" (the first year's revenue from a benefice) should no longer be paid to the pope; that no money raised by the sale of dispensations, indulgences, and other such services should be sent to Rome. In February 1533, Parliament enacted a "Statute of Appeals" directing that all litigation that had previously been referred to Rome for judgment would henceforth come under the jurisdiction of "spiritual and temporal courts within the Realm, without regard to any . . . foreign [authority]."[260] On January 15, 1534, Parliament declared that the appointment of all bishops was a royal, not a papal, prerogative, and removed trials for heresy from clerical to civil courts. On November 11, 1534, came the final step, the Statute of Supremacy. It recognized the king as head of the Anglican Church (*Ecclesia Anglicana*) with full powers over creed, heresy, morals, organizations, and reform.

Bloodshed followed immediately. Three Carthusian priors who expressed their unwillingness to acknowledge any unordained person as head of the Church were seized, and, along with another priest and a friar, they were executed in the most hideous manner. The king's wrath also fell on a variety of clergy across the land, especially on mystics such as George Lazanby. When the pope appointed Bishop John Fisher a cardinal, Henry had him seized and demanded he sign an oath recognizing the king as head of the English Church. When Fisher refused, Henry had his severed head hung from the tower of a bridge and joked about sending it to Rome to get its cardinal's hat.[261] Soon after that, Sir Thomas More's head was hung from the bridge too; this was followed by the closing and looting of the convents and monasteries, yielding huge sums to the Crown.

In 1536 came a Roman Catholic insurrection in the north of England known as the "Pilgrimage of Grace." Led by prominent members of the nobility, several thousand men gathered in Lincolnshire to protest the suppression of the monasteries and the abolition of papal authority. They dispersed when ordered by the king to do so. But the movement spread until at least thirty-five thousand men assembled at Doncaster. They dispersed upon the promise that they would be granted a general pardon, and that a Parliament would be assembled. However, several months later a new uprising took place at Beverley. Although the leaders of the movement had no part in bringing this about and tried to prevent it, they were seized and executed. Thereupon the Crown launched a wave of terror in the northern counties, and many people were hanged on the slightest suspicion of dissidence.[262]

Nor were Protestants exempt from persecution. Henry remained an orthodox Catholic except on matters concerning papal authority, and his agents continued to prosecute heresy charges against outspoken Protestants, sending some of them to the stake. It was not until Henry was succeeded by Edward VI (*1537–1553*) that the Anglican Church became truly Protestant. But upon young Edward's death, Queen Mary I (*1516–1568*) attempted to return the English Church to Rome. Although Protestant polemicists have successfully identified her as "Bloody Mary," it must be said that her efforts spilled substantially less Protestant blood than those of Henry VIII and Edward VI had Catholic blood—in fact, Henry VIII may have shed as much or more Protestant blood than did Mary.[263] Then, with the ascension of Elizabeth I (*1533–1603*) to the throne, the Church was returned to Protestantism. This resulted in considerably more Catholic deaths than the number of Protestants killed during Mary's reign—even without counting the many monks murdered by Elizabethan troops in Ireland. Had the Armada succeeded, our history books might well refer to Elizabeth as "Bloody Bess."

Henry VIII's desire for a divorce was no more than a secondary cause of the English Reformation. Even if we ignore the great popular appeal of Protestant reforms, conflict between the Church and the English Crown had been intensifying for many years. Thus at his coronation in 1509 Henry had refused to swear an oath in support of the "Holy Church" but instead vowed to support the "Holy Church of England." The primary issues were Church wealth and continuing exactions, and papal authority. A. G. Dickens demonstrated that claims concerning the amount of money sent to Rome from English sources has been greatly exaggerated, and that, in fact, following the break with Rome, the Crown took more from English Church income than had ever gone to the pope.[264] But Dickens failed to acknowledge two important factors. First, that nearly all of the Church money sent to Henry VIII's treasury remained within the English economy, unlike money sent to Rome. Second, exaggerated claims about papal exactions were almost universally believed in England at the time of the Reformation, by bishops and the nobility, as well as the public. Indeed, all by himself, through his "enormous wealth and splendid ostentation" and his brutal exercise of Roman authority, Cardinal Wolsey (*1473–1530*) lent dramatic confirmation to antipapal sentiments.

Nevertheless, the English Reformation might very well have been delayed had the pope not thwarted Henry's desires for a divorce. The fact was that the king's petition was well founded in precedent: the pope routinely granted divorces on very flimsy grounds—including one to Henry's sister Queen Margaret of Scotland and another to his brother-in-law the duke of Suffolk. In Henry's case, however, the pope was not free to act because Charles V, the Holy Roman Emperor, held firm military control over Rome and was the nephew of Catherine of Aragon, the wife Henry was seeking to divorce. Charles V had no particular regard for his aunt, but being very sensitive about not having grown up in Spain (although it was his largest kingdom), he was concerned to accommodate Spanish pride in their royal family, certain to be inflamed if the daughter of Ferdinand and Isabella were to be dumped by some mere Englishman. Much history has been made from even more trivial matters.

Elizabeth I's restoration of Protestantism was far from the end of the English Reformation—indeed, it was soon followed by Cromwell's brief but very vigorous reformation of the Anglican Church. However, in this study my interest is largely limited to the brute facts of how and whether a particular place turned Protestant, not in its subsequent religious history.

Swiss Protestantism

The battle to establish Swiss Protestantism was essentially finished before John Calvin even arrived in Switzerland (December 1534). Calvin's major contribution to the spread of Protestantism was to have launched a movement able to attract several million followers outside Switzerland, in France, the Low Countries, and the Rhineland. To see how some parts of Switzerland became Protestant, we must begin with Zwingli.

Zwingli

It was Ulrich Zwingli (*1484–1531*) who gave leadership to the widespread Protestant enthusiasm among the citizens of Zurich and several other Swiss cities.[265] Zwingli was ordained in 1506, and his relatives bought him a parish. From the start he was an enthusiastic admirer of Erasmus and shared his concerns about Church reform. This did not extend to the issue of celibacy, however: Zwingli had a series of affairs with women of the parish and finally acquired a live-in mistress whom he secretly married while still a Roman Catholic priest. Although aspects of his preaching were "Lutheran" before Luther had first been heard from, he responded immediately to the Ninety-five Theses and began to attack indulgences. In fact he persuaded nearby Benedictine monks to remove a sign from their shrine to the Virgin that promised full remission of sins. Reports of these and other efforts reached Zurich, and he was invited to fill a "preachership" (*Prädikaturen*) at a large church in the city. Preacherships were endowed positions meant to satisfy the rapidly growing desire on the part of the educated laity for *sermons* rather than merely a mass—those holding a preachership were often called "people's priests." Preacherships were very prevalent in Germany, especially in the Free Imperial Cities, and in those parts of Switzerland that eventually became Protestant. In fact, a clear link has been demonstrated between the existence of preacherships and the success of Protestantism—holders of preacherships often provided the initial inspiration and leadership for the local Protestant movements. Such was the case in Zurich, as Zwingli began to attract large crowds to hear him proclaim the full Protestant agenda. By 1523 Zurich was officially Protestant, and the next year Zwingli publicly married (or remarried) his mistress Anna Reinhard.

Zwingli was not a proponent of religious tolerance. Under his leadership, Zurich soon outlawed the saying of mass, prohibited citizens from eating fish on Friday, ordered that saints' days no longer be observed, closed monasteries and convents, urged monks and nuns to marry, and prohibited known Catholics from holding public office. As the Protestant movement began to spread from Zurich to other Swiss cities, a group of five Swiss cantons formed a Catholic League to oppose them. When a Protestant missionary from Zurich was burned at the stake in Schwyz, Zwingli led the Zurich Council to declare war. As the opposing forces neared one another at Kappel, negotiations broke out. No battle was fought. The settlement favored the Protestants, as the decision concerning the religious affiliation of a place was to be determined by popular vote. Zwingli was not satisfied, because it did not provide for the freedom of Protestants to preach in Catholic areas (although he was opposed to allowing Catholics a free hand in Protestant areas). Two years later Zwingli forced a war over this issue. In the event, Zwingli marched as chaplain with the Zurich forces of about 1,500 Protestant troops to engage 8,000 Catholics. No miracle took place. Along with more than 500 Zurich troops, Zwingli was killed during the battle—his body was quartered and burned on a manure pile. Protestantism survived in Switzerland because Zwingli's successors had better military sense and were somewhat more flexible concerning religious freedom.

Ultimately, of the fourteen Swiss cantons, five turned Protestant, seven remained Catholic, and two split into Protestant and Catholic areas.[266] Of the six Free Imperial Swiss cities, five[267] embraced Protestantism, and only Freiburg did not. If Geneva and Lucerne are added to create a list of the eight principal cities of Switzerland in this era, six of them turned Protestant, and Lucerne joined Freiburg as the only Catholic cities. I shall return to these patterns in a later section on governance and Protestant success.

Calvin

John Calvin (*1509–1564*) was not only one of the greatest and most prolific Christian theologians and a superb preacher; he was a master strategist of subversive activities, having trained and directed an international network of "secret" missionary-agents who very successfully built a massive "Reformed" underground.[268] Although this is the part of Calvin's career that is central to the concerns of this chapter, it will be useful to briefly place these activities in the context of his biography.[269]

Calvin was born in Picardy, and from childhood he was destined for a clerical career. Hence at age fourteen he was sent to the University of Paris, where two future saints, Francis Xavier (*1506–1552*) and Ignatius Loyola (*1491–1556*), were among his fellow students. Having earned his master's degree, he then went to the University of Orléans to study law. In 1531 Calvin returned to the University of Paris, where he wrote his first book, a study of the Roman Stoic philosopher Seneca. The book appeared in 1532 and was a fitting achievement for a brilliant young Humanist. However, unlike most of the other Humanists with whom he was in contact, including the celebrated Jacques Lefèvre d'Etaples, Calvin converted to Protestantism and thus found it necessary to leave Paris in 1534. He settled in Basel, Switzerland—a bustling Protestant center. There he produced the first edition of his *Institutes of the Christian Religion*—the masterpiece he would revise for the rest of his life. Even before the first edition of the *Institutes* was published, Calvin went to Italy, where he associated with Protestant refugees who had taken shelter at the court of the duchess of Ferrara (daughter of a former king of France). He returned to Basel briefly, then went to France, where he met with sympathetic local intellectuals in Poitiers; finally, in the fall of 1536, while en route to Strassburg, he stopped at Geneva.

Not long before Calvin arrived, Geneva had officially turned Protestant, the elected city council having deposed the prince-bishop. When the prince-bishop appealed to Savoy for help in reestablishing his rule, the town fathers of Geneva called upon Bern, whose ranks of Swiss pikemen sustained Genevan Protestantism. Calvin rapidly gained popularity in Geneva as a preacher. However, when he and Guillaume Farel, who had been a leading agitator during the Protestant ascendancy, began to propose moral legislation, a newly elected city council gave them three days to leave town. Calvin went to Strassburg, where he spent three years ministering to refugee French Protestants—an experience that was crucial to his eventual career as head of the Reformed "underground." Meanwhile, Geneva fell into political and religious chaos and faced renewed pressure to return to Roman Catholicism. The city appealed to Calvin to return from Strassburg and to help provide them with effective leadership. So in 1541 a newly wed Calvin returned in triumph—and his moral ordinances were soon adopted and enforced. He remained in Geneva for the rest of his life.

It is well known that, following in the wake of Lutheranism, Calvinism soon became the primary basis for popular conversions to Protestantism. As will be seen, in many places Lutheranism was from early days a "state church," in that it was adopted by kings and princes as the new, official faith with little regard for what the "people" may have preferred. It was Calvin's "Reformed" brand of Protestantism that rapidly gained several million individual French, Dutch, and German adherents, and a significant number in Italy as well. These converts were not produced by royal edict but were the result of personal enthusiasm, usually in defiance of the state.

A great deal of learned and sophisticated attention has been devoted to the particular theological basis for the greater popular appeal of Calvinism. But even though Calvin was a profound theologian and an exceptionally clear writer, it is unlikely that the theological appeal attributed to his work could explain the conversion of more than one in a hundred of those who became Calvinists. As I noted about the appeal of Lutheranism, at the level of the rank and file, social movements must rely on "slogans." Granted that to be effective, slogans must appeal to individual concerns, thereby creating a climate of opinion favorable to a movement. But to transform favorable sentiments into activities requires face-to-face recruitment. That's how Calvinism really outdid Lutheranism. Not by more effective theology, but by more effective action—by creating huge underground religious networks of individual converts who brought in their friends, relatives, and neighbors, under the guidance of professional, missionary *secret agents.* Consequently, I shall ignore Calvin's remarkable theology and his notable civic career in Geneva, and turn to his underground activities on behalf of the spread of Protestantism. Frankly, I can't understand why Calvin's remarkable career running missionary-agents has been so completely ignored by historians, especially given that Robert M. Kingdon's superb account has been available for nearly fifty years. But virtually no trace of this aspect of Calvin's career or of its immense impact on the success of Reformed Protestantism can be found in the standard works.[270]

It was during his visit to Poitiers that Calvin got his first experience with secret evangelism. Not only did he proselytize in homes, but he held secret services in "a spacious cave near the city."[271] Once reestablished in Geneva, Calvin recognized that he had access to large numbers of men well suited to serve as secret Protestant missionaries behind Catholic lines. They abounded in the constant stream of Protestant refugees (including Calvin) who arrived in Geneva and other Swiss cities from Catholic-controlled territories, especially from France and the Low Countries. At one point there were at least six thousand refugees in the city in addition to the thirteen thousand native Genevans.[272] What Calvin did was select talented and reliable refugees, ordain them and train them not only theologically but also in what modern intelligence agencies call "tradecraft," and send them home to build the Calvinist movement. Responsibility for this operation was vested in the Geneva Company of Pastors.

Training for underground Calvinist missionary-agents stressed the need for secrecy. An important training document was a critical report, detailing the activities of Waldensian preachers (now officially aligned with Calvinism) in Piedmont and Dauphiné, sent back by the first two Calvinist agents dispatched to France. It noted, "[T]hey commonly have the foolish fantasy that it is better to go into the country and preach the Gospel in public, than in secret. We have remonstrated about . . . the great danger that they place not only [on] us but themselves . . . [we reminded them of] the examples of nocturnal assemblies of the primitive church."[273] The Genevan agents were able to convince the Waldensians that armed guards must accompany pastors on their nocturnal trips. They also instituted an individual oath in all Calvinist congregations never to reveal the identities of any fellow Protestants. As for physical security arrangements, services were to be held at night in private homes (or barns for larger groups), the meeting room being heavily curtained, and identities carefully checked at the door. In addition, the missionary-agents used assumed names and often disguised their appearance; elaborate hiding places and escape routes were prepared for their use. Missionary-agents were also instructed in the use of bribes and threats to influence local bailiffs to ignore their activities or to let them out of jail should they be arrested. The night before he was to be executed, one of Calvin's agents "somehow" escaped from prison "without any noise or breaking of doors," whereupon the bailiffs successfully blamed it all on the Devil, testifying that they had seen Satan lead the condemned Calvinist through the walls of the prison.[274]

In addition, the training of agents stressed efforts to win the nobility to their cause, and many of the noble refugees were convinced to return home as covert supporters—it is estimated that 50 percent of French nobles were Calvinists by the time the first French War of Religion broke out in 1562.[275] Of course, since these "subversive" nobles were not trained or directed by the Company, they were not named in its official records, so their number will never be known. Nor do we know how many unordained refugees also went back to their country of origin on their own to missionize. We do know that as religious conflict in France came to a head, during 1561 and 1562, nearly every Calvinist leader in Geneva made at least one surreptitious trip into France.[276]

In any event, despite the records maintained by the Company, it is nearly impossible to know how many missionary-agents Calvin sent out. Robert Kingdon discovered extensive records for eighty-six men, trained and deployed between 1555 and 1562. Clearly, this tally is very incomplete. For example, while these official records show that twelve men were sent out in 1561, other less complete records reveal that an additional hundred went forth that year. In addition, "Swiss cities denuded their pulpits for the sake of the French."[277] The best that can be said, then, is that "hundreds" of ordained missionary-agents were sent forth, in addition to the many lay missionaries and nobles. It is important to realize that the primary role of these agents from Geneva was to recruit local missionaries whose task was to inspire their flocks to convert others, thus constructing a kind of pyramid club of conversion.

Owen Chadwick has offered a specific example of how rapidly these pyramids could grow. In 1559 several citizens from the small town of Castres in the Languedoc went to Geneva to buy Bibles and other religious books. While there they asked to be sent a pastor. In April 1560 Geoffrey Brun arrived in Castres and began holding secret services in a private home. The congregation grew so quickly that after six months Brun returned to Geneva to get an assistant. By February 1561 the assistant was holding separate services in another home. The magistrates ordered him to desist. But after several sessions with Brun, the magistrates joined the congregation. "The flock was now too big to meet in private houses, and so they took over public buildings and released Protestant prisoners by force. Henceforth the town was a Huguenot town."[278]

To assist in Calvinist conversion efforts, printers proliferated, and printing soon became the major industry in Geneva. The presses ran day and night, producing a flood of tracts and pamphlets, as well as books and vulgate Bibles. The city also sustained large paper mills and ink-making plants. Even so, Geneva imported large amounts of paper. Kingdon noted that "[i]t is easy to believe that this propaganda industry absorbed in some way the attention of much of the population of Geneva," not only as printers and paper- and ink-makers, but as authors, editors, and proofreaders.[279] Most of this immense flood of Calvinist publications was sold abroad, making a substantial contribution to the spread of Protestantism. Of course, since most of this material was banned in Catholic-controlled areas, the distribution pipeline operated surreptitiously; some shipments were confiscated, but most went through.

To examine the result of these efforts, let us shift our attention across the border to France.

Protestants in France

Spurred by agents from Geneva, Protestantism was very popular in France, but in the end it could not overcome the brutal opposition of a strong, centralized state.[280]

France began to execute Lutherans as heretics in the early 1520s, and while they were at it, they slaughtered a far larger number of Waldensians. Despite these repressive efforts, Protestantism eventually became such a major force that it could be stamped out only by a series of wars, at the end of which the surviving Protestants were driven into exile. This is a story that can be told either in a long book or in a few paragraphs. Given my limited concerns, the latter option will suffice.

At first the Parisian power structure—the Parlement (high court), the Church, and the University of Paris, with the intermittent blessings of King Francis I (*1494–1547*)—thought that by burning a few heretics, they could defeat Lutheranism. As it happened, they were rather tardy. Henry VIII had created many Lutheran martyrs, the Austrians had done so too, and Charles V had outdone everyone else, burning at least 600 Lutherans in the Low Countries between 1525 and 1539, while the French were still getting underway.[281] Even then, their initial victims weren't real Lutherans. The first was an eccentric monk burned for blasphemy in 1523. In 1526 a young boatman accused of destroying communion wafers was burned during Mardi Gras, and three days later an apprentice attorney was also burned for blasphemy. Later that year, the Parlement finally got it right and burned a young theology student who had fallen into Lutheran views. Once the French effort heated up, during the period 1540–1554 only the Low Countries surpassed France in executing Protestant heretics—an average of 21 per year in the Low Countries versus 18 a year in France, compared with 1.5 per year in Switzerland, and 0.6 in Spain.[282] Many of the French victims were quite prominent, and the others were mostly young scholars. But terror didn't work. Not only did Lutherans continue to appear; they were joined by legions of Calvinist agents who turned out to be far more successful missionaries than the Lutherans. Indeed, the French soon ceased railing against Lutherans, now identifying French Calvinist heretics as "Huguenots" (sworn companions). The Huguenots grew at an incredible rate. In early 1562, an official census placed the number of Huguenot churches in France alone at 2,150, and the number of French congregants is estimated to have been at least three million, or almost 20 percent[283] of the total population. Their numbers were especially formidable because they were not scattered but geographically concentrated.

The easiest way to predict quite accurately the strength of the Huguenots in any French community late in the sixteenth century is to determine how far it was from Paris. Although France had developed an extremely strong, centralized regime, its effective reach tended to attenuate with distance. Consequently, Protestantism flourished in the south of France, where "Huguenot legions sprang almost out of the ground,"[284] along the Channel, and in the "Borderlands" of Lorraine, Alsace, and Franche-Comté. But it wasn't merely distance that impeded the power of Paris in the south. It was here that the earlier, major heretical movements such as the Cathars and the Waldensians had also flourished. Indeed, the tradition of religious dissent had never died in the south—there were still enough Waldensians left in Provence in 1545 to provide more than 2,000 victims for a massacre by royal troops.[285] Moreover, bitterness based on centuries of similarly brutal repressions of religious dissent was part of the southern birthright. So in the Languedoc and in Provence, in Navarre and Dauphiné, across Gascony, Limousin, Lyonnais, Auvergne, and Poitou, the Huguenots became a dominant force.

And just as was true in Germany, the "people" who flocked to the Protestants in France were very disproportionately urban and affluent. As noted, James Tracy estimated that 50 percent of the French nobility were Huguenots. Emmanuel Le Roy Ladurie analyzed a list of Huguenots in Montpellier (in the Languedoc) assembled in 1560 by local Catholic authorities.[286] Of the 561 persons whose occupations were listed, only 27 (4.8 percent) were laborers or peasants. The largest category consisted of shopkeepers and craftsmen (69 percent), followed by members of the learned professions (15.4 percent). Another 8.5 percent were identified as merchants or as "bourgeois," and 2.3 percent were members of the nobility.

By 1560 the Huguenots were too numerous, and too geographically concentrated, to be martyred individually or in small groups, and the execution of heretics virtually ceased in France. Indeed, a group that powerful could be suppressed only by warfare. So in 1562 the French Wars of Religion began.[287] Again and again the loyal Catholic forces attacked. But even when they did well in open battle, they were thwarted by the many strongly fortified cities (such as La Rochelle) under Huguenot control. Consequently, again and again peace treaties were agreed upon. During one of these short intervals of peace, on August 23, 1572, Saint Bartholomew's Day, Catholic conspirators attacked Huguenots in Paris and in other cities where they were not in power—more than 2,000 were massacred in Paris, and at least 3,000 elsewhere. In 1629, after more than sixty years of fighting, the Huguenots were finally defeated. Under the terms of the Peace of Alais they surrendered their political and military independence but retained their religious freedom. The Church remained adamantly opposed, however. Eventually, in 1685, after decades of harassment and some forced conversions, Louis XIV ordered the Huguenots to become Catholics or leave. Many converted, but at least 250,000 left for Holland, England, Prussia, and America.

The Reformation in Spain

Although Protestantism did attract some upper-class Spaniards as well as some intellectuals, especially in the Church, it made virtually no significant headway in Spain. First, because unlike the French, the Spanish moved very effectively to suppress it. Second, because late in the fifteenth century a very vigorous "reformation" had so changed the Spanish Church that "the moral state of the Spanish clergy . . . was immeasurably superior to that of the clergy in any other part of Western Christendom,"[288] with the result that even Erasmus's satires of the clergy went unappreciated in Spain. Or, as Bainton put it, "In Spain originated the Catholic reformation before ever the Protestant had begun."[289]

The two centers of early support for Protestantism in Spain were Valladolid and Seville. In both communities a substantial group of Protestants, made up of clergy, nuns, and "well-born" laity, began to meet and worship in secret. Both groups were exposed to the local inquisitors and tried for heresy. Although, as was typical of the Inquisitions in Spain, most of the "heretics" were treated mildly, in each city a few who refused to recant were executed in public. In Seville, fourteen (including four friars) were executed in the first group, and three months later another eight died (including a nun). In Valladolid, fifteen (including two priests) were executed on Trinity Sunday, and another thirteen died five months later—including four priests and five nuns.[290] While these were not large numbers, the prominence of the victims rendered them chilling examples, and consequently many Spaniards with serious Protestant commitments departed for the Protestant areas in southern France and Holland, while the less committed ceased to dabble.

Reform of the Spanish Church began early in the fifteenth century, but it was toward the end of the century, under the direction of King Ferdinand and Queen Isabella, that truly drastic measures were taken. The ascetic Franciscan monk Ximenez de Cisneros (*1436–1517*), having become a cardinal, imposed strict new standards, going so far as to confiscate monastery lands and endowments. He also purged the clergy—many monks he deemed incorrigible he deported to Morocco. The result was a remarkable increase in popular support for the Church and the lack of the substantial discontent that elsewhere favored Lutheranism and Calvinism.

Italian Protestants

For centuries it was assumed that aside from its impact on a few intellectuals, Protestantism made no headway in Italy, being easily turned aside by the power of the pope and the depth of popular Catholic piety. As recently as 1984 the distinguished Andrea Del Col asserted that except for some scattered Waldensian groups, "in our peninsula, in fact, there were no [Protestant] churches . . . nor was there an organized will to adhere to one."[291]

Not so! Protestantism attracted substantial support in Italy, especially among the privileged, and failed only because of the effective repression imposed by the Spanish, who directly governed most of Italy at this time and exerted considerable pressure on the Papal States.[292] This new interpretation of Italian religious history emerged during the past century as historians began to examine the immense state and ecclesiastical archives that are now open to scholars, a research effort that came to fruition in the recent monograph by Salvatore Caponetto.[293] Caponetto's volume is superb in its detailed treatment of the large cast of Protestant activists and martyrs. Its weakness is the lack of a systematic overview, Caponetto having been content to offer scattered one-line asides, such as his allusion to "the widespread penetration of Lutheran protest at all levels of Italian society, beginning in the 1520s." Caponetto was at his best in tracing the depth and extent of Lutheranism among the Italian clergy, and especially the Augustinians. A "large number of monks" in Italy embraced the teaching of their fellow Augustinians: "masters of theology, superiors in their convents, professors in the most prestigious seats of learning of their order, and leading cultural figures" made up an impressive and lengthy list, all of whom were subjected to "painful and humiliating trials, imprisonment, [and] suspension from teaching and preaching."[294] In the end, most of the Augustinian "Protestants" submitted to Church authority. Lutheranism was also widespread among the Italian upper classes and urban elites, and these groups furnished a full complement of martyrs and a substantial flow of refugees to Switzerland, Germany, and the Huguenot strongholds in southern France.

The fundamental basis for the eventual failure of Protestantism in Italy was not the pope's power or influence but the fact that there was no "Italy" at this time, and all of the once-powerful city-states, save for Venice and the Papal States, were under the control of Spain. And just as they attacked and repressed Protestantism at home and in the Low Countries, the Spanish moved quickly against all signs of Protestant sympathy in Italy. Thus in Spanish-controlled Sicily, by 1560 the Holy Office had prosecuted fifty Protestants.[295] In similar fashion, the Spanish-controlled Neapolitan Inquisition had tried more than twenty Protestants by 1600. Of course, these numbers add up to fewer than 5 percent of the cases brought by these Inquisitions during this period. That might be interpreted as evidence that Protestantism did not appeal to Italians, but that is inconsistent with the reports of widespread initial favorable responses. I interpret these low numbers as showing that by moving very quickly and vigorously against very prominent clergy and officials, the Spanish (and Romans) were able to effectively repress public support, just as they had at Valladolid and Seville. Only in Venice, where Spanish influence was limited, did Protestantism have much opportunity, and there, for a time, it enjoyed considerable success, attracting "lawyers, merchants, patricians, and booksellers [to] various meeting places."[296] But, surrounded by hostile anti-Protestant forces, Venice came under increasing pressure to extradite Protestants to Rome for trial. Rather than do so, however, the Venetians enabled their own Inquisition to proceed against Protestants. Between

1547 and 1585, 767 Venetians were brought to trial for being Protestants, making up 62 percent of all trials held by the Venetian Inquisition in this era. Indeed, during 1580–1582 more than half (59) of all 112 Italians convicted of Protestantism were Venetians—there was only one conviction for Protestantism in Tuscany, another in Naples, and only eleven in the Papal States.[297] It should be noted, however, that the various Italian Inquisitions, like the Spanish Inquisitions, very rarely imposed the death sentence on those convicted of Protestantism. As will be considered at length in Chapter 3, Italian and Spanish inquisitors seldom resorted to capital punishment even in cases of witchcraft, much preferring merely to reconcile "sinners" with the Church. Even so, convictions could carry severe social and economic consequences, and faced with these risks, many Italian Protestants, especially Venetians, fled to Switzerland.[298]

Additional details of the spread of Protestantism, especially throughout Scandinavia, will be provided below and in Chapter 3. But the brief profiles presented above should adequately set the stage for an analysis of why and where Protestantism succeeded.

Explaining Protestant Success

The most fundamental sociological issue concerning Protestantism is *why did it succeed in some places and not in others?* A great deal has been written on this matter, some of it very perceptive and well documented. Nevertheless, a systematic, empirically testable, and general explanation is lacking. I now attempt to provide one.

Theological Appeal

As already noted, the vast literature on why Protestantism succeeded is mainly devoted to its "theological appeal" and emphasizes the popular aspects of doctrine. Clearly, doctrine did matter enormously—it is hard to imagine any other doctrines that could have presented such a profound and popular challenge to Catholic authority. However, I fully agree with Steven Ozment that most of the work done on this topic is unrealistic, stressing intricacies of doctrine that very few of those who became Protestants could possibly have noticed. Of even greater importance is that Protestant doctrine was, during the time in question, essentially *constant* and therefore cannot explain a *variable*—to tell us why some places turned Protestant and others did not. This is not to exclude doctrine from the explanation. As noted above, doctrine was a very *necessary* factor; had Protestant doctrines not had widespread popular appeal, there would have been no Protestant movement. Hence I will stipulate a fundamental causative role for theological appeal—for the popularity of the doctrine that individuals could ensure their salvation through faith alone, without any intercession or interference by the Church. That having been said, the remainder of the explanatory task remains: why was it triumphant here and rejected there?

A host of "materialist" explanations offered for the rise of Protestantism are also based on constants, and I will not stipulate that any of them made a difference. Most of these attribute the "Protestant Reformation" to aspects of social change: to the demise of feudalism, the development of a money economy and the use of credit, the expansion of trade, the rise of industries, new forms of agricultural organization, urbanization, expansion of the bourgeoisie, the declining military significance of heavy cavalry, increased taxes, and population growth, to name only the most commonly proposed causes.[299] All of these things were, in fact, going on. The trouble is that these changes were as prevalent in areas that remained Catholic as they were in those that embraced Protestantism; hence they explain nothing.[300]

Any explanation of the success of Protestantism requires *variables* to distinguish places that turned Protestant from those that did not. I shall argue that three interrelated variables made the difference.

First is the degree of *local Catholic weakness*. The areas most likely to embrace Protestantism were those *where the Roman Catholic Church suffered from a long-standing lack of popular support*. In northern Europe, Catholic weakness stemmed from the Church's failure to have Christianized the general public. In some other areas, long-standing resentment toward the Church was associated with bloody repression of prior movements such as the Cathars and Waldensians. In some places—the "Borderlands," for example—both aspects of weakness existed.

Second, *responsive governance* played a major role. Places were far more likely to become Protestant if their *governments tended to respond to popular preferences*. Places usually remained Catholic to the degree that they were ruled by strong, autocratic regimes. However, this proposition is modified by the third proposition, which explains that in some cases autocrats exerted their power on behalf of Protestantism.

Royal self-interest is the third, and very important, factor that shaped the Protestant Reformation. That is, some regimes had *much to gain in terms of wealth and power from turning Protestant*, while some regimes had far less to gain, having already *minimized Church authority and exactions*. Thus places tended to remain Catholic to the degree that their governing regime had gained substantial, official control over the Church. Aspects of this control were the ability to tax Church property and income, the right to make (or approve) all appointments to high Church offices such as bishop, and the imposition of limits on the jurisdiction of Church courts. In contrast, some regimes lacked these favorable arrangements with the Church and thus stood to gain substantial wealth and authority by supporting the Reformation.

I will assess each of these propositions against the historical record.

Local Catholic Weakness

A map showing the Catholic areas of Europe today looks remarkably like a map showing the boundaries of the Roman Empire. The Romans seldom ventured across the Rhine, and there are few Protestants west or south of that great waterway. This is not coincidental. Rather, as I demonstrated at length in *One True God*, Christian missionizing efforts across the Rhine were superficial in comparison with those within the empire. That is, in its early years Christianity was a mass movement that spread primarily through personal efforts by the rank and file to convert their relatives, friends, and neighbors. However, once Christianity became a highly subsidized state Church, its spirit of volunteerism attenuated; the subsequent spread of the faith was mainly through the baptism of kings, as Christian missionaries concentrated on the nobility and on gaining a monopoly franchise. Once established and supported by law and tithes, the Church did little to evangelize the general population. Consequently, as noted early in the chapter, many people across the Rhine (especially the peasants) treated Christianity as an add-on religion—Christ became part of the mixture of popular religion, along with many elements of paganism. As the great Danish historian Johannes Brøndsted noted, the conversion of royalty made Christianity the "public" faith in Scandinavia, but it was "far more difficult to overcome the complex culture beneath that religion." He quoted an Anglo-Danish monk who wrote in the twelfth century, "As long as things go well and everything is fine, the *Sviar* and *Gautar* seem willing to acknowledge Christ and honor him, though as a pure formality; but when things go wrong," they turn against Christianity and revert to paganism.[301] Or, as was written in the Icelandic *Landnámabók*, Helgi the Lean "was very mixed in his faith; he believed in Christ, but invoked Thor in matters of seafaring and dire necessity." Finally, Brøndsted suggested that to the extent it can be said to have taken place at all, the conversion of Scandinavia occurred "only . . . when Christianity took over old [pagan] superstitions and usages and allowed them to live under a new guise."[302]

I have stressed that a major factor in the success of Protestantism was its popular *support*. Here I want to stress that the very superficial Christianization of Europe beyond the Rhine resulted in a *lack of popular opposition* to Protestantism. Just as there had been little or no popular protest when pagan kings and princes in northern Europe were baptized, there was none when their successors opted for Protestantism. Indeed, what opposition arose was from members of the elites—often *within* royal families. The "people" were passive. As Kenneth Scott Latourette summed up: just as Christianity "was introduced largely under royal auspices and at royal initiative . . . [the shift to Protestantism also] was engineered by kings. It was accomplished more rapidly and encountered even less resistance than had the earlier one."[303]

This was not the case in areas below the Rhine where Christianization had been sustained by rank-and-file efforts. There Protestantism was often embraced by members of the elites but was as frequently opposed, often very actively, by the peasants. As Ladurie noted of the Languedoc, the "rural proletariat, for its part, remained practically impervious to the Reformation . . . [which] remained circumscribed to the urban and artisan classes from which it sprang. It did not migrate and did not spill over into the peasant masses, who remained steadfast in their Catholic beliefs."[304]

In Spain, not only had Christianity gained an early and firm beginning; the commitment of the people had been selectively intensified by centuries as an embattled minority under Muslim rule. Moreover, as noted, the extensive reforms imposed on the Spanish Church preempted many of the proposals that attracted popular support for Protestantism elsewhere in Europe. In addition, Spain was remarkably lacking in an "indigenous bourgeoisie." For example, during Spain's rapid rise as a worldwide imperial power, trade in its major port cities of Cádiz and Seville was monopolized by foreign merchants, most of them Italians. Foreign domination also "prevailed in commerce more generally . . . men of wealth left the field largely to foreign entrepreneurs . . . [preferring] the security of landed rents and government office."[305] Thus those elements of the public most attracted to Protestantism elsewhere were very underrepresented among native Spaniards, making the peasant faith in Catholicism all the more decisive.

An additional reason for a lack of local support for the Church was evident in the case of France: a history of brutal repression of prior "heretical" movements. This fueled the "Protestant Reformation" not only in southern France but also, as mentioned, in the "Borderlands," especially the cities with bloody histories of heresy-hunting.

In any event, a key factor in the success of Protestantism was the relative lack of popular support for Catholicism, whether owing to a lack of essential Christianization, to historical bitterness, or to both. It is possible to test this hypothesis on reasonably satisfactory data.

The sixteen nations of contemporary Western Europe serve as the cases. For each I determined the century in which it is believed to have been Christianized.[306] These vary from the fourth century for Italy to the thirteenth century for Finland.[307] I then subtracted to obtain the number of centuries since Christianization. Based on the assumption that the more recent the Christianization, the more superficial, length of Christianization should be highly correlated with current levels of church attendance (taken from the 1990–1991 World Values Surveys). That prediction is very highly supported by a correlation coefficient (r) of 0.72 (1.0 is perfect correlation). Nations with earlier Christianization have far higher rates of church attendance. Put another way, church attendance is far lower in Protestant than in Catholic nations—and always was.

There also ought to be a high correlation between length of Christianization and remaining Catholic. Since modern nations include many areas that were independent regimes in the sixteenth century, some of which differed as to becoming Protestant or remaining Catholic, it appears to me that the most plausible measure of participation in the Reformation is the current percentage of the population in each nation who are Roman Catholics.[308] These data strongly support the hypothesis—the correlation is 0.89. Thus the longer a place had been "Christianized," the more likely it was to remain Catholic.

On both qualitative and quantitative grounds, there seems to be significant support for the view that variations in the grassroots strength of Catholicism played an essential role in the success or failure of Protestantism.

CHAPTER I

Responsive Governance

It has often been remarked that places became Protestant, remained Catholic, or shifted back and forth, depending on the preferences of their rulers. While there is substantial truth to this claim, it fails to give adequate weight to the fact that Protestantism was a popular movement, and that many places turned Protestant because of the inability or unwillingness of the local government to *resist* public demands. Hence the responsiveness of governance held a vital key to Protestant success: other things being equal, to the extent that local governments responded to popular preferences, they turned Protestant.

Historians have been somewhat inconsistent vis-à-vis this proposition. On the one hand, as will be seen, they fully acknowledge the importance of responsive governance in their discussions of the success of Protestantism in the cities—especially in the Free Imperial Cities.[309] On the other hand, historians have had such contempt for Guy E. Swanson's *Religion and Regime: A Sociological Account of the Reformation* that they have tended to shun the topic—Stanford historian Lewis W. Spitz called Swanson's work "[a] weird attempt, based on several false premises . . . a parade of historical errors gotten up in fine social scientific costuming."[310]

These remarks say as much about Spitz's aversion to sociology as they do about Swanson's study. Nevertheless, despite the subtitle, there is nothing "sociological" whatever about the theoretical superstructure Swanson imposed on his data. It consists of rather simpleminded psychologizing expressed in abstruse jargon. Specifically, Swanson argued that the way that governance influenced whether a place turned Protestant was by creating a mind-set among the residents. That is, by living under autocratic regimes, people came to have a deep psychological preference for autocratic institutions generally, including an autocratic church; hence they preferred Roman Catholicism. However, when they lived under a regime that was at least somewhat responsive to public preferences (Swanson used the term "heterarchic"), people formed psychological preferences for more open institutions; hence they preferred Protestantism. These psychological assumptions are not only dubious; they are entirely superfluous, a judgment shared by many historians, including those who contributed to a special symposium published on Swanson's book in the *Journal for Interdisciplinary History* (1970–1971). It is sufficient and far more plausible simply to propose that popular movements are more apt to be

Monument to Persecution. Southern France is still dotted with the ruins of Cathar fortresses such as this. Here we see not only why the Cathars were difficult to defeat, but that over the centuries everyone in the area was constantly reminded of past massacres initiated by the Church. © David Reed/CORBIS.

thwarted by autocratic than by responsive regimes. However, in discarding Swanson's work, scholars have failed to appreciate the potentially important *empirical results* underlying it all—his quantitative data displaying the direct effects of governance on the success of Protestantism.

Swanson created a data set consisting of 41 European regimes at the time of the "Protestant Reformation." He classified each as to governance and noted which had become Protestant. With his language decoded into conventional terms, Table 1.1 shows his truly impressive results. Of the 21 autocratic regimes, two became Protestant. Of the 20 more responsive regimes, all became Protestant. Unfortunately, Swanson's "cases" are a very mixed bag. Some of them are nations, including England, France, and Spain. Other units are regions such as the "Highlands of Scotland." Still others are Italian city-states such as Florence and Venice. To this, Swanson added all 14 Swiss cantons. In his coding, Swanson ignored matters such as the degree of external coercion, as in the instance of Italian city-states, and brushed aside issues of incomparability. Nevertheless, when only the very comparable 14 Swiss cases are analyzed, all 5 with

TABLE 1.1
Governance and Becoming Protestant

	Responsive Regime	*Autocratic Regime*
Turned Protestant	100%	10%
Remained Catholic	0%	90%
	100%	100%
n =	(20)	(21)

Note: Gamma = 1.00; Kramer's V = 0.907; Prob.< .000.
Source: Calculated from Swanson, 1967:60.

responsive regimes turned Protestant. Of the 9 with autocratic regimes, 7 remained Catholic and 2 very rural cantons split into Protestant and Catholic regions. Even so, an additional criticism of Swanson concerned the validity of his coding of regimes as to their responsiveness. That he placed Denmark, Sweden, and England among the more responsive regimes in Table 1.1, while placing Poland among the most autocratic, suggests that Swanson's coding was influenced by knowledge of which regimes turned Protestant.

Nevertheless, Swanson's thesis seems worth pursuing with better data. As mentioned, discussions of Protestantism and the cities all stress the importance of responsive regimes. Particular emphasis is given to the Free Imperial Cities. Beginning in the thirteenth century, these communities evolved slowly out of the conflict between the burghers of the growing cities and their local feudal lords. By the fourteenth century, many cities, especially in the Germanic areas, gained control over their internal affairs, as even "the most obvious sovereign rights—military and judicial sovereignty—slipped slowly out of the lord's hands."[311] They came to be called "Imperial" because they owed allegiance to the (Holy Roman) Emperor, but they were otherwise free and sovereign. Thus they paid taxes directly to the emperor, but they retained complete control over their own tax systems. The Free Imperial Cities enjoyed freedom in another sense as well, for not only were they not subject to local feudal autocrats; each was governed by a city council. The councils varied in the extent of interests they represented—sometimes they included the artisan guilds and sometimes not. Even so, council members were elected (although not everyone could vote), and there was substantial turnover. As a result, these city councils had to be at least somewhat responsive to public sentiments.

TABLE 1.2
City Governance and Becoming Protestant

	43[a] Significant "Borderland" Cities, 1500	
	Free Imperial Cities	*Not Imperial Cities*
Became Protestant	61%	25%
Remained Catholic	39%	75%
	100%	100%
n =	(31)	(12)

Note: Gamma = 0.652; Kramer's V = 0.326; Prob. < .025.

[a] Aachen, Augsburg, Bamberg, Basel, Bern, Besançon, Coblenz, Colmar, Cologne, Constance, Esslingen, Frankfurt, Freiburg, Geneva, Heidelberg, Heilbronn, Kempton, Lausanne, Lucerne, Mainz, Marburg, Memmingen, Metz, Mulhausen, Munich, Nancy, Nordlingen, Nuremberg, Offenburg, Ravensburg, Regensburg, Reutlingen, Rottenburg, Rottweil, Schwabisch Gmund, Speyer, Strassburg, Stuttgart, Trier, Ulm, Worms, Wurtzberg, and Zurich.

Historians agree that the Free Imperial Cities were unusually apt to accept Protestantism,[312] but there has been no appropriate statistical comparison with similarly situated nonimperial cities. In 1500 there were about sixty-five Free Imperial Cities.[313] Some of them can be ignored because they were so very tiny—some had no more than a thousand residents.[314] Others were isolated far from other Imperial Cities, being surrounded by a powerful duchy or principality that imposed some degree of caution on the city council. In contrast, because they had arisen as trading communities, many of them were clustered in the area along or near the Rhine that historians often refer to as the "Borderlands" (see Chapter 3). In addition, there were many cities in this area that were not Imperial Cities. This provides an opportunity to test the proposition about governance on a set of units of comparable size and similar in terms of cultural heritage and setting. Consequently, I selected all of the significant cities in this "Borderlands" area, ending up with a total of 43. Unlike Swanson, I was not required to assess the nature of each local regime as to its responsiveness, thereby risking some of the errors for which Swanson was pilloried. All I needed to do was compare (12) nonimperial with (31) Free Imperial cities, on the assumption that the latter tended to have more responsive regimes.

Table 1.2 shows the results. The role of responsive governance receives strong support. Nearly two-thirds of the Imperial Cities in this group became Protestant, while three-fourths of the nonimperial Cities remained Catholic.

I am aware that some of these cities later reverted to Catholicism. But I am not attempting to explain the course of the Religious Wars. It is sufficient here to see that, other things being equal, where public pressure was of political significance, Protestantism succeeded. But what about autocratic regimes? Why did some of them turn Protestant too?

Royal Self-Interest

Public opinion was of very little importance in the decision by many autocratic regimes to embrace Protestantism. Indeed, in many instances Protestantism was itself of rather small importance, serving merely to extend religious legitimacy to the "nationalization" of the Church. Since the issue here is why autocratic regimes opted for Protestantism or Catholicism, the discussion is limited to autocratic regimes. Consequently, I will not deal with the success of Protestantism in Holland, but I will touch on the retention of the Spanish Netherlands within the Roman Catholic faith. I begin with regimes that chose to remain Catholic and then assess the situation of those rulers who became Protestants.

STAYING CATHOLIC

In 1296 King Philip of France, desperate for funds to continue the war with England, imposed a tax on Church income. Outraged, Pope Boniface VIII issued a bull forbidding any taxation of the clergy or of Church property. In response, Philip outlawed the export of money or precious metals and prohibited papal collectors from entering France. Subsequently, the papacy moved to Avignon in 1305, partly to be within legal reach of French funds, and remained there until 1378—a period that came to be known as the "Babylonian Captivity," during which all popes were French. However, even after the papacy moved back to Rome, the Church in France remained subordinate to the Crown. Throughout the fifteenth century the king's authority over the Church expanded. At the start of the sixteenth century this eventuated in a substantial reformation of the Church in France (particularly of the monasteries), directed by Cardinal d'Amboise, and empowered by the king. Then, in 1516 the power of the Crown was formalized in the Concordat of Bologna signed by Pope Leo X and King Francis I. The king was acknowledged to have the right to appoint all of the higher posts in the Church in France: the ten archbishops, eighty-two bishops, and the priors, abbots, and abbesses of all of the many hundreds of monasteries, abbeys, and convents. Through these appointments, the king gained control of Church property and income. As Owen Chadwick put it, "When he wanted ecclesiastical money, his methods need not even be devious."[315] This removed a very considerable temptation for the French regime to support Protestantism.

"In Spain, as in France, no Reformation was needed to subordinate the Church to the State."[316] The Spanish Crown had long held the right to nominate archbishops and bishops, to fine the clergy, and to receive a substantial share of the tithe. Spanish control of the Church greatly increased in 1486 when Ferdinand and Isabella gained the right to make all major ecclesiastical appointments, to prohibit appeals from Spanish courts to Rome, and to impose taxes on the clergy.[317] Indeed, it was illegal even to publish papal bulls and decrees in Spain or its possessions without prior royal consent, as will be discussed in Chapter 4. These same conditions prevailed in Portugal. The subordination of the Church to the state increased under Charles V (*1500–1558*), as Spain became the center of the Holy Roman Empire, extending its power to the Netherlands, Austria, portions of southeastern "Germany," and most of the Italian city-states. Although Charles incurred huge costs in defending and attempting to extend his vast holdings, the lure of Church property was more than offset by three factors. First, he was already receiving a substantial portion of Church income. Second, the pope's continuing support was valuable in helping Charles sustain his claims to sovereignty, especially in Spain, where he was always regarded as an "outsider." Third, the immense flow of wealth from the New World reduced the relative value of Church wealth to such an extent that it seemed not worth the risks involved in confiscating it.

As noted, in Italy Protestantism was suppressed by Spanish forces that acted in accord with the favorable arrangements between the Spanish Crown and Church, as these were extended to Spain's Italian holdings. Thus for Protestantism to have succeeded in Italy would have required that it first succeed in Spain.

In early days, Protestantism proved to be popular in Poland and was tolerated by the state, which had long respected the religious rights of Jews and Eastern Orthodox Christians. Eventually, however, Polish Protestantism was suppressed, and a large contingent of Jesuits was brought in to assist in reinstituting Roman Catholic hegemony. Why? Because the ambitions of the restive lower nobility and of the burghers, as well as the factionalism within Protestantism, seemed to threaten the Crown, and because the Church had already surrendered much of its wealth and power to the Polish nobility. Church lands and the clergy were taxed. Only members of Polish noble families could hold higher Church offices, and local landlords controlled the appointment of parish clergy. Thus no windfall profits tempted the Polish Crown to embrace Protestantism. As Robert Wuthnow put it, the Polish nobility "enjoyed sufficient control over the church that they had little incentive to turn toward Protestantism."[318]

To sum up: in none of these places did the Church impose the financial and political burdens it did elsewhere, and royal choices were not tipped in favor of Protestantism by the prospect of immense financial gains.

BECOMING PROTESTANTS

In contrast, in other parts of Europe the enormous value of Church property and the continuing Church financial exactions, in addition to ecclesiastical interference and arrogance, served as powerful temptations and bitter grievances. So long as there had been only one Church, it was risky to challenge papal authority, as Henry IV discovered when he was kept waiting barefoot in the snow by Pope Gregory VII. But now, Protestantism offered an alternative source of religious legitimacy—given the Protestant option, even excommunication was an empty threat. Whatever else may have motivated them, many kings and princes saw Protestantism as an opportunity to greatly increase their wealth and power.[319]

The English had no favorable concordat with Rome when Henry VIII unilaterally usurped the pope's authority. Keep in mind that Henry VIII was not a Protestant. He was quite opposed to central Protestant doctrines, and he continued to burn some Lutherans and Lollards! So Henry could not even pretend to have been motivated by theology. He merely declared an English, rather than Roman, Catholic Church. In so doing, he made the Church the property of the Crown, thereby gaining immense wealth and greatly increasing his annual income. He also eliminated all papal interference in English affairs, ecclesiastical and secular, thus enabling him to take and to shed wives as he saw fit.

In similar fashion, when Luther nailed up his theses, the northwestern German princes and electors had no legal power to stanch the flow of funds to Rome or to limit the expansion of Church lands, a process that continued to eat away their tax bases. By turning Protestant and confiscating Church property and income, as Luther advocated, they reversed their unfavorable situation vis-à-vis the Church, which is precisely what most of them elected to do. This did not, of course, apply to the prince-bishops, since they already owned the Church property and netted most of the Church income, and not one of them opted for Protestantism.

In Denmark, at the dawn of the sixteenth century from a third to half of the tillable land was owned by the Church, and everyone else paid tithes—substantial amounts of which went to Rome. The pope also made all ecclesiastical appointments. In 1534 Christian III became king. As a boy of eighteen, Christian had met Luther at the Diet of Worms and was deeply impressed. He was also impressed with the confiscations of Church property and wealth that were taking place in Germany. Once upon the throne, Christian found himself in dire need of funds and was offended by the arrogance of the Danish bishops. Consequently, he declared Denmark a Protestant state and seized all Church property and tithes, ushering in "an era of prosperity."[320]

Meanwhile, Sweden successfully rebelled against Denmark's rule as Gustavus Vasa drove the Danes out of Sweden and was formally crowned King Gustavus I in 1528. Here, too, the Church had enjoyed unchallenged authority and enormous wealth. When the new king deposed an archbishop and nominated replacements for four empty bishoprics, the pope supported the deposed archbishop and rejected Gustavus's nominees. To this affront was added the fact that the new king was in desperate need of funds. He dealt with both concerns by declaring Sweden to be a Protestant state, and by appropriating "the possessions and revenues of the Church."[321] To strengthen his support among the nobility, he sold them expropriated Church land at bargain prices. Even so, the Church property Gustavus kept increased the Crown lands fourfold.[322]

It is worth noting that in many circumstances it was in the self-interest even of ordinary citizens that Church property be confiscated and Church authority be curtailed. The Free Imperial Cities were severely burdened with extensive, untaxed Church properties, and with large numbers of resident clergy and members of religious orders who refused to perform the duties required of other citizens. In most cities at least one-third of the property belonged to the Church, and as many as one-tenth of the city's residents were clergy or members of religious orders.[323] Virtually everywhere there was substantial conflict between Church and city over special privileges, mainly because of the magnitude of the Church's presence. The clergy exempted themselves from all taxes. This was a daily grievance: in most cities there was a sales tax on many consumer items, such as wine and beer, which was not paid by local priests, monks, and nuns. Everyone else paid property taxes, but not the Church—indeed, everyone else was required to pay tithes to the Church. In similar fashion, when a citizen was accused of a crime, he or she stood trial before the local court and was at great risk of the death penalty. Priests, monks, and nuns could be tried only by a religious court and ran virtually no risk of the death penalty or even of a very severe sentence—murder convictions often resulted in several years of fasting. Nor would the clergy and members of religious orders fulfill such duties as taking their turn standing guard on the city walls, as all other able-bodied men were required to do.[324] Hence all laypeople in these cities had much to gain from Protestantism.

If one extends the mantle of Protestantism to the Hussites, then one could note the substantial benefits the Bohemian Crown and nobility gained by seizing Church lands and assets. Indeed, one could extend this proposition to the noble supporters of many rebellious sect movements, including the Cathars and the Waldensians. But such extensions seem unneeded here.

Once the success of Protestantism depended no longer upon the decisions of regimes but on the outcome of battles, my three propositions are of little relevance. Not wishing to write a history of the Wars of Religion, I have limited my analysis to approximately the period 1517 through 1560. Within this era, the facts strongly support the prediction that those regimes with the most to gain from embracing Protestantism did so, while those regimes having already curtailed Church power and wealth stayed Catholic. France, Spain, Portugal, the Spanish Netherlands, Poland, and the Italian city-states had far less to gain from turning Protestant than did England, northern Germany, and Scandinavia. And that's the way things went, as is shown in Table 1.3.

To sum up: Protestantism succeeded where (1) Catholicism was weak either from lack of prior, effective Christianization or because of longstanding traditions of dissent and resentment; (2) where governments were sufficiently responsive to popular sentiments; and (3) where regimes had a substantial amount to gain from becoming Protestant.

The Catholic Reformation

In recent times historians have tended to dismiss the long-standing interpretation of the Counter-Reformation as a reaction to the Protestant chal-

TABLE 1.3
Royal Self-Interest and Religious Choices, *Autocratic Regimes Only*

	Level of Economic and Political Benefits of Becoming Protestant
Choosing Catholicism	
France	Low
Spain	Low
Portugal	Low
Spanish Netherlands	Low
Poland	Low
Italy	Low
Choosing Protestantism	
England	High
Northwestern German States	High
Denmark	High
Sweden	High

lenge. H. O. Evennett claimed that both the Reformation and the Counter-Reformation "can reasonably be regarded as two different outcomes to the [same] general aspiration toward religious regeneration which pervaded late fifteenth and early sixteenth century Europe." Hence Evennett objected to the term "Counter-Reformation" as implying a "reactionary" movement rather than an "evolutionary adaptation."[325]

There are two very different issues here. I am quite willing to substitute "Catholic Reformation" for "Counter-Reformation." But it is bad history to assert that the changes begun at the Council of Trent[326] (1562–1563) were not provoked by the rapidly rising tide of Protestantism. To hold such a view is to ignore that while the council was in session, France was fighting a bitter civil war to determine whether Catholics or Huguenots would prevail. Indeed, to suppose that the great reforms begun at Trent were due to happen regardless of Protestant agitation is to ignore the fact that the Church of Piety had been trying to achieve a reformation for many centuries, and even reform-minded popes had failed to make any headway.

There is nothing discreditable about admitting that the Catholic Reformation, which had been gestating for so long, required a vigorous Protestant push to be born. What is important is that the Church of Piety did assert its power at Trent. Subsequently, with the aid of such new religious orders as the Jesuits and reinvigorated orders such as the Carmelites, the Church of Piety soon dominated the Roman Catholic Church, and, at long last, the reformers achieved their goals. Simony was ended. Popes and bishops became models of piety. Official, inexpensive, Catholic vulgates were made readily available in all major languages. The Church did undertake to evangelize and educate the rank and file, and continues to do so.

All of these reforms were greatly influenced by what has been called the most significant decision taken at Trent: to establish a network of seminaries to train men for the local priesthood. Previously, the only training most parish priests received was to serve as an apprentice to another priest who had also been an apprentice. Consequently, during the previous centuries many priests had been illiterate or nearly so. Many could not actually say a mass but simply mumbled nonsense syllables. And few knew even elementary points of doctrine—many were unable even to repeat the Ten Commandments or list the Seven Deadly Sins.[327] The decision to establish seminaries (for which bishops were given special authority to divert funds from other activities) soon began to remedy these priestly deficiencies. By the eighteenth century, in most places the Church was staffed by literate men well versed in theology. Perhaps even more important, the seminaries produced priests whose vocations had been shaped and tested in a formal, institutional setting.[328]

This was the positive side of the Catholic Reformation. Unfortunately, perhaps inevitably, the laxity of the Church of Power had benefits that disappeared along with its many shortcomings. Hence many intellectual and economic pursuits that flourished before Trent were soon discouraged or even prohibited for several centuries. This has led to many misperceptions. For example, following Max Weber the view has been widely held that Protestantism gave birth to capitalism and hence to the Industrial Revolution, these being somehow incompatible with Catholic perspectives and policies. In fact, capitalism and industrialization did not suddenly erupt subsequent to the Protestant Reformation. Rather, as Hugh Trevor-Roper explained, they developed gradually, and medieval capitalist enterprises "were as 'rational' in their methods, as 'bureaucratic' in their structure, as any modern capitalism . . . The idea that large-scale industrial capitalism was ideologically impossible before the Reformation is exploded by the simple fact that it existed."[329] However, the repressive activities and policies imposed by the Counter-Reformation resulted in the massive migration of capitalists and of whole industries from Catholic areas, such as Italy and the Spanish Netherlands, into Protestant domains, with the result that Protestant nations soon forged far ahead. As Fernand Braudel put it, "[the Protestant Ethic thesis] is clearly false. The northern countries took over the place that earlier had so long and so brilliantly been occupied by the old capitalist centers of the Mediterranean. They invented nothing, either in technology or in business management."[330]

The same sort of thing happened in science. As will be clear in the next chapter, the rise of Western science was rooted in Scholasticism, and Catholics played as prominent a role as did Protestants in the "Scientific Revolution" of the sixteenth century. But as the Catholic Reformation developed, increasingly severe restrictions were imposed on science, especially in the universities under Church control, and Catholic contributions to science rapidly declined, encouraging incorrect notions about the Protestant roots of science. Of these matters, more later.

Conclusion

The history of reformations and sects did not end in the seventeenth century. I could have greatly extended this chapter by examining how various Protestant and Jewish bodies drifted into laxity over the past several centuries, causing them to externalize a host of sect movements. Indeed, many contemporary Western religious groups,[331] including the Methodists, Episcopalians, Reform Jews, and even Unitarians, are at present undergoing serious reformations, as are many Islamic and Hindu bodies around the world. But I have written enough elsewhere on these more recent developments. In this chapter my aim was to reveal the rather simple underlying mechanisms that generate the desire for reformations and prompt the eruption of sect movements. Although social scientists have been wrong to assert that material motives lie hidden behind all sects and reformations, they have been right to regard these as *generic* phenomena. Sects and reformations are also *inevitable* phenomena because, even if there is only One True God, there can never be only One True Church.

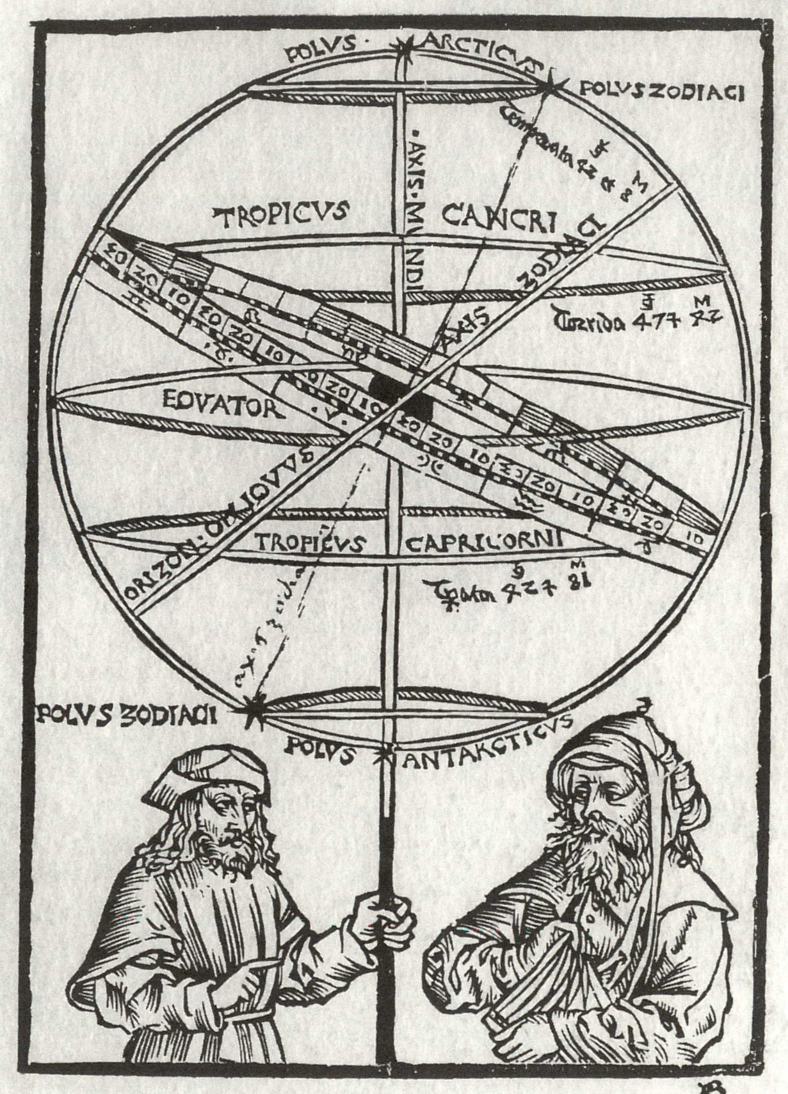

Medieval Globe. This engraving of scholars with a globe, on which the equator, the tropics, the poles, and magnetic north and south are well marked, appeared in a textbook on Ptolemy's cosmology published at the University of Cracow at about the same time that Columbus set out on his first voyage. © Bettmann/CORBIS.

2

God's *Handiwork*: The Religious Origins of Science

The heavens declare the glory of God; and the firmament showeth His handiwork.
—*Psalm 19*

Even children know that in 1492 Christopher Columbus proved that the world is round. They also know that he doggedly pursued backing for his voyage despite years of opposition from the Roman Catholic Church, which ridiculed all dissent from the biblical teaching that the earth is flat. Andrew Dickson White (*1832–1918*), founder and first president of Cornell University, and author of the single most influential book ever written on the conflict between science and theology, offered this summary:

> The warfare of Columbus [with religion] the world knows well: how the Bishop of Ceuta worsted him in Portugal; how sundry wise men of Spain confronted him with the usual quotations from Psalms, from St. Paul, and from St. Augustine; how, even after he was triumphant, and after his voyage had greatly strengthened the theory of the earth's sphericity . . . the Church by its highest authority solemnly stumbled and persisted in going astray . . . the theological barriers to this geographical truth yielded but slowly. Plain as it had become to scholars, they hesitated to declare it to the world at large . . . But in 1519 science gains a crushing victory. Magellan makes his famous voyage. He proves the earth to be round, for his expedition circumnavigates it . . . Yet even this does not end the war. Many conscientious [religious] men oppose the doctrine for two hundred years longer.[1]

Like everyone else, I grew up with this story. It was retold in every account of Columbus's voyage in my schoolbooks, in many movies, and always on Columbus Day.[2] As for A. D. White's immense study, *A History of the Warfare of Science with Theology in Christendom* (in two volumes), when I was young, it was required reading for all budding intellectuals, and I cited it in my second published paper.

Trouble is that almost every word of White's account of the Columbus story is a lie. *Every* educated person of the time, including Roman Catholic prelates, knew the earth was round.[3] The Venerable Bede (*ca. 673–735*) taught that the world was round, as did Bishop Virgilius of Salzburg (*ca. 720–784*), Hildegard of Bingen (*1098–1179*), and Thomas Aquinas (*ca. 1224–1274*), and all four ended up saints. *Sphere* was the title of the most popular medieval textbook on astronomy. Written by the English Scholastic John of Sacrobosco (*ca. 1200–1256*), it transmitted the standard view that all heavenly bodies including Earth were spherical. In the same century as Columbus's voyage, Cardinal Pierre d'Ailly (*1350–1420*), chancellor of the University of Paris, noted that "although there are mountains and valleys on the earth, for which it is not perfectly round, it approximates very nearly to roundness."[4]

As for the "sundry wise men of Spain" who challenged Columbus and advised against funding him, they not only knew the earth was round; they also knew it was far larger than Columbus thought it was. They opposed his plan *only* on the grounds that he had badly underestimated the circumference of the earth and was counting on much too short a voyage. Expressed in modern measures, Columbus claimed that it was about 2,800 miles from the Canary Islands to Japan, when it is actually about 14,000 miles.[5] Had the Western Hemisphere not existed, and Columbus had no knowledge that it did, he and his crew would have died at sea. In any event, Jeffrey Burton Russell found that it was not true that Christian scholars were benighted fanatics clinging to scriptural claims that the earth was flat; rather, during the first fifteen centuries of the Christian era "nearly unanimous scholarly opinion pronounced the earth spherical, and by the fifteenth century all doubt had disappeared."[6] Edward Grant, in his monumental study of medieval cosmology, noted that in none of the Scholastic writings was there any mention of a flat earth except for a few asides to *refute* perceptions of flatness.[7] No contemporary document concerning Columbus, including his own *Journal* and his son's *History of the Admiral*, nor any account of other early voyages including Magellan's, makes any mention of the shape of the earth. Everyone knew.

So why didn't we know they knew? Why do only specialists know now? For the same reason that White's book remains influential despite the fact that modern historians of science dismiss it as nothing but a polemic—White himself admitted that he wrote the book to get even with Christian critics of his plans for Cornell.[8] As will be seen, many of White's other accounts are as bogus as his report of the flat earth and Columbus. The reason we didn't know the truth concerning these matters is that the claim of an inevitable and bitter warfare between religion and science has, for more than three centuries, been the primary polemical device used in the atheist attack on faith. From Thomas Hobbes through Carl Sagan and Richard Dawkins, false claims about religion and science have been used as weapons in the battle to "free" the human mind from the "fetters of faith."

In this chapter, I argue not only that there is no inherent conflict between religion and science, but that *Christian theology was essential for the rise of science*. In demonstration of this thesis I first summarize much recent historical work to the effect that not only did religion not cause the "Dark Ages"; nothing else did either—the story that after the "fall" of Rome a long dark night of ignorance and superstition settled over Europe is as fictional as the Columbus story. In fact, this was an era of profound and rapid technological progress by the end of which Europe had surpassed the rest of the world. Moreover, the so-called Scientific Revolution of the sixteenth century was the normal result of developments begun by Scholastic scholars starting in the eleventh century. Thus my attention shifts to why the Scholastics were interested in science at all. Why did real science develop in Europe at this time? Why did it not develop anywhere else? I find answers to those questions in unique features of Christian theology.

This leads to examination of the outburst of scientific discovery during the late sixteenth and seventeenth centuries, wherein I explore its connections with Protestantism and conclude that it was Christianity, not Protestantism, that sustained the rise of science. As part of this discussion, I show that the leading scientific figures in the sixteenth and seventeenth centuries overwhelmingly were devout Christians who believed it their duty to comprehend God's handiwork. Turning to an assessment of the "Enlightenment," I show it to have been conceived initially as a propaganda ploy by militant atheists and humanists who attempted to claim credit for the rise of science. The falsehood that science required the defeat of religion was proclaimed by such self-appointed cheerleaders as Voltaire, Diderot, and Gibbon, who themselves played no part in the scientific enterprise—a pattern that continues.

Next, I show how the close collaboration between religion and science that characterized much of the nineteenth century was not a "strange interlude." That particular designation goes to the Darwinian Crusade that dominated most popular twentieth-century discussions of religion and science. I argue that, rather than having been a battle between religion and science, the fracas over evolution was and remains largely a conflict between true believers of both varieties—the strident evolutionists being as unscientific as *any* fundamentalists.

I conclude by showing that through it all, professional scientists have remained about as religious as most everyone else, and far more religious than their academic colleagues in the arts and social sciences.

A confession is appropriate here. Having begun this chapter, I immersed myself in recent historical studies, only to find that some of my central arguments have already become the conventional wisdom among historians of science.[9] So I have the comfort of learned opinion on my side but no claim to priority. I might have skipped the chapter entirely, but I am painfully aware that most of what it contains is unknown outside narrow scholarly circles. In fact, if asked, most well-informed people would express their absolute certainty that most of this *could not possibly* be true—early in my career I shared this view. That seemed sufficient reason to write on. But the ultimate justification of this chapter is that, to my knowledge, no one has actually pulled all of the essential themes and findings together to formulate a coherent overall picture of the history of the creative relationship between theology and science.

What Is Science?

Science is not merely technology. A society does not have science simply because it can build sailing ships, smelt iron, or eat off porcelain dishes. ***Science*** is a *method* utilized in *organized* efforts to formulate *explanations of nature*, always subject to modifications and corrections through *systematic observations*.

Put another way, science consists of two components: *theory* and *research*. Theorizing is the explanatory part of science. Scientific theories are *abstract statements* about *why* and *how* some portion of nature (including human social life) fits together and works. However, not all abstract statements, not even all of those offering explanations, qualify as scientific theories; otherwise, theology would be a science. Rather, abstract statements are scientific only if it is possible to deduce from them some definite predictions and prohibitions about what will be observed. And that's where research comes in. It consists of making those observations that are relevant to the empirical predictions and prohibitions. Clearly, then, science is limited to statements about natural and material reality—about things that are at least in principle observable. Hence there are entire realms of discourse that science is unable to address, including such matters as the existence of God.

By "organized," I mean to note that science is not random discovery, nor is it achieved in solitude. Granted that some scientists have worked alone, but not in isolation. From earliest days, scientists have constituted networks and have been very communicative.

Consistent with the views of most contemporary historians as well as philosophers of science, this definition of science excludes all efforts through most of human history to explain and control the material world, even those not involving supernatural means. Most of these efforts can be excluded from the category of science because until recent times "technical progress—sometimes considerable—was mere empiricism," as Marc Bloch put it.[10] That is, progress was the product of observation and of trial and error, but was lacking in explanations—in theorizing. This objection even applies to Nicolaus Copernicus (*1473–1543*), since his heliocentric conception of the solar system was merely a descriptive claim (almost all of it wrong). He had nothing useful to say about *why* planets remain in their orbits around the sun, or moons about the planets. Until Newton there was no *scientific theory* of the solar system. I shall count Copernicus among the founders of modern science only because of his influence on and participation in a network of astronomers whose work soon qualified as truly scientific. But the earlier technical innovations of Greco-Roman times, of Islam, of imperial China, let alone those achieved in prehistoric times, do not constitute science and are better described as lore, skills, wisdom, techniques, crafts, technologies, engineering, learning, or simply knowledge. Thus, for example, even without telescopes the ancients excelled in astronomical observations. But until they were linked to testable theories, these observations remained merely "facts." Charles Darwin expressed this point vividly:

> About thirty years ago there was much talk that geologists ought to observe and not theorize; and I well remember someone saying that at that rate a man might as well go into a gravel-pit and count the pebbles and describe the colours. How odd it is that anyone should not see that all observation must be for or against some view if it is to be of any service![11]

As for the intellectual achievements of Greek or Eastern philosophers, their empiricism was quite atheoretical, and their theorizing was nonempirical. Consider Aristotle (*384–322 B.C.E.*). Although praised for his empiricism, he didn't let it interfere with his theorizing. For example, he taught that the speed at which objects fall to earth is proportionate to their weight—that a stone twice as heavy as another will fall twice as fast.[12] A trip to any of the nearby cliffs would have allowed him to falsify this proposition. He also explained in his *Physics* that the motion of a projectile is due to the push given it by the air closing behind it, paying no heed to the need to open the air in front of it. The superb, and sadly neglected, Scholastic scientist-theologian Jean Buridan (*1300–1358*) dispatched this Aristotelian proposition by observing that, among other things, when a man runs, he "does not feel the air moving him, but rather feels the air in front strongly resisting him."[13]

The same can be said of the rest of the famous Greeks—either their work is entirely empirical, or it does not qualify as science for lack of empiricism, being sets of abstract assertions that disregard or do not imply observable consequences. Thus when Democritus (*ca. 460 B.C.E.–ca. 370 B.C.E.*) proposed the thesis that all matter is composed of atoms, he did not anticipate scientific atomic theory. His "theory" was mere speculation, having no basis in observation or any empirical implications. That it turned out to be "correct" (and most of it did not) does not make his guess any more significant than that of his contemporary Empedocles (*ca. 490 B.C.E.–ca. 430 B.C.E.*), who asserted that all matter is composed of fire, air, water, and earth, or Aristotle's (*384 B.C.E.–322 B.C.E.*) version a century later, that matter consists of heat, cold, dryness, moistness, and quintessence. Indeed, for all his brilliance and analytical power, Euclid (*ca. 300 B.C.E.*) was not a scientist, because, in and of itself, geometry lacks substance, having the capacity only to describe reality, not to explain any portion of it.

Of course, these millennia of technological and intellectual progress were vital to the eventual development of science, but it is the consensus among contemporary historians, philosophers, and sociologists of science that real science arose only once: in Europe. In this regard it is instructive that China, Islam, India, and ancient Greece and Rome had a highly developed alchemy. But only in Europe did alchemy develop into chemistry. By the same token, many societies developed elaborate systems of astrology, but only in Europe did astrology lead to astronomy.

In what follows I will examine the connections between religion and the rise of science in Europe, from its medieval beginnings through its flowering in the sixteenth century. Before doing so, however, I must introduce a very important distinction: I am writing about religion and science, not about *churches* and science.

Institutions and Intellectual Freedom

To say that there was a positive link between religion and science in Western history is surely not to deny that sometimes churches have sought to force conformity to their doctrines. Typically, however, and in almost every instance when blood was shed, these were disputes over *theology*, not between theology and science.

Consider the execution of Giordano Bruno (*1548–1600*), often cited as one of the most shameful examples of the religious repression of science. A. D. White claimed that Bruno "should be mentioned with reverence as beginning to develop again that current of Greek thought . . . [which the] doctors of the Church had interrupted for more than a thousand years."[14] In fact, Bruno was not really a scientist, although he engaged in some speculative astronomy. Rather, he was a renegade monk, a Hermetic sorcerer, and something of a philosopher.[15] His troubles had to do entirely with a heretical theology involving the existence of an infinite number of worlds—a work based entirely on imagination and speculation. The same is true of the other equally infamous case, that of Michael Servetus (*1511–1553*), put to death in Geneva with the acquiescence of John Calvin. Although Servetus did a bit of early work in physiology, he specialized in theology, and it was only for his theological writing that he was condemned.[16] Not only did he have such poor judgment that he sent a copy of his Unitarian views about God to Calvin, but when these views forced him to flee Italy, he foolishly went to Geneva.

Heretical theologies directly threaten the authority of those in control of religious organizations and institutions in a way that science seldom does. Thus even as they pursued heresy, the Spanish inquisitors paid virtually no attention to science per se. In his remarkable recent study, Henry Kamen reported:

> Scientific books written by Catholics tended to circulate freely. The 1583 Quiroga Index had a negligible impact on the accessibility of scientific works, and Galileo was never put on the list of forbidden books. The most direct attacks mounted by the Inquisition were against selected works in the area of astrology and alchemy, sciences that were deemed to carry overtones of superstition.[17]

In contrast, anyone in Spain could have gotten into deep trouble for reading books by Protestants, scientific or not. Even so, most of the books that actually got people in trouble with the inquisitors were not about religion, science, or superstition; they were pornographic.[18] The mention of Galileo anticipates a later discussion of that celebrated and much distorted episode. For now, let me merely propose that *unless checked by other forces, powerful institutions and organizations tend to suppress dissent and nonconformity, and to impose their views and interests on anyone they can.*

Obviously, religious organizations have often demonstrated this principle. But insofar as the suppression of science is concerned, the bloodiest incidents have been recent and have had nothing to do with religion. It was the Nazi Party, not the German Evangelical Church, that tried to eradicate "Jewish" physics, and it was the Communist Party, not the Russian Orthodox Church, that destroyed "bourgeois" genetics and left many other fields of Soviet science in disarray. No one has been prompted by these examples to propose an inherent incompatibility between *politics* and science. By the same token, that there have been conflicts between churches and science does not justify belief in an incompatibility between religion and science. It is, rather, that autocrats often do not tolerate disagreement. With that in mind, let us now journey back to ancient Rome.

THE MYTHICAL "DARK AGES"

In his best-selling *The Discoverers* (1983), the distinguished Daniel Boorstin, University of Chicago professor, Pulitzer Prize winner, and Librarian of Congress, included a chapter entitled "The Prison of Christian Dogma." In it, Boorstin condemned Christianity for imposing an era of general ignorance and fanaticism upon Europe:

> [T]he leaders of orthodox Christendom built a grand barrier against the progress of knowledge . . . After . . . Christianity conquered the Roman Empire and most of Europe . . . we observe a Europe-wide phenomenon of scholarly amnesia, which afflicted the continent from A.D. 300 to at least 1300.[19]

Like the Columbus tale, this is a story many of us were raised on: Rome fell and with that cataclysm came the "Dark Ages." Indeed, the second edition of *Webster's Unabridged Dictionary* (1934) defined the "Dark Ages" as the "earlier part of [the Middle Ages] because of its intellectual stagnation," and the college edition of *Webster's New World Dictionary* of 1958 defined "Dark Ages" as "1. the period from the fall of the Western Roman Empire (476 A.D.) to the beginning of the modern era (c. 1450). 2. The earlier part of the Middle Ages, to about the end of the 10th century . . . the medieval period in Europe, especially the earlier part, [that] was characterized by widespread ignorance."

As to the cause of the "Dark Ages," ever since the start of the eighteenth century historians have proposed that Christianity was the reason, having spread barbarism, superstition, and ignorance across Europe. This interpretation culminated in Edward Gibbon's (*1737–1794*) massive indictment of religion in *The History of the Decline and Fall of the Roman Empire*. In addition to appealing to the French *philosophes* and other antireligious intellectuals of the day, when more narrowly interpreted as an indictment of Roman Catholicism, Gibbon's account was immensely popular among Protestant intellectuals as well. Nevertheless, the phrase "Dark Ages" is of recent origins, probably first used by the British historian Henry Thomas Buckle (*1821–1862*) in his *History of Civilization in England* (1859). Others soon copied Buckle's usage, and by the twentieth century the term was in such general use that few knew it wasn't longstanding. Indeed, some writers seem almost to suggest that people living in, say, the ninth century described their own time as the Dark Ages.

However, modern historians and archaeologists[20] have completely discredited these views, and there was no excuse for Boorstin to have repeated them. By the time his book appeared, even the popular encyclopedias reflected the revised version. Thus *The New Columbia Encyclopedia* (1975) suggested that the term "Dark Ages" is no longer used by historians because this era "is no longer thought to have been so dim." In its entry for the "Dark Ages," the fifteenth edition of *Britannica* (1981) reported that this term "is now rarely used by historians because of the unacceptable value judgment it implies," being a "pejorative" incorrectly denoting this "a period of intellectual darkness and barbarity."

Spurred by the pioneering work of Henri Pirenne (*1862–1935*) and Marc Bloch (*1886–1944*),[21] scholars now realize that Christianity played no role in the defeat of Rome, and that the "Dark Ages" weren't dark. The decline of Rome had many causes, but the actual "fall" was nothing more (or less) than the culmination of several centuries of a shift in military capacity from the Romans to various Germanic groups, such as the Goths, Huns, Vandals, Burgundians, and Franks.[22] Moreover, when the last battles came, Germans made up the larger proportion of the Roman army as well and in that sense had already supplanted the ethnic Romans.[23] However, as a result of the military defeat of Rome, the political and cultural center of Europe shifted northward. It is this shift that was interpreted as a cultural and intellectual decline by those who, many centuries later, equated civilization with the writings of a tiny group of Greco-Roman intellectuals. In a population lacking familiarity with the classical philosophers and poets, they reasoned, how could there be anything but darkness? Moreover, to them, enlightenment was to be found only in books and abstract ideas, and certainly not in machines or in farming practices. Indeed, the "scorn of men of letters for engineers throughout history has kept them, all too often, oblivious to the technology created by those engineers."[24]

Thus only recently have historians realized that while Europe's leading scholars of, say, the eighth century may have written "inferior" Latin, and may not have been well versed in Plato and Aristotle, they were not "barbarians." They certainly were not barbarians morally: both Plato and Aristotle owned slaves, but during the "Dark Ages," Europeans rejected slavery (Chapter 4). And they certainly were not barbarians in terms of technology: beginning early in the "Dark Ages" came "one of the great inventive eras of mankind" as machinery was developed and put into use "on a scale no civilization had previously known."[25] Or, as Lynn White put it, "In technology, at least, the Dark Ages mark a steady and uninterrupted advance over the Roman Empire."[26] Histories of the technological achievements of medieval times are fascinating reading.[27] For the sake of illustration here I will mention only a few.

In 732, during the very depths of the "Dark Ages," Charles Martel (grandfather of Charlemagne) led a Frankish army in the Battle of Tours (or Poitiers) wherein they routed the Saracens—Muslim invaders come north from Spain. As with all successful European armies over the past twenty-five hundred years, Martel's primary force consisted of well-trained infantry formations, and his had better arms and armor than any force fielded by the Romans or the Greeks.[28] Against them the Saracens committed a cloud of cavalry, wearing little or no armor, but superbly mounted and armed with composite bows and the best swords in the world. The Saracen cavalry charged and wheeled and circled, but they could make no dent in the solid ranks of infantry, who inflicted severe casualties upon them with their long pikes. Toward the end of the day the Saracens began to withdraw. It was then that they were slaughtered. Not by the Frankish infantry—men clad in chain-mail armor are ill suited to chase anyone, let alone riders. But at this point came the first-ever appearance on a major battlefield of knights in full armor, who charged at a gallop, putting the full weight of horse and rider behind a long lance.[29] When this wall of force hit the Saracen cavalry, they were routed—their arrows could not penetrate the Frankish armor, and their futile efforts to close and use their swords were forestalled by the long lances of the Frankish knights, and by the irresistible weight of horses charging at full gallop. The difference was stirrups and the Norman saddle. Without stirrups to brace against, a rider attempting to drive home a lance will be thrown off his horse. The ability of a rider to withstand sudden shocks is also greatly enhanced by a saddle with a very high pommel and cantle—the latter being curved to partly enclose the rider's hips.[30] The Romans had no stirrups, nor did the Saracens, and both rode with light, almost flat, pad saddles, or even bareback. So they had no heavy cavalry.

Neither did the Romans or the Saracens know how to harness horses effectively. Before Europeans learned better during the "Dark Ages," horses were harnessed in the same way as oxen. To keep from strangling in such a harness, a horse must keep its head thrown back and can pull only light loads. Fully aware of the problem, Romans responded via legislation! The Theodosian Code decreed severe punishments for anyone "caught harnessing horses to a load in excess of [in modern terms] 500 kilograms."[31] In contrast, during the "Dark Ages" a rigid, well-padded collar was designed that properly places the weight on the horse's shoulders instead of its neck, enabling the horse to pull as much as the ox and to pull it much faster. Having invented the horse collar, European farmers soon switched from oxen to horses, with an immense gain in productivity—a horse could plow more than twice as much per day as an ox.[32]

In addition, it was not until well after the fall of Rome that Europeans developed iron shoes nailed to horses' hooves to protect them from the wear and tear that often causes unshod horses to become lame. The Romans had experimented with various kinds of horse sandals (Nero

Cavalry. Lacking stirrups and having only flat, pad saddles, Roman cavalrymen (shown at left) could only fight with their swords or throw javelins. But, securely mounted in a Norman saddle and braced by his stirrups, the medieval knight could charge his opponents, putting the full weight of his horse behind a long lance. © Bettmann/CORBIS.

had some made of silver), but these fell off if the horse even trotted. With iron shoes firmly attached, horses can travel even on hard surfaces without damage.

Unfortunately, although historians had dimly noted the transformation of agriculture involving the use of the horse, for generations they had no idea why this had come about, nor did they have the slightest notion of why the Romans had not excelled in heavy cavalry. In large part this was because historians seldom rode or harnessed horses and rarely knew anyone who did. Thus it was not until 1931 that these revolutionary technological innovations concerning stirrups, saddles, harnesses, and horseshoes came to scholarly attention through the work of a complete outsider, one who knew relatively less about history, but a great deal more about horses—Lefebvre des Noëttes, a retired French cavalry officer.[33]

Since then there has come a flood of books establishing that long before the end of the Middle Ages, before any "Renaissance," "Enlightenment,"

or "Scientific Revolution," Europe's technology advanced far beyond anything achieved by the ancients: effective waterwheels, mills, camshafts, mechanical clocks, the compass, and so on.[34] Many of these were original inventions. Others came from Asia. But what was most remarkable about the "Dark Ages" was the way in which the full capacities of new technologies were rapidly recognized and widely adopted. Consider gunpowder. The Chinese were the first to use an explosive powder, but it is a misnomer to call their invention gunpowder, since the Chinese did not develop guns and limited its use to fireworks. When knowledge of this Chinese explosive arrived in Europe, probably during the first decade of the fourteenth century, the application to gunnery was immediate—cannon were probably first used in battle during a seige of Metz in 1324.[35] What is certain is that by 1325 "cannon existed all over western Europe."[36]

The rapid adoption of the compass is another compelling example. The claim that the magnetic compass reached Europe from China through Islam is false. Apparently, it was invented independently in both China and Europe, probably in about the eleventh century. The Chinese were satisfied with a very crude compass, a magnetized needle floating in a liquid. This enabled them to determine the north-south axis, which was primarily of magical concern—the Chinese may not have used this device aboard ships until long after Europeans were doing so. In contrast, soon after discovering the floating-needle compass, medieval Europeans added the compass card and then the sight. This allowed mariners not only to know which way was north but to determine their precise heading, which allowed them to set accurate courses in any direction. The temporal clustering of written reports of this new invention demonstrates that it spread among sailors from Italy to Norway in only a few years.[37]

Thus falls forever the first leg of the argument concerning the incompatibility of religion and science. Christianity did not plunge Europe into an era of ignorance and backwardness. Rather, so much technical progress took place during this era that by no later than the thirteenth century, European technology surpassed anything to be found elsewhere in the world.[38] This did not occur because of the "rediscovery" of classical knowledge. There is no more misleading account of Western civilization than the one that starts with classical culture and proceeds directly to the "Renaissance," dismissing the millennium in between as an unfortunate and irrelevant interlude. Western civilization is not the direct descendant of Greco-Roman culture. Instead, it is the product of centuries of interaction between the cultures of the "barbarians" (who, as we have begun to realize, had far more sophisticated cultures than had been acknowledged)[39] and Christianity. In fact, it is far less the case that Christianity "Romanized" the Germans than that the latter "Germanized" Christianity. The subsequent addition of Greco-Roman learning was more decorative than fundamental.[40] For the fact is that the progress achieved during the "Dark Ages" was not limited to technology. Medieval Europe also excelled in philosophy and science. As Lynn White pointed out, by "the late 13th century Europe had seized global scientific leadership."[41]

The Scholastic Beginnings of Science

In many ways the term "Scientific Revolution" is as misleading as "Dark Ages." Both were coined to discredit the medieval Church. The notion of a "Scientific Revolution" has been used to claim that science suddenly burst forth when a weakened Christianity could no longer prevent it, and as the recovery of classical learning made it possible. Both claims are as false as those concerning Columbus and the flat earth. First of all, classical learning did not provide an appropriate model for science. Second, the rise of science was already far along by the sixteenth century, having been carefully nurtured by devout Scholastics in that most Christian invention, the university. As Alfred W. Crosby pointed out, "in our time the word *medieval* is often used as a synonym for muddle-headedness, but it can be more accurately used to indicate precise definition and meticulous reasoning, that is to say, *clarity*" (his emphasis).[42] Granted that the era of scientific discovery that occurred in the sixteenth and seventeenth centuries was indeed marvelous, the cultural equivalent of the blossoming of a rose. However, just as roses do not spring up overnight but must undergo a long period of normal growth before they even bud, so, too, the blossoming of science was the result of centuries of normal intellectual progress, which is why I am unwilling to refer to a "Scientific Revolution" without putting the term in quotation marks. Copernicus provides an unsurpassed example of this point.[43]

The Copernican "Revolution" as Normal Science

All discussions of the "Scientific Revolution" begin with Copernicus, almost as if his use of the word *Revolutions* in the title of his famous work had referred to drastic social changes rather than to celestial orbits. According to popular accounts, Nicolaus Copernicus (*1473–1543*) was an obscure Catholic canon in far-off Poland, an isolated genius who somehow "discovered" that, contrary to what everyone had always believed, the earth revolves around the sun. As A. D. White told it:

> [A]t length appeared, far from the centres of thought, on the borders of Poland, a plain, simple-minded scholar, who first fairly uttered to the modern world the truth—now so commonplace, then so astounding—that the sun and planets do not revolve around the earth, but the earth and planets revolve about the sun.[44]

Then, the popular account continues, the Church made unrelenting efforts to suppress these views, and it was only through the more enlightened auspices of Protestantism that the "truth" survived.

There is far more fiction than fact in this account. First of all, Copernicus received a superb education. He took his first degree at Cracow, one of the greatest universities of that time, and then spent another three and a half years at the University of Bologna, possibly the best university in Europe. Next, he spent about four years at the University in Padua, interrupted by a brief visit to the University of Ferrara, where he received the degree of doctor of canon law. Second, the notion that the earth circles the sun did not come to him out of the blue; rather, Copernicus was *taught* the essential fundamentals leading to the heliocentric model by his Scholastic professors. That is, the heliocentric model was developed gradually by a succession of then-famous (but now sadly neglected) Scholastic scientists over the previous two centuries, their conclusions about mechanics being so well formulated that "Copernicus could not improve upon them."[45] For all the profundity of his contribution, Copernicus is best understood as having added the implicit next step.

The Greeks believed that vacuums were impossible, and that the universe was a sphere filled with transparent matter. Consequently, because of friction, the continuing motion of the heavenly bodies required the continuous application of force. This was reaffirmed by the Christian scholar (and creator of the first Christian calendar) Dionysius Exiguus (*ca. 500–560*), who also proposed that the continuing force was provided by angelic beings who pushed each sphere along. Saint Thomas Aquinas (*1225–1274*) identified God as the Prime Mover but retained the angelic pushers. However, William of Ockham (*ca. 1295–1349*) disputed this view, arguing that a body in motion may not require continuous pushing. This was because he believed space to be a vacuum: once a heavenly body had been set in motion (by the will of God), it encountered no friction and probably would remain in motion. Ockham's views were discussed and extended by his colleagues at Oxford, most notably by Walter Burley (*1275–1357*) and Walter Heytesbury (*1330–1371*), but it was at the University of Paris that Ockham's ideas had the most impact.

Jean Buridan was rector of the University of Paris and a major figure in Scholastic science. Recall his demolition of Aristotle's notion that projectiles are propelled by the air closing in behind them. That was but a fragment of his truly impressive work on mechanics, especially on motion and impetus. The following passage displays his skill at disarming theological critics and his understanding of inertia, thus anticipating Newton's First Law of Motion:

> Also, since the Bible does not state that appropriate intelligences move the celestial bodies, it could be said that it does not appear necessary to posit intelligences of this kind, because it would be answered that God, when He created the world, moved each of the celestial orbs as He pleased, in moving them He impressed upon them impetuses which moved them without His having to move them any more . . . And these impetuses which He impressed in the celestial bodies were not decreased nor corrupted afterwards because

> there was no inclination of the celestial bodies for other movements. Nor was there resistance which could be corruptive or repressive of that impetus.[46]

Buridan also wrote a long discussion on the proposition that the earth turns on its axis, thus creating the appearance that other heavenly bodies such as the sun and moon rise and set. He particularly emphasized that it is more parsimonious to assume that the earth rotates, as this would require far less velocity than would be needed to enable the distant bodies to circle the earth. However, Buridan left his proposition about the earth's revolutions as a hypothetical.

Buridan's successor took impetus theory even further and also extended his discussion of the earth's rotation, noting that "it seems to me that it is possible to embrace the argument . . . that the earth turns rather than the heavens."[47] Nicole d'Oresme (*1325–1382*) was perhaps the most brilliant of all Scholastic scientists, and, after serving as rector of the University of Paris, he completed his career as bishop of Lisieux. His work is remarkably mathematical, thereby setting a high standard for subsequent studies of mechanics and astronomy.[48] The idea that the earth turns had, of course, occurred to many observant people over the centuries, but two objections had always made any motion of the earth seem unlikely. First, why wasn't there a constant and powerful wind from the east, caused by the rotation of the world in that direction? Second, why did an arrow shot straight up into the air not fall well behind (or in front of) the shooter? Since this does not happen, since the arrow comes straight back down, the earth cannot turn. However, building on Buridan's work, Oresme overcame both of these objections. There is no wind from the east because the motion of the earth is imparted to all objects on the earth or close by, including the atmosphere. That also answers the second objection: arrows shot into the air not only have vertical impetus imposed on them by the bow; they also have horizontal impetus conferred on them by the turning earth.

Oresme was succeeded as rector of the University of Paris by Albert of Saxony (*ca. 1316–1390*). He also pursued impetus theory and taught an early approximation of Newton's First Law, noting that this eliminated the need for angelic pushers. "Thus it could be said that the First Cause created the celestial orbs and impressed one such motive quality on each of them, which moves the orb." This initial impression of force remains sufficient because there is no resistance in space and no other force "toward any opposite motion."[49]

As university professors began to teach that sunrise and sunset could be caused by the daily rotation of the earth, it was no longer necessary to assume that the sun circled the earth—the notion of a heliocentric solar system became increasingly plausible and inviting. Then came Nicholas of Cusa (*1401–1464*), who also became a bishop and also taught that the earth turns as a result of "an impetus conferred upon it at the beginning of time." Having noted that, "as we see from its shadow in eclipses, . . . the earth is smaller than the sun" but larger than the moon or Mercury, Nicholas went on to observe (as had Buridan and Oresme) that "whether a man is on the earth, or the sun, or some other star, it will always seem to him that the position he occupies is the motionless centre, and that all other things are in motion."[50] It followed that humans need not trust their perception that the earth is stationary; perhaps it isn't.

All of this prior theorizing was known to Copernicus. Albert of Saxony's *Physics* was among the early printed books, the first edition having been published in Padua in 1493, just prior to Copernicus's becoming a student there.

What, then, did Copernicus contribute? Very little more than to propose a model of the solar system with the sun in the center, circled by the planets. Everything else included in *De revolutionibus orbium coelestium* was wrong! What made the book more than merely a new concept was that Copernicus "express[ed] himself chiefly in mathematics, the native tongue of science."[51] Thus he fully worked out the geometry of his system, providing a method of calculating future positions—essential for setting the date of Easter, the solstices, and the like. However, his system did not yield results more accurate than those produced by the earth-centered system created by Ptolemy in the second century, which had guided Europe's celestial calculations ever since. The Copernican system was no improvement in that respect because he failed to recognize that the planetary orbits are ellipses, not circles. Here he may have been misled by having too much respect for Greek philosophy, which held that the motion of the heavenly bodies must be circular since that is the ideal shape. Consequently, like Ptolemy, Copernicus had to clutter his model with epicycles (loops) in the orbits to obtain reasonably accurate calculations—he ended up with even more loops in his model than had Ptolemy.[52] Indeed, Copernicus failed to progress beyond Ptolemy and the ancient Greeks in that he, too, postulated that the planets did not move through space as such but were encased in "huge rotating spheres" or shells that held them in place.[53] Actually, according to Copernicus it was the *spheres* that rotated

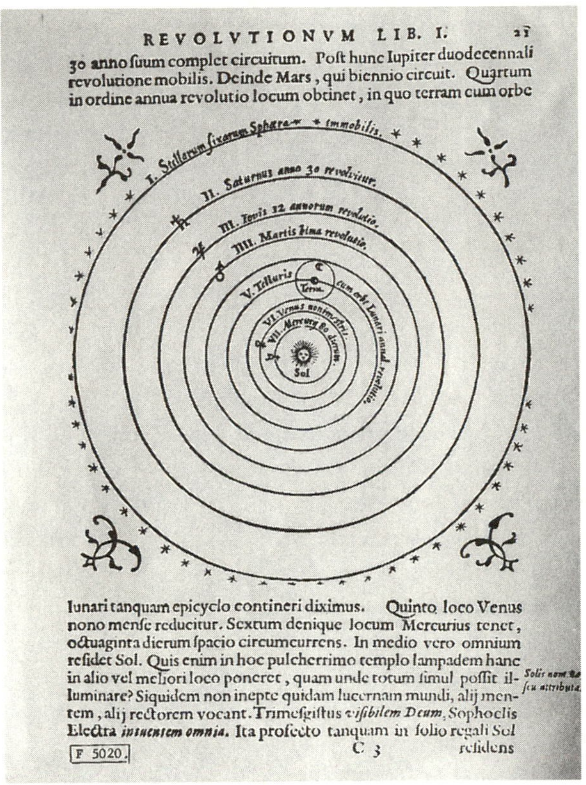

REVOLVTIONVM LIB. I. 21

30 anno ſuum complet circuitum. Poſt hunc Iupiter duodecennali revolutione mobilis. Deinde Mars, qui biennio circuit. Quartum in ordine annua revolutio locum obtinet, in quo terram cum orbe

lunari tanquam epicyclo contineri diximus. Quinto loco Venus nono menſe reducitur. Sextum denique locum Mercurius tenet, octuaginta dierum ſpacio circumcurrens. In medio vero omnium reſidet Sol. Quis enim in hoc pulcherrimo templo lampadem hanc in alio vel meliori loco poneret, quam unde totum ſimul poſſit illuminare? Siquidem non inepte quidam lucernam mundi, alij mentem, alij rectorem vocant. Trimeſgiſtus *viſibilem Deum*, Sophoclis Electra *intuentem omnia*. Ita profecto tanquam in ſolio regali Sol reſidens

Solis nom... ſeu attributa.

F 5020. C 3

The Copernican "Revolution." A diagram of the solar system as it appeared in Copernicus's famous work. The sun is in the center, but the shape of the orbits and the relative distances from the sun are completely inaccurate. © Bettmann/CORBIS.

around the sun—the "Celestial Spheres" in his book's title are not planets, and the circles in his drawings do not designate planetary orbits. Both represent the solid spheres within which he thought the heavenly bodies are embedded.[54]

Thus the "Scientific Revolution" does not begin with Copernicus. As the distinguished I. Bernard Cohen put it, "In short, the idea that a Copernican revolution in science occurred goes counter to the evidence . . . and is an invention of later historians."[55] Many contemporary historians of science agree.[56] If one does not want to acknowledge that the rise of scientific astronomy was begun by Scholastics, then the beginnings of the field must be moved forward in time to the work of Johannes Kepler (*1571–1630*), whose elegant model got everything right that Copernicus had gotten wrong. Even so, Kepler fits far better into a historical model of normal scientific progression, in which Copernicus played a significant role, than into a revolutionary model.

One reason history has paid so little attention to the work that prepared the way for Copernicus is that he failed to acknowledge these debts in his famous book (while Kepler's book gave Copernicus lavish praise). This omission was in no way unusual; it simply was not typical in this era to give much credit to predecessors. Thus for example, Galileo falsely presented the telescope as his own invention, and Newton went to great lengths to erase traces of his debts to Descartes.[57] But the more important reason Copernicus has been presented as a lone genius who revolutionized science is that it suited the ideological agenda of those who were (and remain) determined to impose notions concerning an "Enlightenment" and a "Renaissance" on Western history. Of this, much more later.

Finally, the Protestants did not save the concept of a heliocentric solar system from Catholics bent on suppressing it as a heretical notion. Luther was as appalled by the suggestion that the earth was not the center of the universe as was the pope. The heliocentric model was saved by determined and very devout scholars, both Protestants and Catholics.

Scholastic Universities

From Ockham through Copernicus, the development of the heliocentric model of the solar system was the product of the universities, which, as noted in Chapter 1, were a Christian invention. From the start, the medieval university was a place created and run by scholars and devoted entirely to knowledge. I cannot improve on Marcia L. Colish's description of the Scholastics who founded the university:

> They reviewed past authorities and current opinions, giving [their] analysis of them and [their] reasons for rejecting some and accepting others. Altogether, the methodology already in place by the early twelfth century shows the scholastics' willingness, and readiness, to criticize the foundation documents in their respective fields. More than simply receiving and expanding on the classical and Christian traditions, they set aside ideas from these traditions deemed to have outlived their usefulness. They also freely realigned the authorities they retained to defend positions that these authorities might well

> have thought strange and novel. [Commentaries] were now rarely mere summaries and explications of their author's views. Scholastic commentators were much more likely to take issue with their chosen author or to bring to bear on his work ideas from emerging schools of thought or the scholastic's own opinions.[58]

This intellectual style was encouraged by the governance of the university. Like the trade and craft guilds, the faculty at medieval universities controlled entry to their ranks and set their own standards of competence and achievement. The autonomy of universities often had to be defended, but it strikes the modern reader as quite amazing just how independent, indeed privileged, these medieval institutions managed to be. In the words of Nathan Schachner:

> The University was the darling, the spoiled child of the Papacy and Empire, of king and municipality alike. Privileges were showered on the proud Universities in a continuous golden stream; privileges that had no counterpart, then, before, or since. Not even the sacred hierarchies of the Church had quite the exemptions of the poorest begging scholar who could claim protection of a University. Municipalities competed violently for the honour of housing one within their walls; kings wrote siren letters to entice discontented groups of scholars from the domains of their rivals; Popes intervened with menacing language to compel royalty to respect the inviolability of this favoured institution.[59]

Among these privileges was clerical status. Although they need not be ordained or in holy orders (and most were not), students and faculty were accorded the rights of clergy, including the right to be tried only in an ecclesiastical court (where punishments were usually far milder than in civil courts), and physical attacks on them carried the same severe penalties as were imposed on those who attacked priests. Universities also had the acknowledged right to move elsewhere as their faculties saw fit, which resulted in a potent bargaining position for local economic and political advantages (college towns often paid all faculty salaries).

The autonomy of individual faculty members also benefited from their amazingly frequent moves from one university to another, despite the rather primitive means of transportation and communication. Since all instruction was in Latin, scholars were able to move without regard for linguistic boundaries. And because their degrees were mutually recognized, they were qualified to join any faculty. Indeed, it was a time when all the leading scholars knew of one another—many had actually met and all had many mutual acquaintances. And one gained fame and invitations to join faculties elsewhere by *innovation.* Chapter 1 examined the profound impact of the search for innovations among university theologians, including Wyclif, Hus, Erasmus, Luther, and Calvin. In similar fashion, it was in the universities that Scholastics began the rise of science. As for familiarity with Aristotle, Plato, Euclid, and the other stalwarts of classical learning, it was in the Scholastic universities, not later in the salons of the *philosophes* or during the Italian "Renaissance," that the classics were restored to intellectual importance. In part, this depended on the breaking of the "Greek barrier."

Greek, not Latin, was the intellectual language of classical times. Roman intellectuals actually spoke Greek more often than they did Latin, and therefore the intellectual legacies of Greek learning remained in Greek. Plato, Aristotle, and the like were never really lost or forgotten after the decline of Rome, but they were unreadable in a Europe where only a few scholars knew Greek. This impediment was overcome when, "between 1125 and 1200, a veritable flood of translations into Latin, made Greek . . . [scholarship] available, with more to come in the thirteenth century."[60] Notice that these translations of classical scholarship were not the work of Humanists rebelling against the "long night" of Christian ignorance. The "rediscovery" was accomplished by exceedingly pious Christian scholars in their newly created universities.

Some historians have attributed the revival of classical learning to the fall of Constantinople, which, in 1453, caused many Byzantine scholars to flee to Italy, bringing the ancient authors with them. This claim helps to authenticate the Italian "Renaissance," but it is bad history. Western Scholastics had been reading, translating, citing, and disputing all of the important classical authors for centuries before any émigré Byzantine scholars came west. Indeed, many library catalogs from the twelfth through the fourteen century have survived and reveal substantial classical holdings—"To take one example, the library of Mont-Saint-Michel in the twelfth century contained texts of Cato, Plato's *Timaeus* (in Latin translation), various works by Aristotle and Cicero, extracts from Virgil and Horace."[61] As for the Italian "Renaissance," it was not a "rediscovery" of classical learning. Rather, it was a period of cultural emulation during which people of fashion copied the classical style in manners, art, literature, and philosophy—in Florence, each year Lorenzo de' Medici (*1449–1492*) gave a banquet to celebrate Plato's birthday. Out of this passion for their own ancient days of glory, Italians began to claim that Western history consisted of "two periods of light: antiquity and the Renaissance . . . and between the two . . . crude centuries and obscure times."[62] Thus from stylish enthusiasm and ethnic pride was born the notion of the Dark Ages followed by a dawning of a new enlightenment. But it wasn't so. Scholastics knew and understood the work of Plato, Aristotle, and all the rest.

Scholastic Empiricism

Nor were these devout scholars intimidated by classical learning. We have already seen how Scholastics such as Jean Buridan and Nicole d'Oresme rejected many major claims made by classical writers. The case of Albertus Magnus (*1205–1280*) is also exemplary. Probably no one else did nearly so much to "put Western Christendom in touch with the Aristotelian tradition."[63] But Albertus was not content simply to expound Aristotle. Rather, he supplemented and corrected Aristotle to the best of his ability. Consequently, he attempted to subject Aristotle's empirical claims (and those of others as well) to observational testing when possible, frequently finding them to be in error. Along the way Albertus Magnus became "perhaps the best field botanist of the entire Middle Ages,"[64] instituting a tradition of research leading directly to the breakthroughs in biology and physiology made during the sixteenth and seventeenth centuries.

Albertus was not alone in his commitment to careful empiricism. Consider developments in the study of human physiology. It was the Scholastics, not the Greeks, Romans, Muslims, or Chinese, who based their studies on *human dissection*.[65] Just as everyone has been taught the falsehood about Columbus and the flat earth, hardly anyone knows the truth about dissection and the medieval Church, and for the same reasons.

Human dissection was not permitted in the classical world, which is why Greco-Roman works on anatomy are so faulty. Aristotle's studies were limited entirely to animal dissections, as were those of Celsius and Galen. Celsius claimed that three centuries before his time, several Greek physicians in Alexandria may have dissected a few slaves and criminals. Otherwise "in the classical period the dignity of the human body forbade dissection."[66] Human dissection was also prohibited in Islam. Then came the Christian universities and with them a new outlook on dissection. The starting assumption was that what is unique to humans is a soul, not a physiology. Dissections of the human body, therefore, are not different from studies of animal bodies and have no theological implications. From this assumption two additional justifications of dissection were advanced. The first was forensic. Too many murderers escaped detection because the bodies of their victims were not subjected to a careful postmortem. The second concerned human welfare—that no adequate medical knowledge could be acquired without direct observation of human anatomy.

Thus, in the thirteenth century, local officials (especially in Italian university towns) began to authorize a postmortem in instances when the cause of death was uncertain. Then, late in the century, Mondino de' Luzzi (*ca. 1270–1326*) wrote a textbook on dissection, based on his study of two female cadavers.[67] Subsequently, in about 1315, he performed a human dissection in front of an audience of students and faculty at the University of Bologna. From there, human dissection spread quite rapidly throughout the Italian universities. Public dissections began in Spain in 1391, and the first one in Vienna was conducted in 1404.[68] Nor were these rare occurrences—dissection became a customary part of anatomy classes. In about 1504, Copernicus took part in human dissections during his brief enrollment in medical courses at the University of Padua.[69] The "introduction [of human dissection] into the Latin west, made without serious objection from the Church, was a momentous occurrence."[70]

Nevertheless, A. D. White wrote indignantly about how the great physiologist Andreas Vesalius (*1514–1564*) "risked the most terrible dangers, and especially the charge of sacrilege, founded upon the teachings of the Church" by conducting human dissections. White went on to claim that anyone who dissected a human body at this time risked "excommunication," but that the heroic Vesalius "broke without fear" from "this sacred conventionalism" and proceeded "despite ecclesiastical censure . . . No peril daunted him."[71] All this was alleged to have taken place two centuries *after* human dissection began at the universities where Vesalius learned and then practiced his anatomical craft! This is not a fact only recently brought to light. Writing in the early 1920s, Charles Singer, one of the first historians of medicine, thought it so well known as to need no documentation that "although Vesalius profoundly altered the attitude towards biological phenomena, he yet prosecuted his researches undisturbed by the ecclestiastical authorities."[72]

White also failed to convey the immense fame and recognition Vesalius's work received immediately upon publication. Nor did White deign to report that Charles V, the Holy Roman Emperor, responded to Vesalius's

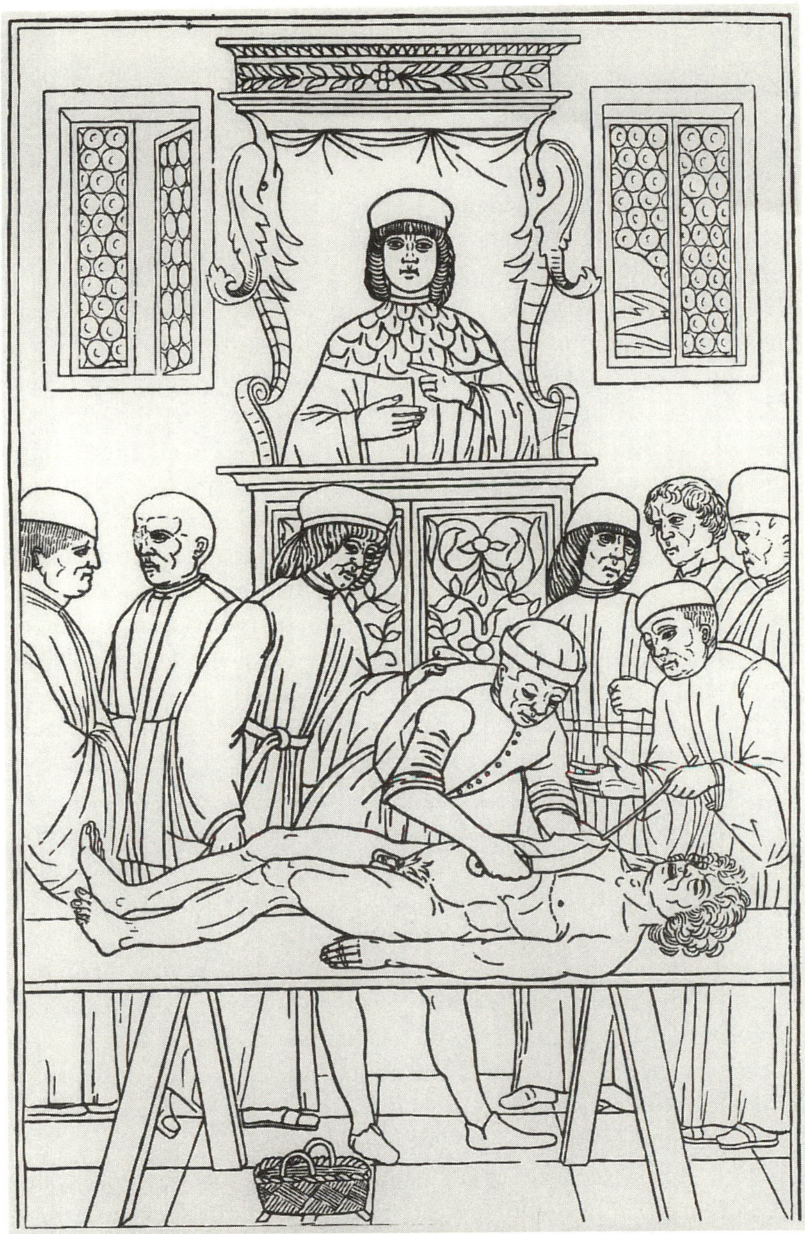

Autopsy. This woodcut published in 1493 shows a postmortem being held in an Italian courtroom. Dissections of the human body, for both legal and scientific reasons, had begun about two centuries earlier without opposition from the Church. © Christel Gerstenberg/CORBIS.

"sacrilege" by ennobling him as a count and awarding him a lifetime pension. Thereafter, the young anatomist took up residence at the court of Phillip II in Spain, and this during the most active period of heresy-hunting by the local inquisitors! As for Vesalius's religious views, he died while returning from a pilgrimage to the Holy Land.[73] Thus we uncover another of White's bogus accounts of the unrelenting religious opposition to science. And, like the tale about Columbus, it has had a deep and twisted effect on our intellectual culture.[74]

The commitment to empiricism was vital to the rise of Western science. Thus, continuing in this tradition, Johannes Kepler produced the first accurate model of the solar system. Long and careful observations prompted Kepler to conceive of the planetary orbits as elliptical, not circular, whereupon entirely accurate orbital calculations could be made quite simply, without a need to assume epicycles. Kepler's breakthrough also made it possible for the first time to accurately explain the seasons, as earth's elliptical orbit placed it at different distances from the sun during the course of the year. Fully scientific astronomy had been achieved.

However, the focus thus far on universities, on innovation, and on empiricism has neglected the truly important question: why were the Scholastics and later Europeans interested in science at all?

At first glance, that would seem a foolish question. Isn't the rise of science a normal aspect of cultural progress, of the rise of civilizations? Not at all. Many quite sophisticated societies did not generate communities of scientists or produce a body of systematic theory and empirical observations that qualify as science. Although China was quite civilized during many centuries when Europeans were still rude savages, the Chinese failed to develop science.[75] Similarly, although in full possession of the whole corpus of Greco-Roman scholarship, and having made some impressive advances in mathematics, Islamic scholars did not become scientists. Once they had mastered the classic texts, Muslim scholars were content with the role of exegetes and added little or nothing of their own. Nor did science arise in ancient India or Egypt. And while classical Greece had considerable learning, it did not have science.

As noted, science consists of an organized (that is, sustained and systematic) and empirically oriented effort to explain natural phenomena—a cumulative process of theory construction and theory testing. This enterprise arose only once. As the historian Edward Grant explained, "it is indisputable that modern science emerged in the seventeenth century in Western Europe and nowhere else."[76] Other leading historians and sociologists of science may date the rise of science somewhat earlier, but all of them agree that it was a development unique to Europe.[77]

The crucial question is: Why?

The Christian Difference

My answer to this question is as brief as it is unoriginal: Christianity depicted God as a rational, responsive, dependable, and omnipotent being and the universe as his personal creation, thus having a rational, lawful, stable structure, awaiting human comprehension.

As Nicole Oresme put it, God's creation "is much like that of a man making a clock and letting it run and continue its own motion by itself."[78] Or, in the words of Psalm 119:89–90: "For ever, O Lord, thy word is settled in heaven. Thy faithfulness is unto all generations: thou hast established the earth, and it abideth." Among the scriptural passages most frequently quoted by medieval scholars is the line from the Wisdom of Solomon (11:20) "[T]hou hast ordered all things in measure and number and weight."

In contrast with the dominant religious and philosophical doctrines in the non-Christian world, Christians developed science because they *believed* it *could* be done, and *should* be done. As Alfred North Whitehead (*1861–1947*) put it during one of his Lowell Lectures at Harvard in 1925, science arose in Europe because of the widespread "faith in the possibility of science . . . derivative from medieval theology."[79] Whitehead's pronouncement shocked not only his distinguished audience but Western intellectuals in general once his lectures had been published. How could this great philosopher and mathematician, coauthor with Bertrand Russell of the landmark *Principia Mathematica* (1910–1913), make such an outlandish claim? Did he not know that religion is the mortal enemy of scientific inquiry?

Whitehead knew better. He had grasped that Christian theology was essential for the rise of science in the West, just as surely as non-Christian theologies had stifled the scientific quest everywhere else. As he explained:

> I do not think, however, that I have even yet brought out the greatest contribution of medievalism to the formation of the scientific movement. I mean the inexpugnable belief that every detailed occurrence can be correlated with its antecedents in a perfectly definite manner, exemplifying general principles.

> Without this belief the incredible labours of scientists would be without hope. It is this instinctive conviction, vividly poised before the imagination, which is the motive power of research:—that there is a secret, a secret which can be unveiled. How has this conviction been so vividly implanted in the European mind?
>
> When we compare this tone of thought in Europe with the attitude of other civilisations when left to themselves, there seems but one source of its origin. It must come from the medieval insistence on the rationality of God, conceived as with the personal energy of Jehovah and with the rationality of a Greek philosopher. Every detail was supervised and ordered: the search into nature could only result in the vindication of the faith in rationality. Remember that I am not talking of the explicit beliefs of a few individuals. What I mean is the impress on the European mind arising from the unquestioned faith of centuries. By this I mean the instinctive tone of thought and not a mere creed of words.[80]

Whitehead ended with the remark that the images of Gods found in other religions, especially in Asia, are too impersonal or too irrational to have sustained science. Any particular "occurrence might be due to the fiat of an irrational despot" God, or might be produced by "some impersonal, inscrutable origin of things. There is not the same confidence as in the intelligible rationality of a personal being."[81]

Indeed, most non-Christian religions do not posit a creation at all: the universe is eternal and, while it may pursue cycles, it is without beginning or purpose, and, most important of all, having never been created, it has no Creator. Consequently, the universe is thought to be a supreme mystery, inconsistent, unpredictable, and arbitrary. For those holding these religious premises, the path to wisdom is through meditation and mystical insights, and there is no occasion to celebrate reason.

In contrast, many central aspects of Christian theology were produced by reasoning. Thus did Tertullian (*ca. 160–225*), one of the earliest Christian theologians, instruct that "reason is a thing of God, inasmuch as there is nothing which God the Maker of all has not provided, disposed, ordained by reason—nothing which He has not willed should be handled and understood by reason."[82] Several centuries later Saint Augustine (*354–430*) held that reason was indispensable to faith: "Heaven forbid that God should hate in us that by which he made us superior to the animals! Heaven forbid that we should believe in such a way as not to accept or seek reasons, since we could not even believe if we did not possess rational souls." Of course, Christian theologians accepted that God's word must be believed even if the reasons were not apparent. Again Augustine: "[I]n certain matters pertaining to the doctrine of salvation that we cannot yet grasp by reason—though one day we shall be able to do so—faith must precede reason and purify the heart and make it fit to receive and endure the great light of reason." Then he added that although it is necessary "for faith to precede reason in certain matters of great moment that cannot yet be grasped, surely the very small portion of reason that persuades us of this must precede faith.[83]

Perhaps the most remarkable aspect of these passages from Augustine is the optimism that one day reason will triumph. In addition to regarding it as the duty of theologians to seek to understand God's will, the weight of opinion in the early and medieval Church was that there was also a duty to understand, the better to marvel at, God's handiwork. As Saint Bonaventure (*1221–1274*) explained, it is the purpose of science that "God may be honored."[84]

Saint Thomas Aquinas (*ca. 1225–1274*) attempted to fulfill Augustine's optimism that some of these "matters of great importance" could be grasped by reason in his monumental *Summa Theologiae*, which remains the definitive explanation of many points of Catholic doctrine. Aquinas argued that because humans lack sufficient intellect to see directly into the essence of things, it is necessary for them to reason their way to knowledge, step-by-step. Thus although Aquinas regarded theology as the highest of the sciences since it deals directly with divine revelations, he advocated the use of the tools of philosophy, especially the principles of logic, in the endeavor to construct theology.[85]

The critical point in all of this is methodological. Centuries of meditation will produce no empirical knowledge, let alone science. But to the extent that religion inspires efforts to comprehend God's handiwork, knowledge will be forthcoming, and science arises as "the handmaiden" of theology. And that's precisely how not only the Scholastic scientists but also those who took part in the great achievements of the sixteenth and seventeenth centuries saw themselves—as in pursuit of the secrets of the Creation. Charles Webster has summed up the consensus among recent historians of science:

> Any truly historical account . . . must pay due attention to the deep interpenetration of scientific and religious ideas. It would seem perverse to deny religious motivation in the numerous cases where this was made explicit

by the scientists themselves, often with painful emphasis. No direction of energy toward science was undertaken without the assurance of Christian conscience.[86]

The Negative Cases

Before ending this discussion, however, I must demonstrate the negative—that the critical religious ideas were lacking in societies that seem otherwise to have had the potential to develop science but did not. Keep in mind that I am arguing only that a particular conception of a Creator was *necessary* for the rise of science, not that it was a sufficient cause. Were a Stone Age culture fully converted to Christianity, one still would not anticipate that they would evolve science anytime soon. Many other cultural and social developments were necessary for the rise of science. Hence negative cases are those in which, if religion is ignored, one might have expected them to become scientific. In my estimation there are three such cases: China, Greece, and Islam.

China

Only three years before his coauthor Alfred North Whitehead proposed that Christianity provided the psychological basis for the pursuit of science, Bertrand Russell found the lack of Chinese science rather baffling. From the perspective of his militant atheism, China should have had science long before Europe. As he explained, "Although Chinese civilization has hitherto been deficient in science, it never contained anything hostile to science, and therefore the spread of scientific knowledge encounters no such obstacles as the Church put in its way in Europe."[87]

But despite Russell's confidence that since it was not afflicted by the Church, China would soon far surpass Western science,[88] he failed to see that it was precisely religious obstacles that had prevented Chinese science. Although through the centuries the common people of China have worshiped an elaborate array of Gods, each of small scope and often rather lacking in character, the intellectuals have prided themselves on following "Godless" religions, wherein the supernatural is conceived of as an essence or principle governing life, but which is impersonal, remote, and definitely not a being. The Tao is an example of an essence; yin and yang represent a principle. Just as small Gods do not create a universe, neither do impersonal essences or principles—indeed, they seem unable to *do* anything. Thus as conceived by Chinese philosophers, the universe simply is and always was. There is no reason to suppose that it functions according to rational laws, or that it could be comprehended in physical rather than mystical terms. Consequently, through the millennia Chinese intellectuals pursued "enlightenment," not explanations. This is precisely the conclusion reached by the Marxist historian Joseph Needham, who devoted most of his career and many volumes to the history of Chinese technology. Having exhausted attempts to discover a materialist explanation, Needham concluded that the failure of the Chinese to develop science was due to their religion, to the inability of Chinese intellectuals to believe in the existence of laws of nature, because "the conception of a divine celestial lawgiver imposing ordinances on non-human Nature never developed." Needham continued: "It was not that there was no order in Nature for the Chinese, but rather that it was not an order ordained by a rational personal being, and hence there was no conviction that rational personal beings would be able to spell out in their lesser earthly languages the divine code of laws which he had decreed aforetime. The Taoists, indeed, would have scorned such an idea as being too naïve for the subtlety and complexity of the universe as they intuited it."[89] Exactly.

Several years ago my friend Graeme Lang dismissed the notion that the influence of Confucianism and Taoism on Chinese intellectuals was the reason that science failed to develop in China; his grounds were that all culture is flexible, and that "if scholars in China had wanted to do science, philosophy alone would not have been a serious impediment."[90] Perhaps. But Lang missed the more basic question: why didn't Chinese scholars *want* to do science? And, with Whitehead and Needham (and many others), I agree that it didn't occur to the Chinese that science was *possible*. Fundamental theological and philosophical assumptions determine whether anyone will attempt to do science.

Greece

For centuries the ancient Greeks seemed on the verge of achieving science. They were interested in explaining the natural world with suitably abstract, general principles. Some of them were careful, systematic observers of nature—although Socrates considered empiricism such as astronomical observations a "waste of time," and Plato agreed, advising his students to approach astronomy through philosophy and to "leave the starry heavens alone."[91] And, like the Scholastics, the Greeks formed coordinated scholarly networks—the famous "schools." But in the end all they achieved were nonempirical, even antiempirical, speculative philosophies, atheoretical collections of facts, and isolated crafts and technologies—they never broke through to real science.

Three factors prevented the Greeks from achieving science. First, their conceptions of the Gods were inadequate to permit them to imagine a conscious Creator. Second, they conceived of the universe not only as eternal and uncreated, but as locked into endless cycles of progress and decay. Third, prompted by their religious conceptions, they transformed inanimate objects into living creatures capable of aims, emotions, and desires—thus short-circuiting the search for physical theories.[92]

To begin with their conception of the Gods—none of the numerous divinities in the Greek pantheon was a suitable creator of a lawful universe, not even Zeus. As were humans, the Gods were subject to the inexorable workings of the natural cycles of all things. Some Greek scholars, including Aristotle *(384–322 B.C.E.)*, did posit a "God" of infinite scope having charge of the universe, but they conceived of this "God" as essentially an essence much like the Tao. Such a "God" lent a certain spiritual aura to a cyclical universe and its ideal, abstract properties, but being an essence, "God" *did* nothing and never had. Plato *(ca. 427–347 B.C.E.)* posited a sort of Godly being called the Demiurge who was the personification of reason. The Demiurge attempted to construct a cosmos that would fully achieve the ideals of the good, the true, and the beautiful, but insofar as this "being" had to work with already existing materials having properties (especially defects) over which the Demiurge had no control, the results fell far short of the intended ideal.

Many scholars doubt that Plato really meant for the existence of the Demiurge to be taken literally.[93] But whether meant as the depiction of a real creator God or as a metaphor, Plato's Demiurge pales in contrast with a God who is not only the master but the Creator of all materials, having made the universe out of nothing. Moreover, Plato proposed that the universe had been created, not in accord with firm operating principles, but in accord with ideals. These consisted primarily of ideal shapes. Thus the universe must be a sphere because that is the symmetrical and perfect shape, and heavenly bodies must rotate in a circle because that is the motion that is most perfect.[94] Composed of a priori assumptions, Platonic idealism was a severe impediment to discovery. For example, the unshakable belief in ideal shapes prevented Copernicus from entertaining the thought that planetary orbits *might not* be circular.

In many ways it is strange that the Greeks sought knowledge and technology at all, having rejected the idea of progress in favor of a never-ending cycle of being. Plato at least proposed that the universe had been created, but most Greek scholars assumed that the universe was uncreated and eternal. Aristotle condemned the idea "that the universe came into being at some point in time . . . as unthinkable."[95] Although the Greeks saw the universe as eternal and unchanging, they did concede the obvious fact that history and culture are ever-changing, *but* only within the strict confines of endless repetition. In *On the Heavens*, Aristotle noted that "the same ideas recur to men not once or twice but over and over again," and in his *Politics* he pointed out that everything has "been invented several times over in the course of ages, or rather times without number"; since he was living in a Golden Age, current levels of technology were at the maximum attainable level. As for inventions, so, too, for individuals—the same persons would be born again and again as the blind cycles of the universe rolled along. According to Chrysippus (*280–207 B.C.E.*) in his now lost *On the Cosmos*, the Stoics taught that the "difference between former and actual existences of the same people will be only extrinsic and accidental; such differences do not produce another man as contrasted with his counterpart from a previous world-age."[96] As for the universe itself, according to Parmenides (*born 515 B.C.E.*) all perceptions of change are illusions, for the universe is in a static state of perfection, "uncreated and indestructible; for it is complete, immovable, and without end."[97] Other influential Greeks, such as the Ionians, taught that although the universe is infinite and eternal, it is also subject to endless cycles of succession. Plato saw things a bit differently, but he, too, firmly believed in cycles: that eternal laws caused each Golden Age to be followed by chaos and collapse.

Finally, the Greeks insisted on turning the cosmos, and inanimate objects more generally, into living things. Entirely in keeping with the animism that anthropologists of religion associate with "primitive" cultures, Plato taught that the Demiurge had created the cosmos as a living thing—writing in *Timaeus* that the world is "a single visible living creature." Hence the world has a soul, and although "solitary," it is "able by reason of its excellence to bear itself company, needing no other acquaintance or friend but sufficient to itself." Indeed, as David C. Lindberg pointed out,

"Plato assigned divinity to the world soul and considered the planets and fixed stars to be a host of celestial gods."[98]

But if mineral objects are animate, one heads in the wrong direction in attempting to explain natural phenomena—the causes of the motion of objects, for example, will be ascribed to *motives*, not to natural forces. The Stoics, particularly Zeno (*490–430* B.C.E.), may have originated the idea of explaining the operations of the cosmos on the basis of its conscious purposes, but this soon became the universal view. Thus, according to Aristotle, celestial bodies move in circles because of their affection for this action. Stanley L. Jaki pointed out that it was only by rejecting Greek, and especially Aristotelian, physics that Scholastic science could progress, by "achieving a depersonalized outlook on nature in which stones were not claimed to fall because of their innate love for the centre of the world."[99]

It is very significant that Greek learning stagnated of its own inner logic. After Plato and Aristotle, very little happened beyond some extensions of geometry. When Rome incorporated the Greek world, it fully embraced and celebrated Greek learning—Greek scholars flourished under the Republic as well as during the reign of the Caesars. But possession of Greek learning did not prompt significant intellectual progress by Romans.[100] The decline of Rome did not interrupt the expansion of human knowledge any more than the "recovery" of Greek learning enabled this process to resume. To the contrary, as will be seen, Greek learning was a *barrier* to the rise of science! It did not lead to science among the Greeks or the Romans, and it stifled intellectual progress in Islam.

Islam

It would seem that Islam has the appropriate God to underwrite the rise of science. But that's not so.[101] Allah is not presented as a lawful creator but has been conceived of as an extremely active God who intrudes on the world as he deems it appropriate. Consequently, there soon arose a major theological bloc within Islam that condemned all efforts to formulate natural laws as blasphemy insofar as they denied Allah's freedom to act. That is, Islam did not fully embrace the notion that the universe ran along on fundamental principles laid down by God at the Creation, but assumed that the world was sustained by his will on a continuing basis. This was justified by a statement in the Qur'ān: "Verily, God will cause to err whom he pleaseth, and will direct whom he pleaseth." Although the line refers to God's determination of the fate of individuals, it has been interpreted broadly to apply to all things.

If God does as he pleases, and what he pleases is variable, then the universe may not be lawful. Contrast this with the Christian conception of God as stated by the early French scientific genius René Descartes (*1596–1650*), who justified his search for natural "laws" on grounds that such laws must exist because God is perfect and therefore "acts in a manner as constant and immutable as possible," except for the rare occurrence of miracles.[102]

Whenever the subject of Islamic science and learning is raised, most historians emphasize that throughout the centuries when Christian Europe knew virtually nothing of Greek learning, that learning was alive and deeply appreciated in Islam. That is certainly true. It is even true that some classical manuscripts reached Christian Europe through Islam, especially as Christian and Muslim intellectuals had contact in Spain. But it is also true that possession of all of this "enlightenment" did not prompt much intellectual progress within Islam, let alone eventuate in Islamic science. Instead, as the devout Muslim historian Caesar E. Farah explained:

> The early Muslim thinkers took up philosophy where the Greeks left off . . . Thus in Aristotle Muslim thinkers found the great guide; to them he became the "first teacher."
>
> Having accepted this *a priori*, Muslim philosophy as it evolved in subsequent centuries merely chose to *continue* in this vein and to enlarge Aristotle rather than to innovate. It chose the course of eclecticism, seeking *to assimilate* rather than *to generate*, with a conscious striving to adapt the results of Greek thinking to Muslim philosophical conceptions, but with much greater comprehensiveness than was achieved by early Christian dogmatics.[103] (Emphasis in the original)

The result was to freeze Islamic learning and stifle all possibility of the rise of an Islamic science, and for the same reasons that Greek learning stagnated of itself: fundamental assumptions antithetical to science. It is very significant that the *Rasa'il*, the great encyclopedia of knowledge produced by early Muslim scholars, fully embraced the Greek conception of the world as a huge, conscious living organism having both intellect and soul.[104] Indeed, according to Jaki, the "Muslim notion of the Creator was not adequately rational to inspire an effective distaste for various types of pantheistic, cyclic, animistic, and magical world pictures which freely made their way into the *Rasa'il*."[105] Nor were outlooks more conducive to science achieved by Ibn Rushd, known to the West as Averroës (*1126–1198*), and his followers, despite their efforts to exclude all Muslim theology from their work, in direct conflict with those who sustained the *Rasa'il*. Instead, Averroës and his followers became intransigent and doctrinaire Aristotelians—proclaiming that his physics was complete and infallible, and if an observation were inconsistent with one of Aristotle's views, the observation was certainly incorrect or an illusion.

As a result of all this, Islamic scholars achieved significant progress only in terms of specific knowledge, such as certain aspects of astronomy and medicine, that did not necessitate any general theoretical basis. And, as time passed, even this sort of progress ceased.

Clearly, then, and contrary to the received wisdom, the "recovery" of Greek learning did not put Europe back on the track to science. Judging from the impact of this learning on the Greeks, the Romans, and the Muslims, it would seem to have been vital that Greek learning was *not* generally available until after Christian scholars had established an independent intellectual base of their own. Consequently, when they first encountered the works of Aristotle, Plato, and the rest, medieval scholars were willing and able to dispute them! As I have tried to make clear, it was in explicit opposition to Aristotle and other classical writers that the Scholastics such as Albertus, Ockham, Buridan, and Oresme advanced toward science. To the extent that he clung to Greek concepts, Copernicus fell far short of founding scientific astronomy. Because medieval scholars outside the sciences (especially those in the arts and in speculative philosophy) had become such ardent admirers of the Greco-Roman "classics," many of the great scientists of the sixteenth and seventeenth centuries often paid lip service to their "debts" to Aristotle and others, but their actual work negated almost everything the Greeks had said about how the world works.

I surely do not mean to minimize the impact of Greek learning on European intellectual life. It had an enormous influence, not only on Scholastic thought, but on many subsequent generations. However, the most antiscientific elements of Greek thought were withstood or, at worst, sequestered in the humanities, while the sciences marched on. For example, the Greek notion that the universe was eternal proved very attractive to many Scholastics. But from the start it was heatedly opposed—Saint Bonaventure ridiculed the notion on logical grounds, and it was included among the condemned propositions in the famous edict issued by the bishop of Paris in 1277.[106] Moreover, not even the most ardent Scholastic supporters of an eternal universe claimed that it was uncreated. Rather, the debate involved very subtle points of theology that affirmed the ability of God to create an eternal universe. No Scholastic Platonists ever proposed a God as limited as the Demiurge. Nor did the idea that the earth and planets were conscious beings gain much credence, let alone such notions as that they went in circles from the joy of doing so. Moreover, even long before Greco-Roman learning was confined to classics departments, it was *not* the philosophy of scientists. While it is true (and constantly cited by classicists) that Newton remarked in a letter to Robert Hooke in 1675, "If I have seen further (than you and Descartes), it is by standing on the shoulders of giants," such high regard for "the ancients" is not expressed or reflected in his work or in his usual presentations of self. Indeed, just as Newton and his peers achieved their breakthroughs in obvious opposition to the Greek "giants," their contemporaries in theology mounted their own assault on Greek learning.[107] For example, Guillaume Budé (*1467–1540*), founder of the Bibliothèque nationale in Paris, condemned Plato and Aristotle for so often writing about things they knew nothing about.[108] Luther took a similar view: "[M]y advice would be that Aristotle's Physics . . . should be altogether discarded, together with all the rest of his books which boast of treating things of nature . . . [for] nothing can be learned from them . . . I venture to say that any potter has more knowledge of nature than is written in these books."[109] Others, including Pierre De La Ramée (*1515–1572*), launched an organized repudiation of the famous Greeks as "fallible individuals, prone to human error, apparently guilty of plagiarisms on many counts," until the "old giants began to look more like modern dwarfs."[110] What the great figures involved in the sixteenth- and seventeenth-century blossoming of science—including Descartes, Galileo, Newton, and Kepler—did confess was their absolute faith in a Creator God, whose work incorporated rational rules awaiting discovery.

To sum up: the rise of science was not an extension of classical learning. It was the natural outgrowth of Christian doctrine: Nature exists because it was created by God. To love and honor God, one must fully appreciate the wonders of his handiwork. Moreover, because God is perfect, his handiwork functions in accord with *immutable principles*. By the full use of our God-given powers of reason and observation, we ought to be able to discover these principles.

These were the crucial ideas, and that's why the rise of science occurred in Christian Europe, not somewhere else.

However, some scholars have argued that not all brands of Christian theology were equally conducive to the rise of science—that it was Protestantism, especially its Puritan variety, that led to the rise of science.

Puritans and the Rise of Science

In 1938 Robert K. Merton's doctoral thesis in sociology at Harvard, submitted in 1935, was published in *Osiris*. In "Science, Technology and Society in Seventeenth Century England," Merton rejected the Marxist and secularist orthodoxies of the day that science was the triumph of irreligion, by proposing that Puritanism had given rise to the "Scientific Revolution." According to Merton, this occurred because the Puritans reasoned (and, presumably, they were the first Christians to do so) that as the world was God's handiwork, it was their duty to study and understand this handiwork as a means of glorifying God. Thus, Merton argued, among Puritan intellectuals in England during the seventeenth century, science was defined as a religious calling. Merton's argument[111] was, of course, an extension of Max Weber's claims about the role of the Protestant ethic in the rise of capitalism and, as will be seen, equally untenable.

To support his thesis, Merton combed the writings of Puritan participants in the "Scientific Revolution," finding they gave overwhelming emphasis to the principle that science consists of the study of God's handiwork for the purpose of more fully appreciating the glory of God. For example, in his last will and testament, Robert Boyle (*1627–1691*) addressed his fellow members of the Royal Society of London, wishing them all success in "their laudable attempts, to discover the true Nature of the Works of God" and "praying that they and all other Searchers into Physical Truths" may thereby add "to the Glory of the Great Author of Nature, and to the Comfort of Mankind." Indeed, since Puritans believed that work was a calling from God, these early scientists were at pains to "justify the ways of science to God."[112]

By assembling many such quotations from seventeenth-century English scientists, Merton made it entirely clear that, far from being a rejection of religion, at least in England the "Scientific Revolution" was made from religious motivations by deeply religious people. Anticipating critics who would propose that these remarks about God by early scientists were no more than the literary conventions of the times or even "calculating hypocrisy," Merton noted how many of these scientists manifested their piety in quite unambiguous actions. Boyle, for example, expended a considerable portion of his limited funds to have the Bible translated into various languages. John Ray left Cambridge because, upon the Restoration, he was unwilling on religious grounds to take the required oaths of loyalty to Charles II. Indeed, Merton dismissed all suspicions of false piety as an "unwarranted extrapolation of twentieth-century beliefs and attitudes to seventeenth-century society." Then, with uncharacteristic candor, he remarked, "Though it always serves to inflate the ego of the iconoclast . . . , 'debunking' can supplant truth with error."[113]

In addition to an analysis of Puritan theology and its implications for the study of God's handiwork, Merton presented quantitative data on the early membership of the Royal Society of London, which he interpreted in support of his claim that Puritans dominated that body, composed of the prominent English scientists of the seventeenth century.

Through the years, Merton's study has received a great deal of attention. As he knew they would, various iconoclasts have indeed suggested that since real scientists know better than to embrace religion, all signs of their piety must be fake. Fortunately, these claims have mainly been ignored by historians and sociologists of science, who have, instead, correctly concentrated on the serious flaws and inferior history of Merton's study.

Scholars now recognize that Merton's claims were much too narrow.[114] The rise of science was neither limited to the efforts of the English nor to Protestants, let alone to Puritans. Thus H. F. Kearney sketched the remarkable intellectual circle centered on Friar Marin Mersenne (*1588–1646*), who, from his convent in Paris, established a correspondence network linking

> the leading scientists of the day, irrespective of religion or nationality . . . It connected Descartes in Holland, Gassendi and Peiresc in Provence, Shickard in Tübingen, Nortensius in Leyden, Galileo in Florence and van Helmont in Brussels . . . Mersenne's correspondence in fact symbolizes the *European* nature of science . . . The intellectual Europe of the age of Galileo took no account of later national boundaries. Nor, curiously enough, do religious differences seem relevant, despite the shadow of the Thirty Years' War.[115]

Of course, this internationalism reflected the European scholarly network that had existed since the rise of universities. Much has been made of the importance of "social networks" for generating and sustaining intellectual innovations, culminating in the extraordinary work on intellectual networks by Randall Collins.[116] There have been many studies of scientific networks, a number of which have followed Merton in examining the Royal Society of London.[117] But, as has been seen, scientific networks had existed in Europe for centuries.

An equally fatal flaw in Merton's thesis is that there was nothing new or Protestant about the belief that science was possible and worthy. As has been established, science was well along before there were any Protestants, and Catholics continued to play a vital role in the scientific blossoming of the sixteenth and seventeenth centuries. Finally, it has been established that Merton's analysis is based on such a broad definition of "Puritan" that essentially no one was excluded—possibly not even Catholics.[118] In Barbara J. Shapiro's pithy summation, "what [Merton] is essentially saying is that Englishmen contributed to English science."[119]

However, not even Merton's most severe critics claim an incompatibility between religion and science. Thus it will be useful to move closer to the individuals who led the rise of science.

Scientific Stars: 1543–1680

Merton analyzed the religious orientation of members of the Royal Society of London in an attempt to support his thesis concerning the role of Puritanism. Subsequently, these data have been reworked a number of times with various results.[120] But, to the best of my knowledge, no one has undertaken anything similar for the full set of scientific stars of this era. Consequently, I created a data set consisting of individual scientists.

How should one define the appropriate population of scientific stars? That is, how shall one decide *when* and *whom*? Historians typically define the era of the "Scientific Revolution" as stretching from the publication in 1543 of Copernicus's *De revolutionibus* to the end of the seventeenth century.[121] Therefore, I selected Copernicus as my first case and included all appropriate cases, beginning with Copernicus's contemporaries and stopping with scientists born after 1680. The "whom" was a bit more difficult. First of all, I limited the set to *active scientists*, thus excluding some well-known philosophers and supporters of science such as Francis Bacon, Joseph Scaliger, and Diego de Zuñiga. Second, I tried to pick only those who made *significant* contributions. To select the cases, I searched books and articles on the history of science, and I also consulted a number of specialized encyclopedias and biographical dictionaries, among which I must mention the several editions of Isaac Asimov's *Biographical Encyclopedia of Science and Technology* for its completeness and lack of obvious biases.[122] Having developed a list of 52 scientists, I then consulted various sources, including individual biographies, to determine the facts that I wished to code for each case. The first fact I coded was nationality, and the results are as follows:

	Number	*Percent*
English*	15	28.9
French	9	17.3
Italian	8	15.4
German	7	13.5
Dutch	5	9.6
Danish	3	5.8
Flemish	2	3.8
Polish	2	3.8
Swedish	1	1.9
	52	100.0

* Including John Napier, the Scottish mathematician.

Clearly, the English did furnish far more than their share of significant early scientists. However, they made up too small a percentage of the total to justify Merton's attribution of the rise of science to the English, let alone to English Puritans.

The second fact I coded was denomination. Was this primarily a Protestant revolution?

	Number
Protestant	26
Catholic	26

Certainly not. Only half of the 52 were Protestants of any sort. Moreover, with the English removed, Catholics outnumbered Protestant scientists 26 to 11, which probably about reflects the difference in the total population of Protestants and Catholics in Europe at this time.

TABLE 2.1
Scientific Stars: 1543–1680

	Total (52)	*Protestant* (26)	*Catholic* (26)
Field			
Physics	28.8%	26.9%	30.8%
Astronomy	28.8%	34.6%	23.1%
Mathematics	23.1%	26.9%	19.2%
Biology/physiology	19.3%	11.6%	26.9%
	100.0%	100.0%	100.0%
Ecclesiastic?			
Yes	28.8%	19.2%	38.5%
Personal Piety			
Devout	61.5%	69.2%	53.9%
Conventionally religious	34.7%	27.0%	42.3%
Skeptic	3.8%	3.8%	3.8%
	100.0%	100.0%	100.0%

Table 2.1 permits examination of the distribution of three other facts I coded, and of cross-tabulations allowing comparisons of Catholics and Protestants. The data show that these 52 early scientists were fairly evenly spread across four fields, but Catholics were a bit more likely to have pursued biological-physiological studies than were Protestants. Slightly over one-fourth (15) of the 52 had ecclesiastical careers as priests, ministers, monks, canons, and the like. Catholics were more than twice as likely as Protestants to have had such a vocation.

The most challenging task was to assess personal piety. It would not do to equate piety with conformity to the prevailing orthodoxy, else one would be forced to argue that Martin Luther and John Calvin were lacking in piety. To code someone as *devout*, I searched for clear signs of especially deep religious concerns. The label of "conventionally religious" was applied to those whose biography offers no evidence of skepticism, but whose piety does not stand out as other than entirely satisfactory to their religious associates. An example is Marcello Malpighi, whose observation of the growth of a chick's heart is regarded as one of the most remarkable achievements of seventeenth-century biology. Malpighi's biography offers no direct evidence of concerns about God of an intensity similar to Boyle's or Newton's. On the other hand, he did retire to Rome to serve as the personal physician of Pope Innocent XII, a very pious Counter-Reformation pontiff, who probably expected a similar level of piety of those around him.[123] If anything, then, I have underrated Malpighi's level of personal piety; similar underestimates may be the real basis for the modest differences shown in Table 2.1 between Catholics and Protestants.

Finally, I reserved the category "skeptic" for anyone about whom we may infer a lack of belief that the world was the work of a *conscious, responsive* God—virtually any French *philosophe* would be so coded.

The most important finding in Table 2.1 is that those who made the "Scientific Revolution" included an unusually large number of devout Christians—more than 60 percent qualified as devout and only two, Edmund Halley and Paracelsus, qualified as skeptics.[124] Given Paracelsus's general exhibitionism, it is difficult to know what he actually did or didn't believe about God. We know he did profess faith in astrology and in the Hermetic form of ritual magic (see Chapter 3). As for Halley, it is likely that he was an atheist.[125] In any event, the proportion of devout is especially striking since, contrary to popular belief, even during the Middle Ages Europeans were not more devout than they are today.[126] Were there any remaining doubt about it, these data make it entirely clear that religion played a substantial role in the rise of science. (The complete list of cases and the code for each on piety is provided in Appendix 2.1.)

Galileo

But what about Galileo? The story of the persecution of Galileo Galilei (*1564–1642*) is nearly as famous as the one about Columbus and the flat earth, although in this instance the conventional version is somewhat more truthful.[127] He was in fact one of the greatest figures in the history of science, and, in his old age, he did run afoul of the Catholic Church, was forced to recant his belief that the earth moves around the sun, and was sentenced to live in seclusion for the last nine years of his life. But there is far more to the story than this, and these overlooked or ignored facts put things in a somewhat different light: that Galileo's troubles stemmed as much from his arrogance as from his scientific views. It happened this way.

Long before he ascended the throne of Peter, when he was still Cardinal Matteo Barberini, Pope Urban VIII (1623 to 1644) knew and liked Galileo. When Galileo published his *Assayer* in 1623, he dedicated it to Barberini, who is reported to have greatly enjoyed the nasty insults it directed at various Jesuit scholars. Indeed, Barberini was prompted to write an adulatory poem on the glory of astronomy. So what went wrong?

Keep in mind that this whole affair took place at a time when the Reformation stood defiant in northern Europe, the Thirty Years' War raged, and the Counter-Reformation was well underway. In these circumstances, the Catholic hierarchy became increasingly sensitive to Protestant attacks that Catholics were unfaithful to the Bible; for many Churchmen, acceptance of the Copernican conception of the solar system was a manifestation of this infidelity.[128] However, the primary issue was Church authority, and as the Counter-Reformation proceeded, the limits of orthodox theology were defined far more narrowly than they had been (Chapter 1). However, most Church leaders, including the pope, were not ready to condemn science and impose an unflinching orthodoxy. Rather, they proposed ways for scientists to sidestep theological conflict. For example, Friar Marin Mersenne advised his network of correspondents that God was free to place the earth anywhere he liked, and it was the duty of scientists to find out where he had put it.[129] Other influential Catholics were more circumspect, noting that there were no theological objections to proposing hypothetical or mathematical conclusions.

In this spirit the pope reassured Galileo that he had nothing to fear as long as he made it clear that he spoke as a mathematician, not a theologian. Specifically, Pope Urban instructed Galileo to acknowledge in his publications that "definitive conclusions could not be reached in the natural sciences. God in his omnipotence could produce a natural phenomenon in any number of ways and it was therefore presumptuous for any philosopher to claim that he had determined a unique solution."[130] It seems a simple enough dodge, akin to the "hypothetical" modifier that the Scholastics had frequently appended to their scientific works. Moreover, for a man who often made false claims to actually have performed research that was at best "hypothetical" (such as dropping weights from the Leaning Tower of Pisa), this surely did not stretch his ethical standards.

When he published his famous *Dialogue concerning the Two Chief World Systems* (in 1632), Galileo did include this formula, but he put it in the mouth of Simplicio, the dullard who voiced all of the "errors," the correction of which was the main thrust of the book. Moreover, he deceived the pope about when the book would appear, so that it came out unexpectedly, touching off a storm of controversy that required response. Understandably, the pope felt betrayed. But Galileo seems never to have understood this and was inclined to blame all his troubles on the Jesuits (who probably played no important role, despite his insults) and on true believers in Aristotle, especially professors (who had also suffered as a group from his acidic humor). Despite all this, the pope did thwart efforts to impose more serious consequences on Galileo. Even so, the scandal caused by Galileo helped to stimulate a general crackdown by the Church on intellectual freedom—albeit too late to prevent Catholic participation in the rise of science.

Although constantly offered as a prime exhibit in the case against religion, what does the Galileo affair actually reveal? It most certainly demonstrates that powerful organizations often do abuse their power. But it also shows that Galileo was not just an innocent victim: not only did he needlessly tempt fate, but he thoughtlessly placed the whole scientific enterprise itself in jeopardy. Beyond that, the case fails to show what most of the opponents of religion hope to gain from their frequent retellings. For the fact is that, despite everything, Galileo had no doubts about God and always regarded himself as a good Catholic. As William Shea noted, "Had Galileo been less devout, he could have refused to go to Rome [when summoned by the Holy Office]; Venice offered him asylum."[131] Thus there is no reason whatever to question his sincerity when he wrote that "the book of nature is a book written by the hand of God in the language of mathematics."[132] Hence the most important lesson here is to recognize that while Pope Urban VIII's religious views may have caused Galileo to suffer for his scientific views, Galileo's science did not suffer because of his own religious views.

Keep in mind that to accept, as I do, that science was the legitimate offspring of Christian theology is not to suppose that such dependency long remained. Once properly launched, science was able to stand on its own and soon developed its own motives and momentum. But, as I plan to show, these are not incompatible with religion. Moreover, when science and religion do appear to collide, questions should usually be raised about the actual scientific and/or religious standing of the matters at issue. The "Enlightenment" offers a revealing case in point.

The "Enlightenment"

The identification of the era beginning in about 1600 as the "Enlightenment" is as inappropriate as the identification of the millennium before it as the "Dark Ages." And both imputations were made by the same people—intellectuals who wished to discredit religion and especially the Roman Catholic Church, and who therefore associated faith with darkness and secular humanism with light. To these ends they sought credit for the "Scientific Revolution" (another of their concepts), even though none of them had played any significant part in the scientific enterprise.

One of the first steps in this effort was to designate their own era as the "Enlightenment," and to claim it was a sudden and complete disjuncture with the past. To this end, the "Dark Ages" were invented. Among the very first ever to do so, Voltaire (*1694–1778*) described medieval Europe as hopelessly mired in "decay and degeneracy."[133] This became the universal theme. Jean-Jacques Rousseau (*1712–1778*) wrote of previous centuries: "Europe had relapsed into the barbarism of the earliest ages. The peoples of this part of the world, so enlightened today, lived some centuries ago in a condition worse than ignorance."[134] A century later, when Jacob Burckhardt[135] (*1818–1897*) popularized the idea of the "Renaissance," the "Dark Ages" were a historical certitude, not to be shaken until late in the twentieth century.

Moreover, it was not enough to blame the "Dark Ages" on Christianity; religion must also be denied any credit for the rise of science. Hence it was necessary to discredit the achievements of the Scholastic era. In keeping with this aim, John Locke (*1632–1704*) denounced the Scholastics as hopelessly lost in a maze of trivial concerns, as "the great mintmasters" of useless terms as an "expedient to cover their ignorance."[136] In similar fashion, one after another of the *philosophes* condemned Catholic scholarship until the word "scholastic" became an epithet—defined as "pedantic and dogmatic" according to any edition of Webster.

With the past out of the way, the central aspect of the campaign by the likes of David Hume, Voltaire, and their associates consisted of wrapping themselves in the achievements of science to authenticate their condemnation of religion in general, and Catholicism very specifically. Franklin L.

Baumer noted that "the Enlightenment was a great Age of Faith." Then he asked, rhetorically, "But faith in what?" Not religion, but "belief in man's power."[137] And the proof of this power was science, which, to paraphrase Laplace, made God an unneeded hypothesis. Never mind that the actual discoveries had been made by "serious and often devout Christians."[138] What mattered was that, in the words of Peter Gay, "science could give the deists and atheists great comfort and supply them with what they wanted—Newton's physics without Newton's God."[139] Indeed, although Voltaire and his circle were careful to acknowledge Newton's commitment to a Creator (albeit only to a remote and impersonal Prime Mover), subsequent generations of "Enlightenment" ideologues took great pains to further minimize Newton's faith.

Newton Deified and Falsified

One of the first actions of those who proclaimed the "Enlightenment" was the "deification of Newton."[140] Voltaire set the example by calling him the greatest man who ever lived.[141] Thus began an unexcelled outpouring of worshipful prose and extravagant poetry. David Hume wrote that Newton was "the greatest and rarest genius that ever rose for the ornament and instruction of the species."[142] As Gay noted, "the adjectives 'divine' and 'immortal' became practically compulsory."[143] For example, in his *Panegyrick on the Newtonian Philosophy* (1750) Benjamin Martin rhapsodized, "Mystery that has been hid from Ages, and from Generations; but is now made manifest to all Nations, by the divine Writings of the immortal Sir Isaac Newton."[144] In 1802 the French *philosophe* Claude-Henri de Saint-Simon (*1760–1825*) founded a Godless religion to be led by scientist-priests and called it the Religion of Newton (his pupil Auguste Comte renamed it "sociology").[145]

However, as the "Enlightenment" became more outspokenly atheistic and more determined to establish the incompatibility of science and religion, a pressing matter arose: what was to be done about Newton's religion? Trouble was that Newton's religious views were not a matter of hearsay or repute. He had, after all, in 1713 added a concluding section to the second edition of his monumental *Principia*, the "General Scholium" (or proposition), which was devoted entirely to his ideas about God. In it, Newton undertook to demonstrate the existence of God, concluding that:

> . . . the true God is a living, intelligent, powerful Being . . .
> . . . he governs all things, and knows all things that are done or can be done.
> . . . He endures forever, and is everywhere present.
> . . . As a blind man has no idea of colors, so have we no idea of the manner by which the all-wise God perceives and understands all things.[146]

Worse yet, Newton had written four letters during 1692–1693 explaining his theology to Richard Bentley. In the "Bentley Letters" Newton ridiculed the idea that the world could be explained in impersonal, mechanical terms. Above all, having discovered the elegant lawfulness of things, Newton believed he had, once and for all, demonstrated the certainty that behind all existence there is an intelligent, aware, omnipotent God. Any other assumption is "inconsistent with my system."[147] Finally, Newton left behind a huge collection of unpublished manuscripts, some of them rewritten several times, which he clearly intended for posthumous release.[148] As we shall see, while these were troubling to those wishing to affirm Newton's absolutely orthodox Anglicanism, they were devastating to those who wished to claim him as the hero of secular rationality. Before we consider the contents of these manuscripts, it will be useful to see how each interest group falsified Newton to history.

The first falsifiers were devout Christians seeking to suppress Newton's mildly heretical views of the Trinity. He did not believe that Jesus was born the actual Son of God. Instead, Newton believed that at the Resurrection Jesus was changed from mortal to immortal, thus *becoming* the Son. Moreover, as will be seen, Newton absolutely believed in the Second Coming. Thus although on purely technical grounds it might be argued that Newton was a non-Trinitarian, he certainly was not a "Unitarian," nor was he any sort of deist—his God was no remote and unconscious "First Cause." Nevertheless, many of Newton's peers thought it best to gloss over and deny even his minor departures from orthodoxy. In doing so, however, they provided an opportunity for those who wished to claim that all of Newton's expressions of faith were insincere.

When Newton died, the Royal Society of London appointed a committee to examine his papers, and they decided, "in view of the theological character of the greater part, that they should not be printed."[149] However, the committee left it to one of their members, Thomas Pellett, to make a fuller assessment and to select items for publication. He found the manuscripts to consist of eighty-two different works, some extremely extensive, adding up to more than four million words. From this trove,

Pellett selected only two very brief works for publication, scrawling "Not Fit to be Printed" on the first page of most of the rest. Control of these papers then passed to Newton's niece Catherine Conduitt (who had lived with him for many years). She decided that most of her uncle's work should be published, but, having ordered that "the papers must be carefully kept," and that nothing could be copied or printed until they had been further examined by the Reverend Arthur Ashley Sykes (1684–1756), Mrs. Conduitt died. The manuscripts were inherited by her uncle, the earl of Portsmouth, whereupon they came to be known as the Portsmouth Collection.[150] When Charles Hutton examined the Collection in the 1790s, he remarked on their extent, noting "there being upwards of four thousand sheets, in folio, besides the bound books etc."[151] But he revealed nothing of their contents. Nor did Samuel Horsley when he produced an edition of Newton's works—"being more anxious to suppress than to make public Newton's heresies."[152] Thus did the *greater part* of Newton's writings remain locked away, all the while being misrepresented by the privileged few who gained access to them. Newton's first biography, written in the 1720s by his friend William Stukeley, portrayed him as almost divine and without any taint of heresy. Nor was his next major biographer, David Brewster,[153] willing to acknowledge Newton's theological excursions, although he was given access to the Collection

Misrepresentations also came from the atheist side, only these were concerned with Newton's *published* writings on religion. As noted, one tactic was to dismiss his various statements about God as insincere, being no more than mere conformity undertaken to avoid trouble with religious authorities and in hopes of preferment. It was asserted, for example, that Newton added the General Scholium only "to allay the suspicion of atheism."[154] Moreover, much was made of the fact that he did this only in 1713 when he was past seventy, and that he should not be judged for actions taken in his dotage. The conformity excuse would not, of course, account for Newton's expressions of faith in the "Bentley Letters," as these had been private communications to a devoted follower. To overcome this problem, although without any legitimate grounds to do so, various writers redated the letters as written subsequent to 1713, rather than in 1692, and dismissed them, too, as the work of a man of diminished intellectual acuity.[155] Indeed, Jean-Baptiste Biot (*1774–1862*) dismissed everything written by Newton after age forty-five as the fantasies of an aging man who had lost his intellectual powers, also claiming that all of Newton's religious writings and interests were subsequent to his mental decline.[156]

Or, as the *philosophe* Baron d'Holbach (*1723–1789*) put it, "the sublime Newton is no more than an infant, when he quits physics and evidence to lose himself in the imaginary regions of theology."[157]

Thus despite clear evidence to the contrary, it came to be the received wisdom in "enlightened circles" that during his vigorous days as a scientist, Newton was at the very most a deist in the mode of Hume, Voltaire, and the *philosophes*. Friedrich Engels (*1820–1895*) claimed that although "Newton still allowed Him the 'first impulse' [he] forbade Him any further interference in his solar system."[158] E. T. Bell wrote in his still popular *Men of Mathematics*, "Newton however did permit his rational science to influence his beliefs to the extent of making him what would now be called a Unitarian."[159] Or as Gerald R. Cragg explained, Newton was "a deist" because he "ignored the claims of revelation."[160]

Meanwhile, Newton's sequestered works ticked on. In 1872 the Portsmouths asked archivists from Cambridge University to catalog the Collection and to keep any papers of scientific value. After categorizing the manuscripts, the archivists found that there was virtually nothing "scientific" among them; hence nearly the entire Collection was returned to the earl of Portsmouth under the terms of the original agreement. Six decades later, an American biographer of Newton consulted the brief inventory that had been drawn up at Cambridge, finding evidence of Newton's enormous theological output, but the actual content of these works remained unknown.[161] Finally, in 1936, faced with confiscatory British inheritance taxes, the current earl of Portsmouth consigned the Collection to Sotheby and Company, the famous London auction house. The Newton manuscripts and papers were offered in 329 lots, making it likely that they would be hopelessly scattered among an international group of dealers. At the time, some Newton scholars assumed that was in fact what happened.[162] But it did not, thanks to a Cambridge economist who used his own funds and careful study of the auction catalog to keep the most important manuscripts together.[163]

John Maynard Keynes (*1883–1946*) was probably the most famous and influential economist of the twentieth century, and the most dedicated collector of Newtonia. According to A.N.L. Munby, the Cambridge librarian and Keynes's biographer, the great economist began his collection in 1905 when he bought a rare first edition of Newton's *Principia* from a Cambridge bookseller for "four shillings, a staggering bargain even in those days."[164] When he learned that the Portsmouth Collection was to be auctioned, Keynes "with characteristic energy and public spirit took upon himself the burden of assembling as much of the material as he could in his own library."[165] Since Newton had carefully recopied the major manuscripts, there were two or more copies of each. Thus Keynes could pick his spots, being careful not to "forfeit the goodwill of the booksellers" who made up the bulk of the other bidders, as he planned to buy many manuscripts from them later. During the sale, which grossed a total of less than £10,000, Keynes bought 38 of the 329 lots offered. Within the next two months he bought 92 more lots. According to Munby, altogether Keynes spent £3,000, or about $15,000—a substantial sum for a professor in those days, but a pittance in terms of value. While Keynes worked to buy the most important of Newton's unpublished works, he corresponded with A. S. Yahuda, a Yale professor who was acquiring Newton's theological manuscripts purchased by American dealers—mainly duplicates of those gathered by Keynes. In his will Keynes bequeathed his entire collection of Newtonia to his college (King's) at Cambridge. The collection assembled by Yahuda is now in the Hebrew National and University Library in Jerusalem.[166]

Because the Sotheby catalog was "a model of learned . . . presentation . . . and must always remain a standard reference book on the shelves of Newtonia scholars,"[167] Keynes knew a great deal about what he was buying. Nevertheless, he was astonished by the content of the manuscripts. They revealed that even during his prime years of scientific achievement, Newton was as interested in theology and Bible prophecy as in physics—he left more than a million words on these topics. For example, in a work on Bible prophecy, begun in the 1670s and with additions and revisions introduced until the month of his death in 1727, Newton calculated, among many other things, that the Second Coming of Christ would occur in 1948, four years after the "end of the great tribulation of the Jews."[168] The documents also revealed that Newton had been deeply involved in astrology and had devoted many years of intensive effort to alchemy, leaving another million words on that topic.[169]

Keynes recognized the historical importance of these papers at once and planned to write about them at length. His first installment was an essay, "Newton, the Man," written for the Royal Society of London's tercentenary celebration of Newton's birth in 1946 (which had been delayed by four years owing to World War II). Unfortunately, Keynes died unexpectedly several months before the event, so his essay was read to the society by his brother Geoffrey. It was Keynes at his eloquent best:

> In the eighteenth century and since, Newton came to be thought of as the first and greatest of the modern age of scientists, a rationalist, one who taught us to think on the lines of cold and untinctured reason. I do not see him in this light. I do not think that any one who has pored over the contents of [these manuscripts] can see him like that. Newton . . . looked on the whole universe and all that is in it *as a riddle*, as a secret which could be read by applying pure thought to certain evidence, certain mystic clues which God had laid about the world to allow a sort of philosopher's treasure hunt . . . He believed that these clues were to be found partly in the evidence of the heavens and in the constitution of elements . . . but also partly in certain papers and traditions handed down . . . in an unbroken chain back to the original cryptic revelation in Babylonia. He regarded the universe as a cryptogram set by the Almighty.

So now we know. The real Isaac Newton was the quintessential student of God's handiwork, believing not only in the existence of physical laws but that similar divine laws governed history as well.[170] Two centuries of efforts to depict Isaac Newton as having been much too sophisticated to believe in God were motivated by precisely the same reasons that underlay the false stories about Columbus, about Vesalius, about the "Dark Ages," about the "Enlightenment" and about the Scholastics. To wit: science stands in opposition to religion. No important scientific work *can* be achieved or even fully understood by minds dominated by "superstition." The "Scientific Revolution" was made by "enlightened men," who thereby enlightened us, making it impossible for an intelligent person to be religious. These are the slogans of one of the longest-running and most effective polemical campaigns in Western history. But while the campaign has had a very significant impact on the intellectual world in general, as evidenced even in dictionaries, strangely enough it seems not to have made much difference to scientists. Not only were those who made the "Scientific Revolution" notable for their piety; that tradition has continued. For example, through most of the nineteenth century, science remained as much a religious as a secular calling—efforts to unravel God's handiwork continued.

"Handiwork" and Nineteenth-Century Science

Perhaps only during the Scholastic era was there such a close and creative relationship between theology and science as obtained during the nineteenth century. Indeed, while early science may have been stimulated by theology, now theology was stimulated by the latest scientific discoveries, finding in them overwhelming proof of basic religious tenets—an approach that was known as "Natural Theology." Its proponents dismissed mere speculation in favor of careful observations of nature. Indeed, "the natural theologian had to be a scientist . . . [it] was a discipline in which Christian philosophy and empirical science merged."[171] Thus where once religion had encouraged the assumption that immutable natural laws existed, now the precision of these laws was used to prove the existence of God. This came to be known as the Design Argument: to discover in the complexity of the world the necessity of a Creator.

No one did more to popularize the Design Argument than did the English Churchman William Paley (*1743–1805*). In his immensely influential *Natural Theology*, Paley considered the implications of finding a stone lying on the ground. If one were asked how the stone came to be there, it might be adequate to answer that perhaps "it had lain there forever." In contrast, "suppose I had found a watch upon the ground." It will not do to suppose that a watch had lain there forever, for, as one examines a watch, any suggestion that it may have come into existence through happenstance becomes absurd—any watch reveals itself as a *creation*. Compared even to the finest watch, the least complex biological organism is a far more sophisticated "machine" and impels us to assume a Creator.[172] In the remainder of his book, Paley explored the complexities of a variety of different biological machines. For, although this may surprise most readers, the fossil evidence of progressive development from simple to complex life-forms, of animals existing long before humans, or evidence of the stars being far older than the earth, *did not* unsettle most Christian theologians! Indeed, there is an immense library of now unread books of Natural Theology that outlined the latest scientific knowledge—particularly in biology, geology, astronomy—and reconciled it with Christian theology. This was not a defensive literature but is more properly described as an enthusiastic celebration of God's handiwork: Paley's image of God as the Divine Watchmaker truly captured the spirit of the times. We will meet Paley again in Chapter 4 because long before he wrote about Natural Theology, he was a vigorous opponent of slavery as utterly incompatible with true Christianity.

During the nineteenth century, astronomical observatories were built in many cities across the United States by public fund-raising campaigns. In nearly every instance these campaigns were organized by and drew mainly upon devout Christians who wished to make it possible for people to observe the wonders of God's handiwork. Leading astronomers were particularly popular lecturers in religious as well as scientific circles—if, in fact, it is possible to distinguish two such circles at this time. The rapidly growing system of American higher education, wherein most scientists were based, was itself almost entirely a religious creation, inspired by denominational competition. Moreover, it was not only theologians who were eager to unite religion and science; similar efforts were typical of the leading scientists of the day. For example, Louis Agassiz (*1807–1873*), among the most important geologists of the nineteenth century and the first to hold an appointment at Harvard, combined the results of his brilliant fieldwork (including pioneering research on the Ice Age) with elegant expressions of the Design Argument. Indeed, in his monumental *Contributions to the Natural History of the United States* (1857–1862), Agassiz argued that attempts to construct biological classification systems were an effort not to impose human understanding on the natural world but to discover the classification system that existed "in the mind of the Creator." In his review of the first volume of Agassiz's *Contributions* James Dwight Dana wrote in the *American Journal of Science* that it had "borne science to a higher level than it had before attained." [173] Dana's own expression of the "harmony" between theology and science, in an essay entitled "Thoughts on Species," was considered so important that it was published simultaneously in both the leading theology journal and the leading science journal of the day.

Although Natural Theology is associated with the nineteenth century, it rested upon a very old tradition of scriptural interpretation. As far back as the first century, Clement I (considered to have been the third pope) taught that the Bible is not only or always to be understood literally; rather, some passages are allegories. Saint Augustine considered this the only acceptable approach to scripture "since divers things may be understood under these words which yet are all true." In fact, Augustine frankly admitted that it is possible for a later reader, with God's help, to grasp a scriptural meaning even though the person who first wrote down the scripture "understood not this." Thus, he continued, it is necessary to "enquire . . . what Moses, that excellent minister of Thy faith, would have his reader understand by those words . . . let us approach together unto the words of Thy book, and seek in them Thy meaning, through the meaning of Thy servant, by whose pen Thou hast dispensed them." Moreover, since God is incapable of either error or falsehood, if the Bible seems to contradict knowledge, that is because of a lack of understanding on the part of the "servant" who recorded God's words.[174]

The Catholic Church has always taught that the meaning of scripture is not invariably literal and is thus subject to interpretation by the Church. In fact, it was by claiming the exclusive right to interpret scripture that the Church placed itself in opposition, not only to those committed to literalism, but also to its own theologians and, in some eras, to science. Moreover, by asserting its interpretive infallibility, the Church made reformations inevitable.

The need to *interpret* the Bible was central to the entire Protestant undertaking, even leading some to assert that people must be their own theologians. But even Protestants committed to a more authoritarian church rejected scriptural literalism. For example, John Calvin clearly asserted the legitimate basis for Natural Theology when he taught that God accommodates his revelations to the limits of human understanding—that "revelation is an act of divine condescension."[175] For example, Calvin explained that the author of Genesis "was ordained to be a teacher of the unlearned and primitive, as well as the learned; so could not achieve his goal without descending to such crude means of instruction." Thus Calvin dismissed such notions as the six days of Creation as not indicative of the actual time involved.[176] In his *Sermons on the Ten Commandments*, Calvin explained:

> Because we are not yet participants in the glory of God, thus we cannot approach him; rather, it is necessary for him to reveal himself to us according to our rudeness and infirmity. The fact remains that since the beginning of the world when God appeared to mortal men, it was not in order to reveal himself as he was, but according to men's ability to support him. We must always keep this in mind: that God was not known by the fathers. And today he does not appear to us in his essence. Rather he accommodates himself to us. That being the case, it is necessary for him to descend according to our capacity in order to make us sense his presence with us.[177]

From the Catholic side, this view was ratified by the Carmelite friar Paolo Antonio Foscarini in his 1615 work on Copernicus: "Scripture speaks according to our mode of understanding."[178]

Hence the rise of science did not catch Christian theologians with their verses down. The only thing new about Natural Theology was the name—indeed, Calvin also wrote at length on the Design Argument. The willingness of scientists to acknowledge a Creator and the equal willingness of theologians to adjust their doctrines to the latest scientific discoveries drove the militant heirs of the "Enlightenment" nearly to distraction. Despite the achievements of the "divine" Newton, the forces of "superstition" not only persisted; they had not even been driven out of the universities. Something had to be done. And it was.

Evolution and Religion

Charles Darwin (*1809–1882*) would be among the most prominent biologists in history even had he not published *The Origin of Species* (1859). But he would not have been deified, nor would he have been substituted for Newton in the campaign to "enlighten" humanity. As will be seen, the battle over evolution is not an example of how "heroic" scientists have withstood the relentless persecution of religious "fanatics." Rather, from the very start it has primarily been an attack on religion by militant atheists who wrap themselves in the mantle of science in an effort to refute all religious claims concerning a Creator—an effort that has also often attempted to suppress all *scientific* criticism of Darwin's work.

Although it has recently become remarkably lively, I would prefer not to participate in the current debate over the logical and empirical status of the theory of evolution. Unfortunately, to adequately understand the real basis of the long-standing conflict over evolution, we must see that the aggressive public certitude of Darwinians has been in almost direct proportion to the shortcomings of the theory. Problems that were obvious even to Darwin have not been overcome after more than 150 years of effort. My reluctance to pursue these matters is based on my experience that nothing causes greater panic among many of my colleagues than any criticism of evolution.[179] They seem to fear that someone might mistake them for Creationists if they even remain in the same room while such talk is going on. As will be seen, that is precisely how "Darwin's Bulldog," Thomas Henry Huxley (*1825–1895*), hoped intellectuals would react when he first adopted the tactic of claiming that the only choice is between Darwin and biblical literalism. Indeed, Richard Dawkins, who holds a chair at Oxford devoted to the public understanding of science, has frankly asserted that "even if there were no actual evidence in favor of Darwinian theory . . . we should still be justified in preferring it over all rival theories," carefully limiting the latter to the crudest possible Creationism and to antique Lamarckian genetics.[180]

However, just as one can doubt Max Weber's Protestant ethic thesis without thereby declaring for Marxism, so, too, one may note the serious shortcomings of Darwinian and neo-Darwinian theory without opting for a six-day Creation or indeed for *any* rival theory—modern physics provides a model of how science benefits from being willing to live with open questions rather than embrace obviously flawed theories. I certainly do not claim that room must be left for a Creator in any adequate theory of biological origins—perhaps a far more adequate and entirely materialistic theory will appear tomorrow. What I am saying is that Darwin's theory, even with all of the subsequent revisions, falls noticeably short of explaining the origin of species. Even so, I raise this issue only because it is needed to demonstrate the thoroughly ideological basis of the Darwinian Crusade, and to thereby show that it does not indicate a basic incompatibility between religion and science. There is, of course, an inherent conflict between "scientific atheism" and religion, which is what is illustrated here.

When a militant Darwinist such as Richard Dawkins claims, "The theory is about as much in doubt as the earth goes round the sun,"[181] he does not state a fact but merely aims to discredit a priori anyone who dares to express reservations about evolution. Indeed, Dawkins has written, "It is absolutely safe to say that, if you meet somebody who claims not to believe in evolution, that person is ignorant, stupid, or insane."[182] Eric Hoffer would have treasured these statements had they been available when he wrote *The True Believer* (1951). Worse yet, Dawkins knows the many serious problems that beset a purely materialistic evolutionary theory, but asserts that no one except true believers in evolution can be allowed into the discussion, which must be held in secret. Thus he chastises Niles Eldredge and Stephen Jay Gould, two distinguished fellow Darwinians, for giving "spurious aid and comfort to modern creationists."[183] Dawkins believes that, regardless of his or her good intentions, "if a reputable scholar breathes so much as a hint of criticism of some detail of Darwinian theory, that fact is seized upon and blown up out of proportion." Dawkins's views have been widely shared. Consequently, while acknowledging that "the extreme rarity of transitional forms in the fossil record" is a major embarrassment for Darwinism, Gould confided that this has been held as a "trade secret of paleontology," and acknowledged that the evolutionary diagrams "that adorn our textbooks" are based on "inference, . . . not the evidence of fossils."[184] Indeed, according to Steven Stanley, another distinguished evolutionist, doubts raised by this problem with the fossil record were "suppressed" for years.[185] Stanley noted that this, too, was a tactic begun by Huxley, who was always careful not to reveal his own serious misgivings in public. As Eldredge summed up, "We paleontologists have said that the history of life supports [the principle of gradual transformations of species], all the while really knowing that it does not."[186] This is not how science is conducted; it is how ideological crusades are run.

Darwinian Theory

To give the greatest possible reassurance to readers, I have been careful to draw my statements about deficiencies of the theory of evolution *only* from well-known, enthusiastic Darwinians.

By Darwin's day it had long been recognized that the fossil evidence showed that, over an immense period of time, there had been a progression in the biological complexity of organisms. In the oldest strata, only simple organisms are observed. In more recent strata, more complex organisms appear. Moreover, following the work of Carolus Linnaeus (*1707–1778*), the biological world has been classified into a set of nested categories. Thus within each genus (mammals, reptiles, etc.) are species (dogs, horses, elephants, etc.), and within each species are many specific varieties, or breeds (Great Dane, poodle, beagle, etc.). The boundaries between species are distinct and firm—one species does not simply trail off into another by degrees. For example, interbreeding is possible among varieties within a species (between, say, poodles and beagles), but not across species (dogs cannot breed with cats). Hence there will be no mixed breeds across species (no dog/cats or horse/cows). What that means is that new species cannot be created by crossbreeding.[187]

These facts were of considerable interest to Natural Theologians and to biologists alike, and everyone realized that they posed two primary questions. The first is about variation *within* species. How is it that there are so many different breeds of dogs, for example? The second question asks about variation *across* species. As more complex creatures appear in the fossil record, where did they come from? That is, how do new species come into existence?

It was well known that selective breeding could create variations *within* species. The immense array of breeds of dogs is the result of centuries of selective breeding wherein humans have picked out dogs showing the greatest amount of the desired trait (short tail, shaggy coat, long legs) and then have bred them until, after many generations of selective breeding, one had Great Danes or Standard Poodles. But how did selective breeding happen in nature without human direction? Here Darwin made a very clever and lasting contribution: the principle of *natural selection*. Just as human breeders select on the basis of desired traits, nature does the same, albeit unwittingly. Three elements are involved. First, organisms within any species vary slightly in many different ways that are inheritable. Second, organisms are subject to a struggle for survival, and those having traits more conducive to survival will be more likely to reproduce.[188] Hence organisms will change by becoming better suited (adapted) to survive. Third, if the conditions governing survival differ from one place (or ecological niche) to another, the result will be different breeds of the same species. This was the easy one.

It would seem impossible for natural selection within existing species to create new species. As Darwin acknowledged, breeding experiments reveal clear limits to selective breeding beyond which no additional changes can be produced. For example, dogs can be bred to be only so big and no bigger, let alone be selectively bred until they are cats. Hence the question of where species come from was the real challenge, and, despite the title of his famous book and more than a century of hoopla and celebration, Darwin essentially left it unanswered.

After many years spent searching for an adequate explanation of the origin of species, in the end Darwin fell back on natural selection, claiming that it could create new creatures, too, if given immense periods of time. That is, organisms respond to their environmental circumstances by slowly changing (evolving) in the direction of traits beneficial to survival until, eventually, they are sufficiently changed as to constitute a new species. Hence new species originate very slowly, one tiny change after another, and eventually this can result in a whole chain of new species, as from lemurs to humans via many intervening species.

Darwin fully recognized that a major weakness of this account of the origin of species involved what he, and others, referred to as the principle of "gradualism in nature." Darwin explicitly rejected the idea that a whole cluster of favorable changes could occur simultaneously, thus producing a new species at one sudden bound. "To admit [such a possibility]," he wrote in *The Origin*, "is, as it seems to me, to enter into the realms of miracle, and to leave those of Science."[189] Linnaeus had pronounced that "nature makes no leaps," and this was the equivalent of Holy Writ for Darwin and his followers. And as Howard Gruber explained, this "posed an alternative of terrible import: nature makes no jumps, but God does."[190] To show that something is of natural, not divine, origins, one must show that it followed an extremely gradual and clear progression from prior forms. And that was the rub. The fossil record was utterly inconsistent with gradualism. As Darwin acknowledged:

> [W]hy, if species have descended from other species by fine gradations, do we not everywhere see innumerable transitional forms? Why is not all nature in confusion instead of the species being, as we see them, well defined?[191]

Darwin offered two solutions. Transitional types are quickly replaced and hence would mainly be observable only in the fossil record. As for the lack of transitional types among the fossils, that was, Darwin admitted, "the most obvious and serious objection which can be urged against the theory."[192] Darwin dealt with this problem by blaming "the extreme imperfection of the geological record." "Only a small portion of the surface of the earth has been geologically explored, and no part with sufficient care."[193] But just wait, Darwin promised, the missing transitions will be found in the expected proportion when more research has been done. Thus began an intensive search for what the popular press soon called the "missing links."

Today, the fossil record is enormous compared to what it was in Darwin's day, but the facts are unchanged. The links are still missing; species appear suddenly and then remain relatively unchanged. As Steven Stanley reported, "The known fossil record . . . offers no evidence that the gradualistic model can be valid."[194] Indeed, the evidence has grown even more contrary since Darwin's day. As the former curator of historical geology at the American Museum of Natural History noted, "Many of the discontinuities [in the fossil record] tend to be more and more emphasized with increased collecting."[195] As Stephen Jay Gould summarized:

> The history of most fossil species includes two features particularly inconsistent with gradualism:
>
> 1. *Stasis*. Most species exhibit no directional change during their tenure on earth. They appear in the fossil record looking much the same as when they disappear; morphological change is usually limited and directionless.
>
> 2. *Sudden appearance*. In any local area, a species does not arise gradually by the steady transformation of its ancestors; it appears all at once and "fully formed."[196]

These are precisely the objections raised by many biologists and geologists in Darwin's time—it was not merely that Darwin's claim that species arise through eons of natural selection was offered without supporting evidence, but that the available evidence was overwhelmingly contrary. Unfortunately, rather than concluding that a theory of the origin of species was yet to be accomplished, many scientists urged that Darwin's claims must be embraced, no matter what. As one of Europe's leading paleontologists, François Jules Pictet, remarked in his 1860 review of *The Origin*:

> We are presented with a theory which on the one hand seems to be impossible because it is inconsistent with observed facts and on the other hand appears to be the best explanation [available].[197]

Ever since, there has been an urgent, if often circumspect, search for a plausible alternative. Ironically, while Thomas Henry Huxley used to regale his audiences with stories of a species springing into existence "without anything to precede it" as proof of the absurdity of Creationism, in private he searched for a biological mechanism by which such leaps could be explained.[198] Huxley was in fact "convinced that new forms came into being not through modification of the details of their morphology but through abrupt, large-scale reorganization of entire anatomical systems."[199] But he couldn't discover a convincing explanation and thus continued his unwavering public condemnations of all criticisms of Darwin's theory. Darwin himself had searched for such a mechanism for many years, and I think it obvious that he fell back on gradualism and natural selection to account for the origin of species only because, finding it necessary to publish to prevent Alfred Russel Wallace from gaining sole credit for the theory of evolution, he had nothing better to offer.

In any event, during the late nineteenth and early twentieth centuries, increasing numbers of biologists attempted to find an evolutionary mechanism capable of fitting the fossil evidence that evolution occurs by sudden leaps.[200] As was Darwin's own work, the earliest of these efforts were based on Jean-Baptiste Lamarck's (*1744–1829*) theory that acquired characteristics can be inherited—that modifications of an organism by its environment are passed along to its offspring. Indeed, Darwin not only knew that it is possible to create a breed of dogs with short tails by selective breeding; he also believed, with Lamarck, that if one surgically shortens the tails of dogs, this will result in a short-tailed breed of dogs—eventually. However, this did not solve the problem. Even by assuming that acquired characteristics are inherited (which was soon rejected by biologists), one ends up with a *gradual* model of evolution by tiny increments, incompatible with a fossil record of new species appearing as if out of nowhere. Then came the rediscovery of the genetic principles of Gregor Mendel (*1822–1884*), and it seemed as if the mechanism for the origin of species had been found.

Darwin knew nothing about genes, let alone about genetic mutations. He agreed with Lamarck that the features of both parents blend to form their offspring. But Mendel showed that genes do not blend. When applied to evolution, this means that gradual changes via natural selection cannot account for new species. Thus at the turn of the century the most prominent biologists, including Hugo de Vries, William Bateson, and Thomas Hunt Morgan, completely (if rather circumspectly vis-à-vis the public) rejected Darwin's theory and searched for a plausible genetic basis for evolution. They thought they found it in the phenomenon of genetic mutations.[201]

A mutation is a change that occurs within a gene of a given organism and which can, therefore, be passed on to that organism's offspring. That is, an actual physical change takes place in a specific gene, thus altering the organism and its genetic potential. In most neo-Darwinian[202] accounts of evolution, mutations are assumed to occur randomly. Many of these minor random mutations will be irrelevant to survival and therefore may or may not persist. Many (perhaps most) will be unfavorable and will disappear, as creatures having this trait will die out. But some traits will be favorable and will persist and spread through a species on the basis of superior rates of survival. But how does this result in a new species? How do slight random mutations change a reptile into a bird or, indeed, a tiny lemur into a human? In keeping with Darwin's views, evolutionists have often explained new species as the result of the accumulation of tiny, favorable random mutations over an immense span of time. But this answer remains inconsistent with the fossil record, wherein creatures appear "as Athena did from the head of Zeus—full-blown and raring to go."[203] Consequently, for most of the past century, biologists and geneticists have tried to discover how a huge number of favorable mutations can occur at one time so that a new species would appear without intermediate types.

In 1940 Richard Goldschmidt proposed the "hopeful monster" solution—"A monstrosity appearing in a single genetic step might . . . produce a new type."[204] He acknowledged that most multiple mutations result in a "hopeless monster," in that the changes are harmful or retrograde. But sometimes new features might be an improvement, hence a "hopeful monster." What Goldschmidt was really up to was inferring a genetic cause from an empirical result. New species pop into view. Since that *must* be the result of evolution, we can only assume that a truly massive, multiple mutation has taken place. In fact, it must happen twice in the same time and place if the monster is to secure a mate. The hopeful monster still stalks the fringes of neo-Darwinism, but it has been dismissed by most biologists as it would have been by Darwin. As the eminent and committed Darwinist Ernst Mayr explained:

> The occurrence of genetic monstrosities by mutation . . . is well substantiated, but they are such evident freaks that these monsters can only be designated as "hopeless." They are so utterly unbalanced that they would not have the slightest chance of escaping elimination through selection. Giving a thrush the wings of a falcon does not make it a better flyer. Indeed, having all of the other equipment of a thrush, it would probably hardly be able to fly at all . . . To believe that such a drastic mutation would produce a viable new type, capable of occupying a new adaptive zone, is equivalent to believing in miracles.[205]

Which is what Darwin said.

A more recent effort to account for the sudden appearance of new species in the fossil record has been suggested by Niles Eldredge and Stephen Jay Gould.[206] This is known as *punctuated equilibrium*. It has never been entirely clear what this principle is, a problem made worse by the fact that the authors, especially Gould, have often changed their minds about what they do mean.[207] In some incarnations it appeared to be a new version of the "hopeful monster"—indeed, Gould published an essay entitled "Return to the Hopeful Monster." The initial version of "punctuated equilibrium" merely asserts that Darwin was wrong to suppose that evolution occurs via a slow accumulation of tiny steps. Since the fossil record shows sudden leaps, that's how evolution occurs—from time to time the *equilibrium* of an unchanging species is *punctuated* by a sudden change. Since Darwin's theory can't handle this, Gould concluded that a new evolutionary principle is needed.[208] But no such principle was suggested. Indeed, Gould was able to write at length about how "punctuated equilibrium theory" reconciles Darwinism with the fossil record, at the same time denying that this theory proposes any "violent mechanism" by which the sudden appearance of a new species occurs. But in not proposing a mechanism, Gould and Eldredge made no progress in solving the problem of the origin of species. In the end, what they argued is that however it happens, new species arise in a very local area and do not spread until they have passed through the intermediate stages. That solves the problem of the "missing links"—they exist in only one small place, and it would take an immense stroke of luck to find them (presumably more luck than is needed to produce the new species itself). But we still don't know why or how such leaps occur. Moreover, even by discussing the urgency of the need for a solution, Gould and Eldredge have stirred up antagonism among peers who realize that any such mechanism is very likely to reopen the door to miracles, just as Darwin feared. In fact, another prominent Darwinian, Daniel C. Dennett, has accused Gould of having such intentions—"my diagnosis, however, is that he [Gould] has all along been hoping for skyhooks[209] [to lift evolution along]."[210]

Indeed, the word "miracle" crops up again and again in mathematical assessments of the possibility that even very simple biochemical chains, let alone living organisms, can occur by a process of random trial and error. For generations, Darwinians have regaled their students with the story of the monkey and the typewriter, noting that given an infinite period of time, the monkey sooner or later is bound to produce *Macbeth* (or all of Shakespeare or the Bible) purely by chance. The moral being that *infinite* time can perform miracles. However, the "monkey" of random evolution does not have infinite time. Even if one makes the wild assumption that life came here from a much older faraway planet, the progression from simple to complex life-forms on Earth took place within a quite limited time.[211] Even more telling is the fact that when competent mathematicians considered the matter, they quickly calculated that even if the monkey's task were reduced to coming up with only a few lines of *Macbeth*, let alone Shakespeare's entire play, the probability is far, far beyond any possibility.[212] The odds of creating even the simplest organism at random are even more remote—Fred Hoyle and Chandra Wickramasinghe[213] calculated the odds as 1 in $10^{40,000}$ (consider that all of the atoms in the known universe are estimated to number no more than 10^{80}). In this sense, then, Darwinian theory does rest on truly miraculous assumptions.

Perhaps the most amazing aspect of the current situation is that while Darwin is treated as a secular saint in the popular media, and the "theory" of evolution is regarded as the invincible challenge to all religious claims, it is taken for granted among the leading biological scientists that the origin of species has yet to be explained. Writing in *Nature* in 1999, Eörs Szathmaŕy began his review of Jeffrey Schwartz's effort to *construct* such a theory:

> The origin of species has long fascinated biologists. Although Darwin's major work bears it as a title, it does not provide a solution to the problem. Does Jeffrey Schwartz give one? I am afraid that, in general, he does not.[214]

When Julian Huxley claimed that "Darwin's theory is . . . no longer a theory but a fact," he surely knew better.[215] But just like his grandfather, Thomas Henry Huxley, he knew that his lie served the greater good of "enlightenment."

The Darwinian Crusade

When *The Origin of Species* was published, it aroused immense interest, but initially it did not provoke antagonism on religious grounds. Darwin's scientific reputation ensured that reviewers took the book seriously and treated its author respectfully. Although many criticized his lack of evidence, none raised religious objections, as even Stephen Jay Gould has acknowledged.[216] Instead, the initial response from those involved in Natural Theology was extremely favorable. Asa Gray (*1810–1888*), the distinguished Harvard botanist, hailed Darwin for having solved the most difficult problem confronting the Design Argument—the many imperfections and failures revealed in the fossil record. Acknowledging that Darwin himself "rejects the idea of design," Gray congratulated him for "bringing out the neatest illustrations of it."[217] Gray interpreted Darwin's work as showing that God has created a few original forms and then let evolution proceed within the framework of divine "laws"—hence the occasional wrong turnings and "errors." Darwin and his immediate supporters found this intolerable—it was precisely in opposition to the Design Argument that his theory was aimed.

Thus when religious antagonism came, it was generated by a social movement which—by constantly proclaiming that, together, Newton and Darwin had evicted God from the cosmos—forced religious leaders to respond. For the heirs of the "Enlightenment," evolution seemed finally to supply the weapon needed to destroy religion. As Richard Dawkins confided, "Darwin made it possible to be an intellectually fulfilled atheist."[218]

The Darwinian Crusade was launched by a group of men led and typified by Thomas Henry Huxley.[219] Like Huxley, some of these crusaders were scientists. But, also like Huxley, since long before the publication of Darwin's theory, they had been activists on behalf of socialism and atheism.[220]

The earliest and most militant proponents of Darwinism made up a virtual Who's Who of socialism.[221] When she wasn't singing hymns praising evolution with George Bernard Shaw at Fabian Society meetings,

Annie Besant was distributing her pamphlet *Why I Am a Socialist*, in which she gave the answer "because I am a believer in Evolution." Alfred Russel Wallace, who is credited as Darwin's codiscoverer of the theory of evolution, was a prominent socialist whose reading of the evolutionary future of humanity led him to be the first to proclaim the coming of that biological paragon of selflessness, "socialist man."[222] Indeed, still to be found in Darwin's library is a first edition of *Das Kapital*, inscribed to "Mr. Charles Darwin. On the part of his sincere admirer, Karl Marx, London 16 June 1873." More than a decade before, when he read *The Origin*, Marx wrote to Engels that Darwin had provided the necessary biological basis for socialism. When he spoke at Marx's burial service, Engels equated the two: "Just as Darwin discovered the law of development of organic nature, so Marx discovered the law of development of human nature."[223] The way was now clear for the revolution and for "scientific atheism."

Indeed, atheism was central to the agenda of the Darwinians.[224] Darwin himself once wrote that he could not understand how anyone could even wish that Christianity were true, noting that the doctrine of damnation was itself damnable.[225] As for Huxley, he expressed his hostility toward religion often and clearly, writing in 1859:

> My screed was meant as a protest against Theology & Parsondom . . . both of which are in my mind the natural & irreconcilable enemies of Science. Few see it but I believe we are on the Eve of a new Reformation and if I have a wish to live thirty years, it is to see the foot of Science on the necks of her Enemies.[226]

As the Oxford historian J. R. Lucas summed up:

> [Huxley] had no love of ecclesiastics and was sure that science must be at odds with religion. Later in his life he [was] still remarkably resistant to the idea that there were clergymen who accepted evolution, even when actually faced with them.[227]

Quite simply, there could be no compromises with faith. For as John Tyndall (*1820–1893*) told the British Association in his 1874 presidential address:

> [T]he basis of the doctrine of evolution consists . . . in its general harmony with scientific thought . . . We claim and we shall wrest from theology, the entire domain of cosmological theory.[228]

That same year, the leading Darwinian in Germany, Ernst Haeckel (*1834–1919*), acknowledged:

> On one side spiritual freedom and truth, reason and culture, evolution and progress stand under the bright banner of science; on the other side, under the black flag of hierarchy, stand spiritual slavery and falsehood, irrationality and barbarism, superstition and retrogression . . . Evolution is the heavy artillery in the struggle for truth. Whole ranks of . . . sophistries fall together under the chain shot of this . . . artillery, and the proud and mighty structure of the Roman hierarchy, that powerful stronghold of infallible dogmatism, falls like a house of cards.[229]

Is it really surprising that religious people, scientists as well as clerics, began to respond in the face of unrelenting challenges issued to them in the name of evolution? It was not as if they were merely asked to accept that life had evolved—Natural Theologians had long taken that for granted and continued to do so.[230] Instead, what the Darwinians demanded was that religionists agree to the untrue and unscientific claim that Darwin had proved that God played no role in the process. Nor were these Darwinian challenges limited to radical circles and peripheral publications. The actual author of the *Times*'s huge review of *The Origin* was none other than Thomas Henry Huxley, who praised the book to the heavens, while denying they existed. How could there not have been religious rejoinders? Indeed, Huxley built his lectures on evolution into a popular touring stage show wherein he challenged various potential religious opponents by name.

Of course, persons of faith felt it necessary to respond. And Huxley was very clever (and lucky) about which ones to emphasize. The most famous among those drawn to respond was William Gladstone (*1809–1898*), four-time prime minister of Britain. Gladstone was a gifted writer and sincere Christian, but he was not a scientist and thereby provided Huxley with an ideal opponent. Even so, Huxley responded to Gladstone mainly with abuse, rather than with science—even he admitted, "I really cannot use respectful language about this intrusion of an utter ignoramus into scientific questions."[231]

In an early draft of this chapter, I assumed that another of Huxley's "victims" was the bishop of Oxford, Samuel Wilberforce (*1805–1873*), who is said to have made an ass of himself in a debate with Huxley during the 1860 meeting of the British Association at Oxford. The original account of this confrontation reported:

I was happy enough to be present on the memorable occasion at Oxford when Mr Huxley bearded Bishop Wilberforce . . . The Bishop arose and in a light scoffing tone, florid and fluent, he assured us that there was nothing in the idea of evolution . . . Then turning to his antagonist with a smiling insolence, he begged to know, was it through his grandfather or his grandmother that he claimed descent from a monkey? On this Mr. Huxley . . . arose . . . and spoke these tremendous words . . . He was not ashamed to have a monkey for an ancestor; but he would be ashamed to be connected with a man who used his great gifts to obscure the truth. No one doubted his meaning and the effect was tremendous.[232]

This anecdote has appeared in *every* distinguished biography of Darwin and of Huxley, as well as in every popular history of the theory of evolution.[233] In his celebrated *Apes, Angels and Victorians*, William Irvine used this tale to disparage the bishop's snobbery.[234] In his prizewinning study, H. James Brix went much further, describing Wilberforce as "naive and pompous," a man whose "faulty opinions" were those of a "fundamentalist creationist," and who provided Huxley with the opportunity to give evolution "its first major victory over dogmatism and duplicity."[235] Every writer tells how the audience gave Huxley an ovation, and nearly everyone has taken pains to identify the bishop as "Soapy Sam."

Trouble is, it didn't happen. The quotation above was the only "firsthand" report of this story, and it appeared in an article entitled "A Grandmother's Tales" written by a nonscholar in a popular magazine[236] thirty-eight years after the alleged encounter! No other account of these meetings, and there were many written at the time, mentioned remarks concerning Huxley's monkey ancestors or claimed that he made a fool of the bishop. To the contrary, many thought the bishop had the better of it, and even many of the committed Darwinians thought it at most a draw.[237] Moreover, as all of the scholars present at Oxford knew, prior to the meeting Bishop Wilberforce had published a review of *The Origin* in which he fully acknowledged the principle of natural selection as the source of variations within species. However, he rejected Darwin's claims concerning the origin of species, and some of these criticisms were sufficiently compelling that Darwin immediately wrote his friend the botanist J. D. Hooker (*1817–1911*) that the review "is uncommonly clever; it picks out with skill all the most conjectural parts, and brings forward well all the difficulties. It quizzes me quite splendidly."[238] In a subsequent letter to the geologist Charles Lyell (*1797–1875*), Darwin complained that Wilberforce's review "is full of errors," but then acknowledged, "By the way, the Bishop makes a very telling case against me."[239] Indeed, several of Wilberforce's comments caused Darwin to make modifications in a later revision of the book.[240] These were the issues that Wilberforce summarized for the British Association and to which Huxley responded.

Even though the account of Huxley's triumph over the supposedly fatuous and snobbish bishop was exposed as fictional more than twenty years ago by J. R. Lucas,[241] this fact has been given so little attention that I almost repeated the fiction—it lives on in Desmond's 1997 biography of Huxley. Yet, judging from their citations, all of the biographers and historians who reported it as fact had read Francis Darwin's collection of his father's correspondence and ought to have wondered why Darwin himself saw merit in "Soapy Sam's" foolishness. Furthermore, Wilberforce's sophisticated review of *The Origin* remains easily accessible in the *Quarterly Review* for July–October 1860. Nevertheless, the tale of the bishop's comeuppance continues to thrive as a revealing "truth" about the incompatibility of religion and science. It's as though Samuel Wilberforce (who took a particularly distinguished first in mathematics at Oxford) must have been wrong and a fool *because* he was a bishop. Indeed, Lucas has suggested that the "most important reason why the legend grew" is that "it is a point of professional pride" for "academics . . . to know nothing outside their own special subject.," They firmly believe that outsiders are necessarily ignorant; hence Huxley "must have succeeded on that occasion." Moreover, "the quarrel between religion and science came not because of what Wilberforce said, but because it was what Huxley wanted; and as Darwin's theory gained supporters, they took over his view of the incident."[242]

The episodes involving Gladstone and Wilberforce reveal several methods frequently used by the Darwinian Crusade to overwhelm its opponents. When possible, focus all attention on the most unqualified and most vulnerable opponents, and when no easy targets present themselves, invent them—as Huxley's celebrated biographer Adrian Desmond admitted, he "made straw men of the 'Creationists.' "[243] Thus even today it is a rare textbook on general biology or on evolution, to say nothing of popular treatments of evolution and religion, that does not reduce "Creationism" to Bishop Ussher's calculations concerning the age of the earth and to William Jennings Bryan's antics during the so-called Scopes Monkey Trial.

James Ussher (*1581–1656*) was a fellow of Trinity College, Dublin, and later served as bishop of Armagh. A Protestant of Calvinist tendencies, Ussher has been credited with calculating that the Creation took place in 4004 B.C.E. In fact, he did not originate this figure, which was only one of many circulating at that time[244]—indeed, Isaac Newton devoted considerable attention to this same matter and reached quite similar conclusions. More to the point, by the time of the Darwinian Crusade, Ussher's date was largely forgotten,[245] and the prevailing view among theologians as well as geologists was that the earth was very old. It was the evolutionists who claimed that Ussher's date was the representative Christian view, the better to discredit their opponents. In fact, serious opposition to evolutionary theory of the truly fundamentalist kind did not arise until more than sixty years after the publication of *The Origin*.[246]

H. James Brix's snide identification of Bishop Wilberforce as a "fundamentalist creationist" was quite incorrect both theologically and linguistically. It was wrong theologically because the bishop did not interpret scripture literally (in his review of *The Origin* Wilberforce specifically condemned all objections to science based on scripture), and it was wrong linguistically because the term "fundamentalist" had not yet been coined. Most people probably assume that fundamentalism is the oldest form of Christianity—that "Old Time Religion" celebrated by the popular revivalist hymn. In fact, the Fundamentalist Movement was born in about 1910 in the United States. In response to the "new criticism" in biblical studies holding sway in the prominent seminaries (Harvard Divinity School had been openly Unitarian for a century), a group of conservative Christian pastors committed themselves to the proposition that everything in the Bible is true as interpreted literally—thus breaking with nearly two thousand years of Christian interpretive tradition. They published their views in twelve booklets called *The Fundamentals*, hence the name.

The Fundamentalist Movement proved to be quite popular and quickly became a major cultural and political factor in American life.[247] Having decided to oppose the teaching of evolution in the schools, the movement succeeded in having laws prohibiting such teaching passed in five southern states including Tennessee. As anyone who has seen the play or movie *Inherit the Wind* knows, as a result of this law, fundamentalist public officials persecuted teachers dedicated to teaching real science. In fact, no prosecutor in Tennessee or anywhere else made any effort to enforce the law, and it would seem that none ever intended to do so.[248] What actually happened was that in 1925 the American Civil Liberties Union ran newspaper ads seeking a volunteer to test the law and managed to recruit John Thomas Scopes, a coach and sometime substitute biology teacher, who was willing to admit to having taught evolution (although he is unlikely to have actually done so) and to force the local prosecutor to act. The ACLU also arranged to have Scopes defended by Clarence Darrow (*1857–1938*), the most prominent defense attorney of the time and author of many atheist tracts. Then came an extraordinary stroke of good luck for the evolutionists. William Jennings Bryan (*1860–1925*), three-time losing Democratic candidate for president, managed to get himself appointed to lead the prosecution. Bryan hoped to parlay the national publicity attracted by the trial into a fourth run for the presidency. Of course, he knew little science, had no particular theological qualifications, and made a fool of himself and thereby of fundamentalism—aided and abetted by an extremely biased press.[249]

The legacy of the "Scopes Monkey Trial" remains so potent that whenever Christians ask that evolution be presented in public schools as "only a theory," they are ridiculed in the press as fundamentalists and Creationists. Julian Huxley and many other Darwinian ideologues claim that, unlike the theories of physics, chemistry, or even sociology, evolution is "fact," not theory. This is philosophical nonsense. *All* scientific theories remain subject to the possibility of future disconfirmation. Indeed, when the great philosopher of science Karl Popper[250] suggested that the standard version of evolution even falls short of being a scientific theory, being instead an untestable tautology, he was subjected to public condemnations and much personal abuse.

Popper's tribulations illustrate another basis for the victory of Darwinism: a successful appeal for a united front on the part of scientists to counter religious opposition has had the consequence of silencing dissent within the scientific community. I have already noted that problems with evolutionary theory have often been "hushed up." But it is worth quoting this remarkably frank admission by the very eminent Everett C. Olson that there is "a generally silent group" of biological scientists "who tend to disagree with much of the current thought" about evolution, but who remain silent, many of them because they "are so strongly in disagreement that it seems futile to" express dissent. He acknowledged that it is "difficult to judge the size and composition of this silent segment," but their "numbers are not inconsiderable" and their "existence is important and cannot be ignored."[251]

Recently the number of such dissenters has become known; Olson's concerns were more than justified. A survey of biologists who are so distinguished as to be listed in *American Men and Women of Science* found that 45 percent acknowledged that the process of evolution is guided by God.[252] A survey of *all* biologists would undoubtedly show that "Evolutionary Creationists" were in the majority! Indeed, the religiousness of modern scientists is not as it is typically portrayed.

The Religiousness of Modern Scientists

Probably the first ever survey of scientists was conducted by Francis Galton (*1822–1911*), who, in 1872, mailed questionnaires to about 190 "English men of science."[253] Galton was Charles Darwin's cousin and one of the founders of quantitative psychology, who had gained fame for his studies of hereditary genius. Galton's survey of scientists is based on one of the most naive and biased questionnaires ever written, nearly as dreadful as the one distributed to English workingmen later in that same decade by Karl Marx.[254] Galton had previously claimed that scientific interest was hereditary, but in this study he wanted to make room for environmental factors as well, having been convinced through correspondence with a Swiss biologist that both nature and nurture were involved. To find out, Galton asked questions such as:

> Measurement round inside rim of your hat?
> How far do your scientific tastes appear to have been innate?
> Has the religion taught in your youth had any deterrent effect on the freedom of your researches?

When Charles Darwin filled out the questionnaire, he wrote "Certainly innate" in answer to the second of the above questions. To the third, he simply responded "No." That answer greatly surprised Galton. Being a militant atheist, Galton expected that not only Darwin but nearly everyone else would answer "Yes." He *knew* science and religion were incompatible. But not only did his cousin reject the opportunity to say so; more than 90 of the 100 who filled out the questionnaire did likewise—Galton seems never to have recognized the ambiguity of the question. He was also badly surprised to discover that nearly every respondent claimed a church affiliation. It is perhaps indicative that although Galton provided exact figures in reporting most of his results (for example, only 13 had a head size under 22 inches and 8 exceeded 24 inches), he was much less forthcoming about his religion results, and the numbers I reported above needed some reconstruction. Moreover, while Galton admitted that many respondents expressed strong religious views, he stressed that "many of those who describe themselves as religiously inclined . . . seem singularly careless of dogma and exempt from mysterious terror."[255] In any event, these findings were so unwelcome that when the pioneering statistician Karl Pearson (*1857–1936*) wrote Galton's biography in three volumes, he was careful to explain the methodological reasons why these data should not be interpreted on behalf of the obviously "erroneous" belief that science and religion are compatible.[256] Nevertheless, when better studies came along, the results were the same.

In 1914 the American psychologist James Leuba sent questionnaires to a random sample of persons listed in *American Men of Science*. Each was asked to select one of the following statements "concerning belief in God" (all italics in the original):

> 1. I believe in a God to whom one may pray in the expectation of receiving an answer. *By "answer," I mean more than the subjective, psychological effect of prayer.*
> 2. I do not believe in God *as defined above.*
> 3. I have no definite belief regarding this question.

Leuba's standard for belief in God is so stringent it would exclude a substantial portion of "mainline" *clergy*,[257] and that was obviously intentional on his part. He wanted to show that men of science were irreligious. To his dismay, Leuba found that 41.8 percent of his sample of prominent scientists selected option one, thereby taking a position many would regard as "fundamentalist." Another 41.5 percent (many of whom, as Leuba acknowledged, no doubt believed in a somewhat less active deity) selected the second option, and 16.7 percent took the indefinite alternative.

Clearly, these results were not what Leuba had expected and hoped for. So he gave great emphasis to the fact that, as measured, believers were not in the majority, and went on to express his faith in the future, claiming that these data demonstrated a rejection of "fundamental dogmas—a rejection apparently destined to extend parallel with the diffusion of knowledge."[258] However, when Leuba's study was exactly repeated in 1996, the results were unchanged.[259] Thus over an eighty-two-year period, there was no decline in a very literal belief in God among scientists.

TABLE 2.2
Religiousness by Scholarly Field

	% Religious Person	*% Regular Attend*	*% Never Attend*	*% Religious Conservative*	*% No Religion*
Mathematics/statistics	60	47	35	40	27
Physical sciences	55	43	38	34	27
Life sciences	55	42	36	36	29
Social sciences	45	31	48	19	36
Economics	50	38	42	26	30
Political science	51	32	43	18	30
Sociology	49	38	43	16	36
Psychology	33	20	62	12	48
Anthropology	29	15	67	11	57

Source: Calculated from the Carnegie Commission Survey of 60,028 American Academics, 1969.

In 1969 the Carnegie Commission conducted a massive survey of more than 60,000 professors—approximately one-fourth of all the college faculty in America and by far the largest survey of its kind. The survey centered on academic issues and political-social attitudes but also included questions concerning religion: "How often do you attend religious services?" "What is your present religion?" "How religious do you consider yourself?" and "Do you consider yourself religiously conservative?"

Table 2.2 summarizes responses to these items across major areas of science. Two rather striking findings challenge claims about the incompatibility of religion and science. First, levels of religiousness are relatively high. Second, social scientists are substantially less religious than those in what must be regarded as the more mature scientific fields.

In most fields a substantial *majority* think of themselves as deeply or moderately religious—only among social scientists (45 percent) is this the minority response. Nor do scientists restrict themselves to tepid faiths—40 percent of faculty in mathematics and statistics characterized themselves as "religiously conservative," as did 34 percent of physical scientists and 36 percent of those in the life sciences. Moreover, scientists attend church at the same level of regularity as the general population—47 percent of mathematicians and statisticians reported attending two or three times a month or oftener, as did 43 percent of physical scientists and 42 percent in the life sciences. The 1973 General Social Survey (which is only four years later than the faculty survey) found that 44 percent of Americans attended at least two or three times a month. Scientists are, however, a bit more likely than the general population to report that they never attend church—about a third in most areas and about half of social scientists, compared with 21 percent in the 1973 GSS. And scientists surpass the general population in the percentage stating their religious preference as "none." Nevertheless, outside the social sciences, only about one in four gave this response.

But perhaps the most striking finding is that on each of these measures, faculty in the "hard" sciences turn out to be far more likely to be religious than are their counterparts in the "softer" social sciences: they attend church more regularly, are more likely to describe themselves as "deeply" or "moderately" religious and to say they are "religiously conservative," and are far more likely to claim religious affiliation. These patterns are evident not only in the simple cross-tabulations shown here but in complex regressions: differences between the social and the natural and physical sciences are extremely robust and withstand controls for individual attributes such as age, gender, race, or religious upbringing. Moreover, these differences across scientific areas have been replicated in other samples of college professors,[260] and even in samples of graduate and undergraduate students.[261] In addition, Steven Bird found that high school students with "fundamentalist" affiliations were no less likely than anyone else to declare scientific majors in college.[262] Furthermore, longitudinal data show that professors and students do not become less religious as they progress through their scientific training; instead, those enrolling in the social sciences are less religious than the general population *before* entering college and graduate school.[263]

Table 2.2 also breaks down the social sciences into specific fields. Here we see an additional feature: it is above all faculty in psychology and anthropology who stand as towers of unbelief. The other social sciences are relatively irreligious, but these two fields are true outliers. Compared to faculty in the physical sciences, psychologists and anthropologists are almost *twice* as likely to not attend church, to not describe themselves as religious persons, and to say they have no religion. These differences are of such magnitude that one can scarcely imagine their not influencing the tone of conversation, instruction, and research in these two fields. Indeed, this sheds a great deal of light on why it is so widely believed that religion and science are incompatible—nearly everything written on the topic during the twentieth century was written by nonscientists or by *social* scientists. It would be difficult to imagine the following quotation in an undergraduate physics or chemistry textbook:

> The evolutionary future of religion is extinction . . . Belief in supernatural powers is doomed to die out, all over the world, as the result of the increasing adequacy and diffusion of scientific knowledge.[264]

But no eyebrows were raised when it appeared in an undergraduate textbook by the very prominent anthropologist Anthony F. C. Wallace.

This contrast between the social and the physical sciences is well illustrated by the following anecdote. In 1940 A. S. Yahuda, the Yale professor who acquired the collection of Newton's manuscripts now in Jerusalem, offered to show Newton's theological works to George Sarton. The eminent Harvard historian declined rather ungraciously on grounds that he was exclusively interested in science.[265] But when Yahuda showed the manuscripts to Albert Einstein, he found them fascinating and wrote a letter in which he expressed his delight in examining Newton's "spiritual workshop."[266] Einstein was also quite given to "God talk."[267] In 1911 Einstein told the Jewish philosopher Martin Buber, "What we [physicists] strive for is just to draw His lines after Him." In 1921, he told a young physicist, "I want to know how God created this world . . . I want to know His thoughts, the rest are details." Moreover, two remarks he frequently made about God became famous: "God is subtle, but he is not malicious," and "God does not play dice with the world."[268] Although some of Einstein's biographers deny that his use of the word "God" had any religious implications,[269] there is no need for me to become involved in that issue. My point is simply that such expressions did not, and do not, raise any eyebrows in the world of the physical and natural sciences, but any social scientist who talked that way would be stigmatized among her or his peers. That's probably why sociologists of science continue to follow Sarton's example. Not only are they not interested in Newton's or Einstein's God talk; they have shown little or no interest in the immense revival of such talk in scientific circles.

On July 20, 1998, the cover of *Newsweek* proclaimed, "Science Finds God." Given the assumptions that have governed intellectual opinions about science and religion for most of the century, the discovery that many sophisticated scientists think a Creator offers the most parsimonious explanation of how it all came to be is news of cover-story magnitude. Yet it was hardly an overnight development. A landmark in the resumption of serious dialogue between science and theology was Ian Barbour's *Issues in Science and Religion* (1966). Ever since, reputable efforts (mostly by scientists) to wed religion and science, such as *God and the New Physics*,[270] have been attracting a large readership. Moreover, these developments could be interpreted as a *return* to the traditional relationship between theology and science. The brilliant new works by theologians such as John Polkinghorne,[271] who is the only ordained member of the Royal Society of London, are in the tradition of Natural Theology—as Polkinghorne fully acknowledges. By the same token, efforts by scientists such as the Nobel laureate in physics Charles Townes[272] to demonstrate that God is a necessary element in any comprehensive explanation of the universe are entirely in keeping with a long tradition, one that the Darwinian Crusade sought to terminate. It might even be legitimate to say that this renewed relationship is a return to "normal" if Albert Einstein was right when he counseled that "[s]cience without religion is lame. Religion without science is blind."[273]

It is *not* my claim that scientists should include God within their cosmologies, or, indeed, that nonbelievers can't do good science—at least not once the system is in place. I *do* argue that religion and science are compatible, and that the *origins* of science lay in theology.

Conclusion

Despite its length, this chapter consists of only two major points. First, science arose only once in history—in medieval Europe. Second, science could only arise in a culture dominated by belief in a conscious, rational, all-powerful Creator. Thus it could be said that the rise of science required an Eleventh Commandment: "Know thou my handiwork."

Appendix 2.1

Roster of Scientific Stars

	Personal Piety
1. *Bayer*, Johann (1572–1625)	Devout
2. Borelli, Giovanni (1608–1679)	Conventional
3. *Boyle*, Robert (1627–1691)	Devout
4. *Brahe*, Tycho (1546–1601)	Conventional
5. *Briggs*, Henry (1561–1630)	Devout
6. Cassini, Giovanni (1625–1712)	Conventional
7. Copernicus, Nicolaus (1473–1543)*	Conventional
8. Descartes, René (1596–1650)	Devout
9. *Fabricius*, David (1564–1617)*	Devout
10. Fallopius, Gabriel (1523–1562)	Devout
11. Fermat, Pierre (1601–1665)	Conventional
12. *Flamsteed*, John (1646–1719)	Devout
13. Galilei, Galileo (1564–1642)	Conventional
14. Gassendi, Pierre (1592–1655)*	Devout
15. *Gellibrand*, Henry (1597–1663)	Devout
16. *Gilbert*, William (1540–1603)	Conventional
17. Graaf, Regnier de (1641–1673)	Conventional
18. *Grew*, Nehemiah (1641–1712)	Devout
19. Grimaldi, Francesco (1618–1663)*	Devout
20. *Guericke*, Otto (1602–1686)	Conventional
21. *Halley*, Edmund (1656–1742)	Skeptic
22. *Harvey*, William (1578–1657)	Conventional
23. Helmont, Jan Baptista van (1577–1644)	Devout
24. Hevelius, Johannes (1611–1687)	Conventional
25. *Hooke*, Robert (1635–1703)	Devout
26. *Horrocks*, Jeremiah (1619–1641)*	Devout
27. *Huygens*, Christiaan (1629–1695)	Devout
28. *Kepler*, Johannes (1571–1630)	Devout

	Personal Piety
29. Kircher, Athanasius (1601–1680)*	Devout
30. *Leeuwenhoek*, Anton (1632–1723)	Conventional
31. *Leibniz*, Gottfried (1646–1716)	Devout
32. Malpighi, Marcello (1628–1694)	Conventional
33. Mariotte, Edme (1620–1684)*	Devout
34. Mersenne, Marin (1588–1648)*	Devout
35. *Napier*, John (1550–1617)	Devout
36. *Newton*, Isaac (1642–1727)	Devout
37. *Oughtred*, William (1575–1660)*	Devout
38. *Papin*, Denis (1647–1712)	Devout
39. Paracelsus (1493–1541)	Skeptic
40. Pascal, Blaise (1623–1662)*	Devout
41. Picard, Jean (1620–1682)*	Devout
42. *Ray*, John (1628–1705)*	Devout
43. Riccioli, Giovanni (1598–1671)	Devout
44. *Roemer*, Olaus (1644–1710)	Conventional
45. Scheiner, Christoph (1575–1650)*	Devout
46. Snell, Willebrord (1591–1626)	Conventional
47. Steno, Nicolaus (1638–1686)*	Devout
48. *Stevinus*, Simon (1548–1620)	Conventional
49. Torricelli, Evangelista (1606–1647)	Conventional
50. Vesalius, Andreas (1514–1564)	Devout
51. Vieta, Franciscus (1540–1603)	Conventional
52. *Wallis*, John (1616–1703)*	Devout

* Ecclesiastic (priest, monk, friar, minister, canon, etc).
Italic type indicates a Protestant.

Satanic Adoration. A standard part of every witches' sabbat was for everyone present to kiss Satan in the anus, as shown in this detail, extracted from a larger engraving published in Fra Francesco Maria Guazzo's *Compendium maleficarum*, a witch-hunter's manual published in 1608.

3

God's *Enemies*: Explaining the European Witch-Hunts

Extreme rationalism may be defined as the failure of reason to understand itself.
—*Abraham Joshua Heschel*

For centuries, nearly all educated Europeans believed that their societies were victimized by a horrible underground of "witches" who had sworn oaths to serve Satan, and who gleefully inflicted suffering, death, and destruction upon their neighbors. The reality of these malefactors was beyond question, having been confessed in elaborate and consistent detail by thousands of "witches" brought to justice in many different places.

These sworn accounts painted a horrifying picture of absolute evil on the prowl. All "witches" were required to regularly attend gatherings where the most extraordinary sacrilegious, criminal, and immoral things took place. The most frequent of these sabbats (or sabbaths) involved only a few "witches" from the immediate neighborhood and were usually held on Friday nights in places such as churchyards, near the local gallows, in graveyards, or at a crossroads. The participants began by praying to the Devil, who was present—sometimes in human form, sometimes as a hideous horned creature. After having reaffirmed his or her renunciation of Christ, each "witch" then kissed the Devil, usually in the anus. This ceremony was followed by a feast, often consisting of a human baby roasted for the occasion. After the meal, there came a blasphemous version of a Christian service. That done, the "witches" recounted their recent achievements in harming others by causing bad weather, blighting crops, sickening cattle and poultry, causing stillbirths, or making people ill, often fatally. Then, by the light of a candle stuck in the rectum of one of their number, who remained on hands and knees, a dance would begin that soon turned into a general orgy in which nothing and no one was forbidden. The climax involved Satan having sex with everyone present, often changing genders to serve males as well as females. Confessed female "witches" agreed that the Devil's penis was painfully rough and his semen icy cold.

Several times a year "witches" from everywhere gathered for a general sabbat. To overcome the huge distances involved, they were provided with magical means of transport, sometimes riding on flying horses, rams, or large dogs, and sometimes they possessed a magic grease that, when rubbed on a pole or broomstick, enabled them to fly. Events at the large sabbats were like those at the regular meetings, but on a far more magnificent scale. The sabbat began as those assembled reaffirmed their vows, including "that they will both in word and deed heap continual insults and revilings on the Blessed Virgin Mary and the other Saints; that they will trample upon and defile and break all the Relics and images of Saints; that they will abstain from using the sign of the Cross . . . that they will never make full confession of their sins to a priest . . . and finally that they will recruit all they can into the service of the devil."[1] At the end of both large and small sabbats, all the "witches" were charged by Satan to depart and do as much harm as possible to their Christian neighbors.

Had Europeans actually been confronted with such a challenge, the only reasonable and decent thing to do would have been to stamp it out, and that's exactly what most reasonable and decent people tried to do. The results were tragic.

Harmful Misconceptions

Few topics have prompted so much nonsense and outright fabrication as the European witch-hunts. Some of the most famous episodes never took place, existing only in fraudulent accounts and forged documents,[2] and even the current "scholarly" literature abounds in absurd death tolls. Andrea Dworkin claimed that nine million European *women* were burned as witches,[3] while Mary Daly was content with "millions" of women.[4] Pennethorne Hughes included both genders in the "number who died as witches," and, having noted that some estimate the total as "nine millions," he added, "It may be many more."[5] Norman Davies[6] devoted only two of the more than thirteen hundred pages in his history of Europe to witchcraft, but that was sufficient to include his confident report that the "craze" had "consum[ed] millions of innocents."[7] It is only by accepting such fantastic statistics that writers can plausibly use words such as "genocide" and "gynocide" and make comparisons to the Holocaust.

As will be seen, real witchcraft trials began at the start of the fourteenth century, but victims were very few until about 150 years later. Hence the conventional dating of the witchcraft era is from about 1450 until 1750, although many of the most ferocious episodes were clustered between about 1550 and 1650. During the entire three centuries, in the whole of Europe it is very unlikely that more than 100,000 people died as "witches." In fact, scholars who have sifted through the actual records with a real concern for numbers agree that the best estimate is that only about 60,000 people—men as well as women—were executed as "witches" in Europe during the entire witch-hunting period.[8] That works out to a total of about two victims per 10,000 population.[9] Even if we were to assume a death toll twice that high, the total is a tiny fraction of what has been claimed.

Of course, witch-hunts were not evenly spread across time and space. Rather, they tended to come in waves and to be concentrated in a few places, so most local episodes were bloodier than the overall statistics suggest. But even most of these episodes were far less deadly than has often been claimed. Theo. B. Hyslop[10] reported that in England from 1600 to 1680, "about forty-two thousand witches were burnt"[11] —the actual death toll in England probably amounted to fewer than a thousand over the entire three centuries.[12] In similar fashion, it was long believed that early in the seventeenth century, 600 witches were executed in the Basque region of Spain. The true figure may be as low as 30 and no higher than 80.[13] Until recently it was also assumed that 99 men, women, and children were burned alive in Mora, Sweden, in 1669.[14] In fact, 17 adults (and no children) were beheaded and *then* burned.[15] Henry C. Lea placed the death toll in Scotland at about 7,500,[16] five times more than the actual number.[17] And so it has gone.

The death of 60,000 innocent people is appalling, but that is no excuse for exaggerating fatalities by orders of magnitude. Nor is there any justification for merely assuming and then asserting that most witch-hunters were sadistic fanatics. If that were true, it might make for an easy explanation, but the facts will not permit it. Hugh Trevor-Roper pointed out that the "most ferocious of witch-burning princes, we often find, are also the most cultured patrons of contemporary learning." As for many of those who took active roles in the actual prosecutions, upon examining their biographies, Trevor-Roper reported "what harmless, scholarly characters they turn out to be!"[18] Granted that several infamous witch-hunters were fanatics who would stop at nothing, but most judges and inquisitors seemed quite concerned to reach fair verdicts. "With few exceptions European criminal courts showed notable restraint and caution in dealing with witchcraft suspects."[19] This is reflected in the fact that the overall conviction rate of those brought to trial for witchcraft was about 50 to 55 percent[20]—low as criminal prosecutions went in those days.[21]

Nor was death the inevitable outcome for those convicted of witchcraft. In many places the penalties for a first offense were very mild—in Spain the norm was reconciliation with the Church without punishment, and it was usually only those who refused to repent who were condemned.[22] In some places, of course, death was the usual sentence given convicted "witches." But here, too, keep in mind that capital punishment was the *usual* penalty for all significant offenses—even at the height of the witch-hunts, many times more thieves and robbers than "witches" were being executed.[23] Indeed, "more women were probably executed for infanticide than for witchcraft."[24] For example, in Rouen, between 1550 and 1590, at the height of the witch-hunts, sixty-six women were burned for infanticide, while three women and six men were burned for witchcraft.[25] Moreover, the use of the stake as a method of execution for witchcraft was chosen not to inflict unusual suffering but "to prevent resurrection of the body."[26] Consequently, "witches" were often strangled before being burned, or wet leaves were placed on the fire so that the victims died of asphyxiation before the flames reached them. In Sweden "witches" were beheaded before being burned. Moreover, many "witches" were not burned, dead or alive. In England and Scotland they were hanged, and in some parts of Germany they were beheaded or drowned.

It should also be noted that, rather than being staffed by religious extremists, the ecclesiastical courts were far more judicious and lenient in dealing with accused witches than were the secular courts.[27] Contrary to its notorious reputation, the consensus among respectable historians is that the Inquisition was initiated in Spain to replace mob actions with judicial process and restraint,[28] with the result that, as Brian Levack pointed out, during "the largest witch-hunt in Spanish history" more than nineteen hundred persons were accused, but most were never charged, and "only eleven individuals were condemned."[29]

It is true that torture was often used to extract confessions from accused witches, and that these brutally compelled confessions, more than anything else, sustained belief in the reality of pacts with the Devil. But torture was generally regarded as a legitimate tool of justice and was also applied to many accused of conventional crimes. Here, too, it was the ecclesiastical courts that were most reluctant to use torture and eventually took the lead in prohibiting its use.

Before taking up explanations of why the witch-hunts occurred, we must distinguish three fundamental activities on which all charges of witchcraft were based: *magic*, *sorcery*, and *satanism*.

Magic, Sorcery, and Satanism

Magic

As will be seen, ordinary magic was widely practiced in this period and was much like magic everywhere, involving simple charms, spells, and potions directed toward controlling weather, fertility, love, health, and wealth. By itself, magic was seldom regarded as a serious misdeed. Although the Church often tried to prohibit it—partly because its intellectuals found magic implausible, and partly because the religious establishment wished to switch the magic "market" to its own offerings—virtually no one got in serious trouble for doing ordinary magic. However, very visible magical practitioners, especially those who did it on a commercial basis, were vulnerable to suspicions that they also did more wicked things. Chief among these were charges that they used their magic to harm others by causing storms, blighting crops, or bringing about miscarriages, stillbirths, and illness. This aspect of magic was often identified as *black magic*, or what scholars and witch-hunters referred to as *maleficia*. We know that *maleficia* was relatively common because, without being subjected to any form of compulsion, many people acknowledged not only doing it but hiring it done.

Sorcery

Sorcery is the most elaborate form of magic, requiring substantial knowledge and training to employ special rites, spells, calculations, and paraphernalia. Alchemy, astrology, divination, and necromancy (the latter three having to do with foretelling the future) were among the arts performed by medieval sorcerers. Most uses of sorcery have the same goals as ordinary magic, but sorcery is regarded as far more powerful and therefore as far more dangerous when employed to harm others. The Church condemned alchemy, astrology, divination, and necromancy as superstitions, but it was *maleficia* that aroused real antagonism among the laity as well as the clergy. As Robin Briggs explained, "Curses and spells employed with malevolence are real dangers when everyone believes in them, so that questions of guilt and innocence are not quite so simple as they may seem."[30] Often enough, people even took credit for harmful events such as bad weather, and it was common for a person to threaten to put hexes on others. The unsophisticated among them were involved only in magic. Sophisticated *maleficia*, such as using wax images to cause illness, required a sorcerer.

There were a substantial number of sorcerers at work in medieval and early modern Europe, and we know some were accused of witchcraft because physical evidence of their trade was admitted as evidence in their trials; physical evidence of *maleficia* was sometimes submitted to the courts as well.[31]

Satanism

As noted in the introduction, sorcery sometimes involves efforts to compel certain primitive supernatural entities to do the sorcerer's bidding. Even so, sorcery remains magic. It is satanism that crosses the line from magic into religion, involving charges of the actual worship of, and collaboration with, *evil* supernatural beings. Magic and sorcery, including the forms involving *maleficia*, are found around the world and are the activities identified as "witchcraft" in the immense and sometimes distinguished anthropological literature on the subject. But that's not what came to define "witches" in Europe. Satanism was the essence of European witchcraft and the grounds for imposing the death penalty. And satanism was a purely European idea, sharply setting "the European concept of witchcraft" apart "from the witch beliefs of other primitive peoples."[32] Thus although the anthropology of witchcraft may be of use even in Europe for understanding village tensions over magic and sorcery, given the unique culture involved, the anthropological literature is irrelevant to grasping why and how Europeans came to believe in satanism.

Sorcery Seminar. Sorcery was a well-established profession in medieval and early modern Europe. Unlike ordinary magic, sorcery required a substantial amount of training—there were many elaborate rites and practices to learn, as these students of the occult are doing. © Bettmann/CORBIS.

And it is this belief that is the issue, for it is no mystery why judges confronted with individuals they truly believed to be active satanists sent them to the gallows or the stake.

Sometimes satanism was the initial charge brought against an individual, but most cases seem to have begun with complaints about magic and sorcery, with charges of satanism emerging out of the process of interrogation. The only evidence in support of the existence of satanism consists of confessions. An objective reader must dismiss these as false, even the few that were volunteered as well as those extracted by torture. As for the consistent agreement on details of sabbats contained in the confessions, as will be seen, the interrogators relied on manuals concerning the discovery of "witches," and these details were precisely those the manuals told them were required to validate confessions. Hence interrogators were instructed to keep up the torture until these specific admissions were forthcoming. Some of the accused already knew these details as part of the public image of witchcraft and were able to produce them without much prompting. But even the ignorant could eventually produce them, having learned them from the detailed questions put to them. In any event, confessions of satanism are invalidated, if for no other reason, because they involve impossible acts, often including flying, slipping through keyholes and up chimneys, changing shapes, taking on animal forms, and having sexual intercourse with Satan.

Eight Faulty Explanations

In addition to grossly exaggerated statistics and the other misconceptions noted thus far, eight quite defective explanations dominate both the popular and the scholarly literature on European witch-hunts. Through clarification and refutation of each of these theories, many essential features of the witch-hunts can be revealed.

Real Witches

Not only the witch-hunters but some modern scholars believe that medieval Europe abounded in *real* satanists. Montague Summers (*1880–1948*), who edited and translated into English many primary sources concerning witchcraft, claimed that people actually sold their souls to Satan, engaged in orgies, flew to sabbats, urinated in baptismal fonts, cooked infants, and all the rest.[33] A less extreme view of the reality of satanism, popularized by Margaret Murray (*1863–1963*), claims that there was a widespread medieval religious underground, based on pre-Christian fertility cults, whose practices resembled those attributed to witches—albeit its members traveled to their gatherings in conventional ways rather than on broomsticks.[34] Thus it is claimed that the witch-hunters were persecuting organized religious rebels who actually engaged in most of the satanic practices for which they were indicted. Murray's work was once very much in vogue—she even wrote the section on witchcraft for many editions of the *Encyclopaedia Britannica*. But reputable scholars now agree with Norman Cohn that Murray's knowledge was at best "superficial and [that] her grasp of historical method was non-existent."[35] Indeed, Murray's dishonesty in excerpting quotations from confessions, in ways clearly intended to mislead by omitting the impossible portions, has been fully exposed, and her work is without merit.[36] It seems worth mentioning that Murray interpreted the burning of Joan of Arc as really having been a ritual sacrifice to ensure good crops,[37] and eventually she claimed that beginning with William the Conqueror, for the next four centuries every king of England was secretly a high priest of the witch cult.[38]

Nevertheless, Murray's views remain popular. Publishers continue to market her books and many others which assert that witchcraft was and is real, usually written by those claiming to be "witches" or by academics who dabble in wiccan groups. Consequently, substantial sections of bookstores are currently devoted to testimonies on behalf of occult powers, and to celebrations of the "reemergence" of witchcraft. The truth is far less sensational but far more interesting: the most learned men and women of the time, firmly committed rationalists, absolutely believed in satanism. It really shouldn't be necessary to point out that they were wrong, that medieval witch-hunters were not chasing real satanists. Nor were they persecuting a witchlike religious underground—had such a thing existed, how did it go undetected for more than a thousand years? Contrary to claims by modern "witches," contemporary wicca is of very recent origins, not of ancient descent.

This is not to say witchcraft was pure fantasy and that "nothing" was going on to generate concern. As will be seen, a substantial proportion of witchcraft charges, especially in early days, involved heresy, and this was an era especially abundant in significant heretical movements. Later in the chapter, I pursue the fact that the geographies of heresy and witchcraft were very similar—"In those areas where heresy was strong, witchcraft too became important."[39] For example, along the Rhine River in Germany and France, heretical movements thrived and witch-hunts were frequent and bloody; in Spain and Italy there was little heresy and very few witchcraft trials. In addition, this is also the geography of episodes of bloody anti-Semitism. I shall argue that anti-Semitic violence, persecution of heretics, and witch-hunts were *collateral* results of conflicts between major religious forces.

A second important factor is the substantiating "background" provided by magic and sorcery, both of which abounded in Europe at this time, and both of which often involved *maleficia*. Thus most claims that someone engaged in *these* practices were true. In the typical case, a person was accused of *maleficia* by neighbors who were motivated by a lengthy list of grievances assembled over many years.[40] These were not flimsy charges based only on suspicions aroused by various misfortunes—hailstorms, sick livestock, the death of newborns, and the like—which were presumed to have been caused by the accused, but were grounded in public knowledge about actual behavior. Many of the accused had provided magical services to those who eventually turned against them. Many others had a long history of public threats to use witchcraft or had bragged of having done so. A typical case was that of Elena Dalok who was brought to court in London in 1493 after repeatedly bragging that she could make it rain at will, and that everyone she cursed had subsequently died.[41] Equally typical is the case of Catarina Servada from the Spanish village of Argelès: "In her conflicts with her husband and neighbours Catarina repeatedly made claims to be a witch and issued threats against those who crossed her."[42] Or, in 1493, Robert Bayly and his wife were charged by their local parish in Somersetshire "as notorious scolds and cursers of their neighbours."[43] This was not cursing in the sense of merely using intemperate language but often involved public invocations of supernatural powers to provide catastrophic results, as when Elizabeth Weeks knelt in a churchyard in Kent and, in front of the congregation, cursed the vicar and his wife, wishing "the Pope and the Devil" to take them.[44]

As these cases demonstrate, there was often a factual basis for accusations, one that could be fully substantiated in court, thus lending an aura of reality to the charge of satanism as well. Moreover, once the culture of satanism had been deduced by theologians and widely publicized, it was to be expected that some people would volunteer confessions of their guilt—just as modern police are frequently presented with false confessions of horrible crimes. No doubt, some people even attempted to become satanists, and a few, having repented, "were sincerely persuaded of their guilt . . . [and] even confessed it to their priests."[45] However, although I agree with Jeffrey Burton Russell that over the years various small groups probably engaged in sex orgies and in many of the sacrilegious acts with which they were charged, I am not persuaded either that such groups were the source of the ideas about satanic gatherings, or that the virtually universal belief in satanic activities rested on these examples. I find the reverse causal order more plausible, that the existence of a vividly imagined culture of satanism stimulated occasional efforts by both individuals and groups to actualize it—as remains the case even in this supposedly more enlightened era. Consequently, while it must be allowed that there was a substantial reality behind belief in witchcraft, there was little substance behind charges of satanism.

Mental Illness

A variant of the claim that "witches" were real argues that the victims suffered from mental illness, which was misinterpreted in these prepsychiatric times.[46] This could be argued only by those unfamiliar with trial transcripts, which clearly reveal the rationality of the overwhelming proportion of victims,[47] as well as the fact that their "delusions" were extracted by coaching and torture and were frequently recanted in court. Moreover, as Nachman Ben-Yehuda[48] noted, the psychopathological interpretation begs the significant question. Since madness did not suddenly appear in the fifteenth century,[49] why should the mentally ill have been labeled as witches only during this era? In fact, mental illness was not mistaken for witchcraft; many records survive of courts distinguishing between the two.[50] For example, a demonology published in 1624 to facilitate the detection of "witches" warned against mistaking various forms of melancholia for witchcraft.[51] Indeed, to the extent that madness may have played any role, it was that sometimes psychotics were taken to be the *victims* of witchcraft—to have been "bewitched." The idea that "witches" were mislabeled psychotics is spurious.[52] This is not to suggest, of course, that many of those selected as "witches" weren't quite peculiar.

Sexism

A third, and equally unfounded, explanation attributes the witch-hunts to *sexism*, to attempts to control women by punishing those who violated

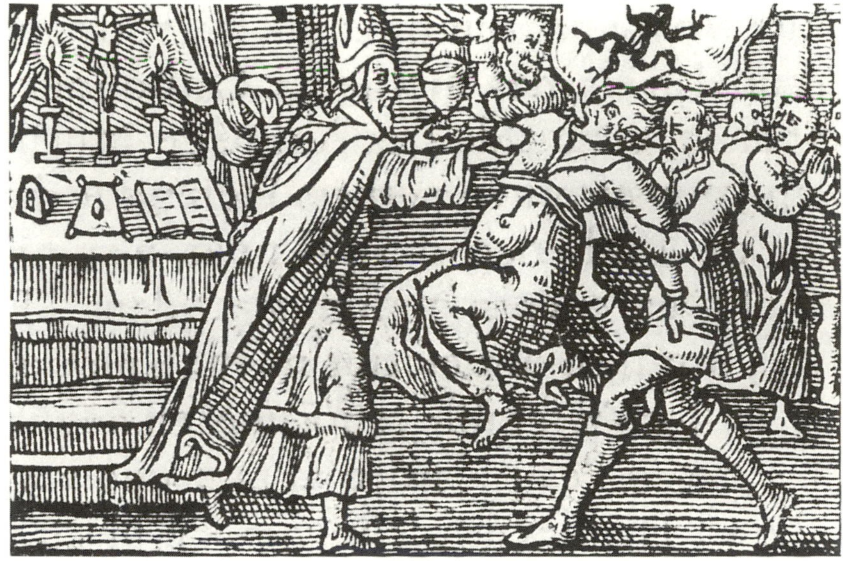

Out! Rather than having been mistaken for witches, mentally ill people were often assumed to be the victims of witchcraft, to be "bewitched" or "possessed" by a demon. In this woodcut created in 1598, a hysterical woman is held by two men as a priest forces her to take the bread and wine of communion to drive out the demon possessing her—seen leaving through her mouth. © CORBIS.

norms governing conventional sex roles.[53] Anne Llewellyn Barstow charged that the witch-hunts occurred because they "gave influential European men the opportunity to punish [women] in a sexually sadistic way," which reveals how "men and women related to each other."[54] It must be granted that the authors of the infamous *Malleus maleficarum* (*Hammer of Witches*)—a fifteenth-century manual for detecting and prosecuting witches—wrote precisely to Barstow's specifications: "All witchcraft comes from carnal lust, which is in women insatiable . . . Wherefore for the sake of fulfilling their lusts they consort even with devils."[55]

A fatal shortcoming of the sexism thesis is that charges of witchcraft were not sex specific, and that most accusations directed at women did not stem from gender conflicts. Based on computations covering the entire era of witch-hunting, about a third of all the victims were men.[56] Admittedly, in some communities the victims were exclusively, or almost exclusively, women. Unfortunately, these cases have received obsessive attention from some writers who simply dismiss as "unrepresentative" those cases wherein the accused were exclusively, or almost exclusively, men. Moreover, later in the chapter, I present the first evidence that among the accused, men were more likely than women to receive severe sentences, including execution. It is true that the *Malleus* claimed that "witches" were almost always women, and this may have contributed to the fact that the percentage of women among the accused rose over time (although the percentage of male victims increased very rapidly at the end of the witch-hunting era). But even in the most intense and ferocious period of witch-hunting, "rich burghers, town-councilors, students, schoolboys, and small children of either sex" were among those indicted, as Norman Cohn explained.[57] Indeed, early in the seventeenth century the prince-bishop of Bamberg had his own chancellor and five burgomasters executed as "witches."[58]

In addition, a very high percentage of women charged with witchcraft were accused by other women, not men—influential or otherwise.[59] Nor will it do to dismiss this fact by claiming that female accusers were patriarchal puppets dancing to male expectations,[60] who attacked women "perceived as outsiders, in hope of being accepted, or tolerated, themselves."[61] What is entirely clear in the many volumes of transcripts is that most accusations brought by women against women stemmed from quarrels among women over women's concerns. As Deborah Willis summarized:

> I take issue especially with the widely held feminist view that assigns the woman accused of witchcraft to the role of rebellious protofeminist and the female accuser to that of patriarchal conformist. Village-level quarrels that led to witchcraft accusations grew out of struggles to control household boundaries, feeding, child care, and other matters typically assigned to women's sphere. In such quarrels, the woman accused of witchcraft was as likely to be the one urging conformity to a patriarchal standard. Her curses and insults were experienced not as violations of proper feminine conduct but as verbal assaults on the other woman's reputation for 'neighborly nurture,' assaults that might also cause harm to loved ones under her care.[62]

Granted that women were more likely than men to be accused. But, as will be seen, their greater vulnerability lay almost entirely in the predominance of women in medical magic (which sometimes evolved into charges of satanism). This gender difference arose not because of deviant behavior but precisely because the *conventional* female role bore responsibility for family health. That also accounts for the fact that females accused of witchcraft tended to be older.[63] It was, of course, older women who had acquired the experience to fill the role of midwife and healer. Women accused as witches are also reported to have been "sharp-tongued, bad-tempered, and quarrelsome."[64] Since charges were usually initiated by neighbors, one would expect that enmity toward the accused would play a significant role. In minor support of the sexism explanation, these personal flaws may have resulted from the unattractive conditions of life faced by older, unmarried women in this era. Keep in mind, however, that the witch-hunters accused very few women of anything, thus ignoring the sex-role violations and disagreeable deportment of millions.

Social Change

The fourth faulty explanation consists of a cluster of sociological claims blaming the whole thing on social change. Thus George Rosen blamed the "tensions and difficulties" caused by "the stress of rapid change." In such times, "fear, uncertainty, suspicion may lead members of the affected group to cast about for some explanation."[65] Paul Tillich agreed, calling this the "age of anxiety."[66] Steven T. Katz listed many changes taking place in Europe during the fourteenth and fifteenth centuries and commented that "it is not difficult to appreciate why Christians were intensely anxious, and how this legitimate concern effervesced as witch hysteria."[67] And the distinguished Michael Walzer proposed "that witchcraft helped solve, in the minds of the people, some of the problems raised by [economic development] and by its impact upon traditional ways of doing things."[68]

Many witchcraft historians allude to the social change thesis, and some even discuss it in unsystematic ways, but the most comprehensive synthesis of these explanations was by Nachman Ben-Yehuda. According to him, the "witch craze" was "a negative reaction" to rapid social change, "in the sense that its purpose was to counteract and prevent change and reestablish traditional religious authority."[69] Ben-Yehuda's essay is a catalog of sociological "causes": urban growth, economic development including the beginnings of the "industrial form of production," expanded trade and a more pronounced division of labor, increased use of money and credit, population growth, the decline of feudalism, the rise of science—all resulting in widespread anomie. As he summed up:

> During the 15th and 16th centuries Europe experienced the painful pangs associated with the emergence of a new social order and the crumbling of an older one . . . The state of powerlessness and anomie experienced by contem-

> porary individuals was further exaggerated by severe climatological and demographic changes which, together with geographical discoveries, created a feeling of impending doom, thus paving the way for the widespread popularity of the craze. The dissolution of the medieval cognitive map of the world gave rise to utopian expectations, magical beliefs, and bold scientific explorations. These conditions created the need for a redefinition of moral boundaries as an attempt to restore the previous social order.[70]

This "explanation" contains almost as many fatal defects as it does parts. But the most important of these is lack of awareness of the episodic and scattered nature of the phenomenon to be explained. There was no *general* "witch craze." As Robin Briggs noted so clearly, "the term 'witch-craze' . . . should be saved for those exceptional [local] cases." Witch-hunting was merely *endemic* in most of Europe most of the time; an *epidemic* of witch-hunting occurred in only a few, notorious, local cases; it "never lasted very long in any specific place and was very restricted geographically . . . Virtually all the significant examples are located between the 1590s and the 1640s."[71] The primary independent variables cited by Ben-Yehuda all followed a long, fairly constant, gradual trend across most of Europe throughout the period in question, but the proposed consequences were sudden, short-term, and local. There is simply no fit between the gradual curves of social change and the sudden spikes of witch-hunting.

In similar fashion, Alan Macfarlane argued that witch-hunts in England were the result of the onset of economic and social individualism that was overwhelming the communal, village-based society.[72] This was a widely shared view of social changes in England at this time, and in Europe as well. Nevertheless, Macfarlane gracefully retracted this entire thesis in a subsequent study in which he found that such changes were not occurring at this time, and that historians had merely assumed that they were. Instead, the development of English individualism long predated the witchcraft trials.[73]

No one would suppose that the witch-hunts occurred in a social vacuum. Of course certain conditions and events were crucial—I will give particular emphasis to major religious conflicts, beginning with the Crusades and ending with the Peace of Westphalia. But it simply will not do to invoke social change (indications of which can nearly always be found), assume an unsettling reaction to whatever changes can be seen, and then assert that these factors caused whatever happened. Such an explanation is so vague as to be consistent with *any* subsequent development—in fact, if nothing happened, that would probably be attributed to social changes producing an age too fearful to act. Blaming "social change" is puerile unless one clearly specifies what changes, and then shows how they directly link to specific outcomes.

Solidarity

In *Wayward Puritans*, Kai T. Erikson offered an eloquent plea on behalf of the functionalist notion that deviance serves to strengthen the moral order—that by detecting and punishing "witches," the people of Salem generated a stronger sense of group solidarity and thereby increased conformity to group norms:

> [Deviance] may actually perform a needed service to society by drawing people together in a common posture of anger and indignation. The deviant individual violates rules of conduct which the rest of the community holds in high respect; and when these people come together to express their outrage over the offense and to bear witness against the offender, they develop a tighter bond of solidarity than existed earlier.[74]

Thus the need for social solidarity was the *root cause* of the witchcraft persecutions. As Erikson explained, "the witchcraft hysteria" was an attempt "by the people of the Bay to clarify their position to the world as a whole, to redefine the boundaries which set New England apart as a new experiment in living."[75]

Erikson's views reflected an approach to deviance that, over the past century or so, has periodically attracted sociologists, partly from their love of the irony that something "good" is caused by something "bad," in this case that witch-hunts (bad) caused increased observance of the norms (good). Notions about the positive latent consequences of deviance may have originated with Emile Durkheim, who claimed that crime was "an integral part of all healthy societies."[76] This view became very fashionable during the 1960s and was commonly understood as the "profound insight" that deviance serves a valuable social function by keeping the mechanisms of social control in good working order; hence "good" people owe their virtue to "bad" people.[77]

This explanation cannot withstand close inspection. First of all, since the need for solidarity would seem to be a constant, it offers no clues as to why "witches," as opposed to murderers or bigamists, say, were selected as the exemplary deviants during this period and not at other times. Second, Travis Hirschi correctly identified this approach as the "exercise theory" of social control—that the more often a group must enforce the norms, the stronger the norms.[78] But, as Hirschi explained, the true irony of this functionalist interpretation is that it rests on the logical contradiction that a society with some deviance will have a lower rate of deviance than a society with no deviance. For example, it follows that a society with a lot of rapes will have stronger norms against rape and hence a greater capacity to prevent rape than a society in which rapes never or seldom occur. A second irony is that behind this notion is a distorted and misunderstood version of deterrence theory—a theory to which those who believe that deviance strengthens solidarity are hotly opposed. Deterrence theory holds that the more certain, rapid, and severe the punishment imposed for an offense, the less frequently that act will be committed.[79] When the theory is applied sequentially, it offers the following account: to the extent that an increase in the incidence of a crime causes public fear and anger, efforts are increased to detect the crime, the punishment is made more severe, and the incidence of that crime will decline. Applied to witchcraft, deterrence theory predicts that an outbreak of witch-burning would result in a decline in the local practice of magic and sorcery, which seems very likely. But the exercise theorists have not made that claim. Rather, they propose that deviance, in and of itself, increases solidarity and conformity.

This brings us to a third fatal flaw: the fact that outbursts of witch-hunting did not increase solidarity, not in Massachusetts or anywhere else. Quite the opposite. As is clear in the sources, some of which will be quoted in subsequent sections, witch-hunts invariably *increased* social tensions and mutual suspicions, raised anxieties about the possibility of being accused, and heightened fears concerning possible revenge by "witches" as yet undetected, or even by Satan himself. Consequently, during witch-hunts people tended to draw apart rather than pull together, which resulted in weakened social solidarity.

A fourth shortcoming is that this sort of functionalism assumes that conscious motives are of little or no relevance to understanding social life. Hence a number of well-known social scientists have proposed that people don't know the real reason they take part in religious rituals such as rain dances or, by extension, witch-hunts. Thus the anthropologists Dan Sperber[80] and Rodney Needham[81] deny the existence of any "interior state" called belief; hence "primitives" can't be concerned with rain Gods and *must* be dancing on behalf of increased solidarity. Indeed, in the absence of "interior states" people have no reasons for *anything* they do, and human behavior is merely a mindless response to social forces. When such assumptions are applied to witchcraft, these functionalists ask us to accept that "society" made people burn "witches," regardless of why they believed they were doing it (if they were capable of belief), or, alternatively, that some people having sufficient sociological insight cynically encouraged others to burn innocent victims for the greater benefit of the group. In fact, people did know why they pursued witches, fully believing that they were the source of great danger.

Greed

A sixth explanation, presented in many studies, places substantial blame for the witch-hunts on *greed*, asserting that witchcraft charges were brought by those seeking to share in the spoils of expropriated wealth.[82] Indeed, Elliot Currie devoted most of an article to the "witchcraft industry," claiming that "in continental Europe [witch-hunting] was a large and complex business which created and sustained the livelihoods of a sizeable number of people."[83] To be sure, court employees were paid for witch trials just as they were paid for all criminal proceedings, and executioners were paid by the job. No doubt, too, there were instances of cynical exploitation of witchcraft charges in pursuit of gain—it was the profit motive that caused King Philip IV of France to fake evidence of satanism and to burn the leading Knights Templars.[84]

Nevertheless, this thesis overlooks several facts. First, the overwhelming majority of victims possessed very little. Second, confiscated property mostly went to the "state," not to their accusers. Third, to the extent that an accused had anything worth confiscating, the courts seldom took more than a small percentage of his or her net worth—in southwestern Germany the average confiscation was about 14 percent.[85] Finally, as Christina Larner pointed out, the cost of a witchcraft prosecution "was nearly always an expense to the local authority rather than a means of revenue."[86] Many other historians have reported the same thing.[87] A typical example is the prosecution of witches in the Basque region of Spain at the start of the seventeenth century. The cost of the prisoners' subsistence alone came to 14,495 reales, while confiscations from those found guilty amounted to 732 reales. This very substantial loss does not even include the costs of the prosecution itself.[88] Indeed, as Keith Thomas pointed out, "in England prosecutions can scarcely ever have had a financial motive."[89] Norman Cohn offered the same judgment for Europe as a whole: "Financial greed and conscious sadism, though by no means lacking in all cases, did not supply the main driving force: that was supplied by religious zeal."[90] Moreover, even if wicked people sometimes sought to gain by lodging accusations of witchcraft, the attribution of greedy motives fails to confront the more fundamental issue: why did the opportunity to denounce others as "witches" exist? How did such an elaborate culture concerning satanism arise? Why did even the leading intellectuals of the time believe that certain people could fly, cast fatal or debilitating spells on others, sicken livestock, and spoil crops? Where did anyone get the idea that there existed a secret underground of lost souls who ate infants, adored incest, and kissed Satan's ass?

Fanatical Clergy

Answers to these questions are proposed by the seventh and eighth explanations, which stress *irrationality.* Much of this is simply anti-Catholicism—the witch-hunts being attributed to "pagan and popish superstitions" by Francis Hutchinson (*1660–1739*) in the first serious history of witchcraft.[91] A more specific "explanation" is that in addition to the normal dose of fanaticism that comes with faith, the fanaticism of the Catholic clergy was goaded to extremes by their repressed sexuality. Thus W. H. Trethowan[92] argued that inhibited sexual desires were the cause of it all: "The persecution of witches, which can be directly attributed to Christian asceticism, was therefore largely a result of the sexual urge being directed from its natural context by divine decree." He continued, "[S]exual desires when inhibited have a strong and sadistic tendency to become a force of destruction." He went on, citing his fellow psychoanalyst Walter Schubart to the effect that the witch-hunts arose from "a fear-laden rejection of women" culminating in "a raging campaign of revenge and annihilation."[93] We are not told, however, why priests were driven to such extremes by their repressed sexual drives only in this era, which would seem to be an instance of the fallacy of using a constant to explain a variable.

Taking somewhat a different tack, Henry Charles Lea (*1825–1909*) proposed that charges of witchcraft were often motivated by priests attempting to pressure women to have sex with them, or to gain revenge on women who spurned them.[94] No doubt this must have happened several times, but the fact remains that charges of witchcraft very seldom originated with a priest; they typically came from neighbors—very often other women. Lea is rightly admired for his careful and energetic efforts to collect original sources, but like so many others who have written on witchcraft, he was an extreme anti-Catholic, and this colored his scholarly generalizations and judgments. In similar fashion, Rossell Hope Robbins claimed that inquisitors were such bloodthirsty fanatics that it was virtually unknown for anyone brought before them to be acquitted: "[A]s all records show, and as even inquisitors admitted, once accused, the chances of escaping death were almost nil."[95] In fact, the various Inquisitions (there were many independent regional and national Inquisitions) were far more likely to acquit or to give mild sentences than were the secular courts.[96] Moreover, as will be seen, in places where the authority of the Inquisitions was greatest, such as in Italy and Spain, most accusations of witchcraft were dismissed without trials, and very few of those convicted were executed. Indeed, in 1550 the Inquisition in Catalonia, soon supported by other Inquisitions in Spain, attacked the evidential basis of witchcraft trials and opposed all further prosecutions—this at a time when the most furious and ferocious period of witch-hunting was just beginning elsewhere.[97] Nevertheless, G. G. Coulton (*1858–1947*) approvingly repeated the misrepresentation that "acquittal was almost unknown to the Inquisition," while basking in Protestant superiority vis-à-vis the "Totalitarian Church."[98]

But it is not only anti-Catholic bias that has shaped many studies of witchcraft. Historians associated with late-nineteenth- and early-twentieth-century "liberalism" wrote in opposition to *all* religion, even if they reserved their most vitriolic attacks for "Papists."[99] As Trevor-Roper summed them up: "The liberal historians . . . write as if the irrationality of the witch-beliefs had always been apparent to the natural reason of man and as if the prevalence of such beliefs could be explained only by clerical bigotry."[100] In fact, these historians seem to have been interested in witchcraft only as it could serve them as a weapon in the battle against faith—many of them were leading proponents of the inevitability of warfare between religion and science. W.E.H. Lecky (*1838–1903*) contrasted credulous, witch-hunting Catholicism with the new spirit of rationalism that had liberated Europe from the "Dark Ages."[101] Jacob Burckhardt, herald of the Renaissance, expressed similar views.[102] Andrew Dickson White, some of whose misrepresentations were exposed in Chapter 2, took the remarkable position that charges of witchcraft were almost entirely based on the refusal of the Catholic Church to accept natural explanations of thunderstorms, which clerics blamed on witches, he asserts, rather than on atmospheric conditions.[103] White's pupil George Lincoln Burr (*1857–1938*) was even more strident, going so far as to suggest that the idea of witchcraft was cynically created by the Inquisition out of the need for new victims when, having run out of heretics to burn, it "turned its idle hands to the extirpation of witches."[104] To which Hugh Trevor-Roper responded, "The picture of the Inquisition using up its idle machinery against witches simply to prevent it from rusting cannot convince us."[105] As for the Inquisition's needing new victims, there were far more real heretics available for persecution at the height of the witchcraft era than ever before—the Wars of Religion raged. Moreover, Protestants proved to be as avid witch-hunters as their Catholic opponents, and it was their combined efforts that carried the witch-hunts to their historic high point. So much, then, for the Catholicity of witchcraft persecution.

But perhaps the most interesting fact, so carefully ignored by many who have tried to use the witchcraft era as the final proof that religion is the relentless opponent of reason and science, is that although these scholars are fond of situating the witch-hunts in the "waning Middle Ages," the really frantic hunting was not part of the Middle Ages at all but occurred during the "Enlightenment." The peak era of witch-hunting took place during "the centuries of Renaissance, Reformation and experimental science," as Trevor-Roper noted.[106] Indeed, "Renaissance humanism did not attack the central presuppositions of the system of witchcraft . . . magic permeated the worldview of much Renaissance humanism."[107] Thus did Erasmus ridicule science, especially astronomy, noting that "nature laughs at their puny conjectures."[108]

Some of the "liberal" historians tried to pass off the magical beliefs of the Enlightenment as a mere holdover of the medieval outlook, or even as the reactionary last gasp of a Church being overwhelmed by progress. As Joseph Hansen explained, the outburst of witchcraft trials was "nothing but the natural dying out of the medieval spirit, which the Reformation only partially pushed aside."[109] But that won't do.[110] The first significant objections to the reality of satanic witchcraft came from Spanish inquisitors, not from scientists! Not only did those who made the "Scientific Revolution" not express opposition to belief in witchcraft; most of them accepted its essential assumptions, and some of them, like Isaac Newton, were themselves very active practitioners of magic and sorcery.[111]

The distinguished philosopher Henry More (*1614–1687*), Newton's close friend and mentor at Cambridge, often attended witchcraft trials, expressed his firm belief in satanism, and even interrogated a young women accused of witchcraft, accepting her confession to having attended witches' sabbats.[112] Joseph Glanvill (*1636–1680*), another of Newton's Cambridge set and a leading member of the Royal Society, wrote *Saducismus Triumphatus, or full and plain evidence concerning witches and apparitions*, in which he argued that only atheists "deny there are spirits or witches."[113] Even a scientist as distinguished as Robert Boyle encouraged witch-hunts.[114] As for Paracelsus, that paragon of religious skepticism and medical innovation observed several witches and pronounced their powers to be genuine, although not satanic.[115] Paracelsus was himself dedicated to Hermetic sorcery and claimed that he had harnessed the energy of the universe by combining alchemy with astrology. In the right circumstances he might well have been tried for witchcraft.[116] As for A. D. White's "martyr" to science, Giordano Bruno, not only was he executed for theological, not scientific, heresy (Chapter 2); he was an equally likely candidate for charges of witchcraft, having also been a devotee of the Hermetic tradition of sorcery.[117]

Even leading *anti*religious voices of the day supported the persecution of witches. Thomas Hobbes (*1599–1679*), the famous English philosopher and outspoken atheist who, in his very influential book *Leviathan*,[118] dismissed all religion as "credulity," "ignorance," and "lies" and Gods as but "creatures of fancy," also wrote in that same book, "[A]s for witches . . . they are justly punished."[119] Or consider Jean Bodin (*ca. 1530–1596*), a bitter enemy of the Church, secret atheist, and "the undisputed intellectual master of the later sixteenth century."[120] Bodin wrote *Colloquium of the Seven about Secrets of the Sublime*, which became the "underground classic" of seventeenth-century atheism. In it Bodin noted that because all of the competing religions claim to be true, "all are refuted by all."[121] Although he seems not to have believed in God, Bodin was a firm believer in demons and the Devil, served as a judge in several witchcraft trials, and advocated burning witches alive in the slowest possible fire. In 1580 Bodin also published *Demonomania of Witches*[122]—"the book which, more than any other, reanimated the witch-fires throughout Europe"[123]—a book that Henry More judged to be "rational and sagacious."[124]

Bodin wrote his book on witchcraft in French to make it more accessible to local judges and prosecutors, but Latin and German editions quickly appeared, and the book was a "best-seller"—by 1604 more than ten editions of the French version had been sold. What Bodin did was to update the *Malleus maleficarum* and adapt it for use in secular courts, while retaining every aspect of the satanist perspective, including cannibalism, infant sacrifices, and sex orgies with the Devil. The scholarly value of Bodin's book today lies in the fact that his arguments demanding death, not only for all witches, but for everyone who doubted any detail of his demonology, march to the clear beat of logic. Ultimately, he appealed not to emotion or superstition (although there is plenty of both), but to *reason*. In this, Bodin was not exceptional. The primary treatises on witchcraft are not wild ravings, albeit they contain a great deal of anger and what we now know to be nonsense. Rather, they are the well-reasoned work of writers who took pride in their logic. This is true even of the *Malleus maleficarum*.[125]

Psychohistory

The eighth false explanation attributes the witch-hunts to episodes of collective madness afflicting Europeans of all religious persuasions. Indeed, the witch "craze" is regarded as the premier instance of outbreaks of "mass psychosis," or what Freud designated "psychical epidemics, of historical mass convulsions."[126] The major proponent of the notion that human groups are often animated by a "collective unconsciousness" akin to hypnotism, which causes each individual group member to "become an automaton," was Gustave LeBon (*1841–1931*), author of *The Crowd*.[127] Indeed, Freud devoted nearly 25 percent of his monograph on group psychology to excerpts from LeBon interspersed with favorable comments.[128] Quoting LeBon—"[G]roups have never thirsted after truth. They demand illusions, and cannot do without them. They constantly give what is unreal precedence over what is real"—Freud then commented, "[T]his predominance of the life of phantasy and of the illusion born of an unfulfilled wish is the ruling factor in the psychology of neuroses . . . a hysterical symptom is based upon phantasy [concerning] an evil intention which was never carried out."[129]

Thus, following Freudian doctrine, George Rosen found the witch-hunts to be classic examples of "collective psychosis, mass delusions, [and] epidemics of hysteria."[130] Indeed, at the end of the first edition of his superb book on the European campaign against heresy and witchcraft, Norman Cohn also ventured into orthodox Freudian psychohistory in "Postscript: Psycho-Historical Speculations." Here he traced the witchcraft "fantasy" to psychological "inner demons" that afflicted European Christians. These were generated in their "innermost selves" by "obsessive fears, and . . . their unacknowledged, terrifying desires." Cohn expanded on this diagnosis by discussing the "unconscious cannibalistic impulses" held by parents "towards their children" and by children "towards a younger sibling."[131]

In my view, application of psychohistory to the witch-hunts amounts to explaining one fantasy with another. Moreover, to banish concerns about "witches" to the realm of psychopathology creates an even deeper mystery: how do such malignant mental states seize large numbers of people who otherwise seem entirely sane? Social science offers no plausible theories to support attributions of mass madness—notions such as "mass hysteria" and the "collective unconscious" were abandoned long ago.[132] Moreover, this sort of psychohistory usually violates a very basic axiom of social science, that it is impossible to judge an action in terms of rationality unless one knows the point of view of the actor. Only if we know what people *think* they are doing can we evaluate *why* they are doing it. In the instance at hand, far too little attention has been paid to what the people persecuting witches actually believed they were doing and why. When sufficient attention is paid to these matters, it becomes clear that the witch-hunters were not driven by irrationality. To the contrary, it was *reason* that led them astray. It is very significant that in 2000, when Norman Cohn produced a revised edition of his famous book, the postscript on psychohistory was omitted—in keeping with the recent and widespread (if overdue) rejection of Freudianism by social scientists.

In what follows I will show that the social construction of witchcraft occurred because of the fundamental faith in reason that has always been the hallmark of Christian theology. It was their efforts to provide a logical explanation of why non-Church magic "worked" that led theologians to confuse magic and religion and to deduce that people *must* be selling their souls to Satan. Because of that error, the persistence of witchcraft trials can be directly attributed to the persistence of magic: *People kept doing magic and the Church kept misinterpreting it as satanism*. Of course, most of the time neither Church nor state was apprised of the magical activities of most practitioners. Magical activities came to official attention only when someone—usually neighbors or clients—brought accusations against an individual. Even then, in the overwhelming majority of cases, neither Church nor state authorities did anything about it, or they dismissed the accusations in perfunctory ways. Only at certain times, in a few places, did real witch-hunts break out. H. C. Erik Midelfort found that there were no more than eighteen incidents wherein more than twenty executions took place in one town during one year in the Baden-Württemberg area, the absolute center of the most ferocious witch-hunting.[133] I will attempt to explain why it all happened when and where it did.

Let me acknowledge at the start that in terms of history I am offering nothing original—each of the primary historical elements of the chapter has been noted by many others. My attempt to contribute consists of fitting these elements together, identifying the significant patterns, and interpreting them according to an original social theory.

The Prevalence of Magic

The classical world was a magical world—astrology, amulets, charms, divination, curses, soothsaying, love potions, healing incantations, and the like, were part of everyday life even among the upper classes in Greco-Roman cities.[134] A great deal of magic was associated with the temples, where in addition to seeking aid from particular Gods and Goddesses, people immersed themselves in sacred pools, bought amulets and charms, consulted astrologers, and patronized oracles. As for the countryside, magic wells, sacred groves, spirit-inhabited rock formations and forest glades were everywhere, and in every village "Wise Ones" dispensed to local needs.

People in the Greco-Roman world also took witchcraft for granted, but it was of the standard variety and did not involve satanism, consisting only of magic or sorcery involving *maleficia*. Many magical curses scratched on lead tablets survive. One of these reads, "I curse Tretia Maria and her life and mind and memory and liver and lungs mixed up together, and her words, thoughts, and memory . . . ," and seven nails had been pounded through the tablet.[135] Magical papyri offering recipes and instructions in "black" sorcery have also been preserved. Greco-Romans, including intellectuals and emperors, often complained of having been "hexed" and otherwise harmed by magicians, and it came to be widely accepted that magicians could (and did) cause death by spells or by poisons—whether magical potions or real drugs.[136] It was also assumed that magicians required corpses for some of their most lethal spells, and that at least a few of them engaged in human sacrifices. That human sacrifices did occur during Druid rites in Britain and in the "barbarian" North lent credibility to these allegations.

Consequently, prefiguring Christian opposition to "superstitions," magic often prompted repressive measures. In 81 B.C.E. the Romans addressed magic under legal provisions against murder and poisoning. This action was aimed at magicians who were believed able to do all manner of wickedness "by the mysterious force of certain incantations." The law banned "impious and nocturnal rites . . . rites involving human sacrifice . . . [and] rites that enchanted, bewitched or bound anyone."[137] The results of this law caused Pliny the Elder (23–79) to write from Britain about the "immense debt owed to the Romans, who swept away the monstrous [Druid] rites, in which to kill a man was the highest religious duty and for him to be eaten a passport to health."[138]

But it wasn't only *maleficia* that caused Romans to be concerned about magic. Astrology and divination, too, upset many of them. Emperor Augustus (63 B.C.E.–14) permitted astrology only on the condition that there be no consultations in private and none concerning anyone's date of death (especially his). Emperor Tiberius (42 B.C.E.–37) expelled astrologers and magicians from Rome in the year 16 to suppress predictions about his reign, especially the date of his death, and this ban was repeated many times during the rest of the century.[139] Details survive of fifteen trials during the first century involving astrologers and their clients. According to Tacitus, the ex-wife of Emperor Caligula (12–41), who next sought to marry Emperor Claudius (10 B.C.E.–54), was accused of "having consulted astrologers, magicians and the oracle of Clarian Apollo about [whether she would be chosen]."[140] For this she was exiled and subsequently forced to commit suicide. She may also have been accused of employing love magic in her quest to become empress once again, as love magic carried the death penalty, although the prohibition was probably ignored except in cases involving high officials or the head of state.

To sum up the situation concerning magic that the Church confronted when it came to power: magic was everywhere. Virtually everyone believed in it. The prevalence of *maleficia* aroused considerable anxiety. And most of the magical practices were of obvious pagan origins. The Church responded in two ways. First, it attempted to prohibit many magical practices. Second, it attempted to Christianize those that seemed too popular to suppress.

Suppressing "Superstition"

The Romans denounced many magical beliefs and practices as "superstition" (*superstitio*), extending the definition to include many "foreign" religions such as Judaism and Christianity. In the beginning, the Church

Head Sorcerer. According to Roman accounts, Druid sorcerers engaged in human sacrifice, displaying the heads of their victims on trees within their sacred groves. Apparently cannibalism was also part of these rituals. © Bettmann/CORBIS.

used the term "superstition" not only to condemn various forms of magic but also in the modern sense that these beliefs and practices were irrational and false. Saint Augustine's (*354–430*) attack on astrology displays both aspects of this use of the term. In the *City of God* (5.1) Augustine noted that twins conceived at the same moment and born at the same time have the same horoscope. Nevertheless, they are often extremely different: "[I]n their actions, in the events which befall them, in their professions, arts, honours, and other things pertaining to human life, also in their very death, there often is so great a difference, that, as far as these things are concerned, many entire strangers are more like them than they are like each other." From this he concluded that astrology is a fraud. But, Augustine continued, astrology is also a heresy as it denies the fundamental doctrine of free will by claiming that any human's fate is predestined in the stars.

Similar arguments were lodged by Christian theologians against most forms of magic and sorcery, including alchemy, necromancy, and love potions.[141] Thus in 1607 the Council of Malines reaffirmed the orthodox definition: "It is superstitious to expect any effect from anything when such an effect cannot be produced by natural causes, by divine institution, or by the ordination and approval of the Church."[142] But perhaps the most astonishing (and far too seldom mentioned) aspect of the Church campaign against superstition was the inclusion of *belief* in witchcraft among the *condemned* superstitions! Saint Boniface (*?–754*), the English missionary to Germany, taught that to believe in "witches" is un-Christian. At that same time, acting on advice from theologians, Charlemagne (*724?–814*) pronounced the death penalty for anyone who burned supposed "witches," as this was a "pagan custom."[143] In the ninth century, Saint Agobard (*779–840*) denied that "witches" could influence the weather. These views denying the reality of witchcraft were made a part of official canon law and came to be known as the *Canon episcopi*. This document proclaimed of anyone who believes that some people "ride on certain beasts . . . in the dead of night to traverse great spaces of the earth" that such a person "is beyond doubt an infidel." The document further advised that "priests throughout their churches should preach with all insistence to the people that they may know this to be in every way false."[144] In conformity to this Church teaching, in the eleventh century the king of Hungary took no notice of "witches" "since they do not exist."[145] For many centuries, that's how things stood.

Christianizing "Pagan" Magic

As mentioned in Chapter 1, in many other matters concerning magic, and especially the survival of pagan folk magic, the Church adopted the strategy of incorporation. In a letter dated 601 and preserved by the Venerable Bede, Pope Gregory the Great advised Abbot Mellitus, who was setting out to missionize in Britain:

> [I] have come to the conclusion that the temples of the idols among that people should on no account be destroyed. The idols are to be destroyed, but the temples themselves are to be aspersed with holy water, altars set up in them, and relics deposited there . . . In this way, we hope that the people, seeing that their temples are not destroyed, may abandon their error and, flocking more readily to their accustomed resorts, may come to know and adore the true God. And since they have a custom of sacrificing many oxen to demons, let some other solemnity be substituted in its place such as a day of Dedication or the Festivals of the holy martyrs whose relics are enshrined there . . . If the people are allowed some worldly pleasures in this way, they will more readily come to desire the joys of the spirit. For it is certainly impossible to eradicate all errors from obstinate minds at one stroke.[146]

Thus began many centuries of Christianizing magical places and practices, and canonizing pagan Gods. As Keith Thomas noted, "The hundreds of magical springs that dotted the country became 'holy wells,' associated with a saint, but they were still employed for magical healing and for divining the future. Their water was sometimes even believed to be peculiarly suitable for use in baptism."[147] Soon the landscape of Britain and Europe was filled with shrines, churches, and abbeys, each with its collection of holy relics, each a potential source of supernatural effects. Often these relics consisted of bones or belongings of local saints or martyrs, but some were thought to have come all the way from the Holy Land—usually via Constantinople. By seeing relics, by touching the caskets and reliquaries in which they were kept, by praying before them for intercession, people sought all manner of results—healing being perhaps primary. Consequently, there was a constant stream of visitors to each site, some drawing pilgrims from afar, some limited to local supplicants.[148] People did not need to depend upon a magician or sorcerer now, since they had access to a full spectrum of supernatural control and benefits through the Church—within *limits*. The Church did not lend its powers to *maleficia*, and it offered no form of love magic. Hildegard of Bingen

(*1098–1179*) provided extensive instructions about how to use mandrake root to suppress sexual urges, including variant recipes for men and women, but nothing to heat the passions.[149]

Although for ease of discussion I sometimes refer to Church "magic," the quotation marks are to remind readers that what the Church offered in place of magic was not magic at all but in fact religion. The holy relics and the incantations employed by priests were thought to work because God caused them to do so (or delegated that power to various saints). As will be seen, this contrast between religion and non-Church magic became critical when Christian theologians began to wonder why non-Church magic "worked." Moreover, the limited range of what the Church offered gave a significant competitive edge to non-Church magic. I will return to these matters. For now, it is important to focus on healing.

The Efficacy of Magic

All magic works—some of the time. Consequently, many who turned to Church "magic" were cured. Moreover, the Church was not content to rely only on shrines and relics to produce medical results; it sanctioned and promulgated many supernatural procedures for treatment of specific problems. Hildegard's mandrake cure for lust at least involved the use of vegetable matter, but many other Church treatments paralleled the tradition of spells and incantations, albeit they remained within the realm of religion. For example, a recommended treatment for someone having a speck in his or her eye was for the cleric to pray:

> Thus I adjure you, O speck, by the living God and the holy God, to disappear from the eye of the servant of God (name of victim), whether you are black, red, or white. May Christ make you go away. Amen. In the name of the Father, and of the Son, and of the Holy Spirit. Amen.[150]

When a woman suffers from menstrual problems, the cure is to write these words on a slip of paper, "By Him, and with Him, and in Him," and then to lay the slip of paper on the woman's forehead.[151]

Of course, since most symptoms usually go away of themselves, these treatments were often followed by the victim's recovery. Trouble was that victims also often recovered when they did not utilize Church "magic" but went to suppliers of traditional magic such as the village "Wise Ones." In fact, treatments by "Wise Ones" were often more successful because the practitioners didn't really know any difference between magic and medicine. Theirs was a repertoire of lore, mostly of empirical origins, usually relying on actual potions and salves rather than incantations, and some of their practices had actual medical benefits. Of even greater significance is that religious healing and folk medicine, magical and otherwise, were far superior to secular medicine, if for no other reason than that they were relatively *in*effective! No woman with menstrual problems ever died from having a slip of paper laid upon her forehead, nor was anyone ever prayed to death. But even as late as the start of the twentieth century, secular medicine very often killed the patient. Physicians were dangerous to health because their techniques were extremely invasive, consisting almost entirely of severe purging and bloodletting.[152] As Robin Briggs explained, "It would have taken some ingenuity to devise better methods of undermining strong constitutions and finishing off weak ones."[153] In addition, although some of their prescriptions were harmless, many of the "medications" used by trained physicians were extremely consequential—mercury was among their favorites.

Secular medicine was made even more lethal by the fact that physicians came into daily contact with many people having serious infections that the physicians then spread to other patients, owing to their ignorance of germs and their consequent failure to wash their hands or clean (let alone sterilize) their instruments as they moved from patient to patient. Even late in the nineteenth century, maternity hospitals were notorious death traps where the attending physicians and nurses carried "childbed fever" from woman to woman. Women were far safer at the hands of a village midwife who had not recently touched an open infection, and, indeed, who had practical rather than "theoretical" knowledge of women's reproductive systems. And most people were far more apt to recover if they employed folk remedies (even when they were of no value) than if they were attended by a physician who purged them, or bled them, treated them with lethal "drugs," or passed them an infection—ironically, the result was that poor peasants enjoyed better medical "treatment" than did the rich. Thomas Hobbes may have condemned witches, but he was correct to note that he would "rather have the advice of . . . an experienced old woman that had been at many sick people's bedsides, than from the learnedst . . . physician."[154]

Hobbes was also quite correct to assume that the alternatives to physicians were experienced old women, because, as noted in the discussion of sexism and witchcraft, the fact is that until recently women bore most of the responsibility for family health care.[155] It was women who bore and cared for infants; hence from earliest childhood men were accustomed to looking to women when they were hurt or ill. Moreover, because they did the cooking and, often, the kitchen-gardening, women learned what was known or believed about herbs and how to transform them into potions and salves. To meet the needs of their families, women shared their medical knowledge and experience; as they got older, those who showed more aptitude and interest emerged as village midwives and healers—often coming to be regarded as "Wise Ones," the European equivalent of witch doctors.[156] Hence any crackdown on medical magic was going to fall primarily on women.

Not only does all magic work some of the time; all magic fails some of the time. The result was a standoff between Church and non-Church medical "magic," as consumers relied alternately on the one and the other as results led them to do. For centuries the Church made little or no effort to enforce a monopoly on magic. Far from suspecting that non-Church magic was of satanic provenance, the Church rejected all notions of witchcraft as heretical. These were also the centuries during which there were no fatal outbursts of anti-Semitism, and the same era when even organized religious heresies were ignored. That bloody anti-Semitism, equally bloody heresy-hunting, and efforts to eliminate non-Church magic all broke out at the same time and together eventuated in witch-hunting is beyond the realm of coincidence.

Religious Conflict

In Chapter 1, I summarized portions of a theory of religious conflict that was presented in detail in *One True God*. I gave primary attention not only to specifying the conditions under which religious groups will be intolerant, but to explaining when and why they condone nonconformity. Then I used the theory to explain the "tranquil" centuries in Europe during which the Church and state, as well as the public, allowed Jews and a variety of heretics to live in peace, albeit the Jews suffered under various discriminatory impositions. The theory also explains why, after so many centuries, toleration of heretics and Jews suddenly ended late in the eleventh century.

Now I will show that the persecution of witches was another aspect of the same basic phenomenon. Indeed, scholars of the witchcraft era often link Jews, heretics, and witches as objects of Christian wrath,[157] but no one has offered a persuasive explanation. Let me briefly restate my version of the dynamic linking these phenomena.

The starting point is that despite acknowledging many lesser supernatural entities, all of the dualistic monotheisms proclaim the existence of One True God. It follows that if there is only one God, anyone who worships other Gods is profoundly wrong, and their religion stands as an affront to the true God. I have long identified such sentiments as **particularism.** It is very difficult to resist eliminating affronts to God or, indeed, to resist forcing people into the true religion for their own salvation!

Fortunately, social life is subject to considerable inertia. Normally, people aren't easily mobilized, especially when they have no direct, personal stake in taking action. This applies to leaders as well as to the general public. Thus while those having a particularistic faith may hold religious nonconformists in contempt, the mere existence of the latter often will not prompt a response. Hence as I explained in Chapter 1, religious nonconformity will be tolerated to the extent that the dissenters are perceived as posing no *institutional threat.*

That they posed no institutional threat helps to explain Church policies allowing Jews to persist in their nonconformity, as circumscribed and inconsistent as these policies were. The same principle explains why this tolerance did not include the Donatists. Such dangerous heretics must be crushed! Why? Because they were led by an elite who controlled much of North Africa, and who posed a direct and serious institutional threat to Trinitarian domination of the Church and state. This is also why the English Protestants were so militant in their hunt for Catholic priests—both groups aspired to a religious monopoly.

This leads to the observation that *religious conflict* will be *maximized* where, other things being equal, *a few powerful and particularistic religious organizations coexist.* Each will pose a clear institutional threat to the other(s), and open religious warfare is to be expected, prevented only by delicate balances of power. Adam Smith saw this very clearly. Religious differences, he wrote, "can be dangerous and troublesome only where there is, either but one sect tolerated in the society, or where the whole of a large society is divided into two or three great sects."[158] As Smith realized, the latter tends to be a very unstable situation, as one group usually wipes out the others or drives them underground. Moreover, such conflicts will tend not to be restricted to the main contenders but to generate a *climate of general religious intolerance* extending to minor religious groups that would ordinarily be tolerated. This leads to the key proposition: *During periods of substantial religious conflict, toleration will be* ***withheld*** *or* ***withdrawn*** *from nonthreatening, but nonconforming religious groups and/or activities.*

As seen in Chapter 1 and pursued at length in *One True God*, it is this proposition that illuminates why the Crusades caused a sudden outbreak of lethal anti-Semitic rampages, not only in Europe, but in Islam as well. It also explains why the Crusades prompted the Church suddenly to become concerned with heresy after virtually ignoring it for centuries. Chapter 1 also traced the evolution of the initial campaign against heretics *within* the Church and examined how the failure of the "Reformation of the Twelfth Century" led to the eruption of a succession of "heretical" mass movements, each of which was defined as inspired by Satan and became the target of bloody campaigns of repression.

Searching for hidden heretics, especially for Waldensians and Cathars, paved the way for witch-hunting. It was the continuing discovery of actual heretical groups that lent substance to the idea that Christendom was riddled with secret satanists.

Heresy as Witchcraft

In some parts of Europe the word for witch was *gazarius*, which is a corruption of *Cathar*, and in many areas it was *wuadensis* or *vaudois*, both being corruptions of *Waldensian*. In the Jura region, the word for witch in local dialects was derived from the word for heretic.[159] This linguistic association reflects the fact that Europeans initially conceived of witchcraft, and became concerned about it, as a function of organized heretical movements. Thus in 1258 Pope Alexander IV advised inquisitors that they "ought not intervene in cases of divination or sorcery unless these *clearly savour* of manifest heresy."[160]

It was in response to Cathar doctrines concerning Satan's immense power and control of worldly affairs that Christian leaders began to worry about actual pacts with the Devil and to condemn the Cathars for satanic dealings. Moreover, it was in response to heresy that the practice of burning people at the stake became common. In 1184 Pope Lucius III endorsed burning heretics by quoting John 15:6: "If a man abideth not in me, he is cast forth as a branch, and is withered; and men gather them, and cast them into the fire, and they are burned." In 1198 Pope Innocent III identified dissenters as guilty of "treason against Christ."[161] And it was the search for Cathars and Waldensians that encouraged belief in witches' sabbats, since these heretics often did, of necessity, meet in secret places, often at night, where they performed heretical rites—to which cynical propagandists and gullible theologians added elaborate claims about orgies and depravity: "kissing cats and frogs, calling up the Devil, and fornicating in an orgy with the lights turned out."[162] Recall from Chapter 1 that the Church nearly always accused heretical groups of sexual improprieties, and this easily carried over into tales about the sexual degeneracy of "witches."

Of course, notions about witchcraft had been around for many centuries, perhaps since the earliest human communities—although these notions were lacking in satanism. Furthermore, the idea that Satan tries to tempt and recruit followers was an old one too—the New Testament tells of the temptation of Christ and reports incidents of possession by evil spirits. Indeed, from early times the Church employed exorcists to deal with that problem. Satanic ties had also often been imputed to the Jews and to various early gnostic heresies, beginning with Simon Magus. Hence there was an orthodox background for satanic suspicions. Then, in the fourteenth century, charges of satanism began to appear in European politics as various high officials, including bishops, were condemned for causing the early death of kings and conspiring against popes.[163] Most of these charges were insincere, as in the many instances when Pope John XXII (1316 to 1334) burned his opponents within the Church, or when Philip IV (*1268–1314*) of France claimed that he had burned grand master of the Knights Templar, Jacques de Molay, and Geoffroi de Charney, preceptor of Normandy, for worshiping the Devil.[164] In some other cases, the prosecutors may have been sincere. Either way, what is important is that the idea of consorting with Satan was becoming credible. Nevertheless, the idea had not yet fully taken hold that ordinary individuals were entering into pacts with the Devil, and fears that Christian society was infiltrated with satanic cells had yet to emerge. But to accept these ideas wasn't much of a stretch from hunting for satanic heretics, especially since the attribution of satanism solved a very perplexing and quite real mystery about magic.

The Problem of Non-Church Magic

For many centuries the Church was content to offer extensive alternatives to the widespread use of magic but made no serious effort to prohibit its continued use. The local priest might suggest that parishioners seek cures at a nearby shrine, but he would not criticize patronage of the town "Wise Ones," who were, in fact, all members of his flock. But as the general climate of tolerance for religious nonconformity faded, the Church became increasingly antagonistic to non-Church magic. Three main tactics were used in this campaign.[165] First, the Church further expanded its own "magic." For example, the list of specialized services available from specific saints ramified; exorcists were identified as specialists in "ecclesiastical medicine," and their numbers greatly increased. The second tactic was to condemn non-Church magic regularly from every pulpit and to try to root it out through confession—local confessors began to chastise "Wise Ones" for use of incantations and clearly magical treatments. The third tactic gave teeth to the second, by prescribing punishments for those who violated the prohibition on magic.

Trouble was that Church substitutes for folk magic often failed, while magical treatments often worked. In a world essentially without medical resources, these facts made recourse to magic virtually irresistible.[166] In fact, the Church could not even get its own clergy to refrain from using and recommending non-Church magic, especially medical magic. As late as the sixteenth century, cases from the archive of Church trials in Modena, translated and analyzed by Mary R. O'Neil, reveal the inability of clergy to resist using prohibited magic in the face of dire need and demands by the populace.[167]

Consider the case of Fra Girolamo Azzolini, a Franciscan exorcist. The charge against him involved a child who had been brought to him with an illness he diagnosed as one he felt incapable of dealing with. He told the mother to take the child to a local sorcerer and to "tell her on my behalf that she should cure this child of yours, and she will do it."[168] Why did Fra Azzolini make such a referral, knowing that it was prohibited? During his trial he admitted that he had suffered from a similar illness, and churchly forms of treatment had failed to cure him. In desperation, his relatives had sent for the sorcerer. When she arrived, she refused to treat him because, she said, "her confessor no longer wanted to absolve her when she did such things." Fra Azzolini replied that if she had performed the remedy before and been absolved, he could assure her that she would be absolved again. The sorcerer accepted this assurance and performed her procedure; Fra Azzolini recovered. In consequence, he faced future cases with the conviction that, if Church methods failed, he knew of a treatment that worked. Fra Azzolini was found guilty, suspended from the practice of exorcism, and exiled from the city. Thus not only the laity but the clergy faced a dilemma when adhering to the Church prohibition might deprive them of a cure. In Modena, between 1580 and 1600, 20 percent of those tried for superstition were priests or friars, four of them exorcists.[169]

A second revealing case from Modena demonstrates the pressure faced by clergy because the Church had not only prohibited magic; it had provided no substitute for love potions, deeming them sinful. Don Gian Battista, a priest of the cathedral, was tried in 1585 for providing a love potion to a local noblewoman. She had requested that he baptize a piece of magnet; she planned to use it to so attract her husband that he would cease consorting with promiscuous women. At first the priest refused, knowing it was a prohibited abuse of a sacrament. He told the court, "Although I had refused her more than ten times, in the end I was obliged by the many importunities of the Signora, and I promised to serve her in this manner."[170]

Deducing Satanism

As these events reveal, Augustinian skepticism no longer prevailed. Those in the Church who opposed magic did not do so because they dismissed it as a fake and a fraud; to the contrary, they believed it worked! That posed a critical question, one that became *the* question insofar as witchcraft was concerned: *Why did magic work?* Given the purely atheoretical nature of magic, as outlined in the introduction, there was no explanatory magical culture for the Christian thinkers to draw upon for an answer. The "Wise Ones" didn't even ask such a question; even the sorcerers ignored these matters. Let me emphasize that the full-blown European conception of satanic witchcraft was not the product of folklore, nor did it have any basis in magical culture. Norman Cohn reported that "[n]owhere, in the surviving [medieval] books on magic, is there a hint of Satanism. Nowhere is it suggested that the magician should ally himself with the demonic hosts, or do evil to win the favour of the Prince of Evil."[171] Rather than having originated in the imaginations of superstitious and illiterate villagers, or among sorcerers, the concept of satanism was *deduced* by leading Church intellectuals. That is, failing to grasp the vital differences between magic and religion, the most sophisticated theologians could not accept the notion that magic "just worked." They knew full well why Church alternatives to magic worked. God and the saints were the active agents; when a Church procedure failed, it was because these supernatural beings decided that it should not work in a given instance. Clearly, however, God and the saints did not cause non-Church magic to work. *Who* then? Asked within the context of dualistic monotheism, the question could have only one answer. Satan is responsible for the evil in the world. Satan is opposed to God. Satan makes magic "work."

No one has traced the deduction of satanism so clearly as Richard Kieckhefer. Having pointed out that "the concern with diabolism arose more from intellectual needs than from psychological grounds," Kieckhefer noted that "[t]he introduction of diabolism can thus more plausibly be construed as resulting from a desire of the literate elite to make sense of the notion of sorcery." He continued:

> Essentially, the [intellectuals] opposed a religious interpretation of sorcery to a magical one. They could not entertain seriously the notion that acts of sorcery and maleficent words or substances had inherent power to bring evil results, without the mediation of demons. There was no place in their worldview for causation that was neither natural nor fully supernatural.
>
> . . . In the mid–fifteenth century, Johannes Wünschelburg argued by analogy with the Church's sacraments and rituals: just as these rites have efficacy as signs, whose use is the bestowal of grace, so also the words and formulas of the sorcerer are merely signs of the devil . . . from the viewpoint of the intellectual elite neither sacraments nor sacramentals could take effect without God's cooperation. Likewise, from their viewpoint, there could be no sorcery without involvement of the devil. One might even suggest that they conceived of sorcery as a kind of negative, diabolical sacrament.[172]

Thus did logic and reason lead the best minds of the time into catastrophic error.

Once deduced, the idea that magic was of Satan, and thus that large numbers of people must be having satanic dealings, spread rapidly and ramified as it did so. It was no longer only heretics who might be engaged in satanism; in every village there might be "witches"—not merely "Wise Ones," but people who flew to witches' sabbats and worshiped His Evil Majesty.

As the creation of theologians and intellectuals, the idea of satanic witchcraft had a very influential institutional base in the rapidly developing universities—the connection between sorcery and satanism was the subject of deliberations by the theological faculty at the University of Paris in 1398.[173] It was in the universities that generations of future judges and

Church officials were instructed in the proliferating literature on satanism. H. C. Erik Midelfort noted that one reason southwestern Germany became the center of the witch-hunt is that the German legal system "permitted university professors [the major proponents of the satanism doctrine] to become full members of the judicial mechanism."[174] Steven T. Katz complained that "[j]urists looked to professors for advice . . . thereby opening the door wide to their pernicious hyperorthodox pedantries."[175] In fact, Jacob Sprenger, coauthor of the *Malleus maleficarum*, was a professor of theology at the University of Cologne. First published in 1486, the *Malleus* was among the earliest printed books, going through many editions and many translations. It would be difficult to exaggerate the impact of this work. Not only did it convince generations of educated people (including Cotton Mather) that "witches" existed; it explained in detail how to find them and how to interrogate them to obtain a valid confession—one that conformed to the "conventional" wisdom concerning the world of satanists. I think it very likely that had the *Malleus*, or something very similar, not been circulated, many local epidemics of witch-hunting would not have happened, and the pursuit of "witches" would not have risen above the very low levels that had prevailed in the fourteenth and fifteenth centuries.

Nevertheless, books do not burn "witches," and the question persists as to why the *Malleus* was a "best-seller." Moreover, the outbursts that inspire use of the term "witch craze" did not begin until several generations after the *Malleus* appeared. Why not sooner, and why didn't witch-hunting occur everywhere? Why was there so much variation in the frequency, duration, and ferocity of the witch-hunts in those locations where they did take place? These are the questions that must be answered.

The Witch-Hunt Time Line

Because local archives of court records are the primary source material, many scholars have published excellent rosters of witchcraft prosecutions, each for a specific community or two.[176] These data have made it possible to calculate such things as the rate of convictions, the distribution of sentences, and the gender of those brought to trial. However, these local studies suffer from several limitations. First, because they are local, they do not include times and places where and when nothing was going on—which seems to have been *most* times and places. Rather, these com-

Satanic Atmosphere. When Christian theologians began to ask why non-Church magic worked, they did so within an environment saturated with images of evil beings. As a typical example, anyone entering through the main portal of the Leon Cathedral need only look up to see what demons do to the damned. Pacts with the devil were credible because no one doubted that Satan and his minions lurked everywhere. © Adam Woolfitt/CORBIS.

munities were selected because they experienced a period of unusually intensive witch-hunting, and the study was usually limited to the period of high intensity. Second, some of these studies (and often the archives on which they are based) omitted all cases that did not end in convictions, or even all cases that did not end in execution, causing severely overstated conviction and execution rates.

Fortunately, these defects do not obscure the overall patterns as to time and place. In combination with comparisons of specific nations and regions, the overall data are sufficient to test the theory presented in subsequent sections. Here I will establish the general time line of witch-hunting in two eras: before and after 1500.

1300–1499

Considerable statistical precision is possible concerning the first two centuries of "witchcraft" trials because Richard Kieckhefer[177] took the time and had the sophistication needed to create a "calendar" of witch trials from 1300 until 1499, in which he attempted to date and locate every known trial and to report the number and gender of the accused, the charges, the verdict/sentence, and other useful information. Given that Kieckhefer's work is now twenty-five years old, and that there has been a spate of new research on the topic, I find it perplexing that nothing has been done to extend his calendar through 1750. Because I am not qualified to undertake such an effort, I have contented myself with turning Kieckhefer's calendar into a quantified database, partly to demonstrate the value of a comprehensive database for the entire era.

Kieckhefer's data begin in 1300 because that's when the first "witchcraft" prosecutions began—aside from those that involved Waldensians or Cathars as defendants. In selecting cases, he included all known trials that involved charges of engaging in magic or sorcery, or having any dealings with the Devil. I narrowed this definition slightly. First, I excluded 12 cases because the charge was defamation brought against persons for having falsely *accused* someone of witchcraft. These were, in effect, antiwitchcraft trials. Second, the early portion of the calendar is dominated by trials (sometimes held in absentia) in which witchcraft was charged quite insincerely as a weapon in struggles for political power. No one involved in the trials of Templars, for example, believed King Philip IV's claim that they were in league with Satan. Nor did anyone really believe the same king when he leveled similar charges against Pope Boniface VIII (1294 to 1303). Insincerity seems equally clear in the many trials initiated by the infamous Pope John XXII (1316 to 1334) at Avignon. These political trials sometimes sent people to the stake and played a significant role in spreading the idea of satanism, but in my judgment they do not qualify as genuine cases. Therefore, I excluded 24 obviously political trials—most of them having occurred in the first half of the fourteenth century. Third, I discarded 15 cases because they involved accusations alone and no trial was held. I also excluded the cases known only from fraudulent sources or based on extremely vague and tenuous sources. In doing so, I was able to follow Kieckhefer's guidance, as he had placed nearly all of these cases in parentheses. I used more recent sources to rescue several of these parenthetical cases and dropped several he had not identified. In the end, I coded 410 trials.

Kieckhefer's appropriately broad definition is reflected in the fact that only 45 percent of the trials involved charges of satanism—27 percent in the fourteenth century, rising to 48 percent in the fifteenth. That accounts for the relatively low rate of death sentences—only 39 percent of trials resulted in executions. But the very low rate of acquittals—only 9 percent—is quite inconsistent with the average rate calculated from various local archives.[178] This inconsistency may be the result of there having been no verdict reported in the sources for 32 percent of the trials. While working closely with the data, consulting new sources as well as those cited by Kieckhefer, I became convinced that the sources were more than eager to report death sentences, and that in most cases when no outcome was reported for a trial, the defendant was probably acquitted. That is, the sources rarely settled for noting that a defendant had been "executed" or "condemned," preferring to report that a defendant was "burned," "hanged," "drowned," "beheaded," "strangled," or, in the case of a mother and daughter convicted of sorcery in Cologne in 1487, "buried alive." Often the sources were also quite specific about noncapital sentences, noting that defendants had been "banished," "fined," "imprisoned," "mutilated," "branded," "whipped," or "purgated." Consequently, when nothing was said other than that someone was tried, I am inclined to believe that's because that person was acquitted. If so, then these data yield an acquittal rate of 41 percent, which is consistent with other results. For the sake of completeness, let me note that an additional 17 percent of trials produced mild sentences such as fines, penances, and banishment, while 3 percent ended in severe punishments such as prison terms, mutilation, and whipping.

Even given Kieckhefer's broad standard for inclusion, there weren't a lot of pertinent trials during these two centuries. As shown in Table 3.1, there were 63 such trials during the fourteenth century and 347 during the fifteenth. Kieckhefer's calendar was based on trials, not defendants. In most entries the number of defendants was provided, there usually being only one. In a few instances of mass trials, however, the number of defendants was unknown, and I entered an estimate of the number, based on context and any available clues, probably erring on the high side. Consequently, the total number of defendants is only approximate. Even so, I calculated that there were only 935 defendants in these two hundred years. Of course, trials and defendants became more numerous as time passed. Still, only 283 defendants stood trial in the whole of Europe during the last 25 years of the fifteenth century, or about 11 a year, with about 4 being executed. Had this rate held, there would have been no "witch craze" to explain. That lay ahead.

TABLE 3.1
Witchcraft Prosecutions 1300–1499

	Number of Trials	*Number of Defendants (Approximate)*
1300–1324	10	17
1325–1349	11	63
1350–1374	9	17
1375–1399	33	90
14th Century	*63*	*187*
1400–1424	30	59
1425–1449	78	170
1450–1474	107	236
1475–1499	132	283
15th Century	*347*	*748*

Source: Data recoded from Kieckhefer, 1976.

TABLE 3.2
Gender of Defendants, 1300–1499

	1300–1399	*1400–1499*	*Total*
Female	50%	66%	63%
Male	32%	24%	25%
Mixed	18%	10%	12%
	100%	100%	100%

Source: Data recoded from Kieckhefer, 1976.

Before turning to the second era, however, I must mention several quantitative findings based on these data. Table 3.2 shows the gender of the defendants. Half the trials in the fourteenth century involved only female defendants, 32 percent had only male defendants, and in 18 percent both men and women stood accused. The proportion of all-female trials rose to 66 percent in the fifteenth century. These percentages are consistent with other findings cited in the section on the sexist theory of witchcraft trials.

TABLE 3.3
Gender and Verdicts, 1300–1499

	Males	*Females*
Death	41%	33%
Acquittal	10%	10%
Severe[a] sentence	6%	1%
Mild[b] sentence	8%	24%
Unknown	35%	32%
	100%	100%

Source: Data recoded from Kieckhefer, 1976.
Note: Prob.< 0.002.
[a] Prison, mutilation, whipping, etc.
[b] Banishment, penance, fine, etc.

However, as far as I know, the gender effects shown in Table 3.3 have not been examined before. Although both genders were equally likely to have been acquitted (or for the outcome of their trials to be unknown), men were more likely than women to have been executed or given severe sentences; women were far more likely to have received mild sentences. These differences are highly significant statistically. It would be worth a lot to know whether these gender differences in sentencing continued in the next era.

1500–1750

Everyone agrees that the eruption of witchcraft trials began early in the sixteenth century, reaching its peak "between the 1590s and 1640s."[179] To encompass this peak, H. C. Erik Midelfort selected 1562 through 1684 as the appropriate period for his celebrated study of the witch-hunts in southwestern Germany. Midelfort found that in this relatively small area, 1,114 people were executed between 1562 and 1600, which is substantially more than had even been brought to trial in all of Europe during the fourteenth and fifteenth centuries. Then, over the next seven decades, 1,839 were executed in this same area.[180] In another fine study, E. William Monter[181] found that in Geneva, 18 people were tried for witchcraft during the first half of the sixteenth century; then 133 went to trial in the second half of the century. During the first half of the seventeenth century, another 153 Genevans were tried. These were substantial numbers given that Geneva's population was only about 19,000 at the time. But then it was over. Only 14 Genevans faced trial after 1649, and only one of these was executed. Meanwhile, to the north in Neuchâtel, Monter found that 77 people were tried for witchcraft from 1568 through 1599, 200 were tried between 1600 and 1649, and another 52 faced charges between 1650 and 1677. Similar curves could be cited for many other locales. Thus everyone agrees that the intense era of witch-hunting occurred between the 1520s and the 1640s, or from the beginnings of Protestantism to the Peace of Westphalia. After that time, some trials still took place and executions continued, but witch-hunting soon dwindled away.

Attempts to explain witch-hunting must be consistent with this time line: a low level of activity, growing out of the hunting down of Cathars and Waldensians, that lasted from 1300 to the early 1500s, then an eruption into a very high level of activity that was sustained into the 1640s, followed by a rapid decline, and then a slow subsiding—there were virtually no trials after 1750. Keep in mind, however, that this is the *overall* time line. It is equally important that a theory of the witch-hunts be consistent with the *low* levels of activity that prevailed in many places and the somewhat *different times* of high intensity in those places where such eruptions occurred.

A Theory of the Witch-Hunts

My explanation of the witch-hunts is an extension of the general propositions concerning monotheism and religious conflict introduced in Chapter 1. Applying the theory to this specific historical phenomenon, we can isolate three major factors that account for when and where the witch-hunts took place.

The Persistence of Magic

Magical activity was the factual basis for the witch-hunts. When, in response to the Crusades, the Church withdrew toleration of nonthreatening religious nonconformity (thus prompting attacks on the Jews and the "rediscovery" of heresy), non-Church magic and sorcery were also condemned. However, for reasons outlined earlier, the need for magic remained so acute that people continued to seek it and to provide it, regardless of Church disapproval. In the beginning, the sanctions imposed on magic were mild. However, once the satanic interpretation of magic came into vogue, magic became a more dangerous commodity. The vast majority of the accusations that led to witchcraft prosecutions began as complaints about harm done by magic. That is, people rarely came forward with charges of satanism; rather, they accused others of magic and sorcery that caused death, illness, storms, and other forms of local misery. Satanic interpretations of such complaints were nearly always imposed by the prosecutors and jurists. Thus if a magical practitioner were brought to the attention of authorities, severe penalties might be imposed. So why did people continue to do magic? Not only from need, or because people pressured them to do so, but also because most of the time, in most places, no one complained to the authorities. Indeed, in many places, priests continued to be very active practitioners of non-Church magic.[182] It is safe to assume that perhaps no more than one out of every several hundred magical practitioners ever got into any trouble, and the chances that any complaints would be lodged depended primarily on perceptions of *maleficia*. Indeed, many convicted as "witches" probably had very little grasp of magic but were fools who claimed to be able to hex and curse their neighbors. Thus the first element in my explanation involves *the continuing practice of magic and sorcery*, combined with *the imputation of satanism to those accused of maleficia*.

Intense and Constant Religious Conflicts

The probability of magical activities' becoming an official matter was immensely influenced by the fact that these were centuries torn by constant, major, bloody religious conflicts and threats—usually taking the form of religious wars between Christians and Muslims or between Catholics and Protestants. These religious wars have essentially been ignored by witchcraft historians on the spurious grounds that witch-hunting was usually suspended when actual fighting took place in a specific area—a matter I will deal with subsequently. Given this neglect, it seems appropriate to sketch the duration, intensity, and extent of these conflicts, because they *did* matter!

I will assess conflicts with Islam first. Considering the impact of the Crusades on both Christian and Muslim intolerance, it must be recognized that this conflict did not end with the Crusades, or even with the "reconquest" of Spain. Instead, the challenge of Islam intensified as armies and navies of the Ottoman Empire invaded the West again and again.

The Crusader Kingdom of Jerusalem lasted for only about two centuries. In 1291 Acre, the last of the major crusader fortress cities in the Holy Land, fell to Islamic forces, whereupon the Muslim counterattack moved beyond the previous historic boundaries of Islam. By 1390 all of Asia Minor was under Muslim rule, except for Constantinople and its immediate vicinity. In 1453 Constantinople fell, and two years later Islamic forces took Athens. From there the attacks on Europe followed two routes. First, there were campaigns against European islands in the Mediterranean, and against European enclaves along the north coast of Africa, as well as against European shipping. Second, sustained efforts were made to invade Europe from the southeast, through the Balkans, Hungary, and Austria.

In 1499 a Venetian fleet was sunk at Lepanto (an island off Greece), which then came under Ottoman rule. The West struck back in 1535 when Charles V, king of Spain and the Holy Roman Emperor, invaded Tunis, freeing thousands of Christian slaves in the process. In 1551 Muslim troops attempted to invade Malta but failed after a long siege; in 1565 they failed again. In 1571 an Ottoman fleet was smashed by Don Juan of Austria off the coast of Lepanto, which then became a Christian island once again. Three years later the Spanish lost Tunis back to Islamic forces. In 1669 Islamic forces conquered Crete. Thus throughout the entire witchcraft era, Christians and Muslims were constantly fighting or preparing to fight on and around the Mediterranean.

However, the Mediterranean theater was secondary to Muslim attacks against eastern Europe, which reached the gates of Vienna three times. These chronic engagements have mostly been ignored in general histories of Europe,[183] but they caused considerable suffering and fear nonetheless, and they are of central importance for explaining the witch-hunts. In 1463, seven years after they conquered Athens, Muslim forces overran Bosnia. In 1492 they invaded Hungary, thus beginning more than two centuries of warfare with the Holy Roman Empire. Again and again the Muslims took Hungary, only to be pushed back. In 1526 they captured the city of Buda and then laid siege to Vienna—only about three hundred miles from Berlin and far closer to the areas in Switzerland and along the Rhine where the most intense witch-hunts took place. Vienna did not fall, but three years later the Muslims returned and again surrounded the city. Again they were defeated, but efforts to drive them out of Hungary failed, despite many campaigns by forces of the Holy Roman Empire. In 1663 a major Muslim push against the empire was turned back with much loss of life on both sides, and the next year Austrian forces defeated Ottoman invaders again. But in 1683 a Turkish army surrounded Vienna once more. Again they were driven back. It wasn't until 1716 that the Ottoman Turks were finally driven out of Hungary and the centuries of fighting ended. These are only the highlights of a conflict that produced a chronic level of fighting and atrocities, punctuated by major battles, throughout the entire witchcraft era.

Even so, the war against the Turks was of far less importance to witch-hunting than were the nearly constant and extremely brutal religious wars intended to stamp out heresies. The Hussite wars lasted for most of the fifteenth century, and armed efforts to root out Waldensian enclaves continued—in 1487 Waldensians were attacked in Dauphiné, and the survivors fled to Piedmont. Then, in quick succession, Martin Luther nailed his Ninety-five Theses to the church door in Wittenberg (1517), while Ulrich Zwingli was preaching in Zurich against Church abuses, and in 1520, the same year that Luther was excommunicated, the Anabaptist movement was launched by Thomas Münzer. Four years later Münzer led the Peasants' Revolt in southern Germany, the same year Zwingli abolished the Catholic mass in Zurich. In 1525 the Peasants' Revolt was suppressed, Münzer was executed, and the surviving Anabaptists settled in Moravia. In 1528, as Ottoman forces were on their way to attack the city, officials in Vienna chose to burn an Anabaptist leader at the stake. Two years later the Protestant princes in Germany formed a league to resist Catholic threats.

In England, Henry VIII took the title of supreme head of the Church of England in 1534, for which he was excommunicated two years later. His attacks on Church property prompted a Catholic rebellion known as the "Pilgrimage of Grace," which was put down after a year, with a very bloody aftermath.

Meanwhile civil war had erupted in 1531 between Protestant Zurich and the Catholic cantons in Switzerland. In Germany, civil war broke out in 1546 between the Protestant Schmalkaldic League and Catholic forces led by Charles V. This was followed by the brief Peace of Augsburg. Then, in France the First War of Religion to suppress the Protestant Huguenots began in 1562. Over the next twenty years there were seven of these wars, interspersed with bloody, undeclared attacks on Huguenots, including the Saint Bartholomew's Day Massacre, during which well-planned mob actions caused at least five thousand Huguenot deaths. Meanwhile, support for the Reformation led to civil war in Scotland, which ended in a Calvinist victory in 1560.

Elsewhere, religious warfare was taking place in the Low Countries as the Spanish army captured several Protestant strongholds. Across the channel "Bloody Mary" had several hundred Protestants burned for heresy. Following her death came priest-hunts, which claimed more lives, and in 1587 Mary Queen of Scots was executed for her involvement in "popish plots." Then, in 1588, the Spanish Armada sailed for England to restore Catholicism. Although the Armada failed, a second attempt was made in 1597 (and was scattered by storms) following an actual landing of Spanish troops in Cornwall in 1595. In 1597 Catholic troops forced the re-Catholicization of upper Austria. The next year Charles XI began persecutions of Catholics in Sweden. In 1601 Spanish troops landed in Ireland and were forced to surrender at Kinsala in 1602. That same year Rudolph II, the reigning Holy Roman Emperor, began persecutions of Protestants.

In 1618 Catholic officials in Bohemia closed all of the Protestant chapels. In response, angry Protestants threw two imperial regents out the window of Hradcany Castle—an act known ever after as the "Defenestration of Prague"—touching off the Thirty Years' War, eventually involving all of the powers of Europe. Collateral actions soon broke out in many places. Catholics slaughtered Protestants in Vatelline in 1620. The Huguenots rebelled in France in 1621, and there was no settlement until 1629. In 1640 the Puritan Revolution broke out in England and lasted for twenty years. In 1641 the Protestants of Ulster were massacred, an event that poisons relations in Northern Ireland to this day.

Then, in 1648, after three decades of intense fighting and atrocities, mainly in Germany and the Low Countries, the Peace of Westphalia was signed. Of course, real and lasting religious peace did not ensue immediately. Protestantism remained illegal in Italy and all Spanish-ruled areas. Serious discrimination against Catholics continued in England. In 1685, Louis XIV expelled the Huguenots from France, forcing large numbers of these French Protestants to flee to Germany, to England, and to America. At this same time, the French expelled all the Jewish families from Bordeaux. Nevertheless, the Religious Wars were over; Protestantism had survived.

For decades, interest in the "Protestant Reformation" among scholars of the witch-hunts was distorted by highly partisan efforts on the part of Protestant historians to demonstrate that witch-hunting was more prevalent in Catholic areas, and by attempts on the part of Catholic historians to show the reverse. This ugly dispute, conducted by scholars having little understanding of the need to compare rates rather than raw numbers, seems to have diverted attention from the true significance of the rise of Protestantism—that by causing religious wars, massacres, and persecutions, *the "Protestant Reformation" was a major cause of the witch-hunts.*

Nevertheless, the causal significance of the "Protestant Reformation" continues to be ignored or at least minimized, even by the most respected historians of witch-hunts. The word "Reformation" does not even appear in the indexes of Jeffrey Burton Russell's[184] or E. William Monter's[185] celebrated studies. In a volume of national case studies of the witch-hunts, edited by Gustav Henningsen and Bengt Ankarloo and including sixteen essays by distinguished contributors, the word "Reformation" appears in only four essays, and each mention is entirely incidental. In his much admired book, H. C. Erik Midelfort[186] was content to rehash the debate as to which side burned more witches. Robin Briggs, another outstanding historian, limited his discussion of the Reformation to tracing how its doctrinal dissent did not extend to rejecting Catholic conceptions of witchcraft.[187] Finally, even after having noted the close correlation between the outbreak of intense witch-hunting and rise of Protestantism, in what many judge to be one of the most comprehensive analyses of the witch-hunts, Brian Levack backed away by cautioning that, of course, "the European witch-hunt actually began almost one hundred years before Luther nailed his ninety-five theses to the castle church at Wittenberg."[188]

In fact, the European witch-hunts began more than *two* hundred years before Luther was born. But so did the Reformation! As Chapter 1 demonstrated, the notion that the chain of events leading directly to the "Protestant Reformation" actually began in the twelfth century (if not sooner) is not a controversial view. Hence, when properly defined, the start of the "Protestant Reformation" preceded the witch-hunting era, and both peaked at precisely the same time. Empirically and theoretically, the "Protestant Reformation" and the witch-hunts are inseparable. Indeed, as will be seen, when Protestants took their Reformation to new regions and nations, they often took witch-hunting with them, or intensified the previous level, fully in keeping with Martin Luther's remark "I should willingly light their stakes myself."[189] By the same token, when Catholics reclaimed an area, they continued the witch-hunts, and they, too, sometimes launched witch-hunts where none had taken place before—in Flanders, for example.[190] For, in all of these brutal religious struggles, "Satan was always on the other side."[191]

Nevertheless, the religious conflicts associated with the "Protestant Reformation," as well as with the Ottoman attacks, were only a *necessary* but not a *sufficient* cause of witch-hunting. A third factor also came into play: effective central governance.

Governance

Witch-hunts *might* have occurred in most European communities. All of them undoubtedly had magical activities going on. Everyone knew about satanism. Very few communities did not have at least some exposure to religious conflicts. But most communities did not succumb to a "witch craze" because *they weren't allowed to do so.*

As will be documented in the case studies below, witch-hunting was prevented in many places because a strong central governmental or ecclesiastical elite suppressed local enthusiasms. Put another way, the witch-hunts occurred in places that Richard S. Dunn characterized as "political vacuums."[192] Most witches were tried by local officials who did not have to answer to higher-level authorities. Where strong central governmental or ecclesiastical power existed, as in France, Spain, and England, witch-hunts were severely controlled. For example, except for the Languedoc and the relatively culturally unassimilated and independent areas of Alsace, Lorraine, and Franche-Comté, all French cases involving accusations of witchcraft were subject to review in Paris, where most of them were overturned. In Spain, the various Inquisitions became so opposed to witchcraft trials that not only did they repeatedly intervene to save the accused when local communities instituted their own trials; they often punished local prosecutors for holding these trials, sometimes severely.[193]

In similar fashion, variations in governance accounted for variations in attacks on Jews and the ability of heretical movements to gain footholds. It was virtually only in the cities along the Rhine, in southwestern Germany, Switzerland, and Alsace and Lorraine, that murderous attacks on Jews took place between 1096 and 1614—attacks that overrode efforts by political and religious authorities to prevent them, and which *were prevented elsewhere*.[194] And it was these same areas that were very hospitable to heresies, again only because Church and state were too weak to prevent them. It was only in the Rhineland, in Cologne and Mainz particularly, that the Cathars had success in Germany during the twelfth century, and it was also primarily in the Rhineland that the Waldensians found support during the thirteenth century—especially in Mainz, Strassburg, Speyer, Worms, and Würzburg.[195] During the thirteenth and fourteenth centuries it was in these same Rhenish towns that the heresy of the Free Spirit flourished—in about 1320 there may have been two thousand members of the Beguines, a female Free Spirit group, living in Cologne.[196] Again in the fifteenth century, it was here that the Hussites found receptive Germans, and such cities as Nuremberg, Mainz, Worms, Speyer, and Regensberg were sites of conflict.[197] And, of course, it was in Speyer that the term "Protestant" was first applied to the followers of Martin Luther, and in Worms that Luther told the Diet "Here I stand." Then, in the next century, it was only in the Rhineland that Calvinism gained a foothold against Lutheran dominance in Germany.[198] Whatever else all this heretical activity may indicate, it clearly reveals the same failure of political and ecclesiastical control that left anti-Semitic mobs unchecked.

Witch-hunting shares this same geography. Historians agree that it was along both sides of the Rhine and in the places that were or became Switzerland that the truly intense "witch crazes" took place.[199] And this was not because people in these places were unusually superstitious; nor were they more prone to anti-Jewish violence because they were more anti-Semitic than other Europeans; nor did they embrace heresy out of some special need for intense religion. No! These things happened in these places, rather than elsewhere, because it was only here that they were not *prevented* from happening. As Brian Levack put it, "witch-hunting was encouraged by *de facto* jurisdictional independence."[200]

The impact of variations in central control can be seen in Table 3.4, which also serves as an introduction to the examination of specific nations and regions. These data are limited to the 1300–1499 era, but major national differences are already apparent. Switzerland—fragmented into the part that was claimed by France, the parts that were German, and the parts struggling to form a Swiss Confederation (a struggle that soon erupted into civil war between Catholic and Protestant areas)—towers over Europe in terms of witchcraft prosecutions. More than a fourth of all trials took place in this small area having only about 650,000 residents. To eliminate differences due merely to population sizes, I have calculated the number of defendants per million residents. Switzerland's rate (376.9) was 6.5 times higher than "Germany's" rate of 57.6; within Switzerland, Basel had a rate more than twice as high as Zurich's. (I have placed quotation marks around Germany in the previous sentence and in the table to

Table 3.4
Location of Prosecutions, 1300–1499

	Number of Trials	*Number of Defendants*	*Population in Millions*[a]	*Defendants per Million Population*
Switzerland	122	245	0.650	376.9
Basel	*4*	*11*	*0.009*	*1,222.2*
Zurich	*6*	*6*	*0.011*	*545.5*
"Germany"	101	311	5.400	57.6
Rhine Region	*62*	*182*		
Nuremberg	*16*	*22*	*0.023*	*956.5*
Frankfurt	*5*	*5*	*0.020*	*250.0*
Strassburg	*3*	*4*	*0.024*	*166.7*
Cologne	*5*	*6*	*0.045*	*133.3*
Low Countries	18	23	1.100	20.9
France	115	232	15.000	15.5
England	24	37	2.500	14.8
Italy	28	85	5.800	14.4
Spain	2	2	7.200	0.3
Total	410	935	37.650	24.8

[a] Sources: Chandler and Fox, 1974; Russell, 1958.

remind readers that in those days Germany was a cultural, but not a political, bloc. I will dispense with the quotation marks in the remainder of the chapter.)

Even though Germany was second highest in terms of defendants per million, its overall rate is somewhat meaningless since German witchcraft trials were so greatly concentrated in the area near the Rhine: nearly two-thirds of all the trials held in Germany, accounting for about 58 percent of all defendants. No population data were available for this region as a whole, but rates can be calculated for four cities in the area. They range from 956.5 defendants per million in Nuremberg to 133 per million in

Cologne. Even so, except for Nuremberg, these rates are well below those in Basel and Zurich. In contrast, France and England, having strong central governments, had very low rates. Italy, where the Inquisitions were powerful, was also low. And Spain, where the Inquisitions also had substantial control, had only two known trials (and two defendants) in two hundred years. As will be seen, these trends held in the sixteenth and seventeenth centuries as well.

To sum up: three factors produced the witch-hunts. One of these was, in part, a constant, since magic continued to be practiced everywhere, throughout the period in question. What varied was the response. There were considerable differences in the efforts made to suppress magic, and, most important, in the willingness to impute satanism to magical practices. Granted that Catholicism was a "universal" faith, but the fact is that in some places the Church showed great reluctance to impute satanism. In general, doubts about satanism and very grave reservations about the credibility of evidence extracted by torture were far more common among political and ecclesiastical elites than among locals. This was particularly important where strong central governance enabled elites to impose their standards. Hence weak governance was a second factor in explaining witch-hunts. The third factor was, of course, religious conflict.

However, each of these three factors was only a *necessary* cause, and only in combination were they a *sufficient* cause.

Magical activity did not always produce witch-hunts, not even where the notion of satanism was widespread—it was not a sufficient cause. But it was a necessary cause—real witch trials (as opposed to those involving only magic or superstition) did not occur when or where this factor was missing.

In similar fashion, religious conflict was only a necessary, not a sufficient, cause of witch-hunting. This means that the witch-hunts would not have occurred (and did not) during the "tranquil" centuries when the lack of any credible institutional threat allowed the Church to ignore religious nonconformity. It also implies that the greater the perceived institutional threat, the less tolerant the major contenders will be, which helps to explain why the Protestants launched their own witch-hunts. It does *not* suggest that the "witches" would be selected mainly from among the partisans of the other contender—that Catholics would mainly have burned Protestant "witches" and vice versa. Granted, there was a tendency to attribute Catholic or Protestant sympathies to those accused of witchcraft, but that was incidental. People got in trouble for doing magic (or being accused of doing magic) at a time when all religious nonconformity was outlawed—the witch-hunts were collateral to the larger conflicts.

However, in that it was only a necessary factor, I do *not* propose that religious conflict always resulted in witch-hunts. Nor do I propose that the intensity of witch-hunts was proportional to the intensity of local religious conflicts. For one thing, when actual fighting was going on in an area, witch-hunting was usually suspended, to be resumed only in more peaceful times.[201] There was nothing special about the suspension of witch-hunts when invaders marched over the horizon; there would undoubtedly have been a substantial decline in all kinds of criminal prosecutions. Indeed, many things slow down or stop during such interludes, from community holiday celebrations to many kinds of commercial transactions. For example, during the twentieth century the American suicide rate fell quite precipitously during every war, including the brief engagement in the Persian Gulf.[202]

The fundamental impact of religious conflict on witch-hunting was its causing the withdrawal of toleration for nonconformity. Once that had occurred, levels of religious conflict were not of continuing importance *except* to *sustain* intolerance. However, even when local levels of intolerance were very high, witch-hunts could be prevented by strong governance. Of course, they did not always occur where governance was weak, as this, too, was only a necessary (but not sufficient) cause of witch-hunting. Consequently, my explanation of the witch-hunts requires that all three factors be present.

The frequency and intensity of witch-hunting will have been highest where and when: (1) Serious efforts were made to *suppress* magic and sorcery, and there was a high probability that *satanism would be imputed* to such activities, *and* (2) there was substantial *conflict* among religious groups representing credible threats to one another's *institutional power*, causing the withdrawal of tolerance for religious nonconformity, *and* (3) *weak* central ecclesiastical and/or political *governance* prevented "national" elites from *curtailing local enthusiasms*.

Applying the Theory

I now examine major cases to determine whether each is adequately consistent with this explanation. Since so many historians have expressed surprise about the relative lack of witch-hunting in southern Europe, that seems the strategic place to begin. In fact, if I can convincingly explain why major witch-hunts *didn't* happen here,[203] I will have gone a long way toward demonstrating the value of my theory. For that reason, I devote more space to the case of Spain than to any other. Next, I briefly show that as in Spain, so also in Italy. Then, having examined France in general, I move to the hotbed of witch-hunting in the area along or near the Rhine River in northern France, southern Germany, and Switzerland—the area often referred to as the "Borderlands."[204] Continuing north, I briefly note the low levels of witch-hunting in the rest of the German area and then analyze events in Scandinavia, in some parts of which witch-hunting was rather intense. I conclude with an analysis of England and Scotland.

Spain

There were comparatively few witchcraft trials in Spain. Even more striking is the fact that hardly any of these resulted in the death penalty. Except for several unusual instances when local, secular courts launched witch-hunts unsanctioned by the Inquisition, few of those accused were brought to trial, and almost all of those who were convicted received mild penalties.[205] Even the virulently anti-Catholic Henry C. Lea agreed that witch-hunting's having been "rendered comparatively harmless" in Spain "was due to the wisdom and firmness of the Inquisition."[206]

Rather than just one Inquisition in Europe, there were a number of quite independent Inquisitions, each holding sway over a particular territory. Two primary Inquisitions operated in Spain, one having jurisdiction over Aragon, the other over Castile. Portugal also had its own Inquisition and will be discussed very briefly at the end of this section.

In Spain, as in many areas, the Inquisition had jurisdiction over all offenses involving heresy, blasphemy, superstition and witchcraft, sexual irregularities (sometimes categorized as "solicitations" and sometimes as "sodomy," although that term was very broadly defined), and "opposition" (interference with the activities of the Inquisition). Table 3.5 is based on 44,701 individuals tried before the Inquisitions of Aragon and Castile, from 1540 through 1700. There are several surprises to be seen.

Many books have been written on the Spanish persecution of the Marranos, Jews charged with heresy for continuing to practice Judaism after having made a formal conversion to Christianity.[207] But virtually no attention has been paid to the Moriscos, Muslims who were also charged with heresy for having made false conversions. Despite this, far more Moriscos

TABLE 3.5
The "Spanish" Inquisitions: Charges and Executions, 1540–1700

	Aragon	*Castile*	*Total*	*Percentage*
Marranos (crypto-Jews)	942	3,455	4,397	9.8
Moriscos (crypto-Muslims)	7,472	3,345	10,817	24.2
Luteranos (Protestants)	2,284	1,219	3,503	7.8
Alumbrados (Illuminati)	61	82	143	0.3
Various other heresies	2,247	771	3,018	6.8
Total Heretics	*13,006*	*8,872*	*21,878*	*49.0*
Propositions and blasphemy	5,888	6,229	12,117	27.1
Bigamists	1,591	1,054	2,645	5.9
Solicitation	695	463	1,131	2.5
Opposition (acts against the Inquisition)	2,139	1,232	3,371	7.6
Superstition and Witchcraft	2,571	961	3,532	7.9
Total	*25,890*	*18,811*	*44,701*	*100.0*
Total executed:			*826*	*1.8*

Source: Adapted from Contreras and Henningsen, 1986.

than Marranos were brought to trial. Indeed, nearly as many were tried for Protestantism or for other heresies as for being secret Jews. All told, these Inquisitions devoted half of their attention to trying heretics.

In contrast, even when witchcraft is combined with the far more common offense of practicing superstitions (magic), trials in this category barely outnumbered trials for Protestantism. Indeed, these statistics caused William Monter to entitle a chapter in his book on the Inquisition in Aragon "Witchcraft: The Forgotten Offense."[208]

But perhaps the greatest surprise is that of these 44,701 persons brought to trial, only 826 (or 1.8 percent) were executed. No data on executions by charges were available in this source, but Table 3.6 lets us see how little risk of execution one faced if tried for superstition or witch-

TABLE 3.6
Number of Executions of Those Convicted by the Inquisition in Aragon, 1540–1640

Marranos	16
Moriscos	181
Protestants	122
Sodomy[a]	167
Superstition and witchcraft	12
Opposition	31
Total	535

Source: Adapted from Monter, 1990.
[a] Very broadly defined to include most sexual irregularities, more often involving bestiality or incest than homosexuality.

craft by the Inquisition in Aragon between 1540 and 1640. During that entire century, only 12 people were executed for witchcraft, out of perhaps ten thousand who were accused and several thousand who were brought to trial. Here, too, we see that it was far safer to be discovered as a secret Jew (16 executions) than a secret Muslim (181 executions)—the latter offense no doubt being greatly exacerbated by several bloody Morisco armed rebellions.

The primary reason that the Spanish inquisitors ignored so many accusations of witchcraft, and were so lenient even with those whom they convicted, was (in keeping with element one in the theory) a very marked reluctance to impute satanism to sorcery and magic. And this, in turn, was the result of a preference among Spanish inquisitors for an empirical rather than a theoretical basis for interpreting what people were really doing.

Magic and sorcery were extremely widespread in Spain, perhaps more so than anywhere except Scandinavia, and the Spanish Inquisitions were as concerned to suppress these "superstitions" as were Church leaders anywhere.[209] However, when they brought people to trial for engaging in non-Church magic, in Spain (and Italy) the inquisitors listened carefully to what the offenders said about what they did and their intentions in doing it. Consequently, they discovered that most of the accused believed they were making legitimate use of Church "magic." That is, the practices and procedures involved were very similar to those authorized for use by the clergy, comparable to the clerical procedures discussed earlier for removing a speck from one's eye or treating menstrual cramps. In pursuit of magical effects they did such things as recite fragments of liturgy, appeal to saints, sprinkle holy water taken from the local church, crumble a communion wafer on an afflicted area, and repeatedly make the sign of the cross. As a result, the accused seemed sincerely surprised to learn they had been doing anything wrong, often remarking that had they had the slightest notion they were sinning, they would not have done it. Indeed, they vehemently denied ever appealing to demons or devils; they had always assumed that they were invoking the power of God.[210] In fact, the only reason these practices did not qualify as Church "magic" was that the practitioners violated the Church's monopoly on divine access: not being ordained, they were not authorized to conduct such activities.

The Spanish inquisitors agreed with their colleagues elsewhere that non-Church magic worked only because of diabolical intervention—it could hardly have been the work of God since these practitioners were not clergy. However, as a result of knowing the true phenomenology involved, the Spanish (and the Italian) Inquisitions drew an extremely significant distinction "between the implicit and explicit invocation of demons."[211] That is, they assumed that most accused of magic were sincere Catholics who truly did not knowingly call upon demons—their invocations were only implicit. While it was wrong for people to have done such things, their guilt deserved only the mildest penalties, often no more than confession and absolution. As explained by Mary O'Neil, the concept of implicit invocation thus "permitted the Inquisition to deal with popular magical practices as a serious but manageable problem for which a restrained and comparatively lenient approach was most appropriate."[212]

The Inquisitions in Aragon and Castile sustained charges of witchcraft and imposed severe punishments only when they confronted seemingly valid evidence of explicit satanic invocations—as in cases of third- and fourth-time offenders or those who defied the court and refused to express contrition. Not surprisingly, such instances were very infrequent, and the inquisitors were seldom willing to impute satanism on less convincing evidence. Of truly major importance was the fact that they were extremely reluctant, and eventually absolutely unwilling, to resort to torture to gain such "evidence."

In contrast, many local, secular authorities in Spain fully embraced the satanic interpretation of magic, were quick to impute it to magical practitioners, and resorted to torture to prove their cases. And it was these "runaway" local witch-hunts that accounted for nearly all of the executions in Spain.[213]

An early example took place in Barcelona in 1549, just as the most ferocious witch-hunts were breaking out in other parts of Europe. An official of the local branch of the Inquisition of Aragon approved the burning of seven women as "witches." The *Suprema* (the ruling body of the Inquisition) was appalled that such a thing could have happened and straightaway sent the inquisitor Francisco Vaca to investigate. Upon arrival he ordered the immediate release of two women still being held under sentence of death. After further investigation he ordered the release of all others under arrest and the return of all confiscated property. His report that the trials had been "illegal and contrary to the rules of the Holy Office," and that the charges were "laughable," prompted the *Suprema* to sack its local representative. After this, both the Aragon and Castile Inquisitions "intervened wherever possible to stop executions."[214] And with few exceptions they succeeded.

One famous exception occurred when a French "witch craze" spread across the border. In 1609 a very serious episode of witch-hunting took place in the Languedoc area of southern France, ending in the burning of eighty "witches." These "executions sent a shiver of terror" across the border in the Basque region of Spain. On Sunday, November 7, 1610, six persons were burned as "witches" by local officials in Logroño. This led to an immediate investigation by the *Suprema*. After interviewing hundreds of people and sorting through all the court records, Alonso de Salazar y Frias reported to the *Suprema* that he could not find the "slightest evidence" of any witchcraft. The *Suprema* took this as proof that it had been correct in its long efforts to suppress witch-hunting. Still, the locals continued to get out of control from time to time. In response, the inquisitors began to impose serious punishment on those involved in these affairs. In 1617 a witchfinder operating in Aragon was arrested after twelve "witches" were hanged in various villages on his say-so. In 1619 another witchfinder employed by local officials was arrested in Catalonia after causing about twenty deaths. The *Suprema* sent him to the galleys for ten years—almost certainly a death sentence.[215]

Thus was witch-hunting minimized in Spain. The inquisitors refused to assume satanism unless driven to do so by substantial and uncoerced evidence, and even then they were extremely reluctant to execute, seeing it as their proper duty to bring the offender back into the good graces of the Church. And in most places, most of the time, the Inquisition could impose its views and procedures on locals, despite the fact that public opinion was often so strongly against them on these matters as to prompt attacks, some of them fatal, on inquisitors or their agents.[216]

As for religious conflict, the Spanish endured centuries of war with Islam—Granada being "reconquered" only in 1492—and Spain was deeply involved in the Wars of Religion, having several times attempted to restore Catholicism to England, and being the major source of troops and funds to battle against Protestantism in the Low Countries and southern Germany. While most of these conflicts were never a direct threat to Spanish life at the local level, they probably generated substantial concern. But by itself religious conflict was not a sufficient cause, and the other two elements were lacking.

In Portugal, which had its own Inquisition and did not become part of Spain until 1580, six "witches" were burned by secular officials in Lisbon in 1559. The Portuguese Inquisition burned a "witch" in Évora in 1626. And that was it! Hence Francisco Bethencourt's assertion that the "witch-craze which affected most central and western European countries . . . did not occur in Portugal."[217] The reasons for the lack of witchcraft executions were precisely the same as in Spain.

Italy

If anything, the various regional Inquisitions in Italy were even less inclined than those in Spain and Portugal to inflict severe sentences on those convicted of witchcraft, carefully observing the rules of canon law, which prescribed that the death penalty should not be imposed for any offense unless the perpetrator had prior convictions, obstinately refused to repent, or had committed an especially heinous crime such as a sex murder. Thus between 1553 and 1588 the inquisitors at Venice had only 4 (of more than 1,000 defendants) executed, none of them for witchcraft. In the Milan jurisdiction, between 1560 and 1630 there were only 7 executions, all of them for heresy. Over a period of more than two hundred years beginning in 1542, the inquisitors in Rome caused 97 executions, few if any of the convicts having been deemed "witches."[218] In the Friuli area, 814 persons were tried for magic and witchcraft by the local Inquisition from 1557 through 1786. So far as is known, none was executed.[219]

Virtually everything that moderated witch-hunts in Spain and Portugal applied in Italy as well. Like their Spanish colleagues, the inquisitors in Italy made full use of the distinction between implicit and explicit invocations, nearly always finding in favor of the former. Consequently, the punishments they imposed were very light, an example being "confession and communion four times a year . . . and recitation of the Rosary every Friday for a year."[220] More severe sentences consisted of the public humiliation of having to stand at the front of one's parish church during a Sunday mass wearing a sign describing one's offense.

It is of interest that Mary O'Neil found that the "most extreme penalties handed out by the Modena Inquisition" were for "love magic." The Inquisition found this especially objectionable for two reasons: the intention was to induce a person to sin, and the perpetrator accepted the heretical notion that the Devil could overcome free will. For those convicted of using love magic, the sentence might be as severe as whipping or banishment. A fascinating sidelight is that most use of love magic was not by men with designs on some otherwise unattainable beauty, but by young, lower-status females seeking to marry upper-class men.[221]

In any event, while magic abounded in Italy, and the Church actively attempted to suppress it, the unwillingness to assume explicit satanism halted the march to the stake. In addition, the regional Inquisitions kept very tight control over all prosecutions for "magical arts," often drawing angry complaints from local officials who wanted greater severity. Finally, of course, most of Italy was remote from the Wars of Religion.

France

France allows us to fully explore the effects of governance while the other two factors remain constant. As in the rest of Europe, magic was everywhere. Religious warfare was chronic from one end of the country to the other. But the central government's control over local affairs varied immensely. For most of the nation, the local courts were tightly controlled by the *Parlement* (High Court) of Paris. On the matter of witchcraft, the *Parlement* imposed the restrained viewpoint held by both ecclesiastical and secular elites—not that witchcraft did not exist, but that trials must meet reasonable standards of evidence and procedure, and that most "witches" should be reconciled with the Church, not killed. But the influence of Paris failed at both the southern and northern borders, and some of the bloodiest episodes in the history of the witch-hunts were the result.

Excluding the border areas, it is estimated that probably fewer than 4,000 persons were executed for witchcraft in France between 1450 and 1750,[222] or about 13 a year (or fewer than one victim per year per million population). As noted, all convictions for witchcraft were subject to review by the Paris *Parlement*. The fact that 75 percent of these convictions were overturned[223] not only directly prevented those particular executions but set standards that discouraged "the entire process of witch-hunting in France."[224] Indeed, the message could not have been clearer when the *Parlement* summonsed three provincial justice officials to Paris, charged them with the murder of an accused witch, and hanged them.[225] Had the French state had this level of authority in the Languedoc in the south and in the northeastern border areas of Alsace, Lorraine, and Franche-Comté, thousands more lives would have been spared.[226] But as Brian Levack explained:

> [T]hese areas were resistant to the efforts of the French monarchy to establish a centralized, absolutist state . . . the main reason for intense witch-hunting in the peripheral regions of France is that courts in these regions operated with greater independence from central government control than did those in the centre of the country . . . and the right of particular localities to prosecute witches without interference from the central government was one of many issues that pitted Louis XIV against the various provinces in his kingdom.[227]

Given that France was torn by chronic and bloody internal religious conflicts as well as external religious wars, that magical practices abounded, and that belief in satanism was virtually universal, only one thing prevented a national bloodbath: strong governance. Unfortunately, along both sides of the Rhine River in France and Germany, and extending into the Alps, there was nothing to prevent the locals from dealing with the "epidemic" of witches as they saw fit. Hence it is now appropriate to focus on the area where events worthy of the name "witch craze" actually occurred.

The "Borderlands"

The area in question consisted of a crazy quilt of relatively autonomous, tiny political units. Most were culturally German, but they had only vague and shifting political ties. As Midelfort described the area:

> [N]o modern definition . . . really fits the geographical facts of the sixteenth and seventeenth centuries. At that time approximately 350 territories formed

> a checkered map of lands held by 250 knights and princes, 25 imperial cities, and some 75 ecclesiastical lords. The territories had no special unity, no capital, and no larger organization to represent them as a whole . . . only individual territories had any real unity.[228]

Consequently, as Levack explained, "political weakness . . . may have been the single most important reason for this high concentration of witchcraft trials in this part of Europe."[229]

Along with the political chaos, these borderlands bore the full burden of the Religious Wars. It was here that Protestant and Catholic armies did much of their fighting, taking and retaking the same places, while inflicting all the horrors of war on the civilian populations: murder, mutilation, rape, arson, vandalism, pillage, starvation, and the spread of disease. In addition, "the region became ecclesiastically unstable, with certain areas changing their religious affiliation more than once" in response to the tides of war or the shifting allegiance of the local ruler.[230]

In these uncertain circumstances, and lacking external constraints, local authorities could do pretty much as they pleased about witches, and what many of them were pleased to do was to hunt them down once and for all. Table 3.4 showed that even before the eruption of witch-hunting took place in the sixteenth century, this region towered above the rest of Europe in its enthusiasm for the practice. That trend continued, and ultimately more than 30,000 "witches" died in this region, making up at least half of the executions for witchcraft in all of Europe.[231] For example, the prince-bishop of Würzburg executed about 900 as "witches" during 1623–1631 at the same time that his cousin, the prince-bishop of Bamberg, burned another 600, including many public officials. Across the Rhine in the Duchy of Lorraine, between 1586 and 1595, Nicholas Remy executed more than 800 at Nancy, and a total of 3,000 may have died in the duchy between 1580 and 1630.[232] Another 10,000 died in the Swiss Confederation, 3,000 of them in the Pays de Vaud.[233]

It will be useful to examine several of these "crazes," in part to reveal aspects not addressed by the theory as to the actual mechanics by which local witch-hunts were generated and spread.

WIESENSTEIG

As the "Protestant Reformation" unfolded, citizens of the small town of Wiesensteig, high in the Swabian Alps, began to invite advocates of reform to lecture there, and the public began to split into factions, some favoring Luther, others Zwingli, and still others Osiander. However, Protestantism did not take a firm hold in Wiesensteig until imposed by the counts of Helfenstein. Count Sebastian von Helfenstein died soon thereafter, and his brother Ulrich eventually returned to Catholicism in 1567, but not before he had launched a major "witch craze." This account is based on Midelfort.[234]

For all practical purposes, Count Ulrich von Helfenstein was the law in Wiesensteig (the town was located in the small county of Helfenstein, constituting the count's ancestral lands). His authority was unchallenged from outside the county especially because of the fluid political situation. In the midst of "religious turmoil [and] fear of war . . . Ulrich lashed out against witches." The precipitating event was an extraordinary hailstorm in 1562 that destroyed the local crops. It was typical in this era for people to blame storms on *maleficia*, especially so the more severe the storm. In the aftermath of such a calamity, fingers tended to be pointed at those already possessed of unsavory reputations—usually toward those known to do magic and possessed of nasty dispositions. In any case, Ulrich was certain that this storm was the work of "witches," and arrested everyone pointed out as a suspect. Torture soon confirmed their guilt, and he quickly had six of them executed, delaying action on the others until their stories could be fully disclosed. The focus of these interrogations was the identity of others they had seen when they attended witches' sabbats. Soon others were implicated, including three citizens of Esslingen, another small town thirty miles away. Officials there were quickly informed that their town harbored many witches too. Midelfort's comments on this are of particular interest:

> Here we see the perfect illustration of why the concept of a witches' sabbath was of such grave structural importance. With information of this sort, a witch panic might spread from an original location to disturb all of the surrounding countryside.

In this instance, however, all three of the persons accused in Esslingen were released. Ulrich was incensed by such "irresponsibility" and soon demonstrated his leadership by executing 41 more "witches" at Wiesensteig. Before the end of the year he had another 20 "witches" burned.

These 67 victims can be credited to Protestant witch-hunting. A few years later, however, Wiesensteig reverted to Catholicism, and, in 1583, "at least 25 were executed there" as witches. Again, around 1605 another

14 were burned, and in 1611 4 female visitors from Württemberg and a man went to the stake in this small town.

ROTTENBURG

Rottenburg was substantially larger than Wiesensteig, having a population of about 2,700. Dwelling in the Neckar River Valley, about fifty miles west of Wiesensteig and twenty-five miles south of Stuttgart, Rottenburgers also showed considerable local interest in Protestantism, but this ended when their Habsburg rulers reimposed Catholicism (this account is also based on Midelfort).[235]

As witch-hunting spread through the region, Rottenburg held off, at least to the extent of not burning anyone. Here, too, it was a bad storm that started some fires and ruined crops that brought on a "witch craze" in 1578, as local resentments led to the identification of seven witches, all of whom were burned. Thus began a chain of accusation, arrest, and torture leading to new accusations, more arrests, more torture, and so on. In fact, it often wasn't necessary to torture the accused to obtain additional suspects, as they proved more than willing to share their fates. In some instances persons fearing they would be accused let it be known that if that happened, they would "take many others" with them and, when the time came, did so.[236] Many writers have blamed the blind fanaticism of prosecutors for their failure to see that they were manufacturing accusations. But these critics miss the similarity to modern prosecutors when they "roll up" criminal conspiracies with grants of immunity to those already implicated. It is more humane to give immunity than to inflict torture, but the ends are the same. In both circumstances prosecutors believe in the reality of a hidden group of evildoers. Because those who prosecuted witches truly believed that they were in the process of uncovering secret cells of satanists, it would have been irresponsible for them not to have pressed those they had caught to reveal others as yet undiscovered. Let this be a reminder that it is quite possible to be responsible, logical, and wrong.

At Rottenburg the process of "uncovering" the community of local satanists kept the executioner busy for thirty-one years, during which a total of 150 persons were burned. Throughout this period the annual toll was quite steady, but there came a sudden peak in 1596 when 36 people were burned for witchcraft. This outburst caused so much interest that both students and professors from the nearby University of Tübingen deserted their classrooms to attend. Professor Martin Crusius noted in his diary on May 7, 1596, "Today ten witches were burned at Rottenburg, four tied to each stake."[237]

As time went on, the social status of the accused began to rise quite remarkably. This started when the accused being tortured to identify others began to name wives of officials and members of the lower nobility. Once begun, the accusations soon spread to officials themselves, and in 1602 the city executive was accused, tortured, and died in jail of his injuries. Such "ladders of accusations" moving up the social scale occurred in many communities, a phenomenon probably connected with the greater visibility of higher-status residents. Envy and old grievances were probably often involved too. In any event, as Midelfort noted, the "attack on high local officials seems often to have shaken communities out of their descent into utter panic." Indeed, as this escalation of status occurred in Rottenburg, the witch-hunt quickly faded away.

Germany

As for the rest of Germany (north and east of the Rhine Borderlands), witch trials were as uncommon here as in France, and political control was about as effective. Granted that even this area lacked a central regime and local courts were not answerable to a *Parlement*, but the political units were far larger, and within these the same quality of central control existed. Recall from Chapter 1 that many of these units turned Protestant or remained Catholic without regard for popular support, based on the political and financial interests of their rulers. It was only effective control that distinguished this area, for both of the other two factors apply. Just as it did along the Rhine, religious conflict abounded, and Protestant and Catholic armies tramped back and forth. And here, too, belief in satanism was unquestioned.

Scandinavia

Witchcraft trials came very late to Scandinavia. But once lit, the fires burned very brightly. It is estimated that, starting late in the seventeenth century, about 1,700 Scandinavians were executed for witchcraft. Given that about 2 million people lived in this region, this yields an execution rate of about 850 per million, far higher than in France or southern Europe. Of course, even in this era "Scandinavia" included several separate nations and relatively autonomous areas. It will be useful to consider some of these independently, starting with the two primary powers: Sweden and Denmark.

SWEDEN

Belief in magic and *maleficia* was universal in Sweden, as it was throughout Europe. In Sweden *maleficia* carried the death penalty if it could be proved that someone had actually been seriously harmed. But it was not until very late in the sixteenth century that references to satanism and to witches' sabbats began to appear in Sweden, having been introduced by Protestant clergy who learned of them in Germany where many of them were educated. At first, opinion was quite divided as to the reality of this form of witchcraft. The idea of "witches" flying to sabbats was consistent with popular beliefs, but "elite tradition was slower to absorb the new ideas."[238] Eventually, notions of satanism prevailed and Sweden's "witch craze" began in 1668.

The first trial produced 18 death sentences, but, 11 of them having been reduced on appeal, 7 "witches" were beheaded and their bodies burned in May 1669. These executions seem to have caused an intense witch-scare that led to dozens of suspects, most of them exposed by self-identified "witchfinders," many of whom were children. Hence, in August 1669, another 29 were sent to the block and then burned. The next year 15 more died. At this point a royal commission was empowered to review cases and supervise prosecutions. From the start, the commission was sharply split. On one side were the three aristocratic members, who regarded the trials as illegal and who doubted the stories of satanism being wrung from defendants. But they were opposed and overruled by the clergy and farmers on the commission. So the executions continued, reaching a peak in 1675 when 100 died. In 1676 a new commission was appointed. It continued to execute "witches" until the members were badly shaken when suddenly several children, upon whose testimony executions had been carried out, confessed to having made it all up. This caused the outlook of the commission to shift so rapidly that not only did witch trials end; official proceedings were initiated against some of the key witnesses from prior trials, and four of them were sentenced to death. After that a few executions occurred in remote areas, but the "craze" was ended forever.[239]

It is significant that notions of witches' sabbats and satanism did not prevail in Sweden until after the adoption of Protestantism—the militant clergy on the royal commission were not Roman Catholics but Lutherans. Moreover, Sweden did not "turn" Protestant in the sense that Protestant agents converted the people to the new faith. In fact, it is not clear that the Swedish masses were ever fully Christianized, let alone Lutheranized. In both instances, religious change in Sweden involved the conversion of the royal house and little else. Sweden was declared to have been Christianized in the eleventh century when the king recognized the Church as the only licit faith, granting it the right to collect tithes. Little or nothing was done to evangelize the masses, and paganism never really died out. As for its becoming a Protestant state, that was accomplished when King Gustavus I, who reigned from 1523 to 1560, switched the state church to Protestantism after feuding with the pope over the appointment of bishops and electing to seize Church wealth. The subsequent transformation from Catholicism to Protestantism was gradual and superficial. Most bishops and clergy shifted over with little conflict. The new church manual distributed in 1571 retained most of the familiar forms, "such as confession, excommunication, and public penance. Many of the parish priests continued in their posts and married their housekeepers or concubines to legitimatize their children."[240] Aside from the fact that the Lutheran Church was now subordinate to the Crown, and the Bible had been translated into Swedish, things were pretty much the same in terms of domestic religious life.

However, having become a Protestant state, Sweden was drawn into the chronic religious warfare of Europe. Indeed, the Swedish army probably saved Protestantism, winning battle after battle, until the Treaty of Westphalia was adopted in 1648. However, this did not mark the end of Swedish war making. Several years after signing the treaty, Charles X launched an attack on Poland, which brought Denmark in against Sweden. Charles soon defeated the Danes and forced Denmark to cede him a number of provinces. But war broke out again in 1658 over Denmark's support of the Netherlands, whereupon England and France came to Denmark's support against Sweden. While negotiating a settlement to these conflicts, Charles X died suddenly in 1660; his five-year-old son became king, but with the actual power vested in a regency until 1672. Under the regents Sweden avoided new wars but developed serious internal conflicts, and the threat of civil war loomed. It was during this moment of high tension and a very weak state, when King Charles XI was only thirteen, that the witch-hunt erupted. And was in 1676, after Charles XI had been in full command for four years, that a new royal commission brought the witch-hunt to an end.

Thus all three conditions of the theory are met. First came the promulgation of satanic interpretations of magic brought by Lutheran clergy. Second came a long period of intense external religious conflict, as Sweden played a leading role in the Thirty Years' War. Third, the witch-hunt broke out during a period of unusually weak governance—elite opinion being such that the hunt would no doubt have been quashed by a strong king.

DENMARK

The Danes were the other major power in Scandinavia, having colonies as far west as Iceland and Greenland. Denmark's episode of "witch" executions occurred much sooner than the one in Sweden and was far milder. More important, it offers a dramatic illustration of the power of governance. Throughout the era, Denmark had strong, centralized governance, and the witch-hunt came and went in response to variations in official policies. Before 1617, legal conceptions of witchcraft in Denmark lacked satanic assumptions. Of equal importance, the legal code prohibited torture (except as part of the sentence imposed after conviction) and rejected denunciations as being insufficient evidence. These rules prevented the snowballing of suspects that created runaway "crazes" in parts of Europe. In 1576 a woman was convicted of *maleficia* by a local jury and sentenced to death. When it was discovered that she had been burned before her sentence was dismissed by the higher court, an additional article was adopted stipulating "that no person found guilty by the jurors was to be executed before the case had been appealed."[241] As a result there were very few "witches" executed in Denmark during the sixteenth century, at a time when many "crazes" were taking place in the Rhine Borderlands.

But in 1617 this changed dramatically. A new ordinance was promulgated that for the first time asserted satanism. It directed that cases of ordinary magic and sorcery were to be treated mildly, and only people known to be in league with the Devil were to be executed. As Jens Christian V. Johansen explained, the "theological aspect of the crime was brought into the forefront for the first time in the legislation: witches . . . were those who had entered into a pact with the devil."[242] Why now? Apparently the king had become very worried about "witches" at this time, under the influence of a particularly militant Lutheran theologian who became bishop of the nation's most important diocese in 1615.[243] In any event, the effect of the new ordinance was immediate and dramatic. Trials began at once, and the number sent to their deaths accelerated from 15 in 1617, to 30 the next year, peaking at 40 in 1620. After that both trials and executions declined rapidly. There seem to have been two major reasons for the decline. First, the suspects about whom there was a local consensus were quickly used up. As Johansen noted, it took "many years to build up this reputation" as a source of *maleficia*.[244] Second, the Danish courts continued to reject torture and implication by others accused of witchcraft, so accusations could not snowball. Both factors greatly reduced the "supply" of potential victims once the initial burst was over. At this point, elite opinion began to shift against satanism—the king's physician, Thomas Bartholin, being an outspoken critic.[245] Consequently, witch trials in Denmark settled into a very low level, eventually fading away—between 1656 and 1685 only one death sentence was pronounced. Then, in 1686 a local witch-hunter managed to have four persons sentenced to the stake. These convictions were overturned by the Supreme Court, and the witch-hunter was suspended. That was the end of it.

ICELAND

Prior to the "Protestant Reformation," there were no witchcraft trials in Denmark's colony of Iceland. Then, "the Reformation was forced upon the Icelanders by the Danish king, certainly not without resistance."[246] Under orders from Christian III, Catholic bishops were deposed and their property seized for the Crown. However, one bishop raised troops and resisted, drawing considerable support from others with nationalist aims. Eventually, Danish forces prevailed, and the bishop and some of his supporters were beheaded.[247]

As Lutheran clergy attempted to impose their new church on public practice, a focal point of conflict was magic and sorcery, which were extremely popular and had met with little opposition under Catholicism. Almost as once, the newly arrived Lutheran clergy demanded a halt to such goings-on and began to bring charges against practitioners. Worse yet, the Lutherans introduced Continental notions linking magic to satanism. Thus in 1625, shortly after the eruption of witchcraft executions in Denmark, the first "witch" was burned in Iceland. The precipitating factors were an unusually cold winter that killed a lot of livestock and an outbreak of plague that killed many people. Suspicion turned to a local sorcerer, who was burned on the authority of a Danish official; the official had been educated in Hamburg and was well-versed in the *Malleus maleficarum*. Before it was over, a total of 22 Icelanders went to the stake—21 men and a woman. All had probably been active sorcerers and may well have been crypto-pagans as well, as elements of paganism remain strong in Iceland even today.[248] In 1686 the decree came from Denmark that all future death sentences must be ratified by the High Court in Copenhagen. That brought executions in Iceland to an end.[249]

NORWAY

Like Iceland, Norway was under Danish control during the days of its witch-hunt. Also like Iceland, Norway had the "Protestant Reformation" imposed on it, and with it came Lutheran clergy educated in Germany and committed to the doctrine of satanism. And, as in Iceland, this led to the redefinition of magic and sorcery as necessitating a compact with the Devil, making a witch-hunt inevitable.[250]

The Norwegian witch-hunt broke out at the same time as the one in Denmark and was conducted "by pastors, judges, and bailiffs born or educated in Denmark and Germany."[251] The Norwegian witch-hunt also peaked at about the same time as the Danish witch-hunt, 69 persons being executed during the 1620s. However, the Norwegian hunt was considerably more deadly and lasted longer than the one in Denmark, tapering off only in the 1680s and taking about 280 lives (or 638 per million). Just as witch-hunting ended in Denmark when the courts were able to assert control over procedures and standards of evidence, these same principles were "exported" to Norway, where the Court of Appeal began not only to void death sentences for witchcraft but to visit outlying areas to interview and release those accused of witchcraft. It was not so much that these judges rejected satanism, although some were beginning to take that view, but that they could see the flaw in accusations and confessions gained by torture or under fear of death. Moreover, Norway was increasingly served by officials and pastors of local origins and education, which moderated the German influence.

But something else had occurred as well. Protestantism had survived! As Hans Eyvind Naess put it: "A Protestant Christianity which had felt itself under siege could now demobilize; earlier militant doctrines began to be questioned."[252] I shall return to this matter at length, later.

FINLAND

During the witchcraft era, Finland was a province of Sweden. Direct German influences caused the Finnish witch-hunt to begin about twenty years earlier, but in both Finland and Sweden the peak came during the 1670s, when 41 Finns were executed as "witches." The end came at the same time as in the rest of Sweden, and for the same reasons. While it lasted, 115 lives were lost, or 329 per million.[253] Half of the victims were men. And, as was common throughout Scandinavia, the majority of the victims were "professional sorcerers" who ran afoul of the satanic assumptions concerning their powers, a viewpoint imported with Protestantism. Indeed, the doctrine of satanism was promulgated by the faculty at Turku Academy, the first university in Finland, founded in 1640. Here German ideas dominated, including those concerning witchcraft. Within several years of its founding, "two dissertations were published at Turku Academy dealing with natural magic, and also discussing compacts with the devil."[254]

To sum up: witch-hunting came to Scandinavia with Protestantism, as militant Lutheran beliefs in satanism collided with an especially active culture of magic and sorcery. The severity of witch-hunts depended upon the strength of central control over local initiatives and the standards of evidence imposed by the central authority. And the witch-hunts ended as the era of intense religious conflict in Europe abated.

England

Only the Spanish and the Italians executed proportionately fewer witches than did the English. C. L'Estrange Ewen[255] estimated that about 1,000 English "witches" went to the gallows, and Brian P. Levack[256] placed the figure at about 500. That works out to at most 200 deaths per million, or as few as 100.

The witch-hunting era in England coincided with the era of "priest-hunting," the latter producing about 260 Catholic "martyrs."[257] Both "hunts" were subsequent to the heresy-hunting that sent about 300 Protestants to the stake during the short reign of "Bloody" Mary—1553–1558.[258] The total numbers of victims of priest-hunting and of witch-hunting are quite comparable if we exclude the 200 whose deaths were caused by Matthew Hopkins, who roamed the eastern counties during 1645 and 1646, "finding" witches. Because Hopkins testified to having seen imps produced by some of his victims, and because he used methods of torture that left no marks in order to circumvent court rules, a very convincing case can be made that Hopkins was a fraud, doing it for the small finder fees he managed to secure from local officials.[259] In any event, Hopkins caused the only true witch "scare" in English history, most of the rest of the cases forming a pattern "of steady and unspectacular annual prosecution."[260] Aside from the cases produced by Hopkins, the peak of English prosecutions came in the 1580s and 1590s during the reign of Elizabeth I (*1533–1603*). After the Hopkins episode (he retired from witch-hunting in 1646 and died the next year), the number of trials declined rapidly, and most of the accused were acquitted. The last "witch" was hanged in England in 1685.

It is crucial to know that not only did England hold rather few witch trials; in most of them the only charge was *maleficia*, not satanism. This might have been the case in many other nations had they not allowed torture, for confessions were the typical basis for expanding original charges concerning *maleficia* into charges of satanism. Indeed, the lack of such confessions in England may explain the lack of interest in the *Malleus maleficarum*, there never having been an English edition (and no English translation until 1928). Keith Thomas noted that "the total absence of an English edition is striking by the side of the thirteen editions on the Continent by 1520 . . . it was issued sixteen times in Germany before 1700 and eleven times in France."[261]

When notions of satanism did gain ground in England, it was by way of Protestant enthusiasts. The Westminster Assembly (1643–1652), called by the Puritans to reform the Church of England, changed the old definition of a witch from one who practices *maleficia* to one who has made a compact with the Devil. In 1645 the assembly also explained, "Some have thought witches should not die unless they had taken away . . . life . . . Though no hurt ensue in this contract at all, the witch deserves present and certain death for the contract itself."[262] Within the year, Matthew Hopkins used this as a warrant for witchfinding. Even so, notions of satanism met resistance, receiving "only reluctant and half-hearted support from the administrative and ruling élite in England."[263]

In addition, the English prohibition of the use of torture prevented snowballing accusations (except when Hopkins cheated), and this minimized group trials. Moreover, with an occasional, idiosyncratic lapse, the English courts enforced the rules of evidence and the principle that the defendant was innocent until proven guilty. Several lapses came from judges who were so agitated about witches that they ignored their duties, and some from judges who gave in to popular demands. Lord Chief Justice North confessed to having allowed the conviction of three innocent women for fear that to have dismissed the charges would have ignited mobs to further witch-hunting. But for the most part the courts kept things under control. In a memorable instance, an English judge responded to charges that the accused flew to witches' sabbats by pointing out that there was no law against flying.[264]

So despite intense, bloody, and local religious conflicts, and even after belief in satanism gained ground, strong governance prevented the worst. That was of no help to the 500 or so unfortunates who died for imaginary crimes, but it saved hundreds who were accused and thousands who might otherwise have been.

Scotland

Things were quite different in Scotland. Although no Scottish "witches" were burned prior to the "Protestant Reformation,"[265] some early advocates of Protestantism went to the stake for heresy, beginning with Patrick Hamilton in 1528. When the Roman Catholic cardinal of Saint Andrews burned the Protestant George Wishart in 1546, a group of Protestant "terrorists" assassinated the bishop and barricaded themselves in a castle awaiting aid from England. Instead, they were taken prisoner by forces sent from France.[266] Among the captives was John Knox (*1514–1572*), who had not taken part in the assassination but had joined the group in the castle. Taken to France, he served a nineteen-month sentence in the galleys and then went to England in 1549. There he served as a chaplain to King Edward VI, but, along with most of the prominent Protestant clergy, Knox had to flee back to the Continent when the militantly Catholic "Bloody" Mary came to the throne. Ending up in Geneva, he became a disciple of John Calvin.

Meanwhile, the Reformation was gathering support in Scotland, greatly encouraged by antagonisms toward French ambitions in Scotland, especially after Mary Queen of Scots was wed to the heir to the French throne in 1558. Knox played a role in building these anti-French sentiments, spending part of 1555 and 1556 preaching in southern Scotland. On December 3, 1557, a group of anti-French nobles formed a Protestant coalition. Civil war soon followed, with both French and English troops taking part. The Protestants won, and in August 1560 the Scottish Parliament adopted a Calvinist confession of faith, drafted by Knox and others.[267]

Three years later, urged on by Calvinist clergy, many of whom were members, the Parliament passed a statute calling for death in all cases of witchcraft. Unlike their English counterparts, the Scottish clergy took the lead in seeking out witches and ensuring that the courts met their obligations to convict and execute.[268] The results were nearly immediate and ferocious. In the end, at least 1,500 were executed in Scotland, or about 750 per million.[269] Not only were the courts guided by the statute of 1563, but even local magistrates had the authority to try witches without any oversight by higher authorities. Furthermore, Scottish courts were not bound by English legal principles. English juries could convict only by unanimous vote; in Scotland, convictions required only a majority of the jurors. England prohibited the use of torture; in Scotland it was a standard part of pretrial interrogations of "witches." The English would not bring charges when the only evidence was an accusation by someone already accused; Scottish prosecutors sought such accusations. Consequently, the well-known snowballing of accusations, resulting in mass trials, was common in Scotland.

As have all the other cases, Scotland meets the terms of my theory. First, an officially sanctioned belief linking satanism and magic was imposed on a very active economy of magic. Second, there was intense religious conflict. Third, in Scotland local control of the courts prevailed, with all the abuses inherent therein.

As we look back over these case studies, it might seem that belief in satanism and the existence of weak courts provide the entire explanation, making religious conflict an unnecessary component of the theory since it seems to have been a constant in this era. But wait. The immense importance of religious conflict is to be seen not only as it *began* the entire affair, by prompting opposition to all perceived forms of religious nonconformity, but also in the *demise* of witch-hunting once a credible and lasting solution had been found to religious conflict. That remark signals the arrival of the last major section of the chapter.

And Then It Ended

By the eighteenth century, witch-hunting had pretty much ceased, except for occasional incidents in remote areas. Standard accounts of why it ended are as unsatisfactory as are those about why it began. We have seen that the notion that witch-hunting was a reactionary movement prompted by fears of impending modernization is unfounded. It is true, of course, that the link between magic and satanism was the product of theological reasoning, but efforts to suppress magic and superstition can hardly be identified as attacks on enlightenment or modernity. Moreover, the most enlightened minds of the time accepted the idea that witches were in league with the Devil. Since witch-hunting did not begin from anxieties about "the dissolution of the medieval cognitive map of the world," it seems equally dubious that its end was caused by the triumph of a modern worldview.

However, the concluding chapters of many studies of the witch-hunts devote much discussion to the arrival of modern times, and how this made belief in witches implausible. Having first offered obligatory praise to the rise of science, many scholars then credit their predecessors—intellectuals who wrote books and articles that were dismissive of satanism—with bringing it all to an end. Clearly, such books were written and read. I am even willing to admit that some of them helped stop the bloodshed. But, as will be seen, the timely intellectual opposition to witch-hunting cannot be represented as the true voice of the "Enlightenment," finally being heard. All of the significant intellectual opposition to witch-hunting that arose soon enough to have mattered came from men who cannot possibly be identified as "modernists." Moreover, books—even those not written by modernists—mattered very little as compared to events in the real world. To conclude this analysis, I will try to weave all of these strands together.

My explanation of why the witch-hunts happened is a macro theory in that it applies primarily to relatively large social units, such as societies and regions, and has little to say about events at the micro level of individuals or small communities. For example, I have said almost nothing about why any particular village experienced a witch-hunt other than it was in an area where that was going on. Nor have I said much about why particular kinds of people were so apt to be designated as witches. I do not regard these as trivial questions and now give them some attention as an essential part of my explanation of why witch-hunting stopped.

Networks and Limits

Having examined all of the known cases of "large" witch-hunts in southwest Germany, H. C. Erik Midelfort made an acute observation. Communities could sustain small witch-hunts more or less indefinitely—year after year a few people could be tried and executed. In contrast, large witch-hunts (defined as more than twenty deaths in a year) could not be sustained but rapidly brought an end to witch-hunting.[270] That is, communities did not return to a low level of executions following a major outburst. Instead, the executions ceased altogether.

Midelfort's explanation for this phenomenon was that large witch-hunts "destroyed all sense of community" and caused everyone to feel at risk. This was a "shattering realization" that refuted the prevailing image of who could be a witch, since now everyone was a potential suspect. I am certain Midelfort was right. Indeed, his observation is entirely consistent with fundamental sociological principles about the nature of group solidarity.

Stripped to the essentials, all communities consist of social networks, structures of relationships among people. These relationships are based on ties of family, neighborhood, friendship, work, and the like. Social networks are the basis of all social life. They provide members with security, emotional satisfaction, and identity. They provide information, attitudes, and social resources. Moreover, networks impose conformity: certain kinds of behavior not only can cost individuals their network ties but can cause the network to impose punishments on them. However, not everyone in any community is part of a network. Always there are isolated individuals or small sets of individuals who don't belong or fit in. The whole of sociology rests on these insights.

In small European villages during the time in question, most people had many strong ties to the local social network, but some were only weakly connected or were virtual isolates. Some were isolated by circumstances. For example, elderly, childless, impoverished widows were often without ties, as were wandering beggars and some elderly spinsters and bachelors. But others were lacking in social ties because of disagreeable personalities, bad habits, lack of character, or unsavory reputations—factors that sometimes isolated an entire family.

The vast literature on the identity of those accused of witchcraft shows that the overwhelming majority of victims were these sorts of isolated, disliked, and disreputable people. Much attention has been given to their greater vulnerability, but the issue of social costs has been largely ignored. To execute isolates puts no strain on social networks. In effect, there is no one to miss them, and perhaps many will be glad they are gone. However, accusations lodged against persons securely embedded in networks will arouse opposition from those who love, respect, or are dependent on those persons. And such accusations will also arouse fears that "no one" is safe.

I suggest that big witch-hunts brought things to an end because they rapidly exhausted the socially "inexpensive" portion of the community, whereupon the social costs of continuing the hunt rapidly rose to unsustainable levels. Suddenly, people who had been willing to stand by as "they" were taken away took a rather different stance when the finger pointed at "us." This is also consistent with the attenuation of witch-hunting as accusations reached persons of higher status.

Support for this interpretation is provided by the remarkable similarity in the death rates that had been reached in many smaller communities at the point when executions subsided. In the eight such communities for which adequate data are available, each of which had experienced a large witch-hunt (none having more than 5,000 residents and most of them far smaller), the "witch crazes" ceased after about *one* person in *twenty* had been killed. Specifically: Miltenburg: 8 percent; Obermarchtal and Oppenau: 7 percent; Gengenbach, Lindheim, Mergentheim, and Rottenburg: 6 percent; and Offenburg: 4 percent.[271]

These findings are consistent with many modern studies about the size of the relatively unattached and disreputable portion of a community, research in both England[272] and the United States[273] placing the number at about 6 percent. I do not suggest that these percentages are precise, but I think they do help us see that there were only a limited number of persons in any community who could *credibly* and *readily* be accused, and that witch-hunts burned out when they began to extend to those firmly embedded in conventional social networks.

Direct evidence of this phenomenon can be found in many accounts of specific cases. For example, Henry Charles Lea, in his posthumously published collection of original materials, quoted a German historian concerning a two-year "witch craze" in the rural Alpine district of Werdenfels:

> The whole population was only 4700, all united together by intermarriages so that there were few families unaffected, especially as women of all classes were involved . . . the special judge finally grew tired of the work and . . . wrote to the authorities at Freising asking that the prosecutions be stopped . . . so the witch-craze came to an end, to the great relief of the population, which had besieged the Freising authorities with petitions to put an end to it.[274]

It must be noted that what I have proposed as "normal" limits were far exceeded in some small villages—in a few, nearly the entire population was wiped out by witch-hunters. But in these episodes, the onslaught was of entirely external origin and far more resembled a slaughter by a conquering army or band of marauders than any judicial proceeding, and pressures from within the village were of no significance. It must also be understood that sometimes substantial witch-hunts resumed when a community was "reclaimed" from Protestantism or vice versa. Such radical religious realignments would result in schisms within the social network(s), thereby re-creating a pool of "inexpensive" victims. Indeed, where the religious realignment involved bloodshed, fatalities would have created isolates out of some people on the losing side.

Larger communities were sometimes able to sustain substantially higher death tolls. For example, in Strassburg, between 1615 and 1635, 18 percent died for "witchcraft." But this is also compatible with network analysis, when several factors are considered. First, large communities consist of more complex and multiple social networks and hence will be slower to respond to attacks on a few members of any given network, and attacks on only one network will not be a direct threat to most residents. Second, larger communities probably contain proportionately more isolated and disreputable people—such people always tend to drift from villages into cities, and cities also produce more such persons.[275] Finally, local autocrats were generally located in the major population center of the area under their jurisdiction. Undoubtedly, in communities ruled by an unusually powerful autocrat, who was particularly excited about witches, greater inroads could be made into the conventional social networks and even into the elites—this could occur even in small communities, as demonstrated by Count Helfenstein's excesses in Wiesensteig. But even autocrats in cities eventually faced social limits. In this regard it is worth quoting a letter written by a priest in Bonn to Count Werner von Salm, in a nearby community:

> [T]hey have begun violent burning of witches in Bonn . . . The victims of the funeral pyres are for the most part male witches. Half the city must be implicated; for already professors, law students, pastors, canons, vicars, and monks have been arrested . . . The Chancellor and his wife and the Private Secretary's wife have already been apprehended and executed . . . A canon of the cathedral named Rotensahe I saw beheaded and burned . . . To sum up, things are in such a pitiful state that one does not know with what people one may talk and associate.[276]

As I read it, serious back pressure was building up in Bonn because the archbishop of Cologne, on whose authority all this was taking place, had exceeded the limits of the pool of relatively isolated people. This probably

Expendable Victims. Communities could engage in witch-burning indefinitely so long as they did not exhaust the supply of socially inexpensive victims. But when a sudden outburst of accusations reached beyond the pool of disreputable or isolated people, the rising social costs rapidly brought an end to local witch-hunting. © Christel Gerstenberg/CORBIS.

played an important role in preventing an even worse catastrophe, since this "craze" was nearly at an end by the time this letter was written.

Of course, no one in any of these communities said that a witch-hunt should end because they had run out of appropriate victims. Rather, as the terror spread to conventional people, and indeed to elites, the basic assumptions of satanism began to come into question. Finding it quite incredible that certain people could be witches, people began to doubt the accuracy of the confessions of witchcraft and the *process* by which they were *extracted*. That was an essential shift.

I will return to the demise of faith in witch-hunting, but let me now shift to the more macro level of analysis and examine the implications of peace and the spread of strong, centralized states.

Peace

In 1648, after more than a century of bloodshed, the Peace of Westphalia was signed. It accepted the right of Protestants to exist and fixed boundaries between Catholic and Protestant territories. It was also agreed that Catholic princes would permit Protestants to worship (in private) within their realms, and that Protestant princes would do likewise for Catholics. However, the agreement covered a very limited area, mostly in Germany. Protestants did not gain real religious freedom in Spain, Portugal, and Italy until well into the twentieth century, and some restrictions still apply. As for France, severe anti-Protestant persecutions continued to the end of the seventeenth century, ceasing only when there were no more Huguenots remaining in the country. In England, too, anti-Catholicism persisted, although the search for secret priests had ended.

Nevertheless, the general level of conflict and, more important, the anxieties associated with these conflicts rapidly declined subsequent to the Peace of Westphalia. This was especially so in Protestant territories. As mentioned in the case study of Norway, suddenly Protestants could feel secure. There would be no more Spanish Armadas; French troops would not intervene in Scotland; neither Catholic nor Protestant forces would prowl along the Rhine; both the Protestant and the Catholic cantons in Switzerland were now secure.

Just as the outbreak of severe religious conflicts brought on the search for witches, the end of the religious wars and the implementation of treaties of toleration brought it to an end. In nation after nation, witch-hunting rapidly collapsed after the Peace of Westphalia. This also marked the end of heresy-hunting: the surviving Waldensians no longer needed to hide. Likewise, the last massacre of Jews (until the twentieth century) occurred in Frankfurt in 1614.

Stronger States

Political settlement also resulted in stronger, more centralized states able to extend their effective authority over local affairs. For example, the powerful state achieved by Louis XIV extended the authority of Paris by annexing the borderlands of Alsace, Lorraine, and Franche-Comté and many of the semi-independent cities such as Strassburg. This had direct and immediate impact. Robin Briggs suggested that witch-hunting in Lorraine might have continued "far longer but for this growth of French influence."[277] In similar fashion, a stronger and expansionist Austria emerged from the Thirty Years' War, able to incorporate portions of the Tyrol.[278] As for Switzerland, authority became far better centralized within the various cantons, and the Peace of Westphalia included formal recognition of the independence of the Swiss Confederation.

A very important result of stronger governance was the rapid spread of prohibitions against the use of torture to gain confessions.[279] Hence the primary mechanism by which witch-hunts proliferated and the only significant source of evidence in favor of satanism was removed. Isolated, peculiar, disreputable, and disagreeable people could no longer be transformed into "witches" out of their own mouths.

Skepticism

As fears of religious conflict faded, and as the prohibition of torture brought an end to the outpouring of lurid new confessions, awareness of the terrible injustices of witch-hunting began to spread quite rapidly among European elites. This was particularly stimulated by the direct experience of some with large witch-hunts that burned out after accusations had extended to obviously solid citizens, thus overturning conceptions about the outward signs of witches. As Keith Thomas pointed out, "one had only to be an eye-witness of a patently unjust accusation to be converted to a belief in the need for exercising greater caution in the future. The leading sceptical writers seem, almost without exception, to have been provoked into publication by personal acquaintance with incidents of this kind."[280]

And just as the witch trials stimulated many intellectual tracts on witches and witchfinding, the demise of these trials soon prompted new learned works denying the existence of witches. Brian Levack hailed these as part of "an intellectual revolution that destroyed scholasticism . . . and . . . dissolved many of the beliefs that lay at the basis of witchcraft prosecutions."[281] However, rather than having caused the end of witch-hunting, these expressions of skepticism came far too late to do more than permit subsequent scholars to falsely exonerate secular intellectuals, and to lay the witch-hunts at the doorstep of the Scholastics and other misguided "believers." In truth, the first significant works of intellectual opposition to witch-hunting came from (1) a Spanish inquisitor in 1549; (2) a German physician who believed in witches, in 1563; (3) a deeply superstitious Englishman who published in 1584; (4) another Spanish inquisitor in 1612; followed in 1631 by (5) a Jesuit who had taken part in burning witches. Everyone else wrote well after witchcraft was a moot issue, when it had become, at most, a target of opportunity.

It was the inquisitor Francisco Vaca who first[282] made a public and unguarded attack on the pursuit of witches, when in 1549 he was sent by the *Suprema* to investigate a witch-burning episode in Barcelona. I have already mentioned this affair in the case study of Spain. Although Vaca did not deny the existence of witches, clearly he thought them to be extremely rare creatures bearing no resemblance to the unfortunates rounded up by local authorities. Hence the report he submitted was described by Henry Kamen to be "one of the most damning indictments of witch persecution ever recorded."[283] And, given its effect on the subsequent policies of the Spanish Inquisitions, it mattered!

The second significant attack on witchcraft trials has been repeatedly cited as evidence that early voices of the Enlightenment were raised in protest. Indeed, E. William Monter called Johan Weyer's book *On Magic*, published in 1563, the "most radical and comprehensive critique of the conventional wisdom about witches and witchcraft to appear in the sixteenth century." Monter went on to claim that "Weyer was the only important sixteenth-century critic to deny the reality of the witch's presumed pact with the Devil."[284] Hardly. Weyer fully accepted the existence of pacts with the Devil; he even claimed to have personally prevented the Devil from flying off with a young virgin.[285] His "critique" consisted of charging that the "old hags" most often convicted of satanic pacts were merely "possessed" and "deceived" by Satan, as only very sophisticated sorcerers could achieve such a diabolical relationship. Thus while surely no early voice of enlightenment (even uncapitalized), Weyer did vigorously condemn torture. "[T]his cruelty is continued until the most innocent are forced to confess themselves guilty." And, having witnessed merciless witch-hunts along the Rhine, he unflinchingly condemned the witch-hunters:

> But when that great searcher of hearts, from whom nothing is hidden, shall appear, your wicked deeds shall be revealed, you tyrants, sanguinary judges, butchers, torturers and ferocious robbers, who have thrown out humanity and do not know mercy. So I summon you before the Great Judge, who shall decide between us, where the truth you have trampled under foot and buried shall arise and condemn you, demanding vengeance for your inhumanities.[286]

The third significant voice raised against witch-hunting was that of Reginald Scot, who published *The Discoverie of Witchcraft* in 1584. Rossell Hope Robbins claimed that "Scot was not writing to advise judges or theologians but to ridicule witchcraft in the eyes of the general public." And he approvingly quoted Henry C. Lea's view that Scot's book "has the honor of being the first of the controversial works which resolutely denied the reality of witchcraft and the power of the Devil."[287] The book did ridicule the idea that the Devil would need such "an unapt instrument" as "a toothless, old, impotent, and unwieldy woman to fly in the air," for "the devil little needs such instruments to bring his purposes to pass."[288] Instead, "the devil indeed enters into the mind, and that way seeketh man's confusion."[289] The issue, then, is not the existence of the Devil but the credibility of claims made concerning his activities. Scot's book is, in fact, a biting attack on the self-fulfilling use of torture to prove satanism, but it is surely not a harbinger of the "new mental outlook" that Levack credits with ending the witchcraft era.[290] Indeed, the book asserts the magical properties of a unicorn's horn and of various gemstones.

Robbin Briggs called Alonso de Salazar y Frias "the astonishingly perceptive Inquisitor."[291] And so he was. Sent by the *Suprema* to investigate the unauthorized burning of six witches in Logroño in 1610, Salazar spent more than a year in the area interviewing the inhabitants and inviting them to repudiate their errors (mostly having to do with magic and superstition). At the end of his mission, Salazar reported that he had reconciled 1,802 persons to the Church. As mentioned in the case study of Spain, he also reported the negative results of his investigation of witchcraft:

> I have not found the slightest evidence from which to infer that a single act of witchcraft has really occurred. Indeed, my previous suspicions have been strengthened by new evidence from the visitation: that the evidence of the accused alone, without external proof, is insufficient to justify arrest.[292]

He went on to suggest that efforts should be made to prevent public discussion and agitation concerning the topic; the preaching of sermons about witchcraft should especially be avoided, because he had discovered "that there were neither witches nor bewitched until they were talked and written about." Neither Salazar nor the *Suprema* declared that there was no such thing as witchcraft, but had their views concerning evidence prevailed further north, tens of thousands of lives would have been spared.

And finally, the Jesuit. Friedrich von Spee lived his whole life in the heartland of "witch crazes." He was born near Cologne, where he attended the Jesuit college, then studied philosophy at Würzburg, after that theology at Mainz, and in 1627 became a professor at Würzburg. Each of these was the site of ferocious witch-hunts. Soon after Father Spee took up his faculty position at Würzburg, there was an extraordinary outburst during which about nine hundred "witches" went to the stake. Father Spee served as the confessor of many accused and accompanied them to their final torment. He quickly recognized the catastrophic results of tortured confessions and wrote a powerful and influential indictment, *Cautio criminalis*, in 1631. As he explained:

> The innocent zealots who encourage witch hunts should realize that, since the tortured have to denounce some persons, trials will become more and more numerous, until at length accusations will encompass them, and in the end everybody will be burned . . . a single innocent person, compelled by torture to confess guilt, is forced to denounce others of whom she knows nothing; so it fares with these, and thus there is scarcely an end to accusers and accused, and, as none dares retract, all are marked for death.[293]

Father Spee's book appeared in sixteen editions (including many translations) during the next century. And it mattered. It is credited with causing Swedish troops to be a moderating influence on witch trials during the Thirty Years' War (the book having been read by Queen Christina), and with having caused the elector of Mainz to put an end to witch trials in areas under his control. Spee's arguments were also adopted and promulgated by the Roman Inquisition.[294] But neither Father Spee nor his colleagues in Rome doubted that Satan was a constant source of human miseries, or thought that witchcraft was impossible. Rather, as Keith Thomas noted, "what influenced them was not a denial of the possibility of witchcraft as such, but a heightened sense of the logical difficulty of proving it to be at work in any particular case."[295]

In contrast, when doubts about the actual existence of witchcraft began to be expressed, it was far too late to matter. For example, Balthasar Bekker is often cited for denying the very existence of the Devil. In *The World Bewitched* he wrote that, as "a monotheist, a believer in but one God," he could not "think there are two gods, the one good, the other bad." He also charged that witchcraft was invented by the Catholics "to fill the pockets of the clergy."[296] But he did not write until 1691. In similar fashion, Christian Thomasius, head of the University of Halle—another who often is cited for disputing the dogmas underlying belief in witchcraft—did not publish until 1701: a full century and a half later than Francisco Vaca.

Finally, it is all well and good to note that the rise of science offered natural explanations for phenomena once credited to active spirits. But, as I made clear in the previous chapter, it is unfortunate "liberal" nonsense to propose that an end to witch-hunting was accomplished by "the triumph of a mechanistic cosmology in late seventeenth-century Europe,"[297] or that this "mechanical philosophy represented a serious threat to current religious belief" and hence discredited "miracles, the efficacy of prayer, the operation of Divine Providence and even the existence of God."[298] Witchcraft beliefs and persecutions did not succumb to the arrival of an age of science and reason. No! Just as their predecessors had deduced satanism as the mechanism behind non-Church magic, it was deeply committed and well-trained Scholastics, responding to the evidence of their senses, who stripped it of its evidential basis.

Why Not in Islam?

Witch-hunts did not occur in Islam despite the fact that Islamic culture is saturated with magic and with belief in devils and evil spirits,[299] and Muslim theology accepts the power of sorcerers to do harm. Indeed, according to Islamic law, death is the appropriate penalty for sorcery.[300] However, belief in satanism and in a widespread and dangerous network of agents of the Devil never developed in Islam, and concerns about witchcraft remained at the level of chronic apprehension associated with belief in witches elsewhere in non-Christian societies. Why? A major factor is that Islam was content to condone the widespread practice of magic, in part because it posed no threat to Muslim political rule, and partly, too, because many of these practices are "embedded in" the Qur'ān.[301] A second important factor is that Muhammad provided individuals with the means to be entirely secure against all forms of magic and sorcery. Muslims believe that by reciting the last several sentences of the Qur'ān following the five daily prayers, they neutralize all evil forces. Finally, Islam failed to develop a satantic perspective for the same reason it failed to develop science: Islamic theologians were not nearly so committed to reason and rationality. Hence while Christian theologians could not settle for the observation that magic simply "worked," their Muslim counterparts could and did. That is the final and fatal irony about European witch-hunts. They were the result of reason and logic applied to a false premise.

Conclusion

In Chapter 2 we saw how theological reasoning yielded one of humankind's finest achievements: the rise of science. Here we have seen how the same process resulted in some of Western society's darkest days, and that it was not fools but some of the finest minds of the time who deduced the culture of witchcraft. The next chapter introduces an additional irony concerning reason and theology: no sixteenth-century figure denounced slavery more bitterly than did Jean Bodin, one of the most vociferous French proponents of witch-hunting. And it was Samuel Sewall, one of the judges who had in 1692 condemned witches in Salem, who later wrote the first theological tract against slavery published in America.

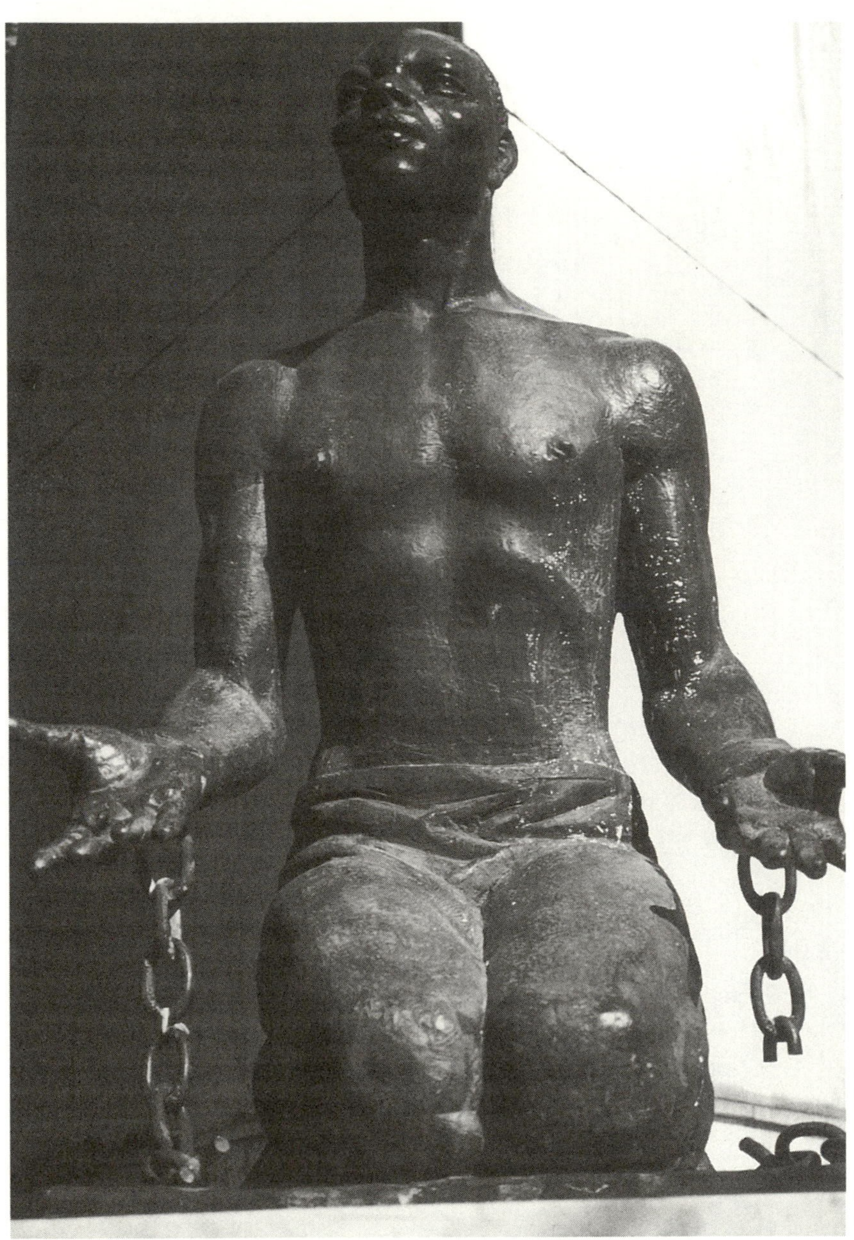

Freedom. This statue of a slave breaking his chains was erected in Ponce, Puerto Rico, to commemorate the abolition of slavery by the Spanish government in 1873. However, the Spanish did not free the slaves in Cuba until 1886. © Macduff Everton/CORBIS.

 4

God's *Justice*: The Sin of Slavery

Indians and all other peoples . . . should not be deprived of their liberty or of their possessions . . . and are not to be reduced to slavery, and whatever happens to the contrary is to be considered null and void.
—*Pope Paul III (June 2, 1537)*

Just as science arose only once, so, too, did effective moral opposition to slavery. Christian theology was essential to both.

This is not to deny that the early Christians condoned slavery. It is to recognize that of all the world's religions, including the three great monotheisms, only in Christianity did the idea develop that slavery was sinful and must be abolished. Although it has been fashionable to deny it, antislavery doctrines began to appear in Christian theology soon after the decline of Rome and were accompanied by the eventual disappearance of slavery in all but the fringes of Christian Europe. When Europeans subsequently instituted slavery in the New World, they did so over strenuous papal opposition, a fact that was conveniently "lost" from history until recently. Finally, the abolition of New World slavery was initiated and achieved by Christian activists.

These are the principal themes to be developed in this chapter, but two other very important matters will be dealt with as well. First, the excesses of political correctness have all but erased awareness that slavery was once nearly universal to all societies able to afford it, and that only in the West did significant moral opposition ever arise and lead to abolition. Unfortunately, the typical discussion of slavery, especially in textbooks, gives the impression that it was a peculiarly European and especially American vice, and no notice is taken of the extent of slavery in times past, or of the substantial amount of slavery that *continues* in many parts of the non-Christian world.[1] Indeed, among the several thousand books on slavery currently in print,[2] there are virtually no scholarly *general* histories or comparative studies of substantial scope. Instead, nearly all of the studies are limited to slavery in the New World, and most are further restricted to one colony or state—many authors concerned themselves with only one town, county, or plantation. Consequently, to assemble this chapter, I was forced to do a great deal of synthesizing.

A second reason I wrote this chapter is that an amazingly influential group of historical revisionists has attempted, not only to deny that religion played the primary role in sustaining the antislavery movement, but to claim that it really played no role at all—that the religious rhetoric of the abolitionists was either "false consciousness" or a mask for economic self-interest.

What follows is an attempt to put the record straight. A sketch of the overall history of slavery will enable me to examine the connection between various religions and slavery in a variety of eras to show why it was that, except for several early Jewish sects, Christian theology was unique in eventually developing an abolitionist perspective. I then examine the social enactment of the theological opposition to slavery into effective social movements. As a revealing contrast, I outline the inability of the irreligious and antireligious philosophers and moralists of the "Enlightenment" to effectively oppose slavery. Finally, I dispatch claims that it was simple economics that killed slavery, and that all the talk about God and sin was irrelevant.

A Brief Survey of Slavery

A slave is a human being who, in the eyes of the law and custom, is the possession, or chattel, of another human being or of a small group of human beings. Ownership of slaves entails absolute control, including the right to punish (often including the right to kill), to direct behavior, and to transfer ownership. The primary ways people become slaves are by birth, by capture, by being sold by parents or relatives, or by judicial proceeding—criminals and debtors have often been sentenced to slavery.

As will be seen, not only has slavery been a nearly universal feature of "civilization"; it was also common in a number of "aboriginal" societies that were sufficiently affluent to afford it—for example, slavery was very prevalent among the Northwest Indians.[3] The existence of slavery is a function of human productivity. When the average person can produce sufficient surplus that it becomes profitable for someone to own him or her—when the *costs* of *maintaining* and *controlling* slaves are more than *offset by their production*—there will be a demand for slaves. In the plantation economies of the New World as in the ancient world, slaves were quite literally the fundamental tools of production. However, when some members of societies are sufficiently affluent, slavery can also exist primarily as a form of *consumption*, wherein slaves are utilized mainly in nonproductive roles as personal servants, concubines, entertainers, and even bodyguards. "Consumption slavery" was the typical form in Islam.

The word "slave" is a corruption of the word "Slav," because Slavic peoples were a common source of European slaves (the Arabic word for slave is also a corruption of the Arabic word for Slav). That fact is of far more than etymological significance, causing us to recognize that often slavery has not involved racial differences. Historically, most slaves have been racially identical with their masters, although usually members of some other community or ethnic group. Thus most Chinese slaves were Chinese, and the rest were Asians. The ancient Athenians mainly enslaved Greeks from other city-states or "foreigners" of similar ethnic stock, and slaves among the North Coast Indians mostly came from nearby tribes—although after the arrival of Europeans in North America, a few of them ended as slaves to the Makah and the Mowachaht.[4]

Although slavery is far older than the pyramids, it has taken similar forms even in very remote societies, because there is an inherent logic to the conditions imposed on slaves.[5] To display the basic aspects of slavery, it seems useful to begin this survey with an assessment of slavery among the tribes of the Northwest Coast of North America.

Slavery among the Northwest Coastal Indians

Generations of anthropologists dismissed slavery among the Northwest Coastal Indians as insignificant and, to the extent that it existed at all, quite unlike "real" slavery such as that of blacks in the American South. Franz Boas noted that "the tribes of the Pacific Coast are divided into a nobility, common people, and slaves," but chose to omit slaves from his analyses "as they do not form part and parcel of the clan."[6] Edward Curtis allowed that slavery "was firmly established among the Coast Salish," but denied that "the harrowing pictures which that word brings before our mind have [any] connection with the institution as it existed among the Indian tribes of this region." He went on to claim that "they labored no more strenuously than the free members of the lower classes," and that "in general it may be said that slaves were very well treated."[7] More recently, Morton Fried[8] argued against applying the word "slave" in this context, it being more accurate to refer to these people as "captives," for "the status called 'slavery' in the Northwest Coast cultures bears little resemblance to that associated with stratified societies."[9] Moreover, these "captives" were "few" in number and consisted mainly of "women and children." Finally, Ronald and Evelyn Rohner had this to say about slavery in their lengthy monograph on the Kwakiutl: "At one time the Kwakiutl also had slaves who were usually war captives from other tribes. Slaves contributed little to the traditional social system except to give prestige to their owners; we give them no further attention."[10]

These glib assurances dominated the conventional wisdom on the subject for so long and to such an extent that no mention of slavery was included in undergraduate textbooks[11] on North American Indians, or in *The Smithsonian Book of North American Indians* published in 1986. Fortunately, from earliest days some scholars told the truth about slavery among various Northwest Coastal tribes: that it was real slavery in all respects, imposing brutal conditions on a substantial number of people.[12] By 1990 even the Smithsonian was ready to acknowledge that the Northwest Indians had real slavery, and to disdain "the standard view . . . that slaves were merely prestige goods" and "lived as well as their masters."[13] Then, in 1997, came the definitive general study, *Aboriginal Slavery on the Northwest Coast of North America*, by Leland Donald. This impressive work documented the following facts.

As for being few in numbers, slaves made up a third of the population in some villages and ranged from 15 to 25 percent in many others. Rather than being of little or no economic significance, "their labor power was important in many subsistence activities," and slave-trading played a substantial role in the economy of some tribes. In all of these Indian cultures, slavery was "regarded as shameful and degrading." Rather than being limited to merely a few captives, slave status was hereditary—"the children of slaves were slaves"—and only very rarely did an owner free a slave. When Boas so imperiously dismissed slaves from his study because they did not belong to any clan, he failed to reveal that for this very reason slaves had no rights or privileges of any kind. They were often traded or given away. "Masters exercised complete physical control over their slaves, and could even kill them if they chose." And they often did choose to kill the old and sick, as well as the rebellious. Finally, slaves were often killed as ritual sacrifices, especially during their master's funeral to provide him with slaves in the next world and to exhibit his wealth to those remaining behind.[14]

So much, then, for efforts to exonerate the "noble savages" of the Northwest. Rather, as enumerated above, all of the fundamental features of slavery were here. As to the economic basis of slavery in these societies, in his classic study H. J. Nieboer argued with eloquence and force that it rested on high levels of natural abundance.[15] Subsistence was very easy to come by along the Northwest Coast, where it required little effort to obtain more food than anyone could eat,[16] where forests of immense cedar trees provided easily shaped logs for boats and dwellings, where the woods and ocean abounded in fur-bearing mammals, and where the climate was mild all year long. As a result of these conditions a slave could be highly productive, and some people could easily afford "consumption slaves."

Greece and Rome: Slave Societies

Chapter 1 sketched how, beginning in about the fifteenth century, the Humanists longed for the glories of Greece and Rome. In asserting the superiority of classical times, most Humanists seemed indifferent to the fact that these were slave societies. Edward Gibbon did call being a slave in Rome "an unhappy condition" but suggested that "cruel treatment" was "almost justified by the great law of self-preservation" in the face of frequent slave "insurrections."[17] Even more revealing is that, in his thousands of pages on Roman history, Gibbon devoted only "a few decorous paragraphs to the subject of slavery."[18] Indeed, to the extent that they acknowledged the existence of slavery at all, most famous Humanists regarded it as the price that had to be paid for the splendor of Greco-Roman culture, a judgment with which Friedrich Engels concurred, writing in 1878 that "without slavery, no Greek state, no Greek art and science."[19] This view persisted among Humanists well into the twentieth century. The influential Joseph Vogt accepted ancient slavery as a necessary evil: "Slavery was essential to the [Greek] . . . devotion to spiritual considerations . . . Slavery and its attendant loss of humanity were part of the sacrifice which had to be paid for this achievement."[20]

It wasn't only the Humanists who shrugged at ancient slavery. Aside from the remark that the cultural legacies of Greece were inseparable from slavery, Engels was far more concerned with recent times. Similarly,

"Marx paid little attention to slavery as such" and virtually none to ancient slavery, other than to agree that it was an "indispensable instrument of production" in the Greco-Roman economies. For that reason Marxist historians ignored the topic too, "as acknowledged by Soviet ancient historians of the early 1960s."[21] As will be seen, the reason Marxists lacked interest in slavery per se is that they considered all labor done for others, including that done for pay, as "slavery"—except, of course, for those employed in socialist enterprises. In any event, study of ancient slavery has been very intermittent and often disfigured by "polemical ferocity."[22]

All early civilizations—including Sumer, Babylon, Assyria, Egypt, China, and India—involved extensive use of slave labor. But, as M. I. Finley explained, the Greeks and Romans achieved the first truly "slave societies," becoming highly dependent upon "the large-scale employment of slave labour in both the countryside and the cities."[23] It will be helpful to sketch the character and extent of classical slavery.

In Greece and Rome, slaves became the primary basis of production as well as a major form of consumption. The reliance on slaves was the result of frequent military victories that "flooded the slave markets of the Mediterranean" with captives.[24] The enclosures at the major Roman markets in Capusa and Delos were capable of handling 20,000 slaves a day and often ran at full capacity.[25] Because of the influx of slaves, small family farms were displaced by large plantations (the Romans called them *latifundia*) worked by huge crews of slaves.

Agricultural slaves were mainly men, and because their owners feared them (since many had been enemy soldiers), they were often kept chained even during work and spent the night in underground prisons. By current American standards, the *latifundia* were not very large—typically ranging from 60 to 150 acres, while the average American farm has nearly 500 acres (an acre is about the size of a football field). But the family farm of this era covered only about 5 acres. Farms were small because, for lack of machinery, Roman and Greek agriculture was extremely labor-intensive. It was estimated that a 60-acre olive orchard required 16 slaves plus additional help during harvest.[26] Over time, however, the *latifundia* got larger, many of them exceeding a thousand acres and some said to be as large a "kingdom." Pliny the Elder (*ca. 23–79*) reported an estate that, at the start of the first century, had 4,117 slaves and 7,200 oxen.[27] In his famous treatise on farming (*De agricultura*) Cato the Elder (*234–149 B.C.E.*) advised that more careful attention be given oxen than slaves, since the latter were better able to care for themselves. Slaves should be well fed so as to maintain their strength, but when they became old or weak, they should be left to perish. Cato also advised against allowing slaves to have wives, because women and children were not worth their upkeep—it was far cheaper to buy a new male slave than to raise one from infancy.[28] Thus the "great hordes" of slaves "dwindled and in large part perished without leaving descendants or trace."[29]

Slaves not only provided Greece and Rome with farm labor but did nearly all of the mining—Athens had more than thirty thousand at work in its silver mines, and Rome maintained hundreds of thousands in its many mines, scattered from Britain to Egypt. Mining consumed slaves at an appalling rate. The Roman historian Diodorus (*?–21 B.C.E.*) wrote that in the mines the slaves were "all in chains, all kept at work continuously day and night . . . there is no indulgence, no respite . . . [they are] kept at their labor by the lash, until overcome by hardships, they die in torments. Their misery is so great that . . . death is welcomed as a thing more desirable than life."[30] As Mary L. Gordon put it in her brilliant essay on the nationality of Roman slaves, "the growth of the empire had a background of human suffering which is unimaginable in its degree and extent . . . [and] if such labour killed [slaves] prematurely, the Roman master of Republican times might say with the concise brutality of Tacitus, *uile damnum*: there were plenty more."[31]

Greek and Roman slaves were also extensively employed in manufacturing and construction. Although there were no factories in this era, there were large shops devoted to making various goods: cooking utensils; armor, shields and weapons; textiles; and the like. And it was primarily slaves who built the famous public buildings such as the Coliseum and the Parthenon.

Of course, in construction, agriculture, and manufacturing, if not in the mines, there continued to be free persons working for hire as well as many who were self-employed. But the economies of the great Greek city-states and the Roman Empire rested on the backs of slaves to such an extent that the slaves involved in production also supported an enormous population of domestic slaves. Everyone kept domestic slaves. Even owners of small farms having only two or three acres kept a house slave or two, and each of the lowest-ranking soldiers in the Roman army owned at least one slave servant, and often more.[32] It is thought that *every* household in Athens and Rome had slaves.[33] And as might be expected, "many owned slaves even when they could not afford them."[34] The Greek sophist Libanius (*314–393*) lamented the severe poverty suffered by the four lec-

Roman Slave Market. A small-time Roman slave dealer eats his lunch while waiting for someone to buy one or more of the seven slaves he is offering for sale—all wearing tags around their necks describing their better features. Clearly, this dealer specialized in "consumption" slaves for domestic service, as only one of his inventory is a male suited to perform hard labor. © Bettmann/CORBIS.

turers in his school—they lived in dreadful lodgings, were deeply in debt and could hardly afford to marry, and were barely able to support three slaves each.[35] When asked how many slaves he had, the Greek poet Xenophanes (*ca. 560–478* B.C.E.) replied, "Two only and I can hardly feed them."[36]

Domestic slaves were often "productive" vis-à-vis the household economy by doing baking, sewing, and weaving, but they were primarily a form of *consumption*, as demonstrated by the incredible overstaffing that was typical.[37] Pliny the Younger (*62–113*) had five hundred slaves in his household, and many senators had more than a thousand, including some eunuchs to attend the women and "cripples" to amuse guests. Social standing was often measured by the number of slaves who accompanied a Roman in public.

In addition to domestic service, slaves provided most of the public entertainment in Rome. Nearly all actors were slaves (there were no actresses, men playing the female roles), and so were almost all of the musicians and prostitutes. In similar fashion, slaves provided the great majority of gladiators, thousands of whom died every year to entertain free Romans.[38]

Finally, these were slave societies in that at least during some periods, slaves outnumbered the free populations in Greece and Rome.

The Decline of Slavery in Christendom

Slavery began to decline in the latter days of the Roman Empire as a direct result of military weakness. No longer were victorious commanders dispatching throngs of prisoners to the slave markets. Since fertility was very low among Roman slaves, owing both to privation and to a lack of women, their numbers rapidly fell, and the shortage of slaves soon caused the conversion of agriculture and industry to reliance on free laborers. As Moses Finley concluded, soon "the world of late antiquity was no longer a slave society . . . slaves no longer dominated large-scale production in the countryside . . . [and] slaves no longer provided the bulk of the property revenues of the elites. Only in the domestic sphere did they remain predominant."[39]

The "fall" of Rome caused a further decrease in slavery, since it had never been a significant feature of Germanic societies.[40] Soon, "in most parts of Western Europe slavery declined and then virtually disappeared with the emergence of the feudal system," persisting "only around the edges of medieval Europe—in Spain, in the vast Moslem world, in the Byzantine Empire, in Kievan Russia."[41] Although this claim would seem obvious, and is ratified by many celebrated historians (Bloch and Finley among them), some find it controversial for various reasons.

For one thing, it is very difficult to say just when slavery died out in Christian Europe (it having continued in pagan areas). As Adam Smith put it, "The time and manner . . . in which so important a revolution was brought about, is one of the most obscure points in modern history."[42] Most medieval historians have simply ducked the issue by ignoring the phenomenon. The words "slave" and "slavery" barely appear in the eight-volume *Cambridge Medieval History* (1911–1936). Norman Davies's huge history of Europe (1996) offers two entries on "slavery" in the index, one fewer than given to Margaret Thatcher, and one more than given to "football" or "Tour de France." The first of Davies's entries on slavery is a one-and-a-half-page account of the slave revolt led by Spartacus in 73 B.C.E., the other an entry of similar length devoted to the first Portuguese purchase of slaves in Africa, followed by a several-paragraph summary of the Atlantic slave trade. Thus Davies not only ignored the decline of slavery but also had nothing to say about slavery in Greece and Rome, or about the European abolition movements of the eighteenth and nineteenth centuries! Even histories with a far narrower scope often do no better. In his revised edition of *The Civilization of the Middle Ages*, Norman F. Cantor mentioned slavery merely to incorrectly assert the unwillingness of early Christianity to condemn slavery, and to implicate the Church in racist views of blacks.[43] As for Joseph Dahmus's *A History of the Middle Ages*, the words "slave" and "slavery" do not appear even once.[44]

Worse yet, some historians who have concerned themselves with European slavery deny that it declined at all. Several justify their claim by citing slavery among the Norse and the Russians, failing to admit that these were not really European societies at the times in question, and by treating scattered, very local, instances of slavery—as in Venice—as somehow typical.[45] Still others reject the decline of slavery by claiming that nothing more took place than a linguistic shift wherein "slave" was replaced by "serf." That is, rather than disappearing, those once called slaves simply came to be called serfs and existed by the millions throughout the medieval period; thus "transformed but still recognizable, slavery persisted in the West from ancient Rome to the encounter with the Americas."[46] Here it is not history but historians who are playing word games. As Marc Bloch noted, the life of medieval serfs "had nothing in common with slavery."[47] Serfs were not chattels; they had rights and a substantial degree of discretion. They married whom they wished, and their families were not subject to sale or dispersal. They paid rent and thus controlled their own time and the pace of their work, "which was generally slow and . . . individualistic."[48] If, as in some places, serfs owed their lords a number of days of labor each year, the obligation was limited and more closely resembled "hired" labor than it did slavery. As Bloch put it, "The slave had been an ox in the stable, always under his master's orders; the . . . serf was a worker who came on certain days and who left as soon as the job was finished."[49] Consequently, although serfs were bound to a lord by extensive obligations, so, too, was their lord bound by obligations to a higher authority, and so on up the line, and all of these were sets of *mutual* obligations—that was the fundamental nature of feudalism.[50]

While no one would argue that medieval peasants were free in the modern sense, they were not slaves, and that brutal institution had essentially disappeared from Europe. That was not the case in societies to the east or south.

Muslim Slavery

During most of the past century, slavery in Islam received as little attention as that among the Indians of the Northwest Coast. In his *Slavery: A World History* (1993) Milton Meltzer didn't even mention Muslim slavery except as part of a brief discussion of *current* slavery at the very end of the book. It is as if, compared with the Atlantic slave trade, Islamic slavery was too insignificant to matter. In truth, Muslim slave-trading began many centuries before Europeans discovered the New World and carried at least as many Africans into bondage, and probably more, as were shipped across the Atlantic.[51] Moreover, long after Western slave-trading had ended, "Arab dhows were [still] furtively moving out of Zanzibar, Mombasa, and other East African ports, following the familiar Indian Ocean routes for the consignment of 'ebony' . . . fated to be sold in the slave marts of Arabia, the Persian Gulf, the Ottoman Empire, and India."[52]

Islamic slavery was overwhelmingly of the "consumer" variety. Early experiments with the use of slave labor on plantations resulted in bloody slave rebellions, and the practice was discontinued—large peasant populations in the agricultural areas of Islam also discouraged the reliance on field slaves. There were some elite military units composed entirely of slaves, mainly whites of Christian origins obtained in childhood. But household servants made up the bulk of Islamic slaves, and a substantial number also became concubines. Consequently, "female slaves were in much greater demand than males,"[53] and very large numbers of male slaves, adult males as well as boys, had their penis and testicles cut off at the time they were captured or purchased. This resulted in extremely high mortality, but the financial losses entailed were more than offset by the premium price paid for eunuchs. Since all forms of mutilation were prohibited by Islamic law, various "nonbelievers" such as Coptic Christians and Jews were used to perform the actual surgery, but usually under the direct supervision of Islamic slave-traders.[54]

Muslims had no particular preference for black slaves and for centuries maintained huge numbers of white slaves. By far the largest number, probably running to several million, were obtained by the *devshirme*, a forced tribute imposed on Europeans in the eastern Mediterranean. Every four

True Bondage. This picture taken in 1900 of a young Moroccan merchant with his new African slave displays two primary features of Islamic slavery. First, it was mainly "consumption" slavery with a marked preference for attractive female slaves and for castrated males to guard them. Second, slavery did not officially end in Muslim nations until quite recently and still continues "unofficially" in some. © Michael Maslan Historic Photographs/CORBIS.

years Ottoman officials passed through every subordinated Christian district and selected the most suitable children, who were taken away and raised as Muslims, and who served as highly prized slaves. In addition, Muslims rounded up large numbers of slaves in Slavic areas of Europe, as well as Europeans captured in battle or taken by pirates. In 1535 when Charles V of Spain invaded Tunis, he freed about 20,000 Christians held as slaves.[55] At the Battle of Lepanto (1571), wherein Christian galleys under the command of Don Juan destroyed a huge Muslim fleet, 15,000 Christian galley slaves were freed, though a far greater number must have drowned.[56]

However, as Islamic forces were pushed out of Europe, Africa became the major source of Islamic slaves. By 1600, it is estimated that more than 7 million Africans had been transported to captivity in Islamic societies.[57] During the next two centuries an additional 2 million were taken away.[58] At the start of the nineteenth century, some nations outlawed the Atlantic slave trade: Denmark in 1803, Great Britain in 1807, the United States in 1808, and Holland in 1818. However, the torrent of slaves into Muslim nations was unabated. The best estimate is that at least 1.2 million were transported between 1800 and 1900.[59] How many slaves Islamic nations imported during the twentieth century is unknown, but it was certainly not a trivial number—slavery was not legally abolished in Saudi Arabia until 1962, and not until 1981 in Mauritania.

It is important to recognize that these statistics mainly reflect the *successful* transporting of blacks from the interior of Africa to a destination within an Islamic nation. Hence the actual number of Africans taken into slavery was much larger because many died "during the long forced marches to the coast or on board the crowded" slave ships.[60] The best estimates are "that 20 to 40 percent of slaves died while being transported to the coast, another 3 to 10 percent died while waiting on the coast, and about 12 to 16 percent of those boarded on ships died during the voyage."[61] That adds up to losses of from 35 to 66 percent of those initially taken as slaves!

It is often claimed that Muslims gave their slaves much better care and treated them with far greater kindness than did slave-owners in the New World. Ronald Segal would have us believe that "the treatment of slaves in Islam was overall more benign," and attributes this to the absence of "Western-style capitalism, with its effective subjugation of people to the priority of profit."[62] And M. A. Salahi claimed that "slaves in the Muslim state enjoyed all their human rights as fellow human beings to their masters. This was true only in the land of Islam."[63] One basis for this claim is that sometimes slaves, especially eunuchs, achieved positions of considerable power and influence. More fundamental is that a comparison between the typical slave in Islam and in the New World is a misleading comparison between house slaves and field slaves. Even so, it is easy to refute the claim that slaves were better off under Islam. Indeed, it is fully sufficient to note how few people of black ancestry one observes in Islamic nations, compared with the New World. Since approximately the same number of Africans arrived at each destination, if the life of slaves in "the land of Islam" was even comparable to that in the New World, then these nations ought to have very substantial black populations. They do not because slave fertility was extremely low in Islam, not only because of the frequent castration of black males, but because infanticide was routinely practiced on infants having any black ancestry.[64]

The end of Islamic slaving (although it still continues on a minor scale) was the direct result of abolition in the West.[65] It was primarily the British navy that embargoed the Muslim slave ships, and British and French colonial troops who intercepted countless slave caravans in Africa, freeing the slaves and sometimes executing the slave-traders on the spot. The very recent abolition of slavery in some Islamic nations was undertaken entirely in response to intense Western pressure.

African Slavery

Just as Western historians long ignored Islamic slavery, there "has been a similar tendency to gloss over the widespread practice of slavery and the extensive traffic in slaves that were carried on in Africa itself."[66] One reason for this neglect is that to focus attention on slavery other than in the New World is to risk nasty attacks on the premise that this somehow minimizes "white" guilt. But the primary reason is that very little has been written about *anything* in Africa. Sources are relatively slim, and so are potential book sales. But the fact remains that slavery and slave-trading were well established in Africa long before the arrival of Europeans, and that both the European and Islamic slave-buyers were dependent on black, African suppliers.[67]

The enslavement of black Africans goes back at least to ancient Egypt. Wall paintings in the tombs of pharaohs depict some slaves as black, in very clear contrast with the Egyptians depicted in the same scenes. Nevertheless, it was slave-owning, not slave-trading, that was the most basic aspect of slavery in black Africa: "many if not all precolonial African societies had systems of slavery" involving the systematic and substantial utilization of slave labor.[68] Hence the onset of slave sales, whether to Egyptian, Islamic, or, eventually, Christian traders, did not depend on innovation any more than it would require new institutions for a society to begin selling agricultural products or other commodities that had long been produced for domestic consumption. Nor is it the case, despite exhortations by radicals such as Walter Rodney, that slave-trading was forced upon Africans by Europeans.[69] It long predated all such contacts. Moreover, long after the export market for slaves largely disappeared, and against the efforts of colonial administrations, local slavery continued (and continues) in many parts of Africa. African slavery was an indigenous institution.

New World Slavery

In 1441, a small Portuguese ship carrying twelve black slaves landed in Lisbon. Africans were a novelty, and their arrival was greeted with great interest, but with no disapproval because, although slavery had long since disappeared in most of Europe, it had not done so in some areas along the Mediterranean. Slavery continued in those parts of Spain and Italy under Moorish (Muslim) rule, and it continued in some Christian areas, especially in Spain, where chronic warfare existed between Christians and Muslims. Christians taken in battle with the Moors were enslaved. Christians reciprocated by enslaving Moorish captives. In Italy, too, contact between Christians and Muslims sustained slavery—merchants in Venice actually sold Europeans (mainly Slavs) to the Moors.

The first shipload of black slaves was soon followed by others, and as black slaves began to appear farther north in Europe, a debate erupted as to the morality and legality of slavery. A consensus quickly developed that slavery was both sinful and illegal—Jean Bodin,[70] that mortal enemy of witches, thundered that slavery was "a thing most pernicious and dangerous," and that having been cast off, it should not be revived. Bodin's views were reasserted by Germain Fromageau, professor at the Sorbonne, who noted that "one can neither, in surety of conscience, buy nor sell Negroes, because in such commerce there is injustice."[71] The principle of "free soil" spread: that slaves who entered a free country were automatically free. That principle was firmly in place in France, Holland, and Belgium by the end of the seventeenth century.[72] Nearly a century later, in

African Slave Traders. As shown in this lithograph of a slave caravan crossing the plains of Africa, black Africans were usually taken into captivity by other black Africans. Slave-trading was a lucrative business in Africa for many centuries before there was any contact with Europeans. © Bettmann/CORBIS.

1761, the Portuguese enacted a similar law, and an English judge applied the principle to Britain in 1772.[73] Although exceptions involving a single slave servant or two, especially when accompanying a foreign traveler, were sometimes overlooked, "beyond a scattering of servants in Spain and Portugal, there were very few true slaves left in Western Europe by the end of the sixteenth century."[74]

Meanwhile, Columbus had sailed to a New World. Suddenly, Portugal and Spain were involved in extensive efforts to control, exploit, and develop their interests in this enormous new region. Doing so required a labor force. Attempts to exploit the indigenous peoples to work plantations or mines were quite unsuccessful. Not only were Indian captives rebellious and obdurate; communicable diseases that Europeans brought with them—especially measles and smallpox—resulted in massive and deadly epidemics, which rapidly reduced the native American populations. In similar fashion, efforts to use workers imported from Europe failed, especially in the West Indies and Brazil, for lack of immunity to the chronic diseases of the tropics. It wasn't long before European colonizers recognized that a suitable labor force, having substantial immunity to tropical diseases, could be purchased, cheaply, on the west coast of Africa.[75]

Europeans seldom participated in slave raids into the African interior. Had that been necessary, it might have greatly minimized the use of black slaves in the new colonies. But the exportation of African slaves had been going on for many centuries, and African dealers were well organized and prepared to offer a seemingly endless supply of prime laborers at a cheap price. To earn huge profits, all the Europeans needed to do was transport them from the coastal African slave centers to the slave markets in the colonies. Usually, the price of slaves in the West Indies was five to six times the going rate in African ports. Between 1638 and 1702, slave prices in West Africa averaged 3.8 British pounds,[76] and the price paid upon arrival in British colonies averaged 21.3 pounds—these prices fluctuated only very slightly over the period.[77] Of course, there were many costs to be subtracted, including the not infrequent loss of an entire ship and its cargo, but most slave merchants expected a profit of 200 to 300 percent in a period of three to four months.[78]

Given an almost inexhaustible demand for slaves in the New World, little wonder that slave ships crowded the Atlantic. From the beginning in about 1510, until the very end when Cuba abolished the slave trade in 1868, approximately 10 million African slaves *reached* the New World slave markets, meaning that at least 15 million (and probably more) began

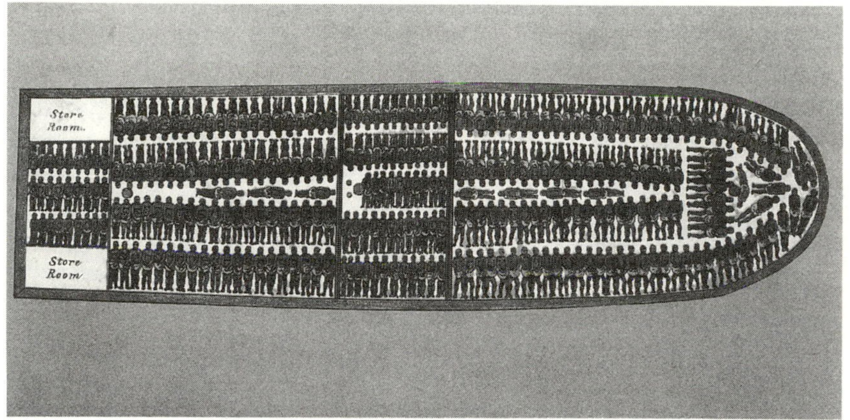

Death Ship. This famous lithograph shows a typical "packing plan" for maximum utilization of the lower deck of a slave transport. At the time a physician criticized this plan, not merely because it forced slaves to lie in their own waste, but because so many died from the lack of oxygen in the foul air. © Bettmann/CORBIS.

the journey from the African interior. Philip Curtin calculated that of the 10 million who survived the trip, about 400,000 went to British North America, 3.6 million went to Brazil, 1.6 million went to Spanish colonies, and the remaining 3.8 million were imported by the British, French, Dutch, and Danish colonies in the Caribbean.[79]

In the New World, slaves overwhelmingly were used as production laborers, mainly on large plantations growing major cash crops, although until 1800 slaves in Spanish areas were mainly used in mining, construction, and general farming. Hence, unlike the Islamic market, in the New World males commanded a far higher price than females, and there was no market for eunuchs. Despite the gender price difference, however, the slave cargoes included substantial numbers of females, and in some colonies slaves were permitted to form "marital" unions, with the result that slave fertility was far higher in parts of the New World than in Islam or the nations of antiquity.

It is difficult to generalize about the conditions imposed on slaves in the New World because there was so much variation across the major slave regions, not only in economics, law, and custom, but also in climate, geography, and endemic diseases. Consequently, I will briefly summarize slavery in the Caribbean, Brazil, and North America.

CARIBBEAN SLAVERY

The territory included in the "Caribbean region" consists of islands such as Cuba, Puerto Rico, Barbados, Martinique, Saint Domingue,[80] Bermuda, the Bahamas, and Jamaica, as well as Guyana, Surinam, and Venezuela on the South American coast. These possessions were divided among the Spanish, British, French, Dutch, and Danes. Most were extreme slave societies, in that slaves constituted the overwhelming majority of the populations. Each had a four-tier system of stratification. At the top was the white elite: plantation owners, managers, merchants, bankers, government officials, and military officers. Beneath them were "poor whites" including overseers, slave-drivers, sailors, and soldiers. Next down the status system were freed slaves and free people of mixed race, the "free coloreds" (there were few persons of either kind in the British colonies). Beneath these three rather small tiers lay the huge mass of slaves.

The basis for the extreme imbalance between slaves and free residents in the Caribbean was that, with exceptions to be noted, these were purely plantation economies, specializing in labor-intensive cash crops: primarily sugar, but with some plantations devoted to rice, indigo, cacao, coffee, cotton, and tobacco. The primacy of sugar had many serious consequences.[81] First of all, it generated very large plantations, as is reflected in the fact that most Caribbean slave-owners had more than 150 slaves (in contrast with North America, where more than 90 percent of slave-owners had fewer than 50). Second, it lent itself to the use of labor gangs of 10 to 20 slaves, each controlled by a driver who was ready to whip laggards. Third, partly because of the intensity of gang labor, and partly because of the environmental conditions suitable for sugarcane (low, swampy areas), mortality was extraordinarily high—in Jamaica the death rate on sugar plantations was 50 percent higher than on coffee plantations.[82] Fourth, a constant and substantial flow of new slaves was necessary since, in addition to high mortality, fertility was well below normal.

Beyond these general conditions, there were very substantial differences in the treatment of slaves in the Caribbean, depending on the nationality of the rulers.

In the **French** colonies the condition of slaves was carefully specified in the *Code Noir* (Black Code) formulated by Jean-Baptiste Colbert (*1619–1683*), Louis XIV's minister of finance. In drawing up the code, finally promulgated in 1685, Colbert was assisted and greatly influenced by leading French Churchmen. Too many historians have noted only Article 3, which prohibited "any public exercise of a religion other than" Roman Catholicism, using it as an opportunity to rail against Catholic "intolerance." Not one of them mentioned that public worship by Roman Catholics was prohibited in British colonies (other than Maryland) at this same time. More important, however, is that these historians ignored the many articles of the code that expanded on the premise that a slave is "a being of God." It was in this spirit that the code required owners to baptize their slaves, provide them with religious instruction, and allow them the sacrament of holy matrimony, which, in turn, became the basis for prohibiting the selling of family members separately. Slaves were also exempted from work on Sundays and holy days (from midnight to midnight), with masters being subject to fines or even to the confiscation of their slaves for violating this provision. Other articles specified minimum amounts of food and clothing that masters must provide, and ordered that the disabled and elderly must be properly cared for, including their hospitalization.

It is surely no surprise that Article 12 prohibited slaves from carrying guns or clubs, or that Article 13 outlawed "slaves belonging to different masters to gather in a crowd." Article 38, which forbade masters to torture their slaves, allowed that they might be whipped. As will be seen, these articles were seized upon by some historians who misrepresented them as the entire *Code Noir*, in an effort to claim that it was devoted solely to "the protection of whites." Peter Gay wrote that the *Code* was "extraordinarily severe—toward the slave, of course."[83] For this fraud to be perpetrated, it is necessary that there be no mention, not only of the many other articles already noted, but of Article 39, which ordered officers of justice "to proceed criminally against the masters and overseers who will have killed their slaves or mutilated them."

It is fashionable to dismiss the *Code Noir* on grounds that often it wasn't fully observed or enforced—David Brion Davis complained that "there is apparently no record of a French master being executed for killing a slave."[84] It strikes me as significant that Davis failed to convey the entire sentence he cited as his source, which reads, "Masters maltreating or killing slaves were liable to prosecution, and there are records of cases having been brought against them, although no master appears to have suffered the death penalty for killing a slave."[85] That puts the issue of enforcement in a rather different light, does it not? Undoubtedly the *Code Noir* was often violated. And undoubtedly masters enjoyed many advantages when the code was interpreted vis-à-vis their actions. But it is equally obvious that legal codes do set standards, and an action is far less likely to occur when explicitly prohibited by law than when left entirely as a matter of choice—there is, after all, a chance of being prosecuted, as some French slave-owners discovered. Granted that the observance of the *Code Noir* varied from one colony to another, and from time to time, but that it did generally mitigate the situation of slaves in most French colonies will be clear in several subsequent discussions.

Surprisingly perhaps, the **Spanish** colonies in the Caribbean did not become true slave societies or develop an extensive system of plantation agriculture until the nineteenth century; as a result, prior to that time there were relatively fewer slaves in Spanish America. The shift to plantations began in the aftermath of the Seven Years' War (1756–1763). Assessing the weakness of their Caribbean colonies, the Spanish court decided to "emulate other European nations' success with slave plantation development in the Caribbean."[86] So the Spanish formed large coffee and sugar plantations in Cuba, Santo Domingo, and Puerto Rico. These plantations required an immense expansion of slavery; nearly a million slaves were imported from Africa during the first half of the nineteenth century, after which the Atlantic slave trade was fully suppressed by international treaties and by the British navy (although slaves continued to be smuggled into Cuba until 1867).

As in French colonies, the Spanish treatment of slaves was greatly influenced by Catholic concerns, but with the effect of far greater leniency. Indeed, toward the end of the eighteenth century, Spain adopted the *Código Negro Español* (Spanish Black Code), based on a thirteenth-century Castilian code formulated to set standards for the treatment of enslaved Moorish prisoners of war. The *Código* not only included most of the provisions of the French *Code Noir*; it was far more liberal in that it guaranteed slaves the right to own property and to purchase their freedom. Specifically, slaves were enabled to petition the courts "to have themselves appraised and to purchase themselves from even unwilling masters or mistresses at their judicially appraised market value."[87] This was greatly facilitated by terms of the code that gave slaves the right to work for themselves on their days off, including the eighty-seven[88] days a year they were at liberty because of not having to work for their owners on Sundays and holy days. In rural areas, slaves were typically permitted to sell the produce raised in their own gardens and keep the proceeds.[89] In contrast, in its original version the *Code Noir* placed serious impediments on manumission, even requiring owners to obtain permission from the government—although "a customary right of self-purchase [soon] began to gain recognition in the French [colonies],"[90] and this eventually led to modification of the code.[91]

Many skeptics have spurned the rights given by the *Código* as merely "symbolic." But how then to account for the fact that in 1817 there were 114,058 free blacks in Cuba alone, many times more than in *all* of the British West Indies?[92] Or that Spanish slaves married (in church) at almost the same rate as whites? As for enforcement of the *Código*, just as the Church had played the major role in its formulation, bishops held frequent synods to "deal with local conditions," during which they "always legislated in favor of the fullest freedom and rights [for slaves] that were permissible" under the *Código*. Meanwhile, "the lower clergy, especially at the parish level, effectively carried this law into practice."[93] They did this, not only by maintaining close contacts with their black parishioners, but by imposing religious definitions on many aspects of the master-slave relationship. Not only were newborn slaves baptized in formal church services that emphasized their "humanity"; church weddings were held for slave couples, and even manumission was made into a religious ceremony held in church.[94]

In contrast, the **British** did not baptize slaves or seek their conversion to Christianity—indeed, several colonial assemblies imposed heavy fines on Quakers for doing so.[95] Moreover, the British had no tradition of slave codes to restrain master-slave relations. In his brutal attack on all non-Marxist historians of slavery, Marvin Harris found it "quite obscure" why this "legal lacuna" could matter "for the course run by slavery."[96] The answer should have been obvious even to so polemical a Marxist. No slave code existed, and Parliament declined to formulate one; thus it was left to the British colonies to enact their own. Since the colonies were fully under the control of a slave-owning "ruling class" (the Church of England did not even pretend to be concerned), the laws enacted were a planter's dream and a slave's nightmare.

In 1661 the plantation owners of Barbados adopted an "Act for the Better Ordering of Slaves." It was soon copied in other British colonies—in Jamaica in 1664, South Carolina in 1696, and Antigua in 1702[97]—and those few historians who mention it sometimes use the designation *Code of Barbados* or *Act of Barbados*. Whatever its title, this code was at least as brutal as any formulated by the Romans.[98] It characterized black slaves as "heathenish, brutish, and an uncertaine, dangerous kinde of people."[99] Masters had the right to "apply unlimited force to compel labor," without penalty, even if this resulted in maiming or death.[100] Thus while the code imposed a fine for "wantonly" killing a slave, this did not apply when slaves were punished for "cause," no matter how insignificant their offense. Consistent with the principle that slaves were private property, the fine was substantially larger if someone wantonly killed someone else's slave.[101] Slaves were specifically denied jury trials: "[B]eing Brutish Slaves, [they] deserve not, from the Baseness of their condition, to be tried by . . . twelve men."[102] However, in the instance of "any offense worthy of Death" the master ought to "bring the culprit before a justice of the peace and two neighbors for formal sentencing."[103] The code also specified that overseers must keep slaves under very close surveillance, including searching their cabins at least twice a month for stolen goods and contraband such as clubs. Slaves were not allowed to marry, and masters were prohibited from setting a slave free, except by a special act of the legislature. This legal restriction on manumission was soon replaced with a tax so heavy as to virtually prohibit it. In the Northern Leeward Islands an owner was required to pay five hundred pounds to the public treasury to free a slave, which was many times a slave's purchase price.[104] A similar tax was imposed on manumission by the legislators on St. Christopher in 1802, with the declared intent of preventing increases in the number of "free Negros," whom they regarded as a "great inconvenience."[105] The planters on Barbados were so concerned to minimize the number of free blacks that they placed an even heavier tax on the freeing of a female slave.

When the code was enacted, the governor of Barbados feared that it might "shock" officials back in England when he sent the document home for review by the government. To his surprise it was quickly approved by the Lords of Trade, who noted that black slaves are "a brutish sort of people and [properly] reckoned as goods and chattels."[106]

Keep in mind that the *Code of Barbados* was adopted in part to *moderate* treatment of slaves in the British colonies! And much moderation was needed. For example, a report from the colony of Nevis in 1675 referred to "severall evill minded persons" who had killed "many" black slaves "frivolously." On Montserrat during the 1690s, a runaway slave was drawn and quartered and "his quarters put up in Publicque places as usual."[107] A visitor to Jamaica during the late 1680s cataloged a whole series of extreme punishments including impaling slaves on stakes up their anus and then slowly burning them alive.[108] In practice, British slave masters were usually rather less brutal than the law allowed, but still most of them treated their slaves far more harshly than was the norm in Catholic colonies.

Thus contrary to all the usual allegations made about "cruel" Spaniards, it was Spain that sustained the most humane slave laws, followed by the French, with the British guilty of enacting by far the most brutal practices into law. As for slave laws not mattering, variations in the severity of legal codes are matched by variations in mortality: slaves had substantially higher death rates in the English colonies than in the Spanish colonies, with the French colonies falling in between the two.[109]

From early times, observers of New World slavery agreed that the Spanish and Portuguese were "undoubtedly the best masters of slaves," as Wadström put it in 1794, and that the English were the worst.[110] Sir Harry Johnston noted that the Portuguese and Brazilians "rival the Spanish for first place in the list of humane slave-holding nations . . . Slavery under the flag . . . of Spain was not a condition without hope, a life in hell, as it was for the most part in the British West Indies."[111] And, of course, Frank Tannenbaum, who is often credited[112] with initiating comparative studies of New World slavery, developed this view in systematic detail in *Slave and Citizen*.[113] This classic study, first published in 1946, was long regarded as the definitive demonstration of the marked contrasts between Spanish and British slavery, "not merely in their effect upon the slave, but even more significantly upon the place and moral status of the freed men."[114] Subsequently, Tannenbaum's judgment was ratified by Stanley M. Elkins, who wrote that in Catholic colonies "the very tension and balance among three kinds of organizational concerns—church, crown, and plantation agriculture—prevented slavery from being carried by the planting class to its ultimate logic."[115] Many other distinguished scholars have expressed similar views.[116]

Of course, revisionists were soon hard at work to show that slaves were certainly no better off under the Spanish or in Brazil, and perhaps they were even worse off. No revisionist was louder than Marvin Harris,[117] or more given to "savage polemical excursions."[118] Harris condemned all notions that aspects of "culture" such as laws or ideals can affect anything, demanding that all historical analysis must be entirely "materialist." He believed it follows that since only class and modes of production *can* make any difference, the French and the Spanish slaves *must have* suffered as greatly as did those owned by the English. Although expressing themselves with much less venom, since the late 1950s Brazilian Marxist historians have also attacked claims that slaves were better off under the Portuguese and the Spanish, which is a complete reversal of the views of earlier Brazilian historians.[119]

The case against the moderating effects of legal and religious culture gained considerable respectability when it was endorsed by David Brion Davis in his Pulitzer Prize–winning *The Problem of Slavery in Western Culture* (1966). Davis condemned as "idealized models" all claims that conditions of servitude were milder in Catholic areas, equating such claims with those made by "Southern apologists" for slavery. He argued instead that "Negro bondage was a single phenomenon, or *Gestalt*, whose variations were less significant than underlying patterns of unity."[120] This pronouncement was followed by pages of examples showing "good" masters in what were alleged to have been "bad" places, and vice versa, and by claims that more humane slave laws were of no consequence owing to dishonest magistrates and sadistic, greedy masters. Finally, Davis concluded that for "lack of detailed statistical information," and because the subject is "too complex," it is impossible "to assume that the treatment of slaves was substantially better in Latin America than in the British colonies, taken as a whole."[121]

Nowhere else did Davis express much interest in statistics, and for him to deny the existence of cultural effects was entirely out of keeping with his whole approach—the remainder of his book is a very traditional history of *ideas*. Indeed, Moses Finley correctly complained that Davis often erred because he was too much the historian of ideas, too little interested in actions and events, and too given to "remaining in the realm of abstractions."[122] I am inclined to attribute Davis's uncharacteristic venture out of the realm of ideas to what has come to be called "political correctness." In the highly charged and polemical context of the 1960s, Davis seems to have been very concerned to avoid the accusations of being "soft" on slavery that were so often heaped upon those who suggested that some slave systems had been less brutal than others—as Fogel and Engerman[123] were soon to discover. The safe position was to assert that slavery was equally inhumane in all of its manifestations. Davis was certainly not alone in opting for safety; it was very typical of the era—as Finley recounted so eloquently.[124]

Another example of this tactic can be found in the distinguished study of the British colonies by Richard S. Dunn, wherein he denied that "Protestant English slavery was more vicious and traumatic than Catholic Spanish and Portuguese slavery." He justified this claim by making an obviously specious comparison, not to the British Caribbean, but to the relatively milder treatment of slaves by the "Protestant English tobacco planters of Virginia or the Protestant English rice planters of Carolina."[125] For many scholars, of course, these are the only comparisons of interest, since nothing is more central to their concerns than slavery in the American South. Even so, when proper comparisons are made among slaves engaged in the same kind of labor (such as growing and processing sugar), in the same physical environments, and where slave-owners (unlike those in the American South) were free from abolitionist pressures, slaves owned by the "Protestant English" were worse off by far.

I have devoted so much attention to this matter only because, as everyone agrees, religion played a far more prominent role in the circumstances of slaves in the Catholic colonies than where Protestants prevailed. To embrace the claim that these religious differences, and the legal differences they inspired, were irrelevant to what actually went on is not only to reject the thesis of this chapter but to ignore common sense.

The **Dutch** played a leading role, second only to the British, in the Atlantic slave trade.[126] However, Dutch planters failed repeatedly in their efforts to run slave plantations. They acquired Surinam from the British in a trade for New Amsterdam, soon renamed New York. But through a series of misjudgments, and hobbled by a high and constant rate of escape by slaves who fled to "maroon" strongholds in the jungle, the Dutch planters never produced a positive balance of trade and experienced frequent bankruptcies. Observers at the time ranked the Dutch with the British as the "worst" slave masters.[127] Of course, the Dutch were also Protestants and like the British allowed the planters to devise their own slave code.

As for the **Danes**, only on St. Croix did they manage to establish large-scale sugar plantations by 1750, but by then the end of slave-trading was in sight—Denmark abolished slave-trading in 1803.[128]

BRAZIL

The Portuguese colony of Brazil was the largest and longest-lived slave society in the New World.[129] Initially, the slaves were native Indians. However, Indian slaves could be captured only by expensive and risky expeditions into the wilderness; the captives were very difficult to control (and often escaped back into the jungle) and suffered very high mortality rates from European diseases. Moreover, Jesuit and Dominican missionaries hotly and effectively opposed the enslavement of Indians, citing papal bulls on the matter (of this, more later). So in 1570 the Portuguese Crown prohibited the enslavement of Indians unless they were captured in a "just war." The Roman Catholic Church was quick to note that attacks on Indians were not just wars. In addition, the Church condemned enslavement of Indians "whether by just or unjust war," as Pope Gregory XIV (1590 to 1591) put it in his bull *Cum sicuti* of 1591.[130] All of these factors caused the Portuguese to turn to Africa for slave laborers, with the added inducement that the African coast is far closer to the coast of Brazil than to any other point in the Western Hemisphere.

From the middle of the sixteenth century until the abolition of slavery in 1888, the Brazilians imported at least 3.6 million slaves from Africa.[131] In addition to very high mortality, very low fertility necessitated this massive importation. Low fertility was the result of a number of factors, including the importation of far more males than females (about 3.2 to 1), brutal living conditions, the harsh climate, and extremely high infant mortality.[132] An unanticipated result of the continuing influx of new slaves from Africa was to reinforce the survival of African culture, which, in turn, shaped "Brazilian culture in general, as is evident in its cuisine, language, music, religion, and many other aspects of life."[133]

Slavery took many curious twists in Brazil. While large numbers of slaves toiled in work gangs on the plantations, many others lived in Brazil's rapidly growing cities—in 1849 Rio de Janeiro had a population of about 200,000, nearly half of whom were slaves, and many others were ex-slaves. But it was often hard to tell the two groups apart—not because ex-slaves lacked freedom, but because many slaves were so unsupervised as to be able to hire themselves out for wages, which was the common source of sums needed to purchase their freedom.[134] Urban slaves also formed their own religious confraternities and took a very visible and active part in public festivities such as Carnival.[135] Unlike the Caribbean colonies, where most slaves were acquired from new overseas shipments, in Brazil there was a very substantial amount of internal slave-trading, and the center of the slave population shifted over time, moving from sugar plantations in northeastern Brazil to coffee-growing areas in the south-central region.[136]

Modern writers are puzzled by laws governing slavery in Brazil, which is hardly surprising since it appears that the Brazilians were quite confused as well. What can be distilled from various bits and pieces of legislation and court decisions are practices apparently influenced by Roman law and the *Código Negro Español*, but often without any specific mention in statutes. For example, the Catholic Church recognized slave marriages as valid, and this was "tacitly accepted in Brazil" but was not recognized "in the civil law." However, the law did acknowledge that an "owner could not sell or alienate a slave in such as way that he or she could not continue the matrimonial life."[137] In general, slaves were permitted to keep a portion of any outside income they gained, and it was common for slaves to buy their freedom, but there were no legal guarantees, and there were no legal formalities involved in manumission. The law did authorize a slave to request to be sold if a master was vicious, yet mutilation, branding, and severe beatings were within the law. Perhaps this legal muddle is partly responsible for the fact that some masters may have felt free to do as they wished—it is claimed that some socially prominent Brazilian planters may have maintained torture chambers on their estates.[138] In any event, there has been a considerable dispute as to whether, compared with other colonies, slaves were treated better or worse in Brazil.[139] As already mentioned vis-à-vis the Spanish colonies, the conclusions drawn depend upon which comparisons one makes. Slaves in Brazil were probably treated considerably better than in the British Caribbean colonies, and they probably fared worse than slaves in the Spanish colonies, and possibly no better than slaves in North America.

NORTH AMERICA

Remarkably few slaves were brought to North America, given the extent of the Southern plantation system at its height and the millions of Americans of African descent. The first black slaves arrived in North America in 1626 when the Dutch landed a small shipment on Manhattan Island. From then until 1808, when it became illegal to import slaves, a total of about 400,000 slaves entered the country. In contrast, an estimated 340,000 slaves were imported by English planters in Barbados, a tiny island having an area of only 166 square miles, or barely a fourth the size of the median American county. Barbados could absorb such a huge number of slaves only because its appalling slave mortality rate was approximately equal to the rate of imports.[140] As another comparison, between 1600 and 1808 an estimated 750,000 slaves were imported by the English colony of Jamaica–at the end of which time there were fewer than half that many persons of African origins or descent alive in the colony.[141]

Thus the most striking feature of slavery in the United States was the rapid, natural population growth. The U.S. Census of 1790, taken before the slave ships stopped debarking, counted 694,224 slaves in America, far more than the total number that were eventually imported. Seventy years later, the Census of 1860 counted 3,950,546 slaves, equally divided between males and females, as well as 482,122 free blacks, for a total eleven times greater than the number brought over from Africa. This is in dramatic contrast with the demography of slavery elsewhere. Unfortunately, it has also often been a very controversial feature of American slavery, because it has been interpreted to mean that the fundamental conditions of slave life in the American South were significantly more favorable than those in other times and places. As noted, some claim that it is immoral and implicitly racist to suggest that there can be *degrees* in the treatment of slaves, since slavery is an absolute evil. But any serious comparative history must confront demographic variations as dramatic as these. American slave-owners probably punished their slaves more severely than did the Spanish or the French, but the health of slaves in the American South benefited greatly from a far more moderate climate and the relative absence of the tropical diseases that beset the Caribbean. Moreover, a whole series of careful and well-documented studies reveal that American slave-owners regarded their slaves as very valuable assets and fed, sheltered, dressed, and worked them accordingly—slave diets in the United States were probably superior to those of the average peasant in most European nations at the time.[142] One need not make any apologies for Southern slave masters to admit that by selfishly pursuing their economic interests, they benefited their chattels.

A major factor in the fundamental shape of American slavery is that it was not based on sugar plantations.[143] In the first part of the eighteenth century, the majority of American slaves were involved in general farming, crafts, and domestic services, while tobacco plantations engaged about a third, and the rest of the plantation slaves grew rice and indigo. Cotton plantations did not become of major importance until about 1800 with the introduction of the cotton gin. Sugar plantations never employed more than 5 percent of American slaves, and that mainly late, and in Louisiana. In comparison with sugar, other crops were not nearly so labor-intensive. Consequently, the demand for slaves was not rapacious; as a result of this, combined with the rapid natural increase of the American slave population, imports were minimized.

Together, these factors had many very significant consequences. First, early on American slaves were overwhelmingly native born: by the 1740s more than half of American slaves were native born; by 1780 about 80 percent of slaves were born here, and many had been here for many generations. In contrast, as late as 1800 about a quarter of the slaves in Jamaica had arrived from Africa during the previous ten years! Second, nearly all American slaves served on small units. The median tobacco plantation had fewer than twenty slaves, and even the larger cotton plantations were small by Caribbean and Brazilian standards, the median spread having only thirty-five slaves. Third, rather than being isolated in large work gangs, American slaves usually had close, constant contact with whites. This was further sustained by the fact that while slaves made up the vast majority of the population of the Caribbean slave societies, even in the Deep South they remained a minority. Fourth, this high level of contact with whites over such an extended period resulted in American slaves' becoming far more fully assimilated into "European" culture—hence the present efforts to recover an African heritage, something that has not occurred in the Caribbean or Latin America.

Many readers will be surprised that the first black slaves brought to America came to New Amsterdam on Dutch ships, and that slavery was not initially restricted to the South. As shown in Table 4.1, in 1790 there were slaves in every state except Massachusetts and Maine, where, owing to their Puritan heritage, slavery was already illegal. While the slave population was concentrated in Southern states, there were significant numbers in New York, New Jersey, Pennsylvania, and Connecticut. Most of the slaves in these Northern states were "consumption slaves," used as personal servants.

The American slave plantations began as part of the British colonial system and were influenced by the *Code of Barbados* rather than by the *Code Noir* or the *Código Negro Español*. However, unlike the British planters in the Caribbean, the Southern planters soon adopted many "reforms" in an effort to forestall the mounting pressure from Northern abolitionists, especially following independence. Thus, for example, Southern courts and legislatures did enact laws against killing slaves. In 1791, North Carolina defined killing a slave as "murder" and subject to pertinent statutes against that crime; in 1816 Georgia held that killing or maiming a slave was the full equivalent of killing or maiming a white person.[144]

In general, however, most Southern courts defined slaves as "real estate," and a few treated them simply as "personal property."[145] This meant that slaves could be inherited, traded, or sold at will, without regard for such concerns as not separating married couples or parents from

TABLE 4.1
Slavery in America, 1790

	Number of Slaves	*Percent of Population*
1. Virginia	292,627	39.1
2. South Carolina	107,094	43.0
3. Maryland	103,036	32.2
4. North Carolina	100,783	25.6
5. Georgia	29,264	35.5
6. New York	21,193	6.3
7. Kentucky[a]	12,430	16.8
8. New Jersey	11,423	6.2
9. Delaware	8,887	15.1
10. Pennsylvania	3,707	0.9
11. Connecticut	2,648	1.2
12. New Hampshire	157	0.1
13. Vermont	17	0.0
14. Maine	0	0.0
15. Massachusetts	0	0.0
Total	694,224[b]	17.7

Source: U.S. Census, 1790.
[a] Still a territory, admitted to statehood in 1792.
[b] Total includes 958 slaves in territories and the newly founded District of Columbia.

children. However, increasingly, Southern courts held that slaves "were property with souls," and evolved principles concerning the "reciprocal duties of slaves and masters and enforced them at law." Hence masters "were obligated to feed, clothe, and provide medical care for slaves, and in many slave jurisdictions they had to provide counsel for slaves on trial for crimes."[146] In a few Southern cities slaves were allowed to hire themselves out (paying a fee to their masters), and sometimes they pursued highly skilled trades. But the courts always upheld the primacy of property rights vis-à-vis slaves.

Moreover, Southerners were as apt as were whites in the British Caribbean to regard "free blacks" as undesirable. Thus the U.S. Census of 1860 reported that in 1849, of more than 3.2 million slaves, only 1,467 had been set free during the year, and of the more than 3.9 million slaves in the nation in 1859, 3,018 were set free that year. Indeed, statistics on free blacks present an opportunity for a "natural experiment" to assess whether and to what extent the *Code Noir* and the *Código Negro Español* made a difference in the lives of slaves. This involves comparing "Catholic" Louisiana with the rest of the "Protestant" South.

Louisiana came under the *Code Noir* in 1724 as the French consolidated their administration. When control of Louisiana shifted to Spain in 1769, the circumstances of slaves were greatly improved owing to the liberal provisions of the *Código Negro Español* concerning the right of slaves to own property and to purchase their freedom. France regained Louisiana in 1802 and sold it to the United States the next year, but by then Catholic norms concerning slavery and the treatment of free blacks were deeply rooted. This is evident in the fact that the U.S. Census of 1830 found that a far higher percentage of the blacks in Louisiana were free (31.2 percent) than in any other slave state. The contrast is especially sharp in comparison to neighboring states having similar plantation economies: Alabama (1.3 percent), Mississippi (0.8 percent), and Georgia (1.1 percent).

However, the contrast between New Orleans and other major cities of the South is even more revealing, as shown in Table 4.2.[147] In New Orleans, more than four of ten black residents were free! Even in Richmond and Norfolk, blacks were far less likely to be free, and these cities are not located in the Deep South. In the Carolina cities the odds of a black's being free varied from 1:10 to 1:20. Elsewhere, very few blacks had gained their freedom. Can such immense differences stem from anything other than the effects of Catholic codes and attitudes toward slavery? Rather than shedding crocodile tears over the lack of "detailed statistical information" to reveal whether Catholic slave codes made a difference, David Brion Davis might better have done the simple calculations shown in Table 4.2—the data have been available for about 170 years.

In keeping with their far greater prevalence, free blacks (as well as slaves) played remarkably prominent roles in the cultural and economic

TABLE 4.2
Free Blacks in Southern Cities, 1830

	Percent of Blacks Who Were Free	*Black Population*
New Orleans, Louisiana	41.7	28,545
Richmond, Virginia	21.1	11,385
Norfolk, Virginia	16.5	11,492
Raleigh, North Carolina	9.3	8,942
Charleston, South Carolina	6.4	56,116
Columbia, South Carolina	5.2	9,534
Savannah, Georgia	4.3	9,901
Augusta, Georgia	3.6	6,481
Nashville, Tennessee	3.9	12,133
Memphis, Tennessee	2.9	2,111
Montgomery, Alabama	1.0	6,515
Selma, Alabama	0.9	7,723
Natchez, Mississippi	1.2	11,077
Vicksburg, Mississippi	0.5	4,505

Source: U.S. Census, 1830.
Note: Atlanta did not exist at this time.

life of New Orleans, and race was often far from decisive in social activities.[148] Indeed, as revealed in nineteenth-century U.S. Census enumerations, although there were black slave-*owners* in some other parts of the South, they were far more common in New Orleans, and only in Louisiana were there large, black-owned plantations having many slaves.[149] In contrast, elsewhere in America—even in the nonslave states—*free* blacks were denied many legal rights, including even the right to testify in court.

This completes what I intended only as a "brief survey" of slavery, meant to provide nothing more than an adequate basis for analyzing the role played by religion in ending this sad history.

CHAPTER 4

Gods and Morality

It has been an axiom among social scientists that religion functions to sustain the moral order. But it's not true, or at least not true in many cases, for only some *kinds* of religions have moral implications. This is not to say that there are societies without moral codes, but that in many, morality has no religious basis and lacks sacred authority. I will pursue this issue at length in the postscript. Here a very brief summary will suffice.

Whether religions generate moral culture depends greatly upon their image of God. Not only are divine essences unable to issue commandments; they cannot sustain any concept of "sin." The Tao does not advise humans to love one another, nor does the "First Cause" tell us not to covet another's spouse. Paul Tillich's "ground of our being" is not a *being* and consequently is incapable of having, let alone expressing, moral concerns.[150] Only *Gods*—conscious supernatural beings—can desire our moral conformity. Even that is not sufficient. Gods can lend sanctions to the moral order only if they are responsive and dependable—if they are concerned about, informed about, and active on behalf of humans. Moreover, to promote virtue among humans, Gods must themselves be virtuous—they must *favor good* over evil. Finally, Gods will be more effective in sustaining moral precepts, the greater their *scope*—that is, the greater the diversity of their powers and the range and duration of their influence.

Besides lacking scope, the many Gods of polytheistic systems are often not conceived of as responsive and dependable, or as necessarily favoring good over evil. Among the Indians of the Northwest Coast, the Gods (such as they were) did not concern themselves with morality, and magic dominated ritual life.[151] Aside from those involved in ascetic sects, most Greeks and Romans believed that their Gods *could* hear their pleas, but that they mostly didn't listen and didn't care. Aristotle taught that the Gods were incapable of real concern for humans—lust, jealousy, and anger, yes, but never affection. Such Gods may require propitiation, and it may sometimes be possible to bargain with them for favors. But they are not to be counted on, and it is quite uncertain that it is even wise to attract their attention. Indeed, the Gods of Greece and Rome (and of polytheisms in general) sometimes kept their word, and sometimes they provided humans with very valuable rewards. But they often lied and did humans great harm for very petty reasons. As William Foxwell Albright put it, "the Olympian deities of Greece [were] charming poetic figures

[but] unedifying examples."[152] It may have been worthwhile to periodically offer such Gods a sacrificial animal or two (especially since the donors feasted on the offering after the ceremony), but they were not worth more. Consequently, they could not ask more.

In contrast, the immense Gods of the monotheisms ask much more and get it. In return for the otherworldly rewards they promise, and to enable humans to avoid the terrible punishments they threaten, these Gods uniformly impose sets of demands. And all of these sets include extensive codes of human conduct, not only toward the sacred, but toward one another. Underlying and reinforcing these moral codes is the concept of *sin*—wrongful thoughts and actions that will bring divine retribution. Some sins will be spelled out in revelations; others will be the products of theology, of study as to the implications of revelations.

Identifying new sins has been a central focus of Jewish, Christian, and Islamic theologians. For example, nowhere in the Bible is suicide prohibited. It was Saint Augustine who *deduced* that it is a sin to take one's own life.[153] Turning to the issue at hand, I propose to show that prior to the rise of monotheism, religions were poorly equipped to impose extensive moral codes, including moral prohibitions of slavery. Nor could philosophers fill the moral gap. Then, I will trace how it was that two early Jewish sects and then medieval Christianity deduced that slavery was a sin—a conclusion subsequently ratified by many popes, then by the Quakers, followed by many other Protestant groups. I complete the section by explaining why Islamic theologians failed to conclude that slavery was sinful.

Polytheism and Slavery

When religions do not underwrite the moral order, social criticism is a secular enterprise left to philosophers, artists, and other intellectuals. Having no concept of sin to put teeth in their judgments and no revelations from which to begin, ancient philosophers were, for the most part, proponents of the status quo. There is no record that any philosopher in Sumer, Babylon, or Assyria ever protested against slavery, "nor is there any expression of the mildest sympathy for the victims of this system. Slavery was simply taken for granted."[154] Indeed, the *Code of Hammurabi* (ca. 1750 B.C.E.) prescribed death for anyone who helped a slave to escape.

Egyptian Slaves. This carving in the base of a colossal statue of Pharaoh Rameses II shows a group of slaves roped together by the neck. The statue stands at the entrance to the Great Temple at Abu Simbel, built more than three thousand years ago. The many Gods of Egypt were not thought to concern themselves with how humans treated one another. © Bettmann/CORBIS.

Nor did the famous Greek philosophers condemn slavery. Plato did oppose enslavement of his fellow "Hellenes" (Greeks) but assigned "barbarian" (foreign) slaves a vital role in his ideal Republic—they would perform all of the productive labor.[155] In fact, the rules Plato laid out concerning the proper treatment of slaves were unusually brutal—"No American slave code was so severe."[156] Moreover, Plato did not believe that becoming a slave was simply a matter of bad luck; rather, in his view, nature creates a "slavish people" lacking the mental capacity for virtue or culture, and fit only to serve. Because slaves have no souls, they have no "human rights," and masters can treat them as they will. Of course, if someone kills a slave belonging to someone else, the owner must be recompensed at twice the dead slave's market value—a principle that reappeared in the *Code of Barbados*.[157] While Plato suggested that slaves should be sternly disciplined, he believed that, to prevent needless unrest, they generally should not be subject to excessive cruelty.[158] As enumerated in his will, Plato's estate included five slaves.

As for Aristotle, he rejected the position advanced by the Sophists that all authority rests on force and therefore is self-justifying, because he sought to condemn political tyranny. But then, how to justify slavery? Here, Aristotle anticipated the Humanists by arguing that without slaves to do the labor, enlightened men would lack the time and energy to pursue virtue and wisdom. He additionally justified slavery by drawing upon Plato's biological claims—slavery is justified because slaves are more akin to dumb brutes than to free men.[159] Left on their own, slaves would be ruled solely by their appetites, causing endless civic harm. The basis for slavery, he wrote, is innate: "From the hour of their birth, some are marked out for subjection, others for rule."[160] Upon his death, Aristotle's personal property included fourteen slaves.

There were some contrary voices among Athenians. The playwright Euripides (*480–406 B.C.E.*) argued that some slaves were more virtuous and intelligent than their masters, thus rejecting the claim that hereditary slavery is in accord with nature. But he also accepted that "there existed some whose nature was fit for slavery."[161] The poet Philemon (*361–262 B.C.E.*) wrote that slave and master are made of the same flesh, and that it is not nature but fate that enslaves the body. And the fourth-century Sophist philosopher Alcidamas taught that "God created us all free; nature makes no slaves."[162] But what God? Sophists could not invoke One True God. Invoking a lesser God made no one tremble.

Monotheism and Slavery

During the twentieth century, most scholars who mentioned the topic took special satisfaction from noting that Judaism, Roman Catholicism, and Islam embraced slavery.[163] Forget for the moment that the medieval Catholic Church did condemn slavery; it is no surprise that theologians suffer from the "blindness" of their times and places. As discussed in Chapter 2, many Christian theologians, including Saint Augustine and John Calvin, have taught that cultural limitations have often made it impossible for people in an earlier time to fully understand a revelation when it was granted them. What is remarkable is that theologians can *ever* rise above these limits. And that is the tale I now tell.

JUDAISM: ESSENES AND THERAPEUTAE

Moses did not come down from the mountain with a commandment forbidding slavery. But, according to the Torah, God did reveal to him a very elaborate moral code vis-à-vis slavery—one that made Jewish slavery far more humane than that of other societies in classical times.

Although Jews were prohibited from enslaving other Jews, and their slaves therefore came from among the "heathen," there were still severe limits on their treatment. Death was decreed for any Jewish master who killed a slave. The Torah also admonished that freedom was to be awarded any slave as compensation for suffering acts of violence: "And if a man smite the eye of his servant, or the eye of his maid, that it perish; he shall go free for his eye's sake. And if he smite out his manservant's tooth, or his maidservant's tooth; he shall let him go free for his tooth's sake" (Exod. 21:26–27). Hebrew law held that children of slaves must not be parted from their parents, nor a wife from her husband. Moreover, in Deut. 23:15–16 Jews were admonished *not* to return escaped slaves: "Thou shalt not deliver unto his master the servant which is escaped from his master unto thee: he shall dwell with thee, even among you . . . thou shalt not oppress him." Indeed, the Talmud advises that the slave be treated as one of the family, allowed to rest on the Sabbath and treated equally: "Do not drink old wine while you give him new wine. Do not sleep on cushions while you let him lie on straw."[164]

Eventually some Jews rejected slavery entirely. Thus the Essenes, the ascetic sect described in Chapter 1, were said to have outlawed slavery.[165] As Philo of Alexandria (*ca. 20 B.C.E.–50*) reported, the Essenes "condemn [slave] masters, not only as unjust, inasmuch as they corrupt the very principle of equality, but likewise as impious, because they destroy the ordinances of nature, which generated them all equally."[166] In similar fashion, the Therapeutae ("healers"), another Jewish sect believed to have lived near Alexandria, also rejected slavery. Philo wrote, "And they do not use the ministrations of slaves, looking upon the possession of . . . slaves to be a thing absolutely and wholly contrary to nature, for nature has created all men free."[167]

Philo does not explain the theology by which either of these groups condemned slavery. Since the Torah clearly accepts slavery, how did they reject it while claiming to be strict observers of the Law? I think the answer is twofold. First, they may not have defined slavery as sinful per se but concluded that true asceticism required many sacrifices including their forgoing being served by others. That is, they rejected slavery as sinful *for them*, rejecting it on the same grounds that they rejected other luxuries and creature comforts. Second, they assumed that as long as they fully observed the Law, they were entirely free to impose even stricter standards. For example, they met kosher precepts by refusing to eat pork and exceeded them by eating no meat of any kind. Similarly, they not only observed the Law concerning humane treatment of slaves; they surpassed it by not reducing anyone to the condition of slavery.

Since the Essenes and the Therapeutae were cloistered groups, regarded as precursors of Christian monastics, it is not certain that they had any expectation that their standards ought to be adopted generally. Consequently, their rejection of slavery may have had no moral significance outside their communities. Whatever the case, so far as I can determine, the Essenes and Therapeutae were the first "societies" (albeit small ones) to prohibit slavery. That the Jews were also among the very first to believe that God took minute interest in the moral behavior of humans is not coincidental.

SAINTS AND POPES

Even some Catholic writers parrot the claim that it was not until 1890 that the Roman Catholic Church repudiated slavery,[168] and a British priest has charged that this did not occur until 1965.[169] Nonsense! As early as the seventh century, Saint Bathilde (wife of King Clovis II) became famous for her campaign to stop slave-trading and free all slaves; in 851 Saint Anskar began his efforts to halt the Viking slave trade. That the Church willingly baptized slaves was claimed as proof that they had souls, and soon both kings and bishops—including William the Conqueror (*1027–1087*) and Saints Wulfstan (*1009–1095*) and Anselm (*1033–1109*)—forbade the enslavement of Christians.[170] Since, except for small settlements of Jews, and the Vikings in the north, *everyone* was at least nominally a Christian, that effectively abolished slavery in medieval Europe, except at the southern and eastern interfaces with Islam where both sides enslaved one another's prisoners. But even this was sometimes condemned: in the tenth century, bishops in Venice did public penance for past involvement in the Moorish slave trade and sought to prevent all Venetians from involvement in slavery. Then, in the thirteenth century, Saint Thomas Aquinas deduced that slavery was a sin, and a series of popes upheld his position, beginning in 1435 and culminating in three major pronouncements against slavery by Pope Paul III in 1537.[171]

It is significant that in Aquinas's day, slavery was a thing of the past or of distant lands. Consequently, he gave very little attention to the subject per se, paying more attention to serfdom, which he held to be repugnant.

However, in his overall analysis of morality in human relationships, Aquinas placed slavery in opposition to natural law, deducing that all "rational creatures" are entitled to justice. Hence he found no natural basis for the enslavement of one person rather than another, "thus removing any possible justification for slavery based on race or religion."[172] Right reason, not coercion, is the moral basis of authority, for "one man is not by nature ordained to another as an end."[173] Here Aquinas distinguished two forms of "subjection" or authority, just and unjust. The former exists when leaders work for the advantage and benefit of their subjects. The unjust form of subjection "is that of slavery, in which the ruler manages the subject for his own [the ruler's] advantage."[174] Based on the immense authority vested in Aquinas by the Church, the official view came to be that slavery is sinful.

It is true that some popes did not observe the moral obligation to oppose slavery—indeed, in 1488 Pope Innocent VIII accepted a gift of a hundred Moorish slaves from King Ferdinand of Aragon, giving some of them to his favorite cardinals. Of course, Innocent was anything but that when it came to a whole list of immoral actions, as noted in Chapter 1. However, laxity must not be confused with doctrine. Thus while Innocent fathered many children, he did not retract the official doctrine that the clergy should be celibate. In similar fashion, his acceptance of a gift of slaves should not be confused with official Church teachings. These were enunciated often and explicitly as they became pertinent.

During the 1430s, the Spanish colonized the Canary Islands and began to enslave the native population. This was not serfdom but true slavery of the sort that Christians and Moors had long practiced upon one another's captives in Spain. When word of these actions reached Pope Eugene IV (1431 to 1447), he issued a bull, *Sicut dudum*. The pope did not mince words. Under threat of excommunication he gave everyone involved fifteen days from receipt of his bull "to restore to their earlier liberty all and each person of either sex who were once residents of said Canary Islands . . . These people are to be totally and perpetually free and are to be let go without the exaction or reception of any money."[175] Pope Pius II (1458 to 1464) and Pope Sixtus IV (1471 to 1484) followed with additional bulls condemning enslavement of the Canary Islanders, which, obviously, had continued. What this episode displays is the weakness of papal authority at this time, not the indifference of the Church to the sin of slavery.

With the successful Spanish and Portuguese invasions of the New World, enslavement of the native peoples and the importation of Africans ensued, and some slavers offered the rationale that this was not in violation of Christian morality, as these were not "rational creatures" entitled to liberty but were a species of animals and therefore legitimately subject to human exploitation. This theological subterfuge by slave-traders was artfully used by Norman F. Cantor to indict Catholicism: "The church accepted slavery . . . in sixteenth-century Spain, Christians were still arguing over whether black slaves had souls or were animal creations of the Lord."[176] Cantor gave no hint that Rome repeatedly denounced New World slavery as grounds for excommunication.

But that is precisely what Pope Paul III (1534 to 1549) had to say about the matter. Although a member of a Roman ecclesiastical family, and something of a libertine in his early years (he was made a cardinal at twenty-five but did not accept ordination until he was fifty), Paul turned out to be a very effective and pious pope who fully recognized the moral significance of Protestantism and initiated the Counter-Reformation. His magnificent bull against New World slavery (as well as similar bulls by other popes) was somehow "lost"[177] from the historical record until very recently.[178] I believe this was due to the extreme Protestant biases of historians, who may also have been scornful of the pope's predicating his attack on the assumption that Satan was the cause of slavery:

> [Satan,] the enemy of the human race, who always opposes all good men so that the race may perish, has thought up a way, unheard of before now, by which he might impede the saving word of God from being preached to the nations. He has stirred up some of his allies who, desiring to satisfy their own avarice, are presuming to assert far and wide that the Indians of the West and the South who have come to our notice in these times be reduced to our service like brute animals, under the pretext that they are lacking in the Catholic faith. And they reduce them to slavery, treating them with afflictions they would scarcely use with brute animals.
>
> Therefore, We . . . noting that the Indians themselves indeed are true men . . . by our Apostolic Authority decree and declare by these present letters that the same Indians and *all other peoples*—even though they are outside the faith—. . . should not be deprived of their liberty or their other possessions . . . and are not to be reduced to slavery, and that whatever happens to the contrary is to be considered null and void. (My italics)[179]

In a second bull on slavery, Paul imposed the penalty of excommunication on anyone, regardless of their "dignity, state, condition, or grade . . . who in any way may presume to reduce said Indians to slavery or despoil them of their goods."[180]

But nothing happened. Soon, in addition to the brutal exploitation of the Indians, Spanish and Portuguese slave ships began to sail between Africa and the New World. And just as overseas Catholic missionaries had aroused Rome to condemn the enslavement of Indians, similar appeals were filed concerning imported black slaves. On April 22, 1639, Pope Urban VIII (1623 to 1644), at the request of the Jesuits of Paraguay, issued a bull *Commissum nobis* reaffirming the ruling by "our predecessor Paul III" that those who reduced others to slavery were subject to excommunication.[181] Eventually, the Congregation of the Holy Office (the Roman Inquisition) even took up the matter. On March 20, 1686, it ruled in the form of questions and answers:

> It is asked:
>
> Whether it is permitted to capture by force and deceit Blacks and other natives who have harmed no one?
>
> Answer: no.
>
> Whether it is permitted to buy, sell or make contracts in their respect Blacks or other natives who have harmed no one and been made captives by force of deceit?
>
> Answer: no.
>
> Whether the possessors of Blacks and other natives who have harmed no one and been captured by force or deceit, are not held to set them free?
>
> Answer: yes.
>
> Whether the captors, buyers and possessors of Blacks and other natives who have harmed no one and who have been captured by force or deceit are not held to make compensation to them?
>
> Answer: yes.[182]

Nothing ambiguous here. The problem wasn't that the Church failed to condemn slavery; it was that few heard and most of them did not listen. In this era, popes had little or no influence over the Spanish and the Portuguese since at that time the Spanish ruled most of Italy (see Chapter 1); in 1527, under the leadership of Charles V, they had even sacked Rome. If the pope had little influence in Spain or Portugal, he had next to none in their New World colonies, except indirectly through the work of the religious orders. In fact, it was illegal even to publish papal decrees "in

Pope Paul III. Although he was celebrated in life for leading the Counter-Reformation, his portrait painted by Titian, it has been nearly forgotten that this son of a wealthy Roman family condemned slavery on pain of excommunication. © Archivo Iconografico, S.A./CORBIS.

the Spanish colonial possessions without royal consent," and the king also appointed all of the bishops.[183] Nevertheless, Urban VIII's bull was read in public by the Jesuits in Rio de Janeiro, with the result that rioters attacked the local Jesuit college and injured a number of priests. In Santos a mob trampled the Jesuit vicar-general when he tried to publish the bull, and the Jesuits were expelled from São Paulo when word spread of their involvement in obtaining the bull.[184] Even so, knowledge of the antislavery bulls and the later ruling of the Inquisition against slavery was generally limited to the clergy, especially the religious orders, and thereby had limited public impact.

Of course, the Spanish and the Portuguese were not the only slavers in the New World. And even had they been published far and wide, papal bulls had no moral force among the British and the Dutch. Thus it must be noted that the introduction of slavery into the New World did not prompt any leading Dutch or English Protestants to denounce it.

However, even though the papal bulls against slavery were hushed up in the New World, the antislavery views of the Church did have a significantly moderating effect in the Catholic Americas by means of the *Code Noir* and *Código Negro Español*. In both cases, the Church took the lead in their formulation and enforcement, thereby demonstrating its fundamental opposition to slavery by trying to ensure "the rights of the slave and his material welfare," and by imposing "obligations on the slave owners, limiting their control over the slave."[185] As Eugene Genovese put it: "Catholicism made a profound difference in the lives of the slaves. [It] imparted to Brazilian and Spanish American slave societies an ethos . . . of genuine spiritual power."[186]

The prevalence of antireligious, and especially anti-Catholic, bias in histories of slavery is well exemplified by the "discussion" of the *Code Noir* in the *Columbia Encyclopedia* (1975) entry for Louisiana: "[T]he *Code Noir*, adopted in 1724, provided for the rigid control of their [slaves'] lives and the protection of whites. Additional provisions established Catholicism as the official religion." And that's it! Not the slightest acknowledgment of the many articles designed to protect slaves. Granted, it was not an emancipation proclamation, but neither was it the *Code of Barbados*.

As an additional instance of the antireligious bias among contemporary historians, consider that in his discussion of the *Code Noir*, Robin Blackburn wrote of the "pretended official policy of encouragement of slave marriages in the French colonies," only to end his sentence with the remarkable admission that it had "limited but not negligible results."[187] He then cited a document from Martinique reporting that half of the slaves of marriageable age were married. Since, given the gender distribution of the slave population, this would have equaled marriage rates in France at that time, it would seem that it was sufficient that support for marriage be "pretended."

Equally remarkable is the fact that so many distinguished historians of slavery barely mentioned the *Code Noir* and ignored the *Código Negro Español* so completely that it does not even appear in the indexes of their well-known works.[188] But if many historians have paid little or no attention to these Church-inspired codes, virtually no one has even mentioned the *Code of Barbados* (under any name), except for the few historians specializing in slavery laws,[189] and several who wrote specifically about the history of slavery in Barbados,[190] although the code was observed in the entire British West Indies. I suggest that the *Code of Barbados* would have received considerable attention had it been produced by Catholics rather than by Protestants.

But perhaps the most revealing omission from all discussions of New World slavery, and especially of the enslavement and mistreatment of indigenous populations, concerns the Jesuit Republic of Paraguay.[191] For more than 150 years (1609–1768), the Jesuits administered an area more than twice the size of France, located south of Brazil and west of the territory ceded to Portugal by the Treaty of Tordesillas (1494). Here, a tiny group of Spanish Jesuits (probably never numbering more than two hundred) founded, protected, educated, and advised a remarkable civilization encompassing at least thirty "Reductions,"[192] or communities, of Guaraní Indians. Not only did arts and industry flourish in the Jesuit republic (cities with paved streets and impressive buildings, symphony orchestras, printing), but a valid attempt was made at representative government. Their purpose in founding the republic, as explained by the Jesuit superior Antonio Ruiz de Montoya in 1609, was to Christianize and "civilize" the Indians so that they could be free subjects of the Crown, equal to the Spaniards, and thus to "bring about peace between the Spaniards and the Indians, a task so difficult that, since the discovery of the West Indies more than a hundred years ago, it still has not been possible."[193]

The republic flourished, but rather than becoming the basis for equality and peace, its existence offended many colonial officials and planters, and provided a tempting plum for expropriation. Nevertheless, the Jesuits managed to forestall and outmaneuver these opposed interests for several generations. But then things began to go sour. The first step in the downfall of the republic came in 1750 when the Portuguese and Spanish signed a new treaty, redividing South America along natural boundaries. As a result, seven of the Reductions fell within Portuguese jurisdiction. Ordered to turn these settlements over to civil authorities, the Jesuits resisted and appealed to the Portuguese and Spanish Crowns to have the Reductions spared. But their opponents were too strong and too unscrupulous, planting rumors and false evidence of Jesuit conspiracies against both Crowns. So in 1754 the Spanish sent troops against the seven Reductions from the west, while the Portuguese advanced from the east. Both forces of European troops were defeated by the Indians, who were quite well trained in military tactics and had muskets and cannons. Although the Jesuits had not participated in the battles, they were blamed as traitors and in response were expelled from Portugal and all Portuguese territories in 1758. Soon additional plots against the Jesuits succeeded in Spain as all members of the order were arrested early in 1667 and deported to the Papal States. In July, colonial authorities were ready to move against the Jesuits in Latin America, and the roundup began in Buenos Aires and Córdoba. But it wasn't until the next year that Spanish troops moved against the final twenty-three Reductions and seized the remaining Jesuits, whereupon even very sick and elderly fathers were tied to mules and transported over mountains in bad weather, many to their deaths. Thus were the Jesuits expelled from the Western Hemisphere. Soon their republic lay in ruins—defeated and looted by civil authorities. Disheartened by their mistreatment and the loss of the Black Robed Fathers, the surviving Guaraní drifted away, many into the cities.

Of course, among the few historians to deal with the Jesuit republic are some who harp against colonialism and Catholicism, condemn the "fanatical" Jesuits for imposing religion and civilization on the "gentle" Indians, and denounce Jesuit efforts to sustain a republic as cruel paternalism and "ruthless exploitation."[194] But even if one were to accept the most extreme version of these claims, one is still faced with sincere and effective efforts by the Jesuits to protect the Indians against the planters and colonial authorities who wished to reduce them to servitude or to eradicate them entirely. To have constructed an advanced Indian civilization in this historical context was quite an extraordinary feat. Moreover, the antagonistic historians at least tell about this significant historical event, while most other historians have simply ignored it. I was able to find only two books on the subject in English written during the past thirty years, one of them translated from Portuguese and both now out of print.[195] So far as I could discover, the only acknowledgment of the subject in the *Encyclopaedia Britannica* was this single sentence under "Paraguay, History of": "During most of the colonial era, Paraguay was known chiefly for the huge Jesuit mission group of 30 *reducciones*." We are not even told what "*reducciones*" are. As for the major works on New World slavery, all of which have bitter (and often anti-Catholic) things to say about the enslavement and abuse of Indians in Latin America: complete silence.

In contrast, considerable attention has been paid by historians to the fact that not all of the Catholic clergy, including not all Jesuits, accepted the claim that slavery was sinful. Indeed, sometimes in the midst of slave societies, clergy themselves kept slaves—during the eighteenth and early nineteenth centuries Jesuits in Maryland were slave-owners.[196] Other clergy were very confused about the issue. For example, the Dominican Bartolomé de Las Casas (*1474–1566*) waged a bitter and quite successful campaign against enslaving Indians, during which he proposed that slaves be brought from Africa instead. Later he came to deeply regret this proposal and expressed doubt as to whether God would pardon him for this terrible sin.[197]

It must also be acknowledged that the Church did not, usually, confront governments head-on over the issue and attempt to force an end to slavery. Granted that popes had threatened excommunication, but in practice the Church settled for attempting to ameliorate the conditions of slaves as much as possible. Thus the Church was unrelenting in its assertion that slavery was only a condition of service, and that those enslaved remained fully human and retained their full equality in the eyes of God. As the prominent Italian Cardinal Hyacinthe Gerdil (*1718–1802*) put it: "Slavery is not to be understood as conferring on one man the same power over another that men have over cattle . . . For slavery does not abolish the natural equality of men . . . [and is] subject to the condition that the master shall take due care of his slave and treat him humanely."[198] As already mentioned, it was in this spirit that the first article of the *Código Negro Español* required all masters to have their slaves baptized and specified serious penalties for masters who did not allow their slaves to attend mass or celebrate feast days. In contrast, the Church of England usually did not recognize slaves "as baptisable human beings."[199] Both views had a profound effect, not only on those in slavery, but on attitudes toward manumission and especially toward ex-slaves.

What is clear is that the common assertion that the Catholic Church generally favored slavery is not true. Indeed, as will be seen, when American Quakers initiated the abolition movement, they found kindred souls not only among other Protestants but among Roman Catholics too.

THE ISLAMIC EXCEPTION

If monotheism has the potential to give rise to antislavery doctrines, why did Islam not turn against slavery too? Indeed, why does slavery persist in some Islamic areas, while having only recently been discontinued in other Muslim nations in response to intense pressure from the West?

To answer this question, we must recognize that theologians work within definite intellectual limits—not just any conclusion is possible given particular cultural materials. For example, it would be quite impossible for Jewish, Christian, or Islamic theologians to deduce that God takes no interest in human sexual behavior. The revealed texts simply will not permit such a conclusion. Nor could Christian theologians deduce that Jesus favored polygamy, at least not without an additional revelation. The fundamental problem facing Muslim theologians vis-à-vis the morality of slavery is that *Muhammad bought, sold, captured, and owned slaves*.[200]

Like Moses, the Prophet did advise that slaves be treated well: "[F]eed them what you eat yourself and clothe them with what you wear . . . They are God's people like unto you and be kind unto them."[201] Muhammad also freed several of his slaves, adopted one as his son, and married another. In addition, the Qur'ān teaches that it is wrong to "compel your slave girls to prostitution" (*24.33*), and that one can gain forgiveness for killing a fellow believer by freeing a slave (*4.92*). As with the Jewish rules about slavery, Muhammad's admonition and example probably often mitigated the conditions of slaves in Islam as contrasted with Greece and Rome. But the fundamental morality of the institution of slavery was not in doubt. While Christian theologians were able to work their way around the biblical acceptance of slavery, they probably could not have done so had Jesus kept slaves.[202] That Muhammad had owned slaves presented Muslim theologians with a fact that no intellectual maneuvering could overcome, even had they desired to do so.

Explaining Abolition Movements

When slaves began to reappear in Europe in the fifteenth century, their presence aroused what can only be called nascent abolition movements. In 1444, when a boatload of African slaves was put on sale in Lagos, Portugal, the crowd became so upset by the sight of families being separated and sold that they stopped the proceedings.[203] When a Dutch slave-trader brought a cargo to the Netherlands in 1596, the local council, prompted by enraged citizens, pronounced all of the slaves to be free—after that, Dutch slavers kept their activities abroad.[204] The sight of slaves on the streets of Paris aroused public disturbances.[205] Upon seeing the slave market in Jamaica early in the eighteenth century, an English admiral wrote an angry and disgusted letter about buyers picking over human beings "as if they had been so many horses."[206]

What these reactions suggest is that direct contact with slavery proved intolerable for many Christians not personally involved in exploiting slaves. Indeed, the fundamental thesis of the remainder of this chapter is this: *Organized opposition to slavery arose only when and where (1) the appropriate moral predisposition was (2) stimulated by the salience of the phenomenon and (3) was not counteracted by perceived self-interest.* The first element explains why indigenous abolition movements have yet to appear in non-Christian nations. The second accounts for the fact that abolition movements were limited to places where people felt some direct responsibility for the existence of slavery, as in the United States, Latin America, and those European nations directly involved in colonial slavery. The third element explains why abolition movements did *not* prosper in the American South or in European colonies.

To fully explore this thesis, I will trace the rise of the abolition movement in the United States. Then, I trace its career in Great Britain and in France. Finally, I explore abolition in Spain and Latin America.

America

On June 19, 1700, Samuel Sewall (*1652–1730*), published *The Selling of Joseph*, the first abolitionist tract written in America. Sewall was an extremely prominent Bostonian—a devout Puritan, a graduate of Harvard, a successful merchant, and a well-known judge who had served on the court during the Salem witchcraft trials, something for which he later offered his public repentance. Despite his social stature, Sewall's attack on slavery "was simply ignored by his contemporaries."[207]

This example demonstrates a fundamental sociological principle: *publications don't launch social movements; people do.* They do so by bringing their friends, relatives, neighbors, and associates together and motivating them to act in coordinated ways—to become an *organization.* This is most easily accomplished when one begins with a group that is already organized.

Consequently, the American abolition movement began not in Boston but fifty-four years later at the Philadelphia Yearly Meeting of the Quakers, prompted by another abolitionist tract. This one was by John Woolman (*1720–1772*), a very pious young man whose moral concerns about slavery surfaced when he was asked by his employer to draw up a bill of sale for a female slave. He did so but experienced unrelieved guilt as a result. Woolman's concerns about slavery grew critical when, while traveling through Virginia, he observed the misery of slaves. Upon his return, he wrote his first tract against the "sin of slavery." However, rather than merely reflecting the opinion of its author, *Some Considerations on the Keeping of Negroes* was officially approved by the Meeting's Overseers of the Press and circulated to everyone in attendance. Woolman's pamphlet[208] was a model of gentle Quaker persuasion. He began by quoting Matt. 25:40: "For as much as ye did it to the least of my brethren, ye did it unto me," with the direct implication that to enslave a "Negro" was to enslave Christ. Although clearly aimed at slaveholding Quakers, it did not single them out but reminded *all* Quakers that "Negroes are our fellow creatures, and their present condition amongst us requires our serious consideration," and that Friends are committed to justice, love, and the betterment of all humankind, not to self-interest. In his final paragraph he expressed his belief that while God has so far not intervened, he sees that "[Negroes] are trodden down and despised, yet he remembers them: he seeth their affliction," and soon God is apt to "humble the most haughty people" who prefer "gain . . . to equity." Subsequently, Woolman devoted his life to spreading the message of abolition, which he based exclusively on religious objections.

It is significant that Woolman had actually written his tract in 1746 but knew better than to bring it forward then because the Overseers of the Press included a majority of slave-owners. By 1754, membership had changed such that only a third of the Overseers were slaveholders. Moreover, the proportion of slave-owners among those sent as representatives to the Yearly Meeting had recently dropped from more than half to only 10 percent.[209] Hence Woolman's message did not confront invincible self-interest but gained considerable acceptance, and by the next year the Meeting agreed to publish a tract of its own, constituting a far more direct attack on slavery: *An Epistle of Caution and Advice, Concerning the Buying and Keeping of Slaves*.

Written by a committee, this statement began by asking whether it was consistent with the Golden Rule to deprive "our fellow creatures of that valuable blessing liberty," or to "grow rich by their bondage." It further proclaimed, "To live in ease and plenty by the toil of those whom violence and cruelty have put in our power, is neither consistent with Christianity nor common justice, and we have good reason to believe draws down the displeasure of Heaven . . . How can we be said to love our brethren and . . . for selfish ends keep them in bondage?"

Then, having pursued some similar lines of concern, the committee got to the clincher: "Finally, brethren, we entreat you in . . . Gospel love, seriously to weigh the cause of detaining them in bondage. If it be for your own private gain, or any motive other than their good, it is much to be feared that the love of God, and the influence of the Holy Spirit is not the prevailing principle in you."[210]

In addition to circulating this tract, the Yearly Meeting also appointed a correspondence committee to inquire of local Meetings whether their members were "clear of importing and buying Negroes"; efforts were to be directed toward convincing those guilty of such actions that they were in the wrong. In response, several local Meetings began to disown such offenders. Next, in 1758 the Yearly Meeting appointed a five-man committee "to visit and treat with all such Friends who have any Slaves" and to report back on their progress. Finally, in the early 1770s, Quaker Yearly Meetings in New England, New York, New Jersey, and Pennsylvania prohibited members from owning slaves, under penalty of exclusion. Thus was launched the American abolition movement.[211]

David Brion Davis was correct to note that a number of non-Quaker voices were also being raised against slavery at this same time, both in America and abroad.[212] But, as Davis recognized, "voices" are not movements. The Quakers were not just a bunch of like-minded people who read and agreed with antislavery tracts. Their approach to abolition was potent because from the start they committed their well-organized and influential religious body to the cause. Their initial aim was to purge themselves of slave-ownership, and in this they were mainly successful. While some Quaker slave-owners abandoned their church rather than comply, most went along, including owners of some extremely large plantations.[213] But just as the Friends hoped eventually to achieve the salvation of all humankind, so, too, did they aim to end slavery everywhere. They came much closer to doing the latter than most sophisticated persons would have anticipated at the time (or than many modern sophisticates are inclined to admit).

One reason for their success was that, despite having begun as a despised sect (between 1659 and 1661 four Quakers who had previously been whipped and driven out of Massachusetts for "heresy" were hanged for having returned), American Quakers had achieved great economic and political power. Many of the wealthiest people of the time were Quakers, some of whom, such as John Pemberton, purchased the freedom of many slaves. Remember, too, that Philadelphia was the largest city in the American colonies and served as the nation's capital until Washington, D.C., was built. Also indicative of Quaker influence: in 1787 the Quaker-inspired Pennsylvania Society for Promoting the Abolition of Slavery was headed by Benjamin Franklin and Benjamin Rush, two of the most respected and influential living Americans. What such people said, mattered. Moreover, the Quakers posed a moral challenge to other Christian organizations. The Puritans could easily ignore Samuel Sewall, but could they let the Quakers monopolize the moral high ground? Surely not, said the Puritan majority in the Massachusetts legislature in 1771 as they outlawed the importation of slaves.

Not to be outdone, many Christian groups and luminaries took up the cause of abolition, and soon abolitionist societies sprang up that were not associated with a specific denomination. But, through it all, the movement (as distinct from those it made sympathetic to the cause) was staffed by devout Christian activists, the majority of them clergy.[214] Indeed, the most prominent clergy of the nineteenth century took leading roles in the abolition movement, including the liberal Congregationalist Lyman Beecher (*1775–1863*), whose daughter wrote *Uncle Tom's Cabin*; the most potent evangelist of the era, Charles Grandison Finney (*1792–1885*), who turned Oberlin College into a key station along the "underground railroad" conveying runaway slaves to Canada; and even John Humphrey Noyes (*1811–1886*), the most prominent "Perfectionist" of them all and founder of the "notorious" Oneida communal group.

In 1833 leading abolitionists formed the American Anti-Slavery Society.[215] Led by the fiery agitator and editor of *The Liberator*, William Lloyd Garrison (*1805–1879*), the group adopted and published a ringing Declaration of Sentiments, filled with religious justifications. Noting that to hold a human being "in involuntary bondage" is, "according to Scripture" stealing, the document proclaimed it a certainty that "the slaves ought instantly to be set free, and brought under the protection of law."

Furthermore, all current laws "admitting the right of slavery, are therefore, before God, utterly null and void . . . an audacious usurpation of Divine prerogative" and "a presumptuous transgression of all the holy commandments." Nevertheless, the group accepted "the sovereignty of each State" and conceded "that Congress . . . has no right to interfere with any slave States." But the declaration maintained that Congress had both the right and the obligation to end slave-trading between states, and to outlaw slavery in all territories. In conclusion, they placed their faith "in the overruling justice of God": "we plant ourselves upon the Declaration of our Independence and the truths of Divine Revelation, as upon the Everlasting Rock."[216]

The American Anti-Slavery Society grew rapidly. Within two years there were 400 local chapters, and by 1838 there were more than 1,000. Although Garrison himself often found it difficult to get along with clergy,[217] they formed the vital spine of his organization. The society spread and grew through the efforts of traveling agents appointed to supervise specific territories, aided by local agents established in major population centers. John A. Auping collected data on all 155 traveling agents and all 149 local agents who served the American Anti-Slavery Society during the period of its great expansion, 1834 through 1840. Eighty-one of the traveling agents, or 52 percent, were ordained ministers. And of the local agents, 111, or 75 percent, were clergy.[218]

Moreover, as abolition sentiments spread, it was primarily the churches (often local congregations), not secular clubs and organizations, that issued formal statements on behalf of ending slavery.[219] The outspoken abolitionism expressed by Northern congregations and denominational gatherings caused major schisms within leading Protestant denominations, eventuating in their separation into independent Northern and Southern organizations; this was the origin of the Southern Baptists, the Southern Methodists, and the Southern Presbyterians. The Congregationalists didn't split because they had no churches south of Connecticut.

The American Roman Catholic Church faced no serious internal conflict over slavery because it had few Southern parishes, and, at least by the start of the nineteenth century, the clergy followed the pope in opposing slavery. At the Congress of Vienna in 1815, Pope Pius VII (1800 to 1823) demanded the suppression of the slave trade. Then, in 1839, Pope Gregory XVI (1831 to 1846) sent an Apostolic Letter to the Provincial Council of American Bishops in which he condemned slavery. It began with a fine example of theological "deduction." In his opening paragraph the pope admitted that the Apostles counseled slaves to obey their masters, but went on to note (as Woolman had also done) that just as Christ declared that whatever was done to the least of all humans, it was done to Him, "it naturally follows" that Christians should treat slaves as their brothers. He then pointed out that "In the process of time, the fog of pagan superstition being more completely dissipated and the manners of barbarous people having been softened, thanks to Faith operating by Charity . . . there are no more slaves in the greater number of Christian nations." Unfortunately, there were "among the Faithful" men who were "shamefully blinded by their desire for sordid gain," and who went to distant countries and there "did not hesitate to reduce to slavery Indians, Negroes and other wretched people." Then, "desiring to remove such a shame from all Christian nations" and "walking in the footsteps of Our Predecessors," the pope demanded an end to slavery.[220]

Subsequently, the American secretary of state, John Forsyth, campaigning in the South during 1840 for the renomination of President Martin Van Buren, identified the pope as an abolitionist to enlist anti-Catholic sentiments. To this, Bishop John England of Charleston, South Carolina, responded that although the Church regarded slavery as sinful, it intended to leave legal issues concerning the matter to the legislative bodies of government. England had reason to be somewhat circumspect, since in 1836 mob violence had forced him to close the school for free blacks he had opened in his diocese the year before.[221] But the bishop's statement failed to defuse the rapidly rising anti-Catholicism—rioting Protestants in Philadelphia during the summer of 1844 burned down the two largest Catholic churches in the city. Indeed, the Catholic Church was so associated with abolition in the eyes of the pro-slavery forces that Charles Finney, the famous evangelist and an early president of Oberlin College, recalled that the school had been boycotted on grounds that its racial views were even "worse than those of Roman Catholicism."[222] Be that as it may, as demonstrated by John Hammond's splendid analysis, Finney's revivals had a profound effect on generating membership in the various antislavery societies, as well as support for the Liberty Party in 1844 and the Free Soil Party in 1848.[223]

The larger point is that the abolitionists, whether popes or evangelists, spoke almost exclusively in the language of Christian faith. And although many Southern clergy proposed theological defenses of slavery, pro-slavery rhetoric was overwhelmingly secular—references were made to "liberty" and "states' rights," not to "sin" or "salvation." This was conclusively demonstrated by Auping, who performed a content analysis of writings by randomly selected samples of prominent abolitionists and defenders of slavery. The abolitionists were many times more likely to invoke God, and the difference persisted even when only clergy were compared.[224] This is hardly surprising, since even the most extreme Marxist historians agree that the abolition movement was initiated and sustained by religious people. Of course, as will be seen, these Marxists also claim that when religious people condemned slavery on religious grounds, they were insincere or victims of false consciousness.

But there is another and far more persuasive tack taken to minimize the importance of religion in abolishing slavery. It is argued that many sincere Christians were quite able to square slavery with theology—as Francis Asbury, first Methodist bishop of the United States, put it in 1798, "Methodists, Baptists, Presbyterians . . . in the highest flights of rapturous piety, still maintain and defend [slavery]."[225] This being the case, the argument goes, it must have been not religion per se but something *else* that prompted some Christians to conclude that it was a sin to hold humans in bondage. But, as Asbury was fully aware, that conclusion misses the point. The case against slavery is theological, not revelational. Had Moses been given a commandment against slavery, then only heretical Jews and Christians could have owned slaves. Or had Jesus proclaimed that no slave master shall enter heaven, there would have been no ambiguity as to what Christians must do. But theology is based on human interpretations, and therefore sincere and brilliant seekers may reach opposite conclusions. Asbury did not propose that those who accepted slavery were ignorant of revelations, but that they had drawn incorrect theological conclusions, that they had neither "a sufficient sense of religion nor of liberty."

Abolition was not inherent in Christian scripture; it was only a *possible* conclusion and one unlikely to be reached except under favorable circumstances. Put another way, I do not propose that monotheism or even Christian culture was a *sufficient* basis for deeming slavery to be a sin. Instead, I propose that it was a *necessary* basis, in that only those religious thinkers working within the Christian tradition were able to reach antislavery conclusions (with the exceptions of the two Jewish sects). But just as I noted that belief in a rational, creator God was a necessary but not sufficient cause for the rise of science (that substantial technological and intellectual progress was needed too), here the *moral potential* for an antislavery conclusion lay within Christian thought, but to bring it to fruition probably required exposure to and perhaps experience with correlative concepts such as freedom and the dignity of the individual—with the general moral and political trends of Western civilization. Indeed, as noted, European Christians had the unique opportunity to live in a "world" without slaves, giving them a vantage point from which to view slavery, free of preconceptions as to its normality.

Keep in mind, too, that I do not suggest that the abolition movement eventually enrolled so many Americans that Lincoln was elected president. Relatively few Americans actually joined any abolition organization, and many factors influenced the rise of the Republican Party and Lincoln's nomination and election in 1860. However, contrary to the revisionist views of such Progressive historical stalwarts as Charles Beard, the Civil War was primarily about slavery, not about the economic interests of the industrial North versus those of the agricultural South. It reveals much about the Progressive historians that none of his peers thought it strange that, as he disdained the religious motives of the abolitionists, Beard blamed religious influences for sustaining Southern pro-slavery opinions.[226] But at least Beard did not deny that emancipation would have been worth fighting for, as did several other distinguished historians of the time, including Avery O. Craven, who blamed the Civil War on reckless moral agitators on both sides, concluding that the war was a needless blunder and slavery not worth fighting over.[227]

Even so, Craven was correct in seeing that the Civil War was not primarily about factory systems versus plantation systems, but about moral visions. Few "Yankee" soldiers had any connection with industry, and most "Rebels" owned no slaves. Blue or Gray, idealism was rampant! And it was for causing this moral confrontation that the abolitionists deserve full credit. Their decades of exhortation, from the pulpit and the public podium, prompted Union regiments to march away singing, "Mine eyes have seen the glory of the coming of the Lord . . ."

The achievement of emancipation in America is a long and complex story, involving intense political crises and compromises and eventually a very bloody war, in which one Union soldier died for every ten slaves who were set free. I have not presumed even to summarize these events in such a short study, being concerned only to provide an adequate account of aspects pertinent to my thesis. To sum up: organized opposition to slavery arose (1) as a matter of conscience among Quakers having (2) personal contact with slavery, but (3) who were not slaveholders, although their moral suasion did cause some Quakers to give up their slaves. Raised to the more general level, (1) abolitionism spread through the Christian churches in the North, sustained by moral indignation, (2) inflamed not only by the existence of slavery in the nearby South but by the testimony of ex-slaves and the predations of agents who captured and, often, kidnapped runaway slaves all across the North. Finally, (3) very few people in the North profited directly from slaves. Thus the abolitionists were well situated to confront slavery from a close, but *external vantage point.* As will be seen, all major abolition movements in Europe and in Latin America enjoyed such a vantage point.

In contrast, although the vast majority of Southerners were active Christians and did not own slaves, most of them regarded slavery as a matter of self-interest, as being basic to the Southern economy and culture, and it was this that stimulated the rise of an intense countermorality in which religion also played the sustaining role.[228] In that fervent spirit they rode off eagerly to defend "Dixie" and the Southern Way of Life.

Finally, the abolitionists knew that theirs was a religious movement, and so did several generations of historians.[229] But during the latter half of the twentieth century, many historians decided they knew better. I leave the Marxist revisionism for later consideration. But it seems appropriate here to clarify misconceptions perpetrated by historians whose failure to see things as they were lay mainly in their antagonism toward religion in general, and the Roman Catholic Church in particular. Once again David Brion Davis can serve as the edifying example.

Davis posed the critical issue concerning the role of religion in abolitionism in two sentences: "For some two thousand years men thought of sin as a kind of slavery. One day they would come to think of slavery as sin."[230] But he made no effort to say *why* this switch took place. Having devoted many pages to demonstrating that those who led the way to abolition overwhelmingly were devout Christians, all of whom said, in one fashion or another, that they were doing it for God, Davis chose not to believe them. In my judgment, Davis reached this conclusion because he failed to grasp the problematic character of theology, and because he denied or overlooked the actual history of Christian responses to slavery. Thus Davis asserted that Christian theologians, and especially the Catholic Church, could not "question the ethical basis of slavery . . . [because] that would be to question fundamental conceptions of God's purpose and man's history and destiny. If slavery were an evil and performed no divinely appointed function, then why had God authorized it in Scripture and permitted it to exist in nearly every nation?"[231]

Liberation. A Yankee soldier cuts the "hobble" chain from this woman who has escaped from slavery, her infant in her arms. Before the Civil War was over, one Union soldier died for every ten slaves set free. © Bettmann/CORBIS.

This argument is plausible only if one fails to see that it *must* have been possible for Christians to question the ethical basis of slavery because *so many of them did so*. As is often the case with academic intellectuals, Davis failed to grasp how creative and subtle theologians can be at finding grounds to justify a desired conclusion—recall the logical elegance of Pope Gregory XVI's Apostolic Letter. Worse yet, because Davis had imputed a monolithic social and moral character to Christianity, whenever he encountered indifference or pro-slavery sentiments on the part of anyone connected to the churches, all stood indicted. Moreover, whenever religious leaders recognized the limits of their power and influence and settled for attempting to humanize the conditions of slavery, Davis disdained their efforts as complicity. By this logic, Christianity could not be given credit for providing the essential moral basis for opposition to slavery unless a huge Ecumenical Conference had been held at which slavery was denounced as a sin by a unanimous vote, accompanied by ordeals of penance for its having been condoned in times past. That not having taken place, Davis was unable to grasp that the conviction that slavery was a sin originated among *some* Christians, *because* they were Christians. It did not trouble them that some other Christians might disagree. Just as none of the thousands of Christian sects and factions that arose through the centuries suffered from doubt because others disagreed with them, so, too, the Christian abolitionists. And, in this case, virtue prevailed.

Great Britain

It was from their American cousins that British Quakers gained enthusiasm for abolition, and they, too, provided the initial religious backbone of the antislavery movement. However, these British forces achieved their goal far sooner than did abolition forces in America. There were two main reasons. First, because nearly all of the British slave-owners lived in distant colonies, their political influence was limited. Second, the British government was far more centralized and far less representative than government in America. Thus party elites could enact laws with considerable impunity in comparison with the United States, where many actions required local, not national, legislation, and where even Congress was an unruly body, often unable to reach any consensus. These are the themes I now pursue.[232]

In 1783, at the request of the Quakers of Philadelphia, the London Meeting for Sufferings was established by British Quakers. Thus, as in America, the Quakers provided a solid organizational basis for British opposition to slavery: volunteers, meeting places, and money. These efforts were greatly amplified in 1787 with the formation of the Society for the Abolition of the Slave Trade, in which other Protestant nonconformists joined with the Quakers. The aged John Wesley (*1703–1791*), founder of Methodism, undertook a preaching campaign against slavery, echoing many of the ideas he had so forcefully expressed in his 1774 abolitionist tract, *Thoughts on Slavery.*[233] Wesley's actions added the substantial resources of his Methodist chapels to the rapidly growing religious coalition for abolition. It was also at this time that the British abolition movement gained its two most important recruits.

William Wilberforce (*1759–1833*) was the father of Bishop Samuel Wilberforce (Chapter 2) and a member of Parliament from Yorkshire. He belonged to a very strict and influential evangelical group within the Church of England known as the Clapham Sect. Probably the only reason these evangelicals did not leave the Church of England was that at this time only members of that denomination had full civil rights, including the exclusive right to serve in the House of Commons. Upon embracing the abolitionists, Wilberforce assumed responsibility for guiding antislavery efforts in the House of Commons, where he enjoyed a close relationship with Prime Minister William Pitt.

Thomas Clarkson (*1760–1846*) attended Cambridge, where he prepared to enter the clergy. Having been ordained a deacon, he competed for an essay prize on the subject "Is it right to make slaves of others against their will?" Grappling with this question led Clarkson to discard "his considerable prospects of ecclesiastical preferment" within the Church of England, to devote his life entirely to the cause of abolition.[234] In his own words, there "never was any cause . . . so great and important . . . never was there one in which the duty of Christian charity could be so extensively exercised; never one, more worthy of the devotion of a whole life towards it."[235] Clarkson soon assumed responsibility for mobilizing public opinion. To this end he built a network of local organizations and activists on the preexisting framework of Quaker congregations, traveling an estimated thirty-three thousand miles on horseback, crisscrossing England again and again between 1787 and 1792. The most visible fruit of all this effort was a petition campaign, calling on Parliament to end the slave trade. During 1786–1787 Clarkson's efforts produced petitions signed by at least sixty thousand English men[236]—eleven thousand from Manchester alone (where about two-thirds of the adult males signed).

These petitions gave Wilberforce powerful ammunition to use in Parliament, and during 1792 it looked as if legislation prohibiting the slave trade would pass the Commons. However, the outbreak of the French Revolution and of war with France thwarted the abolition efforts. In fact, at the height of British outrage over the brutal excesses taking place in France, Wilberforce was briefly accused of radical sympathies. With the defeat of Napoleon's fleet at Trafalgar in 1805, the British seized the French colonies in the Caribbean. At this point a renewed campaign for abolition arose but was unable to gain sufficient votes in Commons to pass a bill abolishing slavery. At this juncture Wilberforce changed tactics and convinced Pitt to impose a ban on the slave trade in the French colonies by administrative decree under his powers to regulate trade in captured territories. Pitt died five months later. When a new government was formed, with Lord Grenville as prime minister and Charles Fox as leader of the House of Commons, it was discovered that a majority in the cabinet favored abolition. So in 1807 a bill abolishing the slave trade throughout the British colonies was approved by overwhelming majorities in both the House of Lords and the House of Commons. Not content with being out of the slave trade themselves, the British used diplomacy and even bribery to cause other nations to sign treaties prohibiting the transportation of slaves from Africa to the New World. More than that, the British formed and financed a special naval squadron to patrol the African coast and enforce these treaties. During the next fifty years, the British navy seized nearly sixteen hundred slave ships, many of them with cargoes of slaves, but even those without slaves on board were taken if they were equipped to transport slaves. Altogether, the British liberated more than 150,000 slaves from ships at sea.[237]

However, ending the slave trade did not abolish slavery in the British colonies; it merely prevented more slaves from being brought in. Hence a new British society was formed to pursue complete abolition: The Society for the Mitigation and Gradual Abolition of Slavery Throughout the British Dominions. Once again Clarkson toured the country renewing and energizing local organizations. A new petition campaign was organized; as political developments came to a head in 1833, the abolitionists produced more than 1.5 million signers, about half of the adult male population of England.[238] These efforts were augmented by the work of Methodist and Baptist missionaries among the slaves in the West Indies—the Church of England still held back. Public opinion in Britain continued to be stirred by reports from the missionaries that "described the threats and harassments they suffered at the hands of planters and lent authenticity to the growing view, not only among Methodists but throughout the evangelical churches that West Indian planters were a corrupt class."[239]

In response, the planters in the colonies warned that emancipation would cost investors in Britain catastrophic losses, and pointed out that everyone in Britain would pay because the price of sugar would rise greatly if it had to be produced by free labor. These appeals carried weight in the House of Lords—in those days the Lords were not a figurehead, and their agreement was needed for all legislation. To gain this agreement, abolitionists in the House of Commons accepted provisions in the Emancipation Act to compensate the planters by an enormous sum—equal to half of the British annual budget. The act thus passed in 1833, a month after the death of William Wilberforce, providing that on August 1, 1834, slavery would cease in all British colonies. The direct cost to individual British citizens was substantial, both in terms of taxes to buy off the planters (and continuing support of naval operations against slave ships) and in a higher cost of living—the price of sugar did rise sharply, as had been predicted. Indeed, the costs of emancipation were so high that Seymour Drescher characterized the British abolition of slavery as voluntary "econocide."[240]

From the beginning to the end, Quakers had played a pivotal role in British abolition organizations, and nearly all of the other leading abolitionists were devout members of nonconformist religious groups—especially the Methodists and Baptists. Nevertheless, revisionist historians have attempted to dismiss religious influences. Their most frequently used argument is that while religious people may have begun the British abolition movement, it succeeded only because it caught on in purely secular quarters, as evidenced by the huge success of the petition campaign. Particular emphasis is given to the overwhelming response of men in Manchester in signing petitions. Manchester was a leading industrial city, and it has been proposed that its workers were somehow "the least parochial in Great Britian," committed to market principles and free trade. Thus it was "Manchester rather than the Quaker religious network [that] pushed Britain across the psychological threshold into the abolitionist era."[241]

There are many flaws in this interpretation. First of all, nothing in its industrial, economic, or cultural makeup distinguished Manchester from several other English cities, aside from its response to the abolition petition. Claims to the contrary are invariably vague and offered without evidence. Second, it presumes that workingmen in Manchester were not influenced by religious motives, as though only clergy and full-time religious activists could be so motivated. But there is no reason to suppose that most people in Manchester so compartmentalized their faith that it had no influence on their "political" judgments. Besides, the petition campaign was presented primarily not as a political matter but as a moral obligation. In addition, it strikes me that the one very significant way that Manchester *was* different was that in 1787, just before the immense local response to the antislavery petitions, John Wesley, the most effective evangelist of the day, preached a revival against slavery in Manchester, and the local Methodists, breaking with the denominational policy of not participating in politics, joined in circulating the petition.[242] It would have been astonishing if these developments had not galvanized local support!

Third, to minimize the importance of those who popularized antislavery attitudes and who circulated the abolitionist petitions, and to credit instead the signers as the true basis of British abolitionism, is to transpose cause and effect. Granted that neither the Quakers nor their nonconformist allies could have achieved the Emancipation Act had they failed to arouse public opinion. But without their organized and effective efforts to shape and arouse public opposition to slavery, nothing would have happened. Finally, claims that abolition was a secular achievement have created a silly and unnecessary "mystery," as is illustrated by Howard Temperley's reflections on the motivations of British abolitionists:

> The British anti-slavery movement has continued to intrigue historians, not the least because of the apparent lack of self-interest on the part of its principal supporters. This is so contrary to conventional views of political behavior that it has given rise to scholarly controversy. Yet in spite of the exercise of much ingenuity, no one has succeeded in showing that those who campaigned for the end of the slave trade and then for the freeing of the slaves stood to gain personally in any tangible way, or that these measures were other than economically costly to the country. In due course Britain's anti-slavery achievements came to be viewed with pride as expressing the nation's commitment to humane and liberal principles.[243]

Temperley's paragraph recapitulates "respectable," recent historiography. After considerable dithering and many flirtations with unfounded Marxist notions that emancipation was indeed an act of economic self-interest, historians have been driven to accept the idea that an immense quotient of idealism was involved. They have come to terms with this conclusion by asserting that these were "liberal principles," thereby averting a return to the "incorrect" belief that the idealism was of religious character. But this requires that we ignore the unanimous testimony of the people who actually accomplished the deed! Those who brought about abolition in Britain quoted not "liberal principles" but the Bible. They talked about sin and about God's saving grace.

France

At first glance it might appear that the abolition movement in France really was based on "liberal principles." However, once allowances are made for the fact that the French abolitionists never appealed for mass support, it was as much of a result of religious concerns as were the American and British movements. Indeed, the three movements were directly connected.[244]

In 1793 Commissioner Léger Félicité Sonthonax of Saint Domingue, an appointee of the revolutionary government of France, declared the abolition of slavery in that colony. He did this in response to the successful slave rebellion that had raged since 1791, and the threats of invasion by the British and the Spanish. His hope was that emancipation would enable him to enlist the support of both ex-slaves and the rebels to help defend the colony. When word of this action reached France, the Jacobin-controlled National Convention not only supported it but abolished slavery in all French colonies. In taking this action members of the convention condemned slavery as a relic of the monarchy and inconsistent with their revolutionary values. That they did not act until four years after the Revolution had occurred, and only when informed of the need for slave allies to defend the colonies, suggests that radical idealism alone might not have sufficed. In any event, in 1802 Napoleon reinstituted slavery in the French colonies. As noted, when the British subsequently took the French colonies in the Caribbean, Pitt prohibited them from importing slaves. However, after the final defeat of Napolean, the Caribbean colonies were returned to France, and the importation of slaves resumed. During the next fifteen years approximately 125,000 new slaves arrived in the French Caribbean.[245] It was not until February 22, 1831, that the French passed an effective law against the slave trade; the abolition of slavery did not occur until 1848.

With British help, an abolition society, the Société des Amis des Noirs (the Society of Friends of Blacks), was founded in France in 1788, just prior to the Revolution. Thomas Clarkson spent considerable time in France helping to form the group, and much of its literature consisted of British pamphlets translated into French. These were appropriate since the French abolitionists also stressed that slavery was wrong on religious grounds. Although the Amis des Noirs never had more than 150 members, many of them were famous, including the philosopher Antoine de Condorcet and the French hero of the American Revolution, the marquis de Lafayette. Unfortunately, as the French Revolution turned on itself, the Amis des Noirs were identified with the Girondist faction and were condemned to death by Robespierre in the spring of 1793—the leaders went to the guillotine, Condorcet committed suicide in prison, and Lafayette fled to Austria. A few survivors resumed meeting later in the decade but were "finally suppressed in 1799 when Napoleon came to power . . . It would be two decades before a society devoted to ending the slave trade and slavery in the French colonies would emerge once again within France."[246]

In 1821 the Société de la Morale Chrétienne (the Society of Christian Morals) was founded. As was evident in its name, the agenda of this group was inspired by religious concerns, and these included abolition of the slave trade. Like the Amis des Noirs, this was a very small group (at its peak it had 338 members), but they composed an even more illustrious elite, including the soon-to-be king, Louis Philippe. They, too, circulated a petition and in 1825 presented it to the government; the petition's 130 signatures were all from people said to be "foremost citizens."[247] In any event, slave-trading was outlawed in 1831, close on the heels of the July Monarchy that brought Louis Philippe to the throne.

The French were soon cooperating fully with the British to capture slave ships sailing from Africa. But, of course, that left slavery intact in the French Caribbean. So in August 1834 French abolitionists formed another group, the Société Française pour l'Abolition de l'Esclavage (French Society for the Abolition of Slavery). It, too, was very small, probably never exceeding 92 members.[248] But it also was a very elite group, made up of leading notables and nobility, and "would operate largely as an appendage to the Chamber of Deputies."[249] Even so, the group had a higher percentage of Protestants than the national average, and nonconformist British abolitionists exerted a considerable influence on the group, despite the fact that the vast majority of members were active Catholics. In addition, more than half of the members were of noble birth, and many of them were well placed in the government. Among them was the distinguished Alexis de Tocqueville (*1805–1859*), recently back from his tour of America. In 1839, on behalf of the Société, Tocqueville submitted an emancipation proposal to the French Chamber of Deputies. It was modeled on the British Emancipation Act and would have provided compensation of 150 million francs to French slave-owners. But the proposal was tabled, and subsequently so were many others of a similar kind.

During the 1840s, with financial support from British abolitionists, the Société began to expand its scope.[250] In 1844 they submitted a new antislavery petition to the government including about 7,000 signatures from Parisians. In response, King Louis Philippe freed all slaves belonging to the Crown. At this point the Catholic Church entered the campaign, calling for immediate emancipation of all French slaves and circulating a new petition. Many of the 11,000 citizens who signed were Catholic priests. Backed by the archbishop of Paris, the Catholic newspaper *L'Univers* joined the battle against slavery, and in 1848 these efforts succeeded when the July Monarchy was replaced by a provisional government prior to the formation of the Second Republic. The emancipation decree passed by the provisional regime freed all slaves within two months of its proclamation and compensated slave-owners at a rate of half the value of each slave, at a cost of 6 million francs in cash and 120 million in 5 percent bonds. Thus, as in Britain, emancipation came at a very substantial cost to all taxpayers.

It has often been remarked that the organized abolition movements in France were tiny and elitist. But in this era France was not a democracy: appeals to popular support not only lacked relevance; they could have severely damaged the cause. From Napoleon on, French governments sought to minimize mobilization of the public, believing, probably correctly, that this was but an invitation to disorder and revolution. Hence mass abolition appeals would have been repressed; success required convincing the French political elite to act. It would be quite wrong to interpret this as evidence that ideals and religious convictions were irrelevant or, at most, window dressing. *Why* did the French elite take this action? It could not have been self-interest, since, as with the British, emancipation of slaves in the French colonies was achieved at a considerable cost that fell most heavily on those who brought it about. Nothing so clearly demonstrates that ideals matter than such an example of idealism in action.

It should also be noted that there is a religious "trail" linking the American, British, and French abolition movements: American Quakers initiated abolitionism among their coreligionists in Britain, whereupon John Wesley's commitment of his British Methodists to abolition influenced American Methodists. Then, it was devout British abolitionists who initiated and partly funded the French abolition movement.

Spain and Latin America

By the time the Sociedad Abolicionista Española (Spanish Abolition Society) was organized in 1865, it was very late in the day. Slaves had been free in the British colonies for more than thirty years, in the French colonies for nearly twenty, and in the Dutch colonies for two; on April 9 of that year, Lee had surrendered to Grant, and all American slaves became free. Only Spanish colonial slavery remained, along with slavery in Brazil, which had by then thrown off Portuguese rule.

Those seeking a secular abolition movement can point to Spain, where religion served as little more than an implicit moral basis and to provide a vocabulary of obligation. Historians of Spanish abolitionism quite properly stress the role of emerging liberal and radical political movements in Spain as well as in the colonies.[251] But these historians fail to give adequate regard to Spain's glaring economic and military weaknesses. It seems very significant that it was antislavery activities in Puerto Rico that prompted the formation of an abolition society in Spain, and that the basis for Puerto Rican abolitionism was mainly its recent economic decline and anxieties about American expansionism. Local interests proposed that "an immediate transition to free labor would benefit the island's" depressed economy.[252] Although this proposal was based on faulty economic reasoning (which the slave-owners spotted at once), it had the effect of linking moral virtue to apparent self-interest. Indeed, visions of a renewed and powerful Spain were an explicit part of Spanish abolitionism, with its dual emphasis on the benefits of free labor and free trade.

Keep in mind that Spanish abolitionists played no role in the emancipation of slaves in most parts of Latin America, because Spain had long since lost its sovereignty over the continent to national liberation movements. Three factors linked most of these liberation movements to emancipation. First of all, aside from Brazil and several continental colonies along the Caribbean, Latin America did not have plantation economies, and slavery was always on a small scale—involved as much in consumption as in production. Second, nearly all who owned slaves opposed the liberation movements. Third, by proclaiming emancipation, liberation movements were able to enlist slaves in their cause—albeit the revolutionary leaders were probably entirely sincere in their opposition to slavery. As Latin American nations gained their independence, they opted for emancipation: Argentina in 1813, Columbia in 1814, Chile in 1823, Central America in 1824, Mexico in 1829, Bolivia in 1831, Ecuador in 1851, and Peru and Venezuela in 1854. Thus when it finally came, Spanish abolition activity was of very reduced scope, applying only to Spain's few remaining colonies, primarily Cuba and Puerto Rico.

The story of how the Spanish government emancipated the slaves in Puerto Rico (1873) and in Cuba (1886) is a complex tale of political turmoil and cycles of liberalization and repression. Through it all, of course, Spain was intensely aware, not only of its status as a slave-owning pariah in the eyes of other European nations, but of its economic and military weaknesses. In fact, a decade after the Spanish Cortes abolished slavery in Cuba, the United States seized all of Spain's Caribbean colonies as well as the Philippines.

Brazil became an independent nation in 1822, when Pedro I (son of King John VI of Portugal) proclaimed himself emperor. As a result, not only were the planters of Brazil the dominant economic and political influence; they could not be overruled by a European regime. Consequently, emancipation came very slowly. When it finally did so in 1888, three factors were involved.[253]

The first factor in ending Brazilian slavery was intense foreign pressure: "Brazilians [were] humiliated by condescending references to their country as the last Christian nation that tolerated slavery, on a level with 'backward' African and Asiatic slaveholding societies."[254] Indeed, it was only in response to British pressures that Brazil agreed to end its involvement in the Atlantic slave trade in 1831. And it was British patrols that eventually halted the illegal importation of slaves by Brazilians by 1853. The fall of the American Southern Confederacy came as a terrific political blow, depriving Brazil of a major ally—had the South won the Civil War, Brazil and the Spanish Caribbean colonies might have joined the Confederacy.[255]

The second factor was an increasingly militant abolition movement, fueled by young men educated abroad and by the very large and rapidly growing number of free blacks, the result of very liberal manumission terms (patterned on the *Código Negro Español*). As early as 1817, about 25 percent of the 2.3 million Brazilians of African descent were free. When emancipation came in 1888, slaves made up only about 5 percent of the total Brazilian labor force.[256]

The third factor was rapid economic development and population growth, which shifted political power away from the planters. Between 1840 and 1890, Brazil's population increased from 4 million to 14 million, a substantial part of the growth being immigrants from Europe.[257] Although cities absorbed much of this growth, immigration also provided a supply of agricultural labor that helped to convert some northern planters to abolitionism.[258] Meanwhile, the sugar and cotton plantations in the northern states fell upon economic hard times, and the active slavery zone shifted to the southern states where coffee was the primary crop—large numbers of slaves were relocated from north to south. Urbanization, industrialization, and a depressed sugar market eroded the political influence of the planters. In the end, the cities and the areas lacking significant dependence on plantations imposed emancipation on the slave-dependent south. Indicative of the reduced influence of the planters, they received no compensation when they were forced to give up their slaves.

Thus was slavery ended in Christendom. It was stopped by moral campaigns stimulated by the salience of the phenomenon—the sense of direct responsibility for its continuation. Of course, most humans not being unreserved moralists, the abolition movements succeeded where moral concerns were not complicated by perceptions of a substantial self-interest in slavery, although in America, Britain, and France people were willing to make considerable personal sacrifices on behalf of freeing the slaves. Nevertheless, in every case, a powerful nonslave area imposed abolition on a weaker slave-owning region. That is, the American abolitionists mobilized the North to free the slaves of the South; abolitionists in slave-free Britain convinced the government to outlaw slavery in its far-flung colonies; it was in metropolitan France that the fate of slavery in the French West Indies was decided; it was in Madrid, not in Havana or San Juan, that emancipation of Spain's Caribbean slaves was accomplished; and it was in Rio that Brazilian slaves were emancipated. In contrast, abolition movements made little or no headway in the southern regions of the United States and Brazil or in Europe's plantation colonies.

The "Enlightenment" and Slavery

It would please many contemporary scholars if the moral arguments for abolition had been a product of the "Enlightenment." Indeed, Peter Gay went so far as to claim that to have been the case, albeit he chided the *philosophes* for having been a bit too vague on the subject.[259] But even Gay's careful selectivity cannot hide the fact that a virtual Who's Who of "Enlightenment" figures fully accepted slavery. Thomas Hobbes (*1588–1679*) and John Locke (*1632–1704*) "openly sanctioned human bondage"[260]—Locke invested in the Atlantic slave trade.[261] Voltaire (*1694–1778*) wrote a nasty comment concerning Christians profiting from slavery, but he supported the slave trade and believed in the inferiority of Africans.[262] Baron Montesquieu (*1689–1755*) took pains to dismiss religious reasons in favor of slavery, only to pronounce it as justified by natural law. Comte de Mirabeau (*1748–1791*) accepted slavery, and so did Edmund Burke (*1729–1797*), who dismissed abolitionists as religious fanatics and explained that "the cause of humanity would be far more benefited by the continuance of the [slave] trade and servitude . . . than by the total destruction of both or either."[263] David Hume (*1711–1776*) did not favor abolition, although his neighbor and close friend Adam Smith (*1723–1790*) was a vehement opponent of slavery on both moral and economic grounds, as will be seen. Indeed, some others associated with the "Enlightenment" also supported abolition, including Denis Diderot (*1713–1784*), Anne-Robert-Jacques Turgot (*1727–1781*), Dr. Samuel

Johnson (*1709–1784*), and, of course, Condorcet (*1749–1794*). But most accepted slavery as a normal part of the human situation.[264] It was not philosophers or secular intellectuals who assembled the moral indictment of slavery, but the very people they held in such contempt: men and women having intense Christian faith, who opposed slavery because it was a sin. Thus, as mentioned in Chapter 2, it was the natural theologian William Paley, not his atheist opponent David Hume, who condemned slavery as an "odious institution" and did so on the basis of Christian "light and influence."[265]

Not only did the intellectuals of the "Enlightenment" fall far short of matching the extent and passion of abolitionist commitment spreading through religious circles at the same time; even had they been unanimously in favor of emancipation, their public support would have counted for far less than that of the Christian abolitionists. The reason is simple: in the course of human events, "voices" count for far less than organizations. The Quakers were few in number,[266] but they were not "voices"; they were *congregations*. They didn't merely express their views; they acted. Their undertakings were well funded, coordinated, well led, and designed to influence public opinion. Churches are always unusually effective in shaping public policy because they do not need to assemble organizations to pursue their aims; they are organizations-in-being. Indeed, abolition was only the most celebrated of many similar and effective religious campaigns—churches played a leading role in the women's suffrage movement and were the essential component of the civil rights movement in the American South.[267]

The Marxist Counterexplanation

Unbeknownst to most Marxist historians, their revisionist explanation of why the slaves "really" were freed is based on the work of the economist they most despise: Adam Smith. But Smith was wrong about the economics of slavery, and, consequently, so were (are) the Marxists.

Smith claimed that slavery is an inefficient mode of production in that slave labor costs more than the labor of free, hired individuals. Slaves have no profit motive but work only to the extent needed to avoid punishment—hence as slowly and carelessly as possible. But free workers can be rewarded in proportion to their production and will therefore exert themselves, mentally and physically. "It appears, accordingly, from the experience of all ages and nations, I believe, that the work done by freemen comes cheaper in the end than that performed by slaves."[268] Hence the wise planter would much prefer a system such as sharecropping to slavery.

As Smith's reputation grew, the conviction spread among intellectuals that slavery was contrary to good business practices—that slave plantations were far less profitable than they would be if they employed free laborers. This soon became the prevailing view among opponents of slavery. So much so that William Lloyd Garrison condemned what he deemed corrupt proposals that the American abolitionists shift the basis of their attack from "Christian duty" to issues of "the pocketbook."[269] On the eve of the Civil War, Hinton Rowan Helper argued that slavery was retarding Southern economic growth,[270] and Frederick Law Olmsted proclaimed Southern slave plantations to be an unprofitable investment.[271] Subsequent to the war this became the accepted academic wisdom on the matter—by the start of the twentieth century every "informed" person knew that Southern slavery had been on its last legs by the time the South seceded, and that had the planters been sober businessmen, not playboys, they would have abandoned slavery long before any war was necessary.

As Marxists took up the matter, these ideas escalated into the claim that it was not moral objections but capitalism that killed slavery! Not that capitalism led to sympathy for those held in bondage, of course. As Howard Temperley put it, "how could a philosophy which extolled the pursuit of individual self-interest have contributed, in the absence of any expectation of economic gain, to the achievement of so praiseworthy an object as the abolition of slavery?"[272] Or, in the words of David Brion Davis, the "paramount question" is this: how "did a seemingly liberal movement emerge and continue to win support from major government leaders in the period from 1790 to 1832, a period characterized both by political reaction and industrial revolution?"[273] The Marxist answer is that abolition was accomplished to replace the unprofitable, outmoded, precapitalist economic institution of slavery: the "real" aim of the abolitionists was to remove an impediment to the further development of capitalism.

The most forceful and original proponent of this view was Eric Williams, an economic historian who served as prime minister of Trinidad and Tobago from 1961 through 1981. He argued that the British attacked slavery in the West Indies because it was "so unprofitable that for this reason alone its destruction was inevitable."[274] Spelled out more fully,

Williams's argument was that the primary aim of emerging capitalism was to lower the cost of labor: being fully aware of Adam Smith's claim that slave labor was more expensive than hired labor, the British capitalists therefore backed abolition. Williams recognized that if he left it at that, his claim was obviously falsified by the fact that slavery in the West Indies was by no means ended by island capitalists seeking to increase their profits. To get around this snag, Williams dismissed the planters as "blind to all considerations and consequences except the maintenance of their diseased system."[275] But how could reduced labor costs in the West Indies benefit capitalists in Britain? By greatly lowering the cost of sugar: as this reduced the cost of living in Britain, employers would be able to reduce the wages of workers. As for religious motivations, Williams dismissed them as obviously insincere because, had they been authentic, the abolitionists would also have campaigned against colonialism and against the capitalist exploitation of free labor. From Williams's perspective, any true opponent of slavery would have fought against "wage slavery."

The economic aspects of Williams's thesis have long since been overwhelmed by the facts. First, it is well established that the planters were not foolish playboys or blind to economic realities; rather, slavery was *very* profitable, and for large-scale, labor-intensive forms of agriculture, slaves were far more productive than hired workers.[276] Second, as already noted and as fully anticipated by those who passed Britain's Emancipation Act, the economic costs of abolition were immense, and the domestic price of sugar rose sharply. Nevertheless, Williams's insistence that the abolitionists *must have been* insincere, self-interested capitalists lingers on. Here, too, David Brion Davis provides the most influential example, albeit his is a somewhat "soft" Marxism.

Davis began by identifying the English Quakers as the "very embodiment of the capitalist mentality . . . in the vanguard of the industrial revolution."[277] As an "entrepreneurial class" their most urgent concern was with "an unruly labor force" and the need for "labor discipline." In effect, abolitionism was the method adopted by Quakers to accomplish that goal:

> To moralists and reformers of other faiths, the Quakers demonstrated that testimony against slavery could be a social correlative of inner purity which seemed to pose no threat to the social order—at least to that capitalist order in which the Quakers had won so enviable a 'stake' . . . [Quaker] antislavery was a highly selective response to labor exploitation. It provided an outlet

London Quakers. A Quaker woman speaks from the balcony to the Friends gathered for their Sabbath Meeting late in the eighteenth century. Despite their commitment to being "plain" people, the wealth of the community is obvious in the way everyone is dressed. In addition to their wealth and influence, the Quakers were a potent force for abolition because they were well organized and deeply committed. © Gianni Dagli Orti/CORBIS.

> for demonstrating Christian concern for human suffering and injustice, and yet thereby gave a certain moral insulation to economic activities less visibly dependent on human suffering and injustice.[278]

Thus "the abolitionist movement helped to clear an ideological path for British industrialists."[279]

Nevertheless, Davis was unwilling to accuse the Quakers of real "insincerity or deliberate deception." Rather, to get around the fact that the Quakers and other Christian abolitionists met all reasonable tests of their sincerity, he claimed that their economic motivation, although real, was *unconscious*. Although the Quakers were oblivious to their true, self-interested motive, sophisticated modern observers can penetrate the "conscious intention" of the abolitionists to see that underneath they truly "reflected the needs and values of the emerging capitalist order."[280]

Here Davis employed the most celebrated dud in the Marxist arsenal: the principle of "false consciousness." Whenever people do not respond to their "economic interests" in accordance with Marxist predictions, this is to be explained as an error or mispercepetion on their part. Thus although the Quakers *should have known* they opposed slavery because they favored the expansion of capitalism, they seem not to have grasped this point, perhaps because they spent too much time in church telling one another religious "fairy tales." As a further explication of this Marxist principle it is appropriate to quote John Ashworth, since he wrote these lines precisely in support of Davis and to elude the plain evidence that the abolitionists were sincere in their idealism. Ashworth defined false consciousness as "the notion that the awareness of historical actors is incomplete, with the result that they misperceive the world around them." This is not merely a matter of self-deception, for it is "society rather than the individual [that] generates false consciousness." He then quoted the assertion of a "Marxist theorist": "[I]t is not the subject that deceives himself, but reality which deceives him." To illustrate this point, Ashworth noted:

> When Marie Antoinette told the peasants of Paris (never mind that the story is probably apocryphal) to eat cake when there was no bread, she was not deceiving herself in thinking they could afford it. Rather the nature of her involvement in society obscured from her the realization that peasants could not in fact afford to eat cake.[281]

Of course, as Ashworth admits, she never said it, and it seems quite inconceivable that she, or anyone else of ordinary intelligence, didn't know that peasants were poor. How appropriate that Ashworth chose to illustrate false consciousness with a false example.

Do people misperceive their situations? Certainly. Do they sometimes have mixed motives? Of course. Do they sometimes unintentionally help those whom they oppose? Undoubtedly. But to admit such human failings falls far short of claiming that reality is whatever Marxist theory leads one to believe—that is pure solipsism. All that I am willing to concede to Marxists on this point is that the principle of false consciousness is a fine example thereof, but I am unable to find another. Instead, I fully agree with Thomas Haskell: "To say that a person is moved by class interest is to say that he *intends* to further the interests of his class, or it is to say nothing at all."[282]

Conclusion

Slavery did not die of its own inefficiency, and emancipation was not a capitalist ploy. As Robert William Fogel put it so well, the death of slavery was "a political execution of an immoral system at its peak of economic success, incited by [people] ablaze with moral fervor."[283] Precisely! Moral fervor is the fundamental topic of this entire book: the potent capacity of monotheism, and especially Christianity, to activate extraordinary episodes of faith that have shaped Western civilization.

Futile Sacrifice. Many modern social scientists would argue that this Egyptian priest wasn't *really* concerned about pleasing the Great God Re. They would propose that the real point of this and similar ceremonies is to build group solidarity, and that despite the sacrifices being offered to the large statue of the God, his "presence" is incidental. I am confident that this priest would find such claims incomprehensible. © Bettmann/CORBIS.

Postscript

Gods, Rituals, and Social Science

> The most obvious basis for religious behavior is the one which any religious actor tells us about when we ask him—and, unlike some anthropologists, I believe him. He believes in superhuman beings and he performs religious ritual in order that he may satisfy them.
>
> —*Melford Spiro*

If it is hard to believe that conceptions of the Gods are ignored in most recently written histories, it is harder yet to understand why Gods were long ago banished from the social scientific study of religion. But that is precisely why I have devoted two volumes to demonstrating the crucial role of the Gods in shaping history and civilization, and to resurrecting and reformulating a sociology of Gods. Now that I have completed this undertaking, it is time to put things in final perspective.

In this postscript I first examine why the social sciences abandoned the Gods and substituted ritual as the fundamental religious aspect. The validity of this switch is easily refuted by compelling evidence that images of the supernatural determine the character and importance of rituals, not the other way around. Then, I show that only religions with adequate conceptions of the Gods are able to support morality, and that ritual participation has little or no independent impact on moral behavior. I end with a brief exhortation.

When Social Science Abandoned God

If asked what the word "religion" means, most religious people will say it's about God or the Gods. Yet, for a century, most social scientific studies of religion have examined nearly every aspect of faith except what people believe about Gods. When and why did we get it so wrong? When Durkheim and the other early functionalists dismissed Gods as unimportant window dressing, emphasizing instead that rites and rituals are the fundamental stuff of religion. In a long review of Part 6 of Herbert Spencer's *Principles of Sociology*, Emile Durkheim condemned Spencer for reducing religion "to being merely a collection of beliefs and practices relating to a supernatural agent." Seen from the perspective of "true" sociology:

> The idea of God which seemed to be the sum total of religion a short while ago, is now no more than a minor accident. It is a psychological phenomenon which has got mixed up with a whole sociological process whose importance is of quite a different order . . . We might perhaps be able to discover what is thus hidden beneath this quite superficial phenomenon . . .
>
> Thus the sociologist will pay scant attention to the different ways in which men and peoples have conceived the unknown cause and mysterious depth of things. He will set aside all such metaphysical speculations and will see in religion only a social discipline.[1]

Fifteen years later Durkheim had not wavered in his conviction that Gods are peripheral to religion, noting that although the apparent purpose of rituals is "strengthening the ties between the faithful and their god," what they really do is strengthen the "ties between the individual and society . . . the god being only a figurative representation of the society."[2] Thus began a new social science orthodoxy: religion consists of participation in rites and rituals—*only.*

I have long suspected that the underlying "insight" that directed our attention away from God and toward ritual had to do with the fact that Durkheim and his circle were militantly secular Jews who, nevertheless, sometimes attended synagogue.[3] In their personal experience, the phenomenology of religion would not have included belief in supernatural beings, but only the solidarity of group rituals. These personal perceptions were then reinforced by their voluminous reading of anthropological accounts of the impassioned ritual life of "primitives" by observers who lacked any sympathy for the objects of these worship services. Indeed, some of the most famous anthropologists advised against paying any attention to the reasons "natives" give for conducting rites. A. R. Radcliffe-Brown called it a "grievous error" to suppose anyone but a sophisticated outside observer can make any sense of ritual activity.[4] Thus it was from his external vantage point that Radcliffe-Brown concluded that although "it is sometimes held that funeral and mourning rites are the result of a belief in a soul surviving death . . . I would rather hold the view that belief in a surviving soul is not the cause but the effect of the rites."[5] By the same logic, cultures are said to "discover" the existence of rain Gods as a result of performing rain dances—never mind how it was that they started doing rain dances in the first place. One must be a highly trained social scientist to believe such things.

This, and a great deal of similar "expert" advice, turned social scientific attention to peripheral matters, giving primacy to what people *did* in the name of religion, which then appeared to be fundamentally irrational to social scientists who, having dismissed the objects of these activities, could not conceive of why people engaged in such actions. If one truly believes that ritual is the essence of religion, then what *is* one to make of people who include very valuable "sacrifices" in their ceremonies, thereby depriving themselves? They must be crazy. Which is, of course, what many social scientists who devoted themselves to explaining "sacrifice" concluded. Royden Keith Yerkes stressed the blind irrationality of sacrifices in traditional societies,[6] while Freud claimed that the irrationality of sacrificial rites was rooted in the Oedipus complex. He argued that the burning of sacrifices commemorates the "original sin" in which the sons in a primal horde rose up and killed and ate their father and then had sex with his wives.[7] This view was ratified at length by Roger Money-Kyrle,[8] and, in his influential textbook, Brian Morris referred to Freud's thesis as "amazing" and "tantalizing."[9]

Eventually this line of analysis "bottomed out" in such absurdities as Rodney Needham's denial of the existence of *any* "interior state" that might be called religious belief[10] and S.R.F. Price's claim that religious belief is a purely Christian invention, so that when "primitives" pray for things, they don't really mean it.[11] Indeed, Dan Sperber offered the amazing solipsism that because it is self-evident that supernatural beings do not exist, it is absurd to interpret religious rituals as efforts to enlist the divine on one's behalf.[12] Even Clifford Geertz went so far as to deny that healing ceremonies conducted by the Navaho are intended to cure the afflicted. Rather, he would have us believe that these rituals merely serve to provide "the stricken person a vocabulary" to relate her or his distress "to the wider world."[13] Never mind that the ceremony consists almost entirely of the chant "May the patient be well."

The notion that religion is not about belief in Gods has also flourished in less extreme forms. Robert Bellah condemned the "confusion of belief and religion" as an instance of the "objectivist fallacy," claiming that the emphasis on belief is found only in "religious traditions deeply influenced by Greek thought—Christianity and Islam."[14] He contrasted these faiths with the religions of the East, being careful to note only those forms in which the supernatural is conceived of not as a being but only as an impersonal, inactive "essence." Consequently, all Bellah really said was that Gods are not central to Godless religions. Bellah also failed to acknowledge that Godless religions are not central to the religious life of the East. As I have often reported, Godless faiths are sustained only by small intellectual elites, and the popular forms of Buddhism, Confucianism, and Taoism abound in Gods. Obviously, when Gods are many and each of quite limited scope, the centrality of any one, or indeed of all of them together, to the religious life will be modest in comparison to the centrality of One True God. But rather than having identified a fallacy, all Bellah did was to dimly perceive that monotheism is different from polytheism, and that both differ greatly from the Godless religions of Eastern philosophers and Western liberals. Perhaps unwittingly, Bellah's work itself stands as evidence that variations in conceptions of the supernatural are the basis from which all comparative analysis of religion as well as magic must begin.

That, of course, is the argument developed in the preceding chapters as well as in *One True God*. But the case that the supernatural, not ritual, provides the core of religion can be demonstrated in several quite specific and dramatic ways. The first of these asks why there is so much variation in the precision needed for the adequate performance of rituals.

Ritual Precision

When magic fails, it is usually assumed that the fault lay with the performance: that incantations were not precisely correct, or that rituals were not done exactly right. The same assumption applies to most ritual actions performed on behalf of the small Gods of polytheism. On the other hand, while there is a correct way to perform the rituals associated with each of the great monotheisms, there is little concern about precision: no sincere Catholic thinks that transubstantiation will not occur during the Mass if the priest gets some of the words wrong or out of order. Indeed, most appeals to Yahweh, Jehovah, or Allah involve a minimum of ritual, often being quite impromptu supplications by ordinary believers.

Recently, a substantial body of anthropological and experimental evidence has been assembled to explain that variations in the importance placed on ritual precision reflect differences in the capacities attributed to the supernatural agents to which (or whom) the rituals are directed.[15] When, as in the case of magic, the supernatural agent is an unconscious entity or is a supernatural creature of very limited capacity (such as a demon or an imp), it will be assumed that each ritual must be performed with extreme precision because the supernatural agency lacks the capacity to know the intent of those performing the ritual and is unable to overlook errors in ritual performance. As Justin Barrett put it, ritual precision is required in dealings with "dumb gods."[16] This same logic applies, if to a somewhat lesser extent, to religions based on Gods of limited scope. They, too, may take note not of the intent of rituals but only of their execution. Indeed, there is a substantial element of *compulsion* in interactions with small Gods, as well as with the creatures that are sometimes invoked by magic (see the introduction). Here, too, the rituals must be perfect; otherwise the supernatural agent will not find them binding. In contrast, the omnipotent Gods of monotheism are thought to be fully aware of the intentions of the supplicant.[17] Consequently, rituals are far less important, and precision is barely an issue when humans deal with Gods conceived of as all-seeing—if the priest errs, Jehovah knows what was meant, and the efficacy of a prayer does not hinge on precise adherence to a sacred formula.

An even more devastating case against the primacy of ritual can be made by close examination of the most popular of all functionalist claims about religion.

Gods, Rituals, and Morality

Religion functions to sustain the moral order. This classic proposition, handed down from the founders, is regarded by many as the closest thing to a "law" that the social scientific study of religion possesses.

In his Burnett Lectures, W. Robertson Smith explained that "even in its rudest form Religion was a moral force, the powers that men revered were on the side of social order and moral law; and the fear of the gods was a motive to enforce the laws of society, which were also the laws of morality."[18] Emile Durkheim, of course, argued that religion exists *because* it unites humans into *moral communities*, and while law and custom also regulate conduct, religion alone "asserts itself not only over conduct but over the *conscience*. It not only dictates actions but ideas and sentiments."[19] And, according to Bronislaw Malinowski, "every religion implies some reward of virtue and punishment of sin."[20]

In one form or another, this proposition appears in nearly every introductory sociology and anthropology text on the market. But it's wrong. Moreover, it wasn't even handed down from the founders, at least not unanimously! Indeed, the founder of British anthropology, Edward Tylor, and the founder of British sociology, Herbert Spencer, both took pains to point out that only *some kinds* of religions have moral implications.

Tylor reported:

> To some the statement may seem startling, yet the evidence seems to justify it, that the relation of morality to religion is one that only belongs in its rudiments, or not at all, to rudimentary civilization. The comparison of savage and civilized religions brings into view . . . a deep-lying contrast in their practical action on human life . . . the popular idea that the moral government of the universe is an essential tenet of natural religion simply falls to the ground. Savage animism [religion] is almost devoid of that ethical element which to the educated modern mind is the very mainspring of practical religion. Not, as I have said, that morality is absent from the life of the lower [cultures] . . . But these ethical laws stand on their own ground of tradition and public opinion, comparatively independent of the animistic beliefs and rites which exist beside them. The lower animism is not immoral, it is unmoral.[21]

Spencer also noted that many religions ignore morality, and he went even further by suggesting that some religions actively encourage crime and immorality: "At the present time in India, we have freebooters like the Domras, among whom a successful theft is always celebrated by a sacrifice to their chief god Gandak."[22]

Although little noticed, this dissenting view has continued among anthropologists. In 1922 J. P. Mills noted that the religion of the Lhotas includes no moral code: "Whatever it be which causes so many Lhotas to lead virtuous lives it is not their religion."[23] In his distinguished study of the Manus of New Guinea, Reo Fortune contrasted the moral aspects of their religion with that of the typical tribe, agreeing that "Tylor is entirely correct in stating that in most primitive regions of the world religion and morality maintain themselves independently."[24] Ruth Benedict also argued that to generalize the link between religion and morality "is to misconceive" the "history of religions." She suggested that this linkage is probably typical only of "the higher ethical religions."[25] Ralph Barton reported that the Ifugaos impute their own unscrupulous exchange practices to their Gods and seize every opportunity to cheat them.[26] Peter Lawrence found that the Garia of New Guinea have no conception whatever of "sin" and "no idea of rewards in the next world for good works."[27] And Mary Douglas flatly asserted that there is no "inherent relation between religion and morality: there are primitives who can be religious without being moral and moral without being religious."[28]

Tylor's observation that not all religions support the moral order should always have been obvious to anyone familiar with Greek and Roman mythology. The Greco-Roman Gods were quite morally deficient (Chapter 1). They were thought to do terrible things to one another and to humans as well—sometimes merely for amusement. And while they were quite apt to do wicked things to humans who failed to propitiate them, the Gods had no interest in anything (wicked or otherwise) humans might do to one another. Instead, the Greek and Roman Gods concerned themselves only with direct affronts. For example, no religious sanctions were incurred by young women who engaged in premarital sex *unless* they immersed themselves in sacred waters reserved for virgins.[29] Because Aristotle taught that the Gods were incapable of caring about mere humans,[30] he could not have concurred that religion serves the function of sustaining and legitimating the moral order. Indeed, classical philosophers would have ridiculed such a proposition as peculiar to Jews and Christians—and they would have been correct.[31] As will be seen, the proposition about the moral functions of religion requires a particular conception of supernatural beings as deeply concerned about the behavior of humans toward one another. Such a conception of the Gods is found in many of the major world faiths, including Judaism, Christianity, Islam, and Hinduism. But it appears to be largely lacking in the supernatural conceptions prevalent in much of Asia, and in animism and folk religions generally.

It would seem to follow, therefore, that the moral behavior of individuals would be influenced by their religious commitments *only* in societies where the dominant religious organizations give clear and consistent expression to divine moral imperatives. Thus, for example, were proper survey data available, they should show that those who frequented the temples in Greco-Roman times were *no more* observant of the prevailing moral codes than were those who were lax in their religious practice. As

Tylor pointed out, this is to suggest, not that societies in antiquity lacked moral codes, but only that these were not predicated on religious foundations. It follows that the moral effectiveness of religions varies according to the moral engagement of their Gods.

Unconscious divine essences are unable to issue commandments or make moral judgments. Thus conceptions of the supernatural are irrelevant to the moral order unless they are *beings*—things having consciousness and desires. Put another way, only beings can desire moral conformity. Even that is not sufficient. Gods can lend sanctions to the moral order only if they are *concerned* and informed about humans, and act on their behalf. Moreover, to promote virtue among humans, Gods must be virtuous—they must *favor good* over evil. Finally, Gods will be effective in sustaining moral precepts, the greater their *scope*—that is, the greater the diversity of their powers and the range of their influence. All-powerful, all-seeing Gods ruling the entire universe are the ultimate deterrent.

Two conclusions follow from this discussion. First, the effects of religiousness on individual morality *are contingent on images of Gods* as conscious, morally concerned beings; religiousness based on impersonal or amoral Gods *will not influence* moral choices. Second, participation in religious rites and rituals will have little or no *independent* effect on morality.

Recently, to test these conclusions, I conducted an elaborate research study based on data for the United States and thirty-three other nations.[32] The results were consistent and overwhelmingly supportive.

In each of twenty-seven nations within Christendom, the greater the importance people placed on God, the less likely they were to approve of buying goods they knew to be stolen; of failure to report that one had accidentally damaged an auto in a parking lot; or of smoking marijuana. The correlations were as high in Protestant as in Roman Catholic nations and whether average levels of church attendance were high or low. Indeed, participation in Sunday services (a measure of ritual activity) was only weakly related to moral attitudes, and these correlations disappeared or became very small when the God "effects" were removed through regression analysis. That is, God matters; ritual doesn't.

The findings are similar for Muslim nations, where the importance placed on Allah is very strongly correlated with morality, but mosque attendance is of no significance. In India, too, concern for the Gods matters, but temple attendance has no detectable effect on morality. But in Japan, where the Gods are conceived of as many, small, and not particu-

Freezing in Hell. Depictions of souls suffering in hell have played a central role in Christian moral instruction. Usually this has involved a fiery fate, but in 1476 Cristoforo de Predis painted this scene in which sinners are being dropped into a cauldron of ice-cold water to freeze for all eternity. © Archivo Iconografico, S.A./CORBIS.

larly interested in human moral behavior, religion is irrelevant to moral outlooks—concern about the God(s), visits to temples, prayer and meditation, all are without any moral effects. Nor are there God or temple effects on morality in China. However, in China prayer does matter, but in the wrong direction! That is, the more often they pray, the more tolerant the Chinese are of immorality. I suggest that this result is due to the fact that in China, "prayer" seldom implies a long-standing, deeply felt relationship with a God, but merely involves requests for favors from various divinities of small scope. As such, praying tends to represent a quite self-centered and self-serving activity, consistent with rapidly shifting from one God to another on the basis of results, or even taking a stick to the statue of a God who fails.[33] Seen in this light, a question about prayer is likely to select those somewhat lacking in terms of a social conscience.

These results show that, in and of themselves, rites and rituals have little or no impact on the major effect universally attributed to religion—conformity to the moral order. Thus it seems necessary to amend the "law" linking religion and morality as follows: *Images of Gods as conscious, powerful, morally concerned beings function to sustain the moral order.*

Conclusion

Clearly, Durkheim made a major error when he dismissed Gods as mere religious epiphenomena. Unfortunately, his error had severe, widespread, and long-lasting consequences, for it quickly became the exclusive sociological view that religion consists of rites and rituals, and that these exist only because their latent function is to integrate societies and to thereby lend sacred sanctions to the norms. In retrospect, it seems remarkable that such a notion gained such rapid acceptance and went unchallenged for so long. Stripped of its functionalist jargon, the basic argument seems to have been that since "we" know there are no Gods, they can't be the real object of religion—the truism that things are real to the extent that people define them as real failed to make any headway in this area of social science.

So, then, let us finally be done with the claim that religion is all about ritual. Gods are the fundamental feature of religions.[34] This holds even for Godless religions, their lack of Gods explaining the inability of such faiths to attract substantial followings. Moreover, it was not the "wisdom of the East" that gave rise to science, nor did Zen meditation turn people's hearts against slavery. By the same token, science was not the work of Western secularists or even deists; it was entirely the work of devout believers in an active, conscious, creator God. And it was faith in the goodness of this same God and in the mission of Jesus that led other devout Christians to end slavery, first in medieval Europe and then again in the New World.

In these ways, at least, Western civilization really was God-given.

Notes

Introduction
Dimensions of the Spiritual

1. Rappaport, 1999:1.
2. In Overmyer, 1993:997.
3. James, [1902] 1958:39–42.
4. Durkheim, [1912] 1995:42.
5. Middleton, 1967:ix.
6. Malinowksi, [1948] 1992:19–20.
7. Middleton, 1967:ix.
8. Benedict, 1938:637.
9. Levack, 1995:6. Also see Peters, 1978.
10. Benedict, 1938:637.
11. Weber, [1922] 1993:28.
12. Swanson, 1960:55.
13. Spencer, 1896:747–48.
14. Russell, 1977:32.
15. Tillich, 1951.
16. Finke and Stark, 1992; Stark, 2001a; Stark and Finke, 2000.

Chapter 1
God's *Truth*: Inevitable Sects and Reformations

1. Bowker, 1997:805.
2. Constable, 1996; Lambert, 1992; Ozment, 1980.

3. This is not to say that it is the *usual* state of affairs within monotheisms, as efforts to impose religious monopolies have been usual.

4. Stark, 1983; Stark and Bainbridge, [1987] 1996; Stark and Finke, 2000, 2002; Stark and Iannaccone, 1994.

5. Weber, [1922] 1993:162.

6. Stark and Bainbridge, [1987] 1996; Stark and Finke, 2000, 2002.

7. Stark and Finke, 2000.

8. Burkert, 1987:10–11.

9. Beard, North, and Price, 1998; Burkert, 1985, 1987; Cumont, 1956; James, 1960; MacMullen, 1981; Von Soden, 1994.

10. Johnson, 1963:542.

11. Allport, 1960:122.

12. See Demerath, 1974.

13. See Bangs, 1972.

14. Finke and Stark, 2001, 1992; Iannaccone, 1992, 1994; Olson and Perl, 2001; Perrin and Mauss, 1993; Stark, 1987, 1996; Stark and Finke, 2000, 2002.

15. Riley, 1997.

16. *Fragments* 11.15, 16.

17. Burkert, 1985.

18. Ibid.:296.

19. Ibid.:297.

20. James, 1960:287.

21. Burkert, 1985:299.

22. Ibid.:303.

23. Tinh, 1982:112.

24. Beard, North, and Price, 1998:289.

25. Johnson, 1963; Niebuhr, 1929; Stark and Bainbridge, 1979, 1985; Stark and Finke, 2000; Troeltsch, [1969] 1931.

26. Stark and Bainbridge, 1985.

27. Stark, 2001a.

28. Lester, 1993:867.

29. Stark, in press.

30. Stark and Bainbridge, 1985, [1987] 1996; Stark and Finke, 2000.

31. Niebuhr, 1929:12.

32. Ibid.:13.

33. Ibid.:15.

34. Ibid.:19.

35. Collins, 1998.

36. Stark, 1965, 1999.

37. Baumgarten, 1997; Blenkinsopp, 1981; Cohen, 1987; Georgi, 1995; Jospe, 1981; Koester, 1982a; Mor, 1992; Neusner, 1990.

38. Hippolytus, *The Refutation of All Heresies* 9.14.

39. Cohen, 1987.

40. Koester, 1982a:230.

41. Cohen, 1987.

42. Ibid.:147.

43. Blenkinsopp, 1981.

44. Cohen, 1987:147.

45. Cohen, 1987; Niebuhr, 1929; Saldarini, 1988.

46. Baumgarten, 1997:47, 51.

47. Williams, 1996.

48. May, 1987–1988; Quispel, 1987; Williams, 1996.

49. *Against Marcion* 4.11.

50. Ibid. 7.17.

51. Rankin, 1995.

52. Johnson, 1976:51.

53. In ibid.

54. Quispel, 1987.

55. Rankin, 1995; Trevett, 1996.

56. *The Refutation of All Heresies* 8.12.

57. Stark, 1996, 2002.

58. Trevett, 1996.

59. Hippolytus, *The Refutation of All Heresies* 8.12.

60. Eusebius, *The Ecclesiastical History* 5.18.

61. Henderson, 1998:10.

62. Ormsby, 1984:92.

63. Dabashi, 1989.

64. Ibn Qudama, 1962:42.

65. The same thing occurred in the United States (Stark, 2001a).

66. Farah, 1994; Henderson, 1998; Hodgson, 1974; Payne, 1959; Rahman, 1981; Waines, 1995.

67. Hodgson, 1974, 1:221.

68. Rahman, 1981.

69. Ibid.:917.

70. Ibid.

71. Glock and Stark, 1966; Stark, 2001a.

72. Hume, 1754, vol. 3.

73. Smith, [1776] 1981:789.

74. Stark, 1983, 2001a; Stark and Bainbridge, [1987] 1996; Stark and Finke, 2000; Stark and Iannaccone, 1994.

75. Fletcher, 1997:19.

76. Duffy, 1997:27.

77. Fletcher, 1997:38.

78. Cheetham, 1983; Duffy, 1997.

79. Stark, in press.

80. Johnson, 1976.

81. Bagnall, 1993; Dodds, 1970; MacMullen, 1984; Stark, 1996.

82. Drake, 1999.

83. in Johnson, 1976:97.

84. MacMullen, 1984:91.

85. In ibid.:101.

86. Brown, 1967; Frend, 1984, 1985; Johnson, 1976; Tilley, 1996.

87. From which the word "traitors" derives.

88. See Tilley, 1996.

89. Frend, 1984:655.

90. Johnson, 1976:85.

91. In Frend, 1984:670.

92. Lambert, 1992:25.

93. *Ecclesiastical History* 1.30

94. Davies, 1996; Jolly, 1996; Milis, 1998.

95. Finke and Wittberg, 2000; Stark and Bainbridge, 1985.

96. Fletcher, 1997; Hannah, 1924; Hickey, 1987; Johnson, 1976; King, 1999; Knowles, 1969; Mayr-Harting, 1993; Smith, 1892.

97. In Duffy, 1997:52.

98. Duffy, 1997; Southern, 1970.

99. Duffy, 1997:57.

100. McBrien, 2000:157.

101. Cheetham, 1983; McBrien, 2000.

102. Cheetham, 1983; Duffy, 1997.

103. Cheetham, 1983:84.

104. Pastor, 1898.

105. Cheetham, 1983.

106. Ibid.:90.

107. Ibid.:87.

108. Costen, 1997; Duffy, 1997; McBrien, 2000; Morris, 1991.

109. In Duffy, 1997:96.

110. All quoted in Moore, 1994:54–55.

111. Chazan, 1986:29.

112. Poliakov, 1965:35.

113. Russell, 1965:103.

114. Brooke, 1971; Costen, 1997; Lambert, 1992; Moore, 1994; Russell, 1965.

115. Russell, 1965:108.

116. Lambert, 1992:25.

117. Stark, 2001a.

118. Chazan, 1986:29.

119. In Poliakov, 1965:48.

120. Constable, 1996.

121. In Payne, 1984:35.

122. Maier, 1994.

123. Ibid.

124. King, 1999; Lambert, 1992; Maier, 1994; Moore, 1995, 1994.

125. Moore, 1994:85.

126. In ibid.

127. In Constable, 1996:34.

128. Lambert, 1992:390.

129. Brooke, 1971; Cheetham, 1983; Costen, 1997; Lambert, 1992; Moore, 1994; Russell, 1965.

130. In Moore, 1994:88.

131. Cheetham, 1983:114.

132. Barber, 2000; Brooke, 1971; Costen, 1997; Lambert, 1998, 1992; Moore, 1994; O'Shea, 2000; Russell, 1965.

133. Lambert, 1998:21.

134. Costen, 1997:65.

135. Lambert, 1998:21.

136. Lambert, 1992:55.

137. Complete text in Russell, 1971:60–68.

138. Lambert, 1998:20.

139. Brooke and Brooke, 1984:99–100.

140. Lambert, 1998:154.

141. Costen, 1997.

142. Ibid.

143. Lenski, 1966.

144. Costen, 1997:70.

145. In ibid.

146. In Barber, 2000:107.

147. Ibid.:109.

148. Brooke, 1971; Cameron, 1984; Lambert, 1992; Moore, 1994; Russell, 1965; Tourn, 1989.

149. Lambert, 1992:69.

150. Ibid.:149, 170.

151. In Johnson, 1976:251.

152. Lambert, 1992:147.

153. Leff, 1967:376.

154. Lerner, 1972:3.

155. Cohn, 1961; Lambert, 1992; Leff, 1967; Lerner, 1972.

156. Cohn, 1961:164.

157. Lambert, 1992.

158. Cohn, 1961.

159. It was not called the "Black Death" until several centuries later (Ziegler, 1971).

160. Cartwright and Biddiss, 1972; Ziegler, 1971.

161. Ziegler, 1971.

162. Tuchman, 1979:115.

163. In Marx and Engels, 1964:98.

164. In ibid.:99–100.

165. In Russell, 1965:231.

166. Cohn, 1961:xiii.

167. Stark and Bainbridge, 1985.

168. Tourn, 1989:49.

169. As late as 1617, Saint Vincent de Paul discovered that his local priest knew no Latin, not even the words of absolution (Delumeau, 1977).

170. Cobban, 1988; Colish, 1997; Daly, 1961; Haskins, 1923; Schachner, 1938.

171. Recently, some historians have identified universities in Ireland as early as the sixth century. The most famous of these was at Clonmacnois, and it drew scholars not only from Ireland and England but from the Continent as well. Indeed, Irish scholars were widely admired at that time and were especially welcome in the cathedral schools of Europe. However, these Irish institutions seem to have been destroyed during the Norse occupation.

172. Grant, 1996; Lindberg, 1992.

173. Grant, 1996; Russell, 1958.

174. Colish, 1997:266.

175. Collins, 1998.

176. Colish (1997:268) called theology at this time "the most high-risk discipline."

177. Aston, 1984; Dickens, 1991; Lambert, 1992; McFarlane, 1952; McSheffrey, 1995; Plumb, 1986.

178. Lambert, 1992:228.

179. Fines, 1995.

180. Dickens, 1991.

181. Lambert, 1992; Plumb, 1986.

182. McSheffrey, 1995.

183. McFarlane, 1952:180.

184. Dickens, 1991:48.

185. Bartos, 1986; Dickens, 1991; Kaminsky, 1967; Lambert, 1992; Ozment, 1980.

186. Luther, 1915 [1520]:141.

187. In Duffy, 1997:121.

188. Cheetham, 1983:184.

189. Cheetham, 1983; Duffy, 1997; McBrien, 2000.

190. Duffy, 1997:146.

191. Ibid.:135.

192. McBrien, 2000.

193. Cheetham, 1983:199.

194. Collins, 1903:378.

195. Dickens, 1991:18.

196. In Lea, 1902:672.

197. Pastor, 1898, 5:457.

198. Swanson, 1995. If that number seems excessive, that there were so many priests in one archdiocese reflects the overchurching that the laity found so burdensome.

199. King, 1999.

200. In Lea, 1902:674.

201. *Epistle* 94.

202. In Durant, 1957:20–21.

203. Chadwick, 1972.

204. Duffy, 1997.

205. Coulton, 1938a.

206. Johnson, 1976:267.

207. Hayes, 1917.

208. Durant, 1957.

209. Ozment, 1975.

210. Schwiebert, 1950:312.

211. Dickens, 1991.

212. In Lambert, 1992:73.

213. Ibid.:240.

214. Eisenstein, 1979; Hirsch, 1967.

215. Ozment, 1980.

216. Ibid.

217. Dickens, 1966:51.

218. Johnson, 1976:271.

219. This meaning is close to the way the term is used today by antireligious groups such as the American Humanist Association.

220. Smith, [1923] 1962:1.

221. In Schwiebert, 1950:275.

222. In fact, Aquinas wrote excellent Latin. But it was not the flowery, poetic style prized by Valla and other Humanists. Alfred Crosby (1997:65) described Aquinas's prose as "a bony minimum stripped of alliteration, figures of speech, or even metaphor, except where tradition demanded otherwise. (He could not very well reject the poetry of the Psalms, but he did criticize Plato for extravagance of language.) His reasoning and language are almost mathematical: our translators sometimes use algebraic letter symbols as the best means to express in twentieth century English what he wrote in thirteenth century Latin."

223. Bainton, 1969; Durant, 1957; Erasmus, [1500s] 1996; Huizinga, [1924] 1957; Moeller, 1972; Ozment, 1980; Phillips, 1949; Smith, [1923] 1962.

224. Chadwick, 1972:32.

225. See Bainton, 1969.

226. Chadwick, 1972:32.

227. Huizinga, [1924] 1957:85.

228. The appropriate comparison is with the "inside" jokes that ethnic, racial, and religious groups tell about themselves, jokes that would be regarded as very offensive coming from outsiders. Erasmus was, technically, a monk.

229. Monter, 1999:56.

230. Durant, 1957:291.

231. Bainton, [1952] 1985.

232. Ibid.; Chadwick, 1972; Durant, 1957; Elton, 1999; Holborn, 1982, 1969; Kittelson, 1986; Luther, [1520] 1915; McNally, 1969; Moeller, 1972; Oberman, 1992; Ozment, 1975, 1980; Rupp, 1981, 1951; Schwiebert, 1950; Tracy, 1999.

233. Oberman 1992:149.

234. In ibid.

235. Chadwick, 1972:42; also Duffy, 1997:153, and Schwiebert, 1950:310.

236. In Oberman, 1992:188.

237. Schwiebert, 1950:314.

238. McNally, 1969.

239. In Eisenstein, 1979:306–7.

240. Aston, 1968:76.

241. Eisenstein, 1979.

242. In Durant, 1957:352.

243. Luther, [1520] 1915:157.

244. Ibid.:84.

245. Ibid.:138.

246. Ibid.:139.

247. Rupp, 1981:192.

248. Ozment, 1980; Stark, 1999.

249. Brady, 1978; Monter, 1967; Ozment, 1975; Rörig, 1969; Strauss, 1967; Tracy, 1999.

250. Christman, 1982.

251. Pollard, 1903:159.

252. See his remarkable "Nativity Sermons," some of which have been collected by Roland H. Bainton (1997).

253. Chadwick, 1972; Collinson, 1967; Dickens, 1991; Duffy, 1992; Durant, 1957; Fines, 1981; Hoyle, 2001; MacCulloch, 2000; O'Day, 1986; Scarisbrick, 1984; Tracy, 1999.

254. Dickens, 1991:13–14.

255. O'Day, 1986.

256. Fines, 1981.

257. Dickens, 1991:326.

258. *Letters and Papers of Henry VIII*, number 6385.

259. Dickens, 1991:128.

260. In Durant, 1957:547.

261. Ibid.:550.

262. Bush, 1999; Dickens, 1991; Dodds and Dodds, [1915] 1971; Hoyle, 2001.

263. Monter, 1999.

264. Dickens, 1991.

265. Durant, 1957; Ozment, 1980; Potter, 1976; Walton, 1967.

266. Protestant: Basel, Bern, Geneva, Schaffhausen, and Zurich; Catholic: Freiburg, Lucerne, Schwyz, Solothurn, Unterwalden, Uri, and Zug; split: Appenzell, Glarus.

267. Basel, Bern, Lausanne, Schaffhausen, and Zurich.

268. Kingdon, 1956, 1981.

269. Bouwsma, 1988; Cottret, 2000; Kingdon, 1956, 1972, 1981; Monter, 1967; Ozment, 1980; Parker, 1975.

270. I was alerted to this by a paragraph in the article on Calvin the *The Encyclopaedia Britannica*, which was written by Kingdon.

271. Kingdon, 1956:56.

272. Bainton, [1952] 1985.

273. In Kingdon, 1956:56.

274. Ibid.:57.

275. Tracy, 1999.

276. Kingdon, 1956.

277. Chadwick, 1972:156.

278. Ibid.:156–57.

279. Kingdon, 1956:94.

280. Durant, 1957; Holt, 1995; Ladurie, 1974; Monter, 1999; Rörig, 1969; Tracy, 1999.

281. Monter, 1999.

282. Ibid.

283. Kingdon used 20 million as the estimated population of France. Later studies have revised that downward to 16 million.

284. Durant, 1957:505.

285. Monter, 1999.

286. Ladurie, 1974:158–60.

287. Dunn, 1979; Holt, 1995; Kingdon, 1956.

288. Collins, 1903:400.

289. Bainton, [1952] 1985:131.

290. Collins, 1903:400.

291. In Caponetto, 1999:xvi.

292. Bainton, [1952] 1985; Caponetto, 1999; Collins, 1903; Durant, 1957; Tracy, 1999.

293. The first Italian edition appeared in 1992, followed by a revision in 1997, and then by a fine English translation in 1999.

294. Caponetto, 1999:14.

295. Monter and Tedeschi, 1986.

296. Tracy, 1999:390.

297. Monter and Tedeschi, 1986.

298. Caponetto, 1999; Collins, 1903; Tracy, 1999; Trevor-Roper, [1969] 2001; Williams, 1972.

299. Brady, 1978; Durant, 1957; Engels, [1873] 1964; Ozment, 1980; Swanson, 1967; Tracy, 1999; Weber, [1904–1905] 1958; Wuthnow, 1989.

300. Becker, 2000; Braudel, 1977; Jere Cohen 1980; Delacroix and Nielsen, 2001; Fischoff, 1968; Hamilton, 1996; Samuelsson, [1957] 1993.

301. Brøndsted, 1965:312.

302. Ibid.:306–7.

303. Latourette, 1975:732.

304. Ladurie, 1974:159–60.

305. Wuthnow, 1989:105–6.

306. Barrett, 1982; Brøndsted, 1965; Davies, 1996; Jones, 1968; Roesdahl, 1980; Sawyer, 1982; Shepherd, 1980.

307. Austria, ninth; Belgium, seventh; Denmark, eleventh; Finland, thirteenth; France, sixth; Germany, ninth; Great Britain, ninth; Iceland, eleventh; Ireland, fifth; Italy, fourth; Netherlands, eighth; Norway, eleventh; Portugal, fourth; Spain, fourth; Sweden, twelfth; Switzerland, eighth.

308. Data provided by the 1996 *Catholic Almanac*.

309. Moeller, 1972; Ozment, 1975; Pollard, 1903; Rörig, 1969; Tracy, 1999.

310. Spitz, 1969:145.

311. Rörig, 1969:25.

312. Steven Ozment (1975:124–25) proposed a three-step process by which cities became Protestant. The process began (1) with the arrival of Protestant preachers and agitators who (2) managed to assemble a dedicated public following that (3) won the "grudging support and final sanction by government." Ozment noted that the reluctance of city council members to declare for Protestantism often reflected not their religious opposition but a preference for proper procedures and orderly change. Of course, some city councils refused to take step three.

313. Moeller, 1972.

314. Rörig, 1969.

315. Chadwick, 1972:26.

316. Durant, 1957:639.

317. Bush, 1967; Hill, 1967.

318. Wuthnow, 1989:90.

319. Chadwick, 1972; Duffy, 1992; Durant, 1957; Latourette, 1975; Ozment, 1975, Roberts, 1968; Tracy, 1999.

320. Latourette, 1975:735.

321. Ibid.:737.

322. Roberts, 1968.

323. Ozment, 1975.

324. Moeller, 1972; Ozment, 1975; Tracy, 1999.

325. Evennett, 1968:3–9.

326. Trent was a small town in northern Italy.

327. Chadwick, 1972; Duffy, 1987; Gentilcore, 1992; Thomas, 1971.

328. Mullett, 1999.

329. Trevor-Roper, [1969] 2001:20–21.

330. Braudel, 1977:66.

331. A case could be made that the post–Vatican II changes introduced by Pope John Paul II constitute a reformation.

Chapter 2
God's *Handiwork*: The Religious Origins of Science

1. White, 1896, 2:108–9.

2. It also provides the opening line of that great standard by George and Ira Gershwin, "They All Laughed" (1936): "They all laughed at Christopher Columbus, when he said the world was round."

3. Grant, 1971, 1994; Hamilton, 1996; Russell, 1991.

4. In Grant, 1994:619.

5. Russell, 1991:10.

6. Ibid.:26.

7. Grant, 1994.

8. Brooke and Cantor, 1998:18; also see Lindberg and Numbers, 1986; Russell, 1991.

9. Albeit a small, very vocal minority of religion-baiters persists.

10. Bloch, [1940] 1961:83.

11. Darwin and Seward, 1903, 1:195.

12. *On the Heavens*.

13. In Clagett, 1961:536.

14. White, 1896, 1:57

15. Yates, 1964, 1979.

16. As Theodore K. Rabb (1975:274) put it, "The Servetus case seems irrelevant to a discussion of Protestant opposition to science, because surely nobody has questioned that both Calvin and those who led the outcry . . . were interested only in the punishment of doctrinal heresy. To suggest another issue is to raise a straw man."

17. Kamen, 1997:134.

18. Monter and Tedeschi, 1986.

19. Boorstin, 1983:100.

20. In its fiftieth anniversary issue, published in September 1998, *Archaeology* ran a lengthy article entitled "The Not-So-Dark Ages," summarizing the findings of an immense number of excavations which demonstrate that this era was far more "civilized" than had been admitted in previous generations, and confirmed the historical reassessment crediting this era with having laid the "foundations of modern European culture" (Hodges, 1998:61).

21. Bloch [1940] 1961; Pirenne, [1922] 1955; [1936] 1958.

22. Ferrill, 1986; Grant, 1978; Luttwak, 1976; Wolfram, 1997.

23. Ferrill, 1986; Wolfram, 1997.

24. Gimpel, 1976:x.

25. Ibid.:viii, 1.

26. White, 1940:151.

27. Especially Gies and Gies, 1994; Gimpel, 1976; White, 1962.

28. Hanson, 2001.

29. Montgomery, 1968; White, 1962.

30. Hyland, 1994.

31. Gimpel, 1976:32.

32. Smil, 2000; White, 1962.

33. Gimpel, 1976:32.

34. Gies and Gies, 1994; Gimpel, 1976; White, 1940, 1962.

35. Hime, 1915; Manucy, 1949; Partington, [1960] 1999.

36. Barclay and Schofield, 1981:488.

37. Hitchins and May, 1951; May and Howard, 1981; Needham, 1954–1984.

38. White, 1967.

39. I was taught that when Julius Caesar conquered Britain, the natives were semisavages who painted themselves blue. Yet Caesar's own account reveals that he had to fight and win a long and closely contested naval battle to cross the Channel. People possessed of a navy able to challenge the Romans could hardly have been rude savages.

40. Dawson, 1950.

41. White, 1967:1203.

42. Crosby, 1997:65.

43. Armitage, 1951; Brooke, 1991; Clagett, 1961; Cohen, 1985a; Crosby, 1997; Gingerich, 1975; Grant, 1994, 1996; Jaki, 1986; Mason, 1962; Neugebauer, 1975; Rosen, 1971.

44. White, 1896:121.

45. Grant, 1996:169.

46. In Clagett, 1961:536.

47. In Grant, 1994:642.

48. Oresme, [ca. 1350–1360] 1968, 1971.

49. In Grant, 1994:550.

50. Danielson, 2000: 98; Mason, 1962:120–21.

51. Crosby, 1997:104.

52. Cohen, 1985a; Gingerich, 1975; Neugebauer, 1975.

53. Cohen, 1985a:107.

54. Cohen, 1985a; Gingerich, 1975; Rosen, 1971.

55. Cohen, 1985a:106.

56. Gingerich, 1975; Jaki, 2000; Rosen, 1971.

57. Jaki, 2000.

58. Colish, 1997:266.

59. Schachner, 1938:3.

60. Grant, 1996:23.

61. Pernoud, 2000:24.

62. Ibid.:21.

63. Lindberg, 1992:230.

64. Ibid.

65. Grant, 1996; Porter, 1998.

66. Porter, 1998:56.

67. Mason, 1962.

68. Porter, 1998.

69. Armitage, 1951.

70. Grant, 1996:205.

71. White, 1896, 2:50.

72. Singer, [1925] 1970:129.

73. O'Malley, 1964; Porter, 1998.

74. Movies and stories concerning "body snatchers" often suggest that their nefarious activities were necessary because of prohibitions on dissection. In fact, body snatching did take place in various times and places—not, however, because human dissection was forbidden, but because of a lack of bodies: families were reluctant to offer their loved ones to disrespectful treatment, or to forgo the comfort of visits to a grave site.

75. Dorn, 1991; Huff, 1993; Lang, 1997; Needham, 1954–1984.

76. Grant, 1996:168.

77. Ben-David, 1990; Cohen 1985a; Collins, 1998; Dorn, 1991; Grant, 1996; Huff, 1993; Jaki, 2000; Kuhn, 1962.

78. In Crosby, 1997:83.

79. Whitehead, [1925] 1967:13.

80. Ibid.:12.

81. Ibid.:13.

82. *On Repentance* 1.

83. In Lindberg and Numbers, 1986:27–28.

84. *De reductione artium ac theologiam.*

85. Grant, 1996; Meyer, 1944.

86. Webster, 1986:213.

87. Russell, 1922:193.

88. The quotation from Russell continues, "I have no doubt that if the Chinese get a stable government and sufficient funds, they would, within the next thirty years, begin to produce remarkable work in science. It is quite likely that they might outstrip us . . ."

89. Needham, 1954–1984, 1:581.

90. Lang, 1997:18.

91. In Mason, 1962:36–37.

92. Grant, 1994, 1996; Jaki, 1986; Lindberg, 1992; Mason, 1962, as well as the cited original sources.

93. Lindberg, 1992.

94. Mason, 1962.

95. Lindberg, 1992:54.

96. In Jaki, 1986:114.

97. Full text in Danielson, 2000:14–15.

98. Lindberg, 1992:42.

99. Jaki, 1986:105.

100. Lindberg, 1992; Mason, 1962.

101. Farah, 1994; Hodgson, 1974; Jaki, 1986; Nasr, 1993; Waines, 1995.

102. *Oeuvres* 8:61.

103. Farah, 1994:199.

104. Nasr, 1993.

105. Jaki, 2000:207.

106. Grant, 1994.

107. Baker, 1952.

108. Kinser, 1971.

109. Luther, [1520] 1915:146.

110. Eisenstein, 1980:321.

111. Given Merton's obsession with matters of priority, I find it very peculiar that he was never forthcoming about the extent of his debt to Dorothy Stimson's prior publication of a relationship between Puritanism and the rise of science. It may be that he wrote his thesis without knowledge of her prior work. But, for all the reasons he advanced in his own writings about priority, he should have clearly

stated the facts when he published in 1938, and he certainly needed to do so in later republications of the key excerpt of his thesis. A very tardy discussion of the matter by Bernard Cohen, one of Merton's greatest admirers, in Clark, Modgil, and Modgil (1990) was not very enlightening. Some historians now attribute the thesis jointly to Merton and Stimson, also without mention of priority (cf. Hunter, 1982; Shapiro, 1968). However, since these same historians reject the thesis, this may have become as insignificant as a dispute about the first claim concerning the existence of phlogiston.

112. Merton, 1938:447, 450–51.

113. Ibid.:445.

114. Merton's thesis strongly appealed to the anti-Catholic biases of the time. It was an era of very open anti-Catholicism. Indeed, it has been said that in those days anti-Catholicism was the anti-Semitism of liberal intellectuals. Remarkably strident anti-Catholicism was common in the respectable magazines and journals of the 1930s—indeed, until the 1960s.

115. Kearney, 1964:259–60.

116. Collins, 1998.

117. Hunter, 1982, 1989.

118. Kearney, 1964; Rabb, 1965.

119. Shapiro, 1968:288.

120. Feuer, 1963; Hunter, 1982, 1989; Shapiro, 1968.

121. Cohen, 1985a.

122. In contrast, the *Random House Webster's Dictionary of Scientists*, in addition to displaying every sin of political correctness, trivializes the word "scientist" by the inclusion of a flock of entries such as "Fixx, James 1932–1984. US popularizer of jogging."

123. Cheetham, 1983.

124. Some historians have attempted to identify Pierre Gassendi as a skeptic despite his having been a Catholic priest. This seems entirely unfounded, as Sylvia Murr (1993) has demonstrated convincingly.

125. Brooke, 1991; Jaki, 2000.

126. Stark, 1999.

127. Brooke and Cantor, 1998; Langford, 1971; Shea, 1986.

128. Ironically, part of Galileo's troubles stemmed from renewed efforts to crack down on astrologers, whose claims to predict the future had long been denounced as dangerous superstition (see Chapter 3). Some Churchmen mistakenly equated the claim that the earth moved with doctrines that fate was ruled by the motion of heavenly bodies.

129. Brooke and Cantor, 1998:20.

130. Ibid.:110.

131. Shea, 1986:132.

132. *Confessions* 12.23–24.

133. *Works* 1:23.

134. Rousseau, *Works* 3:183.

135. Burckhardt was also the first to claim that Constantine's conversion was insincere, a mere pose assumed out of his lust for power. Fortunately, later historians have dismissed this claim, but they have yet to fully detect the similar biases at work in his study of the Renaissance.

136. *Essay concerning Human Understanding* 3.9.

137. Baumer, 1960:67.

138. Gay, 1966:23.

139. Gay, 1969:145.

140. Ibid.:130.

141. *Letters concerning the English Nation*, Letter 12.

142. Hume, *History of England*, vol. 8.

143. Gay, 1969:131.

144. In Hindle, 1956:80.

145. Manuel, 1974:53.

146. Cajori's translation: Newton, 1934:543–47.

147. In Hurlbutt, 1985:7.

148. Before his death, Newton destroyed a vast collection of papers. Many of the manuscripts he carefully saved he also recopied, as authors did in those days to provide a clean manuscript for the printer.

149. McLachlan, 1941:165.

150. Christianson, 1984; More, 1934.

151. McLachlan, 1941:167.

152. Ibid.

153. Brewster, 1855, 1871.

154. Hurlbutt, 1985:14.

155. In Brewster, 1871:242–45.

156. Ibid.:206; Manuel, 1968, 1974.

157. In Buckley, 1987:310.

158. Marx and Engels, 1964:192.

159. Bell, 1937:96.

160. Cragg, 1964:13.

161. More, 1934.

162. McLachlan, 1941:172.

163. Hall, 1992; Munby, 1952.

164. Munby, 1952:48.

165. Ibid.:41.

166. In addition, there is a very major collection of Newton's scientific manuscripts at Oxford and another in the Babson College Archives, in Wellesley, Massachusetts.

167. Munby, 1952:41.

168. White, 1997:158–62.

169. Dobbs, 1975, 1991.

170. Over the past four decades, Newton's theological, alchemical, astrological, and other esoteric manuscripts and notes have been studied with great care, and much has been published—although there remains more to come (cf. Castillejo, 1981; Dobbs, 1975, 1991; Hall and Hall, 1962; McLachlan, 1950).

171. Hovenkamp, 1978:ix.

172. Paley, [1803] 1809:5.

173. Dana, 1858:341.

174. *Confessions* 12.

175. McGrath, 1999:11.

176. In ibid.

177. Calvin, [ca. 1555] 1980:52–53.

178. In McGrath, 1999:12.

179. I was advised by several colleagues that to criticize evolutionary theory would damage my "career." This merely hardened my resolve to suffer no more of this arrogant occultism.

180. Dawkins, 1986:287.

181. Dawkins, 1976:1.

182. Dawkins, 1989:34.

183. Dawkins, 1986:241, 251.

184. Gould, 1980:181.

185. Stanley, 1981:104.

186. Eldredge, 1986:145.

187. Some might claim that there are rare exceptions such as when a horse and an ass are bred to produce a mule. But, as in the case of mules, the offspring of such crossbreeding are sterile hybrids.

188. Here I am giving orthodox and neo-orthodox Darwinians a break, since they have not been able to define fitness as other than a relatively higher rate of reproduction, hence making the theory tautological: those that reproduce at a higher rate will reproduce at a higher rate.

189. Darwin, 1993:316.

190. Gruber, 1981:125–26.

191. Darwin, 1993:212.

192. Ibid.:406.

193. Ibid.:414.

194. Stanley, 1979:39.

195. Newell, 1959:267.

196. Gould, 1980:182.

197. In Hull, 1973:146.

198. Desmond, 1997:459.

199. Schwartz, 1999:3.

200. Ruse, 1999; Schwartz, 1999.

201. Schwartz, 1999.

202. This term ("neo" means new) is applied to all evolutionary studies based on Mendelian genetics.

203. Schwartz, 1999:3.

204. Goldschmidt, 1940:390.

205. Mayr, 1970:253.

206. Eldredge, 1971; Eldredge and Gould, 1972; Gould and Eldredge, 1993.

207. Dennett, 1995.

208. Gould, 1980.

209. A skyhook is a magical device, a hook attached to a cable that reaches into the sky and is able to raise and lower loads despite not being hooked to a crane or other mechanical device. When I was in the army, the term was in common usage, and a sergeant might say, "Unless the chaplain can pray us down a skyhook, we ain't never going to lift that sucker."

210. Dennett, 1995:298.

211. Indicative of the unscientific character of the Darwinian Crusade, Carl Sagan (1975:82) responded to the fact that "the time available for the origin of life seems to have been short, a few hundred million years at most," as proof that evolution must be much faster and statistically much more probable than we had thought.

212. Dawkins (1986) "solves" this problem by introducing an unidentified editor who lets the monkey know each time it has a correct letter in the correct space, thus providing for a quite rapid accomplishment of the lines. I find this remarkable in someone who essentially makes his living from atheism, since any educated Creationist would gladly embrace this version of "directed" evolution.

213. Hoyle and Wickramasinghe, 1981.

214. Szathmaŕy, 1999.

215. Huxley, 1960:1.

216. Gould, 1977:7.

217. In Barrow and Tipler, 1986:85.

218. Dawkins, 1986:6.

219. Desmond, 1997; Eiseley, 1958; Irvine, 1955.

220. Desmond, 1997.

221. Ibid.; MacKenzie and MacKenzie, 1977; Wilson, 1999.

222. Desmond, 1997:245.

223. McLellan, 1987:3n.

224. Wilson, 1999.

225. Barlow, [1958] 1993.

226. In Desmond, 1997:253.

227. Lucas, 1979:329.

228. Tyndall, 1874:44.

229. In Gould, 1977:77.

230. A survey of students at five leading American Protestant divinity schools, conducted in the late 1920s, found that 94 percent agreed "[t]hat the idea of evolution is consistent with belief in God as Creator," and only 5 percent agreed "[t]hat the creation of the world occurred in the manner and time recorded in Genesis" (Betts, 1929).

231. In Desmond, 1997:544.

232. Sidgwick, 1898:433–34.

233. Brix, 1984; Dennett, 1995; Desmond, 1997; Desmond and Moore, 1991; Irvine, 1959; Richards, 1987; Wilson, 1999.

234. Irvine, 1959:6.

235. Brix, 1984:15, 135.

236. *Macmillan's Magazine*, October 1898.

237. Brooke and Cantor, 1998; Cohen, 1985b:597.

238. Darwin, 1896, 2:117–18.

239. Ibid.:124–25.

240. Cohen, 1985b.

241. Lucas, 1979.

242. Ibid.:329–30.

243. Desmond, 1997:256.

244. Rudwick, 1986:302.

245. That it was remembered at all was due to its being included in a marginal note in some editions of the King James Version of the Bible.

246. Numbers, 1986.

247. Finke and Stark, 1992.

248. Larson, 1997.

249. Ibid.

250. Popper, 1957, 1962, [1976] 1996.

251. Olson, 1960:523.

252. Larson and Witham, 1997; Witham, 1997.

253. Galton, 1875; Hilts, 1975.

254. Reprinted in Bottomore and Rubel, 1956.

255. Galton, 1875:97.

256. Pearson, 1914–1930.

257. A cross-sectional sample of Protestant ministers in Chicago in the late 1920s revealed that, while all expressed their belief "[t]hat God exists," only 64 percent agreed "[t]hat prayer has the power to change conditions in nature." The same study also surveyed students at five theological schools, of whom only 21 percent agreed with the item on prayer (Betts, 1929). In a 1968 sample of Protestant clergy in California, only 45 percent of pastors of the United Church of Christ could agree to the statement "I know God really exists and I have no doubts about it" (Stark et al., 1971). Of Methodist clergy, 52 percent agreed. Notice that this item is much less stringent than the one used by Leuba, since clergy were free to define God as they wished. Given that the majority of these same clergy doubted the divinity of Jesus, one must suppose that many of them asserted their beliefs in a rather remote and vague conception of God, not one who hears and answers prayers.

258. Leuba, [1916] 1921:280.

259. Larson and Witham, 1997.

260. Leuba [1916] 1921, 1934; Thalheimer 1973.

261. Feldman and Newcomb, 1970.

262. Bird, 1993.

263. Wuthnow, 1985:191.

264. Wallace, 1966:265.

265. This is not surprising, for Sarton remained a staunch supporter of A. D. White and his claim that religion is the natural enemy of science (see Sarton, 1955).

266. Manuel, 1974:27.

267. Regis, 1987:24.

268. Clark, 1971:18–19; Regis, 1987:24.

269. Clark, 1971; Snow, 1967.

270. Davies, 1983.

271. Polkinghorne, 1998.

272. Townes, 1995.

273. Einstein, 1954:46.

Chapter 3
God's *Enemies*: Explaining the European Witch-Hunts

1. Guazzo [1608] 1972:16.

2. The most important of these is Étienne-Léon de Lamothe-Langdon's three-volume history of the French Inquisition (1829), which claimed that at least a thousand witchcraft trials and huge numbers of executions had occurred in Toulouse and Carcassonne between 1320 and 1350. He included lengthy excerpts from official court records. Subsequent scholars treated this as the "most important single body of sources for early European witch trials" (Kieckhefer, 1976:16). I find it incredible that nearly 150 years passed before anyone wondered how there could have been so many trials here when there were virtually none taking place elsewhere, or about the fact that all of the original documents cited by Lamothe-Langdon had "disappeared' before anyone else could see them, or about the anachronistic use of terms that did not come into use until far later than the alleged date of the documents, or the fact that Lamonthe-Langdon was known to have produced a number of other forgeries, such as fake memoirs by eighteenth-century celebrities. It was not until the mid-1970s that witchcraft scholars caught on. Norman Cohn (1975, 2000) and Richard Kieckhefer (1976) are to be congratulated for exposing this rat who caused a great deal of scholarly effort to be wasted on efforts to account for things that never happened.

3. Dworkin, 1974.

4. Daly, 1978.

5. Hughes, 1952:195.

6. Davies, 1996:567.

7. The total of nine million deaths can be traced back to Matilda Joslyn Gage, in *Woman, Church and State*, an early feminist work published in 1893. Gage appears simply to have intuited this figure, offering no basis for it whatever. It has since lived on, often without specific citation—Andrea Dworkin (1974:130) merely calls her all-female version of it "the most responsible estimate." Indeed!

8. Briggs, 1998; Katz, 1994; Levack, 1995.

9. Assuming an average population total of 35 million for Europe during these three centuries (Russell, 1958) and that, given prevailing life expectancy, the population would have turned over three times a century, 315 million people were at risk of execution for witchcraft.

10. Hyslop, 1925:4.

11. Moreover, "witches" were hanged, not burned, in England.

12. Ewen, 1929; Levack, 1995; Thomas, 1971.

13. Henningsen, 1980.

14. Robbins, 1959.

15. Ankarloo, 1990.

16. Lea, 1906–1907.

17. Larner, 1981.

18. Trevor-Roper, [1969] 2001:141–43.

19. Briggs, 1996:8.

20. Katz, 1994; Levack, 1995.

21. In the most carefully studied and documented of all witch-hunts, 162 persons were accused of witchcraft in Salem, Massachusetts. Of these, 76 were tried, 30 were convicted, and 20 were executed (Levack, 1995).

22. Ibid.; Kamen, 1993, 1997; Katz, 1994.

23. Weisser, 1979.

24. Briggs, 1998:262.

25. Monter, 1999.

26. Hansen, 1969:12.

27. Levack, 1995.

28. Haliczer, 1990; Hamilton, 1981; Henningsen, 1980; Kamen, 1997, 1993.

29. Levack, 1995:92.

30. Briggs, 1989:65.

31. Levack, 1995.

32. Thomas, 1971:438.

33. Summers, 1926, 1927.

34. Murray, 1921, [1933] 1970; also Hughes, 1952; Rose, 1962.

35. Cohn, 1975:109.

36. Briggs, 1998; Cohn, 1975, 2000; Kieckhefer, 1976; Parrinder, 1958; Robbins, 1959; Rose, 1962; Russell, 1972; Thomas, 1971; Trevor-Roper, [1969] 2001.

37. Murray, 1921.

38. Murray, 1954.

39. Russell, 1972:40.

40. Briggs, 1989.

41. Kittredge, 1929:130.

42. Kamen, 1993:238–39.

43. Thomas, 1971:511.

44. Ibid.:508.

45. Monter, 1976:199.

46. Alexander and Selesnick, 1966; Bromberg, 1959; Cartwright and Biddiss, 1972; Freud, [1921] 1959; Sarbin, 1969; Zilboorg, 1935.

47. Midelfort, 1972; Spanos, 1978.

48. Ben-Yehuda, 1981.

49. Although some psychiatric historians suggest that it did, based on circular reasoning from the eruption of witchcraft accusations (see Alexander and Selesnick, 1966).

50. Rosen, 1968.

51. Monter, 1976.

52. Spanos, 1978.

53. Barstow, 1995; Hughes, 1952; Larner, 1984.

54. Barstow, 1995:12.

55. Krämer and Sprenger, [1487] 1928:47.

56. Briggs, 1998; Levack, 1995.

57. Cohn, 1975:xiii.

58. Midelfort, 1972; Trevor-Roper, [1969] 2001.

59. Briggs, 1998; Holmes, 1993.

60. Larner, 1984.

61. Barstow, 1988:17–18.

62. Willis, 1995:13.

63. Levack, 1995.

64. Ibid.:152. Also see Cohn, 2000; Monter, 1976; Thomas, 1971.

65. Rosen, 1968:7.

66. Tillich, 1952:48.

67. Katz, 1994:416n.

68. Walzer, [1963] 1969:140.

69. Ben-Yehuda, 1980:14.

70. Ibid.:24–25.

71. Briggs, 1998:401–2.

72. Macfarlane, 1970.

73. Macfarlane, 1978.

74. Erikson, 1966:4.

75. Ibid.:67.

76. Durkheim, [1895] 1958:67.

77. Coser, 1962; Erikson, 1962, 1966; Homans, 1950.

78. Hirschi, 1973.

79. Gibbs, 1975.

80. Sperber, 1975.

81. Needham, 1972.

82. Currie, 1968; Lea, [1887] 1955; Robbins, 1959.

83. Currie, 1968:21.

84. Cohn, 1975; Read, 1999.

85. Midelfort, 1972.

86. Larner, 1981:116.

87. Henningsen, 1980; Midelfort, 1972; Thomas, 1971.

88. Henningsen, 1980.

89. Thomas, 1971:457.

90. Cohn, 2000:233.

91. Hutchinson, 1720.

92. Trethowan (1963:341) expresses his amazement that there is "a remarkable resemblance" between the discussions of the "psychopathology" of impotence in the *Malleus maleficarum* and those accepted by him and his fellow Freudians. To anyone but a true believer, that might have been a cause for reflection as to the scientific worth of psychoanalysis.

93. Ibid.:343.

94. Lea, 1867.

95. Robbins, 1959:270.

96. Katz, 1994; Levack, 1995; Monter and Tedeschi, 1986.

97. Kamen, 1993, 1997.

98. Coulton, 1938a:119, 324.

99. Russell, 1972.

100. Trevor-Roper, [1969] 2001:162.

101. Lecky, [1865] 1903.

102. Burckhardt, [1885] 1990.

103. This claim was as fraudulent as those concerning belief in a flat earth or Church opposition to human dissections. For example, in 1619 Pere Gil, rector of the Jesuit College in Barcelona, expressed the orthodox Catholic view that all claims that "witches" could cause bad weather were heretical superstitions, since only God could intervene in the natural causes of storms (Kamen, 1993:241). White was correct that many witches were condemned for causing hailstorms and other bad weather, but this was the work of local, secular courts, or of ignorant and isolated clergy, and was contrary to Church doctrine.

104. Burr, 1897:1.

105. Trevor-Roper, [1969] 2001:163.

106. Ibid.:90.

107. Monter, 1976:29.

108. *In Praise of Folly.*

109. In Midelfort, 1972:30.

110. William Shakespeare (*1564–1616*) believed in witches, and so did his audiences (Harris, 1980; Willis, 1995). Albrecht Dürer (*1471–1528*) did his best to draw accurate portraits of witches revealing their monstrous souls.

111. White, 1997, and Chapter 2.

112. Robbins, 1959.

113. In Ibid.:224.

114. Briggs, 1998.

115. Monter, 1976.

116. Midelfort, 1974; Pagel, 1958.

117. Yates, 1964, 1979.

118. Hobbs, [1651] 1956, 21.

119. Hobbes did not believe that witches truly possessed supernatural powers, but he assumed that they believed they did and tried to use these powers, and therefore were guilty. This leaves his atheism intact but does not qualify him as "enlightened."

120. Trevor-Roper, [1969] 2001:113.

121. In Preus, 1987:9.

122. Amazingly, having gone on at length about his book on political theory, now largely forgotten and ignored, both the *Encyclopaedia Britannica* and the *New Columbia Encyclopedia* fail to mention this, his most influential book by far, in their articles on Bodin.

123. Trevor-Roper, [1969] 2001:112.

124. In Robbins, 1959:54.

125. Feyerabend, 1983.

126. In Jones, 1953:184.

127. LeBon, [1896] 1960.

128. Freud, [1921] 1959.

129. Ibid.:17.

130. Rosen, 1968:5.

131. Cohn, 1975.

132. Turner and Killian, 1987.

133. Midelfort, 1972.

134. Beard, North, and Price, 1998; Cumont, [1912] 1960, [1911] 1956; MacMullen, 1981.

135. In Kieckhefer, 1989:19.

136. Beard, North, and Price, 1998; MacMullen, 1981.

137. Beard, North, and Price, 1998:233.

138. *Natural History* 30.13.11.3.

139. Beard, North, and Price, 1998.

140. *Annals* 12.22.

141. Condemnations of love potions, as interfering with freedom of choice and hence being a form of rape, are indistinguishable from contemporary objections to the "date rape drug."

142. In Thomas, 1971:49.

143. Trevor-Roper, [1969] 2001:85.

144. In Russell, 1972:76–77.

145. Trevor-Roper, [1969] 2001:85.

146. *Ecclesiastical History* 1.30.

147. Thomas, 1971:48.

148. Brooke and Brooke, 1984.

149. *Physica* 1.56.

150. In Kieckhefer, 1989:3.

151. In ibid.:4.

152. Porter, 1998.

153. Briggs, 1998:70.

154. In Thomas, 1971:14.

155. Briggs, 1998; Levack, 1995; Russell, 1972; Thomas, 1971.

156. Briggs, 1998.

157. See Russell, 1972:148.

158. Smith, [1776] 1981:792–93.

159. Monter, 1976; Russell, 1972.

160. Text in Kors and Peters, 1972:79.

161. Russell, 1972:151.

162. Ibid.:126–27.

163. Kieckhefer, 1976.

164. Read, 1999.

165. O'Neil, 1984.

166. Thomas, 1971.

167. O'Neil, 1981, 1984, 1987.

168. O'Neil, 1981:19.

169. O'Neil, 1984.

170. O'Neil, 1981:11.

171. Cohn, 1975:169.

172. Kieckhefer, 1976:79–80.

173. Ibid.:22.

174. Midelfort 1981:30.

175. Katz, 1994:417.

176. Henningsen, 1980; Larner, Lee, and McLachlan, 1977; Macfarlane, 1970; Midelfort, 1972; Monter, 1976.

177. Kieckhefer, 1976.

178. Katz, 1994; Levack, 1995.

179. Briggs, 1998:402.

180. Midelfort, 1972.

181. Monter, 1976.

182. O'Neil, 1981, 1984; Kamen, 1993.

183. Norman Davies (1996) gave considerable coverage to the decline of the Ottoman Empire in the nineteenth and twentieth centuries, but none to these important campaigns.

184. Russell, 1972.

185. Monter, 1976.

186. Midelfort, 1972.

187. Briggs, 1989, 1998.

188. Levack, 1995:102.

189. In Delumeau, 1977:171.

190. Trevor-Roper, [1969] 2001.

191. Katz, 1994:420.

192. Dunn, 1979:295.

193. Kamen, 1993, 1997.

194. Stark, 2001a.

195. Kieckhefer, 1979.

196. Cohn, 1961; Johnson, 1976; Kieckhefer, 1976.

197. Kieckhefer, 1976.

198. Holborn, 1982.

199. Briggs, 1989, 1998; Levack, 1995; Midelfort, 1972; Monter, 1976.

200. Levack, 1995:196.

201. Briggs, 1998; Levack, 1995; Midelfort, 1972; Monter, 1976.

202. Stark, 1998.

203. Robin Briggs (1989:20) suggested that we "regard the whole [witch-hunt] phenomenon as a natural result of powerful tendencies within both Christianity and the development of a higher civilization, and concentrate on explaining why things were not a great deal worse, rather than why they happened at all."

204. Monter, 1976.

205. Contreras and Henningsen, 1986; Given, 1997; Haliczer, 1990; Henningsen, 1980; Kamen, 1993, 1997; Levack, 1995; Monter, 1990.

206. Lea, 1906–1907, 4:206.

207. Gitlitz, 1996; Netanyahu, 1999.
208. Monter, 1990.
209. Kamen, 1993, 1997.
210. O'Neil, 1987.
211. Ibid.:90.
212. Ibid.
213. Henningsen, 1980; Kamen, 1993, 1997; Levack, 1995; Monter, 1990.
214. Kamen, 1997:237–38.
215. Kamen, 1993, 1997.
216. Kamen, 1993.
217. Bethencourt, 1990:404.
218. Monter and Tedeschi, 1986.
219. Ginzburg, 1983.
220. O'Neil, 1987:94.
221. O'Neil, 1987.
222. Levack, 1995.
223. Ibid.:97.
224. Ibid.:199.
225. Briggs, 1989.
226. Ibid.
227. Levack, 1995:198.
228. Midelfort, 1972:8.
229. Levack, 1995:193.
230. Ibid.:200.
231. Levack, 1995; Monter, 1976.
232. Briggs, 1989.
233. Levack, 1995.
234. Midelfort, 1972:88–90.
235. Ibid.:90–94.
236. Briggs, 1989:92.
237. He did not teach mathematics.
238. Ankarloo, 1990:290.
239. Ankarloo, 1990.
240. Latourette, 1975:738.
241. Johansen, 1990:341.
242. Ibid.
243. Johansen, 1990.
244. Ibid.:348.
245. Naess, 1990.

246. Hastrup, 1990:386; Vésteinsson, 2001.

247. Latourette, 1975.

248. Stark, 2001a; Swatos and Gissurarson, 1997.

249. Hastrup, 1990.

250. Naess, 1990.

251. Ibid.:381.

252. Ibid.

253. Heikkinen and Kervinen, 1990.

254. Ibid., 323–26.

255. Ewen, 1929.

256. Levack, 1995.

257. Thomas, 1971.

258. Lambert, 1992; Latourette, 1975.

259. Robbins, 1959; Thomas, 1971.

260. Thomas, 1971:451.

261. Ibid.:440.

262. In ibid.:441.

263. Levack, 1995:201.

264. Thomas, 1971.

265. Levack, 1995.

266. Latourette, 1975.

267. Ibid.

268. Larner, 1981, 1984.

269. Larner, 1981, 1984; Levack, 1995.

270. Midelfort, 1972:191.

271. Midelfort, 1972; Lea, [1939] 1956, vol. 3.

272. Farrington, 1988.

273. Wolfgang, Figlio, and Sellin, 1972.

274. Lea, [1939] 1956, 3:1125.

275. Fischer, 1975.

276. In Robbins, 1959:220–21.

277. Briggs, 1989:59.

278. Barraclough, 1982.

279. Levack, 1995.

280. Thomas, 1971:576.

281. Levack, 1995:240.

282. I am sure others must have objected to witch-hunting earlier, but they are not mentioned in the literature. I omit Michel de Montaigne because his "attack" in the essay "Of Cripples" is so elliptical, amounting to little more than the line,

so revered by the proponents of the thesis that it was the Humanists who saved Europe from more witch-hunts, that "it is putting a high price on one's conjectures to have a man roasted alive because of them."

283. Kamen, 1993:238.
284. Monter, 1976:32–33.
285. Robbins, 1959.
286. In Robbins, 1959:540.
287. Ibid.:454.
288. Scot, [1584] 1972:7–8.
289. I modernized the spelling.
290. Levack, 1995:239.
291. Briggs, 1998:407.
292. In Kamen, 1997:274.
293. In Robbins, 1959:480.
294. Midelfort, 1972.
295. Thomas, 1971:573.
296. All in Robbins, 1959:45.
297. Monter, 1976:39.
298. Levack, 1995:241.
299. Zwemer, 1921.
300. Abdurrahman, 2000.
301. Zwemer, 1921.

Chapter 4
God's *Justice*: The Sin of Slavery

1. Bales, 1999.
2. A subject search through Amazon books produced 2,680 titles.
3. Donald, 1997.
4. Ibid.
5. Patterson, 1982.
6. Boas, 1897:338.
7. Curtis, 1913:74.
8. Fried, 1967:220–23.
9. And what competent sociologist would agree that any societies are *not* stratified?
10. Rohner and Rohner, 1970:79.
11. During the 1990s, the leading high school textbook for American history, *Rise of the American Nation* (Harcourt, Brace, Jovanovich), flatly asserted that

slavery was unknown in North American until introduced by Europeans (Carroll and Shiflett, 2002).

12. See Macleod, 1925, 1928; Nieboer, 1910; Ruby and Brown, 1993; Ruyle, 1973; Siegel, 1945.

13. Suttles and Jonaitis, 1990:87.

14. Donald, 1997:33–34.

15. Nieboer, 1910.

16. During a stay on Debob Bay, an inlet of Puget Sound, my wife and I gathered more than a dozen large crabs in less than fifteen minutes at low tide, using only our bare hands and a sack. The local oysters were so abundant that we could gather them as rapidly as we could pick them up. A crude digging stick sufficed us to obtain a variety of clams. Easily trapped ducks and geese abounded, and the sea was full of fish, including magnificent salmon. An array of wild berries grew all over. If these conditions prevail in modern times, it is impossible to imagine the abundance of the area even a century ago.

17. Gibbon, [1776] 1994, 1:67.

18. Finley, 1980:22.

19. In ibid.:12.

20. Vogt, 1974:25.

21. Finley, 1980:41–42.

22. Ibid.:11.

23. Ibid.:67.

24. Boak and Sinnigen, 1965:157.

25. Grant, 1978:140.

26. Boak and Sinnigen, 1965.

27. Meltzer, 1993.

28. Grant, 1978; Jones, 1956.

29. Gordon, 1924:102.

30. In Meltzer, 1993:150–51.

31. Gordon, 1924:102.

32. Jones, 1956.

33. Meltzer, 1993.

34. Finley, 1981:101.

35. *Oratio XXXI* 11.

36. In Meltzer, 1993:76.

37. Jones, 1956.

38. Barton, 1993; Beacham, 1999; Finley, 1981; Gordon, 1924.

39. Finley, 1980:149.

40. Thompson, 1957.

41. Davis, 1966:31, 37.

42. Smith, [1776] 1981:389.

43. Cantor, 1993.

44. Dahmus, [1968] 1995.

45. Meltzer, 1993; Phillips, 1998.

46. Bensch, 1998:231.

47. Bloch, [1940] 1961:260.

48. Fogel, 1989:25.

49. Bloch, 1975:23.

50. Bloch, [1940] 1961, 1975; Dahmus, [1968] 1995; Davis, 1966; Pelteret, 1995.

51. Austen, 1979; Curtin, 1969; Gordon, 1989; Lewis, 1990; Lovejoy, [1983] 2000; Mauny, 1970; Segal, 2001; Thomas, 1997.

52. Gordon, 1989:4.

53. Ibid.:57.

54. Gordon, 1989; Lewis, 1990; Lovejoy, [1983] 2000; Segal, 2001.

55. Grun, 1982.

56. Hanson, 2001.

57. Lovejoy, [1983] 2000.

58. Austen, 1979.

59. Ibid.

60. Gordon, 1989:149.

61. Cohn, 1998:290.

62. Segal, 2001:5.

63. Salahi, 1995:375.

64. Gordon, 1989; Lewis, 1990.

65. Lewis, 1990.

66. Gordon, 1989:5.

67. Lovejoy, [1983] 2000; Manning, 1990; Thornton, 1998a.

68. Thornton, 1998b:27.

69. Rodney, 1984.

70. *Les Six Livres de la République.*

71. In Elkins, [1959] 1976:69.

72. Watson, 1989.

73. This was the famous Somersett decision. I find it difficult to explain why so many historians insist that this was the first great step toward abolition, when there were far earlier European precedents of which the English court seems to have been fully aware. David Brion Davis ([1975] 1999:505) covers his flank by admitting that "seeming precedents" for the Somersett decision could be found

in French law, but dismisses these by noting that "the Code Noir of 1685 authorized chattel slavery in the colonies," which has nothing whatever to do with the free soil principle in France itself. In the same sentence in which he acknowledges "seeming precedents" Davis wrote that "the British were contemptuously amused by pretensions of liberty in Bourbon France," which would seem adequate evidence of his fundamental anti-Catholic and Anglophile biases.

74. Blackburn, 1998:62.

75. Diamond, 1998; McNeill, 1976.

76. I omitted one African price since it was an order of magnitude higher than the other twelve and was based on only one source.

77. Bean, 1975.

78. Thomas, 1997.

79. Curtin, 1969.

80. Later separated into Haiti and the Dominican Republic.

81. Fogel, 1989.

82. Higman, 1976.

83. Gay, 1969:411. He did go on to admit that "its promulgation marked the beginning of some constraint on masters."

84. Davis, 1966:258.

85. Goveia, 1969:132.

86. Scarano, 1998:140.

87. Schafer, 1994:2–3.

88. Fifty-two Sundays and thirty-five holy days.

89. Tannenbaum, [1946] 1992.

90. Turley, 2000:58.

91. Goveia, 1969.

92. Schmidt-Nowara, 1999.

93. Klein, 1969:145.

94. Klein, 1967; Meltzer, 1993; Thomas, 1997; Turley, 2000.

95. Dunn, 1972.

96. Harris, 1964:70.

97. Dunn, 1972.

98. Beckles, 1989; Dunn, 1973; Goveia, 1969; Sheridan, 1974; Watson, 1989.

99. In Dunn, 1972:239.

100. Fogel, 1989:36.

101. Dunn, 1972.

102. Goveia, 1969:126.

103. Dunn, 1972:243.

104. Johnston, 1910:231.

105. Mathieson, 1926:38–40.

106. Ibid.:245.

107. Ibid.:244.

108. Craton, 1998; Dunn, 1972.

109. Beckles, 1989; Curtin, 1969; Dunn, 1972.

110. In Elkins, [1959] 1976:77.

111. Johnston, 1910:89.

112. Actually, Manoel de Oliveira Lima (1914) and Gilberto Freyre (1922) anticipated Tannenbaum.

113. Tannenbaum, [1946] 1992.

114. Ibid.:88.

115. Elkins, [1959] 1976:71.

116. See Genovese, 1969b; Goveia, 1969; Klein, 1967, 1986.

117. Harris, 1963, 1964.

118. Genovese, 1969b.

119. See Schwartz, 1992.

120. Davis, 1966:228–29.

121. Ibid.:243.

122. Finley, 1969:260.

123. Fogel and Engerman, 1974.

124. Finley, 1980.

125. Dunn, 1972:225.

126. Emmer, 1998.

127. Elkins, [1959] 1976:77.

128. Green-Pedersen, 1971, 1981.

129. Conrad, 1993, 1983, 1974; Drescher, 1988; Karasch, 1987; Schwartz, 1998, 1992, 1985; Toplin, 1972, 1981.

130. Panzer, 1996:30.

131. Curtin, 1969.

132. Conrad, 1974.

133. Schwartz, 1998:101.

134. Karasch, 1987.

135. Schwartz, 1998.

136. Turley, 2000.

137. Watson, 1989:98.

138. Boxer, 1962; Davis, 1966.

139. See Davis, 1966.

140. Curtin, 1969; Dunn, 1972.

141. Higman, 1976.

142. Fogel, 1989; Fogel and Engerman, 1974.

143. Fogel, 1989.

144. Cobb, [1858] 1968.

145. Morris, 1996.

146. Morris, 1998:257.

147. Data for cities are reconstructed from county data.

148. Ingersoll, 1999.

149. Foner, 1970; Genovese, 1974; Koger, 1985; Menn, 1964; Mills, 1977.

150. Tillich, 1951.

151. Suttles, 1990.

152. Albright, 1957:265.

153. *The City of God* 1.17–23.

154. Mendelsohn, 1949:123.

155. Schlaifer, 1936.

156. Davis, 1966:66.

157. The emphasis on "classical" education in Britain makes it probable that at least some of the legislators were aware of this Grecian principle.

158. Schlaifer, 1936.

159. Ibid.

160. *Politics* 1.1254.

161. Schlaifer, 1936:199.

162. In Meltzer, 1993:96.

163. See Blackburn, 1998; Davis, 1966; Meltzer, 1993.

164. In Meltzer, 1993:44.

165. The Dead Sea scrolls, which most authorities associate with the Essenes, include legal codes that did permit slavery of nonbelievers (Vermes, 2000).

166. *Every Good Man Is Free* 79.

167. *On the Contemplative Life* 70.

168. See Hurbon, 1992; Noonan, 1993.

169. Maxwell, 1975.

170. Attwater and John, 1995; Thomas, 1997.

171. Brett, 1994; Panzer, 1996.

172. Brett, 1994:57, 78.

173. *Summa* q.3, a.3.

174. Ibid. q.92, a, 1–2.

175. In Panzer, 1996:8.

176. Cantor, 1993:38.

177. Auping, 1994; Panzer, 1996.

178. Stanley M. Elkins ([1959] 1976:69) knew of these bulls, having written, "[T]he papacy itself would denounce it [slavery] in various ways in 1462, 1537, 1639, 1741, 1815, and 1839." But that was it! No quotations. No indication of contents or contexts. Nothing. Frank Tannenbaum also knew of these bulls: "The slave trade had been condemned by Pius II on October 7, 1462, by Paul III on May 29, 1537, by Urban VIII on April 2, 1639, by Benedict XIV on December 20, 1741, and finally by Gregory XVI on December 3, 1839. The grounds of the condemnation were that innocent and free persons were illegally and by force captured and sold into slavery, that rapine, cruelty, and war were stimulated in the search for human beings to be sold at profit." A bit fuller treatment than Elkins gave it, but very little, nonetheless. However, even Elkins gave far more coverage to papal bulls against slavery than have most historians. The only entry for "pope" in the index of David Brion Davis's celebrated intellectual history of slavery in Western culture (Davis, 1966) is the British poet Alexander Pope. Precisely the same can be said of Robin Blackburn's extensive study (1998). As for Milton Meltzer (1993), his index doesn't even include Alexander Pope. Nor is any mention made of popes in Drescher and Engerman's encyclopedic *A Historical Guide to World Slavery* (1998), although there are lengthy sections devoted to "Moral Issues" and to "Religion."

179. Panzer, 1996:19–21.

180. Ibid.:22.

181. Ibid.:33.

182. Ibid.: Appendix C.

183. Latourette, 1975:944.

184. Delumeau, 1977; Genovese, 1974.

185. Auping, 1994:13.

186. Genovese, 1974:179.

187. Blackburn, 1998:291.

188. Blackburn, 1998; Davis, 1966, [1975] 1999; Drescher and Engerman, 1998; Meltzer, 1993; Turley, 2000.

189. Goveia, 1969; Morris, 1996; Schafer, 1994; Watson, 1989.

190. Beckles, 1989; Dunn, 1979.

191. Abou, 1997; Boxer, 1962; Caraman, 1975; Furneaux, 1969; Graham, 1901; Mörner, 1965.

192. The meaning here is similar to that used in cooking, as in reducing a sauce, based on the fact that the Jesuits had concentrated the Guaraní in far denser settlements than those they had inhabited before.

193. In Abou, 1997:65.

194. Garay, [1900] 1965; Madariaga, [1948] 1965; see a summary in Caraman, 1975.

195. Abou, 1997; Caraman, 1975.

196. Murphy, 2001.

197. Hanke, 1951.

198. In Fox, 1913:40.

199. Fiske, 1899:108.

200. Lewis, 1990; Watt, 1961, 1965.

201. In Gordon, 1989:19.

202. I should qualify this assertion by noting the ability of many Protestant theologians to "get around" the fact that Jesus drank wine.

203. Saunders, 1982.

204. Drescher, 1987.

205. McCloy, 1961.

206. Leslie, 1740.

207. Yazawa, 1998:3.

208. Woolman, [1754] 1969.

209. Soderlund, 1985.

210. In Brookes, 1937:475–77.

211. Soderlund, 1985.

212. Davis, 1966.

213. Soderlund, 1985.

214. Auping, 1994; Barnes, [1933] 1964; Strong, 1999.

215. Kraditor, 1967; Mayer, 1998; Nye, 1955.

216. In Ruchames, 1963:78.

217. Mayer, 1998.

218. Auping, 1994.

219. Barnes, [1933] 1964; Strong, 1999.

220. In Auping, 1994:109–10.

221. Auping, 1994.

222. Finney, [1876] 1960:344.

223. Hammond, 1974.

224. Auping, 1994.

225. Asbury, 1958, 2:151.

226. Beard, 1927.

227. Craven, 1942.

228. Fox-Genovese and Genovese, 1987; Mathews, 1977.

229. Ahlstrom, 1972; Anstey, 1975; Barnes, [1933] 1964; Coupland, 1933; Fogel, 1989.

230. Davis, 1966:90.

231. Ibid.:91.

232. Anstey, 1975; Blackburn, 1988; Clarkson, 1808; Drescher, 1987; Eltis, 1987, Temperley, 1998; Walvin, 1981.

233. Green, 1964; Smith, 1986.

234. Anstey, 1975:249.

235. Clarkson, 1808, 1:228–29.

236. Since women were unable to vote, it was thought that their opinions would carry little weight with elected officials.

237. Eltis, 1987.

238. My calculation based on population data from Mitchell, 1962.

239. Fogel, 1989:219.

240. Drescher, 1977.

241. Drescher, 1987:71–72.

242. Drescher, 1987; Green, 1964; Smith, 1986.

243. Temperley, 1998:14.

244. Blackburn, 1988; Daget, 1980; Drescher, 1987; Jennings, 2000.

245. Blackburn, 1988.

246. Jennings, 2000:3–4.

247. Daget, 1980:72.

248. Jennings, 2000.

249. Ibid.:54.

250. Jennings, 2000.

251. Blackburn, 1988; Klein, 1986; Schmidt-Nowara, 1999.

252. Schmidt-Nowara, 1999:7.

253. Conrad, 1993, 1983, 1974; Drescher, 1988; Karasch, 1987; Schwartz, 1998, 1992, 1985; Toplin, 1972, 1981.

254. Drescher, 1988:21.

255. Fogel, 1989.

256. Conrad, 1993; Schwartz, 1998.

257. Merrick and Graham, 1979.

258. Toplin, 1972.

259. Gay, 1969:410.

260. Davis, 1966:391.

261. Gay, 1969.

262. Seeber, 1937.

263. In Davis, 1966:398.

264. Davis, 1966.

265. Paley, [1785] 1827, 87–88.

266. Even in the United States in 1776 they made up only 10 percent of all congregations (Stark and Finke, 1988).

267. Branch, 1988; Fogel, 2000; Morris, 1984.

268. Smith, [1776] 1981:99.

269. In Thomas, 1963:326.

270. Helper, 1857.

271. Olmsted, 1861.

272. Temperley, 1977:105.

273. Davis, [1975] 1999:348–49.

274. Williams, [1944] 1994:135.

275. Ibid.

276. Conrad and Meyer, 1958; Easterlin, 1961; Fogel and Engerman, 1974.

277. Davis, [1975] 1999:233.

278. Ibid.:251.

279. Ibid.:467.

280. Ibid.:350.

281. Ashworth, 1992:182.

282. Haskell, 1992:117.

283. Fogel, 1989:410.

Postscript
Gods, Rituals, and Social Science

1. Durkheim, [1886] 1994:19.

2. Durkheim, [1912] 1995:227.

3. Strenski, 1997.

4. Radcliffe-Brown, 1939:25.

5. Radcliffe-Brown, 1952:155.

6. Yerkes, 1952:4.

7. Freud, [1912–1913] 1950.

8. Money-Kyrle, 1929.

9. Morris, 1987:159.

10. Needham, 1972.

11. Price, 1984.

12. Sperber, 1975:5.

13. Geertz, 1966:19–20.

14. Bellah, 1970:220.

15. Barrett, in press, 2000; Barrett and Lawson, 2001; Lawson and McCauley, 1990.

16. Barrett, in press.
17. They are "smart Gods" according to Barrett.
18. Smith, 1889:53.
19. Durkheim, [1886] 1994:21.
20. Malinowski, 1935:viii.
21. Tylor, [1871] 1958:446.
22. Spencer, 1896, 2:808–9.
23. Mills, 1922:121.
24. Fortune, 1935:357.
25. Benedict, 1938:633.
26. Barton, 1946.
27. Lawrence, 1964.
28. Douglas, 1975:77.
29. MacMullen, 1981:58.
30. Ibid.:53.
31. MacMullen, 1981; Meeks, 1993; Stark, 1996.
32. Stark, 2001b.
33. Chen, 1995; Green, 1988; Lang and Ragvold, 1993.
34. However, this does not mean that the effects of images of God will always outweigh those of religious participation, if for no other reason than that such things as voting or fertility may be more a result of "social" exposure to a particular group than the product of a purely "religious" influence.

Bibliography

Abdurrahman, Abdullah K. 2000. "Magic and Fortune-Telling." *Al Jumuah* 12/13:1–5.

Abou, Sélim. 1997. *The Jesuit "Republic" of the Guaranís (1609–1768)*. New York: Crossroad Publishing Company.

Agassiz, Louis. 1857–1862. *Contributions to the Natural History of the United States*. London: Trübner and Co.

Ahlstrom, Sidney E. 1972. *A Religious History of the American People*. New Haven: Yale University Press.

Albright, William Foxwell. 1957. *From the Stone Age to Christianity: Monotheism and the Historical Process*. 2d ed. Garden City: NY: Doubleday.

Alexander, Franz G., and Sheldon T. Selesnick. 1966. *The History of Psychiatry*. New York: Harper and Row.

Allport, Gordon W. 1960. *The Individual and His Religion*. New York: Macmillan.

Anderson, Robert D. 1970. "The History of Witchcraft: A Review with Some Psychiatric Comments." *American Journal of Psychiatry* 126:1727–35.

Ankarloo, Bengt. 1990. "Sweden: the Mass Burnings (1668–76)." InAnkarloo and Henningsen, 1990:285–317.

Ankarloo, Bengt, and Gustav Henningsen, eds. 1990. *Early Modern European Witchcraft*. Oxford: Clarendon Press.

Anstey, Roger. 1975. *The Atlantic Slave Trade and British Abolition, 1760–1810*. London: Macmillan.

Armitage, Angus. 1951. *The World of Copernicus*. New York: Mentor Books.

Armstrong, Karen. 1993. *Muhammad: A Biography of the Prophet*. San Francisco: Harper.

Asbury, Francis. 1958. *The Journal and Letters of Francis Asbury.* Edited by Elmer T. Clark, Manning J. Potts, and Jacob S. Payton. 3 vols. Nashville: Abingdon Press.

Ashworth, John. 1992. "The Relationship between Capitalism and Humanitarianism." In *The Antislavery Debate: Capitalism and Abolitionism as a Problem of Historical Interpretation*, edited by Thomas Bender, 180–99. Berkeley and Los Angeles: University of California Press.

Asimov, Isaac. 1972. *Asimov's Biographical Encyclopedia of Science and Technology.* Garden City, NY: Doubleday.

Aston, Margaret. 1984. *Lollards and Reformers: Images and Literacy in Late Medieval Religion.* London: Hambledon.

———. 1970. *The Fifteenth Century: The Prospect of Europe.* London: Thames and Hudson.

———. 1968. *The Fifteenth Century: The Prospect of Europe.* New York: Harcourt, Brace and World.

Attwater, Donald, and Catherine Rachel John. 1995. *The Penguin Dictionary of Saints.* 3d ed. London: Penguin.

Auping, John A. 1994. *Religion and Social Justice: The Case of Christianity and the Abolition of Slavery in America.* Mexico City: Universidad Iberoamericana.

Austen, Ralph A. 1979. "The Trans-Saharan Slave Trade: A Tentative Census." In *The Uncommon Market: Essays in the Economic History of the Atlantic Slave Trade*, edited by Henry A. Gemery and Jan S. Hogendorn, 23–76. New York: Academic Press.

Bagnall, Roger S. 1993. *Egypt in Late Antiquity.* Princeton: Princeton University Press.

Bailey, Edward. 1998. *Implicit Religion: An Introduction.* London: Middlesex University Press.

Bainton, Roland Herbert, ed. 1997. *Martin Luther's Christmas Book.* Minneapolis: Augsburg Fortress Publishers.

———. [1952] 1985. *The Reformation of the Sixteenth Century.* Enl. ed. Boston: Beacon Press.

———. 1969. *Erasmus of Christendom.* New York: Scribner's.

Baker, Herschel. 1952. *The Wars of Truth.* Cambridge: Harvard University Press.

Bales, Kevin. 1999. *Disposable People: New Slavery in the Global Economy.* Berkeley and Los Angeles: University of California Press.

Bangs, Carl. 1972. "Deceptive Statistics." *Christian Century* 89:852–53.

Barber, Malcolm. 2000. *The Cathars in Languedoc.* New York: Addison Wesley Longman.

Barclay, Brig. Cycil Nelson, and Vice Adm. Brian Betham Schofield. 1981. "Gunnery." *Encyclopaedia Britannica*, 488–98. 15th ed. Chicago: University of Chicago Press.

Barlow, Nora, ed. [1958] 1993. *The Autobiography of Charles Darwin*. New York: W. W. Norton.

Barnes, Gilbert. [1933] 1964. *The Antislavery Impulse, 1830–1844*. New York: Harcourt, Brace & World.

Barraclough, Geoffrey, ed. 1998. *HarperCollins Atlas of World History*. Ann Arbor, MI: Borders Press.

———. 1982. *The Times Concise Atlas of World History*. London: Times Books.

Barrett, David B. 1982. *World Christian Encyclopedia*. Oxford: Oxford University Press.

Barrett, Justin L. In press. "Smart Gods, Dumb Gods, and the Role of Social Cognition in Structuring Ritual Intuitions." *Journal for the Scientific Study of Religion*.

———. 2000. "Exploring the Natural Foundations of Religion." *Trends in Cognitive Sciences* 4:29–34.

Barrett, Justin L., and E. Thomas Lawson. 2001. "Ritual Intuitions: Cognitive Contributions to Judgments of Ritual Efficacy." *Journal of Cognition and Culture* 1:183–201.

Barrow, John D., and Frank J. Tipler. 1986. *The Anthropic Cosmological Principle*. Oxford: Oxford University Press.

Barstow, Anne Llewellyn. 1995. *Witchcraze: A New History of European Witch Hunts*. San Franciso: Pandora.

———. 1988. "On Studying Witchcraft as Women's History: A Historiography of European Witch Persecutions." *Journal of Feminist Studies in Religion* 4:17–18.

Barton, Carlin A. 1993. *The Sorrows of the Ancient Romans: The Gladiator and the Monster*. Princeton: Princeton University Press.

Barton, Ralph. 1946. "The Religion of the Ifugaos." *American Anthropologist* 40:4.

Bartos, F. G. 1986. *The Hussite Revolution, 1424–37*. New York: Eastern European Monographs.

Bastide, Roger. 1978. *African Religions in Brazil*. Baltimore: Johns Hopkins University Press.

Baumer, Franklin L. 1960. *Religion and the Rise of Scepticism*. New York: Harcourt Brace.

Baumgarten, Albert I. 1997. *The Flourishing of Jewish Sects in the Maccabean Era: An Interpretation*. Leiden: Brill.

Beacham, Richard C. 1999. *Spectacle Entertainments of Early Imperial Rome.* New Haven: Yale University Press.

Bean, Richard N. 1975. "British-American and West African Slave Prices." In *Historical Statistics of the United States*, 1174. Washington, DC: Bureau of the Census.

Beard, Charles A. 1927. *The Rise of American Civilization.* New York: Macmillan.

Beard, Mary, John North, and Simon Price. 1998. *Religions of Rome*, vol. 1, *A History.* Cambridge: Cambridge University Press.

Becker, George. 2000. "Educational 'Preference' of German Protestants and Catholics: The Politics behind Educational Specialization." *Review of Religious Research* 41:311–327.

———. 1991. "Pietism's Confrontation with Enlightenment Rationalism: An Examination of the Relationship between Ascetic Protestantism and Science." *Journal for the Scientific Study of Religion* 30:139–58.

———. 1984. "Pietism and Science: A Critique of Robert K. Merton's Pietism-Science Hypothesis." *American Journal of Sociology* 89:1065–90.

Beckford, James A. 1984. "Holistic Imagery and Healing in New Religious and Healing Movements." *Social Compass* 31:259–71.

Beckles, Hilary. 1989. *White Servitude and Black Slavery in Barbados, 1627–1715.* Knoxville: University of Tennessee Press.

Bell, E. T. 1937. *Men of Mathematics.* New York: Simon and Schuster.

Bellah, Robert N. 1970. *Beyond Belief.* New York: Harper & Row.

———. 1964. "Religious Evolution." *American Sociological Review* 29:358–74.

Ben-David, Joseph. 1990. "Puritanism and Modern Science: A Study in the Continuity and Coherence of Sociological Research." In *Puritanism and the Rise of Modern Science*, edited by I. Bernard Cohen, 246–61. New Brunswick, NJ: Rutgers University Press.

Benedict, Saint. [ca. 520] 1981. *The Rule of St. Benedict in English.* Collegeville, MN: The Liturgical Press.

Benedict, Ruth. 1938. "Religion." In *General Anthropology*, edited by Franz Boas, 627–65. New York: C. D. Heath.

Bensch, Stephen P. 1998. "Historiography: Medieval European and Mediterranean Slavery." In Drescher and Engerman, 1998:229–31.

Ben-Yehuda, Nachman. 1981. "Problems Inherent in Socio-Historical Approaches to the European Witch Craze." *Journal for the Scientific Study of Religion* 20:326–38.

———. 1980. "The European Witch Craze of the Fourteenth to Seventeenth Centuries: A Sociologist's Perspective." *American Sociological Review* 86:1–31.

Berger, Peter. 1967. *The Sacred Canopy*. Garden City, NY: Doubleday.

Bethencourt, Francisco. 1990. "Portugal: A Scrupulous Inquisition." In Ankarloo and Henningson, 1990:403–22.

Betts, George Herbert. 1929. *The Beliefs of Seven Hundred Ministers*. New York: Abingdon Press.

Beyer, Peter. 1994. *Religion and Globalization*. London: Sage.

Bird, Steven. 1993. "Religion and Modernity in the United States: A Rational Choice Analysis of Conflict and Harmony." Ph.D. diss., Purdue University.

Blackburn, Robin. 1998. *The Making of New World Slavery: From the Baroque to the Modern 1492–1800*. London: Verso.

———. 1988. *The Overthrow of Colonial Slavery, 1776–1848*. London: Verso.

Blenkinsopp, Joseph. 1981. "Interpretation and the Tendency to Sectarianism: An Aspect of Second Temple History." In *Jewish and Christian Self-Definition*, vol. 2, edited by E. P. Sanders, 1–26. Philadelphia: Fortress Press.

Bloch, Marc. 1975. *Slavery and Serfdom in the Middle Ages*. Berkeley and Los Angeles: University of California Press.

———. [1940] 1961. *Feudal Society*. 2 vols. Chicago: University of Chicago Press.

Boak, Arthur E. R., and William G. Sinnigen. 1965. *A History of Rome to A.D. 565*. New York: The Macmillan Company.

Boas, Franz. 1897. "The Social Organization and Secret Societies of the Kwakiutl." In *Report of the United States National Museum for 1895*, 371–738. Washington, DC: U.S. Government Printing Office

Boorstin, Daniel J. 1983. *The Discoverers*. New York: Random House.

Bossy, John. 1985. *Christianity in the West 1400–1700*. New York: Oxford University Press.

Bottomore, T. B., and Maximilien Rubel. 1956. *Karl Marx: Selected Writings in Sociology and Social Philosophy*. London: Watts and Co.

Bouwsma, William James. 1988. *John Calvin: A Sixteenth Century Portrait*. New York: Oxford University Press.

Bowker, John, ed. 1997. *The Oxford Dictionary of World Religions*. Oxford: Oxford University Press.

Boxer, Charles R. 1963. *Race Relations in the Portuguese Empire, 1415–1825*. Oxford: Oxford University Press.

———. 1962. *The Golden Age of Brazil, 1695–1750*. Berkeley and Los Angeles: University of California Press.

Brady, Thomas A. 1978. *Ruling Class, Regime and Reformation at Strasbourg, 1520–1555*. Leiden: Brill.

Branch, Taylor. 1988. *Parting the Waters: America in the King Years, 1953–63*. New York: Simon and Schuster.

Braudel, Fernand. 1977. *Afterthoughts on Material Civilization and Capitalism*. Baltimore: Johns Hopkins University Press.

Brett, Stephen F. 1994. *Slavery and the Catholic Tradition*. New York: Peter Lang.

Brewster, David. 1871. *The Life of Sir Isaac Newton*. New York: Harper & Brothers.

———. 1855. *Memoirs of the Life, Writings and Discoveries of Sir Isaac Newton*. 2 vols. Edinburgh: T. Constable & Co.

Briggs, Robin. 1998. *Witches and Neighbors: The Social and Cultural Content of European Witchcraft*. New York: Penguin Books.

———. 1989. *Communities of Belief: Cultural and Social Tensions in Early Modern France*. Oxford: Clarendon Press.

Brix, H. James. 1984. *Theories of Evolution*. Springfield, IL: Charles C. Thomas.

Bromberg, Walter. 1959. *The Mind of Man: A History of Psychotherapy and Psychoanalysis*. New York: Harper and Row.

Brøndsted, Johannes. 1965. *The Vikings*. Baltimore: Penguin Books.

Brooke, Christopher. 1971. *Medieval Church and Society*. London: Sidgwick & Jackson.

Brooke, John, and Geoffrey Cantor. 1998. *Reconstructing Nature: The Engagement of Science and Religion*. Oxford: Oxford University Press.

Brooke, John Hedley. 1991. *Science and Religion: Some Historical Perspectives*. Cambridge: Cambridge University Press.

Brooke, Rosalind, and Christopher Brooke. 1984. *Popular Religion in the Middle Ages: Western Europe 1000–1300*. London: Thames and Hudson.

Brookes, George. 1937. *Friend Anthony Benezet*. Philadelphia: University of Pennsylvania Press.

Brown, Peter. 1967. *Augustine of Hippo: A Biography*. Berkeley and Los Angeles: University of California Press.

Bruckner, Aleksander. 1979. "The Polish Reformation in the Sixteenth Century." In *Polish Civilization: Essays and Studies*, edited by Mieczyslaw Giergielewicz. New York: New York University Press.

Buckley, Michael J., S.J. 1987. *At the Origins of Modern Atheism*. New Haven: Yale University Press.

Burckhardt, Jacob. [1885] 1990. *The Civilization of the Renaissance in Italy*. New York: Penguin.

Burkert, Walter. 1987. *Ancient Mystery Cults*. Cambridge: Harvard University Press.

———. 1985. *Greek Religion*. Cambridge: Harvard University Press.

Burr, George Lincoln. 1897. *Translations and Reprints from the Original Sources of Europe History*. Philadelphia: University of Pennsylvania Press.

———. 1890. *The Literature of Witchcraft.* New York: G. P. Putnam's Sons.

Bush, M. L. 1999. *The Defeat of the Pilgrimage of Grace.* Hull: University of Hull Press.

———. 1967. *Renaissance, Reformation, and the Outer World, 1450–1660.* London: Blandford Press.

Calvin, John. [ca. 1555] 1980. *John Calvin's Sermons on the Ten Commandments.* Grand Rapids, MI: Baker Bookhouse.

Cameron, Euan. 1984. *The Reformation of the Heretics: The Waldenses of the Alps, 1480–1580.* Oxford: Oxford University Press.

Cantor, Norman F. 1993. *The Civilization of the Middle Ages.* Rev. ed. New York: HarperCollins.

Caponetto, Salvatore. 1999. *The Protestant Reformation in Sixteenth-Century Italy.* Kirksville, MO: Truman State University Press.

Caraman, Philip. 1975. *The Lost Paradise: The Jesuit Republic in South America.* New York: Dorset Press.

Carroll, Vincent, and David Shiflett. 2002. *Christianity on Trial: Arguments against Anti-Religious Bigotry.* San Francisco: Encounter Books.

Cartwright, Frederick F., and Michael D. Biddiss. 1972. *Disease and History.* New York: Crowell.

Castillejo, David. 1981. *The Expanding Force in Newton's Cosmos: "As Shown in His Unpublished Papers".* Madrid: Ediciones de Art y Bibliofilia.

Chadwick, Owen. 1972. *The Reformation.* Rev. ed. London: Penguin.

Chandler, Tertius, and Gerald Fox. 1974. *Three Thousand Years of Urban Growth.* New York: Academic Press.

Chazan, Robert. 1996. *In the Year 1096: The First Crusade and the Jews.* Philadelphia: The Jewish Publication Society.

———. 1986. *European Jewry and the First Crusade.* Berkeley and Los Angeles: University of California Press.

Chee-Beng, Tan. 1994. "Chinese Religion: Continuity, Transformation, and Identity with Special References to Malaysia." In *Religions sans frontières?* edited by Roberto Cipriani, 257–89. Rome: Dipartimento per L'Informazione e Editoria.

Cheetham, Nicolas. 1983. *Keepers of the Keys: A History of the Popes From St. Peter to John Paul II.* New York: Scribner's.

Chen, Hsinchih. 1995. "The Development of Taiwanese Folk Religion, 1683–1945." Ph.D. diss., University of Washington.

Christianson, Gale E. 1984. *In the Presence of the Creator: Isaac Newton and His Times.* New York: The Free Press.

Christman, Miriam. 1982. *Lay Culture, Learned Culture: Books and Social Change in Strasbourg, 1480–1599*. New Haven: Yale University Press.

Clagett, Marshall. 1961. *The Science of Mechanics in the Middle Ages*. Madison: University of Wisconsin Press.

Clark, Jon, Celia Modgil, and Sohan Modgil, eds. 1990. *Robert K. Merton: Consensus and Controversy*. New York: Falmer Press.

Clark, Ronald W. 1971. *Einstein: The Life and Times*. New York: World.

Clarkson, Thomas. 1808. *The History of the Rise, Progress and Accomplishment of the Abolition of the African Slave Trade by the British Parliament*. 2 vols. Philadelphia: James P. Parke.

Clendenin, Daniel B., ed. 1995. *Eastern Orthodox Theology: A Contemporary Reader*. Grand Rapids, MI: Baker Books.

Clough, Bradley S. 1997. "Buddhism." In *God*, edited by Jacob Neusner, 56–84. Cleveland: The Pilgrim Press.

Cobb, Thomas R. R. [1858] 1968. *Inquiry into the Law of Negro Slavery in the United States of America*. New York: Negro Universities Press.

Cobban, Alan B. 1988. *The Medieval Universities: Their Development and Organization*. Berkeley and Los Angeles: University of California Press.

Codrington, R. H. 1891. *The Melanesians*. Oxford: Oxford University Press.

Cohen, I. Bernard. 1985a. *Revolution in Science*. Cambridge: Harvard University Press, Belknap Press.

———. 1985b. "Three Notes on the Reception of Darwin's Ideas on Natural Selection (Henry Baker Tristram, Alfred Newton, and Samuel Wilberforce." In *The Darwinian Age*, edited by David Kohn, 589–607. Princeton: Princeton University Press.

Cohen, Jere. 1980. "Rational Capitalism in Rennaissance Italy." *American Journal of Sociology* 85:1340–55.

Cohen, Shaye J. D. 1987. *From the Maccabees to the Mishnah*. Philadelphia: Westminster Press.

Cohen, William B. 1980. *The French Encounter with Africans: White Response to Blacks, 1530–1880*. Bloomington: Indiana University Press.

Cohn, Norman. 2000. *Europe's Inner Demons*. Rev. ed. Chicago: University of Chicago Press.

———. 1975. *Europe's Inner Demons*. New York: Basic Books.

———. 1961. *The Pursuit of the Millennium* 2d ed. New York: Harper Torchbooks.

Cohn, Raymond L. 1998. "Mortality in Transport." In Drescher and Engerman, 1998:290–92.

Coleman, James S. 1990. *Foundations of Social Theory*. Cambridge: Harvard University Press, Belknap Press.

———. 1956."Social Cleavage and Religious Conflict." *Journal of Social Issues* 12:44–56.

Colish, Marcia L. 1997. *Medieval Foundations of the Western Intellectual Tradition, 400–1400*. New Haven: Yale University Press.

Collingwood, R. G. 1940. *An Essay in Metaphysics*. London: Oxford.

Collins, Randall. 1998. *The Sociology of Philosophies: A Global Theory of Intellectual Change*. Cambridge: Harvard University Press.

Collins, W. E. 1903. "The Catholic South." In *The Cambridge Modern History*, 2:377–415. Cambridge: Cambridge University Press.

Collinson, Patrick. 1967. *The Elizabethan Puritan Movement*. London: Jonathan Cape.

Condorcet, Marquis de. 1955. *Sketch for a Historical Picture of the Progress of the Human Mind*. London: Weidenfeld & Nicholson.

Conrad, Alfred H., and John R. Meyer. 1958. *The Economics of Slavery and Other Studies in Econometric History*. Chicago: Aldine.

Conrad, Robert. 1993. *The Destruction of Brazilian Slavery 1850–1888*. 2d ed. Malabar, FL: Krieger Publishing Company.

———. 1983. *Children of God's Fire: A Documentary History of Black Slavery in Brazil*. Princeton: Princeton University Press.

———. 1974. "Nineteenth-Century Brazilian Slavery." In *Slavery and Race Relations in Latin America*, edited by Robert Brent Toplin, 146–75. Westport, CT: Greenwood Press.

Constable, Giles. 1996. *The Reformation of the Twelfth Century*. Cambridge: Cambridge University Press.

Contreras, Jaime, and Gustav Henningsen. 1986. "Forty-four Thousand Cases of the Spanish Inquisition (1540–1700): Analysis of a Historical Data Bank." In Henningsen and Tedeschi, 1986:100–129.

Coser, Lewis A. 1962. "Some Functions of Deviant Behavior and Normative Flexibility." *American Journal of Sociology* 68:172–81

Costen, Michael. 1997. *The Cathars and the Albigensian Crusade*. New York: St. Martin's Press.

Cottret, Bernard. 2000. *Calvin: A Biography*. Grand Rapids, MI: Eerdmans.

Coulton, G. G. 1938a. *Medieval Panorama*. Cambridge: Cambridge University Press.

———. 1938b. *Inquisition and Liberty*. London: W. Heinemann.

Coupland, Reginald. 1933. *The British Anti-Slavery Movement*. London: Thornton, Butterworth.

Cragg, Gerald R. 1964. *From Puritanism to the Age of Reason.* Cambridge: Cambridge University Press.

Craton, Michael. 1998. "British Caribbean." In Drescher and Engerman, 1998:125–32.

Craven, Avery O. 1942. *The Coming of the Civil War.* Chicago: University of Chicago Press.

Crosby, Alfred W. 1997. *The Measure of Reality: Quantification and Western Society, 1250–1600.* Cambridge: Cambridge University Press.

Cumont, Franz. [1912] 1960. *Astrology and Religion among the Greeks and Romans.* New York: Dover.

———. [1911] 1956. *Oriental Religions in Roman Paganism.* New York: Dover Publications.

Currie, Elliot P. 1968. "Crime without Victims: Witchcraft and Its Control in Renaissance Europe." *Law and Society Review* 3:7–32.

Curry, Patrick. 1999. "Magic vs. Enchantment." *Journal of Contemporary Religion* 14:401–12.

Curtin, Philip D. 1969. *The Atlantic Slave Trade: A Census.* Madison: University of Wisconsin Press.

Curtis, Edward S. 1913. *The North American Indian*, vol. 9. Norwood, MA: Plimpton Press.

Dabashi, Hamid. 1989. *Authority in Islam: From the Rise of Mohammad to the Establishment of the Umayyads.* New Brunswick, NJ: Transaction Publishers.

Daget, Serge. 1980. "A Model of the French Abolitionist Movement and Its Variations," In *Anti-Slavery, Religion, and Reform*, edited by Christine Bolt and Seymour Drescher, 64–79. Folkestone, UK: W. Dawson.

Dahmus, Joseph. [1968] 1995. *A History of the Middle Ages.* New York: Barnes & Noble.

Daly, Lowrie J. 1961. *The Medieval University, 1200–1400.* New York: Sheed and Ward.

Daly, Mary. 1978. *Gyn/Ecology: The Metaethics of Radical Feminism.* Boston: Beacon Press.

Dana, James Dwight. 1858. "Agassiz's Contributions to the Natural History of the United States," *American Journal of Science* 75:341.

Danielson, Dennis Richard. 2000. *The Book of the Cosmos: Imagining the Universe from Heraclitus to Hawking.* Cambridge, MA: Perseus Publishing.

Darwin, Charles. 1993. *The Origin of Species.* 6th ed. New York: The Modern Library.

Darwin, Francis, ed. 1896. *The Life and Letters of Charles Darwin.* 2 vols. New York: D. Appleton and Company.

Darwin, Francis, and A. C. Seward, eds. 1903. *More Letters of Charles Darwin.* 2 vols. New York: Appleton and Company.

Davie, Grace. 1994. *Religion in Britain since 1945: Believing without Belonging.* Oxford: Blackwell.

Davies, Norman. 1996. *Europe: A History.* Oxford: Oxford University Press.

Davies, Paul. 1983. *God and the New Physics.* London: J. M. Dent & Sons.

Davis, David Brion. [1975] 1999. *The Problem of Slavery in the Age of Revolution 1770–1823.* New York: Oxford University Press.

———. 1966. *The Problem of Slavery in Western Culture.* Ithaca, NY: Cornell University Press.

Dawkins, Richard. 1996. *Climbing Mount Improbable.* New York: W. W. Norton

———. 1989. Review of *Blueprints*, by Donald Johanson and Maitland Edey. *New York Times*, April 9, 34.

———. 1986. *The Blind Watchmaker: Why the Evidence of Evolution Reveals a Universe without Design.* New York: W. W. Norton.

———. 1976. *The Selfish Gene.* Oxford: Oxford University Press.

Dawson, Christopher. 1950. *Religion and the Rise of Western Culture.* New York: Sheed & Ward.

Delacroix, Jacques, and François Nielsen. 2001. "The Beloved Myth: Protestantism and the Rise of Industrial Capitalism in Nineteenth-Century Europe." *Social Forces* 80:509–53.

Delumeau, Jean. 1977. *Catholicism between Luther and Voltaire: A New View of the Counter-Reformation.* Philadelphia: Westminster Press.

Demerath, N. J., III. 2000. "The Varieties of Sacred Experience: Finding the Sacred in a Secular Grove." *Journal for the Scientific Study of Religion* 39:1–11.

———. 1974. *A Tottering Transcendence: Civil vs. Cultic Aspects of the Sacred.* Indianapolis: Bobbs-Merrill.

Demerath, N. J., III, Peter Dobkin Hall, Terry Schmitt, and Rhys H. Williams, eds. 1998. *Sacred Companies: Organizational Aspects of Religion and Religious Aspects of Organizations.* New York: Oxford University Press.

Demerath, N. J., III, and Phillip E. Hammond. 1969. *Religion in Social Context.* New York: Random House.

Dennett, Daniel C. 1995. *Darwin's Dangerous Idea: Evolution and the Meanings of Life.* New York: Touchstone (Simon & Schuster).

Derrida, Jacques. 1972. *Marges de la philosophie.* Paris: Éditions de Minuit.

Desmond, Adrian. 1997. *Huxley: From Devil's Disciple to Evolution's High Priest.* Reading, MA: Addison-Wesley.

Desmond, Adrian, and James Moore. 1991. *Darwin.* London: Michael Joseph.

Diamond, Jared. 1998. *Guns, Germs, and Steel.* New York: W. W. Norton.

Dickens, A. G. 1991. *The English Reformation*. 2d ed. University Park: Pennsylvania State University Press.

———. 1966. *Reformation and Society in Sixteenth Century Europe*. New York: Harcourt, Brace & World.

Dickson, D. Bruce. 1990. *The Dawn of Belief*. Tucson: University of Arizona Press.

Dobbs, Betty Jo. 1991. *The Janus Faces of Genius: The Role of Alchemy in Newton's Thought*. Cambridge: Cambridge University Press.

———. 1975. *The Foundations of Newton's Alchemy: or "The Hunting of the Greene Lyon"*. Cambridge: Cambridge University Press.

Dodds, E. R. 1970. *Pagan and Christian in an Age of Anxiety*. New York: Norton.

Dodds, Madeleine Hope, and Ruth Dodds. [1915] 1971. *The Pilgrimage of Grace, 1536–1537 and the Exeter Conspiracy, 1538*. 2 vols. London: F. Cass.

Donald, Leland. 1997. *Aboriginal Slavery on the Northwest Coast of North America*. Berkeley and Los Angeles: University of California Press.

Dorn, Harold. 1991. *The Geography of Science*. Baltimore: Johns Hopkins University Press.

Douglas, Mary. 1975. *Implicit Meanings: Essays in Anthropology*. London: Routledge & Kegan Paul.

Drake, H. A. 1999. *Constantine and the Bishops: The Politics of Intolerance*. Baltimore: Johns Hopkins University Press.

Drescher, Seymour. 1988. "Brazilian Abolition in Comparative Perspective." In *The Abolition of Slavery and the Aftermath of Emancipation in Brazil*, 21–54. Durham: Duke University Press.

———. 1987. *Capitalism and Antislavery: British Mobilization in Comparative Perspective*. New York: Oxford University Press.

———. 1977. *Econocide: British Slavery in the Era of Abolition*. Pittsburgh: University of Pittsburgh Press.

Drescher, Seymour, and Stanley L. Engerman, eds. 1998. *A Historical Guide to World Slavery*. New York: Oxford University Press.

Duffy, Eamon. 1997. *Saints and Sinners: A History of Popes*. New Haven: Yale University Press.

———. 1992. *The Stripping of the Altars: Traditional Religion in England 1400–1580*. New Haven: Yale University Press.

———. 1987. "The Late Middle Ages: Vitality or Decline." In *Atlas of the Christian Church*, edited by Henry Chadwick and G. R. Evans, 86-95. New York: Facts on File.

Dulles, Avery, S.J. 1992. *Models of Revelation*. Maryknoll, NY: Orbis Books.

Dunn, Richard S. 1979. *The Age of Religious Wars, 1559–1715*. 2d ed. New York: W. W. Norton.

———. 1973. *Sugar and Slaves: The Rise of the Planter Class in the British West Indies, 1624–1713*. New York: W. W. Norton.

———. 1972. *Sugar and Slaves*. Chapel Hill: University of North Carolina Press.

Durant, Will. 1957. *The Reformation*. New York: Simon and Schuster.

Durkheim, Emile. [1912] 1995. *The Elementary Forms of Religious Life*. Translated by Karen E. Fields. New York: The Free Press.

———. [1886] 1994. "Review of Part VI of the *Principles of Sociology* by Herbert Spencer." *Revue philosophique de la France et de l'étranger* 21:61–69. Translated and published by W.S.F. Pickering in *Durkheim on Religion*, 13–23. Atlanta: Scholars Press.

———. [1895] 1958. *The Rules of Sociological Method*. Glencoe, IL: The Free Press.

Dworkin, Andrea. 1974. *Woman Hating: A Radical Look at Sexuality*. New York: Dutton.

Eagleton, Terry. 1996. *The Illusions of Postmodernism*. Oxford: Blackwell.

Easterlin, Richard A. 1961. "Regional Income Trends, 1840–1850." In *American Economic History*, edited by Seymour Harris, 525–47. New York: McGraw-Hill.

Eichhorn, Werner. 1959. "Taoism." In *The Concise Encyclopaedia of Living Faiths*, edited by R. C. Zaehner, 385–401 Boston: Beacon.

Einstein, Albert. 1954. *Ideas and Opinions*. New York: Crown.

Eiseley, Loren. 1958. *Darwin's Century: Evolution and the Men Who Discovered It*. Garden City, NY: Doubleday.

Eisenstein, Elizabeth L. 1979. *The Printing Press as an Agent of Change*. Cambridge: Cambridge University Press.

Eldredge, Niles. 1986. *Time Frames*. New York: Simon & Schuster.

———. 1971. "The Alloptric Model and Phylogeny in Paleozoic Invertebrates." *Evolution* 25:156–67.

Eldredge, Niles, and Stephen Jay Gould. 1972. "Punctuated Equilibria: An Alternative to Phyletic Gradualism." In *Models in Paleobiology*, edited by T.J.M. Schopf, 82–115. San Francisco: Freeman, Cooper.

Eleta, Paula. 1997. "The Conquest of Magic over Public Space: Discovering the Face of Popular Magic in Contemporary Society." *Journal of Contemporary Religion* 12:51–67.

Elkins, Stanley M. [1959] 1976. *Slavery: A Problem in American Institutional and Intellectual Life*. Rev. 3d ed. Chicago: University of Chicago Press.

Ellison, Christopher G., and Jeffrey S. Levin. 1998. "The Religion-Health Connection: Evidence, Theory, and Future Directions." *Health Education and Behavior* 25:700–720.

Eltis, David. 1987. *Economic Growth and the Ending of the Transatlantic Slave Trade*. New York: Oxford University Press.

———. 1981. "The Impact of Abolition on the Atlantic Slave Trade." In *The Abolition of the Atlantic Slave Trade*, edited by David Eltis and James Walvin, 155–76. Madison: University of Wisconsin Press.

Elton, Geoffrey R. 1999. *Reform and Reformation, England 1517–1559*. Oxford: Blackwell.

Emmer, Pieter. 1998. "Dutch Caribbean." In Drescher and Engerman, 1998:142–46.

Engels, Friederich. [1873] 1964. "Dialectics of Nature." In Marx and Engels, 1964:152–1193.

———. [1850] 1964. "The Peasant War in Germany." In Marx and Engels, 1964:97–118.

Erasmus, Desiderius. [1500s] 1996. *Collected Works of Erasmus*. Edited and translated by Craig R. Thompson. Toronto: Toronto University Press.

Erikson, Kai T. 1966. *Wayward Puritans: A Study in the Sociology of Deviance*. New York: Wiley.

———. 1962. "Notes on the Sociology of Deviance." *Social Problems* 9:309–14.

Evans-Pritchard, Sir Edward. 1967. *The Zande Trickster*. Oxford: Clarendon Press.

———. 1965. *Theories of Primitive Religion*. Oxford: Clarendon Press.

Evennett, H. O. 1968. *The Spirit of the Counter Reformation*. Cambridge: Cambridge University Press.

Ewen, C. L'Estrange. 1929. *Witch Hunting and Witch Trials*. London: Kegan Paul, Trench, Trübner.

Farah, Caesar E. 1994. *Islam: Beliefs and Observances*. 5th ed. Hauppauge, NY: Barron's.

Farrington, David P. 1988. "Social, Psychological and Biological Influences on Juvenile Delinquency and Adult Crime." In *Explaining Criminal Behavior*, edited by Wouter Buikhuisen and Sarnoff A. Mednick, 68–89. Leiden: Brill.

Feldman, Kenneth A., and Theodore M. Newcomb. 1970. *The Impact of College on Students*. San Francisco: Jossey-Bass.

Ferrill, Arthur. 1986. *The Fall of the Roman Empire: The Military Explanation*. London: Thames and Hudson.

Feuer, Lewis. 1963. *The Scientific Intellectual*. New York: Basic Books.

Feyerabend, Paul. 1983. *Science in a Free Society*. London: Verso.

Fines, John. 1995. *Who's Who in the Middle Ages*. New York: Barnes & Noble.

———. 1981. *Biographical Register of Early English Protestants and Others Opposed to the Roman Catholic Church, 1525–1558*. Appleford, Abingdon, Oxfordshire: Sutton Courtenay Press.

Finke, Roger, and Rodney Stark. 2001. "The New Holy Clubs: Testing Church-to-Sect Propositions." *Sociology of Religion* 62:175–89.

———. 1992. *The Churching of America—1776–1990: Winners and Losers in Our Religious Economy.* New Brunswick, NJ: Rutgers University Press.

Finke, Roger, and Patricia Wittberg. 2000. "Organizational Revival from Within: Explaining Revivalism and Reform in the Roman Catholic Church." *Journal for the Scientific Study of Religion* 39:154–170.

Finley, M. I. 1981. *Economy and Society in Ancient Greece*. New York: Viking Press.

———. 1980. *Ancient Slavery and Modern Ideology.* New York: Viking Press.

———. 1969. "The Idea of Slavery: Critique of David Brion Davis's *The Problem of Slavery in Western Culture*." In *Slavery in the New World: A Reader in Comparative History*, edited by Laura Foner and Eugene D. Genovese, 256–61. Englewood Cliffs, NJ: Prentice-Hall.

Finney, Charles G. [1876] 1960. *An Autobiography.* Old Tappen, NJ: Fleming H. Revell Company.

Fischer, Claude S. 1975. "Toward a Subcultural Theory of Urbanism." *American Journal of Sociology* 80:1319–-1341.

Fischoff, Ephraim. 1968. "The Protestant Ethic and the Spirit of Capitalism: The History of a Controvery." In *The Protestant Ethic and Modernization: A Comparative View*, edited by S. H. Eisenstadt, 67–86. New York: Basic Books.

Fiske, Amos. 1899. *The West Indies*. New York: G. P. Putnam's Sons.

Fletcher, Richard. 1997. *The Barbarian Conversion: From Paganism to Christianity.* New York: Henry Holt.

Fogel, Robert William. 2000. *The Fourth Great Awakening and the Future of Egalitarianism*. Chicago: University of Chicago Press.

———. 1989. *Without Consent or Contract: The Rise and Fall of American Slavery.* New York: W. W. Norton.

Fogel, Robert William, and Stanley L. Engerman. 1974. *Time on the Cross: The Economics of American Negro Slavery.* 2 vols. Boston: Little, Brown.

Foner, Laura. 1970. "The Free People of Color in Louisiana and St. Domingue: A Comparative Portrait of Two Three-Caste Societies." *Journal of Social History* 3:406–30.

Fortune, Reo F. 1935. "Manus Religion." *Memoirs of the American Philosophical Society* 3.

Fox, James J. 1913. "Slavery, Ethical Aspect of." In *The Catholic Encyclopedia*, 14:40.

Fox-Genovese, Elizabeth, and Eugene D. Genovese. 1987. "The Divine Sanction of Social Order: Religious Foundations of the Southern Slaveholder's World View," *Journal of the American Academy of Religion* 55:211–33.

Frazer, James G. [1922] 1950. *The Golden Bough*. New York: Macmillan.

Frend, W.H.C. 1985. *The Donatist Church: A Movement of Protest in Roman North Africa*. Oxford: Clarendon Press.

———. 1984. *The Rise of Christianity*. Philadelphia: Fortress Press.

———. 1965. *Martyrdom and Persecution in the Early Church*. Oxford: Blackwell.

Freud, Sigmund. [1927] 1961. *The Future of an Illusion*. Garden City, NY: Doubleday.

———. [1921] 1959. *Group Psychology and the Analysis of Ego*. New York: W. W. Norton.

———. [1912–1913] 1950. *Totem and Taboo: Some Points of Agreement between the Mental Lives of Savages and Neurotics*. New York: W. W. Norton.

Freyre, Gilberto. 1922. "Social Life in Brazil in the Middle of the Nineteenth Century." *Hispanic American Historical Review* 5:597–628.

Fried, Morton H. 1967. *The Evolution of Political Society*. New York: Random House.

Furneaux, Robin. 1969. *The Amazon: The Story of a Great River*. London: Hamilton.

Gage, Matilda Joslyn. [1893] 1980. *Woman, Church and State*. Watertown, MA: Persephone Press.

Gallup International. 1984. *Human Values and Beliefs*. London.

Galton, Francis. 1875. *English Men of Science: Their Nature and Nurture*. New York: D. Appleton and Company.

Garay, Blas. [1900] 1965. "The Guaraní Misions—A Ruthless Exploitation of the Indians." In Mörner, 1965:63–78.

Gay, Peter. 1969. *The Enlightenment: An Interpretation*. New York: W. W. Norton.

———. 1966. *The Enlightenment: The Rise of Modern Paganism*. New York: W. W. Norton & Company.

Geertz, Clifford. 1973. *The Interpretation of Cultures*. New York: Basic Books.

———. 1966. "Religion as a Cultural System." In *Anthropological Approaches to the Study of Religion*, edited by Michael Banton, 1–46. London: Tavistock Publications.

Genovese, Eugene D. 1974. *Roll, Jordan, Roll: The World the Slaves Made*. New York: Pantheon Books.

———. 1969a. *The World the Slaveholders Made: Two Essays in Interpretation*. New York: Vantage Books.

———. 1969b. "Materialism and Idealism in the History of Negro Slavery in the Americas." In *Slavery in the New World: A Reader in Comparative History*, edited by Laura Foner and Eugene D. Genovese, 238–55. Englewood Cliffs, NJ: Prentice-Hall.

Gentilcore, David. 1992. *Bishop to Witch*. Manchester: Manchester University Press.

Georgi, Dieter. 1995. "The Early Church: Internal Migration of New Religion." *Harvard Theological Review* 88:35–68.

Gibbon, Edward. [1776] 1994. *The History of the Decline and Fall of the Roman Empire*. 6 vols. London: Allen Lane, The Penguin Press.

Gibbs, Jack P. 1975. *Crime, Punishment, and Deterrence*. New York: Elsevier.

Gies, Frances, and Joseph Gies. 1994. *Cathedral, Forge, and Waterwheel: Technology and Invention in the Middle Ages*. New York: Harper Collins.

Gimpel, Jean. 1976. *The Medieval Machine: The Industrial Revolution of the Middle Ages*. New York: Penguin Books.

Gingerich, Owen. 1975. " 'Crisis' versus Aesthetic in the Copernican Revolution." *Vistas in Astronomy* 17:85–93.

Ginzburg, Carlo. 1991. *Ecstasies: Deciphering the Witches' Sabbath*. New York: Pantheon Books.

———. 1983. *The Night Battles: Witchcraft and Agrarian Cults in the Sixteenth and Seventeenth Centuries*. New York: Penguin.

Gitlitz, David M. 1996. *Secrecy and Deceit: The Religion of the Crypto-Jews*. Philadelphia: The Jewish Publication Society.

Given, James B. 1997. *Inquisition and Medieval Society: Power, Discipline, and Resistance in Languedoc*. Ithaca, NY: Cornell University Press.

Glock, Charles Y., and Rodney Stark. 1966. *Christian Beliefs and Anti-Semitism*. New York: Harper and Row.

Godwin, Joscelyn. 1981. *Mystery Religions in the Ancient World*. San Francisco: Harper & Row.

Goldenweiser, Alexander A. "Review of *Les Formes élémentaires de la view religieuse, le système totémique en Australie*." *American Anthropologist* 17:719–35.

Goldman, Marion. 1999. *Passionate Journeys: Why Successful Women Joined a Cult*. Ann Arbor: University of Michigan Press.

Goldschmidt, Richard. 1940. *The Material Basis of Evolution*. New Haven: Yale University Press.

Goody, Jack. 1961. "Religion and Ritual: The Definitional Problem." *British Journal of Sociology* 12:142–64.

Gordon, Mary L. 1924. "The Nationality of Slaves under the Early Roman Empire." *Journal of Roman Studies* 14:93–111.

Gordon, Murray. 1989. *Slavery in the Arab World*. New York: New Amsterdam Press.

Gould, Stephen Jay. 1989. *Wonderful Life: The Burgess Shale and the Nature of History*. New York: W. W. Norton.

———. 1983. *Hen's Teeth and Horse's Toes*. New York: W. W. Norton.

———. 1980. *The Panda's Thumb*. New York: W. W. Norton.

———. 1977. *Ontogeny and Phylogeny*. Cambridge: Harvard University Press, Belknap Press.

Gould, Stephen Jay, and Niles Eldredge. 1993. "Punctuated Equilibrium Comes of Age." *Nature* 366:223–27.

Goveia, Elsa V. 1969. "The West Indian Slave Laws of the Eighteenth Century." In *Slavery in the New World: A Reader in Comparative History*, edited by Laura Foner and Eugene D. Genovese, 113–37. Englewood Cliffs, NJ: Prentice-Hall.

Graham, R. B. Cunninghame. 1901. *A Vanished Arcadia: Being Some Account of the Jesuits in Paraguay, 1607–1776*. London: Heinemann.

Grant, Edward. 1996. *The Foundations of Modern Science in the Middle Ages: Their Religious, Institutional, and Intellectual Contexts*. Cambridge: Cambridge University Press.

———. 1994. *Planets, Star, and Orbs: The Medieval Cosmos, 1200–1687*. Cambridge: Cambridge University Press.

———. 1971. *Physical Science in the Middle Ages*. New York: Wiley.

Grant, Michael. 1978. *A History of Rome*. London: Faber and Faber.

Gray, Asa. 1876. *Darwiniana*. New York: D. Appleton and Company.

Green, Ronald M. 1988. *Religion and Moral Reason: A New Method for Comparative Study*. New York: Oxford University Press.

Green, Vivian Hubert Howard. 1964. *John Wesley*. London: Nelson.

Green-Pederson, Svend E. 1981. "Slave Demography in the Danish West Indies and the Abolition of the Danish Slave Trade." *In The Abolition of the Atlantic Slave Trade*, edited by David Eltis and James Walvin, 231–57. Madison: University of Wisconsin Press.

———. 1971. "The Scope and Structure of the Danish Negro Slave Trade." *Scandinavian Economic History Review* 19:149–97.

Greil, Arthur L., and Thomas Robbins, eds. 1994. *Between Sacred and Secular: Research and Theory of Quasi-Religion*. Greenwich, NJ: JAI Press.

Gruber, Howard. 1981. *Darwin on Man: A Psychological Study of Scientific Creativity*. 2d ed. Chicago: University of Chicago Press.

Grun, Bernard. 1982. *The Timetables of History*. New York: Simon and Schuster.

Guazzo, Fra Francesco Maria. [1608] 1972. *Compendium Maleficarum*. New York: Dover Publications.

Haliczer, Stephen. 1990. *Inquisition and Society in the Kingdom of Valencia, 1487–1834*. Berkeley and Los Angeles: University of California Press.

Hall, A. Rupert. 1992. *Isaac Newton: Adventurer in Thought*. Cambridge: Cambridge University Press.

Hall, A. Rupert, and Marie Boas Hall. 1962. *The Unpublished Scientific Papers of Isaac Newton*. Cambridge: Cambridge University Press.

Hamilton, Bernard. 1981. *The Medieval Inquisition*. New York: Holmes and Meier.

Hamilton, Richard F. 1996. *The Social Misconstruction of Reality: Validity and Verification in the Scholarly Community*. New Haven: Yale University Press.

Hammond, John L. 1974. "Revival Religion and Antislavery Politics." *American Sociological Review* 39:175–86.

Hanke, Lewis. 1951. *Bartolomé de las Casas: An Interpretation of His Life and Writings*. The Hague: M. Nijhoff.

Hannah, Ian C. 1924. *Christian Monasticism: A Great Force in History*. London: George Allen & Unwin.

Hansen, Chadwick. 1969. *Witchcraft at Salem*. New York: George Braziller.

Hanson, Victor Davis. 2001. *Carnage and Culture: Landmark Battles in the Rise of Western Power*. New York: Doubleday.

Harnack, Adolph von. 1908. *The Mission and Expansion of Christianity in the First Three Centuries*. Translated by James Moffatt. 2 vols. New York: G. P. Putnam's Sons.

Harris, Anthony. 1980. *Night's Black Agents: Witchcraft and Magic in Seventeenth Century English Drama*. Manchester: Manchester University Press.

Harris, Marvin. 1964. *Patterns of Race in the Americas*. New York: Walker & Company.

———. 1963. *The Nature of Cultural Things*. New York: Random House.

Harrison, Jane E. 1912. *Themis: A Study of the Social Origins of Greek Religion*. Cambridge: Cambridge University Press.

Haskell, Thomas L. 1992. "Capitalism and the Origins of the Humanitarian Sensibility." Parts 1 and 2. In *The Antislavery Debate: Capitalism and Abolitionism as a Problem in Historical Interpretation*, edited by Thomas Bender, 107–60. Berkeley and Los Angeles: University of California Press.

Haskins, Charles Homer. 1923. *The Rise of Universities*. New York: Henry Holt.

Hastrup, Kirsten. 1990. "Iceland: Sorcerers and Paganism." In Ankarloo and Henningsen, 1990:383–401.

Hayes, Carlton, J. H. 1917. *Political and Social History of Modern Europe*. 2 vols. New York: Macmillan.

Hegel, George Wilhelm Friedrich. [1840] 1996. *Lectures on the Philosophy of Religion*.Vol. 1, *Introduction and the Concept of Religion*. Berkeley and Los Angeles: University of California Press.

Heikkinen, Antero, and Timo Kervinen. 1990. "Finland: The Male Domination." In Ankarloo and Henningsen, 1990:319–38.

Helper, Hinton Rowan. 1857. *The Impending Crisis in the South: How to Meet It*. New York: Burdick Brothers.

Henderson, John B. 1998. *The Construction of Orthodoxy and Heresy: Neo-Confucian, Islamic, Jewish, and Early Christian Patterns*. Albany: State University of New York Press.

Henningsen, Gustav. 1980. *The Witches Advocate: Basque Witchcraft and the Spanish Inquisition (1609–1614)*. Reno: University of Nevada Press.

Henningsen, Gustav, and John Tedeschi. 1986. *The Inquisition in Early Modern Europe: Studies on Sources and Methods*. DeKalb: Northern Illinois University Press.

Herodotus. [ca. 450 B.C.] 1987. *The History*. Translated by David Grene. Chicago: University of Chicago Press.

Hickey, Anne Ewing. 1987. *Women of the Roman Aristocracy as Christian Monastics*. Ann Arbon, MI: UMI Research Press.

Higman, Barry W. 1976. *Slave Population and Economy in Jamaica, 1807–1834*. Cambridge: Cambridge University Press.

Hill, Christopher. 1967. *Reformation to the Industrial Revolution, 1530–1780*. London: Penguin Books.

Hilts, Victor L. 1975. *A Guide to Francis Galton's "English Men of Science"*. Philadelphia: American Philosophical Society.

Hime, Henry W. L. 1915. *Origin of Artillery*. London: Longmans, Green and Co.

Hindle, Brooke. 1956. *The Pursuit of Science in Revolutionary America, 1735–1789*. Chapel Hill: University of North Carolina Press.

Hirsch, Rudolph. 1967. *Printing, Selling and Reading, 1450–1550*. Wiesbaden: Harrassowitz.

Hirschi, Travis. 1973. "Procedural Rules and the Study of Deviant Behavior." *Social Problems* 21:159–73.

Hitchins, H. L., and William E. May. 1951. *From Lodestone to Gyro-Compass.* London: Hutchinson's Scientific and Technical Publications.

Hobbes, Thomas. [1651] 1956. *Leviathan.* Vol. 1. Chicago: Henry Regnery Company.

Hocking, William Ernest. 1932. *Re-thinking Missions: A Laymen's Inquiry after One Hundred Years* (report of the Commission of Appraisal, Laymen's Foreign Missions Inquiry). New York: Harper & Brothers.

———. 1912. *The Meaning of God in Human Experience: A Philosophic Study of Religion.* New Haven: Yale University Press.

Hodges, Richard. 1998. "The Not-So-Dark Ages." *Archaeology* 51 (September/October): 61–78.

Hodgson, Marshall G. S. 1974. *The Venture of Islam.* Vols. 1 and 2. Chicago: University of Chicago Press.

Holborn, Hajo. 1982. *A History of Modern Germany: The Reformation.* Princeton: Princeton University Press.

———. 1969. "Luther and the Princes." In *Luther, Erasmus and the Reformation,* edited by John C. Olin, James D. Smart, and Robert E. McNally, S.J., 67–867. New York: Fordham University Press.

Holdrege, Barbara. 2000. "What's beyond the Post?" In *A Magic Still Dwells: Comparative Religion in the Postmodern Age,* edited by Kimberly C. Patton and Benjamin C. Ray, 77–91. Berkeley and Los Angeles: University of California Press.

Holmes, Clive. 1993. "Women: Witnesses and Witches." *Past and Present* 140:45–78.

Holt, Mack P. 1995. *The French Wars of Religion, 1562-1629.* Cambridge: Cambridge University Press.

Homans, George C. 1950. *The Human Group.* New York: Harcourt Brace.

Horton, Robin. 1964. "Ritual Man in Africa." *Africa* 34:85–104.

———. 1962. "The Kalabari World-View: An Outline and Interpretation." *Africa* 32:197–220.

Hovenkamp, Herbert. 1978. *Science and Religion in America 1800–1860.* Philadelphia: University of Pennsylvania Press.

Hoyle, Fred, and Chandra Wickramasinghe. 1981. *Evolution from Space.* London: J. M. Dent & Sons.

Hoyle, R. W. 2001. *The Pilgrimage of Grace and the Politics of the 1530s.* Oxford: Oxford University Press.

Huff, Toby. 1993. *The Rise of Early Modern Science: Islam, China, and the West.* Cambridge: Cambridge University Press.

Hughes, Pennethorne. 1952. *Witchcraft.* London: Longmans, Green.

Huizinga, Johan. [1924] 1957. *Erasmus and the Age of Reformation.* London: Phaidon Publishers.

Hull, D. L. 1973. *Darwin and His Critics.* Cambridge: Harvard University Press.

Hume, David. 1754. *The History of England.* 6 vols. London: A. Millar.

Hunter, Michael. 1989. *Establishing the New Science: The Experience of the Early Royal Society.* Woodbridge, Suffolk: Boydell Press.

———. 1982. *The Royal Society and Its Fellows 1660–1700.* Chalfont St. Giles: The British Society for the History of Science.

Hurbon, Laennec. 1992. "The Church and Afro-American Slavery." In *The Church in Latin America*, edited by Enrique Dussel. Maryknoll, NY: Orbis Books.

Hurlbutt, Robert H., III. 1985. *Hume, Newton, and the Design Argument.* 2d ed. Lincoln: University of Nebraska Press.

Hutchinson, Francis. 1720. *An Historical Essay concerning Witchcraft.* 2d ed. London: R. Knaplock.

Huxley, Julian. 1960. "The Emergence of Darwinism." In *Evolution after Darwin*, edited by Sol Tax, 1:1-22. Chicago: University of Chicago Press.

Hyland, Ann. 1994. *The Medieval Warhorse: From Byzantium to the Crusades.* London: Grange Books.

Hyslop, Theo. B. 1925. *The Great Abnormals.* New York: George H. Doran.

Iannaccone, Laurence R. 1995. "Risk, Rationality, and Religious Portfolios." *Economic Inquiry* 33:285–95.

———. 1994. "Why Strict Churches Are Strong." *American Journal of Sociology* 99:1180–1211.

———. 1992. "Sacrifice and Stigma: Reducing Free-Riding in Cults, Communes, and other Collectives." *Journal of Political Economy* 100(2):271–292.

———. 1990. "Religious Practice: A Human Capital Approach." *Journal for the Scientific Study of Religion* 29:297–314.

Ibn Qudama, 1962. *Ibn Qudama's Censure of Spectulative Theology.* London: Luzac.

Ingersoll, Thomas N. 1999. *Mammon and Manon in Early New Orleans: The First Slave Society in the Deep South, 1718–1819.* Knoxville: University of Tennessee Press.

Irvine, William. 1959. *Apes, Angels, and Victorians: Darwin, Huxley, and Evolution.* New York: Meridian Books.

———. 1955. *Apes, Angels, and Victorians.* New York: McGraw-Hill.

Jaki, Stanley L. 2000. *The Savior of Science.* Grand Rapids, MI: Eerdmans.

———. 1986. *Science and Creation.* Edinburgh: Scottish Academic Press.

James, E. O. 1960. *The Ancient Gods*. New York: G. P. Putnam's.

James, William. [1902] 1958. *The Varieties of Religious Experience*. New York: Mentor Books.

Jennings, Lawrence C. 2000. *French Anti-Slavery: The Movement for the Abolition of Slavery in France, 1802-1848*. Cambridge: Cambridge University Press.

Johansen, Jens Christian V. 1990. "Denmark: The Sociology of Accusations." In Ankarloo and Henningsen, 1990:339–65.

Johnson, Benton. 1963. "On Church and Sect." *American Sociological Review* 28:539–549.

Johnson, Paul. 1976. *A History of Christianity*. New York: Atheneum.

Johnston, Sir Harry Hamilton. 1910. *The Negro in the New World*. London: Methuen & Co.

Jolly, Karen Louise. 1996. *Popular Religion in Late Saxon England*. Chapel Hill: University of North Carolina Press.

Jones, A.H.M. 1956. "Slavery in the Ancient World." *Economic History Review*, 2d ser., 9:185–99.

Jones, Ernest. 1953. *Life and Works of Sigmund Freud*. Vol. 1. New York: Basic Books.

Jones, Gwyn. 1968. *A History of the Vikings*. London: Oxford University Press.

Jospe, Raphael. 1981. *Great Schisms in Jewish History*. Denver: KATV Publishing.

Kaelber, Lutz. 1998. *Schools of Asceticism: Ideology and Organization in Medieval Religious Communities*. University Park: Pennsylvania State University Press.

Kamen, Henry. 1997. *The Spanish Inquisition: An Historical Revision*. London: Weidenfeld & Nicolson.

———. 1993. *The Phoenix and the Flame: Catalonia and the Counter Reformation*. New Haven: Yale University Press.

Kaminsky, Howard. 1967. *A History of the Hussite Revolution*. Berkeley and Los Angeles: University of California Press.

Karasch, Mary. 1987. *Slave Life in Rio de Janeiro, 1880–1850*. Princeton: Princeton University Press.

Karmiris, John. 1973. "Concerning the Sacraments." In Clendenin, 1995:21–31.

Katz, Steven T. 1994. *The Holocaust in Historical Context*. Vol. 1. New York: Oxford University Press.

Kearney, Hugh F. 1964. *Origins of the Scientific Revolution*. London: Longmans.

Keynes, John Maynard. 1947. "Newton the Man." In Royal Society, *Newton Tercentenary Celebrations*, 27–34. Cambridge: Cambridge University Press.

Khomiakov, Aleksei. 1895. "The Church Is One." In *Russia and the English Church in the Last Fifty Years*, edited by W. J. Birbeck, 201–37. London: Rivington.

Kieckhefer, Richard. 1989. *Magic in the Middle Ages*. Cambridge: Cambridge University Press.

———. 1979. *Repression of Heresy in Medieval Germany*. Philadelphia: University of Pennsylvania Press.

———. 1976. *European Witch Trials: Their Foundations in Popular and Learned Culture*. Berkeley and Los Angeles: University of California Press.

King, Peter. 1999. *Western Monasticism: A History of the Monastic Movement in the Latin Church*. Kalamazoo, MI: Cistercian Publications.

Kingdon, Robert M. 1981. "Calvin, John." *Encyclopaedia Britannica*. 15th ed. Chicago: University of Chicago Press.

———. 1972. "The Control of Morals in Calvin's Geneva." In *The Social History of the Reformation*, edited by Lawrence P. Buck and Jonathan W. Zophy. Columbus: Ohio State University Press.

———. 1956. *Geneva and the Coming of the Wars of Religion in France, 1555–1563*. Geneva: Librairie E. Droz.

Kinser, Samuel. 1971. "Ideas of Temporal Change and Cultural Process in France 1470–1535." In *Renaissance: Studies in Honor of Hans Baron*, edited by A. Molho and J. Tedeschi, 703–57. DeKalb: Northern Illinois State University Press.

Kittelson, James M. 1986. *Luther the Reformer*. Minneapolis: Augsburg.

Kittredge, George Lyman. 1929. *Witchcraft in Old and New England*. Cambridge: Harvard University Press.

Klaaren, Eugene M. 1977. *Religious Origins of Modern Science*. Grand Rapids, MI: Eerdmans.

Klein, Herbert S. 1986. *African Slavery in Latin America and the Caribbean*. New York: Oxford University Press.

———. 1969. "Anglicanism, Catholicism, and the Negro Slave." In *Slavery in the New World: A Reader in Comparative History*, edited by Laura Foner and Eugene D. Genovese, 138–69. Englewood Cliffs, NJ: Prentice-Hall.

———. 1967. *Slavery in the Americas: A Comparative Study of Virginia and Cuba*. Chicago: University of Chicago Press.

Knowles, David. 1969. *Christian Monasticism*. New York: McGraw-Hill.

Koester, Helmut. 1982a. *History, Culture and Religion of the Hellenistic Age*. Vol. 1 1 of *Introduction to the New Testament*. New York: Walter de Gruyter.

———. 1982b. *History and Literature of Early Christianity* Vol. 2 of *Introduction to the New Testament*. New York: Walter de Gruyter.

Koger, Larry. 1985. *Black Slaveowners: Free Black Slave Masters in South Carolina, 1790–1860*. Columbia: University of South Carolina Press.

Kors, Alan C., and Edward Peters. 1972. *Witchcraft in Europe: A Documentary History*. Philadelphia: University of Pennsylvania Press.

Kraditor, Aileen. 1967. *Means and Ends in American Abolitionism: Garrison and His Critics on Strategy and Tactics, 1834–1850*. New York: Pantheon.

Krämer, Heinrich, and Jacob Sprenger. [1487] 1928. *Malleus Maleficarum*. London: J. Rodker.

Kuhn, Thomas S. 1962. *The Structure of Scientific Revolutions*. Chicago: University of Chicago Press.

Ladurie, Emmanuel Le Roy. 1978. *Montaillou: The Promised Land of Error*. New York: George Braziller.

———. 1974. *The Peasants of Languedoc*. Urbana: University of Illinois Press.

Lambert, Malcolm. 1998. *The Cathars*. Oxford: Blackwell.

———. 1992. *Medieval Heresy*. Oxford: Blackwell.

Lang, Graeme. 1997. "State Systems and the Origins of Modern Science: A Comparison of Europe and China." *East-West Dialogue* 2:16–31.

Lang, Graeme, and Lars Ragvold. 1993. *The Rise of a Refugee God: Hong Kong's Wong Tai Sin*. Oxford: Oxford University Press.

Langford, Jerome L. 1971. *Galileo, Science, and the Church*. Rev. ed. Ann Arbor: University of Michigan Press.

Larner, Christina. 1984. *Witchcraft and Religion: The Politics of Popular Belief*. Oxford: Blackwell.

———. 1981. *Enemies of God: The Witch-Hunt in Scotland*. London: Chatto & Windus.

Larner, Christina, Christopher Lee, and Hugh McLachlan. 1977. *A Source Book of Scottish Witchcraft*. Glasgow: University of Glasgow Press.

Larner, John. 1999. *Marco Polo and the Discovery of the World*. New Haven: Yale University Press.

Larson, Edward J. 1997. *Summer for the Gods: The Scopes Trial and America's Continuing Debate over Science and Religion*. New York: Basic Books.

Larson, Edward J., and Larry Witham. 1997. "Scientists Are Still Keeping the Faith." *Nature* 386 (3 April): 435.

Latourette, Kenneth Scott. 1975. *A History of Christianity*. Vol. 2. Rev. ed. San Francisco: HarperSanFrancisco.

Lawrence, Peter. 1964. *Road Belong Cargo: A Study of the Cargo Movement in South Madang District, New Guinea*. Manchester: Manchester University Press.

Lawson, E. Thomas, and Robert N. McCauley. 1990. *Rethinking Religion: Connecting Cognition and Culture*. Oxford: Oxford University Press.

Lea, Henry C. [1939] 1956. *Materials toward a History of Witchcraft*. New York: Thomas Yoseloff.

———. [1887] 1955. *A History of the Inquisition of the Middle Ages*. 3 vols. New York: Russell & Russell.

———. 1906–1907. *A History of the Inquisition in Spain*. 4 vols. New York: Macmillan.

———. 1902. "The Eve of the Reformation." In *The Cambridge Modern History*, 1: 653–92. Cambridge: Cambridge University Press.

———. 1867. *An Historical Sketch of Sacerdotal Celibacy in the Christian Church*. Philadelphia: J. B. Lippincott.

LeBon, Gustave. [1896] 1960. *The Crowd: A Study of the Popular Mind*. New York: Viking Press.

Lecky, W.E.H. [1865] 1903. *History of the Rise and Influence of the Spirit of Rationalism in Europe*. New York: D. Appleton and Company.

Leff, Gordon. 1967. *Heresy in the Later Middle Ages: The Relation of Heterodoxy to Dissent*. Manchester: Manchester University Press.

Lenski, Gerhard E. 1966. *Power and Privilege*. New York: McGraw-Hill.

Lerner, Robert. 1972. *The Heresy of the Free Spirit in the Later Middle Ages*. Notre Dame, IN: University of Notre Dame Press.

Leslie, Charles A. 1740. *A New History of Jamaica . . . in Thirteen Letters*. London: J. Hodges.

Lester, Robert C. 1993. "Buddhism: The Path to Nirvana." In *Religious Traditions of the World*, edited by H. Byron Earhart, 847–971. San Francisco: HarperSanFrancisco.

Leuba, James H. 1934. "Religious Beliefs of American Scientists." *Harper's Magazine* 169:291–300.

———. [1916] 1921. *The Belief in God and Immortality*. Chicago: Open Court Publishing Co.

Levack, Brian P. 1995. *The Witch-Hunt in Early Modern Europe*. 2d ed. London: Longman.

Levine, Donald N. 1995. *Visions of the Sociological Tradition*. Chicago: University of Chicago Press.

Lévi-Strauss, Claude. 1966. *The Savage Mind*. London: Weidenfeld & Nicholson.

Lewis, Bernard. 1990. *Race and Slavery in the Middle East*. Oxford: Oxford University Press.

Lima, Manoel de Oliveira. 1914. *The Evolution of Brazil Compared with That of Spanish and Anglo-Saxon America*. Stanford: Stanford University Press.

Lindberg, David C. 1992. *The Beginnings of Western Science*. Chicago: University of Chicago Press.

———. 1978. *Science in the Middle Ages*. Chicago: University of Chicago Press.

Lindberg, David C., and Ronald L. Numbers, eds. 1986. *God and Nature: Historical Essays on the Encounter between Christianity and Science*. Berkeley and Los Angeles: University of California Press.

Linton, Ralph. 1936. *The Study of Man: An Introduction*. Englewood Cliffs, NJ: Prentice-Hall.

Lofland, John, and Rodney Stark. 1965. "Becoming a World-Saver: A Theory of Conversion to a Deviant Perspective." *American Sociological Review* 30:862–75.

Lovejoy, Paul E. [1983] 2000. *Transformations in Slavery: A History of Slavery in Africa*. Cambridge: Cambridge University Press.

Lucas, J. R. 1979. "Wilberforce and Huxley: A Legendary Encounter." *Historical Journal* 22:313–30.

Luckmann, Thomas. 1967. *The Invisible Religion*. New York: Macmillan.

Luther, Martin. [1520] 1915. *Works*. Vol. 2. Philadelphia: Muhlenberg Press.

Luttwak, Edward N. 1976. *The Grand Strategy of the Roman Empire*. Baltimore: Johns Hopkins University Press.

Lyon, Bryce. 1972. *The Origins of the Middle Ages*. New York: W. W. Norton.

Lyotard, Jean-François. 1993. "Answering the Question: What Is Postmodernism?" In *Postmodernism: A Reader*, edited by Thomas Docherty, 27–42. New York: Columbia University Press.

MacCloud, William Christie. 1928. "Economic Aspects of Indigenous American Slavery." *American Anthropologist* 30:632–50.

———. 1925. "Debtor and Chattel Slavery in Aboriginal North America." *American Anthropologist* 27:370–80.

MacCulloch, Diarmaid. 2000. *Tudor Church Militant: Edward VI and the Protestant Reformation*. London: Penguin.

Macfarlane, Alan. 1978. *The Origins of English Individualism*. Oxford: Blackwell.

———. 1970. *Witchcraft in Tudor and Stuart England*. New York: Harper and Row.

MacKenzie, Norman, and Jeanne MacKenzie. 1977. *The Fabians*. New York: Simon and Schuster.

MacLeod, William. 1928. "Economic Aspects of Indigenous American Slavery." *American Anthropologist* 30:632–50.

———1925. "Debtor and Chattel Slavery in Aboriginal America." *American Anthropologist* 27:370–80.

MacMullen, Ramsay. 1984. *Christianizing the Roman Empire*. Hew Haven: Yale University Press.

———. 1981. *Paganism in the Roman Empire*. New Haven: Yale University Press.

Madariaga, Salvador. [1948] 1965. "The Fall of the Jesuits—The Triumph of the Philosophers." In Mörner, 1965:33–52.

Maier, Christoph. 1994. *Preaching the Crusades: Mendicant Friars and the Cross in the Thirteenth Century*. Cambridge: Cambridge University Press.

Malinowski, Bronislaw. [1948] 1992. *Magic, Science and Religion*. Prospect Heights, IL: Waveland Press.

———. 1935. *The Foundations of Faith and Morals*. Oxford: Oxford University Press.

Mandelbaum, David G. 1966. "Transcendental and Pragmatic Aspects of Religion." *American Anthropologist* 68:1174–91.

Manning, Patrick. 1990. *Slavery and African Life: Occidental, Oriental, and African Slave Traders*. Cambridge: Cambridge University Press.

Manucy, Albert C. 1949. *Artillery through the Ages*. Washington DC: U.S. Government Printing Office.

Manuel, Frank E. 1974. *The Religion of Isaac Newton*. Oxford: Clarendon Press.

———. 1968. *A Portrait of Isaac Newton*. Cambridge: Harvard University Press, Belknap Press.

Marx, Karl. [1857–1858] 1964. *Pre-Capitalist Economic Formation*. New York: International Publishers.

Marx, Karl, and Friedrich Engels. 1964. *On Religion*. Atlanta: Scholars Press.

Mason, Stephen F. 1962. *A History of the Sciences*. Rev. ed. New York: Macmillan.

Mathews, Donald G. 1977. *Religion in the Old South*. Chicago: University of Chicago Press.

Mathieson, William Law. 1926. *British Slavery and Its Abolition*. London: Longmans, Green & Co.

Mauny, Raymond. 1970. *Les Siècles obscurs de l'Afrique noire*. Paris: Fayard.

Mauss, Marcel. 1950. *A General Theory of Magic*. London: Routledge & Kegan Paul.

Maxwell, John F. 1975. *Slavery and the Catholic Church*. Chichester, UK: Ross.

May, Gerhard. 1987–1988. "Marcion in Contemporary Views: Results and Open Questions." *The Second Century* 6:129–51.

May, William E., and John L. Howard. 1981. "Compass." *Encyclopaedia Britannica*. 15th ed. Chicago: University of Chicago Press.

Mayer, Henry. 1998. *All on Fire: William Lloyd Garrison and the Abolition of Slavery*. New York: St. Martin's Press.

Mayr, Ernst. 1970. *Populations, Species and Evolution*. Cambridge: Harvard University Press.

Mayr-Harting, Henry. 1993. "The West: The Age of Conversion (700–1050)." In *The Oxford History of Christianity*, edited by John McManners, 101–29. Oxford: Oxford University Press.

McBrien, Richard P. 2000. *Lives of the Popes*. San Francisco: Harper San Francisco.

McCloy, Shelby. 1961. *The Negro in France*. Lexington: University of Kenntucky Press.

McFarlane, K. B. 1952. *John Wycliffe and the Beginnings of English Nonconformity*. London: English Universities Press.

McGrath, Alister E. 1999. *Science and Religion*. Oxford: Blackwell.

McGuire, Meredith. 1988. *Ritual Healing in Suburban America*. New Brunswick, NJ: Rutgers University Press.

McLachlan, Herbert. 1950. *Sir Isaac Newton's Theological Manuscripts*. Liverpool: Liverpool University Press.

———. 1941. *The Religious Opinions of Milton, Locke and Newton*. Manchester: Manchester University Press.

McLellan, David. 1987. *Marxism and Religion*. New York: Harper & Row.

McNally, Robert E., S.J. 1969. "The Reformation: A Catholic Reappraisal." In *Luther, Erasmus and the Reformation*, edited by John C. Olin, James D. Smart, and Robert E. McNally, S.J., 26–47. New York: Fordham University Press

McNeill, William H. 1976. *Plagues and Peoples*. Garden City, NY: Doubleday.

McSheffrey, Shannon. 1995. *Gender and Heresy: Women and Men in Lollard Communities, 1420–1530*. Philadelphia: University of Pennsylvania Press.

Meeks, Wayne. 1993. *The Origins of Christian Morality: The First Two Centuries*. New Haven: Yale University Press.

———.1983. *The First Urban Christians*. New Haven: Yale University Press.

Meltzer, Milton. 1993. *Slavery: A World History*. New York: Da Capo Press.

Mendelsohn, Isaac. 1949. *Slavery in the Ancient Near East*. New York: Oxford University Press.

Menn, Joseph Karl. 1964. *The Large Slave-Owners of Louisiana—1860*. New Orleans: Pelican Publishing Co.

Merrick, Thomas D., and Douglas H. Graham. 1979. *Population and Economic Development in Brazil, 1800 to the Present*. Baltimore: Johns Hopkins University Press.

Merton, Robert K. 1938. "Science, Technology and Society in Seventeenth Century England." *Osiris* 4 (pt. 2): 360–632.

Meyer, Hans. 1944. *The Philosophy of St. Thomas Aquinas*. St. Louis: B. Herder.

Michelet, Jules. 1939. *Satanism and Witchcraft: A Study in Medieval Superstition*. New York: The Citadel Press.

Middleton, John, ed. 1967. *Magic, Witchcraft, and Curing*. Austin: University of Texas Press.

Midelfort, H. C. Erik. 1981. "Heartland of the Witchcraze: Central and Northern Europe." *History Today* 31:27–31.

———. 1974. "Were There Really Witches?" In *Transition and Revolution: Problems and Issues of European Renaissance and Reformation History*, edited by Robert M. Kingdon, 189–205. Minneapolis, MN: Burgess Publishing Company.

———. 1972. *Witch-Hunting in Southwestern Germany*. Stanford: Stanford University Press.

Milis, Ludo J. R., ed. 1998. *The Pagan Middle Ages*. Rochester, NY: Boydell Press.

Miller, Alan S., and Satoshi Kanazawa. 2000. *Order by Accident: The Origins and Consequences of Conformity in Contemporary Japan*. Boulder, CO: Westview Press.

Mills, Gary. 1977. *The Forgotten People*. Baton Rouge: Louisiana State University Press.

Mills, J. P. 1922. *The Lhota Nagas*. London: Macmillan.

Mintz, Sidney W. 1969. "Slavery and Emergent Capitalism." In *Slavery in the New World: A Reader in Comparative History*, edited by Laura Foner and Eugene D. Genovese, 27–37. Englewood Cliffs, NJ: Prentice-Hall.

Mitchell, B. R. 1962. *Abstract of British Historical Statistics*. Cambridge: Cambridge University Press.

Moeller, Bernd. 1972. *Imperial Cities and the Reformation: Three Essays*. Philadelphia: Fortess Press.

Mone, Franz Joseph. 1839. *Anzeiger für Kunde der teutschen Vorzeit*. Jahrgang 8. Karlsruhe, 1839.

Money-Kyrle, Roger. 1929. *The Meaning of Sacrifice*. London: Hogarth Press.

Monter, E. William. 1999. *Judging the French Reformation: Heresy Trials by Sixteenth Century Parlements*. Cambridge: Harvard University Press.

———. 1990. *Frontiers of Heresy: The Spanish Inquisition from the Basque Lands to Sicily*. Cambridge: Cambridge University Press.

———. 1976. *Witchcraft in France and Switzerland: The Borderlands during the Reformation*. Ithaca, NY: Cornell University Press.

———. 1967. *Calvin's Geneva*. New York: Wiley.

Monter, E. William, and John Tedeschi. 1986. "Towards a Statistical Profile of the Italian Inquisitions, Sixteenth to Eighteenth Centuries." In Henningsen and Tedeschi, 1986:130–57.

Montgomery, Field-Marshall Viscount (Bernard). 1968. *A History of Warfare.* New York: World.

Moore, R. I. 1995. *The Birth of Popular Heresy.* Toronto: University of Toronto Press.

———. 1994. *The Origins of European Dissent.* Toronto: University of Toronto Press.

Mor, Menachem. 1992. *Jewish Sects, Religious Movements, and Political Parties.* Omaha, NE: Creightenon University Press.

More, L. T. 1934. *Sir Isaac Newton: A Biography.* New York: Scribner's.

Mörner, Magnus. 1965. *The Expulsion of the Jesuits from Latin America.* New York: Knopf.

Morris, Aldon D. 1984. *The Origins of the Civil Rights Movement: Black Communities Organizing for Change.* New York: Free Press.

Morris, Brian. 1987. *Anthropological Studies of Religion: An Introduction.* Cambridge: Cambridge University Press.

Morris, Colin M. 1991. *The Papal Monarchy: The Western Church from 1050 to 1250.* Oxford: Oxford University Press.

Morris, Thomas D. 1998. "United States Law." In Drescher and Engerman, 1998:255–60.

———. 1996. *Southern Slavery and the Law, 1619–1860.* Chapel Hill: University of North Carolina Press.

Mullett, Michael A. 1999. *The Catholic Reformation.* London: Routledge.

Munby, A.N.L. 1952. "The Keynes Collection of the Work of Sir Isaac Newton at King's College, Cambridge." *Notes and Records of the Royal Society of London* 10:40–50.

Murphy, Thomas. 2001. *Jesuit Slaveholding in Maryland, 1717–1838.* New York: Garland.

Murr, Sylvia. 1993. "Gassendi's Scepticism as a Religious Attitude." In *Scepticism and Irreligion in the Seventeenth and Eighteenth Centuries*, edited by Richard H. Popkin and Arjo Vanderjagt, 12–30. Leiden: Brill.

Murray, Alexander. 1972. "Piety and Impiety in Thirteenth-Century Italy." *Studies in Church History* 8:83–106.

Murray, Margaret. [1933] 1970. *The God of the Witches.* Oxford: Oxford University Press.

———. 1954. *The Divine King in England.* Oxford: Oxford University Press.

———. 1921. *The Witch-Cult in Western Europe.* Oxford: Oxford University Press.

Naess, Hans Eyvind. 1990. "Norway: The Criminological Context." In Ankarloo and Henningsen, 1990:367–82.

Nasr, Seyyed Hossein. 1993. *An Introduction to Islamic Cosmological Doctrines*. Albany: State University of New York Press.

Needham, Joseph. 1954–1984. *Science and Civilization in China*. 6 vols. Cambridge: Cambridge University Press.

Needham, Rodney. 1985. *Exemplars*. Berkeley and Los Angeles: University of California Press.

———. 1972. *Belief, Language and Experience*. Chicago: University of Chicago Press.

Netanyahu, B. 1999. *The Marranos of Spain: From the Late Fourteenth to the Early Sixteenth Century, According to Contemporary Hebrew Sources*. 3d ed. Ithaca, NY: Cornell University Press.

Neugebauer, O. 1975. *A History of Ancient Mathematical Astronomy*. 3 vols. New York: Springer-Verlag.

Neusner, Jacob, ed. 1990. *The Pharisees and Other Sects*. New York: Garland.

Newell, Norman D. 1959. "The Nature of the Fossil Record." *Proceedings of the American Philosophical Society* 103:264–85.

Newton, Sir Isaac. 1934. *Principia*. Translated by Florian Cajori. 2 vols. Berkeley and Los Angeles: University of California Press.

Nieboer, H. J. 1910. *Slavery as an Industrial System: Ethnological Researches*. The Hague: Martinus Nijhoff.

Niebuhr, H. Richard. 1929. *The Social Sources of Denominationalism*. New York: Henry Holt.

Nock, Arthur Darby. 1933. *Conversion: The Old and the New in Religion from Alexander the Great to Augustine of Hippo*. Oxford: Clarendon.

Noonan, John T., Jr. 1993. "Development in Moral Doctrine." *Theological Studies* 54: 666–77.

Norbeck, Edward. 1961. *Religion in Primitive Society*. New York: Harper.

Numbers, Ronald L. 1986. "The Creationists." In Lindberg and Numbers, 1986:391–423.

Nye, Russell B. 1955. *William Lloyd Garrison and Humanitarian Reformers*. Boston: Little Brown.

Oberman, Heiko A. 1992. *Luther: Man between God and the Devil*. New York: Image Books.

O'Day, Rosemary. 1986. *The Debate on the English Reformation*. London: Methuen.

O'Keefe, Daniel Lawrence. 1982. *Stolen Lightning: A Social Theory of Magic*. New York: Vintage Books.

Olmsted, Frederick Law. 1861. *The Cotton Kingdom*. New York: Mason Brothers.

Olson, Daniel V. A., and Paul Perl. 2001. "Variations in Strictness and Religious Commitment within and among Five Denominations." *Journal for the Scientific Study of Religion* 40:757–64.

Olson, Everett C. 1960. "Morphology, Paleontology, and Evolution." In *Evolution after Darwin*, edited by Sol Tax, 1:523–45. Chicago: University of Chicago Press.

O'Malley, Charles Donald. 1964. *Andreas Vesalius of Brussels, 1514–1564*. Berkeley and Los Angeles: University of California Press.

O'Neil, Mary R. 1987. "Magical Healing, Love Magic and the Inquisition in Late Sixteenth Century Modena." In *Inquisition and Society in Early Modern Europe*, edited by Stephen Haliczer, 88–114. London: Croom Helm.

———. 1984. "*Sacerdote ovvero strione*: Eccelsiastical and Superstitious Remedies in Sixteenth Century Italy." In *Understanding Popular Culture: Europe from the Middle Ages to the Nineteenth Century*, edited by Steven L. Kapland, 53–83. Berlin: Mouton Publishers.

———. 1981. "Discerning Superstition: Trials of Clerics and Exorcists in Sixteenth Century Italy." Paper presented at the International Congress on Medieval Studies, Kalamazoo, Michigan.

Oresme, Nicole. [1359–1360). 1971. *The Kinematics of Circular Motion (Tractatus de commensurabilitate vel incommensurabilitate motuum celi*). Translated by Edward Grant. Madison: University of Wisconsin Press.

———. [ca. 1350–1360] 1968. *The Geometry of Qualities and Motions (Tractatus de configurationibus qualitatem et motuum*. Translated by Marshall Clagett. Madison: University of Wisconsin Press.

Ormsby, Eric L. 1984. *Theodicy in Islamic Thought*. Princeton: Princeton University Press.

O'Shea, Stephen. 2000. *The Perfect Heresy: The Revolutionary Life and Death of the Medieval Cathars*. New York: Walker & Company.

Overmyer, Daniel L. 1993. "Religions of China: The World as a Living System." In *Religious Traditions of the World*, edited by H. Bryon Earhart, 975–1073. San Francisco: HarperSanFrancisco.

Ozment, Steven. 1980. *The Age of Reform 1250–1550: An Intellectual and Religious History of Late Medieval and Reformation Europe*. New Haven: Yale University Press.

———. 1975. *The Reformation in the Cities*. New Haven: Yale University Press.

Pagel, Walter. 1958. *Paracelsus: An Introduction to Philosophical Medicine in the Era of the Renaissance*. New York: Karger.

Paley, William. [1803] 1809. *Natural Theology*. 12th ed. London: J. Faulder.

Paley, William. [1785] 1827. *The Principles of Moral and Political Philosophy.* 1st American ed. Bridgeport, CT: M. Sherman.

Panzer, Joel S. 1996. *The Popes and Slavery.* New York: Alba House.

Parker, T.H.L. 1975. *John Calvin: A Biography.* London: Dent.

Parrinder, Geoffrey. 1983. *World Religions.* New York: Facts on File.

———. 1958. *Witchcraft: European and African.* London: Penguin.

Parsons, Talcott. 1951. *The Social System.* Glencoe, IL: The Free Press.

Partington, J. R. [1960] 1999. *A History of Greek Fire and Gunpowder.* Baltimore: Johns Hopkins University Press.

Pastor, Ludwig. 1898. *The History of the Popes.* 14 vols. St. Louis: B. Herder.

Pásztor, János. 1995. "The Theology of the Serving Church and the Theology of Diaconia in the Protestant Churches and Their Consequences in Hungary during the Time of Socialism." *Religion in Eastern Europe* 15:6:22–35.

Patterson, Orlando. 1982. *Slavery and Social Death: A Comparative Study.* Cambridge: Harvard University Press.

Payne, Robert. 1984. *The Dream and the Tomb: A History of the Crusades.* New York: Stein and Day.

———. 1959. *The History of Islam.* New York: Barnes and Noble.

Pearson, Karl. 1914–1930. *Life, Letters, and Labours of Francis Galton.* 3 vols. Cambridge: Cambridge University Press.

Pelikan, Jaroslav. 1996. *Mary though the Centuries: Her Place in the History of Culture.* New Haven: Yale University Press.

Pelteret, David A. E. 1995. *Slavery in Early Mediaeval England: From the Reign of Alfred until the Twelfth Century.* Woodbridge, Suffolk: Boydell Press.

Peregrine, Peter. 1996. "The Birth of the Gods Revisited: A Partial Replication of Guy Swanson's (1960) Cross-Cultural Study of Religion." *Cross-Cultural Research* 30:84–122.

Pernoud, Régine. 2000. *Those Terrible Middle Ages! Debunking the Myths.* San Franciso: Ignatius Press.

Perrin, Robin D., and Armand L. Mauss. 1993. "Strictly Speaking . . . : Kelley's Quandary and the Vineyard Christian Fellowship." *Journal for the Scientific Study of Religion* 32:125–35.

Peters, Edward. 1978. *The Magician, the Witch, and the Law.* Philadelphia: University of Pennsylvania Press.

Phillips, Margaret Mann. 1949. *Erasmus and the Northern Renaissance.* London: Hodder & Stoughton.

Phillips, William D., Jr. 1998. "Europe: Middle Ages." In Drescher and Engerman, 1998:197–200.

Pike, Ruth. 1962. "The Genoese in Seville and the Opening of the New World." *Journal of Economic History* 22:348–78.

Pirenne, Henri. [1936] 1958. *A History of Europe from the End of the Roman World in the West to the Beginnings of the Western States*. New York: Doubleday Anchor.

———. [1922] 1955. *Mohammed and Charlemagne*. New York: Barnes and Noble.

Plumb, Derek. 1986. "The Social and Economic Spread of Rural Lollardy: A Reappraisal." *Studies in Church History* 23:111–30.

Poliakov, Léon. 1965. *The History of Anti-Semitism: From the Time of Christ to the Court Jews*. Vol. 1. New York: Vanguard Press.

Polkinghorne, John. 1998. *Belief in God in an Age of Science*. New Haven: Yale University Press.

Pollard, A. F. 1903. "National Opposition to Rome in Germany." In *The Cambridge Modern History*, 1:142–73. Cambridge: Cambridge University Press.

Popper, Karl. [1976] 1996. "Darwinism as a Metaphysical Research Program." Reprinted in *But Is It Science?* edited by Michael Ruse, 144–76. Amherst, NY: Prometheus Books.

———. 1962. *Conjectures and Refutations: The Growth of Scientific Knowledge*. London: Routledge & Kegan Paul.

———. 1957. *The Poverty of Historicism*. London: Routledge & Kegan Paul.

Porter, Roy. 1998. *The Greatest Benefit to Mankind: A Medical History of Humanity*. New York: W. W. Norton.

Potter, G. H. 1976. *Zwingli*. Cambridge: Cambridge University Press.

Preus, J. Samuel. 1987. *Explaining Religion*. New Haven: Yale University Press.

Price, S.R.F. 1984. *Rituals and Power: The Roman Imperial Cult in Asia Minor*. Cambridge: Cambridge University Press.

Quispel, Gilles. 1987. "Gnosticism: Gnosticism from Its Origins to the Middle Ages." In *The Encyclopedia of Religion*, edited by Mircea Eliade, 5:566–74. New York: Macmillan.

Rabb, Theodore K. 1975. "Religion and the Rise of Modern Science." *Past and Present*, no. 31. Reprinted in *The Intellectual Revolution of the Seventeenth Century*, edited by Charles Webster, 262–79. London: Routledge & Kegan Paul, 1974.

Radcliffe-Brown, A. R. 1952. *Structure and Function in Primitive Society*. Glencoe, IL: The Free Press.

———. 1939. *Taboo*. Cambridge: Cambridge University Press.

Radin, Paul. [1937] 1957. *Primitive Religion*. New York: Dover Books.

———. 1956. *The Trickster*. London: Routledge & Kegan Paul.

Rahman, Fazlur, 1981. "Islam." *Encyclopaedia Britannica*, 911–26. 15th ed. Chicago: University of Chicago Press.

Rahner, Karl. 1975. "Theology. I. Nature." In *Encyclopedia of Theology: The Concise "Sacramentum Mundi"*, edited by Karl Rahner. New York: Seabury.

Ranke, Leopold von. [1878] 1966. *History of the Popes*. 3 vols. New York: F. Unger.

Rankin, David. 1995. *Tertullian and the Church*. Cambridge: Cambridge University Press.

Rappaport, Roy A. 1999. *Ritual and Religion in the Making of Humanity*. Cambridge: Cambridge University Press.

Read, Piers Paul. 1999. *The Templars*. New York: St. Martin's Press.

Regis, Ed. 1987. *Who Got Einstein's Office: Eccentricity and Genius at the Institute for Advanced Study*. Reading, MA: Addison-Wesley.

Reichard, Gladys A. 1950. *Navaho Religion*. 2 vols. New York: Pantheon Books.

Richards, Robert J. 1987. *Darwin and the Emergence of Evolutionary Theories of Mind and Behavior*. Chicago: University of Chicago Press.

Riley, Gregory J. 1997. *One Jesus, Many Christs*. San Francisco: HarperSan Francisco.

Robbins, Rossell Hope. 1959. *The Encyclopedia of Witchcraft and Demonology*. New York: Crown.

Roberts, Keith A. 1995. *Religion in Sociological Perspective*. Belmont, CA: Wadsworth.

Roberts, Michael. 1968. *The Early Vasas: A History of Sweden, 1523–1611*. Cambridge: Cambridge University Press.

Rodney, Walter. 1984. *How Europe Underdeveloped Africa*. Washington, DC: Howard University Press.

Roesdahl, Else. 1980. "The Scandinavians at Home." In *The Northern World*, edited by David M. Wilson, 145–58. New York: Harry N. Abrams.

Rohner, Ronald P., and Evelyn C. Rohner. 1970. *The Kwakiutl: Indians of British Columbia*. New York: Holt, Rinehart and Winston.

Roper, Lyndal. 1994. *Oedipus and the Devil: Witchcraft, Sexuality and Religion in Early Modern Europe*. London: Routledge.

Rörig, Fritz. 1969. *The Medieval Town*. Berkeley and Los Angeles: University of California Press.

Rose, Elliot. 1962. *A Razor for a Goat*. Toronto: University of Toronto Press.

Rosen, Edward. 1971. *Three Copernican Treatises*. 3d ed. New York: Octagon Books.

Rosen, George. 1968. *Madness in Society: Chapters in the Historical Sociology of Mental Illness*. Chicago: University of Chicago Press.

Ross, Thomas W. 1985. "The Implicit Theology of Carl Sagan." *Pacific Theological Review* 18:24–32.

Ruby, Robert H., and John A. Brown. 1993. *Indian Slavery in the Pacific Northwest.* Spokane, WA: Clark.

Ruchames, Louis. 1963. *The Abolitionists: A Collection of Their Writings.* New York: Putnam.

Rudwick, Martin J. S. 1986. "The Shape and Meaning of Earth History." In Lindberg and Numbers, 1986:296–321.

Rupp, Ernest Gordon. 1981. "Luther, Martin." *Encyclopaedia Britannica,* 188–96. 15th ed. Chicago: University of Chicago Press.

———. 1951. *Luther's Progress to the Diet of Worms, 1521.* Chicago: University of Chicago Press.

Ruse, Michael. 1999. *Mystery of Mysteries: Is Evolution a Social Construction?* Cambridge: Harvard University Press.

Russell, Bertrand. 1922. *The Problem of China.* London: George Allen & Unwin.

Russell, J. C. 1958. *Late Ancient and Medieval Population. Transactions of the American Philosophical Society* 48:3:3–152. Philadelphia: The American Philosophical Society.

Russell, Jeffrey Burton. 1991. *Inventing the Flat Earth: Columbus and Modern Historians.* New York: Praeger.

———. 1977. *The Devil: Perceptions of Evil from Antiquity to Primitive Christianity.* Ithaca: Cornell University Press.

———. 1972. *Witchcraft in the Middle Ages.* Ithaca, NY: Cornell University Press.

———. 1965. *Dissent and Reform in the Early Middle Ages.* Berkeley and Los Angeles: University of California Press.

———, ed. 1971. *Religious Dissent in the Middle Ages.* New York: Wiley.

Ruyle, Eugene R. 1973. "Slavery, Surplus and Stratification on the Northwest Coast." *Current Anthropology* 14:603–31.

Sagan, Carl. 1975. "The Search for Extraterrestrial Intelligence." *Scientific American* 232:5):80–89.

Salahi, M. A. 1995. *Muhammad: Man and Prophet.* Shaftesbury: Element.

Saldarini, Anthony J. 1988. *Pharisees, Scribes and Sadducees in Palestinian Society: A Sociological Approach.* Wilmington, DE: M. Glazier.

Samuelsson, Kurt. [1957] 1993. *Religion and Economic Action: The Protestant Ethic, the Rise of Capitalism, and the Abuse of Scholarship.* Toronto: University of Toronto Press.

Sarbin, Theodore. 1969. "The Scientific Status of the Mental Illness Metaphor." In *Changing Perspectives in Mental Illness*, edited by S. C. Plag and R. B. Edgerton, 9–31. New York: Holt, Rinehart and Winston.

Sarton, George. 1955. "Introductory Essay." In *Science, Religion, and Reality*, edited by Joseph Needham. New York: George Braziller.

Saunders, A. C. de C. M. 1982. *A Social History of Black Slaves and Freedmen in Portugal 1441–1555*. Cambridge: Cambridge University Press.

Sawyer, P. H. 1982. *Kings and Vikings: Scandinavia and Europe AD 700–1100*. London: Methuen.

Scarano, Franciso A. 1998. "Spanish Caribbean." In Drescher and Engerman, 1998:137–42.

Scarisbrick, J. J. 1984. *The Reformation and the English People*. Oxford: Blackwell.

Scarre, Geoffrey. 1987. *Witchcraft and Magic in Sixteenth and Seventeenth Century Europe*. London: Macmillan.

Schachner, Nathan. 1938. *The Mediaeval Universities*. New York: Frederick A. Stokes.

Schafer, Judith Kelleher. 1994. *Slavery, the Civil Law, and the Supreme Court of Louisiana*. Baton Rouge: Louisiana State University Press.

Schlaifer, Robert. 1936. "Greek Theories of Slavery from Homer to Aristotle." *Harvard Studies in Classical Philology* 47:165–204.

Schmidt-Nowara, Christopher. 1999. *Empire and Slavery: Spain, Cuba, and Puerto Rico, 1822–1874*. Pittsburgh: University of Pittsburgh Press.

Schwartz, Jeffrey H. 1999. *Sudden Origins: Fossils, Genes, and the Emergence of Species*. New York: Wiley.

Schwartz, Stuart B. 1998. "Brazil." In Drescher and Engerman, 1998:100–105.

———. 1992. *Slaves, Peasants, and Rebels: Reconsidering Brazilian Slavery*. Urbana: University of Illinois Press.

———. 1985. *Sugar Plantations in the Formation of Brazillian Society: Bahia, 1550–1835*. New York: Cambridge University Press.

Schwiebert, E. G. 1950. *Luther and His Times: The Reformation from a New Perspective*. St. Louis: Concordia Publishing House.

Scot, Reginald. [1584] 1972. *The Discoverie of Witchcraft*. New York: Dover.

Seeber, Edward D. 1937. *Anti-Slavery Opinion in France during the Second Half of the Eighteenth Century*. Baltimore: Johns Hopkins University Press.

Segal, Ronald. 2001. *Islam's Black Slaves: The Other Black Diaspora*. New York: Farrar, Straus and Giroux.

Shapiro, Barbara J. 1968. "Latitudinarism and Science in Seventeenth-Century England." *Past and Present*, no. 40. Reprinted in *The Intellectual Revolution of the Seventeenth Century*, edited by Charles Webster, 286–316. London: Routledge & Kegan Paul, 1974.

Shapiro, Herman. 1964. *Medieval Philosophy: Selected Readings from Augustine to Buridan*. New York: Modern Library.

Shea, William R. 1986. "Galileo and the Church." In Lindberg and Numbers, 1986:114–35.

Sheler, Jeffery L. 1999. *Is the Bible True? How Modern Debates and Discoveries Affirm the Essence of the Scriptures*. San Francisco: HarperSanFrancisco.

Shepherd, William R. 1980. *Shepherd's Historical Atlas*. Rev. 9th ed. Totowa, NJ: Barnes & Noble.

Sheridan, Richard B. 1974. *Sugar and Slavery: An Economic History of the British West Indies, 1623–1775*. Aylesbury, UK: Ginn and Company.

Sidgewick, Isabella. 1898. "A Grandmother's Tale." *Macmillan's Magazine* 78:425–35.

Siegel, Bernard J. 1945. "Some Methodological Considerations for a Comparative Study of Slavery." *American Anthropologist* 47:357–92.

Singer, Charles. [1925] 1970. "Historical Relations of Religion and Science." In *Science Religion and Reality*, edited by Joseph Needham, 87–148. Port Washington, NY: Kennikat Press.

Sio, Arnold A. 1969. "Interpretations of Slavery: The Slave Status in the Americas." In *Slavery in the New World: A Reader in Comparative History*, edited by Laura Foner and Eugene D. Genovese, 96–112. Englewood Cliffs, NJ: Prentice-Hall.

Smart, Ninian. 1984. *The Religious Experience of Mankind*. 3d ed. New York: Scribner's.

Smil, Vaclav. 2000. "Horse Power." *Nature* 405 (May 11): 125.

Smith, Adam. [1776] 1981. *An Inquiry into the Nature and Causes of the Wealth of Nations*. 2 vols. Indianapolis: Liberty Fund.

Smith, I. Gregory. 1892. *Christian Monasticism: From the Fourth to the Ninth Centuries of the Christian Era*. London: A. D. Innes and Co.

Smith, Jonathan Z. 1978. *Map Is Not Territory: Studies in the History of Religions*. Leiden: Brill.

Smith, Preserved. [1923] 1962. *Erasmus: A Study of His Life, Ideals and Place in History*. New York: Ungar.

Smith, W. Robertson. 1889. *The Religion of the Semites: Fundamental Institutions*. Edinburgh: Adam and Charles Black.

Smith, Warren Thomas. 1986. *John Wesley and Slavery*. Nashville: Abingdon Press.

Snow, C. P. 1967. *Variety of Men*. New York: Charles Scribner's Sons.

Snow, David A., and Richard Machalek. 1983. "The Convert as a Social Type." In *Sociological Theory, 1983*, edited by Randall Collins, 259–88. San Francisco: Jossey-Bass.

Snow, David A., and Cynthia L. Phillips. 1980. "The Lofland-Stark Conversion Model: A Critical Reassessment." *Social Problems* 27:430–447.

Soderlund, Jean R. 1985. *Quakers and Slavery: A Divided Spirit*. Princeton: Princeton University Press.

Southern, R. W. 1970. *Western Society and the Church*. Harmondsworth: Penguin Books.

Southwold, Martin. 1978. "Buddhism and the Definition of Religion." *Man*, n.s., 13:362–79.

Spanos, N. P. 1978. "Witchcraft in Histories of Psychiatry: A Critical Analysis and an Alternative Conceptualization." *Psychological Bulletin* 85:417–39.

Spencer, Herbert. 1896. *Principles of Sociology*. Rev. ed. 2 vols. New York: D. Appleton and Company.

Sperber, Dan. 1975. *Rethinking Symbolism*. Cambridge: Cambridge University Press.

Spitz, Lewis W. 1969. "Recent Studies of Luther and the Reformation." In *Luther, Erasmus and the Reformation*, edited by John C. Olin, James D. Smart, and Robert E. McNally, S.J., 134–50. New York: Fordham University Press.

Stanley, Steven M. 1981. *The New Evolutionary Timetable*. New York: Basic Books.

———. 1979. (1998 reprint.) *Microevolution: Pattern and Process*. Baltimore: Johns Hopkins University Press.

Stark, Rodney. In press. "Upper Class Asceticism: Social Origins of Ascetic Movements and Medieval Saints." *Review of Religious Research*.

———. 2002. "Physiology and Faith: Addressing the 'Universal' Gender Difference in Religiousness." *Journal for the Scientific Study of Religion* 41:495–507.

———. 2001a. *One True God: Historical Consequences of Monotheism*. Princeton: Princeton University Press.

———. 2001b. "Gods, Rituals, and the Moral Order." *Journal for the Scientific Study of Religion* 40:619–36.

———. 2001c. "Reconceptualizing Religion, Magic, and Science." *Review of Religious Research* 43:101–20.

———. 2000. "Religious Effects: In Praise of 'Idealistic Humbug.' " *Review of Religious Research* 41:289–310.

———. 1999. "Secularization, R.I.P." *Sociology of Religion* 60:249–73.

———. 1998. *Doing Sociology: A Global Perspective*. 3d ed. Belmont, CA: Wadsworth.

———. 1996. *The Rise of Christianity: A Sociologist Reconsiders History.* Princeton: Princeton University Press.

———. 1987. "How New Religions Succeed: A Theoretical Model." In *The Future of New Religious Movements*, edited by David G. Bromley and Phillip E. Hammond, 11–19. Macon, GA: Mercer University Press.

———. 1983. "Religious Economies: A New Perspective." Conference on New Directions in Religious Research, University of Lethbridge.

———. 1965. "A Taxonomy of Religious Experience." *Journal for the Scientific Study of Religion* 5:97–100.

Stark, Rodney, and William Sims Bainbridge. 1997. *Religion, Deviance, and Social Control.* New York: Routledge.

———. [1987] 1996. *A Theory of Religion.* Republished ed. New Brunswick, NJ. Rutgers University Press.

———. 1985. *The Future of Religion: Secularization, Revival, and Cult Formation.* Berkeley and Los Angeles: University of California Press.

———. 1979. "Of Churches, Sects, and Cults: Preliminary Concepts for a Theory of Religious Movements." *Journal for the Scientific Study of Religion* 18:117–31.

Stark, Rodney, and Roger Finke. 2002. "Beyond Church and Sect: Dynamics and Stability in Religious Economies." In *Sacred Markets and Sacred Canopies: Essays on Religious Markets and Religious Pluralism*, edited by Ted G. Jelen. Lanham, MD: Rowman & Littlefield.

———. 2000. *Acts of Faith: Explaining the Human Side of Religion.* Berkeley and Los Angeles: University of California Press.

———. 1988. "American Religion in 1776: A Statistical Portrait." *Sociological Analysis* 49:39–51.

Stark, Rodney, Bruce D. Foster, Charles Y. Glock, and Harold E. Quinley. 1971. *Wayward Shepherds: Prejudice and the Protestant Clergy.* New York: Harper and Row.

Stark, Rodney, and Laurence R. Iannaccone. 1994. "A Supply-Side Reinterpretation of the 'Secularization' of Europe." *Journal for the Scientific Study of Religion* 33:230–52.

Ste. Croix, G.E.M. de. 1981. *The Class Struggle in the Ancient Greek World, from the Archaic Age to the Arab Conquest.* London: Duckworth.

Strauss, Gerald. 1967. "Protestant Dogma and City Government: The Case of Nuremberg." *Past and Present* 36:38–58.

Strenski, Ivan. 1997. *Durkheim and the Jews of France.* Chicago: University of Chicago Press.

Strong, Douglas M. 1999. *Perfectionist Politics: Abolition and Religious Tension of American Democracy.* Syracuse: Syracuse University Press.

Summers, Montague. 1927. *The Geography of Witchcraft.* London: Kegan Paul.

———. 1926. *The History of Watchcraft and Demonology.* London: Kegan Paul.

Suttles, Wayne, ed. 1990. *Handbook of North American Indians.* Vol. 7, *Northwest Coast.* Washington DC: Smithsonian Institution.

Suttles, Wayne, and Aldona Jonaitis. 1990. "History of Research in Ethnology." In Suttles, 1990:73–87.

Swanson, Guy E. 1967. *Religion and Regime: A Sociological Account of the Reformation.* Ann Arbor: University of Michigan Press.

———. 1960. *The Birth of the Gods.* Ann Arbor: University of Michigan Press.

Swanson, R. N. 1995. *Religion and Devotion in Europe, c.1215–c.1515.* Cambridge: Cambridge University Press.

Swatos, William, Jr., ed. 1998. *Encyclopedia of Religion and Society.* Walnut Creek, CA: AltaMira Press.

Swatos, William H., Jr., and Loftur Reimar Gissurarson. 1997. *Icelandic Spiritualism: Mediumship and Modernity in Iceland.* New Brunswick, NJ: Transaction Publishers.

Szathma{{racute}}y, Eörs. 1999. "When the Means Do Not Justify the End." *Nature* 399 (June 24): 745.

Tannenbaum, Frank. [1946] 1992. *Slave and Citizen.* Boston: Beacon Press.

Tawney, Richard H. [1922] 1962. *Religion and the Rise of Capitalism: A Historical Study.* Gloucester, MA: P. Smith.

Temperley, Howard. 1998 "Abolition and Anti-Slavery: Britain." In Drescher and Engerman, 1998:10–15.

———. 1977 "Capitalism, Slavery, and Ideology." *Past and Present* 75:94–118.

Thalheimer, Fred. 1973. "Religiosity and Secularization in the Academic Professions." *Sociology of Education* 46:183–202.

Thomas, Hugh. 1997. *The Slave Trade: The Story of the Atlantic Slave Trade, 1440–1870.* New York: Simon and Schuster.

Thomas, John L. 1963. *The Liberator: William Lloyd Garrison, a Biography.* Boston: Little Brown.

Thomas, Keith. 1971. *Religion and the Decline of Magic.* New York: Scribner's.

Thompson, E. A. 1957. "Slavery in Early Germany." *Hermathena* 89:17–29.

Thornton, John. 1998a. *Africa and Africans in the Making of the Atlantic World, 1400–1800.* 2d ed. Cambridge: Cambridge University Press.

———. 1998b. "Africa: An Overview." In Drescher and Engerman, 1998:27–32.

Tilley, Maureen A. 1996. *Donatist Martyr Stories: The Church in Conflict in Roman North Africa.* Liverpool: University of Liverpool Press.

Tillich, Paul. 1952. *The Courage To Be*. New Haven: Yale University Press.

———. 1951. *Systematic Theology*. Vol. 1. Chicago: University of Chicago Press.

Tinh, Tran Tam. 1982. "Sarapis and Isis." In *Jewish and Christian Self-Definition*, edited by Ben F. Meyer and E. P. Sanders, 3:101–17. Philadelphia: Fortress Press.

Tökés, László. 1990. "The Possible Role of Rumania's Churches on the Social Renewal of the Country." *Occasional Papers on Religion in Eastern Europe* 10:5:29–32.

Toplin, Robert Brent. 1981. *Freedom and Prejudice: The Legacy of Slavery in the United States and Brazil*. Westport, CT: Greenwood Press.

———. 1972. *The Abolition of Slavery in Brazil*. New York: Atheneum.

Tourn, Giorgio. 1989. *Your Are My Witnesses: The Waldensians across Eight Hundred Years*. Cincinnati: Friendship Press.

Townes, Charles H. 1995. *Making Waves*. Woodbury, NY: American Institute of Physics Press.

Tracy, James D. 1999. *Europe's Reformations, 1450–1650*. Lanham, MD: Rowman & Littlefield.

Trethowan, W. H. 1963. "The Demonopathology of Impotence." *British Journal of Psychiatry* 109:341–47.

Trevett, Christine. 1996. *Montanism: Gender, Authority and the New Prophecy*. Cambridge: Cambridge University Press.

Trevor-Roper, H. R. [1969] 2001. *The Crisis of the Seventeenth Century: Religion, the Reformation, and Social Change*. Indianapolis: Liberty Fund.

Troeltsch, Ernst. [1912] 1931. *The Social Teaching of the Christian Churches*. 2 vols. New York: Macmillan.

Tuchman, Barbara W. 1979. *A Distant Mirror: The Calamitous Fourteenth Century*. New York: Ballantine Books.

Turley, David. 2000. *Slavery*. Oxford: Blackwell.

Turner, Ralph H., and Lewis M. Killian. 1987. *Collective Behavior*. 3d ed. Englewood Cliffs, NJ: Prentice-Hall.

Tyler, Stephen A. 1986. "Post-Modern Ethnography: From Document of the Occult to Occult Document." In *Writing Culture*, edited by James Clifford and George Marcus. Berkeley and Los Angeles: University of California Press.

Tylor, Edward Burnett. [1871] 1958. *Religion in Primitive Culture*. New York: Harper and Brothers.

Tyndall, John. 1874. *Presidential Address to the British Association*. Melbourne: George Robertson.

Vermes, Geza. 2000. *The Dead Sea Scrolls: A Selection of Original Manuscripts*. London: Folio Society.

Vésteinsson, Orri. 2001. *The Christianization of Iceland*. Oxford: Oxford University Press.

Vogt, Joseph. 1974. *Ancient Slavery and the Ideal of Man*. Oxford: Oxford University Press.

Von Soden, Wolfram. 1994. *The Ancient Orient*. Grand Rapids, MI: Eerdmans.

Voyé, Liliane, and Karel Dobbelaere. 1994. "Roman Catholicism: Universalism at Stake." In *Religions sans frontières?* edited by Roberto Cipriani, 83–113., Rome: Dipartimento per L'Informazione e Editoria.

Waines, David. 1995. *An Introduction to Islam*. Cambridge: Cambridge University Press.

Wallace, Anthony F. C. 1966. *Religion: An Anthropological View*. New York: Random House.

———. 1956. "Revitalization Movements." *American Anthropologist* 58:264–81.

Walton, Robert. 1967. *Zwingli's Theocracy*. Toronto: University of Toronto Press.

Walvin, James. 1981. "The Public Campaign in England against Slavery." In *The Abolition of the Atlantic Slave Trade*, edited by David Eltis and James Walvin, 63–79. Madison: University of Wisconsin Press.

Walzer, Michael. [1963] 1969. "Puritanism as a Revolutionary Ideology." In *Studies in Social Movements: A Social Psychological Perspective*, edited by Barry McLaughlin, 118–54. New York: The Free Press.

Watson, Alan. 1989. *Slave Law in the Americas*. Athens: University of Georgia Press.

Watt, W. Montgomery. 1965. *Muhammad at Medina*. London: Oxford University Press.

———. 1961. *Muhammad: Prophet and Statesman*. London: Oxford University Press.

Weaver, Mary Jo (with David Brakke and Jason Bivins). 1998. *Introduction to Christianity*. 3d ed. Belmont, CA: Wadsworth.

Weber, Max. [1922] 1993. *The Sociology of Religion*. Boston: Beacon Press.

———. [1891] 1976. *The Agrarian Sociology of Ancient Civilisations*. London: Humanities Press.

———. [1904–1905] 1958. *The Protestant Ethic and the Spirit of Capitalism*. New York: Charles Scribner's Sons.

———. 1946. *From Max Weber: Essays in Sociology*. Edited by H. H. Gerth and C. Wright Mills. New York: Oxford University Press.

Webster, Charles. 1986. "Puritanism, Separatism, and Science." In *God and Nature: Historical Essays on the Encounter between Christianity and Science*, edited by David C. Lindberg and Ronald L. Numbers, 192–217. Berkeley and Los Angeles: University of California Press.

Weightman, Simon. 1984. "Hinduism." In *A Handbook of Living Religions*, edited by John R. Hinnells, 191–236. London: Penguin Books.

Weisser, Michael R. 1979. *Crime and Punishment in Early Modern Europe*. Atlantic Highlands, NJ: Humanities Press.

White, Andrew Dickson, 1896. *A History of the Warfare of Science with Theology in Christendom*. 2 vols. New York: D. Appleton and Company.

White, Lynn, Jr. 1967. "The Historical Roots of Our Ecologic Crisis." *Science* 155:1203–7.

———. 1962. *Medieval Technology and Social Change*. Oxford: Oxford University Press.

———. 1954. "The Spared Wolves." *Saturday Review of Literature* 37 (November 13).

———. 1940. "Technology and Invention in the Middle Ages." *Speculum* 15:141–56.

White, Michael. 1997. *Isaac Newton: The Last Sorcerer*. Reading, MA: Addison-Wesley.

Whitehead, Alfred North. [1925] 1967. *Science and the Modern World*. New York: The Free Press.

Williams, Eric. [1944] 1994. *Capitalism and Slavery*. Chapel Hill: University of North Carolina Press.

Williams, George H. 1972. "The Two Social Strands in Italian Anabaptism, ca. 1526–ca.1565." In *The Social History of the Reformation*, edited by Lawrence P. Buck and Jonathan W. Zophy, 156–207. Columbus: Ohio State University Press.

Williams, Michael Allen. 1996. *Rethinking "Gnosticism": An Argument for Dismantling a Dubious Category*. Princeton: Princeton University Press.

Willis, Deborah. 1995. *Malevolent Nurture: Witch-Hunting and Maternal Power in Early Modern England*. Ithaca, NY: Cornell University Press.

Wilson, A. N. 1999. *God's Funeral*. New York: W. W. Norton.

Wilson, Bryan. 1975. *Magic and the Millennium*. Frogmore, UK: Paladin.

Winter, J. Alan. 1977. *Continuities in the Sociology of Religion*. New York: Harper & Row.

Witham, Larry 1997. "Many Scientists See God's Hand in Evolution." *Washington Times*, April 11, A8.

Wolfgang, Marvin E., Robert M. Figlio, and Thorsten Sellin. 1972. *Delinquency in a Birth Cohort*. Chicago: University of Chicago Press.

Wolfram, Herwig. 1997. *The Roman Empire and Its Germanic Peoples*. Berkeley and Los Angeles: University of California Press.

Wood, Betty. 1997. *The Origins of American Slavery: Freedom and Bondage in the English Colonies*. New York: Hill & Wang.

Woolman, John. [1754] 1969. *The Works of John Woolman*. Facsimile reprint. Miami: Mnemosyne Publishing Co.

Wuthnow, Robert. 1989. *Communities of Discourse*. Cambridge: Harvard University Press.

———. 1985. "Science and the Sacred." In *The Sacred in a Secular Age*, edited by Phillip E. Hammond, 187–203. Berkeley and Los Angeles: University of California Press.

Yates, Frances A. 1979. *The Occult Philosophy in the Elizabethan Age*. London: Routledge & Kegan Paul.

———. 1964. *Giordano Bruno and the Hermetic Tradition*. Chicago: University of Chicago Press.

Yazawa, Mel. 1998. *The Diary and Life of Samuel Sewall*. Boston: Bedford Books.

Yerkes, Royden Keith. 1952. *Sacrifice in Greek and Roman Religions and Early Judaism*. New York: Scribner's.

Yinger, J. Milton. 1957. *Religion, Society and the Individual*. New York: Macmillan.

Ziegler, Philip. 1971. *The Black Death*. New York: Harper Torchbooks.

Zilboorg, Gregory. 1935. *The Medical Man and the Witch during the Renaissance*. Baltimore: Johns Hopkins University Press.

Zwemer, Samuel M. 1921. *The Influence of Animism on Islam: An Account of Popular Superstitions*. New York: Macmillan.

Index

Page references in bold indicate an illustration; page references followed by *t* indicate a table.